Lowe's Transport Manager's and Operator's Handbook 2022

52nd edition

Lowe's Transport Manager's and Operator's Handbook 2022

David Lowe with Glen Davies

First published in Great Britain as *The Transport Manager's Handbook* in 1970 by Kogan Page Limited
Nineteenth edition published as *The Transport Manager's and Operator's Handbook* in 1989
Forty-first edition published as *Lowe's Transport Manager's and Operator's Handbook* in 2010
Fifty-second edition published in Great Britain and the United States in 2022

2nd Floor, 45 Gee Street	8 W 38th Street, Suite 902	4737/23 Ansari Road
London	New York, NY 10018	Daryaganj
EC1V 3RS	USA	New Delhi 110002
United Kingdom		India
www.koganpage.com		

© David Lowe, 2022

ISBNs

Hardback   978 1 3986 0576 3
Paperback   978 1 3986 0528 2
Ebook   978 1 3986 0577 0
ISSN   2399-5114

British Library Cataloguing-in-Publication Data

A CIP record for this book is available from the British Library.

Typeset by Hong Kong FIVE Workshop
Print production managed by Jellyfish
Printed and bound by CPI Group (UK) Ltd, Croydon CR0 4YY

CONTENTS

Biographical Notes **xiv**

Introduction by Glen Davies xvi

01   **Goods Vehicle O-Licensing** 1
Administration of Licensing System 2
The Vehicle O-Licensing System 3
O-Licences Not for Sale 4
Exemptions from O-Licensing 4
The Vehicle User 7
Rental of Vehicles 9
Hire and Contract Hire 10
Leasing 10
Restricted and Standard O-Licences 11
Requirements for O-Licence 12
Licence Application 21
Additional Vehicles 36
Licence Variation 38
Transfer of Vehicles 38
Notification of Changes 39
Subsidiary Companies 39
Temporary Derogation 39
Production of O-Licences 40
TCs' Powers of Review 40
Penalties against O-Licences 41
The Upper Transport Tribunal 44
Northern Ireland Licensing 47
Use of Light Commercial Vehicles 49
Foreign Vehicles in the UK 50

02   **Professional Competence** 52
Who May Become Professionally Competent? 52
Proof of Professional Competence 53
Examinations 54
Transfer of Qualifications 62

Driver CPC 62
Minimum Training and Qualification Requirements 66

03   Goods Vehicle Drivers' Hours and Working Time 68
Which Rules Apply? 68
European Union and AETR Rules 69
GB Domestic Rules 81
Mixed EU/AETR and GB Domestic Rules 83
AETR Rules 84
Working Time 85
The Regulations 85
The National Minimum Wage 87
Self-Employment 88
Tax Relief on Driver Allowances 89
Enforcement and Penalties 91
Reporting of Illegal Operations 91

04   Drivers' Hours Records – GB Domestic Rules 93
Exemptions from Written Record Keeping 94
Record Books 94

05   Drivers' Hours Records – EU/AETR rules 98
Legal Requirements for Tachographs 98
Exemptions 99
Employers' Responsibilities 102
Drivers' Responsibilities 104
Tachograph Calibration, Sealing and Inspection 105
Tachograph Breakdown 108
Use of Analogue Tachographs 109
The Analogue Tachograph Instrument 114
Chart Analysis 118
Digital Tachographs 118
Typical Digital Equipment 129
Production of Digital Records 129
Smart Tachographs 133
Offences 134
Production of Records 135

06 Driver Licensing and Licence Penalties 136

Driver Licensing 136
Driving Licences 138
Vehicle Categories/Groups for Driver Licensing 142
Application for Licences and Vocational Entitlements 148
Medical Requirements for Vocational Entitlements 150
Licence Fees and Validity 158
Production of Driving Licences 161
International Driving Permits 161
Exchange of Driving Licences 162
Driving Licence Penalty Points and Disqualification 164

07 Driver Testing and Training 177

Driving Tests 177
Large Goods Vehicle Driver Apprenticeship 191
Specialist Training 192
Continuing Professional Development 194

08 Vehicle Registration, HGV Road User Levy, Excise Duty and Trade Licences 196

Vehicle Registration 196
HGV Road User Levy 200
Vehicle Tax 201
Trade Licences 215
Recovery Vehicles 218
Rebated Heavy Oil (Red Diesel) 220
Oil Storage 221

09 Insurance (Vehicles and Goods in Transit) and Conditions of Carriage 222

Motor Vehicle Insurance 222
Fleet Insurance 228
Additional Insurance Cover 229
Goods in Transit Insurance 231
Conditions of Carriage 233
Security 236

10 Road Traffic Law 237

Speed Limits 240
Lighting-Up Time 244

Stopping, Loading and Unloading 244
Tramways 246
Motorway Driving 247
Hazard Warning Flashers 251
Temporary Obstruction Actions 252
Lights During Daytime 253
Parking 253
Lorry Routes and Controls 254
London Safer Lorry Scheme 258
Bus Lanes 259
High-Occupancy Vehicle (HOV) Lanes 260
Level Crossings 260
Level and Tram Crossings 260
Weight-Restricted Roads and Bridges 261
Owner Liability 261
Fixed Penalties 262
Civil Enforcement Officers 267
Pedestrian Crossings 267
Builders' Skips 267
Abandoned Motor Vehicles 268
Retention and Disposal of Seized Vehicles 268
Wheel Clamps 269
Overloaded Vehicles 269
Road Traffic Collision Procedure 270
Road Humps – Traffic Calming 271
Sale of Unroadworthy Vehicles 271
Seat Belts 272
Stowaways 274
Smuggling 278
Use of Radios and Telephones in Vehicles 280
Traffic and Weather Reports 280

11   Goods Vehicle Dimensions and Weights 282
Definitions 283
Length 283
Width 290
Height 290
Authorized Weight Regulations 292
ISO Container Dimensions and Weights 296
Weight Offences 297

12 Construction and Use of Vehicles 301
Definitions of Vehicles 301
International Vehicle Classifications 302
Constructional and Maintenance Requirements 303
Use of Vehicles 338
Trailer and Semi-Trailer Coupling and Uncoupling 341
Type Approval 341
Responsibility for Compliance 344
Responsibility for Type Approval 345
The Standards Checked 345
Arrangements for First Licensing of Vehicles 345
Alteration to Vehicles 346

13 Vehicle Lighting and Marking 348
Obligatory Lights 348
Side Marker Lamps 353
End-Outline Marker Lamps 354
Lighting Switches 354
Visibility of Lights and Reflectors 354
Direction Indicators 354
Optional Lamps 355
Warning Beacons 356
Swivelling Spotlights (Work Lamps) 357
Rear Retro-Reflectors 357
Side Retro-Reflectors 357
Front Retro-Reflectors 358
Vehicle Markings 358

14 Goods Vehicle Plating, Annual Testing and Vehicle Inspections 371
Annual Testing 371
Plating of Goods Vehicles and Trailers 384
Enforcement Checks on Vehicles 390
Inspection Notices and Prohibitions 396
Northern Ireland Certification of Vehicles 399

15 Light Vehicle (MOT) Testing 404
Vehicle Classes 405
The Test 407
Vehicle Defect Rectification Schemes 410

16   Vehicle Maintenance and Maintenance Records 411
The Choice: In-House or Contract Out 413
In-House Maintenance 414
Vehicle Servicing 415
Cleaning of Vehicles 416
Maintenance Records 416
Driver Defect Reports 416
Inspection Reports 417
Service Records 417
Maintenance Planning 418

17   Safety – on the Road and at Work 419
Road Safety 419
Vehicle Safety 420
Load Safety 421
Distribution of Loads 421
Workplace Transport Safety 422
Health and Safety at Work 425
The COSHH Regulations 2002 (as Amended) 433
The Reporting of Injuries, Diseases and Dangerous Occurrences
    Regulations 2013 (RIDDOR) 434
Vehicle Batteries 438
Risk Management 441
Fire Safety 442
First Aid 444
Workplace Safety Signs 447
Vehicle Reversing 448
Safe Tipping 450
Sheeting Loads 451
Safe Parking 452
Work at Height 452
Noise at Work 453
Forklift Truck Safety 453
Freight Container Safety Regulations 454
Operation of Lorry Loaders 455
Safety in Dock Premises 456
Health and Safety Enforcement 456

18   Loads – General, Livestock, Food, etc 459

Load Dimensions 459

Carriage of Livestock 460

Food 465

Sand and Ballast Loads 468

Landfill Tax 468

Solid Fuel Loads 469

ISO Containers 469

Fly-Tipping 469

19   Loads – Abnormal and Projecting 470

Abnormal Indivisible Loads 470

Special Types Vehicles 470

ESDAL Abnormal Load Notification 477

Escorts 477

High Loads 478

Projecting Loads 479

Lighting on Projecting and Long Loads 481

20   Loads – Dangerous Goods and Waste 483

Dangerous Goods by Road – UK 483

ADR 483

Definition and Classification of Dangerous Goods 484

Responsibilities 489

Exemptions 492

Transport Information and Documentation 495

Information to be Displayed on Containers, Tanks and Vehicles 497

Emergency Procedures 502

Security Provisions 504

Enforcement 507

Carriage of Explosives 508

Class 7: Radioactive Substances 508

Driver Training 508

Dangerous Goods Safety Advisor (DGSA) 510

Controlled and Hazardous Waste 511

Packaging Waste 515

21   Light Vehicles 516

Vehicle Roadworthiness 516

Vehicle Tax 516

Insurance 516

Fuel 517

Construction and Use Regulations 517

Drivers' Hours and Records 519

Speed Limits 520

Seat Belts 520

22   Vehicle Fuel Efficiency 522

Fuel and Vehicle 522

Fuel and Tyres 524

Fuel and the Driver 524

Fuel and Fleet Management 525

Fuel Efficiency Checklist 527

Energy Efficiency Best Practice Programme 528

Reducing Fuel Bills 529

23   Digital Communications and Technology 531

Information Management Systems 531

Mobile Communications Devices 532

Tachograph Analysis 534

Online Services 535

Intelligent Transport Systems 537

Data Protection (GDPR) 537

24   Transport and the Environment 540

Impact of Transport 540

Possible Solutions 542

Alternative Fuels 544

25   International Operations 546

Operators 546

Drivers 547

Vehicles 548

Cross-Border Readiness 548

Ways to Move Goods Across a Border 551

Pre-Notification 554

UK and EU Customs Procedures 556

Customs Procedures by Country 557

New Registration Rules 560

UK Licence for the Community 561

International Permits 562

International Carriage of Goods by Road – CMR 565

Cabotage 576

The TIR Convention 576

Carnets de Passage en Douane 579

Road Tolls 579

European Lorry Restrictions 582

Miscellaneous Requirements 582

Index 587

BIOGRAPHICAL NOTES

David Lowe FCILT

David Lowe was a freelance writer and lecturer who was actively involved with the road transport industry for many years.

He was the original author of *Lowe's Transport Manager's and Operator's Handbook*, now in its 52nd year of annual publication. His many other works included two best-selling titles for CPC students: *A Study Manual of Professional Competence in Road Haulage* (12 editions), *1001 Typical CPC Questions and Answers* (three editions), *Goods Vehicle Costing and Pricing Handbook* (four editions), *The Tachograph Manual* (two editions) and *The European Road Freighting Handbook* (1994), all published by Kogan Page. Two other works, *The Dictionary of Transport and Logistics* and *The Pocket Guide to LGV Drivers' Hours and Tachograph Law*, were published by Kogan Page in 2002 and 2006 (third edition) respectively.

He wrote extensively for the transport press, including *Commercial Motor*, and also wrote a number of successful operator and driver handbooks for *Headlight* magazine. He was the author of the Chartered Institute of Purchasing and Supply (CIPS) graduate diploma study guides *Distribution* and *Storage and Distribution in Supply Chains* published in 2000 and 2003 respectively. Another of his works, *Intermodal Freight Transport*, was published by Elsevier in 2005.

With his detailed practical knowledge of UK and European transport law, David Lowe was an acknowledged expert at explaining complex legal issues in layman's terms. He understood what the transport manager and small fleet operator needed to know, and he told them in no uncertain terms what they must and must not do to stay on the right side of the law.

He was a Chartered Fellow of the Chartered Institute of Logistics and Transport, a Freeman of the City of London and a Freeman of the Worshipful Company of Carmen. He was also a past winner of the Carmen's prestigious Herbert Crow silver medal award for 'consistent achievement for over thirty years as an outstanding freelance writer specializing in transport and logistics'.

Glen Davies FCILT

Glen Davies has been employed in logistics and transport all his working life. He is an independent consultant supporting a range of organizations on freight policy, city logistics and road transport management, specifically, improving operational efficiency while minimizing the impacts of road risk and vehicle emissions. Alongside his consultancy work he is Managing Director at The Driver Handbook, bringing driver communications into the 21st century. In 2020, he was appointed Editor of *Lowe's Transport Manager's and Operator's Handbook*, where he brings a new perspective to a well-matured publication.

His 23-year Army career provided him with first-hand operational experience in logistics and transport at all levels: from driving trucks aged 17, to his final operational responsibility for capability, compliance and safety across a 9,000-vehicle fleet. During this time Glen's roles have also included trainer, driving examiner, auditor, road safety officer and collision investigator. In 2007, he was employed by Transport for London for his industry-leading knowledge to lead the freight safety and environmental programmes; develop, manage and commercialize the Fleet Operator Recognition Scheme; and work with vehicle manufacturers, operators and regulators to establish the world's first direct vision standard for HGVs.

Now, as a consultant, Glen's work is varied; he is active in both public and private organizations in the UK and beyond. While happy in any logistics sector, he has carved a niche in the complexity of construction logistics planning and management. He helps organizations lead the way, and even informs policy on road safety and environmental standards, ensuring the operating benchmark is not just about legal compliance. He also specializes in technology projects that generate operational efficiency, minimize negative impacts and create new ways of working.

Glen is a Chartered Fellow of the Chartered Institute of Logistics and Transport, a Freeman of the City of London and a Liveryman of the Worshipful Company of Carmen.

INTRODUCTION
BY GLEN DAVIES

The 52nd edition of the *Lowe's Transport Manager's & Operator's Handbook* is published at the end of an extremely turbulent year. But one thing you can be sure of is this handbook is an essential and highly regarded set of structured references that will guide you through the legislative minefield of transport and logistics.

Alongside the COVID-19 pandemic, changes to The Highway Code and the roll out of local Clean Air Zones and the HGV Safety Permit Scheme, one of the main complexities is the post-Brexit era and the ending of the transition period on 31 January 2021. The most significant changes are reflected in Chapter 25 – International Operations, but there are many other European regulations that remain applicable across UK domestic operations. Many EU/EC rules have been retained in UK law through Section 3 of the European Union (Withdrawal) Act 2018 and various Statutory Instruments have been amended to make them suitable as UK law, ie removing references to 'Member States', 'the EU' and 'EC'. Statutory Instrument titles are unchanged, but they are now referred to as 'retained' rules.

The UK and EU also have the Trade and Cooperation Agreement (TCA) in place, which applies to journeys between the UK and EU. It contains rules that are identical to European rules with regards to driving times, rest/breaks, tachographs and record keeping. The UK is applying the requirements of the TCA via retained rules and Part VI of the Transport Act 1968. The retained rules therefore apply to both national journeys within the UK and international journeys between the UK and EU.

So, if you are ever asked why we still operate to EU drivers' hours rules, now you know.

Another area for transport managers to keep pace with is technology. Never has there been a more powerful influence on fleet operations than the effect of the technological revolution. The fleet sector isn't new to technology though and there are many digital forerunners that are now firmly entrenched in fleet operations. Take the term 'telematics' for example, which was first coined in France in 1978. Honda launched the first vehicle navigation system in 1981, the first HGV telematics system was launched in 1982 and I was first introduced to fleet management software sometime in the 1990s. Even government services are moving towards digital. The Government Digital Service was established in 2011, which has led to automated driver licence checking, paperless vehicle tax, DVSA Digital, Earned Recognition and remote enforcement.

We have started to recognise how automation can lead to a safer, more efficient and less impacting operation. It can make the world smaller, make it easier to keep an eye on and enable instant communications. The role of the transport manager is developing from a tactical day-to-day doer to a forward-thinking strategic analyst. Digital systems deliver immense value. They enable us to connect, collaborate and communicate. Imagine a day without a computer or smart phone in the office – nice not to have the emails but imagine everything you do digitally done instead on paper and by landline.

The digitized workplace is the new norm and technology is a basic tool of the trade. Our expectations are high, the expectations of the people who work for us are high and if we are to attract and retain young talent into the profession, we must be progressive. Millennials are now the largest generation in the workplace. They are tech-savvy, open to change and they can't stand the phrase, 'that's the way we've always done it'. The post-millennial generation, Generation Z, is already coming through, and they don't even know a world without technology, the internet and social media.

So how far are we from a truly paperless office? We have finally started to digitize walkaround checks, defect reporting, scheduling, tachograph analysis and licence checks, but what about the information we provide to drivers – policies, procedures, instructions in writing, risk assessments, toolbox talks? Technology won't solve the driver shortage, but it will make the profession much more attractive to Generation Z.

Which leads me nicely into the HGV driver shortage. The UK Government has been steadfast on its driver shortage position and I have to say I agree to an extent. The driver shortage is not a new phenomenon. Yes, it has been aggravated by COVID-19 and Brexit but it has been a problem for at least the past decade. Admittedly, there is a backlog of driving test applications and a shortage of examiners, and it is government's role to address this, but making HGV driving an attractive profession is primarily the haulage industry's problem to solve. We should look to the passenger sector's approach, which has an ongoing programme of driver succession. It actively recruits category B (car) drivers and trains them to drive category D (PCV). It doesn't rely on the military, agencies, individuals, charities or government to fund vocational licence acquisition. It takes ownership of the driving profession and invests in people. It accepts that some drivers will leave within five years but many stay in the profession for life. I am pleased to say that there are some haulage operators that do this, but the industry needs a widespread, coordinated and sustained effort of attracting, recruiting and training new drivers into the profession to ensure the driver shortage doesn't continue for the next decade.

Goods Vehicle O-Licensing

The Operator Licence (O-Licence) is the regulatory requirement to operate heavy goods vehicles and public service vehicles in the UK. Similar systems operate throughout Europe. The O-Licence aims to ensure the safe, fair and legal operation of most goods and passenger vehicles. O-Licence details are available online (with a PIN and password from the Central Licensing Office). Applicants may also use the online facility when applying for an O-Licence.

While other aspects of GB and Northern Ireland legislation apply to goods vehicles, the O-Licence provides a legal framework for transport operations. Failure to observe the undertakings, requirements and conditions of an O-Licence can lead to severe penalties for companies and individuals. Similar licensing controls apply to goods vehicle operations in Northern Ireland.

Trade or business users of most goods vehicles and vehicle combinations (vehicles with trailers) over 3,500 kg gross vehicle weight must hold an O-Licence, whether they are used for carrying goods in connection with the operator's main trade or business as an own-account operator, or are used for carrying goods for hire or reward. Certain goods vehicles, including those used exclusively for private purposes, are exempt from the licensing requirements. Details of vehicles exempt from requiring an O-Licence can be found in the Exemptions from O-Licensing section further on in the chapter.

Note: Exemptions are always under review and there are proposals to introduce O-Licences for goods vehicles under 3,500 kg. Electrically powered vans are now able to operate at weights up to 4,250 kg without requiring an O-Licence.

The O-Licence system is regulated by the Goods Vehicle (Licensing of Operators) Act 1995 (as amended). This Act states that no person may use a goods vehicle on a road for hire or reward or in connection with any trade or business carried on by him except under an O-Licence.

The O-Licence system is regulated by the following EU and UK regulations:

- EC Regulation 1071/2009/EC;
- The Road Transport Operator Regulations 2011 (SI 2632/2011/EC).

Section 3 of the European Union (Withdrawal) Act 2018 and various statutory instruments made changes to make EU rules suitable as UK law.

Other Relevant Legislation

Other relevant legislation includes:

- The Goods Vehicles (Licensing of Operators) Act 1995
- The Goods Vehicles (Licensing of Operators) Regulations 1995 (SI 1995/2869) (as amended)
- The Goods Vehicle Operators (Qualifications) Regulations 1999 (SI 1999/2430) (as amended)
- The Road Transport Operator Regulations 2011 (SI 2011/2632)
- The Road Transport Act 2013
- The Road Transport (Vehicle Registration) Regulation 2017
- The Road Transport (Driver Licensing) Regulation 2017
- The Road Vehicles (Authorised Weights) and (Construction and Use) Regulations 2017
- EU Regulation 1071/2009 establishing common rules concerning conditions to be complied with to pursue the occupation of road transport operator
- EU Regulation 1072/2009 on common rules for access to the international road haulage market
- The Goods Vehicles (Community Licences) Regulations 2011 (SI 2011/2633)

There are also guides, advice and 13 Senior Traffic Commissioner statutory documents available at GOV.UK.

Administration of Licensing System

The aim of the O-Licensing system is to ensure a safe, fair and legal operation. It is administered on a regional (ie Traffic Area) basis throughout Great Britain. (Northern Ireland's Road Freight Vehicle O-Licensing system is dealt with separately by the Driver and Vehicle Agency – part of the Department of the Environment.)

Each Traffic Area has its own Traffic Commissioner (TC) and Traffic Area Offices (TAOs), see Appendix I.

TCs are independent regulators for HGV and PSV operations, their management and professional drivers. Collectively, they are a non-departmental tribunal and licensing authority, sponsored by the Department for Transport (DfT).

There is a 'Senior' TC, and 'Lead' TCs are appointed where operators hold operating licences in more than one Traffic Area. Where this is the case, the Lead TC will be the person that the operator in question will need to deal with and who will make final decisions. Lead TCs also have a team to deal with operators who hold licences in more than one Traffic Area, known as the Multiple Licence Holder (MLH) team.

O-Licence application administration is now centralized at:

Central Licensing Office
Hillcrest House
386 Harehills Lane
Leeds LS9 6NF

The Central Licensing Office (CLO) supports the TCs and their role as the independent licensing authority.

Figures for the year ending March 2021 showed that there were 369,287 goods vehicles authorized on 69,528 O-Licences in Great Britain, of which 35,505 were restricted licences, 25,091 were standard national licences and 8,932 were standard international licences.

Source: Traffic Commissioners for Great Britain Annual Report to the Secretary of State 2020–2021 (for the year ending 31 March 2021)

The Vehicle O-Licensing System

The Vehicle O-Licensing system (VOL) is a web-based portal to apply for and manage O-Licences. VOL provides enforcement agencies with 'real-time' data to help inform enforcement activities.

VOL reduces the application process from nine weeks to seven weeks and enables goods vehicle operators to add and remove vehicles from their licence at any time. It also reduces the time taken to add a vehicle to a licence from 14 days to a few minutes. Operators can:

- register online to check their own licence details held on the Driver and Vehicle Standards Agency (DVSA)'s O-Licence computer system;
- transfer vehicles between licences they hold in different areas;
- track the progress of licence applications;
- set up access for other members of their staff, allowing greater access to records and transactions for larger companies;
- pay licence fees and renew licences.

VOL also includes a template for advertising changes to its licences in local newspapers.

O-Licences Not for Sale

O-Licences are issued only to applicants who meet strict criteria. As such, O-Licences are *not* transferable between operators and may *not* be borrowed, used on loan or sold, with or without the vehicles to which they relate, by any person other than the authorized holder.

Exemptions from O-Licensing

There are a number of categories of vehicle which are exempt from O-Licence requirements.

Light Vehicles

The principal exemption applies to 'light' vehicles identified as follows.

Rigid vehicles are 'light' if:

- they are plated and the gross plated weight is not more than 3.5 tonnes;
- they are unplated and have an unladen weight of not more than 1,525 kg.

A combination of a rigid vehicle and a drawbar trailer is 'small' if:

- both the vehicle and the trailer are plated, and the total of the gross *plated* weights is not more than 3.5 tonnes (this is increased to 4.25 tonnes for alternatively fuelled vehicles);
- either the vehicle or the trailer is not plated, and the total of the *unladen* weights is not more than 1,525 kg.

NB: *The text throughout this* Handbook *will refer to 3.5 tonnes as the relevant total gross plated weight, as these sized vehicles make up over 95 per cent of these types of vehicles.*

Operators engaged in 'own-account' work with vehicles that do not exceed 3.5 tonnes gross plated weight used in combination with trailers that have an unladen weight that does not exceed 1,020 kg remain out of the scope of the O-Licence regulations.

Articulated vehicles are 'small' if:

- the semi-trailer is plated, and the total of the *unladen* weight of the tractive unit and the plated weight of the semi-trailer is not more than 3.5 tonnes;

- the semi-trailer is not plated, and the total of the *unladen* weights of the tractive unit and the semi-trailer is not more than 1,525 kg. However, this exemption does not apply if other people's goods are carried for hire or reward.

Older Vehicles

Also included in the exemptions are pre-1 January 1977 vehicles which have an unladen weight not exceeding 1,525 kg and a gross weight greater than 3.5 tonnes.

Other Exemptions

Regulations list the following further specific exemptions from O-Licence requirements:

1 Vehicles licensed as agricultural tractors used solely for handling specified goods, and any trailer drawn by them.

2 Dual-purpose vehicles and any trailer drawn by them.

3 Vehicles used on roads only for the purpose of passing between private premises in the immediate neighbourhood and belonging to the same person (except in the case of a vehicle used only in connection with excavation or demolition), provided that the distance travelled on the road in any one week does not exceed in aggregate 9.654 km (ie 6 miles).

4 Motor vehicles constructed or adapted primarily for the carriage of passengers and their effects and any trailer drawn by them while being so used.

5 Vehicles being used for funerals.

6 Vehicles being used for police, fire brigade and ambulance service purposes.

7 Vehicles being used for fire-fighting or rescue work at mines.

8 Vehicles on which a permanent body has not yet been built carrying goods for trial or for use in building the body.

9 Vehicles being used under a trade licence.

10 Vehicles used in the service of a visiting force or headquarters.

11 Vehicles used by or under the control of HM Armed Forces.

12 Trailers not constructed for the carriage of goods but which are used incidentally for that purpose in connection with the construction, maintenance or repair of roads.

13 Road rollers or any trailer drawn by them.*

14 Vehicles used by the Maritime and Coastguard Agency (MCA) or the Royal National Lifeboat Institution (RNLI) for the carriage of lifeboats, life-saving appliances or crew.

15 Vehicles fitted with permanent equipment (ie machines or appliances) so that the only goods carried are:

(a) for use in connection with the equipment;

(b) for threshing, grading, cleaning or chemically treating grain or for mixing by the equipment with other goods not carried on the vehicle to make animal fodder;

(c) mud or other matter swept up from the road by the equipment.

16 Vehicles while being used by a local authority for the purpose of enactments relating to weights and measures or the sale of food or drugs.

17 Vehicles used by a local authority under the Civil Defence Act 1948.

18 Steam-propelled vehicles.

19 Tower wagons or any trailer drawn by them provided that any goods carried on the trailer are required for use in connection with the work on which the tower wagon is used.

20 Vehicles used on airports under the Civil Aviation Act 1982.

21 Electrically propelled vehicles.*

22 Showmen's goods vehicles and any trailer drawn by such vehicles.

23 Vehicles first registered prior to 1 January 1977 which are not over 1,525 kg unladen weight and are plated for more than 3,500 kg but not more than 3,556.21 kg (3.5 tonnes).

24 Vehicles used by a highway authority in connection with weigh-bridges.

25 Vehicles used for emergency operations by the water, electricity, gas and telephone services.

26 Recovery vehicles.*

27 Incomplete vehicles (with no fixed body).

28 Vehicles used for snow clearing or the distribution of grit, salt or other materials on frosted, ice-bound or snow-covered roads and for any other purpose connected with such activities. *NB: This exemption is not restricted solely to local authority-owned vehicles.*

29 Vehicles going to or coming from a test station and carrying a load which is required for the test at the request of the Secretary of State for Transport (ie by the test station).

At the time of writing, vehicles such as road rollers, recovery vehicles and electrically powered vehicles are still under review as to whether or not they should lose their exemptions.

Exemption for Private Vehicles

Exemptions also apply to vehicles used privately (ie for carrying goods for solely private purposes and not in any way connected with a business activity) and by voluntary organizations.

Non-Exempt Vehicles

All other conventionally powered goods-carrying vehicles over 3.5 tonnes gross weight not specifically shown as exempt in the list above must be covered by an O-Licence. This includes such vehicles that are only temporarily in the operator's possession, or are hired from another operator without a driver, or borrowed on a short-term basis, if they are used in connection with a business (even a part-time business).

No Exemption for Fast Agricultural Tractors

Fastrac-type agricultural tractors capable of pulling substantial loads at speeds of up to 40 mph on public roads must be specified on an O-Licence if used for hire or reward haulage work. The agricultural exemption mentioned above applies only when such machines are used by farmers in connection with their own agricultural business.

The Vehicle User

An O-Licence must be obtained by the 'user' of the vehicle for all the vehicles to which the regulations apply. The 'user' may be the operating company or the owner or hirer of the vehicle. If the vehicle was hired without a driver, the hirer is the 'user'. The term 'user' means:

- a company or organization that is responsible for the operation of a vehicle that is either owned, leased or hired to it;
- an owner-driver who uses a vehicle in connection with their own business as long as they are responsible for the success or failure of the business;
- the owner of a vehicle employing a driver and paying the driver's wages;
- the borrower or hirer of a vehicle either without a driver and they themselves drive it or paying the wages of a driver employed to drive it.

In general, the person or company that pays the driver's wages is the 'user' of a vehicle, and it is this person (or company) or the nominated 'competent person' (usually a transport manager) who is responsible for holding an O-Licence and for the safe condition of the vehicle on the road and for ensuring that it is operated in accordance with the law. The driver, although an employee, is the user of the vehicle in the context of certain legislation (eg the Road Vehicles (Construction and Use) Regulations 1986, as amended) and is responsible for its safe condition on the road.

Agency Drivers

Dependence on agencies for the supply of temporary drivers can cause difficulty in interpretation of the term 'user' and in deciding who should hold the O-Licence: the vehicle owner, or the agency which employs the driver.

The status of the vehicle 'user' in these circumstances is determined by driver agencies getting operators to sign agreements. The vehicle operator technically becomes the employer of the driver and consequently the operator remains the legal 'user' of the vehicle. Usually, the agency asks the hirer to sign an agreement whereby the agency becomes the 'agent' of the operator for these purposes in paying the driver's wages.

This practice has been proved in court to be legally acceptable on the grounds that the Transport Act 1968 section 92(2) states that 'the person whose servant or agent the driver is, shall be deemed to be the person using the vehicle'. The driver is considered to be the employee of the hirer because the hirer gives instructions and directs the activities of the driver who is temporarily in their employ. The key issue here is who controls how the drivers do their job. This must be the 'user' of the vehicle and the holder of the O-Licence. However, there can be difficulties when a court interprets it such that because the agency actually 'pays' the driver then the driver is a servant of the agency and not the hirer.

Operators employing agency drivers need to take extreme care to ensure the true 'status' of any agency drivers used and are advised to discuss this matter with the supplying agency in order to agree an acceptable position.

With agency drivers, the operator has no sound means of establishing whether the driver is legally qualified to drive or whether they have already exceeded the permitted driving hours on previous days and whether they have had adequate rest periods, other than to be able to download information held on the driver's 'digi' tacho card. Reputable agencies usually go to considerable lengths to ensure that drivers are properly licensed and have complied with the driving hours rules in all respects. It is worth also remembering that the use of casually hired or temporary drivers (whose backgrounds and previous experiences may not be fully known) can result in jeopardy of the contract of insurance covering the use of vehicles and there could also be serious security risks as well as possible O-Licence penalties for infringements of the law.

Operators who use agency drivers should be aware that they may be held liable for negligence or driving offences. They are also liable for ensuring the health and safety of hired drivers, and must inform them of the legal requirements of vehicle operations, such as the 'hours' law, tachographs, safe loading and vehicle checks. Operators also need to ensure that they obtain copies of agency drivers' records for duties performed while under their control.

Rental of Vehicles

Rental of vehicles on a short-term basis of a few days or a few weeks does not impose onerous contractual obligations on the hirer. The mechanical condition of the vehicle is the hirer's responsibility while under their control.

O-Licence Provisions

Hiring does involve other legal obligations in respect of the vehicle itself and its use. If the vehicle is over 3.5 tonnes gross plated weight and has been rented for use in connection with a trade or business, then the person or firm renting it must hold an O-Licence and there must be a margin on that licence to cover the renting of one or more additional vehicles.

There is no need to advise the TC of details of the vehicle unless it is to be retained on hire for more than one month, after which time the TC must be notified so an O-Licence disc can be issued. If the vehicle is rented for a shorter period and then returned to the rental company to be replaced by another vehicle, the TC does not have to be notified if the combined total of the two rental periods exceeds one month unless both are part of the same rental agreement.

If a vehicle over 3.5 tonnes is rented for use in a Traffic Area different from the one in which the O-Licence is held, then an O-Licence must be obtained in that other Traffic Area before a vehicle is permitted to operate from a base there.

Whether or not the rented vehicle comes within the scope of O-Licence, the person or firm renting it carries the user responsibility for its safe mechanical condition when it is on the road. Consequently, if vehicle faults result in prosecution, the user (not the rental company) will have to pay any fines imposed and the user's O-Licence will be put in jeopardy (even if the vehicle is not specified on the O-Licence). Careful selection of a reputable rental company with high maintenance standards is therefore essential.

Hire and Contract Hire

Hiring vehicles (or more specifically contract hire), as opposed to rental, implies a longer-term arrangement with a more rigid agreement as to the obligations of the parties involved. Hiring arrangements vary considerably since the vehicle provider and the customer draw up a contract to incorporate the services required. There are two principal forms of contract hire: vehicles supplied with drivers and vehicles supplied without drivers.

The important difference is that in the former case the contract hire company, as the employer of the driver, is the 'user' of the vehicles in law and therefore holds the O-Licence and shoulders the legal responsibilities previously described, while the hirer merely operates the vehicles exclusively to suit requirements. However, in the latter case the hirer is the 'user' and O-Licence holder and, as with vehicles purchased and leased with own-employee drivers at the wheel, the hirer carries the full legal responsibilities.

Advantages of Contract Hire

Full contract hire with driver is advantageous to the operator, because it removes the burden of:

- capital expenditure on an ancillary activity;
- a range of legal responsibilities while providing the right vehicles for exclusive use.

A further financial advantage can arise for a firm operating its own fleet but wishing to switch to contract hire. Contract hire companies will usually purchase a whole existing fleet and then contract-hire it back to the operator, thus still giving the resources to meet transport needs and yet providing an immediate refund of the capital tied up in vehicles. This proposition can be used to advantage in relieving cash-flow pressure.

Leasing

Leasing is a totally different concept from outright purchase or hire purchase in that the operator (ie the lessee) never actually owns the vehicle but has the full use of it as though it were their own. It is also a different concept from rental and hiring arrangements in that it is purely a financial means of acquiring vehicles. In other words, those putting up the money are not transport or vehicle operators, they are finance houses.

Several different forms of leasing are available (basically divided by the assumption of risk, with the lessee taking the risk with a pure finance lease and the lessor retaining the risk with an operating lease) and legislation governing leasing arrangements is subject to change.

The general concept of leasing is that a finance house (ie the lessor) purchases a vehicle, for which the operator has specified the requirements and negotiated the price and any available discount from the supplier, and then it spreads the capital cost, interest charges, overhead costs and its profit margin over a period of time to determine the amount of the periodic repayments.

Where leasing is purely a financial arrangement, the advantages and disadvantages from an operational viewpoint are the same as for outright purchase. Because in principle the lessee operates the vehicle as though it is owned, and employs the driver, the full weight of legal responsibility applies to the lessee so they need to have a full transport back-up of administration and operational staff, maintenance facilities and policies for selection of the correct vehicles and for replacement at the most economic intervals. Where maintenance is included in the leasing package, this allows the operator to more accurately forecast expenditure, develop quotations and form operating budgets.

Clearly, while both contract hire and leasing enable operators to avoid major capital expenditure, there are costs involved with both options. While these costs may mean additional expenditure for the operator, they are usually fixed costs, or largely fixed costs, and this often enables operators to more accurately produce charge-out rates and operating cost tables.

Restricted and Standard O-Licences

There are three main types of O-Licence and, in exceptional circumstances, a temporary licence, known as an interim licence or interim authorization, may be granted (see the section on Interim Licences later in this chapter).

1 **Restricted licences:** available only to own-account operators who carry nothing other than goods in connection with their own trade or business, which is a business other than that of carrying goods for hire or reward. These licences cover both national and international transport operations with own-account goods. Restricted O-Licence holders must not use their vehicles to carry goods for hire or reward or on behalf of customers' businesses – even if it is done only as a favour or is seen as being part of the service provided to a customer and even if no charges are raised (see below).

2 **Standard licences (national transport operations):** for hire or reward (ie professional) hauliers, or own-account operators who also engage in hire or reward operations, but restricted solely to national transport operations (ie operations exclusively within the UK). Own-account holders of such licences may also carry their own goods (but not goods for hire or reward) on international journeys.

3 Standard licences (national and international transport operations): for hire or reward (ie professional) hauliers, or own-account operators who also engage in hire or reward carrying, on both national and international transport operations.

Standard Licences for Own-Account Operators

Own-account operators may voluntarily choose to hold a standard O-Licence for national or both national and international transport operations instead of a restricted licence, provided they are prepared to meet the necessary additional qualifying requirements (principally the professional competence qualification – see Chapter 2 – and the need for a status of 'good repute'). Among the reasons which may influence them to take this step is the desire to carry goods for hire or reward to utilize spare capacity on their vehicles, especially on return trips. Such a requirement may also arise because a firm is involved in carrying goods for associate companies on a reciprocal or integrated working basis, which does not come within the scope of activities that are permitted under O-Licence between subsidiary companies and holding companies (see the section on Subsidiary Companies later in this chapter), or firms may find themselves in the position where they carry goods in connection with their customers' businesses, as opposed to their own.

Firms holding restricted O-Licences may not carry goods on behalf of customers (ie in connection with the trade or business of the customer rather than in connection with their own business) or other firms even if such operations are described as being a 'favour' or 'part of the service' to the customer and involve no payment whatsoever. This may occur, for example, when a vehicle delivers goods to a customer and the customer then asks the driver to drop off items on their return journey because they are 'going past the door' and their own vehicle is not available. Such activities would be illegal under the terms of a restricted O-Licence, and if two convictions for such an offence are made within five years, the licence must be revoked by the TC.

Requirements for O-Licence

In order to obtain an O-Licence, applicants must satisfy certain conditions.

Restricted Licences

Applicants must be:

- fit and proper;
- of appropriate financial standing.

Standard Licences (National Transport Operations)

Applicants must be:

- of good repute;
- of appropriate financial standing;
- professionally competent, or must employ a person who is professionally competent.

Standard Licences (National and International Transport Operations)

Applicants must be:

- of good repute;
- of appropriate financial standing;
- professionally competent, or must employ a person who is professionally competent.

Other Legal Requirements

Licence applicants also need to:

- declare any relevant convictions (usually related to previous vehicle operation);
- satisfy legal requirements relating to the suitability and environmental acceptability of their operating centres;
- satisfy legal requirements relating to the suitability of their vehicle maintenance facilities or arrangements; and
- declare their ability and willingness to comply with the law in regard to vehicle operating as demonstrated by signing the undertakings on the O-Licence application form.

Good Repute

For a TC to be able to grant a standard O-Licence, they must determine that the applicant is of good repute or no licence will be granted.

An individual is *not* of good repute if they have been convicted of more than one serious offence or of road transport offences concerning:

- pay and employment conditions in the profession (ie of road haulier);
- drivers' hours and rest periods;

- O-Licensing;
- weights and dimensions of goods vehicles;
- vehicle maintenance;
- road and vehicle safety;
- protection of the environment;
- rules concerning professional liability;
- rules relating to the contravention of provisions contained within traffic orders.

For the purposes of the standard O-Licence scheme, this means that the applicant for a licence (ie an individual) must not have a record which includes more than one conviction for serious offences or conviction for road transport offences during the previous five years (excluding convictions that are spent – see below) relating to the above issues. Similarly, to be a fit and proper person in order to obtain a restricted O-Licence means that there should not be a past record of such offences.

If it is a limited liability company applying for a licence and the company, or any director, has relevant convictions on their record (ie for serious offences; the term used is 'relevant' offences and these may include prosecutions for issues such as breaches of Health and Safety Regulations, etc, as listed below), then the TC may use discretion in deciding whether the firm, or director, is of good repute.

It should be noted that the TC will not necessarily refuse to grant a licence to an applicant who has had relevant or transport-related convictions – but must if the convictions are for more than one serious offence, which affects the applicant's good repute – but will consider the number and seriousness of the convictions before making a grant. For example, a licence may be issued for a shorter period to give the applicant an opportunity to demonstrate compliance, or a licence may be granted for fewer vehicles than the number requested. If, during the currency of a licence, an O-Licence holder is convicted of offences related to goods vehicle operations, the TC may call the operator to a public inquiry (PI) and determine whether they are still a fit and proper person or of good repute, and whether they should be allowed to continue holding an O-Licence.

In the case of partnership applications for licences, if one of the partners is considered not to be of good repute, then the TC will be bound to conclude that the partnership firm is not of good repute and, on that basis, may also refuse to grant a licence.

The relevant offences for which conviction damages a person's good repute are those specified in Regulation 1071/2009/EC Article 6(1)(2) and Annex IV, as follows:

- commercial law;
- insolvency law;

- pay and employment conditions in the profession;
- road traffic;
- professional liability;
- trafficking in human beings or drugs;
- the driving time and rest periods of drivers, working time and the installation and use of recording equipment;
- the maximum weights and dimensions of commercial vehicles used in international traffic;
- the initial qualification and continuous training of drivers;
- the roadworthiness of commercial vehicles, including the compulsory technical inspection of motor vehicles;
- access to the market in international road haulage or, as appropriate, access to the market in road passenger transport;
- safety in the carriage of dangerous goods by road;
- the installation and use of speed-limiting devices in certain categories of vehicle;
- driving licences;
- admission to the occupation of road transport operator;
- live animal transport.

Under Regulation 1071/2009/EC, the most serious infringements for the purposes of Article 6(2) are as follows:

1 (a) Exceeding the maximum six-day or fortnightly driving time limits by margins of 25 per cent or more.

(b) Exceeding, during a daily working period, the maximum daily driving time limit by a margin of 50 per cent or more without taking a break or without an uninterrupted rest period of at least 4.5 hours.

2 Not having a tachograph and/or speed limiter, or using a fraudulent device able to modify the records of the recording equipment and/or the speed limiter or falsifying record sheets or data downloaded from the tachograph and/or the driver card.

3 Driving without a valid roadworthiness certificate if such a document is required under Community law and/or driving with a very serious deficiency of, among other things, the braking system, the steering linkages, the wheels/tyres, the suspension or chassis that would create such an immediate risk to road safety that it leads to a decision to immobilize the vehicle.

4 Transporting dangerous goods that are prohibited for transport or transporting such goods in a prohibited or non-approved means of containment or without identifying them on the vehicle as dangerous goods, thus endangering lives or the environment to such extent that it leads to a decision to immobilize the vehicle.

5 Carrying passengers or goods without holding a valid driving licence or carrying by an undertaking not holding a valid Community licence.

6 Driving with a driver card that has been falsified, or with a card of which the driver is not the holder, or which has been obtained on the basis of false declarations and/or forged documents.

7 Carrying goods exceeding the maximum permissible laden mass by 20 per cent or more for vehicles the permissible laden weight of which exceeds 12 tonnes, and by 25 per cent or more for vehicles the permissible laden weight of which does not exceed 12 tonnes.

Committing any of the seven offences listed above, besides any fines imposed by the courts, may result in:

- the operator's Operator Compliance Risk Score (OCRS) being seriously affected (see Chapter 14);
- loss of good repute for the operator and/or transport manager;
- if appropriate, a premises check of the undertaking;
- a record of the offence(s) being made in the National Electronic Register (see the section National Electronic Registers found later in this chapter);
- revocation, suspension, curtailment or loss of the O-Licence.

Serious Offences

A serious offence is an offence committed in the UK that results in one of:

- a sentence of more than three months' imprisonment;
- a community service order of more than 60 hours;
- a fine exceeding level four on the standard scale (currently £2,500).

If committed abroad, the seriousness of the offence would be determined by assessing the punishment relative to UK standards.

Criminal Offences

The following are recorded as criminal offences and can be accessed by the police and TCs to determine a person's good repute:

- falsifying records (eg tachograph charts or records);
- forgery (eg of insurance documents or a driving licence);

- fraudulent use or display of an official document (eg an O-Licence disc);
- aiding and abetting any of the above.

Spent Convictions

The Rehabilitation of Offenders Act 1974 exists to support the rehabilitation of reformed offenders. Under the Act, following a specified period of time, all cautions and convictions (except those resulting in prison sentences of over 30 months) are regarded as 'spent'. As a result, the offender is regarded as rehabilitated. Spent convictions do not have to be declared on the licence application form.

Under the Rehabilitation of Offenders Act 1974, the rehabilitation period is determined by the type of disposal administered or the length of the sentence imposed.

Rehabilitation periods that run beyond the end of a sentence are made up of the total sentence length plus an additional period that runs from the end of the sentence, commonly called the 'buffer periods'. Other rehabilitation periods start from the date of conviction or the date the penalty was imposed. The 'buffer periods' are halved for those who are under 18 at date of conviction (save for custodial sentences of six months or less, where the 'buffer period' is 18 months).

The rehabilitation periods for sentences with additional 'buffer periods' which run from the end date of the sentence are shown in the table below:

Sentence/disposal	Buffer period for adults (18 and over at the time of conviction or the time the disposal is administered). This applies from the end date of the sentence (including the licence period)	Buffer period for young people (under 18 at the time of conviction or the time the disposal is administered). This applies from the end date of the sentence (including the licence period)
Custodial sentence* of over 4 years, or a public protection sentence	Never spent	Never spent
Custodial sentence of over 30 months (2½ years) and up to and including 48 months (4 years)	7 years	3½ years
Custodial sentence of over 6 months and up to and including 30 months (2½ years)	4 years	2 years

Sentence/disposal	Buffer period for adults (18 and over at the time of conviction or the time the disposal is administered). This applies from the end date of the sentence (including the licence period)	Buffer period for young people (under 18 at the time of conviction or the time the disposal is administered). This applies from the end date of the sentence (including the licence period)
Custodial sentence of 6 months or less	2 years	18 months
Community order or youth rehabilitation order**	1 year	6 months

*Custodial sentence includes a sentence of imprisonment (both an immediate custodial sentence and a suspended sentence), a sentence of detention in a young offender institution, a sentence of detention under section 91 of the Powers of Criminal Courts (Sentencing) Act 2000, a detention and training order, a sentence of youth custody and a sentence of corrective training.

**In relation to any community or youth rehabilitation order which has no specified end date, the rehabilitation period is two years from the date of conviction.

The following table sets out the rehabilitation period for sentences which do not have 'buffer periods' and for which the rehabilitation period runs from the date of conviction:

Sentence/disposal	Rehabilitation period for adults (18 and over at the time of conviction or the time the disposal is administered)	Rehabilitation period for young people (under 18 at the time of conviction or the time the disposal is administered)
Fine	1 year	6 months
Conditional discharge	Period of the order	Period of the order
Absolute discharge	None	None
Conditional caution and youth conditional caution	3 months, or when the caution ceases to have effect if earlier	3 months
Simple caution, youth caution	Spent immediately	Spent immediately
Compensation order	On the discharge of the order (ie when it is paid in full)	On the discharge of the order (ie when it is paid in full)
Binding over order	Period of the order	Period of the order
Attendance centre order	Period of the order	Period of the order

Sentence/disposal	Rehabilitation period for adults (18 and over at the time of conviction or the time the disposal is administered)	Rehabilitation period for young people (under 18 at the time of conviction or the time the disposal is administered)
Hospital order (with or without a restriction order)	Period of the order	Period of the order
Referral order	Not available for adults	Period of the order
Reparation order	Not available for adults	None

Financial Standing

The requirement for financial standing means the applicant being able to prove to, or assure, the TC that sufficient funds (ie money) are readily available to maintain the vehicles authorized to be covered by the licence to the standards of fitness and safety required by law. (The requirement to have sufficient funds to cover authorized vehicles means that an operator with five vehicles, with an O-Licence authorizing 10 vehicles, will need to be able to prove sufficient financial reserves for all 10 authorized vehicles.)

Levels of financial reserves are quoted in euros as €9,000 for the first authorized vehicle and €5,000 for each additional authorized vehicle.

Due to the fluctuations in exchange rates, TCs review financial standing annually.

As at 1 January 2021, the levels of financial reserves for a standard national or standard international O-Licence are:

- first authorized vehicle: £8,000;
- each additional authorized vehicle: £4,500.

For a restricted O-Licence, the levels of financial reserves are:

- first authorized vehicle: £3,100;
- each additional authorized vehicle: £1,700.

Financial standing, comprising both capital and reserves, must be available to the operator at all times and must be demonstrated on the basis of annual accounts certified by an auditor or duly accredited person.

It is important to realize that the requirement for minimum levels of capital and reserves applies to the total number of vehicles authorized on an O-Licence, not just to the vehicles currently specified. In the case where an operator has a significant margin between the number of authorized vehicles and those actually specified, they may wish to consider decreasing this margin to reduce the amount of financial resources they have to prove to the TC. The number of authorized vehicles on an O-Licence can be reduced using VOL.

Financial standing can be established by means of confirmation or assurance from a bank or from other properly qualified institutions that such funds are available, in the form of a bank guarantee, pledge or security, or by similar means. The operator does not need to actually hold the reserves but must have agreed access to them.

Financial standing relates to an average balance over the life of the licence and does not relate to a single day when a bank balance may have been artificially boosted by a temporary injection of funds.

Failure to pay fines, other penalties and business debts as well as non-payment of vehicle tax will suggest to the TC that an operator has cash-flow problems and is therefore unlikely to meet the legal requirement for financial standing.

Assessment of Financial Standing

At the five-yearly review of a licence, the TC may carry out a 'wealth' check to determine whether the required reserves have been available during the previous five years. If they have not, the licence holder will be deemed to be no longer of the required financial standing and the licence may be revoked.

The TC has powers to:

- ask for evidence of financial standing;
- inquire into the finances of applicants;
- require applicants to declare any past bankruptcy or financial failures.

The firm's balance sheet within the audited accounts will be looked at to determine its liquidity (ie its capability of paying its debts as they fall due). The TC will examine the relevant financial ratios such as current assets to current liabilities, which should exceed 0.5 (meaning that the applicant can only pay half their creditors). However, any ratio between 0.5 and 1.0 may indicate a problem and must be referred to the TC to ensure that there are arrangements in place to cover any deficit.

Where an operator becomes unable to meet the financial standing requirements, the TC can allow a 'period of grace' of up to six months for the operator to resolve the issue.

In complex cases, usually involving companies where, perhaps, funds are moved between one subsidiary and another, and there is cross-accounting and suchlike, the TCs can call on financial experts (assessors) to help determine the true position of an applicant.

Operating Centres

The vehicle operating centre is defined as the place where the vehicle is 'normally kept', ie the place where the vehicle is regularly parked when it is not in use. Sufficient space must be available to park all the vehicles and trailers on the O-Licence. However, places where vehicles are parked occasionally, even if on a regular basis, in circumstances that are exceptional to the normal conduct of the business are not considered to be operating centres.

Where operators regularly permit drivers to take vehicles home with them, the place where the drivers park vehicles near to their home becomes the vehicle operating centre. This place must be declared on the O-Licence application form.

In these circumstances an operator could have to declare a number of separate operating centres in addition to the normal depot or base and could face environmental representation against each of these places and have restrictive environmental conditions placed on the licence in respect of their use.

TCs expect licence applicants to be able to show that their proposed operating centre is both suitable in environmental terms and sufficiently large to accommodate all the vehicles authorized to be based there.

Where an operating centre may be overcrowded at times, leading to vehicles (including staff cars, etc) having to park outside on a road or roads in the area, or wait for periods outside in order to enter, this may also affect the suitability in relation to residents making representations about the centre affecting their use and enjoyment of their land, or vehicles causing an obstruction.

Operating centres are subject to review as to their continued suitability at five-yearly intervals – at the TC's discretion.

Licence Application

Applications for O-Licences are made using VOL and are based on where the operator keeps their vehicles. The application will be by the relevant TC for each Traffic Area in which the operator has vehicles based. These bases will be the operating centres for the vehicles. One O-Licence will be sufficient to cover any number of vehicles operating at one centre and any number of operating centres in any one Traffic Area. If operating centres are required in different Traffic Areas then separate O-Licences will be required for each Traffic Area. (A list of Traffic Area Office addresses is to be found in Appendix I.)

Undertakings

During the application process, applicants make a number of commitments – undertakings – concerning the minimum standards that they have agreed to maintain.

The undertakings relate to running a compliant, safe and fair operation. If at some time during the licensed period the TC finds that these undertakings have not been fulfilled, they may revoke, suspend or curtail the licence. The basis on which the applicant makes the undertakings is that they promise the following:

I, or the licensed operator, undertake to make proper arrangements so that:

1 the laws relating to the driving and operation of vehicles used under this licence are observed;

2 the rules on drivers' hours and tachographs are observed, proper records are kept and these are made available on request;

3 vehicles and trailers are not overloaded;

4 vehicles operate within speed limits;

5 vehicles and trailers, including hired vehicles and trailers, are kept in a fit and serviceable condition;

6 drivers report promptly any defects or symptoms of defects that could prevent the safe operation of vehicles and/or trailers, and that any defects are recorded in writing;

7 records are kept (for 15 months) of all driver reports which record defects, all safety inspections, routine maintenance and repairs to vehicles, and that these are made available on request;

8 in respect of each operating centre specified, the number of vehicles and the number of trailers kept there will not exceed the maximum numbers authorized at each operating centre (which will be noted on the licence);

9 an unauthorized operating centre is not used in any Traffic Area.

10 Furthermore, I will notify the TC of any convictions against myself, or the company, business partner(s), the company directors, nominated transport manager/s named in this application, or employees or agents of the applicant for this licence and, if the licence is issued, convictions against the licence holder or employees or agents of the licence holder.

11 I will ensure that the TC is notified within 28 days of any other changes, for example a change to the proposed maintenance arrangements, a change in the financial status of the licence holder (eg if placed in liquidation or receivership), or a change to limited company status or partnership, that might affect the licence, if issued.

For standard licence holders only:

1 I must be able to prove that I have a formal arrangement for access at all times to at least one vehicle registered or in circulation in GB. This could be by specifying a vehicle for use under an O-Licence or by demonstrating on request that I (the

licence holder) have a vehicle available – so vehicles may be either wholly owned or held under a hire purchase, hire/leasing arrangement or other type of formal arrangement.

2 I have an establishment in GB with premises in which I keep core business documents. These include (as a minimum) accounting and personnel management documents and data on driving time and rest. I understand that the use of a PO box or third-party address is not permitted.

Nominating Transport Managers

Applicants must list all of the transport managers they propose to name on the licence. This must include their personal details and provide information about other employments and details of convictions. They should also submit a signed contract of employment in order to confirm their employment. The transport manager's original proof of professional competence must accompany the application.

There are a minimum number of hours that must be spent by a nominated transport manager in order for them to be able to satisfy the TC that they have control over the fleet or fleets under their charge:

Vehicles	Guideline hours (per week)
2 or less	2–4
3–5	4–8
6–10	8–12
11–14	12–20
15–29	20–30
30 and above	30 full-time*
More than 50	Full-time and additional assistance is required

NB: Additional hours may be required for fleets with trailers.
*When a single person is in control of 30 or more vehicles, the TCs expect the operator to provide details on how the person will administer 'effective and continuous' control of the fleet.

Additional Information

The following supplementary information is required during the online application process:

- operating centre advertisement;
- vehicle and driver safety and compliance information;

- financial evidence;
- safety inspector details;
- licence history, convictions and penalties.

Environmental Information

If the TC receives representations from the local community following publication of the applicant's operating centre proposals in the local newspaper, the applicant is contacted for further information. The TC will consider the application in the light of information from both the applicant and the community.

Date for Applications

Most O-Licence applications are processed within seven weeks (nine weeks if using GV79). These time periods are not guaranteed and it may take longer, and applicants should be aware that it is illegal to start operating vehicles until their licence has actually been granted. Where there is an urgent need to start operations before a licence is granted through the normal processes, application can be made to the TC for an interim licence (see below), although the granting of an interim licence is unlikely if the applicant is unable to show any previous experience of having held, or holding, an O-Licence.

Offences while Applications Are Pending

Applicants for licences have a duty to advise the TC if, in the period of time between the application being submitted and it being dealt with by the TC, they are convicted of a relevant offence or declared bankrupt, etc, which they would have had to include on the application form had the conviction, etc, been made before the application was made. Failure to notify the TC is an offence and it could jeopardize any licence subsequently granted.

Advertising of Applications

Applicants for O-Licences who are seeking a new licence, or variation of an existing licence, are required to arrange for publication of an advertisement (following a specified format to contain the necessary information for potential environmental representors – see Figure 1.1) in a local newspaper (or newspapers). If more than one operating centre is specified in the application, separate advertisements must be placed for each in the respective local newspapers. The sole purpose of the advertisement is to give local residents an opportunity to make representations against proposals to use a particular place as a goods vehicle operating centre.

Figure 1.1   Format which must be used for O-Licence newspaper advertisements

Advertisement	**Goods Vehicle Operator's Licence**

Your name (name of operator)   ►

Your trading name (if any)   ►

trading as _____

Your full correspondence address   ►
(as stated in Section 1)

of _____

Full address of first operating centre   ►
including postcode. If there is a unit
number you must also include this.
This must be the same as the
address given in Section 10.

is applying for a licence to use

Enter the total number of vehicles   ►
and trailers to be kept at this
address.   These must match the
numbers given in Section 10.

as an operating centre for _____ goods vehicles
and _____ trailers

If you are applying for two operating   ►
centres and the same newspaper
can be used for both, you should
enter the details here.

and to use

If you are only putting one operating
centre in this advert then you
should strike through this section.

as an operating centre for _____ goods vehicles
and _____ trailers

All advertisements must finish with   ►
this section and you must not
amend any of the wording
otherwise you will have to place a
fresh advertisement.

Owners or occupiers of land (including buildings)
near the operating centre(s) who believe that their
use or enjoyment of that land would be affected
should make written representations to the Traffic
Commissioner at Hillcrest House, 386 Harehills
Lane, Leeds, LS9 6NF, stating their reasons, within
21 days of this notice. Representors must at the
same time send a copy of their representations to
the applicant at the address given at the top of this
notice. A Guide to Making Representations is
available from the Traffic Commissioner's office.

The advertisement need appear only once but it must be published not more than 21 days before and not more than 21 days after the licence application is made. There is no specified minimum or maximum size requirement for the advertisement but the TCs advise that it 'should not be too small and should be easy to read'.

Normally the advertisement will appear in the public or official notices section of the newspaper.

Proof that the advertisement has appeared – and is published correctly (which many are not) – must be included in the application.

Schedule 4 Application Procedure

This procedure can be used by a TC to allow an operating centre to be accepted without the need to put an advert in a local paper. This would apply, for example, when transferring an operating centre currently on one O-Licence to another.

However, there are particular circumstances that must be taken into consideration. These include:

- The operating centre is an existing, properly authorized centre being given up by the original operator.
- The new operator must use it on the same terms as the original licence holder.
- The applicant may specify only up to the total number of vehicles already specified at the operating centre of the original operator.
- Any conditions that apply to the operating centre concerned are transferred with it.

Such approval of the Schedule 4 procedure is allowed at the discretion of the TC.

Interim Licences

The TC may grant an interim licence pending a decision on the full licence application. A grant of an interim licence should not be taken as a guarantee that a full-term licence will be granted by the TC. A licence would not be granted to an applicant for a standard O-Licence if they cannot demonstrate professional competence. Neither will a grant of an interim licence normally be considered before the statutory 21-day waiting period for environmental representations and objections has expired.

Interim licences are not granted for any fixed period. Normally they remain in force until the TC has made their decision on the grant of a full licence or, alternatively, until they are revoked. Applications are made using VOL.

Duration of Licences

Operators' licences are valid indefinitely and remain so unless the operator contravenes the terms under which the licence was granted, or fails to renew or pay the necessary fees by the due dates. Under normal circumstances the only reason for making a new application, and being subject to the risk of objection or environmental representation, is when a major variation of a licence is necessary in order to add to the number of authorized vehicles or to change an existing, or to add a new, operating centre on the licence.

Licence Fees and Discs

Application fees and administrative charges:

Application fee for a licence (GV79) or for a major (publishable) variation (GV81)	£257 (Payment to accompany application)
Fee payable for the issue of a licence	£401 (Payment within 15 working days of issue)
Charge for the continuation of an existing licence	£401 (Payment before the end of the month preceding the end of the five-year period)
Fee payable for the issue of an interim licence or direction	£68 (Payment within 15 working days of issue)
Major change to a licence	£257 (Payment to accompany application)

All fees paid are *non-refundable*.

Termination of Licences for Unpaid Fees

Failure to pay any of the fees will result in a licence being automatically terminated from the date on which the fee was due. In this event, the vehicle operation will have to cease and a new licence will have to be applied for before recommencing is permitted.

Licence Discs

O-Licence discs, issued on the grant (or variation) of a licence, must be displayed on the vehicle (normally on the windscreen) in a clearly visible position and in a water-proof container. Licence discs are coloured to differentiate between restricted and standard licences and between standard national and standard international licences:

- restricted licence – orange;
- standard licence, national – blue;
- standard licence, international – green;

- interim licence – issued in the colour appropriate to the type of licence applied for with the word 'INTERIM' across the face of the disc;
- copy discs – with the word 'COPY' in red across the face of the disc.

Goods vehicles' licence discs are not interchangeable between vehicles or between operators. They are valid only when displayed on the vehicle whose registration number is shown on the disc and when that vehicle is being 'used' by the named operator to whom it was issued. Heavy fines are imposed on offenders who loan and borrow discs (this is fraudulent use and is a serious offence); their own O-Licence may be jeopardized and the vehicle insurance could be invalidated.

Licence Surrender/Termination

The O-Licence itself and all vehicle windscreen discs must be returned to the TC on the change of type, surrender or termination of an O-Licence.

EU Community Licences/UK Licences for the Community

All UK holders of standard international O-Licences are issued (automatically) with a UK Licence for the Community to be kept at their main place of business together with certified copies equalling the total number of vehicles authorized on their O-Licence (a certified copy must be carried on each vehicle when undertaking journeys from the UK to the EU and/or cross-border journeys within the EU) – more information on Community Licensing is in Chapter 25.

Maintenance Facilities/Arrangements

Satisfactory arrangements must be in place for maintaining vehicles in a safe and legal condition and for keeping maintenance records – more information is in Chapter 16. Vehicles must also be subjected to safety inspections at regular intervals of time or mileage and any person carrying out the safety inspections must be capable of doing so to a professional standard.

O-Licence applicants must give details of their proposed periods between safety inspections and submit the documentation that will be used for the inspections. In general terms, inspections should be based on a time interval only, but high-mileage vehicles, older vehicles or vehicles undertaking arduous operations may also be considerations for the TC. A minimum safety inspection frequency of six weeks is mandatory for vehicle trailers which are more than 12 years old, irrespective of either light work or low annual mileage. The TCs also seek assurances that operators are using a driver defect reporting system and planning inspections for a forward look of six months.

Drivers' Hours and Records

The TC will consider whether there are satisfactory arrangements for ensuring that the law relating to drivers' hours and records (including tachographs) will be complied with.

Overloading

The TC will want to be sure that arrangements are made to prevent the overloading of vehicles and that vehicle weight limits in general will be observed.

Professional Competence Requirements

Applicants for a standard O-Licence must be professionally competent. This may be the applicant themselves or an employee holding a Certificate of Professional Competence. The named professionally competent person must be:

- genuinely linked to the undertaking – ie being a direct employee, a director or a shareholder (ie internal transport manager), or engaged under contract (ie external transport manager);
- carrying out the functions of a transport manager in an adequate manner;
- able to prove that they have effective control over the vehicles under their charge;
- able to 'exercise continuous and effective management of the vehicles on a day-to-day basis'.

The key points that the TC will take account of are as follows:

- whether the nominated transport manager is 'internal' or 'external';
- the number of O-Licences that the transport manager will be responsible for (maximum of four);
- the amount of time that the external transport manager will spend carrying out their duties;
- the number of operating centres and authorized vehicles an external transport manager is responsible for, both on that licence and on any other licences;
- the location of the transport manager in relation to the O-Licence and the operating centres on that licence;
- any other employment or activities in which the nominated transport manager is engaged which may restrict their ability to devote sufficient time to the duties of a transport manager on that licence;
- the terms upon which the nominated transport manager is to be employed.

In order to further ensure that nominated transport managers carry out their duties effectively and in accordance with the law, a proposed transport manager's contract of employment form has been devised (see Figure 1.2), which must be completed by the O-Licence holder and the appointed transport manager as they may be required to produce it 'upon request'.

Number of Qualified Persons

There is no restriction under the regulations (see Chapter 2) on the number of people in a transport department or organization who may be professionally competent and consequently hold certificates of competence.

In determining how many qualified persons must be named on a standard O-Licence, the TC will take account of the management structure of applicant firms and the size of the fleet (see above), but generally there will need to be a minimum of one qualified person per O-Licence. The TC may require the names of more qualified persons to be specified if they consider it appropriate in view of a division of responsibilities for the operation of vehicles under the licence, or if vehicles specified on the licence are located at different operating centres within the Traffic Area.

Part-Time (ie 'External') Managers

Increasingly, TCs are questioning the role of part-time and agency-provided professionally competent transport managers. There is concern that such managers are not in a position to meet the statutory requirement for managers whereby they should have 'continuous and effective responsibility' for the fleet for which they are named.

Travel

The distance that a part-time transport manager needs to travel to each site they may be responsible for is also a factor as the TC needs to ensure that they are able to attend each centre within a reasonable time, if required.

Financial Standing

In addition to these points, the TC is required to establish details of the applicant's financial standing (a bank statement, a bank manager's letter of reference or an accountant's certificate of solvency may be requested, for example, or other evidence of the availability of funds) because this has a bearing on the applicant's ability to operate and maintain vehicles in a safe condition and in compliance with the law (see also the section Assessment of Financial Standing). While considering an applicant's financial status for this purpose, the TC also has the authority to call for the services of an assessor from a panel of persons appointed by the Secretary of State for Transport, if appropriate, due to the complexity of the financial structure of the applicant's business or affairs.

Figure 1.2 Transport manager – contract of employment

TRANSPORT MANAGER – CONTRACT OF EMPLOYMENT

Surname	First name(s)	Date of birth

Home address

(Postcode)

Address of place of work (if not the same as operating centre)

(Postcode)

Which operating centres will the nominated TM be responsible for?

All? Yes ☐ No ☐

If no, please list individual operating centres (by first address line only)

How many hours a week is the TM contracted to work?

Will the TM be responsible for vehicles on any other licences (in *any* Traffic Area)?

Yes ☐ No ☐

If yes, please list details below

Licence number	Vehicles/trailers authorized	Hours worked per week

Declaration: In accordance with the requirements of the Goods Vehicles (Licensing of Operators) Act 1995, we declare that .... will carry out all necessary checks on the operation of the licence holder's business. We also confirm that we understand the requirements placed on both of us by the above Act.

We understand that these responsibilities include:

- the method of control of drivers' hours;
- the maintenance of the licence holder's vehicles, including the inspection of vehicles at the appropriate time, the action taken to remedy defects found and the recording of these events;
- the reporting and recording of vehicle defects by drivers;
- the method of compilation and the accuracy of all records kept;
- the making of arrangements to ensure that the licence holder's vehicle/s are not overloaded.

Signature (Licence Holder)   **date**

Signature (Transport Manager)   **date**

Suitability of Operating Centres

An operating centre is defined as 'a place where a vehicle is usually kept'. TCs must inquire into and be satisfied that the place or places to be used as vehicle operating centres are suitable, cause no danger to the public, are environmentally acceptable and sufficiently large to accommodate all the vehicles authorized on the licence (or requested in the application). Local residents have rights (as described below) to make representations about the environmental consequences of the use of places for transport depots or vehicle operating centres and the TCs are bound to listen to these representations and make appropriate decisions about the application depending on the weight of the argument on either side – residents or operator. In particular, the TC, when considering the suitability of premises, will take account of the following:

- whether danger to the public may be caused where vehicles first join (or last leave) a public road;
- whether danger to the public may be caused on roads (other than public roads) along which vehicles are driven between the operating centre and a public road;
- the nature or use of any other land in the vicinity of the operating centre and the effect which the granting of the licence would be likely to have on the environment of that land;
- how much granting a licence which is to materially change the use of an existing (or previously used) operating centre would harm the environment of the land in the vicinity of the operating centre;
- for a new operating centre, any planning permission (or planning application) relating to the operating centre or the land in its vicinity;
- the number, type and size of the authorized vehicles (including trailers) which will use the operating centre;
- the parking arrangements for authorized vehicles within and near to the operating centre;
- nature and times of use of the operating centre;
- nature and times of use of equipment at the operating centre;
- how many vehicles would be entering or leaving the operating centre, and how often.

Reviews of Operating Centres

TCs are given powers to review all operating centres, normally at five-yearly intervals counting from the date when the licence was first issued – in certain circumstances more frequent reviews may be carried out. Where the TC decides to review an operating centre they must give two months' notice in writing. Once the period has passed for the TC making a decision to review an operating centre, the licence holder can rest assured that they are safe for another five years, unless they operate outside the terms of their licence, fail to pay fees or apply for a major variation of the licence.

When carrying out the review of a centre, which will most likely be as a result of written complaints by local residents (who may now write in at any time rather than just when a licence application/variation advertisement appears), the TC will be concerned to ensure that it remains environmentally suitable, meets road safety considerations and can accommodate all the vehicles authorized on the licence, or that their parking causes no adverse effect on the local environment.

When carrying out the review, the TC may decide that no action is required, but they have powers to act if necessary. For example, if an operating centre is found to be unsuitable they may attach conditions or vary any existing conditions for road safety or environmental reasons. However, the licence holder is given the opportunity to make representations about the effect that such conditions would have on their business before they are attached. The TC also has the power to remove an operating centre from a licence for non-environmental reasons (eg on the basis of road safety considerations), or because the operating centre is environmentally unsuitable by reason (only) of the parking of vehicles used under the licence at or near the centre.

Applications and Decisions

When an application for a new O-Licence or a variation of an existing licence is received by the TC, details of the application (ie the name of the applicant and the number of vehicles and trailers included in the application) will be published in a Traffic Area notice called *Applications and Decisions (As and Ds)*. As its name implies, this notice will also contain details of licences granted by the TC and details of public inquiries to be held. The notice is published either weekly or fortnightly by all Traffic Areas and may be inspected at Traffic Area Offices or purchased as an individual copy or on a regular basis. It is by means of this notice that statutory objectors (see below) are able to know when applications have been made, against which they may wish to object. They can do this within 21 days of publication of the relevant As and Ds notice. As and Ds are also available for download from the GOV. UK website by typing in 'Applications and Decisions'.

Objections to the Application

Applications for O-Licences are open to statutory objection by certain bodies listed below (and only by these listed bodies – no other individual or organization has this statutory right).

Objections to applications can only be made on the grounds that the applicant does not meet the essential qualifying criteria for the grant of a licence. The bodies may also object on environmental grounds (for example that the operating centre is environmentally unsuitable).

The bodies which may make statutory objection to an O-Licence application are:

- the police;
- a local authority (but not a parish council or community council);
- a planning authority;
- the British Association of Removers (BAR);
- Logistics UK;
- the Road Haulage Association (RHA);
- the GMB;
- the National Union of Rail, Maritime and Transport Workers (RMT);
- the Transport and General Workers' Union (TGWU);
- the Union of Shop, Distributive and Allied Workers (USDAW);
- the United Road Transport Union (URTU).

If any of these bodies do make a statutory objection they are required to send a copy of their objection to the applicant and one to the TC (within 21 days of the publication of details of the application). Failure to send a copy to the applicant renders the objection invalid.

Representations by Local Residents

Local residents are able to make representations individually against O-Licence applications and variations on environmental grounds. Group action is not permitted (although a group of individual representors may appoint a joint spokesperson or legal representative to put forward their case), nor is representation by any environmental pressure group, political or other campaigning body. Similarly, parish councils have no right of objection unless they own/occupy land within the vicinity of an operating centre, in which case they may make representation as the owner/occupier of the land.

The grounds for representation include noise, vibration, fumes and visual intrusion, but could include obstruction. They do not include road safety matters. The grounds must be stated precisely in the written representation.

One of the facts that has been difficult to establish in connection with this is a definition of the term 'within the vicinity'. It has been shown that residents living along an access road to a vehicle operating centre can be considered to be in the vicinity and adverse environmental effects of vehicles travelling along the road could be taken account of by the TC in consideration of any environmental representations against a licence application. Each TC is left to make their own determination of whether a representor lives 'within the vicinity', but as a general rule if a representor can see, hear or smell a vehicle operating centre from their property then they will be considered to be 'in the vicinity'.

Those wishing to make a representation must do so in writing (or have their solicitor do so on their behalf), within a period of 21 days from the date of publication of the advertisement, to the TC at the Traffic Area Office address given in the advertisement. They must also send a copy of their representation to the licence applicant. Their letter must clearly state the 'particulars' of the matters forming the basis of their representation so that both the TC and the licence applicant may be fully aware of the specific grounds on which the representation is made. Failure to be specific as to the facts in this letter, failure to send a copy to the licence applicant or failure to submit the representation within the specified timescale will render the representation invalid.

Normal action is for the TC to call a public inquiry (PI) to give all parties an opportunity to make their cases. Both sides submit evidence and make statements to the presiding TC who will often make a ruling at the time but, in some cases, may need time to clarify details or consider wider issues.

While representors have no direct right of appeal should their case against use of the operating centre fail, they are able to join together with any statutory objectors in making an appeal. Operators do have a right of appeal through the Transport Tribunal (see later). The rights of 'representation' are not to be confused with the rights of objection, described later.

Grant or Refusal of a Licence

The TC has power to grant an O-Licence to an applicant if they consider that all the necessary requirements are met. Alternatively, they may refuse to grant a licence or grant a licence for fewer vehicles or operating centres than the number applied for if they doubt the ability of the applicant to comply with the law with more vehicles, to properly maintain more vehicles or to adequately finance the operation of more vehicles. Environmental conditions can be imposed on any licence granted and the name put forward for the professionally competent person (in the case of standard licence applications) can be refused if it is believed that the person is not of good repute.

Licence Grant with Conditions

The case made by those raising valid environmental representations may influence the TC either to refuse the application altogether on the grounds that the operating centre is not environmentally suitable or, alternatively, to grant the licence but with environmental conditions attached. To prevent or minimize any adverse effects on the environment, the TC may place conditions or restrictions on the scope of the licence, including:

- the number, type and size of authorized vehicles (including trailers) at any operating centre for maintenance or parking;
- parking arrangements for authorized vehicles (including trailers) at or in the vicinity of the centre(s);
- the times when the centre(s) may be used for maintenance or movement of any authorized vehicle;
- how authorized vehicles enter and leave the operating centre(s) (including routes used).

As an alternative to imposing environmental conditions on the licence, the TC may seek undertakings from the operator that they will follow certain practices in order to reduce environmental disturbance of local residents (eg control the number of vehicle movements into and out of the centre, times of operation, etc).

Licence holders who find they have breached environmental conditions on their licence through unforeseen circumstances must notify the TC.

Where operators find that environmental conditions placed on their licence prove too onerous to allow them to run their businesses effectively, they should apply to the TC to vary the conditions rather than ignore the conditions and become liable to a licence penalty.

Additional Vehicles

Seeking a Margin

An applicant can request authorization for any additional vehicles during the licence period. Doing this at the point of application, the operator saves the problems of making a new application when wanting to add or hire-in vehicles on a temporary basis to meet trading peaks.

If additional vehicles were requested and the request was granted at the time of making the original application, the operator will have a 'margin' for extra vehicles on the licence. The TC will need to be notified (online through VOL) from the date of actually acquiring the additional vehicles – not the date of putting them into service.

- Authorized vehicles – the maximum number of vehicles/trailers that the licence is actually granted to cover.

- Specified vehicles – the actual vehicles which the operator has in possession and which are specified on the licence by registration number.
- Margin – the difference between the numbers of authorized and specified vehicles on the licence; in other words, the vehicles still to be acquired by the operator whether on a permanent or a temporary basis.

Hired Vehicles

If an operator plans to hire extra vehicles without drivers during the currency of a licence, whether for a short period (a day, a few days or even one or two weeks) or on a long-term contract, they must be covered by the operator's O-Licence and the operator will need to have applied for a sufficient margin of additional vehicles on the licence to cover these. If vehicles are hired within the margin, the TC must be notified and an O-Licence disc obtained for display on the vehicle.

Number of Extra Vehicles

When making the request for additional vehicles on the initial application for an O-Licence, the number which may be requested is not limited in any way but it is recommended that it should be in reasonable proportion to the number of vehicles already operated (or initially required) and, most importantly, it should only be of a number which the applicant can maintain, and prove they can maintain (both physically and financially), on the same basis as the remainder of the fleet. If the request for additional vehicles relates to vehicles that are to be hired rather than owned, it must be remembered that the person who hires a self-drive vehicle is fully responsible for the mechanical condition of the vehicle in so far as safety and legal requirements are concerned.

Replacement Vehicles

If for some reason an authorized vehicle ceases to be used, the TC must be advised of the fact, but if at that time or later another vehicle is acquired to replace it, the operator must use VOL to make the change within one month of *acquiring* the replacement vehicle. This means within one month from the date of the vehicle coming into the operator's possession. Vehicles which are not removed from the licence (even when standing in a yard or workshop smashed or cannibalized) are still counted as specified vehicles and cannot be replaced by others within the authorized number on the licence until they are removed by notifying the TC. The windscreen discs from the vehicle(s) being replaced need to be physically returned to the Central Licensing Office.

Surrender of Licence

VOL is also used when an operator wishes to surrender their licence. This requires the operator to make a declaration to that effect.

Licence Variation

An application must be made through VOL (allowing seven weeks' notice) if an O-Licence holder wishes to:

- change the type of licence held or to notify a change;
- change the nominated transport manager;
- amend the total number of vehicles/trailers authorized;
- change operating centres (ie by adding another centre or stopping the use of a centre); or
- remove a condition or undertaking recorded on the licence (including conditions on the use of operating centres).

These changes all involve the need to advertise the application in local newspapers, as described in the previous section Advertising of Applications, and a copy of the published advertisement must be uploaded to VOL. Information about vehicle maintenance arrangements or change to any of the environmental conditions or undertakings is required. Reasons must be given as to why this change or removal is requested.

Transfer of Vehicles

If a vehicle is transferred from the Traffic Area in which it is licensed to another Traffic Area for more than three months, it must be removed from the original licence and specified on a licence in the new Traffic Area. Transfers for less than three months are permitted without the need for notification to the TC provided an O-Licence with a sufficient margin to cover the transferred vehicles is already held.

If the operator does not hold an O-Licence in the other Traffic Area, or holds a licence in the area but it does not have a sufficient margin to accommodate the transferred vehicles, then an application for a new licence or a variation of the existing licence must be made to the TC for that Traffic Area.

Notification of Changes

Licence holders should notify the TC through VOL, within 28 days, of any changes in the legal entity of their business, such as a change of name, address, ownership, if a new partnership has been formed, a limited company formed or the constitution of the partnership has been changed. The TC must also be informed if the proprietor or persons concerned in the business die, or if the business becomes bankrupt or goes into liquidation.

Other changes which must be notified in writing are those in maintenance facilities or arrangements and any breach of environmental conditions which the TC placed on the licence. Failure to notify the TC of such changes can have the same result as making false statements or failing to fulfil intentions stated in the original application – namely the risk of licence suspension, curtailment or revocation.

The TC expects to be notified of some changes 'as soon as possible'; other changes may be subject to a 28-day notification period. Operators are advised to seek clarification on timescales for any change they intend to make, or have just made, from their local Traffic Area Office or by contacting the DVSA customer service centre.

Subsidiary Companies

A holding company can include in its O-Licence application vehicles belonging to any subsidiary company in which it owns more than a 50 per cent shareholding. But associate companies (ie where the shareholding arrangement is less than 50 per cent) owned by the same holding company cannot have vehicles specified on each other's licences and separate divisions of a company are not permitted to hold separate licences unless they are separate entities in law.

The vehicles of any subsidiary company acquired during the currency of the holding company's O-Licence can, if desired, be included in the holding company's licence either within its existing licence margin or by a change to the licence on VOL.

Temporary Derogation

Should the nominated professionally competent person die or become legally incapacitated, there are provisions in place to enable a standard O-Licence to remain in force for up to six months to allow a replacement person to be appointed. This may be extended by a further three months if the TC feels it is appropriate.

The TC may also defer revocation of, or refusal to grant, a licence in the event of the death or incapacity of a nominated professionally competent person.

Should the licence holder die or become legally incapacitated, another person may be authorized to carry on the business during the changeover period.

The TC must be notified of any cases 'as soon as possible'. The person carrying on the business will be considered to be the licence holder while the required changes are made.

Production of O-Licences

Licence holders must produce their O-Licence (form OL 1 and vehicle disc form OL 2) for examination when required to do so by the police, DVSA officers or the TC. The holder has 14 days in which to present the licence, either at one of the operating centres authorized on the licence or at their principal place of business in the Traffic Area. In the case of production to the police, this can be at a police station of the holder's choice, also within 14 days.

TCs' Powers of Review

TCs have statutory powers (under the Goods Vehicles (Licensing of Operators) Act 1995, section 36) to review, vary or revoke any decision they have previously made to grant or refuse:

- an application for an O-Licence;
- an application for the variation of an O-Licence requiring publication.

These powers to review a previous decision apply only in the following circumstances:

- if, within two months, the TC has given notice to the applicant or the licence holder that they intend to review the decision;
- if, within two months, a person with interest in the decision has requested the TC to review it;
- where neither of the above situations applies, if the TC considers that there are exceptional circumstances to justify a review.

Normally the TC will only decide to review previous decisions where they are satisfied that a procedural requirement was not complied with in making the decision; for example, where an environmental representation or statutory objection was overlooked, or a decision was made under the wrong section of the Act.

The authority for TCs to review their own decisions eliminates many of the situations which would have previously required appeal to the Transport Tribunal.

Penalties against O-Licences

Penalties

The maximum fine which may currently be imposed by a court for running vehicles without an O-Licence is £5,000. Failure to notify the TC of certain information about relevant convictions incurred by the licence holder or by a professionally competent transport manager can result in fines of up to £2,500.

The TCs also have the power to revoke, suspend or curtail an O-Licence for the following reasons:

- contravention by the licence holder of the provision, in the case of standard O-Licences, regarding professional competence requirements;
- failure to notify the TC of changes in the business;
- convictions for failure to maintain vehicles in a fit and serviceable condition;
- contravention of speed limits, overloading or offences in connection with loading or unloading vehicles in restricted parking or waiting areas;
- failure to ensure that drivers are correctly licensed;
- convictions relating to the use of rebated (duty-free) fuel oil in vehicles (see Chapter 8);
- failure to keep records relating to vehicle inspections and repairs and driver defect reports;
- falsely stating facts on applications for O-Licences and not fulfilling statements of intent or environmental conditions placed on the licence;
- if the licence holder becomes bankrupt or, in the case of a company, goes into liquidation;
- if a place not listed on the licence is used as a vehicle operating centre.

Offences are committed, for which prosecution and a court appearance may follow, if a:

- windscreen licence disc is not displayed;
- change of address is not notified;
- licence is not produced for examination on request;
- duplicate windscreen disc is not returned if the original is found;
- disc is not returned when a vehicle is disposed of;
- subsidiary company featured on a holding company licence is disposed of and the TC is not advised.

The TCs can take action against HGV drivers caught speeding. They can impose a driving licence suspension or penalties on HGV licence categories and penalize O-Licence holders whose drivers persistently and wilfully exceed speed limits. Evidence is obtained during routine enforcement checking of tachograph records, where recordings showing frequent instances of driving above 100 kph are clear evidence of breach of the 60 mph maximum speed limit for vehicles exceeding 7.5 tonnes maximum laden weight.

The licence holder may be called to a PI to explain why the offences occurred and what corrective action is being taken. The TC may issue a warning or impose a penalty. This could be suspension, curtailment or revocation.

Curtailment (vehicles removed from a licence) is the most commonly imposed penalty and this implies removal of one or more authorized vehicles from the licence for any period up to the expiry of the licence. Suspension involves suspension of the whole licence and this may be combined with premature termination so the TC can review the whole operation under the provisions for consideration of a new licence application. As with premature termination of an existing licence, the need to apply for a new licence places the operator at risk of objection and environmental representation. The TC can direct that a vehicle on a licence which has been suspended or limited may not be used by another operator for a maximum of six months during the period of suspension.

Revocation of Licences for Smuggling and People Trafficking

Licence holders convicted of smuggling or people trafficking risk losing their O-Licences. Where O-Licensed vehicles are involved in cross-Channel smuggling or people-trafficking activities, HM Revenue & Customs passes details of the operators involved to the TCs for action, which could include revocation of licences.

Tough new measures to combat smuggling include financial penalties levied in order for an operator to recover confiscated vehicles, and permanent confiscation in the case of repeated smuggling offences. Drivers caught smuggling or people trafficking may also lose their driving licences and in serious cases individuals risk a prison sentence on conviction.

NB: An HM Revenue & Customs hotline is available for reporting excise duty, fraud and smuggling: 0800 788 887. Alternatively, it is possible to call Crimestoppers on 0800 555111.

Revocation of Licences for Using Unlicensed Sub-contractors

It is essential for O-Licensed hauliers to check carefully that any sub-contractor used is correctly licensed (as well as determining that they are using roadworthy vehicles and comply with the law on such matters as drivers' hours and tachographs). The use of an unlicensed operator may result in prosecution for aiding, abetting, counselling or procuring that operator to use a vehicle for hire or reward without an O-Licence. This is a criminal offence carrying a maximum fine of £5,000 on conviction and could result in loss of the principal contractor's O-Licence.

National Electronic Registers

One of the key provisions in Regulation 1072/2009/EC (Article 16) was the requirement for all EU member states to establish a National Electronic Register of data relating to road transport undertakings. In the UK this was undertaken by the DVSA. The essential data in the register are as follows:

1 the name and legal form of the undertaking (ie whether sole trader, partnership or limited company);

2 the address of the business;

3 the names of the transport managers designated to meet the conditions of good repute and professional competence or, as appropriate, the name of a legal representative;

4 the type of authorization (ie O-Licence), the number of vehicles it covers and, where appropriate, the serial number of the Community licence and of the certified copies;

5 the number, category and type of serious infringements, as referred to in Article 6(1)(2) – see the Good Repute section earlier in this chapter, which have resulted in a conviction or penalty during the last two years;

6 the name of any person declared to be unfit to manage the transport activities of an undertaking, as long as the good repute of that person has not been re-established, and the rehabilitation measures applicable (eg additional training).

The relevant data above must be available upon request or directly accessible to all competent authorities of EU member states and the requested information must be provided within 30 working days of receipt of the request.

Data concerning an undertaking whose O-Licence has been suspended or withdrawn must remain in the National Electronic Register for two years from the expiry of the suspension or the withdrawal of the licence, and must thereafter be removed immediately.

Protection of Personal Data

Data protection is governed by the Information Commissioner's Office (ICO) and any organization that holds or processes personal information must comply with the

Data Protection Act 2018, which is the UK's implementation of the General Data Protection Regulation (GDPR). GDPR applies to personal data held electronically and paper records.

Organizations have to ensure that personal data are gathered legally and under strict conditions, and those who collect and manage them are obliged to protect them from misuse and exploitation, as well as to respect the rights of data owners – or face penalties for not doing so. GDPR applies to any organization operating within the EU (and those outside of the EU that offer goods or services to customers or businesses in the EU).

For more information go to ICO.ORG.UK.

The Upper Transport Tribunal

Inquiries and Appeals

A public inquiry (PI) enables a TC to seek more information prior to determining whether a licence should be granted. In the event of a representation on environmental grounds or an objection being made, the TC may hold a PI at which the parties (applicant, objectors or those making representations) will have an opportunity to state their case further. If the application is refused in whole or in part, or if environmental conditions are attached to a licence, the applicant has rights of appeal against the TC's decision to the Administrative Appeals Chamber of the Upper Tribunal, using form UT12, within 28 days of the decision being made.

If the appellant is not made aware of the TC's decision within 21 days because the decision is not published for some reason, the appeal must be received by the Upper Tribunal within 49 days after the actual date the appellant receives the decision.

An existing licence will remain in force while an appeal is being heard and the TC may allow a revoked or suspended licence to continue during this time. If the TC refuses this, the Tribunal can be asked to allow it to do so.

Statutory objectors also have a right of appeal to the Tribunal if an application for a licence is granted and they still feel that their objection is valid. Those individuals making representations on environmental grounds have *no* similar right of appeal if their case fails.

It should be noted that the Tribunal is the *only* source of appeal in regard to O-Licence matters.

Public Inquiries

PIs are presided over by the TC or their deputy and are open to members of the general public, other operators, interested parties and the press.

TCs may restrict general attendance at a PI to protect an operator's business, particularly in regard to personal matters, commercially sensitive information and other information obtained in confidence.

Verbal evidence is given to the TC by the applicant or by their legal representative if they have one. Any advice, if it is required, should be sought from an experienced transport lawyer who fully understands the legal basis of the whole licensing system as well as the intricacies of the PI system.

TCs must give at least 21 days' written notice of public inquiries both to operators and to other parties entitled to attend, and similar notice if they intend to vary the time or place of the inquiry. However, given the consent of all parties, this requirement can be varied.

Appeals to the Administrative Appeals Chamber of the Upper Tribunal

The Tribunal is a completely independent judicial body supported administratively by the Ministry of Justice. The Tribunal is made up of legally qualified legal members and non-legal members, who have experience in transport operations and its law and procedure.

An appeal on form UT12 for England and Wales should be sent to:

Upper Tribunal
Administrative Appeals Chamber
5th Floor
7 Rolls Building
Fetter Lane
London
EC4A 1NL
Telephone: 020 7071 5662
Email: adminappeals@hmcts.gsi.gov.uk

An appeal on form UT12 for Scotland should be sent to:

Upper Tribunal
Administrative Appeals Chamber
George House
126 George Street
Edinburgh
EH2 4HH
Telephone: 0131 271 4310
Email: UTAACmailbox@scotland.gsi.gov.uk

For Northern Ireland the details are:

Tribunal Hearing Centre
2nd Floor
Royal Courts of Justice
Chichester Street
Belfast
BT1 3JF
Telephone: 028 9072 4823
Email: tribunalsunit@courtsni.gov.uk

Appeals may be made against a TC's decision to refuse to grant an O-Licence if:

- they attach environmental conditions to an O-Licence;
- a licence is granted authorizing fewer vehicles than the number applied for;
- a licence is granted for a shorter period than that applied for;
- an existing licence is withdrawn, suspended or prematurely terminated by the TC.

Should the decision not be published, or not be released to the appellant, after a period of 21 days following the date the decision was made, the appellant has a further 49 days to lodge an appeal.

Where a TC makes a disciplinary decision against an O-Licence (ie suspension, curtailment or revocation) and the licence holder wishes to appeal, they can apply for a 'stay' of the decision until the appeal is heard, in order to keep vehicles operating. Otherwise they would have to observe the decision irrespective of the consequences (financial and operational) on their business. An initial request for a 'stay' of the decision is made direct to the TC, but failing this an application must be made immediately to the Tribunal giving details of the decision and the reason for requesting the 'stay'. Application for a 'stay' of the decision cannot be made if there is no intention to appeal.

Appeals to the Tribunal must be in writing and should be sent to the Tribunal stating the decision against which the appeal is made, the grounds for the appeal, and the names and addresses of every person to whom a copy of the appeal has been sent. Advice and relevant forms can be obtained by contacting the relevant Tribunal at the address above or by downloading them from the HM Courts & Tribunals Service website.

Copies of the appeal must be sent to the TC and to all objectors if the appeal is being made by a licence applicant, or to the applicant if the appeal is being made by an objector to the decision.

Although the Tribunal has the powers and status of a High Court, its proceedings are conducted informally and appellants may represent themselves or be represented by any person they choose (there are no wigs and gowns, even for barristers present). However, in the best interests of the applicant, they should be legally represented at an appeal by a solicitor or barrister experienced in transport law to ensure that their case is fully and correctly made.

When an appeal is heard, the Tribunal examines the transcript of the PI or the TC's statement of their reasons for the decision against which the appeal is lodged and then may ask further questions of the applicant or their advocate. No oath has to be taken and there is no protection by privilege. The proceedings are open to the public and the press. Tribunal appeal decisions may be announced at the hearing or later. All parties will be sent a full statement of the decision usually within three weeks of the hearing.

Generally, Tribunal decisions will fall into one of three categories: either to uphold the TC's decision, to change the decision, or to refer the matter back to the TC with a direction that they should reconsider their decision but taking account of legal guidance from the Tribunal. In exceptional circumstances the Tribunal may review its decision subject to a request to do so made within 14 days of the appeal hearing. Decisions of the Tribunal are binding from the date they are given; in other words, they have immediate effect.

Further appeals against decisions of the Tribunal may be made to the Court of Appeal or the Court of Session in Scotland but only on points of law, not on the original decision of the TC or the subsequent ruling of the Tribunal. The address is:

The Civil Appeals Office
Room E307
3rd Floor East Block
The Royal Courts of Justice
Strand
London WC2A 2LL
Monday to Friday, 10 am to 4.30 pm
Telephone: 020 7947 6000

Information on applying to the Court of Session in Scotland is available under the Rules of the Court of Session, which can be found at: www.scotcourts.gov.uk.

No fees are payable in respect of appeals but costs may be awarded against frivolous, vexatious, improper or unreasonable appeals.

Further details of the appeals procedure can be found in a free publication giving guidance on appeals to the Tribunal, and can be downloaded from its website at www.justice.gov.uk/about/hmcts.

Northern Ireland Licensing

Goods vehicle operators in Northern Ireland do not need to obtain a short-term O-Licence prior to entry into Great Britain. Similarly, there is no need for Great

Britain operators to obtain a short-term licence prior to entry into Northern Ireland. A goods vehicle operating on a current O-Licence issued in Great Britain or a road freight O-Licence issued in Northern Ireland is permitted to carry goods throughout the UK.

Goods vehicles from Northern Ireland engaging in own-account operations for which a road freight O-Licence is required in the Province must, while operating in Great Britain, carry a document showing details of their load and route in Great Britain.

Vehicles based and registered in England, Wales and Scotland must comply with all the normal legal requirements (eg vehicle condition, excise duty, insurance and observance of traffic rules) set out in this *Handbook* when operating in Northern Ireland, but particularly so in regard to O-Licences (Chapter 1), professional competence (Chapter 2), drivers' hours and record-keeping regulations (Chapters 3 and 4), tachographs (Chapter 5), driver licensing and testing (Chapters 6 and 7) and plating and testing (Chapter 14). It should be noted that in regard to road traffic and road traffic offences there are differences between the Northern Ireland requirements and those on the British mainland. A separate edition of the *Highway Code* (new edition and e-edition, 2019) is published for Northern Ireland and is free to download at the nidirect.gov.uk website.

Vehicles based and operated in Northern Ireland now also benefit from VOL and are under the supervision of the Central Licensing Office in Leeds but must comply with the law as it applies in the Province, which is substantially similar to that applicable in the rest of the United Kingdom. Further information may be obtained from:

DfI Central Licensing Office
PO Box 180
Leeds
LS9 1BU
Telephone: 0300 200 7831 (NI Direct)
Email: niclo@dvsa.gov.uk

Conditions for Grant of O-Licence

Under the statutory requirements for the grant of a standard road freight O-Licence, an operator has to have premises in Northern Ireland where business documents are kept and which satisfy the issuing authority that the operator is:

- of good repute;
- of appropriate financial standing;

- professionally competent or employs a full-time manager who is professionally competent and of good repute;
- declaring all previous convictions and penalties.

The requirements of good repute and appropriate financial standing are as stated in detail in this chapter of this *Handbook*. The professional competence requirement in Northern Ireland is as explained in Chapter 2.

For a restricted licence in Northern Ireland the applicant only has to show evidence of good financial standing and declare all previous convictions and penalties.

The criteria relating to the holding of a licence, the validity of a licence (continuous) and most of the exemptions from licensing in Northern Ireland now align with those in the rest of the UK. The main difference is that the licensing regime is controlled and administered by the Department for Infrastructure (DfI) and not the DVSA.

Northern Ireland Penalties for Illegal Use

Making a false statement to obtain the grant of a road freight O-Licence or a road freight vehicle licence is an offence punishable on conviction by a fine or imprisonment for up to six months, or both. The O-Licence could also be suspended or revoked. Use of a motor vehicle on a road for the carriage of goods for reward without a road freight vehicle licence can result in a fine, which increases for subsequent convictions. Enforcement officers of the Northern Ireland Driver & Vehicle Agency (NIDVA) have been empowered to issue fixed penalty notices, some of which attract penalty points on driver licences, for certain driver and vehicle offences (see https://www.nidirect.gov.uk/information-and-services/motoring).

Use of Light Commercial Vehicles

While operators of Light Commercial Vehicles (LCV) are not subject to the O-Licence regime, they do have certain obligations. First, if they tow a trailer for hire and reward only with such a vehicle, the combined weight of both vehicle and trailer (if over 1,020 kg unladen) could exceed the 3.5 tonne weight threshold above which an O-Licence would be needed, and the provisions of the EU or British drivers' hours rules and the relevant record-keeping or tachograph requirements may apply (see Chapters 3, 4 and 5). Second, if they also operate (or plan to operate in the future) larger vehicles which are within the scope of an O-Licence, their conduct will be taken into account at application.

The TCs have made the point that when an operator applies to renew an O-Licence the TCs would consider any relevant convictions in respect of smaller vehicles belonging to the operator and could call the operator to a PI to explain why the O-Licence should not be revoked or curtailed. LCV operators still have to ensure that vehicles are not overloaded and that they are kept in safe mechanical order under other regulations; they must be tested annually after they become three years old (four years old in Northern Ireland). Drivers of these vehicles are required to observe the drivers' hours regulations.

Foreign Vehicles in the UK

Vehicles entering Great Britain from EU member states under valid Community licences do not need a UK O-Licence. Vehicles from certain non-EU countries where a bilateral agreement exists are exempt from the requirement to hold an O-Licence under the Goods Vehicles (Licensing of Operators) (Temporary Use in Great Britain) Regulations 1996 and this is likely to be the preferred option for all EU vehicles post-Brexit, providing we negotiate further bilateral agreements.

Other foreign vehicles entering Great Britain under an ECMT (European Conference of Ministers of Transport) permit do not need an O-Licence provided the permit is being carried on the vehicle.

Impounding of HGVs

Principally, impounding applies to vehicles used for hire or reward carriage without an O-Licence in force. Such vehicles are fitted with an immobilization device (ie a clamp), either on the spot or after removal to a more suitable site, and will be marked by an immobilization notice warning against any attempt to remove the device or move the vehicle except under proper authorization. Impounded vehicles may be returned to their owner provided specified conditions are met, and loads returned to their owner where title is established. Ultimately, however, without satisfactory compliance with requirements for the release of a vehicle and its load, they will be disposed of by sale or by destruction. Obstruction of authorized examiners in the course of vehicle impounding will lead to a fine at level 3 (maximum £1,000) on conviction.

An appeals procedure via the TCs initially and the Transport Tribunal subsequently allows operators to apply for the return of an impounded vehicle, although this may be unsuccessful depending on the circumstances.

Impounding of Rental/Hired Vehicles

The law is clear in that the regulations permit the seizing of vehicles hired, rented or leased to unlicensed operators. The TCs too have made it clear that such firms have a duty to ensure that any hiring arrangement they enter into in relation to relevant (ie over 3.5 tonne) vehicles is with an O-Licensed operator. The situation becomes more complex where a vehicle is leased to an unlicensed operator by a vehicle leasing company subject to a finance arrangement with a third party (such as a bank or loan company), which is therefore the statutory owner of the vehicle. In such cases, it becomes necessary for the legal owner to make application to the TC for the return of the vehicle on the basis that it, the legal owner, did not know that the vehicle had been, or was being, used without an O-Licence in accordance with the Goods Vehicles (Licensing of Operators) Act 1995 (section 2). An application for the return of a vehicle in these circumstances has to be made within 21 days of the notification of the impounding being published in the *London Gazette* or *Edinburgh Gazette* (in which all vehicle impoundings are published).

Professional Competence

02

The Certificate of Professional Competence (CPC) applies to both transport managers (Transport Manager CPC) and to HGV drivers (Driver CPC). However, these are two totally different qualifications.

Transport Manager CPC

Transport Manager CPC demonstrates competence of the legal, environmental, economic and operational requirements to run a safe and efficient goods vehicle operation, both nationally and internationally for hire and reward.

Under the Goods Vehicles (Licensing of Operators) Act 1995 (section 13 and schedule 3), operators wishing to carry goods for hire or reward or in connection with another business are required to demonstrate professional competence to hold a standard O-Licence. Own-account operators on a restricted O-LO-Licence are not required to demonstrate professional competence.

Standard O-Licence operators must nominate a person who is professionally competent and who is responsible for the licensed operation. This person must have 'continuous and effective responsibility' for the management of the transport operation and a direct reference to the O-Licence application. This person may be the applicant, if suitably qualified, or it may be a person employed as transport manager by the applicant and who is professionally competent.

A part-time transport manager is acceptable as long as the vehicle thresholds are not exceeded. The employment requirement does not necessarily mean that the person concerned must devote all of their working time to the transport management function; they may have other duties and responsibilities in the organization.

Where the fleet is 30 vehicles or more, the applicant is expected to explain how the fleet will be managed by describing the roles and responsibilities of the competent person.

Who May Become Professionally Competent?

Any individual may become professionally competent if they meet the necessary qualifying conditions or pass official examinations. A company or a corporate body cannot be classed as being professionally competent. There is no pre-qualifying standard and no requirement that the person should have any previous experience in the transport industry in any capacity. It is open to anybody to become professionally competent.

Once nominated, the transport manager must be engaged in 'effectively and continuously' managing the transport activities of the undertaking.

Proof of Professional Competence

Proof that a person is professionally competent and is therefore able to satisfy the requirements of the O-Licence is dependent on holding one (or more) of the following:

- an 'acquired rights' certificate (replaced 'grandfather rights' certificates in 2013);
- an official CPC examination pass certificate;
- a membership (or exemption) certificate from one of the recognized professional institutes, which confers exemption;
- a certificate issued by an EU member state which fulfils the 'mutual recognition' requirements of EC Directive 77/796 as amended by EC Directive 89/438 that the UK has decided to recognize.

Please visit https://ciltuk.org.uk for more information on the Transport Manager CPC.

Qualification by Exemption

New entrants to the industry may obtain the professional competence qualification if they satisfy certain exemption criteria.

The exemption qualifications are normally based on holding current and valid membership of one or more of a number of professional bodies at certain levels, as mentioned above.

For All Hire and Reward Operations

- Fellow or Member of the CILT by examination and/or formal accreditation in Road Freight Transport.
- Fellow, Member or Associate Member of the Society of Operations Engineers.
- Fellow or Associate of the Institute of the Furniture Warehousing and Removing Industry (IFWRI), or, from 13 May 1995, Fellow or Associate of the British Association of Removers.
- Associate of the Institute of Transport Administration by examination.

There are no grounds for obtaining professional competence by exemption other than those detailed above. Valid membership of the relevant body (ie subscription paid, etc) is sufficient to confirm professional competence but, if required, the institutes will issue a confirmatory certificate or statement (ie not a certificate of competence of the type issued under grandfather rights, or rather acquired rights).

Examinations

Examinations for Transport Manager CPC are held at CILT-approved training centres throughout the UK.

CILT Examination System (from March 2012)

The CILT(UK) Transport Manager CPC consists of one unit made up of four modules. Each of the four modules focuses on a specific area of competence relevant to the role of a Transport Manager.

Multi Format Response Paper

Multi Format Response Paper 1 is a closed book assessment. The objective is to test basic recall of core knowledge across all elements of the syllabus.

Case Study Assessment

Case Study Assessment Paper 2 is open book. Only learning material supplied by a learners' CILT(UK) Accredited Learning Partner is admissible in the test. Questions relate to case studies which are pre-published in this syllabus and each assessment contains detailed contextual and quantifiable elements in the form of scenarios, giving further context to the case study. The questions focus on application in the workplace.

Examination Syllabus

Study Facilities

Study for the CPC examinations may be undertaken at courses organized by the CILT or their approved training providers. These can be trade associations, commercial training providers or technical colleges.

The study may involve full-time or part-time attendance, supported by distance, online or e-Learning..

Self-study books are also available for those who may not be able to commit to formal study.

The Council Directive Syllabus

The syllabus for road haulage operations published in Regulation 1071/2009/EC and effective since 4 December 2011 is detailed below. It is still in force within the UK and it shows the assessment objectives and (in brackets) the depth of knowledge required for the examination.

A. *Civil Law*

Candidates must:

1 be familiar with the main types of contract used in road transport and with the rights and obligations arising therefrom (*Contracts: legal obligations; sub-contracting; legal duties of agents, employers and employees and the elements comprising a contract*);

2 be capable of negotiating a legally valid transport contract, notably with regard to conditions of carriage (*Legal obligations: capacity to contract; specific performance; liability; lien; laws of agency*);

3 be able to consider a claim by their principal regarding compensation for loss of or damage to goods during transportation or for their late delivery, and to understand how such claims affect their contractual responsibility (*Performance: general and specific liabilities of principal, sub-contractors and agents for the performance of a contract. Compensation: for losses relating to damage. Settlements: interim and full payments*);

4 be familiar with the rules and obligations arising from the CMR Convention on the Contract for the International Carriage of Goods by Road (*CMR liability and unwitting CMR: CMR notes to CMR convention. Successive carriers. Limits of liability. Relevance of insurance*);

5 be familiar with the different categories of transport auxiliaries (*freight forwarders, warehousing and distribution services, groupage services, clearing houses*), their role, their functions and, where appropriate, their status.

B. *Commercial Law*

Candidates must:

1 be familiar with the conditions and formalities laid down for plying the trade, the general obligations incumbent upon transport operators (registration, keeping records) and the consequences of bankruptcy (*Trading law relating to: sole traders and partnerships; partnership agreements; rights and duties of partners; powers of partners; partners as agents; dissolution of partnerships. Company law: registered* *companies (private and public); AGMs; liquidation. Documentation: prospectus, memorandum of association; articles of association; certificate of incorporation);*

2 have appropriate knowledge of the various forms of commercial company and the rules governing their constitution and operation (*Types of business organization: sole traders; partnerships; private and public limited companies*).

C. Social Law

Candidates must be familiar with:

1 the role and function of the various social institutions that are concerned with road transport (trade unions, works councils, shop stewards, labour inspectors) (*Role of: employment tribunals; trade unions; ACAS; CAC; HSE; arbitrators. Employees' rights: trade union membership and activities*);

2 the employers' social security obligations (*Relevant parts of current legislation relating to: health and safety; discrimination; employment protection; employment rights*);

3 the rules governing work contracts for the various categories of worker employed by road transport undertakings (form of the contracts, obligations of the parties, working conditions and working hours, paid leave, remuneration, breach of contract) (*Contracts of employment: content of written statement; time limits for the issue of contracts. Employment rights: of full- and part-time employees; of self-employed; of agency staff; transfer of undertakings; remuneration and itemized pay statements; holiday entitlement; statutory payments; agency staff; dismissal and unfair dismissal; notice to terminate employment; working time regulations*);

4 the rules applicable to driving time, rest periods and working time, and in particular the provisions of EU Regulation, Regulation (EC) 165/2014 (this Regulation replaced the old EEC Regulation 3821/85 in March 2015) No 561/2006, Directive 2002/15/EC and Directive 2006/22/EC, and the practical measures for applying those provisions; practical arrangements for implementing these regulations (*Community regulations: the working week; driving time; breaks; daily and weekly rest periods; emergencies. Domestic hours' law: the working week; driving time; rest periods; emergencies, working time. Tachograph legislation and operation: points of law; the records; driver and employer responsibilities; enforcement and inspection; calibration and sealing; malfunctions*);

5 the rules applicable to the initial qualification and continuous training of drivers (ie the Driver CPC), and in particular those deriving from Directive 2003/59/EC.

D. Fiscal Law

Candidates must be familiar with the rules governing:

1 VAT on transport services (*VAT – national operations: income threshold and registration; zero-rated goods and services; VAT returns; reclaiming VAT. Turnover tax – international operations: registration for VAT; applying VAT; submitting returns; reclaiming VAT*);

2 motor vehicle tax (*Calculation of vehicle tax: basis for calculating motor vehicle taxation on general vehicles and vehicles used in special operations and conditions applied to them*);

3 taxes on certain road haulage vehicles and tolls and infrastructure user charges (*Domestic operation: HGV Road User Levy, toll roads and bridges and the basis on which calculation is made. International operation: rules governing tolls and taxation of vehicles on international journeys*);

4 income tax (*Corporate taxation. Status: rules governing the status of employees and the self-employed and the imposition of income tax regulations. Employers' responsibilities: deduction and collection of income tax and National Insurance from employees; payment of income tax and National Insurance to HM Revenue & Customs*).

E. Business and Financial Management of the Undertaking

Candidates must:

1 be familiar with the laws and practices regarding the use of cheques, bills of exchange, promissory notes, credit cards and other means or methods of payment (*National operation – payment methods: cash; cheques; credit cards; promissory notes; bills of exchange; debit systems and credit transfer. International operation: banking and payment systems, including the electronic transfer of funds*);

2 be familiar with the various forms of credit (bank credit, documentary credit, guarantee deposits, mortgages, leasing, renting, factoring) and with the charges and obligations arising from them (*Different forms of credit: overdrafts; loans; documentary credit; guarantee deposits; mortgages; leases; rents; factoring*);

3 know what a balance sheet is, how it is set out and how to interpret it (*Determine: fixed assets; net current assets; current assets; long-term liabilities; current liabilities. Interpretation: calculate and interpret*);

4 be able to read and interpret a profit and loss account (*Determine: direct and indirect costs; gross (or operating or trading) profit; net profit*);

5 be able to assess the company's profitability and financial position, in particular on the basis of financial ratios (*Determine: capital employed and return on capital employed; return on sales and assets turnover; working capital; cash flow. Use of ratios: current ratio (working capital ratio); quick ratio (liquidity ratio or acid test ratio)*);

6 be able to prepare a budget (*Construct budgets from data supplied. Use of budgets: to monitor and control performance, budgetary control, variance analysis*);

7 be familiar with their company's cost elements (fixed costs, variable costs, working capital, depreciation, etc), and be able to calculate costs per vehicle, per kilometre, per journey or per tonne (*From data supplied: identify and/or calculate fixed costs, variable costs, overhead costs, depreciation. Determine: time and distance costs*);

8 be able to draw up an organization chart relating to the undertaking's personnel as a whole and to organize work plans (*Prepare an organization chart for an: organization, department, function, unit or depot. Organizing, planning and measuring work*);

9 be familiar with the principles of marketing, publicity and public relations, including transport services, sales promotion and the preparation of customer files (*Market research (primary and secondary); segmentation; product promotion, sales and publicity. Customer: relations; research files*);

10 be familiar with the different types of insurance relating to road transport (liability, accidental injury/life insurance) and with the guarantees and obligations arising therefrom (*EHIC; insurance: risk assessment; cover; claims, risk management and improvement of risk. Types of insurance: fidelity; goods in transit; employers' liability; public liability; professional negligence; motor; plant; travel; health; property; consequential loss; cash in transit. Risks: guarantees; obligations; liability and role of trustees*);

11 be familiar with the applications of electronic data transmission in road transport (*Legislation: Data Protection Act. Hardware and software: electronic vehicle status monitoring; electronic data transmission; real-time information systems; customer information systems; depot readers; GPS; route and load planning systems; vehicle and staff scheduling; data analysis; data information systems*);

12 be able to apply the rules governing the invoicing of road haulage services and know the meaning of Incoterms (agreed trading terms with legal definitions, eg EXW, DAP, DAT, DDP, etc).

NB: Incoterm stands for International Commercial Terms, which are overseen by the International Chamber of Commerce (ICC). The ICC produces several books and guides on the latest Incoterms being used (Incoterms 2010, which were last updated in February 2018).

F. Access to the Market

Candidates must be familiar with:

1 the occupational regulations governing road transport for hire or reward, industrial vehicle rental and sub-contracting, and in particular the rules governing the official organization of the occupation, admission to the occupation, authorizations for intra- and extra-Community road transport operations, inspections and sanctions (*National operation: role of TCs and enforcement agencies; statutory procedures concerning operator licensing; requirements for vehicle maintenance; regulations governing domestic operation. International operation: statutory procedures concerning operator licensing; regulations governing international operations*);

2 the rules for setting up a road transport undertaking (*Rules for setting up a road transport undertaking: statutory procedures and rules concerning operator licensing*);

3 the various documents required for operating road transport services and be able to introduce checking procedures for ensuring that the approved documents relating to each transport operation, and in particular those relating to the vehicle, the driver and the goods or luggage, are kept both in the vehicle and on the premises of the undertaking (*Documents and their administration: operator licences and vehicle discs; vehicle authorizations; tachograph records; waybills/ consignment notes; driving entitlement; maintenance documents; insurance documents; systems for document checking and control procedures*);

4 the rules on the organization of the market in road haulage services, on freight handling and logistics (*Quality regulation and its role in competitive markets; third country traffic, cabotage; through traffic and own-account operations*);

5 planning international journeys; common transit; community transit; TIR, ATA carnets; carnets de passage en douane; border crossing formalities; Schengen agreement passports and visa controls (*Anti-smuggling, immigration controls; restricted goods; required documents for certain goods*).

G. Technical Standards and Aspects of Operation

Candidates must:

1 be familiar with the rules concerning the weights and dimensions of vehicles in the member states of the European Union and the procedures to be followed in the case of abnormal loads that constitute an exception to these rules (*Terms used to identify the differing weight conditions. Statutory limits: weights and dimensions. Formulas used for various calculations concerned in weights and* *dimensions of vehicles. Main rules and most common weights and dimensions used internationally*);

2 be able to choose vehicles and their components (chassis, engine, transmission system, braking system, etc) in accordance with the needs of the undertaking (*Vehicle specifications that will improve road safety and economy, and reduce impact on the environment. Vehicle specifications to be taken into account for international operations*);

3 be familiar with the formalities relating to the type approval, registration and technical inspection of these vehicles (Main provisions within current legislation relating to C&U (Construction and Use), type approval, plating and testing and safety. Powers of enforcement agencies);

4 understand what measures must be taken to reduce noise and to combat air pollution by motor vehicle exhaust emissions (*Main provisions of the C&U Regulations; EU directives and environmental legislation, EGR, hush kits, low-noise tyres*);

5 be able to draw up periodic maintenance plans for the vehicles and their equipment (*Maintenance programmes: planned preventative; methods of maintenance; operator's obligations and liabilities to maintain vehicles and equipment in a safe, roadworthy condition; responsibility for vehicles whose maintenance is contracted out; record keeping*);

6 be familiar with the different types of cargo-handling and cargo-loading devices (tailboards, containers, pallets, etc) and be able to introduce procedures and issue instructions for loading and unloading goods (load distribution, stacking, stowing, blocking and chocking) (*Risk analysis and safe operations: requirements for various loads and procedures to ensure safe operations*);

7 be familiar with the various techniques of 'piggy-back' and roll-on/roll-off combined transport (*Safety requirements; vehicle specifications charging methods*);

8 be able to implement procedures for complying with the rules on the carriage of dangerous goods and waste, notably those arising from:

(a) Directive 2008/68/EC with regard to the transport of dangerous goods by road;

(b) Regulation (EC) 2006/1013/EC on the supervision and control of shipments of waste within, into and out of the European Community, including IMDG (International Maritime Dangerous Goods) requirements;

9 be able to implement procedures for complying with the rules on the carriage of perishable foodstuffs, notably those arising from the Agreement on the International Carriage of Perishable Foodstuffs and on the Special Equipment to be used for such Carriage (ATP) (*Procedures to ensure correct compliance with legislation and best practice*);

10 be able to implement procedures for complying with the rules on the transport of live animals (*National and international: procedures to ensure correct compliance with legislation and best practice*).

H. Road Safety

Candidates must:

1 know what qualifications are required for drivers – driving licences, medical certificates, certificates of fitness (*Vocational entitlements: different categories, types and qualifications for driving licences and entitlements. Procedures: relating to the issue, renewal, revocation and production of licences and removal of entitlements. Disciplinary matters: procedures and appeals. Driving tests: scope and conduct and sequence of theory and driving tests. International Driving Permits: issue and validation*);

2 be able to take the necessary steps to ensure that drivers comply with the traffic rules, prohibitions and restrictions in force in the different member states of the European Union – speed limits, priorities, waiting and parking restrictions, use of lights, road signs (*Traffic regulations: signs and signals; variation in weights, dimensions and speed of road haulage vehicles in EU member states and non-member countries. Restrictions: imposed on the movement and speeds of road haulage vehicles*);

3 be able to draw up drivers' instructions for checking their compliance with the safety requirements concerning the condition of the vehicles, their equipment and cargo, and concerning preventive measures to be taken (*Write instructions for inspection, defect reporting and the safe use of vehicles and equipment, including cargo*);

4 be able to lay down procedures to be followed in the event of an accident and to implement appropriate procedures for preventing the recurrence of accidents or serious traffic offences (*Accident procedures: introduce measures to inform appropriate authorities and personnel of accidents; take appropriate action to minimize further dangers and to relieve suffering. The use of European Accident Statements*);

5 be able to implement procedures to properly secure goods;

6 have elementary knowledge of the layout of the road network in the EU member states.

Both awarding bodies state that new legislative measures will not be included in the examination for at least three months from the date of implementation.

Those wishing to study for the examinations should ensure that they have an up-to-date syllabus, covering either road haulage or passenger transport operations, from the CILT or OCR (Oxford, Cambridge and RSA Examinations).

From the above syllabus it is clear that there will be some major amendments required to the details within this syllabus, not least in relation to UK vehicles operating abroad and the multiple references to the UK as an EU member state.

Transfer of Qualifications

Provisions are in place that allow mutual recognition of Transport Manager CPC between Great Britain (GB), Northern Ireland (NI) and the European Union (EU).

Anyone in GB seeking mutual recognition and applying to operate in NI or the EU must request a Certificate of Qualification from the TC confirming good repute, professional competence and, where relevant, the financial standing.

Where a person seeking a Certificate of Qualification is not, or has not been, an O-Licence holder in the UK, the TCs will have no knowledge of their experience, good repute or financial standing and will be unable to issue a certificate. In these cases, application can be made to the Secretary of State (ie for the DfT), who is empowered to issue a certificate to such a person on payment of the requisite fee.

Rights of Transport Managers

In order to protect the rights of individuals, TCs are not permitted to examine and rule upon Transport Managers' good repute or professional competence unless they have been notified at least 28 days in advance that this is to happen (and for what reason) and have had an opportunity to make personal representation to the TC (at a public inquiry if necessary and represented by a solicitor if they so wish) concerning any allegations made about them.

Driver CPC

Driver CPC is a qualification for PSV and HGV drivers administered by the DVSA. It was introduced by the EU Driver Training Directive (2003/59/EC) and applies across the EU. Its aim is to improve road safety, reduce environmental impact and maintain high standards of driving.

New drivers obtain their Driver CPC by passing a series of initial qualification tests with both theory and practical sections. Existing drivers maintain their Driver

CPC with 35 hours of periodic training every five years. Each periodic training session must be at least seven hours.

Exemptions to Driver CPC apply to drivers of the following vehicles:

- vehicles with a maximum authorized speed not exceeding 45 kph;
- vehicles used by, or under the control of, the armed forces, civil defence, the prison service, the fire service and forces responsible for maintaining public order;
- vehicles undergoing road tests for technical development, repair or maintenance purposes, or new or rebuilt vehicles which have not yet been put into service;
- vehicles used in states of emergency or assigned to rescue missions;
- vehicles used in the course of driving lessons for any person wishing to obtain a driving licence or a CPC;
- vehicles used for non-commercial carriage of passengers or goods for personal use;
- vehicles carrying material or equipment to be used by drivers in the course of their work, within 100 km of the driver's base, provided that driving the vehicle is not the driver's principal activity;
- vehicles going to, and returning from, a pre-booked test at a DVSA test centre or an Authorized Test Facility (ATF).

Initial Training

Initial training applies to drivers who acquire their entitlement to drive vehicles in categories C1, C1E, C or CE. Drivers complete Driver CPC initial training alongside their vocational licence test before they are allowed to drive HGVs on the public highway.

All parts of the vocational licence acquisition process are now considered to be Driver CPC initial training. There are four parts:

- DCPC part 1 – theory: As soon as a driver has their provisional licence they can book the part 1 theory test of the Driver CPC. The test is made up of two parts, a) multiple choice and b) hazard perception. Both parts are booked separately but can be taken on the same day.
- DCPC part 2 – case studies: Drivers can book the part 2 case studies test of the Driver CPC as soon as they have got their provisional licence. The Driver CPC part 2 case study test can be taken before or after the Driver CPC part 1 theory test (but must be taken within two years of each other).
- DCPC part 3 – driving ability: Drivers must have passed the Driver CPC part 1 theory test before they can book the Driver CPC part 3 test. The practical test will

last about 1 hour and 30 minutes and includes vehicle safety questions, practical road driving and off-road exercises.

- DCPC part 4 – practical: Drivers must have passed the Driver CPC part 2 test before they can book the Driver CPC part 4 test. Drivers are tested on being able to:
  - load the vehicle following safety rules and keep it secure;
  - stop trafficking of illegal immigrants;
  - assess emergency situations;
  - reduce physical risks to themselves or others;
  - do a walkaround vehicle safety check.

Fees for Theory and Practical Tests

Module 1a Theory Test = £26

Module 1b Theory Test = £11

Module 2 Theory Test Case Studies = £23

Module 3 Practical Test = £115 (£141 weekends and bank holidays)

Module 4 Practical Demonstration Test = £55 (£63 weekends and bank holidays)

Periodic Training

All HGV drivers must complete 35 hours of training every five years. The training must be delivered by an approved training centre, and each course must be of at least seven hours' duration (this can be split into two 3.5-hour sessions but these must both be completed within a 24-hour period). The training is recorded and uploaded to the DVSA by the training provider who pays a £1.25 fee for each hour of training per driver (£8.75 per seven-hour training session).

There is no restriction on when a driver should undertake the training within the five years, but good practice is one seven-hour training session per year. The training objective can be to provide 'up-skilling' in general to improve overall driver performance and safety awareness, or specific training to account for new technological developments in vehicle design, for example, or operating 'best practices' as and when they occur.

Drivers can take up to two hours of each seven-hour course as e-learning. Drivers can access an e-learning part of a course to gain underpinning knowledge before attending the face-to-face session. The process for training approval is the same as for classroom training and training providers must:

- use an e-learning system;
- verify the identity of the driver;
- prove drivers have participated;
- provide devices on site for those who do not have their own;
- be able to demonstrate that the e-learning has been completed in full.

Training, Testing and Certification

Driver CPC periodic training and certification are provided by approved training centres delivering approved training courses. Approval for trainers, training centres and training courses is granted by the Joint Approvals Unit for Periodic Training (JAUPT) – see Appendix II for contact details.

Minimum Age for Driving HGVs

The minimum age for driving HGVs is 18 years, but this applies only to drivers holding a Driver Qualification Card (DQC) who have completed initial training, or to young drivers being trained to acquire a Driver Qualification Card.

Availability of Training

A list of approved training centres can be found on the JAUPT website at: jaupt.org.uk.

Certification

Drivers are issued a DQC by the DVLA to evidence their Driver CPC. The DQC must be carried when they are driving an HGV and must be 'produced upon request' when requested by an enforcement officer. Failure to show a DQC to the authorities can lead to a fixed penalty fine or even the driver being prosecuted, fined and having their licence endorsed.

DQCs include a photograph of the driver, the driving licence number, validity dates and licence entitlements. Drivers can check up on their personal accumulated training hours by enquiry to the DVSA. Employers can also check up on accumulated training hours provided they have the employee's permission.

Enforcement, Offences and Penalties

All HGV drivers must carry their DQC when driving professionally and may be asked to produce this at the time of a roadside check. Enforcement of Driver CPC is conducted by the DVSA and police.

Offences and Penalties

Drivers failing to produce a valid DQC when driving professionally can be issued with a fixed penalty fine of £50 and can be fined up to £1,000 if the DQC has expired. The more serious offence is failure to have undergone the mandatory 35 hours of periodic training within the past five years.

When driving abroad, drivers must carry their driving licence and their DQC. They risk an on-the-spot penalty if caught in breach of this requirement. Foreign drivers operating in the UK face similar penalties.

Minimum Training and Qualification Requirements

List of Subjects

The content of Driver CPC periodic training courses must match the syllabus.

Individual courses don't have to cover the full syllabus but must focus on specific aspects. The content of each course must be equivalent to at least a Level 2 National Vocational Qualification.

Syllabus

The specific syllabus learning points are listed below; the detail under each learning point can be found at GOV.UK.

1 Advanced training in rational driving based on safety regulations

   1.1 To know the characteristics of the transmission system in order to make the best possible use of it.

   1.2 To know the technical characteristics and operation of the safety controls in order to control the vehicle, minimize wear and tear and prevent disfunctioning.

   1.3 Ability to optimize fuel consumption. Optimization of fuel consumption by applying know-how as regards points 1.1 and 1.2.

   1.4 Ability to load the vehicle with due regard for safety rules and proper vehicle use.

2 Application of regulations

2.1 To know the social environment of road transport and the rules governing it.

2.2 To know the regulations governing the carriage of goods.

3 Health, road and environmental safety, service, logistics

3.1 To make drivers aware of the risks of the road and of accidents at work.

3.2 Ability to prevent criminality and trafficking in illegal immigrants.

3.3 Ability to prevent physical risks.

3.4 Awareness of the importance of physical and mental ability.

3.5 Ability to assess emergency situations.

3.6 Ability to adopt behaviour to help enhance the image of the company.

3.7 To know the economic environment of road haulage and the organization of the market.

Disability awareness, dangerous goods transportation and livestock transportation are also permitted within the syllabus.

All courses must make reference to the safety of vulnerable road users, such as cyclists and pedestrians, where relevant, and managing road risk should be included in at least one training session during the five-year period.

Only approved training centres can deliver Driver CPC periodic training and apply to have courses approved.

Training must be relevant to the driver's role, and drivers should not be allowed to attend repeated training courses during a periodic training cycle. Driver CPC is the minimum legal training requirement for drivers; if a driver needs to repeat a subject it should be delivered additionally outside of the scope of Driver CPC.

Driver CPC is an EU-derived qualification, therefore UK DQCs issued before 31 December 2020 should be valid within the EU until their expiry date.

Should DQCs issued in the UK after 31 December 2020 not be recognized by EU member states, then UK drivers will be treated as 'third country drivers' in the countries concerned, the outcome of which will depend on any new rules in place at the end of the transition period.

Goods Vehicle Drivers' Hours and Working Time

03

The rules on drivers' hours and working time are in place to ensure drivers are adequately rested in the interest of road safety, to improve driver working conditions and to avoid unfair competition. However, the rules are long and complex. Each regulation is complex in itself but this is compounded when they interact with each other. Different working time rules apply to an HGV driver depending on whether they are operating on GB domestic drivers' hours or EU drivers' hours.

Which Rules Apply?

The rules cover maximum limits on driving time and working time and minimum requirements for breaks and rest periods. HGV operators and drivers must understand drivers' hours and working time rules to ensure they are complied with – in particular, which rules apply to them depending on the nature of the transport operation. TC Statutory Document No 6 – Vocation Driver Conduct states that 'drivers are expected to fully acquaint themselves with the relevant legislation before undertaking employment as a professional driver'. The main rules that apply are:

- EU rules on drivers' hours (Regulation (EC) 561/2006);
- GB domestic rules on drivers' hours (Transport Act 1968);
- The Road Transport (Working Time) Regulations 2005 (Directive 2002/15/EC);
- The Working Time (Amendment) Regulations 2003 (Statutory Instrument 1684 2003).

There is also the European Agreement Concerning the Work of Crews of Vehicles Engaged in International Road Transport – AETR rules (Accord Européen sur le Transport Routier). AETR rules are the same as EU rules and are recognized by EU member states and AETR signatories.

AETR rules now also apply to Norway, Iceland, Liechtenstein and Switzerland.

Since Brexit, the application of drivers hours' rules is now a bit more complex. EC 561/2006 (and EU 165/2014 Tachographs in road transport) has been retained in UK law through Section 3 of the European Union (Withdrawal) Act 2018 and various Statutory Instruments have been amended to make them suitable as UK law (e.g. removing references to Member States, the EU and EC). Statute titles are unchanged but are now referred to as 'retained' rules.

The UK and EU have the Trade and Cooperation Agreement (TCA), which applies to journeys between the UK and EU. It contains rules that are identical to EC 561/2006 and EU 165/2014 as regards driving times, rests/breaks, tachographs and record keeping etc.

The UK is applying the requirements of the TCA via the retained rules and Part VI of the Transport Act 1968. The retained rules therefore apply to both national journeys within the UK and international journeys between the UK and EU.

European Union and AETR Rules

Regulation (EC) No 561/2006 provides a common set of EU rules for maximum daily and fortnightly driving times, as well as daily and weekly minimum rest periods. The scope includes road haulage and passenger operations, international and national, long and short distance, hire and reward, employees and self-employed.

The regulation applies to the UK, EU member states, European Economic Area (EEA) countries and Switzerland. EEA countries and Switzerland form the European Free Trade Association (EFTA) – it is likely that the UK will operate under EEA status after the Brexit transition period.

Vehicles Covered

EU/AETR rules apply if the gross weight of a goods vehicle or vehicle combination is more than 3.5 tonnes, unless a specific EU-wide exemption or a national derogation applies. Where the gross weight of a goods vehicle or vehicle combination is under 3.5 tonnes or operating under an exemption or derogation then GB domestic drivers' hours rules apply.

Exemptions from EU and AETR rules

There are a number of specific EU-wide exemptions to the EU rules and national governments are permitted to apply derogations within their own country.

International Exemptions (Under EU/AETR regulations)

1 Vehicles used for the carriage of passengers on regular services where the route covered by the service in question does not exceed 50 km.

2 Vehicles with a maximum authorized speed not exceeding 40 km per hour.

3 Vehicles owned or hired without a driver by the armed services, civil defence services, fire services, and forces responsible for maintaining public order when the carriage is undertaken as a consequence of the tasks assigned to these services and is under their control.

4 Vehicles, including vehicles used in the non-commercial transport of humanitarian aid, used in emergencies or by road rescue operations.

5 Specialized vehicles used for medical purposes.

6 Specialized breakdown vehicles operating within a 100 km radius of their base.

7 Vehicles undergoing road tests for technical development, repair or maintenance purposes, and new or rebuilt vehicles which have not yet been put into service.

8 Vehicles or combinations of vehicles with a maximum permissible mass not exceeding 7.5 tonnes used for the non-commercial carriage of goods.

9 Commercial vehicles which have an historic status according to the legislation of the member state in the countries in which they are being driven, and which are used for the non-commercial carriage of passengers or goods.

National Derogations

1 Passenger vehicles constructed to carry not more than 17 persons including the driver.

2 Vehicles used by public authorities to provide public services which are not in competition with professional road hauliers.

3 Vehicles used by agricultural, horticultural, forestry or fishery* undertakings, for carrying goods within a 100 km radius of the place where the vehicle is normally based, including local administrative areas – the centres of which are situated within that radius.

Vehicle must be used to carry live fish or to carry a catch of fish which has not been subjected to any process or treatment (other than freezing) from the place of landing to a place where it is to be processed or treated.

4 Vehicles used for carrying animal waste or carcasses not intended for human consumption.

5 Vehicles used for carrying live animals no more than 100 km from farms to local markets and vice versa, or from markets to local slaughterhouses.

6 Vehicles specially fitted for and used:

- as shops at local markets and for door-to-door selling;

- for mobile banking, exchange or savings transactions;

- for worship;

- for the lending of books, records or CDs;

- for cultural events or exhibitions.

7 Vehicles (not exceeding 7.5 tonnes gross vehicle weight (gvw)) operated by 'universal service providers' (currently only Royal Mail).

8 Vehicles (not exceeding 7.5 tonnes gvw) carrying materials or equipment for drivers' use in the course of their work within a 100 km radius of their base, provided the driving does not constitute their main activity and does not prejudice the objectives of the regulations.

9 Vehicles operating exclusively on islands not exceeding 2,300 sq km not linked to the mainland by bridge, ford or tunnel for use by motor vehicles (this includes the Isle of Wight, Arran and Bute).

10 Vehicles (not exceeding 7.5 tonnes gvw) used within a 100 km radius of base for the carriage of goods propelled by natural or liquefied gas or by electricity.

11 Vehicles used for driving instruction (but not if carrying goods for hire or reward).

12 Vehicles used for milk collections from farms, for the return of milk containers to farms or for the delivery of milk products which are to be used for animal feed.

13 Vehicles used in connection with sewerage, flood protection, water, gas, electricity maintenance services, road maintenance and control, door-to-door household refuse collection or disposal, telegraph or telephone services, radio and television broadcasting and the detection of radio or television transmitters or receivers.

14 Agricultural and forestry tractors used exclusively for agricultural and forestry work within 100 km radius of base.

15 Vehicles used by the RNLI for hauling lifeboats.

16 Vehicles manufactured before 1 January 1947.

17 Steam-propelled vehicles.

18 Specialized vehicles used for transporting circus and funfair equipment.

19 Vehicles used exclusively on roads inside hub facilities such as ports, airports, interports and railway terminals.

20 Vintage vehicles (ie over 25 years old) not carrying more than nine persons including the driver, not being used for profit, and being driven to or from a vintage rally, museum, public display or a place where they have been or are to be repaired, maintained or tested.

NB: In exemption 2 above relating to vehicles used by public authorities, the exemption applies only if the vehicle is being used by:

a *a health authority in England and Wales, a health board in Scotland or a National Health Service (NHS) Trust:*

  - *to provide ambulance services in pursuance of its duty under the NHS Act 1977 or NHS (Scotland) Act 1978;*

  - to carry staff, patients, medical supplies or equipment in pursuance of its general duties *under the Act;*

b *a local authority to fulfil social services functions, such as services for old persons or for physically and mentally handicapped persons;*

c *HM Coastguard or lighthouse authorities;*

d *harbour authorities within harbour limits;*

e *airports authority within airport perimeters;*

f *the British Railways Board, any holder of a rail network licence that is wholly owned by the Crown, Transport for London, and a Passenger Transport Executive or local authority for maintaining railways;*

g *the British Waterways Board for maintaining navigable waterways.*

Exemption for Military Reservists

An exemption from EU/AETR drivers' hours rules is available to military reservists who drive HGVs for a living, which enables them to take part in weekend military training without breaching the rules on weekly rest requirements. It allows a driver who finishes normal driving duties on a Friday to complete a 34-hour period of military training and then resume normal driving duties again on a Monday morning – providing specified safeguards are met. The exemption applies to 15 days' annual camp and 10 weekend training sessions per annum – a total of 35 days; and weekend training is not allowed to take place on consecutive weeks (other than during the 15-day annual camp).

The following safeguards are imposed to ensure that road safety is not jeopardized:

- A regular daily rest period of 11 hours must be taken between the end of weekend training and start of work for the primary employer.

- A 45-hour weekly rest period must be taken no later than at the end of the sixth day following a period of weekend training.

Further details can be found in The Reserve Land Forces Regulations at GOV.UK.

EU and AETR rules

Certain terminology is used throughout the regulations. It is important to know the correct interpretation and definition of specific terms to ensure the rules are applied:

- 'Vehicle' means a motor vehicle, tractor, trailer or semi-trailer or a combination of these vehicles, defined as follows:
    - a 'motor vehicle' is any self-propelled vehicle travelling on the road, other than a vehicle permanently on rails, and normally used for carrying passengers or goods;
    - a 'tractor' is any self-propelled vehicle travelling on the road, other than a vehicle permanently running on rails and specially designed to pull, push or move trailers, semi-trailers, implements or machines;
    - a 'trailer' is any vehicle designed to be coupled to a motor vehicle or tractor;
    - a 'semi-trailer' is a trailer without a front axle coupled in such a way that a substantial part of its weight and the weight of its load is borne by the tractor or motor vehicle.
- 'Driver' means any person who drives the vehicle, even for a short period, or someone who is carried in a vehicle as part of their duties to be available for driving if necessary.
- 'Break' means any period during which a driver may not carry out any driving or any other work and which is used exclusively for recuperation.
- 'Other work' means all activities which are defined as working time in Article 3(a) of Directive 2002/15/EC except 'driving', including any work for the same or another employer, within or outside of the transport sector.
- 'Rest' means any uninterrupted period during which a driver may freely dispose of their time.
- 'Daily rest' means the daily period during which drivers may freely dispose of their time and covers a 'regular daily rest period' and a 'reduced daily rest period':
    - 'Regular daily rest period' means any period of rest of at least 11 hours. Alternatively, this regular daily rest period may be taken in two periods, the first of which must be an uninterrupted period of at least three hours and the second an uninterrupted period of at least nine hours.
    - 'Reduced daily rest period' means any period of rest of at least nine hours but less than 11 hours.
- 'Weekly rest period' means the weekly period during which drivers may freely dispose of their time and covers a 'regular weekly rest period' and a 'reduced weekly rest period':
    - 'Regular weekly rest period' means any period of rest of at least 45 hours.

- – 'Reduced weekly rest period' means any period of rest of less than 45 hours, which may, subject to the conditions laid down in Article 8(6) (ie relating to compensated rest), be shortened to a minimum of 24 consecutive hours.
- 'A week' means the period of time between 0000 hrs on Monday and 2400 hrs on Sunday.
- 'Driving time' means the duration of driving activity recorded automatically or semi-automatically by the recording equipment.
- 'Daily driving time' means the total accumulated driving time between the end of one daily rest period and the beginning of the following daily rest period or between a daily rest period and a weekly rest period.
- 'Weekly driving time' means the total accumulated driving time during a week.
- 'Maximum permissible mass' means the maximum authorized operating mass (ie weight) of a vehicle when fully laden.
- 'Multi-manning' means the situation where, during each period of driving between any two consecutive daily rest periods, or between a daily rest period and a weekly rest period, there are at least two drivers in the vehicle to do the driving. For the first hour of multi-manning, the presence of another driver or drivers is optional but for the remainder of the period it is compulsory.
- 'Driving period' means the accumulated driving time from when a driver commences driving following a rest period or a break. The driving period may be continuous or broken.

Employers' Responsibilities

Under the EU/AETR rules, employers have specific responsibilities:

- They must organize drivers' work in such a way that the requirements of the regulations are not broken (ie on driving times, breaks and rest periods, etc).
- They must make regular checks of tachograph records (see Chapter 5) to ensure the regulations are complied with.
- Where they find any breaches of the law by drivers, they must take appropriate steps to prevent any repetition.

Employers should ensure their drivers do understand how the law in this respect applies to them and how to comply with its detailed provisions. The court expects the employer to have instructed the driver in the law's requirements and might well convict the employer for 'failing to cause' the driver to conform to the law (or for permitting offences).

Driving Limits

Goods vehicle drivers are restricted in the amount of time they can spend driving before taking a break and the amount of driving they can do between any two daily rest periods (or a daily and a weekly rest period), in a week and in a fortnight. The maximum limits are as follows:

- driving before a break: 4½ hours;
- daily driving normally: 9 hours;
- extended driving on two days in week only: 10 hours;
- weekly driving: 56 hours (6 daily driving shifts);
- fortnightly driving: 90 hours.

Break Periods

Drivers must take a break or breaks if in a day the aggregate of their driving time amounts to 4½ hours or more. If drivers do not drive for periods amounting in aggregate to 4½ hours in the day, there is no requirement for them to take a break during that day under drivers' hours regulations but they may be required to take a break under the rules of the Road Transport Directive (RTD) (see below).

Breaks do not contribute to a daily rest period, and during breaks the driver must not carry out any 'other work'. However, periods of time driving to or from a vehicle when the vehicle is neither at the driver's home nor at the employer's operating centre, known periods of waiting time, time spent riding as a passenger in a vehicle or time spent on a ferry or train are either counted as 'other work' for these purposes or they may be recorded as 'periods of availability' (POA) if POA criteria apply (see below).

The requirement for taking a break is that immediately the 4½-hour driving limit is reached a break of 45 minutes must be taken, unless the driver commences a rest period at that time (see below). This 45-minute break may be replaced by a break of at least 15 minutes followed by a break of at least 30 minutes, each distributed over the driving period or taken during and immediately after this period, so as to equal at least 45 minutes and taken in such a way that the 4½-hour limit is not exceeded.

A break period which was otherwise due in accordance with this requirement does not have to be taken if immediately following the driving period the driver commences a daily or weekly rest period, so long as the 4½ hours' aggregated driving is not exceeded.

Rest Periods

Rest is an uninterrupted period during which the driver 'may freely dispose of their time'. Daily rest periods, and particularly rest periods which are compensating for previously reduced rest periods, should not be confused with, or combined with, statutory break periods required to be taken during the driving day, as described above.

Time spent by drivers on weekend training courses (eg Driver CPC, ADR, etc), is classed as 'other work', even where there is no direct payment of wages by the employer.

Daily Rest Periods

Drivers are required to observe a regular, a reduced or a split daily rest period. Daily rest periods are to be taken once in each 24 hours, commencing at the time when the driver activates the tachograph following a weekly or daily rest period. Where the daily rest is taken in two separate periods (see below), the calculation must commence at the end of a rest period of not less than nine hours. Thus, in each 24-hour period as defined here, one or other of the following daily rest periods must be taken:

- regular daily rest: 11 hours;

or alternatively,

- reduced rest: 9 hours – may be taken no more than three times between any two weekly rest periods;
- split rest: where the daily rest period is not reduced (as above), the rest may be split and taken in two separate periods during the 24 hours, provided:
  - the first period is at least three hours;
  - the last period is at least nine hours.

Split Daily Rest

When a regular daily rest period is split into two or three separate periods (shown above to be permitted under the rules), the minimum nine-hour period must be the last portion of the rest.

Multi-Manned Vehicles

Where a vehicle is operated by a two-man crew, the daily rest period requirement is that each must have had a minimum of nine hours' rest in each period of 30 hours, counting from the end of a daily or weekly rest period.

NB: In the case of multi-manning, it should be noted that the hours law applies to the crew members from the commencement of the journey (or their day's work if that commenced earlier) but for the first hour the presence of another driver is optional. This allows the first driver to pick up the second driver up to one hour after leaving base.

Daily Rest on Vehicles

Daily rest periods may be taken on a vehicle provided:

- the vehicle has a bunk so the driver (but not necessarily a mate or attendant) can lie down; and
- the vehicle is stationary for the whole of the rest period.

Drivers on a multi-manned vehicle cannot be taking part of their *daily rest period* on the bunk while a co-driver continues to drive the vehicle. The driver could, however, be taking a *break* at this time while the vehicle is moving, with the tachograph chart recording other work. It is permissible for the co-driver to book a POA when not driving, instead of a break or other work. This can only be applied when all the POA qualifying conditions exist to do so.

Daily Rest on Ferries/Trains

Normal 11-hour daily rest periods which are taken when a vehicle is carried for part of its journey on a ferry crossing or by rail may be interrupted, not more than twice, by other activities (such as embarkation or disembarkation) provided:

- the interruption must be 'as short as possible' and in any event must not be more than one hour;
- during both parts of the rest (ie in the terminal and on board the ferry/train) the driver must have access to a bunk or couchette.

NB: For vehicles arriving at, or departing from, ports, driving within port areas within the UK is now classed as driving and not duty. Embarkation and disembarkation driving times need to be recorded using the 'ferry flag' option in the rest mode and reset to straight rest once embarkation or disembarkation has been completed. On an analogue tachograph these activities need to be recorded manually.

Weekly Rest Period

After six successive 24-hour periods, a regular weekly rest period totalling 45 hours must be taken. A weekly rest period which begins in one fixed week and continues into the following week may be attached to either of these weeks but not to both.

While the normal weekly rest period is 45 hours as described above, this may be reduced to a rest period of at least 24 hours whether at base or away from base.

Reduced weekly rest periods must be compensated (ie made up) by an equivalent amount of rest period time taken *en bloc* and added to another rest period of at least nine hours' duration before the end of the third week following the week in which the reduced weekly rest period is taken.

Within the EU some member states insist that weekly rests taken in a vehicle must be taken at a safe and secure site, and that only two weekly rests may be taken 'back to back' by a driver, with the third weekly rest needing to be taken either at home or in a hotel, etc. However, reduced weekly rests will always be allowed to be taken in the vehicle cab.

Compensated Rest Periods

When reduced weekly rest periods are taken, the compensated time must be attached to another rest period of at least nine hours' duration and must be granted, at the request of the driver, at the vehicle parking place or at the driver's base. Compensation in this respect *does not* mean compensation by means of payment; it means the provision of an equivalent amount of rest time taken on a later occasion, but by the end of the third following week in the case of compensated weekly rest periods.

Summary of EU Rules

The following summarizes the EU rules applicable to both national and international goods vehicle operations:

- Maximum daily driving: 9 hours (10 hours on two days in week).
- Maximum weekly driving: 56 hours.
- Maximum fortnightly driving: 90 hours.
- Maximum driving before a break: 4½ hours.
- Minimum breaks after driving: 45 minutes or one break of at least 15 minutes and one of at least 30 minutes each to equal 45 minutes.
- Minimum daily rest (normally): 11 hours.
- Reduced daily rest: 9 hours on up to three days per week between any two weekly rest periods.
- Split daily rest: a regular daily rest period may be split into two periods – the first at least three hours, the other at least nine hours. This gives a minimum total rest of 12 hours.
- Minimum weekly rest (normally): 45 hours once each fixed week.
- Reduced weekly rest: 24 hours (any reduction must be made up *en bloc* by the end of the third following week).
- Rest on ferries/trains: normal daily rest (11 hours) may be interrupted not more than twice:

– no more than one hour between parts;
– drivers must have access to a bunk or couchette for both parts of rest.

Amending Regulation to (EC) No 561/2006

An amendment to EU rules took effect in 2020 and a summary of the changes is below.

Weekly rest periods for drivers on international operations

An HGV driver engaged in international operations may take two consecutive reduced weekly rest periods whilst overseas. The driver must take at least four weekly rest periods in any four consecutive weeks, and at least two must be regular weekly rest periods.

Any reduction in weekly rest period shall be compensated by an equivalent period of rest taken *en bloc* before the end of the third week following the week in question. Where two reduced weekly rest periods have been taken consecutively, the next weekly rest period must be preceded by a rest period taken as compensation for the two reduced weekly rest periods.

Return home every four weeks

Operators must organize drivers' work in such a way that the drivers are able to 'return home' at least every four consecutive weeks, in order to spend at least one regular weekly rest period or a compensated weekly rest period.

Where drivers take two consecutive reduced weekly rest periods, operators must organize drivers' work in such a way that the driver is able to return before the start of the regular weekly rest period of more than 45 hours taken in compensation. Operators must document how they fulfil this obligation.

Ban on taking weekly rest in the vehicle

Regular and compensated weekly rest periods must not be taken in a vehicle. They shall be taken in suitable gender-friendly accommodation with adequate sleeping and sanitary facilities. Any costs for accommodation outside the vehicle shall be covered by the operator.

Rests and breaks for drivers when on a ferry or train

Where a driver takes a regular or reduced daily rest period whilst accompanying a vehicle transported by ferry or train on a journey scheduled for at least eight hours, the rest period may be interrupted no more than twice by other activities and not exceeding one hour in total. During the rest period the driver must have access to a sleeper cabin, bunk or couchette at their disposal.

Any time spent travelling to pick up or return a vehicle in scope of EU rules from a location that is not the driver's home or the operating centre where the driver is normally based is not counted as a rest or break unless the driver is on a ferry or train and has access to a sleeper cabin, bunk or couchette.

Records of all other work

A driver must record any time spent as other work, including driving a vehicle commercially but out of scope of EU rules, and any periods of availability. The record must be entered either manually on a record sheet or printout or as a manual entry on the tachograph.

A new definition of 'non-commercial carriage'

'Non-commercial carriage' means any carriage by road, other than carriage for hire or reward or on own account, for which no direct or indirect remuneration is received and which does not directly or indirectly generate any income for the driver of the vehicle or for others, and which is not linked to professional or commercial activity.

Double-manning drive and break rules

A driver engaged in multi-manning may take a break of 45 minutes in a vehicle driven by another driver provided the driver taking the break is not involved in assisting the driver driving the vehicle.

Exceeding daily and weekly driving limits in order to get home

In exceptional circumstances (and providing road safety is not jeopardized), for a driver to reach their operating centre or home (to take a weekly rest period), they may:

- exceed the daily and weekly driving time by up to one hour;
- exceed the daily and weekly driving time by up to two hours, provided that an uninterrupted break of 30 minutes was taken immediately prior to the additional driving.

Any extension must be compensated by an equivalent period of rest taken *en bloc* with any rest period, by the end of the third week following the week in question.

Unforeseen Circumstances

It is permitted for the driver to depart from the EU/AETR rules to enable them to reach a suitable stopping place when an unforeseen circumstance, such as an emergency, arises where the driver needs to ensure the safety of persons, the vehicle or its load, providing road safety is not jeopardized. The nature of and reasons for departing from the rules in these circumstances must be shown on the tachograph chart or on a printout from a digital tachograph. The driver should note the reasons when they reach a suitable stopping place.

Prohibition on Certain Payments

The EU/AETR rules prohibit any payment to wage-earning drivers in the form of bonuses or wage supplements related to distances travelled and/or the amount of goods carried unless such payments do not endanger road safety.

GB Domestic Rules

The Transport Act 1968 includes drivers' hours rules for drivers of goods vehicles that are exempt from EU rules. These are known as GB domestic rules and apply to goods vehicle drivers whose activities are exempt from EU rules. GB domestic rules only include limits on daily driving and daily duty.

Exemptions and Concessions

The British domestic rules apply to drivers of all goods vehicles which are exempt from the EU regulations as described earlier, but with the following further exceptions which are totally exempt from all hours rules control:

- the armed forces;
- police and fire brigade services;
- driving off the public road system;
- driving for purely private purposes (ie not in connection with any trade or business).

The British domestic rules do not apply:

- to a driver who on any day does not drive a relevant vehicle;
- to a driver who on each day of the week does not drive a vehicle within the rules for more than four hours (note: this exemption does not apply to a driver whose activities fall within the scope of the EU/AETR rules within that fixed week).

Driving and Duty Definitions

For the purposes of the British domestic rules:

- Driving means time spent behind the wheel actually driving a goods vehicle and the specified maximum limit applies to such time spent driving on public roads. Driving on off-road sites and premises such as quarries, civil engineering and building sites and on agricultural and forestry land is counted as duty time, not driving time. If unsure about whether or not a particular road is classed as 'off-road', drivers should be advised to comply with the British domestic rules.

- Duty time is the time drivers spend working for their employer and includes any work undertaken, including the driving of private motor cars, for example, and non-driving work which is not driving time for the purposes of the regulations. The daily duty limit does not apply on any day when a driver does not drive a goods vehicle.

Summary of British Domestic Rules

- Maximum daily driving: 10 hours.
- Maximum daily duty: 11 hours.
- Continuous duty: No specified limit.
- Daily spreadover: No specified limit.
- Weekly duty: No specified limit.
- Breaks during day: No requirement specified.
- Daily rest: No specified requirement (but a minimum of 13 hours so as not to exceed the daily 11-hour duty limit).
- Weekly rest: No specified requirement.

A driver operating under GB domestic rules may be required to take a break under The Working Time (Amendment) Regulations.

Drivers who drive for less than four hours a day for an entire 'fixed week' (midnight Sun/Mon – midnight Sun/Mon) are exempt from the daily duty limit but if on any one day of the fixed week they do drive for more than four hours, then the 11-hour daily duty limit will apply for every day of that fixed week.

Emergencies

GB domestic hours' rules may be suspended when an emergency situation arises. This is defined as an event requiring immediate action to avoid danger to life or health of one or more individuals or animals, serious interruption in the maintenance of essential public services for the supply of gas, water, electricity, drainage, or of telecommunications and postal services, or in the use of roads, railways, ports or airports, or damage to property. Details of the emergency should be entered by drivers on their record sheet when the limits are exceeded. Where a British domestic driver uses a tachograph instead of a record sheet, these details should be added to the tachograph record.

Light Goods Vehicles

Drivers of goods vehicles not exceeding 3.5 tonnes gross weight fall within the scope of GB domestic rules and must observe the daily limits on driving (10 hours) and duty (11 hours). However, only the 10-hour daily driving limit applies when such vehicles are used:

- by doctors, dentists, nurses, midwives or vets;
- for any service of inspection, cleaning, maintenance, repair, installation or fitting;
- by a commercial traveller, and carrying only goods used for soliciting orders;
- by an employee of the AA, the RAC or the Royal Scottish Automobile Club (RSAC);
- for the business of cinematography or of radio or television broadcasting.

There is no legal requirement for drivers of goods vehicles not exceeding 3.5 tonnes gross weight to maintain records of their driving or working time. However, if a trailer is attached to a vehicle not exceeding 3.5 tonnes gross weight, taking the gross combination weight to over 3.5 tonnes, then either EU/AETR rules or GB domestic rules apply dependent on the nature of the operation.

Mixed EU/AETR and GB Domestic Rules

It is possible that a goods vehicle driver may be engaged in transport operations which come within the scope of both the EU/AETR drivers' hours rules and GB domestic hours' rules on the same day or week. The driver may conform strictly to the EU/AETR rules throughout the whole of the driving/working period or take advantage of the more liberal British domestic rules where appropriate. The driver must be aware of the following points:

- Time spent driving under the EU/AETR rules cannot count as an off-duty period for the British rules.
- Time spent driving or on duty under the British rules cannot count as a break or rest period under the EU/AETR rules.

riving under the EU/AETR rules counts towards the driving and duty limits for the British rules.

- If any EU/AETR rules driving is done in a week, the driver must observe the EU/AETR daily and weekly rest period requirements for the whole of that week.
- Where a driver drives under both EU/AETR rules and British rules on the same day, both sets of rules must be complied with. The important point here is that it would limit the total duty time to the 11-hour limit under British rules and not allow the driver to take advantage of the longer duty time available under the EU/AETR rules.

AETR Rules

AETR rules are the same as EU rules and recognized by EU member states and AETR signatories.

AETR Countries

Albania	Monaco
Andorra	Montenegro
Armenia	Russia
Azerbaijan	San Marino
Belarus	Serbia
Bosnia and Herzegovina	Turkey
Kazakhstan	Turkmenistan
Liechtenstein	Ukraine
Macedonia	*United Kingdom
Moldova	Uzbekistan

UK drivers who are currently subject to EU rules will operate on AETR rules after the Brexit transition period.

When undertaking journeys to AETR signatory countries, EU drivers must follow the AETR rules for the whole journey, including any EU countries where the journey may begin, or any that may be passed through, if permitted to do so by the EU country concerned. The AETR rules not only align with the EU rules, they also recognize the digital tachograph.

As the whole journey requires a single set of rules to be followed, the AETR rules for a UK driver operating within the EU would apply.

Working Time

The Working Time Regulations (1998) implemented the European Working Time Directive into GB law. This introduced a number of provisions to control working time for most employees in the interest of improving work environments and ensuring better protection for workers by limiting maximum weekly working hours, setting minimum daily and weekly rest periods and minimum in-work breaks, setting minimum annual holidays and requiring regular health checks for night workers. It also specified a maximum 48-hour working week and limited night working in any 24-hour period.

However, mobile and non-mobile workers in the transport sector were exempt from the Working Time Regulations (1998) and they are now covered by two separate complementary working time regulations:

- **The Road Transport (Working Time) Regulations 2005** applies to all mobile workers whose work is subject to EC and AETR drivers' hours rules.

- **The Working Time (Amendment) Regulations 2003** (incorporating the Horizontal Amending Directive to the original directive) applying rules for drivers operating on GB domestic drivers' hours and non-mobile workers in the transport sector.

The Regulations

Drivers operating in scope of EU/AETR drivers' hours are in scope of The Road Transport (Working Time) Regulations 2005. Drivers operating in scope of GB domestic drivers' hours are in scope of The Working Time (Amendment) Regulations 2003.

The Working Time (Amendment) Regulations 2003

Commonly known as the Working Time Directive (WTD), The Working Time (Amendment) Regulations 2003 ensured that all employed road transport personnel, 'non-mobile workers' and other exempt employment categories were in scope of the rules. It applies all the restrictions of the original WTD to non-mobile workers and ensures mobile workers are entitled to:

- a 48-hour average working week;

- 5.6 weeks' paid annual holiday;

- health assessments for night workers;

- an uninterrupted 20-minute rest break if they work more than 6 hours;
- provision for 'adequate rest'.

Under these regulations, workers are allowed to opt out of the 48-hour average working week.

Non-mobile workers are entitled to an uninterrupted period of rest of 11 hours a day and a minimum of one day off a week, while mobile workers are entitled to adequate rest.

Adequate rest means that drivers should have regular rest periods. These should be sufficiently long and continuous to ensure that they do not injure themselves, fellow workers or others and that they do not damage their health, either in the short term or long term.

The Road Transport (Working Time) Regulations 2005

Commonly known as the Road Transport Directive (RTD), The Road Transport (Working Time) Regulations 2005 applies to all mobile workers whose work is subject to EC and AETR drivers' hours rules. Under these regulations:

- employers are required to limit average weekly working time to a maximum of 48 hours, including overtime, calculated over successive periods of 17 weeks (ie four months), or for the period of employment where this is less than 17 weeks;
- the opt-out clause which would have allowed non-mobile workers to exceed the average 48-hour working week has now been withdrawn by the European Parliament;
- employers are required to limit night working to no more than eight hours in 24 hours taken as an average over a 17-week reference period. For night workers (ie those who work for at least three hours at night) whose work involves special hazards or heavy physical or mental strain, the limit is a straight eight hours in 24 hours with no averaging out;
- employers are required to provide free health assessments for night workers and the opportunity for employees to transfer to day work if their health is affected by night working;
- employers are required to allow workers a daily rest period of at least 11 consecutive hours in each 24-hour period and an uninterrupted rest break of at least 20 minutes when their daily work exceeds six hours;
- employers are required to allow workers a weekly rest period of not less than 24 hours in each seven days;
- employers are required to allow workers who have been employed continuously for 13 weeks to have at least four weeks' paid annual leave, which may not be

exchanged for payment in lieu except where it occurs on termination of the employment;

- employers are required to keep records of workers' hours of work that are adequate to show that the legal requirements are complied with, and retain these records for at least two years from the date on which they were made.

The Road Transport (Working Time) Regulations set more restrictive standards for young workers and exempt certain special classes of worker such as Crown servants, the police, trainees and agricultural workers.

Record Keeping

Irrespective of which working time rules apply, employers must keep records of employee working time and provide copies of such records to their employees when asked for them. There is no officially prescribed system for record keeping or special format for individual records, but records must be kept for two years. This means that if tachograph records are used to record working time details, they must be retained for two years in accordance with working time rules rather than 12 months under drivers' hours rules.

Health Assessments

Employers will be required to provide free health assessments for night workers. Employers have a duty to determine exactly who is a night worker for this purpose and provide the health assessment accordingly. The assessment should include a questionnaire devised and monitored by a qualified health professional and, where necessary, be backed up by a medical examination.

Enforcement

The RTD is generally enforced by the DVSA, most likely when they are checking compliance with the EU drivers' hours and tachograph rules, or as a result of complaints made to them. The WTD is enforced by the Health and Safety Executive (HSE).

The National Minimum Wage

Until April 2022, workers (other than self-employed persons) aged 23 years and over must be paid a minimum 'Living Wage' rate of £8.91 per hour. Workers aged 21–23 years of age must be paid at least £8.36 per hour, and workers aged from

18 to 20 years at least £6.56 per hour. The development rate for under 18-year-olds is £4.62 per hour and the apprentice rate is £4.30 per hour. The minimum wage applies to most workers in the UK, including agency workers (eg agency drivers), part-time and casual workers and those paid on a commission basis. These rates are updated annually.

Assessing Minimum Pay

For the purposes of assessing minimum pay, payments to employees comprising bonuses, incentives and performance-related awards count as part of the pay package, but other allowances not consolidated into an employee's pay are not counted. Similarly, overtime payments and shift payments do not count. Benefits in kind, such as the provision of overnight subsistence, meals, uniforms and workwear allowances, are also excluded. Gross pay, with all deductions and reductions subtracted, should be divided by the number of hours worked to determine whether the resulting hourly pay rate at least matches, if not exceeds, the national minima stated above.

Enforcement and Penalties

Enforcement of the minimum and living wage provisions is by HM Revenue & Customs and by the employees themselves, who have a right to complain if they are not being paid the National Minimum/Living Wage levels.

Employers obviously need to keep accurate records of the hours worked and hourly rates paid to employees in case such information is called into question later – for a minimum of three years. An employee (or any other qualifying worker) may make a written request for access to their own records, and this must be allowed within 14 days unless extended by agreement. Should a dispute arise, the burden of proof is on the employer to show that the National Minimum/Living Wage has been paid, not on the employee to prove that it has not.

Refusal to pay the National Minimum/Living Wage is a criminal offence carrying a maximum fine of up to £5,000 on conviction. Dismissal of an employee who becomes eligible for the National Minimum/Living Wage or for a higher rate of pay will constitute unfair dismissal, with no qualifying period to be served by workers to secure protection against this form of unfair dismissal.

Self-Employment

To satisfy HMRC, a self-employed person needs to meet a series of 'tests' under which the self-employed person:

- decides, broadly, how and when specified work is to be carried out, the actual hours worked and when breaks and holidays are taken, and is not subject to the disciplinary provisions of an employer;

- provides their own tools and equipment and is free to send another person (or sub-contractor) in their place to carry out work where necessary;

- has no entitlement to payment for public or annual holidays or sickness, is not included in an employer's pension scheme, and has no rights to claim redundancy payments, unfair dismissal or any entitlement to unemployment benefit if services are no longer required;

- takes financial risk with the aim of making a profit, is responsible for paying their own income tax and National Insurance contributions, and charges for the services provided by submitting an invoice;

- is free to work for other employers as required (a self-employed person who works for only one employer is likely to be considered to be an employee of that employer).

Tax Relief on Driver Allowances

Sleeper Cab Allowances

The amount paid to drivers for overnight subsistence varies considerably from area to area but HM Revenue & Customs has agreed that HGV drivers can be paid night-out allowances on a tax-free basis amounting to £34.90 per night where the vehicle does not have a sleeper cab, reducing to £26.20 per night where a sleeper cab is available. These levels of payments are considered by HMRC to reimburse a driver and do not prevent an employer from paying an additional allowance, although any additional allowance will normally be subject to tax. Payment of such amounts is subject to the employer being satisfied that:

- the individual did necessarily spend the night away from home and normal place of work and that a sleeper cab was used;

- the employee necessarily incurred extra expense in doing so;

- the amounts paid are no more than reasonable reimbursement of the average allowable expenses of the driver (ie for payment of an evening meal, breakfast, washing facilities and the upkeep of bedding).

Owner-drivers are dealt with differently for tax purposes and may *not* claim such night-out allowances against their tax liability.

These payments should only be made where the employee does actually spend the night away and incurs extra expense. If the bunk in a sleeper cab is used, the allowable amount is only that required to meet the expenses incurred, not the full night-out allowance.

HM Revenue & Customs may refuse claims for tax-free payments of night-out allowances above the general limit. Employers who have paid in excess of this amount (or a locally agreed rate) without deduction of tax may find themselves liable to meet the tax due on the additional amounts paid, except where it can be proved that the expense was genuinely incurred (by production of a valid receipt); alternatively, they should include it as part of the wages within PAYE.

Records Retained for Tax Purposes

Where tachograph records are used to justify payment of night-out and other subsistence expenses to drivers, these become part of the tax record and as such must be retained for six years instead of the normal one year.

Personal Incidental Expenses

Employee drivers may be paid additional amounts by way of 'personal incidental expenses' in relation to genuine expenditure (eg newspapers, laundry and calls home) during a qualifying absence (ie when working away from home) up to a tax-free limit, without any tax or National Insurance consequences for the employer up to the value of £5 per day if in the UK, or £10 per day outside the UK (source: GOV. UK).

Benchmark Scale Rate Payments

Where an employee has to spend money as a result of a business journey in the UK, and incurs an allowable expense while on that journey, employers are allowed to make the following subsistence payments, in relation to travel time:

Minimum journey time	Maximum amount of meal allowance
5 hours	£5
10 hours	£10
15 hours (and ongoing at 8 pm)	£25

Enforcement and Penalties

In the UK, enforcement of drivers' hours rules is undertaken by both the police and the DVSA. Besides prosecution for infringements and the penalties, provisions brought in by the Transport Act 2000 authorize DVSA enforcement officers to detain drivers found to be in breach of the drivers' hours rules.

Where it is determined during a roadside check that a UK or foreign driver has not taken sufficient break or rest periods, they will be prohibited from continuing the journey. In the case of break-period infringements, the delay at the roadside will be until a full 45-minute break-period has been taken. Where breaches of the daily or weekly rest-period requirements are detected, the driver and the vehicle will be escorted by the police to a suitable parking area (eg service area or truck stop) where the driver will have to remain until a full 11-hour daily rest or at least a minimum 24-hour weekly rest has been taken, if entitled to a reduced weekly rest. Otherwise they will have to take a full 45-hour weekly rest.

Where the infringement results in the driver being notified of a prosecution, the enforcement officers may now look at 'historic' evidence of earlier infringements recorded on the tachograph going back for a period not exceeding 28 days, and these offences may also be taken into account in relation to the intended prosecution.

The vehicle operator may send a relief driver to take over the vehicle and continue its journey, but this driver will be subject to scrutiny by the DVSA to ensure that they have sufficient time available within legal limits to drive the vehicle.

UK-based employers of convicted drivers also risk prosecution and heavy fines for similar offences. Additionally, they may have penalties imposed against their 'O' licences by the TCs.

It is also a specific requirement within the rules that employers must make periodic checks to ensure the rules are observed (normally by tachograph analysis) and must take appropriate action if they discover breaches of the law to ensure there is no repetition of offences.

In both mainland Europe and the UK, 'historic offences' are also often allowed to be taken into account and breaches of the rules detected in roadside checks may result in drivers incurring heavy on-the-spot fines which must be paid immediately, otherwise the vehicle may be impounded and the driver held until the fine is paid.

Reporting of Illegal Operations

Under the Public Interest Disclosure Act 1998, employees are protected if they report corruption, wrongdoing or danger at work, or if they are unduly pressured by an unscrupulous employer to break the law.

For example, in the context of the drivers' hours, where drivers are encouraged or pressured to breach the driving hours or tachograph rules, they would have protection under the Act if they reported such matters either to the DVSA or to the TC.

The Act entitles workers to unlimited compensation if their employer penalizes them for exposing breaches of the law or unsafe practices. The United Road Transport Union (URTU) also provides a confidential hotline service for drivers on helplines accessed through its website: urtu.com.

Drivers' Hours Records – GB Domestic Rules

04

Most drivers of goods vehicles over 3.5 tonnes gross weight must keep records of the time they spend driving, working and on rest breaks. When within the scope of the EU or AETR drivers' hours rules, the record-keeping requirement is based on the mandatory use of tachographs, as described in Chapter 5.

When outside the scope of the EU or AETR rules then the GB domestic (ie 1968 Transport Act – as amended) drivers' hours rules normally apply (see Chapter 3), and the driver of such a vehicle is required to keep written records capable of accurately capturing a driver's activities.

Drivers operating under GB domestic rules may use tachographs instead of written records. Where this is done, the rules on tachograph operation and inspection/calibration apply.

To summarize the main record-keeping alternatives, these are as follows:

- Goods vehicles not exceeding 3.5 tonnes gross vehicle weight – NO RECORDS.*

- Goods vehicles over 3.5 tonnes gross vehicle weight (including the weight of any trailer drawn) operating within EU rules – TACHOGRAPH RECORDS (ie either analogue or digital).

- Goods vehicles over 3.5 tonnes gross vehicle weight exempt from EU rules – WRITTEN RECORDS (but subject to further exemption in certain cases).

- Goods vehicles over 3.5 tonnes gross vehicle weight exempt from both EU and British domestic rules (eg military vehicles, etc) – NO RECORDS.

Currently records are required when driving in Germany. Note also that alternatively fuelled vehicles are able to operate up to 4,250 kg in the UK without the need for a tachograph.

Exemptions from Written Record Keeping

Written records do not have to be kept in the following cases:

- by drivers of vehicles being operated by, or under the control of, the armed forces, the police or the fire brigade;
- by drivers of goods vehicles who do not drive on public roads;
- by drivers who do not drive in connection with a business or commercial activity;
- by drivers voluntarily using an EU/AETR tachograph for record-keeping purposes which has been calibrated and sealed at a DVSA-approved tachograph centre.

Record Books

Ready-printed record books can be purchased or firms can have their own version. In the latter case it is important that the specific requirements of the regulations are observed in both the format and the printing of the book.

The book must be a minimum size of A6 (105 mm × 148 mm). It must comprise a front sheet on which is entered relevant information, a set of instructions for the use of the book, and a number of individual weekly record sheets with facilities for completing these in duplicate (ie with carbon paper or carbonless copy paper) and for the duplicate sheet to be detached for return to the employer when completed.

Weekly record sheets in the book must follow the format set out in the regulations, with appropriate spaces for entries to be made under the following headings:

- Driver's name
- Period covered by sheet: week commencing... week ending...
- Registration number of vehicle(s)
- Place where vehicle(s) based
- Time of going on duty
- Time of going off duty
- Time spent driving
- Time spent on duty
- Signature of driver
- Certification by employer (ie signature and position held)

Issue and Return of Record Books

Operators must issue their drivers with record books when they are required to drive vehicles under GB domestic driving hours regulations and where records must be kept. Before issuing the book, the employer must complete the front cover to show the firm's name, address and telephone number.

The driver should complete the front cover with surname, first name(s), date of birth and home address, and the date of first use. When completed, the date of the last entry (ie date of last use) should also be included. There is space to record the name and address of a second employer.

Books issued by an operator to a driver must be returned to the operator when complete (subject to the requirement for the driver to retain it for two weeks after use) or when the employee leaves that employment. They must not be taken to a new employer. Any unused weekly sheets and all duplicates must be included when the book is returned.

Two Employers

Where a driver works for two operators, the first employer must issue the record book as described (completed weekly record sheets and completed record books must be returned to this employer), and the second employer must write or stamp the company details on the front cover of the record book with a statement that the holder is also a driver in their employment. When the driver does part-time driving work for another employer, they must disclose to each employer, if requested, details of working and driving times with the other employer. Similarly, when a driver changes to a new employer, the former employer must give the new employer details of the driver's previous driving and working times, if requested.

Record Book Entries

The driver must make entries on the weekly sheet for each day on which a record is required (instructions on the correct use of the book are printed inside the cover). Care must be taken to ensure that an exact duplicate of the entry is made simultaneously (ie two separately written repeat entries are *not* acceptable even if no carbon paper is available). When completing a daily sheet the driver must enter all the required details under each of the headings. If vehicles are changed during the day, the driver must write in the registration number for each vehicle. The sheet must be signed before being returned to the employer.

The driver can enter any remarks concerning entries, or point out corrections which should be made, in the appropriate box at the foot of the record. The employer may also use this space if required for making comments regarding the record. This space may also be used for recording the name of a second driver.

Corrections

Entries in the record book must be in ink. Mistakes may only be corrected by writing an explanation or showing the correct information in the remarks space. Sheets must not be mutilated or destroyed.

Return and Signing of Record Sheets

On completion of the weekly sheet, and after it has been signed by the driver, the duplicate copy must be given to the employer within seven days of the date of the last entry on the sheet, and then within a further seven days the employer must have examined and signed the duplicate sheet. However, if in either case it is not reasonably practicable to do so, these actions must be carried out as soon as possible.

Retention and Production of Record Books

Drivers should carry a record book at all times when working and produce it for inspection at the request of an authorized examiner. The book should be shown to the employer at the end of every week or as soon as possible after the week so it can be examined and countersigned. Following completion of their book, drivers must keep it for a further 14 days (available for inspection by the enforcement authorities) before returning it to their employer.

Completed record books must be retained by the employer for not less than 12 months. As stated earlier, if the books are to be used to record compliance with a Working Time Directive then they need to be retained for a minimum of 24 months, not 12.

Records for Germany

In Germany, foreign drivers of goods vehicles between 2.8 tonnes and 3.5 tonnes gross weight must use either a tachograph or an AETR-type log book. Failure to produce a record, carry a log book or comply with the required driving and rest rules could result in delays and penalties.

Figure 4.1 Simplified record sheet for British domestic transport operations

WEEKLY RECORD SHEETS

WEEKLY SHEETS

1. DRIVER'S NAME			2. PERIOD COVERED BY SHEET WEEK COMMENCING (DATE) .... TO WEEK ENDING (DATE)				
DAY ON WHICH DUTY COMMENCED	REGISTRATION NO OF VEHICLE(S) 3.	PLACE WHERE VEHICLE(S) BASED 4.	TIME OF GOING ON DUTY 5.	TIME OF GOING OFF DUTY 6.	TIME SPENT DRIVING 7.	TIME SPENT ON DUTY 8.	SIGNATURE OF DRIVER 9.
MONDAY							
TUESDAY							
WEDNESDAY							
THURSDAY							
FRIDAY							
SATURDAY							
SUNDAY							
10. CERTIFICATION BY EMPLOYER			I HAVE EXAMINED THE ENTRIES IN THIS SHEET SIGNATURE .... POSITION HELD				

Drivers' Hours Records – EU/ AETR rules

05

Tachographs must be capable of producing a record of drivers' working activities, breaks, rests and driving practices to ensure that legal requirements – especially observance of the drivers' hours rules – have been met.

There are two types of tachograph recording systems: an analogue system for vehicles registered before May 2006, and a digital system for vehicles registered after May 2006.

Legal Requirements for Tachographs

Tachographs must be fitted and used in most goods vehicles and other vehicles used for the carriage of goods over 3.5 tonnes permissible maximum weight (with certain exemptions as listed in the following section of this chapter). The law applies to:

- any goods vehicle over 3.5 tonnes gvw,* or a combination of a goods vehicle and goods-carrying trailer which together exceed 3.5 tonnes permissible maximum weight;
- any other vehicle (such as off-road vehicles and 4 × 4s) used for the carriage of goods, which when towing a trailer has a combined permissible maximum weight exceeding 3.5 tonnes.

Note: The 4,250 kg weight limit for alternatively powered vehicles means that these vehicles are currently also exempt from the need for a tachograph.

In particular, it should be noted that:

- Vehicles carrying postal articles exceeding 3.5 tonnes permitted maximum weight, while exempt from EU drivers' hours rules, must be fitted with tachographs.
- There is no exemption for short-distance operations, infrequent-use vehicles or occasional driving under the EU rules. Once a relevant vehicle is on the highway, the law applies in full.

This means that a tachograph instrument must normally be installed in the vehicle and that whoever drives it must keep a tachograph record and observe the EU/AETR drivers' hours rules in full, both for the day on which the driving takes place and for the week in which that day falls. It should also be noted that vehicles which are exempt from the tachograph rules are not necessarily exempt from record-keeping requirements (for example, those operating under the British domestic hours rules). See Chapter 4 for details of activities where written records must be kept.

There are a number of specific requirements relating to analogue tachographs:

- The tachograph instrument must conform to the technical specification laid down in the EU regulation 165/2014.
- The instrument must be calibrated and officially sealed at an approved calibration centre to ensure that accurate (ie legally acceptable) records are made.
- The instrument must be used in accordance with the regulations, with individual responsibilities being observed by both employer and driver.
- Electronic tachographs must be capable of detecting interruptions in the power supply.
- Driving time must be recorded automatically.
- Facilities must be provided for the removal and subsequent refitting, by an approved centre, of recording equipment seals to enable speed limiters to be fitted.
- Cables connecting electronic tachographs to the transmitter (ie sender unit) must be protected by a continuous steel sheath (ie a tamper-proof armoured cable).

Exemptions

There is no requirement for the fitment and use of tachographs in vehicles in the following list, or in vehicles used in connection with the particular transport operations specified in the exemption list.

Changes in regulations (ie the Community Drivers' Hours and Recording Equipment (Amendment) Regulations 1998 – effective from 24 August 1998) brought within the scope of the tachograph rules those vehicles which are not in themselves considered to be goods vehicles (eg four-wheel-drive off-road vehicles) and therefore were previously exempt from the rules. However, when such vehicles are drawing a trailer for the carriage of goods for commercial purposes, and the combined weight of the towing vehicle and trailer exceeds 3.5 tonnes, the fitment and use of tachographs as described in this chapter is necessary and the driver must observe the EU drivers' hours rules as set out in Chapter 3.

National and International Exemptions

1 Vehicles not exceeding 3.5 tonnes gross weight, including the weight of any trailer drawn.

2 Passenger vehicles constructed to carry not more than nine persons, including the driver.

3 Vehicles on regular passenger services on routes not exceeding 50 km.

4 Vehicles with legal maximum speed not exceeding 40 kph (approx 25 mph).

5 Vehicles used by the armed services, civil defence, fire services, or forces responsible for maintaining public order (ie police).

NB: Item 4 above includes certain works trucks and industrial tractors which have a statutory 30 kph speed limit imposed upon them, but this does not include forklift trucks, which may come within the scope of the rules. Vehicles used for private waste collection (ie not on behalf of local authorities) on journeys exceeding a 100 km radius from the place where they are normally based must be fitted with a fully calibrated tachograph.

6 Vehicles used in emergencies or rescue operations, including humanitarian aid.

7 Specialized vehicles used for medical purposes.

8 Vehicles transporting circus and funfair equipment.

9 Specialized breakdown vehicles operating within 100 km of their base.

10 Vehicles undergoing road tests for technical development, repair or maintenance purposes, and new or rebuilt vehicles which have not yet been put into service.

11 Vehicles used for non-commercial carriage of goods for personal use (ie private use).

12 Vehicles used for milk containers or milk products intended for animal feed.

Further Derogations in National Operations Only

13 Vehicles with between 10 and 17 seats used exclusively for the non-commercial carriage of passengers.

14 Vehicles used by public authorities to provide public services which are not in competition with professional road hauliers.

15 Vehicles used by agricultural, horticultural, forestry or fishery* undertakings for carrying goods within a 100 km radius of the place where the vehicle is normally based, including local administrative areas the centres of which are situated within that radius.

*To gain this exemption the vehicle must be used to carry live fish or to carry a catch of fish which has not been subjected to any process or treatment (other than freezing) from the place of landing to a place where it is to be processed or treated.

16 Vehicles used for carrying animal waste or carcasses not intended for human consumption.

17 Vehicles used for carrying live animals from farms to local markets and vice versa, or from markets to local slaughterhouses within a radius of 100 km.

18 Vehicles used in connection with sewerage; flood protection; water, gas and electricity services; highway maintenance and control; refuse collection and disposal; telephone and telegraph services; carriage of postal articles*; radio and television broadcasting; detection of radio or television transmitters or receivers.

*This does not apply to vehicles operated by universal service providers (only Royal Mail at the present time within the UK), which must have a tachograph fitted in spite of operating under GB domestic rules.

19 Vehicles specially fitted for and used:
  – as shops at local markets and for door-to-door selling;
  – for mobile banking, exchange or savings transactions;
  – for worship;
  – for the lending of books, records or CDs;
  – for cultural events or exhibitions.

20 Vehicles (not exceeding 7.5 tonnes gvw) carrying materials or equipment for drivers' use in the course of their work within a 100 km radius of their base, provided the driving does not constitute their main activity and does not prejudice the objectives of the regulations.

21 Vehicles operating exclusively on islands not exceeding 2,300 sq km not linked to the mainland by bridge, ford or tunnel for use by motor vehicles (this includes the Isle of Wight, Arran and Bute).

22 Vehicles used to collect sea coal, due to the effect of salt water on the equipment.

23 Vehicles (not exceeding 7.5 tonnes gvw) used for the carriage of goods propelled by natural or liquefied gas or by electricity.

24 Vehicles used for driving instruction (but not if carrying goods for hire or reward).

25 Tractors used after 1 January 1990 exclusively for agricultural and forestry work.

26 Vehicles used by the RNLI for hauling lifeboats.

27 Vehicles manufactured before 1 January 1947.

28 Steam-propelled vehicles.

29 Vintage vehicles (ie over 25 years old) not carrying more than nine persons including the driver, not being used for profit, and being driven to or from a vintage rally, museum, public display or a place where they have been or are to be repaired, maintained or tested.

NB: *In the exemption above relating to vehicles used by public authorities, the exemption applies only if the vehicle is being used by:*

a *a health authority in England and Wales, a health board in Scotland or a National Health Service (NHS) Trust:*

- to provide ambulance services in pursuance of its duty under the NHS Act 1977 or NHS (Scotland) Act 1978;

- to carry staff, patients, medical supplies or equipment in pursuance of its general duties under the Act;

b *a local authority to fulfil social services functions, such as services for old persons or for physically and mentally handicapped persons;*

c *HM Coastguard or lighthouse authorities;*

d *harbour authorities within harbour limits;*

e *airports authority within airport perimeters;*

f *any holder of a rail network licence, Transport for London, holders of network licences wholly owned by HM Government, a Passenger Transport Executive or local authority for maintaining railways;*

g *Canal & River Trust for maintaining navigable waterways.*

Declaration of Exemption

When presenting a vehicle for the goods vehicle annual test which the operator believes is exempt from the tachograph regulations in accordance with the list above, a 'Declaration of Exemption' form V112G must be completed. Forms can be downloaded from the GOV.UK website.

Employers' Responsibilities

The employer needs to determine whether the transport operation and vehicles fall within scope of the EU tachograph requirements – by reference to the exemption list above – and take appropriate steps regarding the fitment and calibration of instruments as described in this chapter. They must also instruct drivers accordingly. Additionally, the employer must:

- ensure that the tachograph is sealed and calibrated in accordance with the rules (see below);

- organize drivers' work in such a way that they are able to comply with both the drivers' hours and tachograph rules;

- ensure that drivers understand the tachograph requirements and use the equipment properly to provide accurate records;

- supply drivers with sufficient numbers of the correct type of tachograph charts (ie one chart for the day, one spare in case the first is impounded by an enforcement officer, plus any further spares which are necessary to account for any charts that become too dirty or damaged to use), and ensure that completed charts are collected from drivers no later than 42 days after use;

- periodically check completed charts to ensure that the law has been complied with (ie that drivers have made a chart for the day, that they have completed it fully and properly, and that they have observed the driving hours rules) and if breaches of the law are found, the employer must take appropriate steps to prevent their repetition;

- retain completed charts for 12 months for inspection by DVSA examiners, if required;

- give copies of the record to drivers concerned who request them.

A number of court cases have highlighted the extent of employer responsibilities for tachograph operation as follows:

- It has been made clear that employers who do not check tachograph records are permitting drivers' hours offences and can be prosecuted and convicted accordingly.

- Employers can be charged with failing to use the tachograph in accordance with the regulations in cases where drivers are unable to produce charts to show their driving and other work activities (eg when requested to do so in a roadside check).

- Where employers allow drivers to take their tractive units home after their day's work, they must ensure that such driving is recorded on a tachograph chart and is counted as part of drivers' legally permitted driving and working time for that day – it is not part of their rest period.

- Employers who do not take action against drivers found to have repeated infringements when their tachograph records are analysed can be held to account by the Traffic Commissioners for having a system of analysis that in itself does nothing to reduce infringements or improve compliance.

Drivers' Responsibilities

Drivers of vehicles operating within the EU rules must observe the tachograph requirements. This means understanding what the law requires and how to comply with it. The specific responsibilities of the driver in regard to the law are as follows:

- Drivers using tachograph charts must ensure that a proper record is made by the instrument, that is:
  - that they enter the correct personal details, places of start and finish of duty, the vehicle registration number (VRN), date and time and odometer readings of any change of vehicle;
  - that it is a continuous record;
  - that it is a 'time right' record (ie recordings are in the correct 12-hour section of the chart – daytime or night-time hours – and that the time recorded is that of the country of origin, if on an international journey).
- In the event of instrument failure or in circumstances where no vehicle is available when drivers are working, they must make manual recordings of their activities on the chart 'legibly and without dirtying' it.
- Drivers must produce for inspection on request by an authorized inspecting officer a current chart/record for that day plus the charts relating to the previous 28 days (see section below on Production of Charts/Records).
- Drivers must return completed charts and/or records to their employer no later than 42 days after use.
- Drivers must allow any authorized inspecting officer to inspect the charts and tachograph calibration plaque, which is usually fixed inside the body of the instrument.

In cases where drivers take their vehicle home at the end of their working shift, this time must be recorded on the tachograph chart and counted as part of the daily maximum driving time and the drivers' day's work – it is not part of their rest period.

Production of Charts/Records

When driving vehicles with analogue tachographs the driver must be able to produce:

- the record sheet (ie chart/s) for the current day and those used in the previous 28 calendar days.

Two-Crew Operation

A two-man tachograph must be fitted when another driver assists with driving and both drivers must use it to produce records as follows:

- The person who is driving must have the chart located in the uppermost (ie number 1) position in the instrument and use the number 1 activity mode switch.

- The person who is riding passenger must have their chart in the rearmost (ie number 2) position and use the number 2 activity mode switch to record other work activities, or break or rest periods. Only time-group recordings are made on this chart; driving, speed and distance traces are *not* produced on the second-man chart.

NB: *The second person on a double-manned vehicle operation must insert the chart in the second position of the instrument from the commencement of the journey, or at the time they board the vehicle, not when commencing driving.*

Tachograph Calibration, Sealing and Inspection

To make legally acceptable records, tachograph installations in vehicles must be calibrated initially at an approved tachograph centre (a list of DfT-approved tachograph fitting and calibration centres can be found at GOV.UK). Analogue tachographs must be inspected every two years and fully recalibrated every six years or after repair at an approved centre. Digital tachographs must be recalibrated after two years, following any repair, if the UTC (Universal Time Coordinated) time is incorrect by more than 20 minutes, if the VRN is changed or if the circumference of the tyres is changed.

The DVSA specifies and approves the premises (and the display of approved signs), equipment, staff (including their training) and procedures for the installation, repair, inspection, calibration and sealing of tachographs. Such centres must be approved to BS 5750 Part 2 before they can gain DVSA approval. No other work-shops or individuals are permitted to carry out this work.

Tachograph Installation Offences

It is an offence for any unauthorized person to carry out work on tachograph instal-lations. It is also an offence (maximum fine £5,000) for a vehicle operator to obtain and use a tachograph instrument repaired by a firm which is not BS 5750 approved.

Calibration

The calibration process requires the vehicle to be presented in normal road-going trim, complete with body and all fixtures, unladen, and with tyres complying with legal limits as to tread wear and inflated to the manufacturer's recommended pressures. At the centre, the necessary work on the analogue installation is carried out to within specified tolerances.

The regulations specify tolerances within which the tachograph installation must operate and are valid for temperatures between 0 °C and 40 °C, as follows:

Table 5.1 Calibration process

	On bench test	On installation	In use
Speed	3 kph	4 kph	6 kph
Distance	1%	2%	4%
Time	In all cases, ±2 minutes per day with a maximum of 10 minutes per seven days		

NB: *In the case of both speed and distance figures shown above, the tolerance is measured relative to the real speed and to the real distance of at least 1 km.*

Sealing of Analogue Tachographs

Approved centres seal analogue tachograph installations after calibration or two-yearly inspections with their own official seals (each of which is coded differently) and details of all seals are maintained on a register by the DVSA. The seals are of the Customs type whereby a piece of wire is passed through each of the connecting points between the vehicle and the tachograph itself and then a lead seal is squeezed tight onto the wire with special pliers which imprint the centre code number in the metal. Attempts to remove any of the seals or their actual removal will show and will need to be accounted for.

The purpose of sealing is to ensure that there is no tampering with the equipment or any of its drive mechanism or cables which could either vary the recordings of time, speed or distance or inhibit the recording in any way. Such tampering is illegal and once seals are broken the installation no longer complies with the law and legally acceptable records cannot be made.

Besides the seals inside the body of the instrument head, the following points are sealed:

- the installation plaque;
- the two ends of the link between the recording equipment and the vehicle;
- the adaptor itself and the point of its insertion into the circuit;
- the switch mechanism for vehicles with two or more axle ratios;

- the links joining the adaptor and the switch mechanism to the rest of the equipment;
- the casings of the instrument;
- any cover giving access to the means of adapting the constant of the recording equipment to the characteristic coefficient of the vehicle.

Seal Breakage

Obviously, there are occasions when certain of the seals have to be broken of necessity to carry out repairs to the vehicle and replacement of defective parts (eg the vehicle clutch or gearbox). The only seals which may be broken in these circumstances are as follows:

- those at the two ends of the link between the tachograph equipment and the vehicle;
- those between the adaptor (ie the tachograph drive gearbox) and the point of its insertion into the circuit;
- those at the links joining the adaptor and the switch mechanism (ie where the vehicle has a two-speed rear axle) to the rest of the equipment.

With the introduction of statutory speed limiters, operators are permitted to break tachograph seals for the purpose of fitting such devices, but the seals must be replaced at an approved tachograph centre within seven days.

While it is permitted to break the particular seals listed above for other authorized purposes (eg in connection with vehicle maintenance), a written record must be kept of the seal breakage and the reason for it. The installation must be inspected or recalibrated and fully sealed following repair or seal breakage as soon as 'circumstances permit' and before the vehicle is used again.

DVSA vehicle examiners check that all tachograph head seals are intact when vehicles are submitted for their annual goods vehicle test.

Analogue Tachograph Calibration Plaques

When an analogue tachograph has been inspected or recalibrated, the approved centre must fix, either inside the tachograph head or near to it on the vehicle dashboard in a visible position, a plaque giving details of the centre, the 'turns count' and the calibration date. The plaque is sealed and must not be tampered with or the sealing tape removed. When an instrument is subjected to a two-year inspection or recalibration a new plaque must be fitted.

The normal sequence for plaques is that one will show the initial calibration date, the next (two years later), which is fitted alongside the first plaque, will show the date of the two-year inspection and a third plaque will show the second two-year inspection. After a further two years, a six-year recalibration of the installation will be due and at this time all the previous plaques will be removed, the new calibration plaque will be fitted and the procedure described above starts again. In between times, following certain repairs, a 'minor work' plaque may be fitted but this does not alter the sequence of dates for the two-year inspection and the six-year recalibration plaques.

The two-year and six-year periods referred to above for inspections and calibrations are counted to the actual day/date, not to the end of the month in which that day/date falls.

Tachograph Breakdown

If analogue tachograph equipment becomes defective, drivers must continue to record manually on the chart all necessary information regarding their working, driving, breaks and rest times, which is no longer being recorded by the instrument. There is no requirement to attempt to record speed or distance.

Once a vehicle has returned to base with a defective tachograph it should not leave again until the instrument is in working order and has been recalibrated (if necessary) and the seals replaced. If it cannot be repaired immediately, the vehicle can be used so long as the operator has taken positive steps (which they can satisfactorily prove later if challenged by the enforcement authorities – see below) to have the installation repaired as soon as reasonably practicable.

If a vehicle is unable to return to base within *one week* (ie seven days), counting from the day of the breakdown, arrangements must be made to have the defective instrument repaired and recalibrated as necessary at an approved centre en route within that time.

Defence

There is a defence in the regulations against conviction (ie not against prosecution) for an offence of using a vehicle with a defective tachograph. This has the effect of allowing subsequent use of a vehicle with a defective tachograph provided steps have been taken to have the installation restored to a legal condition as soon as circumstances permit and provided drivers continue to record their driving, working and break period times manually on a tachograph chart. In such circumstances it will be necessary to satisfactorily prove to the enforcement authorities – and to the court if they proceed with prosecution – that a definite booking for the repair had already been made at the time the vehicle was apprehended and that this appointment was for the repair to be carried out at the earliest possible opportunity.

It is also a defence to show that at the time it was examined by an enforcement officer the vehicle was on its way to an approved tachograph centre to have necessary repairs carried out. However, this defence will fail if drivers did not keep written records of their activities in the meantime.

Use of Analogue Tachographs

Drivers are responsible for ensuring that the tachograph instrument in their vehicle functions correctly throughout the whole of their working shift in order that a full and proper recording for a full 24 hours can be produced. They must also ensure that they have sufficient quantities of the right type of charts (see below) on which to make recordings.

NB: *Some prolonged activities away from the vehicle may need to be recorded manually.*

Time Changes

Drivers must ensure that the time at which the instrument clock is set and consequently recordings are made on the chart, agrees with the official time in the country of registration of the vehicle. This is a significant point for British drivers travelling in Europe, who may be tempted to change the clock in the instrument to the correct local European time rather than having it indicate and record the time in Britain.

Dirty or Damaged Charts

If a chart becomes dirty or damaged in use, it must be replaced and the old chart should be securely attached to the new chart. Care must be taken not to mark either chart so that any recordings are further damaged or obscured, etc.

Completion of Centre Field

Drivers must enter on the centre field of their chart for that day the following details:

- surname and first name (not initials);
- the date and place where use of the chart begins;
- VRN;
- the distance recorder (odometer) reading at the start of the day.

At the end of a working day, drivers should then record the following:

- the place and date where the chart is completed;
- the closing odometer reading;
- by subtraction, the total distance driven – in kilometres (it is not a legal requirement for the driver to carry out this calculation).

Making Recordings

When the centre field has been completed, the chart should be inserted in the tachograph, ensuring that it is the right way up (it should be impossible to fit it wrongly) and that the recording will commence on the correct part of the 24-hour chart (day or night). The instrument face should be securely closed. The activity mode switch (number 1) should be turned as necessary throughout the work period to indicate the driver's relevant activities: driving, other work, break or rest periods.

Recording Rules

Regulation 561/2006/EC specifies in Article 26 that the use to which the tachograph crossed hammers and rectangle symbols are put must, from 1 May 2006, be as follows:

 use to record 'other work' (ie any activity other than driving) done for both the driving employer and any other employer outside of transport;

 use to record 'periods of availability' as defined in EU Directive 2002/15/EC – The Road Transport Directive Other Work and Overtime Recordings.

Drivers must record *all* periods of work on their tachograph charts. This makes it clear that work undertaken for the employer after the daily driving shift has been completed (eg in a yard, warehouse, workshop or office), and whether deemed part of the normal day or overtime working, must be recorded on the chart for that day – ie either by the instrument if this is convenient or otherwise manually.

Where manual recordings are entered onto the tachograph to record other work, etc, they are permitted to be either on the front or rear of the chart providing that they do not deface or obscure any details made by the recording equipment.

Overnight Recordings

At the end of a shift the driver can leave the chart in the instrument overnight to record the daily rest period or, alternatively, it can be removed and the rest period recorded manually on the chart. If the driver is scheduled to start work later on the following day, there will be an overlap recording on the chart, which is illegal. It is also recommended that the driver manually enters the start and finish times of every daily duty on the chart, as this will effectively provide an accurate 24-hour record. The driver must not make an entry that could obscure a part of the chart where the machine trace will be made.

Vehicle Changes

If the driver changes to another vehicle during the working day, he must take the existing chart with him and record details of the time of change, the registration number of the further vehicle(s) and distance recordings in the appropriate spaces on the chart. The driver then uses that chart in the next vehicle to record continuing driving, working activities and break periods. This procedure is repeated no matter how many different vehicles (except those not driven on the public highway) are driven during the day, so the one chart shows all of the driver's daily activity. If the chart and the instrument are not compatible, a new chart must be used by the driver. The charts used by the driver must be kept together to show a complete day's work.

Mixed Tachographs

There are still various makes and models of analogue tachograph currently available in the UK that need different charts and they cannot all be interchanged. At the end of each day all charts used should be put together to present a comprehensive (and legal) record for the whole day. However, there are some charts now available on the market suitable for dual use in different makes of tachograph. It is the employer's duty to issue drivers with the correct charts (ie with matching type-approval numbers to those on the tachograph instrument in use) in sufficient numbers for the schedule which the driver has to operate.

There are also different tachographs for use in vehicles with different speed limits. This means that, while most tachographs are designed to be fitted with charts capable of recording up to 125 kph, there are charts capable of recording up to 140 kph and even 180 kph. It is the operator's responsibility to issue the correct type of chart to the driver but it is also the driver's responsibility to ensure that a proper record is made, and using a differently calibrated chart in a differently calibrated tachograph head would certainly not produce a proper record.

Manual Records

Drivers are responsible for ensuring that the instrument is kept running while they are in charge of the vehicle, and should it fail or otherwise cease making proper records they should remove the chart and continue to record their activities manually. They must also make manual recordings on the chart of work done or time spent away from the vehicle (for example, periods during the day spent working in the yard, warehouse or workshop). Manual recordings must be made legibly and in making them the chart must not be 'dirtied'.

Records for Part-time Drivers

The rules on the use of tachographs apply equally to part-time or occasional drivers such as yard and warehouse staff, office people and even the transport manager. The rules also apply fully even if the driving on the road is for a very short distance or period of time; a five-minute drive without a tachograph chart in use would be sufficient to break the law and risk prosecution. Vehicle fitters and other workshop staff who drive vehicles on the road for testing in connection with repair or main-tenance are exempt from the need to keep tachograph records when undertaking such activities, but this exemption *does not* apply to them when using vehicles for other purposes (eg collecting spare parts, ferrying vehicles back and forth, taking replacement vehicles out to on-road breakdowns, taking and collecting vehicles to and from goods vehicle test stations, etc).

Retention, Return and Checking of Tachograph Charts

Drivers must retain and be able to produce, on request by authorized examiners (including the police), completed tachograph charts for the current day and for the previous 28 days.

Charts must be returned by drivers to their employer no later than 42 days after use, and on receiving the charts the employer must periodically check them to ensure that the drivers' hours and record-keeping regulations have been complied with. Failure by an operator to check charts for possible offences by drivers can lead to charges of 'permitting' the commission of certain tachograph and drivers' hours offences (should such offences be proven) – in one case a transport manager was held to be 'reckless' because his chart-checking system was not sufficiently thorough. Charts must then be retained, available for inspection if required, for a period of one year (see below).

Where drivers have more than one employer in a week (eg as with agency drivers), they must return the tachograph charts to the employer who first employed them in that week. This provision clearly presents a problem for those firms which regularly employ agency drivers and which may find difficulty in securing the return of charts for driving work done with their vehicles, and operators should try to include this requirement when considering using a driver agency.

Retention of Charts for Tax Records

Where tachograph charts are used by employers to justify payment of driver night-out and other subsistence expenses for tax purposes, then the charts constitute part of the legal recording system for tax purposes and as such must be retained for six years instead of the normal one-year period.

Retention of Charts for Working Time Records

Where tachograph charts are used by employers to record compliance with either the Road Transport Directive (RTD) or the Horizontal Amending Directive (HAD), they must be retained for two years.

Non-Driving Days (All Tachographs)

Drivers must make records for work completed on any non-driving days, within a working week, when they have undertaken some driving that comes within the scope of the EU drivers' hours rules, since their last weekly rest.

For example, a driver who drives a vehicle within the scope of the EU rules on a Monday and then works in a warehouse from Tuesday to Friday of the same week, must complete non-driving records for the work completed from Tuesday to Friday.

The driver can make the record in a number of ways by:

- making manual records on a tachograph chart;
- making manual records on a printout from a digital tachograph;
- using the manual input facility on a digital tachograph;
- making manual records in a domestic log book for days when they are working under the domestic drivers' hours rules and a record is legally required.

Records for non-driving days do not need to be complex. They may merely show the name of the driver, the date and the start and finish of the shift. The driver should always carry these records on the vehicle (for the previous 28 days) to be able to produce them to enforcement officers for the relevant period.

Official Inspection of Charts

An authorized inspecting officer may require any person to produce, for inspection, any tachograph chart or record on which recordings have been made. This includes:

- any charts for the current day and for the previous 28 *calendar* days;
- any legally required manual records made in the previous 28 days.

They may also enter a vehicle to inspect a chart or a tachograph instrument (they should be able to read the recordings relating to the nine hours prior to the time of their inspection) and the calibration plaques and detain a vehicle for this purpose. At any reasonable time they can enter premises in which they believe vehicles or tachograph charts are kept and inspect the instruments in such vehicles and the completed charts. By serving a notice in writing, charts can be requested to be produced at a Traffic Area Office on giving at least 10 days' notice. Where a chart is suspected of showing a false entry, the chart may be seized (but not for reasons other than evidence of a false entry, or an entry intended to deceive or an entry altered for such purposes) and retained for a maximum period of six months, after which time, if no charges for offences have been made, the chart should be returned. If not, the person from whom it was taken can apply to a magistrate's court to seek an order for its return.

In practice, TCs regularly ask operators to provide batches of tachograph charts covering one or more of their vehicles for a short period or possibly some months, either on a routine basis or following investigations into, or leads about, hours' law or tachograph infringements – and where it is suspected that drivers are regularly exceeding speed limits. These charts are then analysed for contraventions of the law.

Cases have been reported where the police have demanded that operators should send, by post, tachograph charts required for inspection. This is an illegal practice: there is no provision in the law which allows random collection of charts by the police or demands for charts to be submitted by post. Only in cases where an on-the-spot examination reveals possible offences can the police then request copies of the relevant chart for that day, other charts for that week and for the last day of the previous week. DVSA enforcement officers, on the other hand, may take random selections of charts away for examination.

It is an offence to fail to produce records for inspection as required or to obstruct enforcement officers in their request to inspect records or tachograph installations in vehicles.

The Analogue Tachograph Instrument

An analogue tachograph is a cable or electronically driven speedometer incorporating an integral electric clock and a chart-recording mechanism. It is fitted into the vehicle dashboard or in some other convenient visible position in the driving cab. The instrument indicates time, speed and distance and permanently records this information on the chart, as well as the driver's working activities. The following information can be determined from a chart:

- varying speeds (and the highest speed) at which the vehicle was driven;
- total distance travelled and distances between individual stops;
- times when the vehicle was being driven and the total amount of driving time;
- times when the vehicle was standing and whether the driver was indicating other work, break or rest period during this time.

Recordings

Recordings are made on special circular charts, each of which covers a period of 24 hours (Figure 5.1), by three styli. One stylus records distance, another records speed and the third records time-group activities as determined by the driver turning the activity mode switch on the head of the instrument (ie driving, other work, break and rest period). The styli press through a wax recording layer on the chart, revealing the carbonated layer between the top surface and the backing paper. The charts are accurately pre-marked with time, distance and speed reference radials, and when the styli have marked the chart with the appropriate recordings these can be easily identified and interpreted against the printed reference marks.

Figure 5.1   A typical tachograph chart showing recordings of times, distance and speed

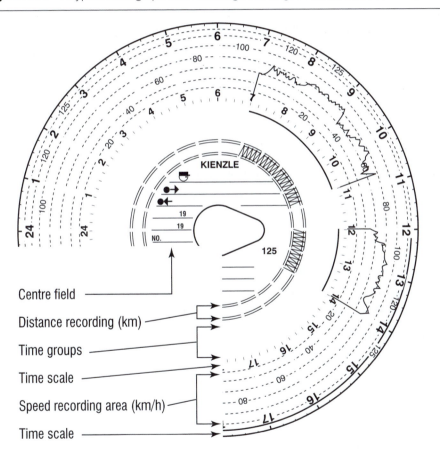

Movement of the vehicle creates a broad running line on the time radial, indicating when the vehicle started running and when it stopped. After the vehicle has stopped, the time-group stylus continues to mark the chart but with an easily distinguishable

thin line. The speed trace gives an accurate recording of the speeds attained at all times throughout the journey, continuing to record on the speed base line when the vehicle is stationary to provide an unbroken trace except when the instrument is opened. The distance recording is made by the stylus moving up and down, each movement representing five kilometres travelled; thus, every five kilometres the stylus reverses direction, forming a 'V' for every 10 kilometres of distance travelled. To calculate the total distance covered, the 'V's are counted and multiplied by 10 and any 'tail-ends' are added in, the total being expressed in kilometres.

When a second chart is located in the rear position of a two-man tachograph, only a time recording of the second activities (ie other work, break or rest) is shown. Traces showing driving, vehicle speed or distance cannot be recorded on this chart.

Precautions against interference with the readings are incorporated in the instrument. It is opened with a key and a security mark is made on the chart every time the instrument is opened and/or when the power supply is interrupted. When checking the chart it can be easily established at what time the instrument was opened or the power interrupted and thus whether this was for an authorized reason or not. Interference with the recording mechanism to give false readings, particularly of speed, can be determined quite simply by an experienced chart analyst.

Faults

Listed below are some of the faults which may occur:

- failure of the cable drive at the vehicle gearbox;
- failure of the cable drive at the tachograph head;
- failure of the adaptor/corrector/triplex gearbox;
- cable breaking or seizure;
- electrical faults affecting lights in the instrument or the clock;
- incorrect time showing on the 24-hour clock (eg day-shift work becomes shown against night hours on the charts);
- failure of the tachograph head;
- damage to the recording styli;
- failure of the distance recorder;
- damage to charts because of incorrect insertion.

Fiddles

A key feature of tachograph recordings is that careful observation will show results of the majority of faults in recordings as well as fiddles and attempts at falsification of recordings by drivers. The main faults likely to be encountered will show as follows:

- Clock stops – recordings continue in a single vertical line until the styli penetrate the chart.

- Styli jam/seize up – recordings continue around the chart with no vertical movement.

- Cable or electronic drive failure – chart continues to rotate and speed and distance styli continue to record on base line and where last positioned, respectively. Time-group recordings can still be made but no driving trace will appear.

Attempts at falsification of charts will appear as follows:

- Opening the instrument face will result in a gap in recordings.

- Interrupting the power supply will lead to incomplete records being produced.

- Winding the clock backward or forward will leave either a gap in the recording or an overlap. In either case the distance recording will not match up if the vehicle is moved.

- Stopping the clock will stop the rotation of the chart, so all speed and distance recordings will be on one vertical line (see above how faults in instruments show on charts).

- Restricting the speed stylus to give indications of lower-than-actual speed will result in flat-topped speed recordings, while bending the stylus down to achieve the same effect will result in recordings below the speed base line when the vehicle is stationary.

- Written or marked-in recordings with pens or sharp pointed objects are readily identifiable by even a relatively unskilled chart analyst.

EU Instruments and Charts

Tachographs may only be used for legal record-keeping purposes if they are type-approved and comply with the detailed EU specification, which indicates to the driver, without the instrument being opened, that a chart has been inserted and that a continuous recording is being made. They also enable the driver to select, by an activity mode switch on the instrument, the type of recording which is being made, that is:

- driving time;
- other work time;
- break or rest period.

Two-man instruments are also provided with a means of simultaneously recording the activities of a second crew member on a separate chart located in the rear position in the instrument.

The charts must also be type-approved as indicated by the appropriate 'e' markings printed on them. It is illegal to use non-approved charts or charts which are not approved for the specific type of instrument being used. Care should be taken that charts used have accurate time registration.

Chart Analysis

Analysis of the information recorded on tachograph charts can provide valuable data for determining whether drivers have complied with the law on driving, working, break and rest period times, and have conformed to statutory speed limits. The data can also be extremely useful as a basis for finding means of increasing the efficiency of vehicle operation and for establishing productivity monitoring and payment schemes for drivers.

Many fleet operators use and rely upon the services of tachograph analysis agencies for checking their charts for conformity with the law. However, it should be noted that should such firms fail to recognize and notify the operator of deficiencies in their records, it is the operator who is at risk and their licence, not the analysis company. Generally, also, the checking carried out by such firms is for standard hours' law infringements only, which are mainly picked up by computerized analysis and may not include identification of other irregularities, false entries or fraudulent recordings. Similarly, such analysis may not identify driver abuse of vehicles or frequent and excessive speeding.

Tachograph manufacturers supply accessories to enable detailed chart analysis to be carried out. For operators, an important point relating to chart analysis is that where infringements are detected and the driver informed, it is not sufficient to simply file the record away, as remedial actions are expected where infringements exist. In short, operators need to ensure that drivers improve their compliance and that the number and types of infringements reduce over time.

Digital Tachographs

It is important to note that despite the introduction of the digital tachograph from May 2006 in all new goods vehicles over 3.5 tonnes gross weight (apart from those specifically exempt under the legislation), existing analogue tachographs fitted to goods vehicles will remain valid and effective until such time as the vehicle reaches the end of its useful life or the analogue tachograph instrument itself ceases to function. In the latter case, where the vehicle exceeds 12 tonnes maximum weight, the replacement tachograph fitted must be of the digital type. On this basis, it is clear that analogue (or chart-type) tachographs will continue in use for at least a few more years.

A driver who has failed to obtain a digital 'smart card' cannot legally drive a vehicle fitted with a digital tachograph unless the driver in question is specifically exempted, as in the case of a driver operating under British domestic driving rules and using a 'log book'.

The Regulations

Regulation 561/2006/EC, which is outlined here, was introduced for a number of reasons, including:

- to prevent infringement and fraud in application of the driving hours rules;
- to monitor automatically driver performance and behaviour;
- to overcome problems of monitoring compliance due to the numbers of individual record sheets (charts) that have to be held in the vehicle cab;
- the need to introduce advanced recording equipment with electronic storage devices and personal driver cards to provide an indisputable record of work done by the driver over the last few days and the vehicle over a period of several months;
- to devise a system which ensures total security of the recorded data.

Definitions for Digital Tachographs and Ancillaries

The digital equipment features a number of key components defined in the technical Annex of the Regulation, as follows:

- *Recording equipment* means the total equipment intended for installation in road vehicles to show, record and store automatically or semi-automatically details of the movement of such vehicles and of certain work periods of their drivers. This equipment includes cables, sensors, an electronic driver information device, one (two) card reader(s) for the insertion of one or two driver memory card(s), an integrated or separate printer, display instruments, facilities for downloading the data memory, facilities to display or print information on demand, and facilities for the input of the places where the daily work period begins and ends.

- *Data memory* means an electronic storage system built into the recording equipment, capable of storing at least 365 calendar days from the recording equipment. The memory should be protected in such a way as to prevent unauthorized access to and manipulation of the data and detect any such attempt.

- A '*driver card with memory*' means a removable information transfer and storage device allocated by the authorities of the member states to each individual driver for the purposes of identification of the driver and storage of essential data. The format and technical specifications of the driver card must meet the requirements laid down in the technical annex to the regulations.

- A *'control card'* means a removable data transfer and storage device for use in the card reader of the recording equipment, issued by the authorities of the member states to competent authorities to get access to the data stored in the data memory or in the driver cards for reading, printing and/or downloading.

- A *'company data card'* means a removable data transfer device issued by the member state's authorities to the owner of vehicles fitted with recording equipment. The company data card allows for displaying, downloading and printing of the data.

- A *'workshop data card'* means a removable data transfer device for use by vehicle and equipment manufacturers and authorized personnel operating in a DVSA-approved workshop. It is valid for one year and allows the equipment to be tested and calibrated and data to be downloaded.

- *Downloading* means the copying of a part of or a complete set of data stored in the data memory of the vehicle or in the memory of the driver card, but which does not alter or delete any stored data, allows for the origin of downloaded data to be authenticable and to be kept in a format that can be used by any authorized person, and ensures that any attempts to manipulate data are detectable.

Function and Use of Digital Instruments

The regulations require digital instruments to be able to record, store, display and print out specified statutory information as follows.

Recording and Storing in the Data Memory

The instrument is required to record and store:

- Distance travelled by the vehicle with an accuracy of 1 km.

- Speed of the vehicle:
  - momentary speed of the vehicle at a frequency of 1 second for the last 24 hours of use of the vehicle;
  - exceeding the authorized speed of the vehicle, defined as any period of more than 1 minute during which the vehicle speed exceeds 90 kph for N3 vehicles or 105 kph for M3 vehicles (with time, date, maximum speed of the over-speeding, average speed during the period concerned).

- Periods of driving time (times and dates), with an accuracy of one minute.

- Other periods of work or of availability (times and dates) with an accuracy of one minute.

- Breaks from work and daily rest periods (times and dates) with an accuracy of one minute.

- For electronic recording equipment, which is equipment operated by signals transmitted electrically from the distance and speed sensor, any interruption exceeding 100 milliseconds in the power supply of the recording equipment (except lighting), in the power supply of the distance and speed sensor, and any interruption in the signal lead to the distance and speed sensor, with date, time, duration and driver card issue number.

- The driver card issue number with times and dates of insertion and removal.

- For each driver card that is inserted for the first time after it was used in another item of recording equipment:
  - current driving time since the last break or rest period;
  - driving time for the day after the last rest period of at least eight hours;
  - driving times for the day between two rest periods of at least eight hours for the preceding 27 calendar days, with date, time and duration;
  - total of the driving times for the current week and the preceding week and the total of the driving times of the two completed preceding weeks;
  - rest periods of at least eight hours' duration for the day and the preceding 27 calendar days, in each case with date, time and duration;
  - the VRN of the vehicles driven.

- Date, time and duration of driving without an inserted or a functioning driver card.

- Data recorded on the places at which the daily work period began and ended.

- Automatically identifiable system faults of the recording equipment with date, time and driver card issue number.

- Faults in the driver card with date, time and driver card issue number.

- Workshop card number of the authorized fitter or workshop with date of at least the last installation inspection and/or periodic inspection of the recording equipment.

- Control card number with date of control card insertion and type of control (display, printing, downloading). In the case of downloading, the period downloaded should be recorded.

- Time adjustment with date, time and card issue number.

- Driving status (single/crew driving – driver/co-driver).

Storage on the Driver Card

The driver card must be capable of storing:

- the essential data for a period of at least the last 28 days combined with the VRN identification of the vehicle driven and the data as required above;
- the events and faults mentioned above with the VRN identification of the vehicle driven;
- the date and time of insertion and removal of the driver card and distance travelled during the corresponding period;
- the date and time of insertion and removal of the co-driver card with issue number.

Data must be recorded and stored on the driver card in such a way as to rule out any possibility of falsification.

Recording and Storing for Two Drivers

Where vehicles are used by two drivers, the driving time must be recorded and stored on the driver card of the driver who is driving the vehicle. This means that the cards need to be changed over from their slots on the vehicle unit (VU) when the drivers change over. The equipment must record and store in the data memory and on the two driver cards simultaneously, but distinctly, details of the information listed above.

Recording Driver Walkaround

Increasingly, DVSA examining officers are checking on recordings of the time that drivers spend doing their daily walkaround checks of the vehicle before starting out on their journey. Where no such recording is shown, their assumption is that no such check was carried out, which could lead to further enquiries by the DVSA. Conversely, if drivers insist they did check their vehicle, this may lead the examiner to allege that they have failed to keep a proper record or have falsified their record, both of which are offences for which prosecution may follow.

Recording Multi-Drop Deliveries

For tachograph recording purposes, a minute is defined as 'the same type of activity as the longest activity within the minute'. This means that if a driver records driving for 25 seconds within a minute and 'other work' for 35 seconds within that same minute, the whole minute will be recorded as 'other work'. This is accepted by the authorities as being acceptable for recording the activities of drivers who need to stop and start the vehicle repeatedly during their periods of duty.

Displaying or Printing for an Authorized Examiner

The equipment must be capable of displaying or printing, on request, the following information:

- Driver card issue number, expiry date of the card.
- The surname and first name of the driver who is the cardholder.
- Current driving time since the last break or rest period.
- Driving time for the day after the last rest period of at least eight hours.
- Driving times for the day between two rest periods of at least eight hours for the preceding 27 calendar days on which the driver has driven, with date, time and duration.
- Total of the driving times for the current week and the preceding week and the total times for the two completed preceding weeks.
- The other periods of work and availability.
- Rest periods of at least eight hours' duration for the day and the preceding 27 days, in each case with date, time and duration.
- VRN identification of vehicles driven for at least the last 28 calendar days, with the distance travelled per vehicle and day, time of first insertion and last removal of the driver card and the time of change of vehicle.
- Time adjustment with date, time and card issue number.
- Interruption of power supply to the recording equipment, with date, time, duration and driver card issue number.
- Sensor interruption, with date, time, duration and driver card issue number.
- The vehicle identification number (VIN) and/or VRN identification of the vehicle driven.
- Driving without driver card as defined above for the last 28 calendar days.
- Details of the information stored concerning the driver.
- Recorded data on the places where the daily work period began and ended.
- The automatically identifiable system faults of the recording equipment, with date, time and driver card issue number.
- The faults in the driver card, with date and time and driver card issue number.
- Control card number, with date of control card insertion and type of control (display, printing, downloading). In the case of downloading, the period downloaded should be recorded.
- Exceeding the authorized speed as defined above, with date, time and driver card issue number for the current week and in any case including the last day of the previous week.

- Summary reports to permit compliance with the relevant regulations to be checked.

Figure 5.2 shows a list of the pictograms used in digital tachographs, both on screen and on the printouts, while Figure 5.3 is a sample printout with an explanation of the coding (both courtesy of Siemens VDO).

Smart Cards

Crucial to the whole system is the driver ('smart') card, often referred to as a 'digi-card', which is personal to the individual and carries identification information and other essential data. It has a capacity to store relevant data on driving and working times, breaks and rest periods covering at least 28 days, and comprises the legal record in place of the current tachograph chart. The card itself is tamper-proof, and strict regulatory systems are established by national governments to prevent fraudulent issue, use and transfer of cards within their territories. Cards are valid for five years, after which time they should be renewed by application to the DVLA no later than 15 days before the expiry of the card.

Once issued, a digi-card must be able to be produced by the driver, even when driving a vehicle with an analogue tachograph, in order to allow the enforcement authorities to make a full check on the driver's activities. Failure to produce the card upon request could lead to the driver being prosecuted.

The plastic card is similar in size to a photocard driving licence or credit card, with a microchip embedded in it. There are four different cards:

- driver cards – which drivers insert at the commencement of their journeys to record driving and working activities (see Figures 5.4 and 5.5);
- company cards – for use by vehicle operators to protect and download the data;
- workshop cards – available only to approved tachograph calibration centres;
- control cards – for use only by DVSA examiners and the police for carrying out enforcement activities.

Before commencing a journey the driver is required to insert the driver card into the 1st (driver) or 2nd (co-driver) slot on the front of the VU. Where the vehicle has two drivers (ie multi-crewing), the DfT has advised that both drivers must insert their respective driver cards into the VU when they start using the vehicle. While the vehicle is moving, time spent as the second driver will be recorded as a period of availability and the mode cannot be changed to other work or to a break until the vehicle comes to rest. The time setting (and all manual entries) must be in UTC (Universal Time Coordinated), which replaced Greenwich Mean Time (GMT), and must remain so both in the UK and throughout Europe. The 'centre field' details,

Figure 5.2   Pictograms used in digital tachographs

Basic pictograms	Pictograms list	Pictogram combinations
People	**Actions**	▯ ● Control pace
⌂ Company		● → Location begin
▯ Controller	Control	→ ● Location end
o Driver	Driving	☉→ From time
⊤ Workshop/	Inspection/	→ ☉ To time
test station	calibration	
⊟ Manufacturer		>> Overspeed

Activities	**Duration**	**Cards**
▨ Available	Current availability	o▤ Driver card
	period	⌂▤ Company card
o Drive	Continuous driving	▯▤ Control card
	time	⊤▤ Workshop card
⊢ Rest	Current rest period	
⚹ Work	Current work period	**Driving**
‖ Break	Cumulative break	o o Crew driving
	time	o │ Driving time for one week
? Unknown		o ‖ Driving time for two weeks

Equipment	**Functions**	**Print-outs**
1 Driver slot		24h ▤▼ Daily driver activities from driver card
2 Co-driver slot		print-out
▤ Card		24h ⊟▼ Daily driver activities from VU print-out
☉ Clock		! ✕ ▤▼ Events and faults from driver card
▢ Display		print-out
⊥ External storage	Downloading	! ✕ ⊟▼ Events and faults from VU print-out
÷ Power supply		⊤☉▼ Technical data print-out
▼ Printer/	Printing	>>▼ Overspeed print-out
print-out		
⊓ Sensor		**Faults**
⊟ Vehicle/		✕▤ 1 Card fault (driver slot)
vehicle unit		✕▤ 2 Card fault (co-driver slot)
		✕▢ Display fault

Miscellaneous

!   Event
✕   Fault
●   Location
🔒   Security
>   Speed
☉   Time
Σ   Total/summary

Qualifiers

24h   Daily
│   Weekly
‖   Two weeks
→   From or to

Figure 5.3   Example of a typical printout from a digital tachograph

```
Driver Activities Card Daily Print-Out
+---------------------------+
|▼ 15/10/1997 15:15 (UTC)|    1  Printing - Date & Time (UTC)
|-----------▼-----------|       Delimiter Print-out general information
|# DavidFish             |    2  Controller - Name
|#■B/4803992633          |       Controller - Card Number
|                        |
|#→ .................... |    3  Control Place (Hand written)
|                        |
|                        |
|□ WALSTER               |    5  Driver - Last Name
|  Nick D.               |       Driver - First Name
|□■GB/135798642          |    6  Driver Card - Number
|  14/05/2004            |       Driver Card - Expiry Date
|                        |
|▲ XAD1117483A           |    7  Vehicle - VIN
|  B/PV1772              |       Vehicle - Nation + VRN
|                        |
|Tacho-Manufacturer      |    8  Tachograph - Manufacturer Name
|Tacho-Part-Number       |       Tachograph - Part Number
|T Workshop-Name         |       Last Inspection/Calibration - Workshop Name
|T■GB/159482637          |       Workshop Card Number
|T 05/03/1997            |       Date
|-----------□-----------|        Delimiter driver information
|■▼14/10/1997            |    4  Type of Print-Out (Card) & Enquiry date
|                        |
|? 00:00  06:17  06h18   |    9  Card not inserted. Activity unknown
|------------------|        10  Card insertion
|▲ B/PV1772             |        Insertion in VRN No
|  42000 km              |        Odometer at card insertion
|⊙ 14:12  16:03  01h52   |   11  Detailed activities
|✳ 16:04  18:00  01h57   |
|ʜ 18:01  18:01  00h01   |
|  81111 km; 111 km      |   12  Odometer, Distance travelled at Card withdrawal
|                        |
|? 18:02  23:59  05h58   |    9  Card not inserted. Activity unknown
|-----------Σ-----------|        Summary information
|→✳06:19 F               |   13  Start daily work time Country/Region Odometer
|✳→18:00 E   CAT         |        End daily work time Country/Region Odometer
|                        |
|  ⊙ 04h59  374 km       |   14  Activity totals
|  ✳ 03h42  ▨ 00h11      |
|  ʜ 01h14  ? 13h54      |
|                        |
|□2 05h25                |   15  Duration of crew status
|-----------!■✕---------|    16  Delimiter Cards Events and Faults
|!S12/09/1997 18:24      |        Event Security breach attempt and VRN number
|B/PV1772                |        of the vehicle in which this event/fault occurred
|!↯12/09/1997 18:23      |        Event Power supply interruption and VRN
|B/PV1772                |        number of the vehicle in which this event/fault
|                        |        occurred
|-----------!▲✕---------|    17  Delimiter Vehicle Unit Events and Faults
|!л05/09/1997 06:35      |        Event Sensor interruption
|□■IT/836254363          |        Driver Card Number
|✕▲21/08/1997 12:45      |        Fault VU
|□■---                   |        No card inserted
|✕▼21/08/1997 12:46      |        Fault Printer
|□■---                   |        No card inserted
|-----------------------|
|                        |
|□ .................... |    18  Driver's signature if applicable
|                        |
|# .................... |    19  Controller's signature if applicable
+---------------------------+
```

Figure 5.4   Front view of driver 'smart' card

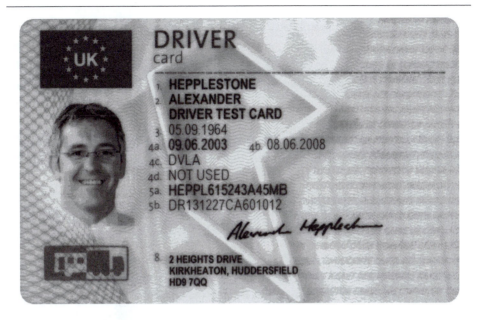

Figure 5.5   Rear view of driver 'smart' card

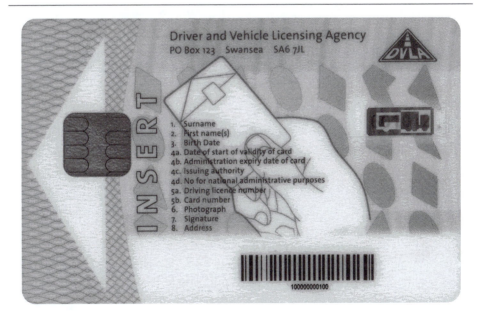

with digital instruments, will be recorded automatically by the tachograph – ie driver name, VRN, start and finish odometer readings and name of place code.

In the same way that drivers and co-drivers currently record their different activities – driving, other work, break and rest – by changing the mode switch and by swapping the position of charts in the tachograph head, with digital tachographs the mode switch will have to be turned and digital smart cards will need to be swapped between driver and co-driver slots in the instrument when double-manning a vehicle.

Details of time spent working away from the vehicle that are currently written on the rear of the tachograph chart (ie record sheet) will have to be input manually into the digital tachograph. However, time spent embarking and disembarking ferries where this interrupts a driver's daily rest can be entered using the 'ferry flag' facility. The system will also record details of any faults, interference, errors and over-speeding that occur.

NB: To select the 'Ferry Flag' the driver needs to select the ferry/train mode on the digital tachograph. Actions then depend upon the particular journey. For example, if the ferry crossing is going to be part of the driver's daily rest, the driver needs to select daily rest while in the ferry queue and then select the ferry mode for actual embarkation. Embarkation will automatically be shown as driving. Once on the ferry the driver needs to select rest mode again and the record will have been made.

If the driver has finished their daily rest while on the ferry, the tachograph should be used as if the driver was starting the working day as usual. However, if the driver needs to finish their daily rest immediately following disembarkation, they need to select ferry mode immediately prior to disembarkation, disembark, park up and re-select rest mode.

Note also that ferry mode is to be used when these circumstances apply to train journeys.

All this information will be stored for at least 28 days on the driver's personal smart card and for at least a year in the VU. It is also worthy of note that the driver's digi-card is planned to be merged with the driver's driving licence to form a single card to be used in future 'smart' tachographs.

Recording Rules

The crossed hammers, used to record 'other work' (ie any activity other than driving) done for both the driving employer and any other employer outside of transport.

The rectangle, used to record 'periods of availability' as defined in EU Directive 2002/15/EC – The Road Transport Directive – and as described in the section 'The Road Transport (Working Time) Regulations 2005' in Chapter 3.

Fees for Digital Tachograph Cards (ie Digi-Cards)

Applications for new or replacement driver digi-cards are made using form D777B and applications for new or replacement company cards are made using form D779B.

The following table of fees has been set by the DVLA for digital tachograph 'smart' cards.

Table 5.2   Table of fees

Transaction	Driver card	Company card	Workshop card	Control card
Card application	£32	£32	£0	£0
Renewal after 5 years	£19	£19	£0	£0
Replacement – lost/stolen	£19	£19	£0	£0
Exchange	£0	£32	£0	£0
Malfunction	£0	£0	£0	£0

NB: *Further information on digital tachographs can be found on the official Government website: www.gov.uk/tachographs*

Typical Digital Equipment

Typical equipment comprises a recording unit (ie the VU) incorporating a mass memory fitted into the vehicle instrument panel. This is connected to an intelligent sensor to enable transmission of 'driving' pulses to the recording unit and to the instrument cluster for displaying road speed, time and distance travelled. Connections are provided (ie data interfaces) to allow readout of the stored data via a PC or laptop, and for it to be printed out. Various warning functions are incorporated and a keypad connection can be made to input additional commands and relevant data.

Production of Digital Records

Operator Responsibility for Digital Records

Operators should follow the guidance given by the DVSA in its Safe Operator's Guide, which is summarized below. In particular, it is important that the operator can show that drivers are keeping to the hours and record-keeping regulations by having a good monitoring and control system in place. Digital tachographs require the electronic downloading of data from driver digi-cards and from the tachograph. The downloading and monitoring system should cover the following requirements, which are the responsibility of the transport manager or a delegated person.

Inspection and Calibration

Digital tachographs need to be inspected every two years. At the time of inspection they must also be calibrated.

Issue of Tachograph Record Print Rolls

- Record the quantity and type of print rolls* (see below) issued (ie make and type-approval number).
- Record the driver's name and date of issue.

*Drivers must have a spare print roll available to use should the roll in the printer be removed and retained by the enforcement authorities or if the roll in the printer is completely used up, in the same way as drivers using analogue tachographs need to have at least one spare chart. Should the print roll be removed by the enforcement authorities and the driver does not have a replacement, they will be unable to continue to drive until a replacement roll has been fitted.

Return of Record Sheets and Printouts

- Record the date and time of chart returns and/or printouts.
- Record other relevant details (eg damaged or defaced charts and missing records).

Checking and Downloading of Driver Digi-Cards

- Download data from driver digi-cards at regular intervals – ie at a maximum of 28-day intervals and sufficiently often that no data are lost (NB: digi-cards generally hold up to 28 days' data, overwriting the oldest records when the card is full).
- Routinely check and download digi-cards, particularly for agency and part-time drivers, to ensure that the cards are valid and that drivers have adequate time to complete their duties.

Locking in and out of Digital Tachographs with a Company Card

Company cards allow operators to download data from the digital tachograph, which should be done routinely within the legal maximum time, ie at a maximum of 90-day intervals, to ensure that data are complete and accurate and to enable operators to take timely action to remedy any problems. The DVSA recommends that data are downloaded before the maximum 90-day limit to ensure no data are lost. This download will identify all driving activities, driver cards used and driving where no card has been used, and any 'events' or 'faults' recorded by the instrument. Company cards can also be used to 'lock out' third parties who may want unauthorized access to the records produced.

Analysing Digital Data

Software is needed to analyse data. Alternatively, analysis can be carried out remotely by a third party.

Records of Analysis of Driver Record

Records should be kept of the analysis and the results from both analogue and digital tachographs, particularly why journeys were not completed as scheduled, breakdowns, traffic delays, etc, and whether the driver has endorsed the back of the chart or the printout as appropriate.

Lists of Faults and Offences

Lists should be kept of all drivers' hours and records of offences, occurrences of tachograph faults and instances of speeding found during analysis. A procedure should be in place to bring these promptly to the attention of the person running the operation (ie the CPC holder) and the drivers. The monitoring and control system should also include informing the drivers of any issues and the drivers in question acknowledging that they have been informed.

Monitoring and Training of Drivers

A system should be in place to interview drivers when offences are discovered, with a view to arranging suitable training programmes and, where necessary, imposing sanctions.

Repairing Tachographs

Adequate procedures should be in place for ensuring that tachograph malfunctions are dealt with, bearing in mind that it is an offence to use a vehicle with a defective tachograph. Any breakdown of the equipment must be dealt with as soon as possible but, in any case, the repairs must be carried out en route within seven days if the vehicle is not going to return to base within that time.

Storing Record Sheets and Printouts

It is a legal requirement that tachograph records (both charts and printouts) are kept for at least one year* from the date they were made – filed in date order under either the driver's name or the VRNs.

As noted above, this may be extended to two or even six years depending upon the purpose for which the records are kept.

Storing Digital Data

This data must be stored in its downloaded format (in accordance with the technical data in Regulation 1360/2002/EC) and operators are legally required to ensure that the downloading equipment used (by themselves or by contracted outside agencies) can fulfil this requirement. The data may be stored remotely from the operating centre (eg at the premises of an analysis company), provided it can be made readily available on request (eg by email transfer if necessary).

Production of Digital Records

Drivers working with digital tachographs must be able to produce for inspection on request by an inspecting officer:

- their digital tachograph card;
- any printouts and manual records for the current day and for the previous 28 calendar days;
- any analogue tachograph charts relating to the use of such instruments during this period.

Drivers who fail to produce these may find themselves prohibited from driving for a period of time and fined. These actions will also be recorded against the OCRS and may result in vehicles being pinpointed more frequently during roadside enforcement checks.

Signing of Digital Records

In instances where a smart card malfunctions, drivers are required by law to produce two copies of the digital printout from the tachograph each day, one at the beginning of the journey and the other at the end. These copies must be annotated to show the date and driver's name or driver's licence number, and they must sign each copy. If the printer is also malfunctioning then a written record needs to be kept, but this too must be signed at the start and end of duty.

Return of Records

Digital records must be returned by the driver to the employer or the vehicle operator, normally within 28 days but this may vary according to circumstances. Where this is not possible, the enforcement authorities will require evidence that the employer/operator has adequate alternative systems in place for controlling drivers' compliance with the driving hours and working time regulations.

Smart Tachographs

All new vehicles from June 2019 are fitted with smart tachographs. They are designed to reduce record falsification and improve the overall administration of drivers' hours and driver activity. The smart functions include:

- a Global Positioning System (GPS), which allows the location of the vehicle to be determined when away from base and also allows tracking throughout a journey;
- the capability to be linked to the vehicle telematics systems, enabling the operator to determine exactly what activities the driver is performing at any given time.

In relation to GPS, smart tachographs automatically record the vehicle's position at various times of the day. These include:

- at the starting location of the daily work period;
- every three hours of accumulated driving;
- at the location where the daily work period finishes.

The smart tachograph also automatically records the country in which the vehicle is located and operating. This can help in cases where the true location of a vehicle may need to be proven.

Enforcement authorities can access data held by the tachograph without stopping the vehicle. This in turn allows them to target enforcement activities to non-compliant operations.

Data that can be accessed include:

- the latest attempted security breach;
- the longest interruption of the power supply;
- sensor faults;
- motion data errors;
- vehicle motion recording conflicts;
- driving without a valid card;

- crew member card insertion while driving;
- time adjustment data;
- calibration data including dates of the two most recent calibrations;
- vehicle registration data;
- speed recorded by the tachograph.

In order to comply with data protection legislation and to protect drivers, the data captured do not include details about typical drivers' hours offences, such as failing to take a break or exceeding the daily driving limit. In addition, the data can only be retained for a total of three hours unless some sort of offence or irregularity is detected. Even where this is detected, the data cannot, by themselves, lead to automatic penalties but they can be used towards further action being taken.

Offences

It is an offence to use or cause or permit the use of a vehicle which does not have a fully calibrated tachograph installed, and for drivers to fail to keep records by means of a tachograph (or manually if the instrument is defective) or to make false recordings. Further, it is an offence for drivers to fail to return used charts to their employer within 42 days after use of an analogue tachograph or 28 days for a digital tachograph, or to fail to notify their first employer of any other employer for whom they drive vehicles to which the regulations apply.

In many cases, offences committed by drivers result in charges against the employer for 'causing' or 'permitting' offences. For example, where tachograph records go missing and cannot be produced for examination by the enforcement authorities, the employer may be charged with any one of three (or even all three) relevant offences: namely, failing to cause the driver to keep a record, failing to preserve the record or failing to produce the record. There are three types of offence:

- missing mileages when charts are compared;
- use of illegal/cloned digi-cards by drivers;
- interference with tachograph systems.

Penalties can be a fine of up to level 4 on the standard scale (currently £2,500) and conviction for such offences can jeopardize both the employer's 'O' licence (by seriously impacting on the OCRS) and the driver's HGV driving entitlement. Conviction for the more serious offences of making false entries on a tachograph chart and forgery can result in level 5 fines of up to £5,000 (per offence) or imprisonment for up to two years.

Heavy penalties are also likely for operators and LGV drivers found guilty in UK courts of forging tachograph entries relating to international journeys. Fines may be in excess of the current level 5 standard scale maximum of £5,000, and custodial sentences longer than those available to the courts under other legislation.

The courts have ruled that in cases where a driver or transport operator claims not to have known that the tachograph instrument in a vehicle had been fitted with a device intended to interfere with its operation (ie a trip device to aid the production of false records), this was no excuse and an offence of 'strict liability' was committed, to which there is no defence.

Tachograph Records as Evidence

Tachograph records going back up to 28 days may be used as evidence of further infringements or offences by drivers facing prosecution for drivers' hours-related offences identified at roadside checks. This 'historic offence' provision means not only that fixed penalty notices can be issued for previous offences committed by UK drivers, but also that fixed penalty notices can be issued to foreign drivers who have committed earlier offences while in the UK. In addition, the TCs may impose short-term LGV driving bans on drivers found from their records to have regularly exceeded maximum speed limits.

Note: Clearly, analogue tachographs are being replaced by both digital and fourth-generation tachographs but there is no set date, as yet, for them to be statutorily replaced by the newer technology.

Production of Records

Under digital tachograph legislation (ie Regulation 561/2006/EC – Article 26), drivers must be able to produce records (ie charts or digital printouts) to the enforcement authorities (eg the DVSA and the police) as follows:

- When driving vehicles with digital tachographs or a combination of both digital and analogue types:
  - record sheets (ie charts) for the day of driving with the analogue instrument and for the previous 28 days;
  - any manual record and printout made by a digital instrument during the current week and for the previous 28 days.

Driver Licensing and Licence Penalties 06

Driver Licensing

Any person wishing to drive a motor vehicle on a public road in the UK or within Europe must hold a licence showing a driving entitlement (either full or provisional) for the relevant category of vehicle. Specifically in the case of HGVs, drivers must hold a licence showing a relevant vocational driving entitlement.

It is an offence to drive, or to cause or permit another person to drive, a vehicle on the road without a valid driving licence. It is the responsibility of the employer of any person required to drive for business purposes to ensure that, irrespective of their function, status or seniority, they are correctly licensed to drive company vehicles.

In the case of HGVs, the driving licence categories are C1, C and CE.

Checking Licences

Operators should check drivers' licences on a regular basis – initially when giving a driver a job and then at least once every three to six months..

Licence checks can be made in several different ways:

1 Online by using the 'View or Share Driving Licence' system at GOV.UK. This allows drivers to gain access to their driving licence details and share them with an employer.

2 A telephone service where the driver calls 0300 790 6801 to give permission for the check and the employer then calls 0906 139 3837 to get the information.

3 A postal service using form D888/1, completed by the driver, to request the information.

4 The DVLA Access to Driver Data (ADD) service, which is a business-to-business facility allowing employers to access live licence data relating to drivers, with their permission.

To check licences of non-UK nationals, drivers can contact DVLA on 0300 790 6801 to give permission for the check by allowing the employer to call the same number within seven days of permission being granted, or the operator can call the same number with the driver involved in the conversation.

With the 'View or Share Driving Licence' system, it works in the following way. A driver can view their driving licence, including the vehicle categories they are entitled to drive and any endorsements or penalty points that they may have, by using the free View Driving Licence service. This can be found at GOV.UK. Once the site is accessed the driver needs to enter:

- their driving licence number;
- their National Insurance number; and
- their home address postcode.

Should the driver then wish to share the details, they select the 'Share your information' tab and click on the 'Get a code' box. This code enables the person the driver wishes to share the details with to access the information on a single occasion any time up to 21 days after the code has been issued.

Invalidation of Insurance

Driving without a valid driving licence can invalidate insurance cover and could result in any accident or damage claim being refused by the insurance company under the terms of its policy contract.

Licensing Provisions

The licensing provisions described in this chapter are principally contained in:

- the Road Traffic Act 1988;
- the Road Traffic (Driver Licensing and Information Systems) Act 1989;
- the Road Traffic (New Drivers) Act 1995;
- the Third European Directive on Driving Licences (3EUD) (2006/126/EC);

and the following regulations:

- the Motor Vehicles (Driving Licences) (Large Goods and Passenger Carrying Vehicles) Regulations 1990 (which deal with entitlements to drive HGVs over 7.5 tonnes gross weight and passenger-carrying vehicles that are used for hire and reward operations), plus a number of subsequent amendments;
- the Motor Vehicles (Driving Licences) Regulations 1999;
- the Motor Vehicles (Driving Licences) Amendment Regulations (updating fees);
- the Motor Vehicles (Driving Licences) (Amendment) Regulations 2018.

For driver licensing purposes:

- a heavy goods vehicle is a motor vehicle (not being a medium-sized goods vehicle) which is constructed or adapted to carry or haul goods and its permissible maximum weight exceeds 7.5 tonnes;
- a medium-sized goods vehicle is defined as one having a permissible maximum weight exceeding 3.5 tonnes but not exceeding 7.5 tonnes;
- a large passenger-carrying vehicle is a vehicle constructed or adapted to carry more than 16 passengers;
- a small passenger-carrying vehicle is a vehicle which carries passengers for hire or reward and is constructed or adapted to carry more than eight but not more than 16 passengers.

Driving Licences

Vocational licences show, where appropriate, provisional driving entitlements and include a clear list of entitlements. They operate using universal medical requirements for drivers and universal periods of validity for licences of five years, with universal validity for photographs of 10 years.

The DVLA no longer issues paper driving licences. An EU directive required all member states to issue driving licences in a card format containing the licence holder's photograph and signature. Because of this the paper 'counterpart' licence was no longer relevant, because any endorsements on the licence could not be viewed. This means that drivers hoping to hire vehicles need to get proof of their entitlement to do so by contacting the DVLA to download a copy of their licence details which shows endorsements, or not. This is done by accessing the 'View or Share Driving Licence' system mentioned previously.

Organ Donor Option

It is the responsibility of the potential donor to ensure that their wishes to donate are recorded. It should be noted that in Scotland and Wales, organ donor consent is assumed unless the person actually physically opts out of the scheme.

The Issuing Authority

Responsibility for the issue of vocational driving entitlements rests with the DVLA, Swansea. However, the TCs retain a disciplinary role in regard to vocational entitlements, as described in the section 'Penalties against Vocational Entitlements' to be found later in this chapter.

All applications in connection with driver licensing (ie for both ordinary and vocational driving entitlements) should be addressed to the DVLA, Swansea followed by the appropriate postcode, ie:

- SA99 1BN for replacement licences; and

- SA99 1DH for licence renewal.

A full list of DVLA postcodes (including vehicle-related issues) is available on the DVLA website, but also see below.

Online licence applications are encouraged by the DVLA and are quick and simple. They can be made using the website at www.gov.uk/browse/driving/driving-licences.

Further information on driver licensing can be obtained from the Customer Services Unit, DVLA, Swansea SA6 7JL (tel: 0300 790 6801 for general enquiries about driver licensing).

- Changes to a V5C = DVLA SA99 1BA

- First Registration = DVLA SA99 1BE

- Enforcement Enquiries = DVLA SA99 1AH

- Medical Enquiries = DVLA SA99 1TU

- Applications using V11 or V890 = DVLA SA99 1AR

- Vehicle and Driver Record Enquiries = DVLA SA99 1BP

- Replacement Driving Licences = DVLA SA99 1BN

- Renewal of Driving Licences (10 years) = DVLA SA99 1DH

- Trade Licensing = DVLA SA99 1DZ

- Trade Disposals = DVLA SA99 1BD

- Trade Personalized Number Plates = DVLA SA99 1DP

- Private Personalized Number Plates = DVLA SA99 1DS

Minimum Age for Drivers of Small, Medium and Large Vehicles

Certain minimum ages are specified by law for drivers of small, medium and large motor vehicles, as follows.

Small Goods Vehicles

- Small goods vehicles not exceeding 3.5 tonnes maximum authorized mass (MAM) and alternatively fuelled small goods vehicles up to 4.25 tonnes MAM (including the weight of a trailer not exceeding 750 kg MAM):

Category B   *17 years**

*16 if receiving a Disability Living Allowance (ie mobility allowance)

- Small goods vehicles not exceeding 3.5 tonnes MAM (including the weight of a trailer exceeding 750 kg MAM):

  Category BE   *17 years*

NB: *To take advantage of the increased weight allowance to 4.25 tonnes, drivers need to have undertaken at least five hours of training in an alternatively fuelled vehicle of that size. The training must be delivered by either an instructor on the National Register of LGV Instructors or an instructor on the National Vocational Driving Instructors Register.*

Medium Goods Vehicles

- Medium-sized goods vehicles constructed or adapted to transport goods, which exceed 3.5 tonnes MAM but not 7.5 tonnes MAM (including the weight of a trailer not exceeding 750 kg MAM):

  Category C1   *18 years**

  *17 if member of the armed services

- Combinations of vehicles where the towing vehicle is in subcategory C1 and its trailer has a MAM of more than 750 kg MAM, provided that the MAM of the combination thus formed does not exceed 12,000 kg and the MAM of the trailer does not exceed the unladen mass of the towing vehicle. (If drivers passed Category B test prior to 1 January 1997 they will be restricted to a total weight not more than 8,250 kg.)

  Category C1E   *21 years* ***

  *17 if member of the armed services

  ** 18 if:

  – having passed a driving test for this category and Driver CPC initial qualification;

  – learning to drive or taking a driving test for this category or Driver CPC initial qualification;

  – undergoing a national vocational training course to obtain a Driver CPC initial qualification.

Large Goods Vehicles

- Vehicles over 3,500 kg MAM with a trailer up to 750 kg MAM:

Category C   *21 years* ***

*17 if member of the armed services

** 18 if:

– having passed a driving test for this category and Driver CPC initial qualification;

– learning to drive or taking a driving test for this category or Driver CPC initial qualification;

– undergoing a national vocational training course to obtain a Driver CPC initial qualification.

- Vehicles over 3,500 kg MAM with a trailer over 750 kg MAM:

Category CE   *21 years* ***

*17 if member of the armed services

** 18 if:

– having passed a driving test for this category and Driver CPC initial qualification;

– learning to drive or taking a driving test for this category or Driver CPC initial qualification;

– undergoing a national vocational training course to obtain a Driver CPC initial qualification.

NB: Drivers with vocational entitlement to drive medium and large goods vehicles who have passed their vocational tests since 19 January 2013 need to renew their vocational entitlements every five years irrespective of their age at the time of passing the test. The medical requirements for these renewals entail 'self-certification' declarations by drivers up until the age of 45, after which time full medicals will be required.

Road Rollers

A person under 21 but not less than 17 years old may drive a road roller if it:

- is propelled by means other than steam;
- has an unladen weight of not more than 11,690 kg;*
- is fitted with metal or hard rollers;
- is not constructed or adapted to carry a load other than water, fuel, accumulators and other equipment used for the purpose of propulsion, loose tools, loose equipment and any object which is specially constructed for attachment to the vehicle so as to increase, temporarily, its unladen weight.

* If this weight is exceeded, the minimum age for driving a roller is 21 years.

Agricultural Tractors

A person under 17 but over 16 may drive an agricultural tractor only if it is:

- of the wheeled type;
- not more than 2.45 metres wide including the width of any fitted implement;
- specially licensed for excise duty purposes as an agricultural machine;
- not drawing a trailer other than one of the two-wheeled or close-coupled four-wheeled type which is not more than 2.45 metres wide.

Sixteen-year-olds must not drive an agricultural tractor on a road unless they have passed the appropriate test.

Tracked Vehicles

A person under 21, but over 17, may drive a tracked machine providing that the MAM of the machine does not exceed 3,500 kg.

Vehicle Categories/Groups for Driver Licensing

Categories are used to denote the sizes and types of vehicles that may be driven. Licences also show moped and motorcycle categories but these are not included in detail as they do not relate to vehicles. A list of the categories is below:

Category	Vehicle type
Cars and light vans	
B	Motor vehicles not exceeding 3.5 tonnes mass and with not more than eight seats (excluding the driver's seat) including drawing a trailer not exceeding 750 kg mass. Including combinations of Category B vehicles and a trailer where the combined weight does not exceed 3.5 tonnes and the weight of the trailer does not exceed the unladen weight of the towing vehicle.* Note also the concession to 4.25 tonnes, above. *Additional categories covered: F, K, P*
BE	Motor vehicles in Category B drawing a trailer over 750 kg where the combination does not come within Category B.
Medium goods vehicles	
C1	Medium goods vehicles between 3.5 tonnes and 7.5 tonnes (including drawing trailer not exceeding 750 kg) – maximum weight of the combination must not exceed 8.25 tonnes.
C1E	Medium goods vehicles between 3.5 tonnes and 7.5 tonnes and drawing a trailer over 750 kg but does not exceed the unladen weight of the towing vehicle – maximum weight of the combination must not exceed 12 tonnes. *Additional category covered: BE*

Category	Vehicle type

Large goods vehicles

| C | Large goods vehicles over 3.5 tonnes (but excluding vehicles in categories D, F, G and H) including those drawing a trailer not exceeding 750 kg. |
| CE | Large goods vehicles in Category C drawing a trailer exceeding 750 kg. Some CE licences, where the holder was previously qualified to drive vehicles in old HGV class 2 or 3, show a restriction limiting driving to drawbar combinations only. This is coded as a Restriction 102. *Additional category covered: BE* |

Minibuses

| D1 | Passenger vehicles with between 9 and 16 seats including drawing trailer not exceeding 750 kg. |
| D1E | Motor vehicles in Category D1 drawing a trailer over 750 kg – the weight of the trailer must not exceed the unladen weight of the towing vehicle and the maximum weight of the combination must not exceed 12 tonnes. *Additional category covered: BE* |

Passenger vehicles

| D | Passenger vehicles with more than eight seats including drawing a trailer not exceeding 750 kg. |
| DE | Passenger vehicles in Category D drawing a trailer over 750 kg. *Additional category covered: BE* |

Other vehicles

A	Mopeds, motorcycles and tricycles.
F	Agricultural or forestry tractors but excluding any vehicle in Category H.
G	Road rollers.
H	Track-laying vehicles steered by their tracks.
K	Mowing machine or pedestrian-controlled vehicle with up to three wheels and not over 410 kg.
L	Electrically propelled vehicles.

*The concession relating to trailers in Category B (above) came as part of the 2013 EU Directive, which now allows post-1997 Category B drivers to pull trailers, exceeding 750 kg, under some circumstances, providing the drawing vehicle has a MAM of less than 3,500 kg. For example, if a Category B driver, who passed their driving test after 1 January 1997, drives a van with a MAM of 2,300 kg they can now tow a trailer up to a combination weight of 3,500 kg. This means that the driver could tow a 1,200 kg MAM trailer. This provision is not available for drivers driving vehicles with a MAM of 3,500 kg, who are still restricted to drawing trailers not exceeding 750 kg MAM. In any case it is worthy of note that if the trailer MAM cannot be accurately determined, the DVSA recommends that the trailer weight should not exceed more than 70 per cent of the weight of the drawing vehicle.

NB: In the above table, vehicle/trailer weights, unless otherwise specified, are to be taken as the MAM, which is the same as the permissible maximum weight (pmw) for the vehicle/trailer – commonly referred to as the 'gross weight'.

Restricted Category for Pre-1997 Drivers

Drivers of goods vehicles with trailers in Category C1E who passed their Category B test prior to 1 January 1997 are restricted to a total combination weight of 8,250 kg. The restriction is marked on the driver's licence with the code 107. Driving a combination up to the 12-tonne limit requires an additional test.

NB: A full list of licence restrictions and information codes can be found on the GOV.UK website at: www.gov.uk/driving-licence-codes.

Restricted Categories for Post-1997 Drivers

Since 1 January 1997, new drivers passing the car and light vehicle test (ie with vehicles not exceeding 3.5 tonnes pmw) for the first time are not permitted to drive vehicles above this weight without securing additional driving categories on their licence. It is stressed that this restriction to 3.5 tonne driving applies *only* to those who first pass their test since this date; it will not be applied retrospectively to existing licence holders – their existing entitlements are preserved.

Drivers who pass their car test (ie Category B) are not permitted to:

- drive minibuses (in Category D1);
- drive medium-sized goods vehicles (in Category C1); or
- tow large (ie over 750 kg) trailers (in categories BE, C1E and D1E).

They must take a further test if they wish to drive such vehicles or vehicle combinations.

Any driver wishing to drive a vehicle towing a heavy trailer (ie one with a gross weight over 750 kg) must not drive a combination exceeding 3,500 kg MAM without first having passed a test in the associated rigid vehicle towing an appropriate trailer. Learner drivers in categories B, C1, C, D1 and D cannot drive a vehicle towing a trailer of any size.

Towed and Pushed Vehicles

A person who steers a vehicle being towed (whether it has broken down or even has vital parts missing, such as the engine) is 'driving' the vehicle for licensing purposes and therefore needs to hold valid driving entitlement covering that category of vehicle. Conversely, it has been held that a person pushing a vehicle from the outside (ie with both feet on the ground) is not 'driving' a vehicle, nor are they 'using' the vehicle.

Incomplete Vehicles

Drivers of incomplete goods vehicles comprising a chassis and cab only (ie before bodywork is fitted) and of articulated tractor units not yet fitted with a fifth-wheel coupling must (from 1 January 1998) hold either a Category C1 driving entitlement for such vehicles weighing between 3.5 and 7.5 tonnes, or a Category C entitlement for such vehicles weighing over 7.5 tonnes. Prior to this date, incomplete vehicles could be driven on a Category B licence covering motor cars and light vans.

Tractor Units

Drivers of heavy (ie over 3.5 tonnes) articulated tractor units with no semi-trailer attached need hold only a Category C driving entitlement.

Learner Drivers

Learner drivers must hold a provisional driving entitlement to cover them while driving under tuition.

Full Category C (rigid HGV) entitlement holders can use this entitlement in place of a provisional entitlement for learning to drive vehicles in Category CE (ie drawbar combinations and articulated vehicles). But it should be noted that full entitlements in categories B and C1 *cannot* be used as a provisional entitlement for learning to drive vehicles in categories C or CE respectively. A proper provisional entitlement for these classes is required.

Learner drivers must be accompanied, when driving on public roads, by the holder of a full entitlement covering the category of vehicle being driven (see also below) and must not drive a vehicle drawing a trailer, except in the case of articulated vehicles or agricultural trailers. (*NB: Full licence holders must have held the licence for three years.*)

An 'L' plate of the approved dimensions must be displayed on the front and rear of a vehicle being driven by a learner driver (see Chapter 7). Learners driving in Wales may alternatively display a 'D' plate.

Learner drivers of Category B vehicles are allowed to drive on motorways in order to gain 'high speed' driving skills. However, there are some rules which must be obeyed. First, the car must be fitted with dual controls and the driver must be having a lesson with an official, approved driving instructor (ADI). It is the instructor who must assess whether or not the learner driver in question is safe to drive if motorway instruction is planned. However, learner drivers seeking a licence for Category C1, C and CE vehicles and who hold full entitlements in licence categories B, C1 or C, as appropriate, may drive such vehicles on motorways while under tuition as a normal part of their training.

Compulsory Re-Tests for Offending New Drivers

Newly qualified drivers who tot up six or more penalty points on their licence within two years of passing the test revert to learner status (ie with the display of 'L' plates and the need to be accompanied by a qualified driver) and have to re-pass both the theory test and the practical driving test before regaining a full licence.

Supervision of 'L' Drivers

Qualified drivers who supervise learner drivers in cars and in light, medium and large goods vehicles must:

- be at least 21 years old;
- have held a full driving entitlement for a continuous period of at least three years (excluding any periods of disqualification);
- for accompanying learner vocational drivers, have held a relevant entitlement (ie for the type of vehicle on which they are supervising) for at least three years;
- have passed a test for the category of licence being taught. Drivers acquiring an entitlement by 'grandfather rights' cannot supervise learner drivers.

Contravention of these requirements could lead to prosecution of the supervising driver and, on conviction, a fine, penalty points and possibly licence disqualification.

Exemptions from Vocational Licensing

Exemptions from the need to hold a vocational driving entitlement (ie in categories C1, C or CE) apply when driving certain vehicles, as follows (in most cases such vehicles may be driven by the holder of a Category B licence):

1 Steam-propelled vehicles.
2 Road construction vehicles used or kept on the road solely for the conveyance of built-in construction machinery.
3 Engineering plant, but not mobile cranes.*
4 Works trucks.
5 Industrial tractors.
6 Agricultural motor vehicles which are not agricultural or forestry tractors.
7 Digging machines.
8 Vehicles used on public roads only when passing between land occupied by the vehicle's registered keeper and which do not exceed an aggregate of 9.7 km in a calendar week.

9   Vehicles, other than agricultural vehicles, used only for the purposes of agriculture, horticulture or forestry, between areas of land occupied by the same person and which do not travel more than 1.5 km on public roads.

10 Vehicles used for no purpose other than the haulage of lifeboats and the conveyance of the necessary gear of the lifeboats being hauled.

11 Vehicles manufactured before 1 January 1960 used unladen and not drawing a laden trailer.

12 Articulated goods vehicles with an unladen weight not exceeding 3.05 tonnes.

13 Vehicles in the service of a visiting military force or headquarters as defined in the Visiting Forces and International Headquarters (Application of Law) Order 1965.

14 Any vehicle being driven by a police constable for the purpose of removing it to avoid obstruction to other road users or danger to other road users or members of the public, for the purpose of safeguarding life or property, including the vehicle and its load, or for other similar purposes.

15 Breakdown vehicles which weigh less than 3.05 tonnes unladen, provided they are fitted with apparatus for raising a disabled vehicle partly from the ground and for drawing a vehicle when so raised, used solely for the purpose of dealing with disabled vehicles, and carrying no load other than a disabled vehicle and articles used in connection with dealing with disabled vehicles.

16 A passenger-carrying vehicle-recovery vehicle other than an articulated vehicle with an unladen weight of not more than 10.2 tonnes, which belongs to the holder of a PSV 'O' licence, when such a vehicle is going to or returning from a place where it is to give assistance to a damaged or disabled passenger-carrying vehicle or giving assistance to or moving a disabled passenger-carrying vehicle or moving a damaged vehicle.

17 A mobile project vehicle, which is defined as a vehicle exceeding 3.5 tonnes pmw constructed or adapted to carry not more than eight persons in addition to the driver and which carries mainly goods or burden comprising play or educational equipment for children or articles used for display or exhibition purposes.

Drivers of mobile cranes must hold a full vocational entitlement covering vehicles in Category C1 for driving cranes between 3.5 and 7.5 tonnes and Category C for driving cranes over 7.5 tonnes pmw (applicable since 1 January 1999).

Application for Licences and Vocational Entitlements

Applications for driving licences have to be made to Swansea on form D1 for ordinary licences and forms D2 and D4 for vocational licences. Forms are obtainable from main post offices or online at GOV.UK

Health Declaration

Applicants for ordinary licences (Group One) are asked to declare information about their health, particularly as to whether they have:

- had an epileptic event (ie seizure or fit);
- sudden attacks of disabling giddiness, fainting or blackouts;
- severe mental handicap;
- had a pacemaker, defibrillator or anti-ventricular tachycardia device fitted;
- diabetes controlled by insulin;
- angina (heart pain) while driving;
- had a major or minor stroke;
- Parkinson's disease;
- any other chronic neurological condition;
- a serious problem with memory;
- serious episodes of confusion;
- had any type of brain surgery, brain tumour or severe head injury involving hospital inpatient treatment;
- any severe psychiatric illness or mental disorder;
- continuing or permanent difficulty in the use of arms or legs which affects the ability to control a vehicle safely;
- been dependent on or misused alcohol, illicit drugs or chemical substances in the previous three years (excluding drink-driving offences);
- any visual disability which affects both eyes (short/long sight and colour blindness do not have to be declared);
- Obstructive Sleep Apnoea Syndrome (OSAS) (this does not have to be reported unless the driver shows symptoms such as daytime sleepiness).

In addition, Group Two applicants for vocational entitlements (unless submitting a medical report – form D4 – see below) are required to state whether they have:

- sight in only one eye;
- any visual problems affecting either eye;
- angina;
- any heart condition or had a heart operation;
- OSAS.

Applicants for vocational licences must be able to demonstrate visual acuity of at least Snellen 6/7.5 in at least one eye and Snellen 6/6.0 in the other eye.

Where licence applicants have previously declared a medical condition, they are required to state what the condition is, whether it has worsened since it was previously declared and whether any special controls have been fitted to their vehicle since the last licence was issued.

The DVLA's Considerations for Vocational Entitlements

Applicants for vocational driving entitlements must meet specified conditions as follows:

- They must be fit and proper persons.
- They must meet laid-down eyesight requirements.
- They must satisfy a medical examination and specifically must not:
  - have had an epileptic attack in the previous 10 years (see below); or
  - suffer from insulin-dependent diabetes.

The decision as to whether or not an applicant will be granted a vocational driving entitlement rests entirely with the DVLA and in making this decision it will take into account any driving convictions for motoring offences, drivers' hours and record offences, and offences relating to the roadworthiness or loading of vehicles against the applicant in the four years prior to the application, and any offence connected with driving under the influence of drink or drugs during the 11 years prior to the application. The applicant has to declare such convictions on the licence application form (D2) but the DVLA has means of checking to ensure that applicants have declared any such convictions against them.

TCs' Powers in Respect of Vocational Entitlements

Although vocational licences are issued by the DVLA, TCs have powers to consider the fitness of persons applying for or holding them. This allows a TC to call licence applicants or holders to provide information on their conduct and may refuse, suspend or disqualify a person from holding such an entitlement.

Date for Vocational Applications

Application for a vocational driving entitlement should be made not more than three months before the date from which the entitlement is required to run. Reminders will be sent out by the DVLA to existing licence/entitlement holders two months prior to the expiry date of their existing licence/entitlement.

Medical Requirements for Vocational Entitlements

Strict medical standards for vocational entitlement holders ensure that those wishing to drive HGVs are safe to do so and are not suffering from any disease or disability (especially cardiovascular disease, diabetes mellitus, epilepsy, neurosurgical disorders, excessive sleepiness, nervous or mental disorders, vision problems, or the excessive use of prescribed medicines or illicit drugs, for example) which would prevent them from driving safely.

UK applicants for vocational driving entitlements must satisfy medical standards on first application and subsequently. They must undergo a medical examination and have their doctor complete the medical certificate portion of the application form D4 not more than four months before the date when the entitlement is needed to commence.

For drivers who passed their vocational test before 19 January 2013, a further examination and completed medical certificate is required for each five-yearly renewal of the entitlement after reaching the age of 45 years. After reaching the age of 65 years a medical examination is required for each annual renewal of the entitlement. Further medical examinations may be called at any time if there is any doubt as to a driver's fitness to drive.

The form D4 requests applicants' consent to allow the DVLA's medical advisor to obtain reports from their own doctor and any specialist consulted if this helps to establish their medical condition.

Drivers passing their test after 19 January 2013 will still need an initial medical examination using form D4 but will then 'self-certificate' their medical condition every five years until attaining the age of 45, when full medicals will be required.

Driving Following Medical Disqualification

Where an application for a full driving licence is made following the revocation of a licence or the refusal of its renewal on medical grounds, the applicant may be required to take a driving test (or an 'on-road assessment') to determine whether they are fit to regain their licence. A provisional licence may be granted for this purpose (ie to authorize driving on the road), but its use is restricted to driving only during the period preceding and while taking the test, and its authority ceases immediately upon conclusion of the test or assessment.

Medicals for Category C1 Drivers

Since 1 January 1997 new drivers of vehicles over 3.5 tonnes gross weight (ie covered by driving licence Category C1) require the same medical examination that previously applied only to over 7.5 tonnes vocational licence holders and must follow the same regime as described above for subsequent medical examinations.

Medical Examination Fees

Doctors charge a fee for conducting such medical examinations, which the candidate must pay. These examinations are not available on the National Health Service in the UK – current fees are around £120 to £200. The medical fee for licence/entitlement renewal can be claimed as an allowable expense for income tax purposes.

Diabetes

Some drivers with insulin-dependent diabetes may be allowed to drive HGVs, although there is often a requirement that the driver needs to renew the licence more frequently than would otherwise be the case. Diabetes sufferers where the diabetes is controlled by diet and who are 'stable' are not normally affected by driver licensing restrictions, but see below.

Rules for Diabetics

Note: Advice for HGV and coach/bus drivers with diabetes is as follows.

If they are NOT insulin treated but there is a change in their condition they need to inform the DVLA if they:

- have suffered two episodes of severe hypoglycaemia within the last 12 months (the term 'severe' is normally interpreted as suffering hypoglycaemia where assistance was needed from a second person);
- have developed impaired awareness of hypoglycaemia;
- are experiencing visual problems.

In cases where the driver is reliant on insulin, they:

- need to have three months of continuous blood glucose readings available on a memory meter every time they apply for a licence;
- must test their blood glucose no more than two hours before the start of the first journey and every two hours through the day (they will also need to test their blood glucose and record the readings at least twice a day even when not driving).

Finally, because most insulin-treated Group 2 licence holders need to renew their vocational entitlements every 12 months, there is now a set three-year routine to be followed. This is outlined below:

- First application or Year One – self-declaration, GP examination and independent diabetologist examination.
- Year Two – self-declaration and independent diabetologist examination.
- Year Three – self-declaration, GP examination and independent diabetologist examination.

Following the cycle above, it simply repeats itself. For full information visit the diabetes and driving pages on GOV.UK.

Epilepsy

A person will now be prevented from holding a vocational entitlement *only* if they have a 'liability to epileptic seizures'. An applicant must satisfy the DVLA that:

- they have not suffered an epileptic seizure during the 10 years prior to the date when the entitlement is to take effect;
- no epilepsy treatment has been administered during the 10 years prior to the starting date for the entitlement; and
- a consultant nominated by the DVLA has examined the medical history and is satisfied that there is no continuing liability to seizures.

Car, light vehicle and certain other drivers (ie in licence categories A, B, BE, F, G, H, K, L and P), but not vocational drivers, who suffer from epilepsy can obtain a licence to drive such vehicles provided:

- they have been free from an epileptic attack during the period of one year from the date the licence is granted; or,
- if not free from such an attack, they have had an asleep-attack more than three years before the date on which the licence is granted and have had attacks only while asleep between the date of that attack and the date when the licence is granted; and
- the DVLA is satisfied that driving by them will not cause danger.

Coronary Health Problems

Drivers who have suspected coronary health problems are permitted to retain their vocational driving entitlements while medical enquiries are made. The DVLA says that ECG exercise tests will be undertaken no earlier than three months after a coronary event and, providing the driver displays no signs of angina or other significant symptoms, they are allowed to keep their driving entitlement while investigations are made, but subject to the approval of their own doctor.

Drivers who have suffered, or are suffering from, the following heart-related conditions must notify the DVLA:

- heart attack (myocardial infarction, coronary thrombosis);
- coronary angioplasty;
- heart valve disease/surgery;
- coronary artery bypass surgery;
- angina (heart pain);
- heart operation (other than a heart transplant).

The DVLA's Drivers Medical Branch has the following advice for heart sufferers:

- Following a heart attack or heart operation, driving should not be recommenced for at least one month following the attack or operation. Driving may be resumed after this time if recovery has been uncomplicated and the patient's own doctor has given their approval.
- A driver suffering from angina may continue to drive (whether or not they are receiving treatment) unless attacks occur while driving, in which case they must notify the DVLA immediately (see below) and *stop driving*.
- A driver who suffers sudden attacks of disabling giddiness, fainting, falling, loss of awareness or confusion must notify the DVLA immediately (see below) and *stop driving*.

Any driver who has doubts about their ability to continue to drive safely is advised to discuss the matter with their own doctor, who has access to medical advice from the DVLA.

Alcohol and Drug-Related Problems

Persons with repeated convictions for drink-driving or drug-driving offences may be required to satisfy the DVLA (with certification from their own doctor) that they do not have an 'alcohol/drug problem' before their licence is restored to them.

Note: Operators checking licences held by some non-UK, EU drivers may see a Restriction 69. This restriction means that the driver has been convicted of drinking and driving in an EU member state and needs to have a breathalyser fitted into the vehicle, which must be used before they are allowed to take the vehicle on the public road.

Other Medical Conditions

Other conditions which may cause failure of the driver's medical examination include:

- sudden attacks of vertigo ('dizziness');
- OSAS;
- heart disease which causes disabling weakness or pain;
- a history of coronary thrombosis;
- the use of hypertensive drugs for blood pressure treatment;
- serious arrhythmia;
- severe mental disorder;
- severe behavioural problems;
- alcohol dependency;
- inability to refrain from drinking and driving;
- drug abuse and dependency;
- psychotropic medicines taken in quantities likely to impair fitness to drive safely.

A licence will be refused to a driver who is liable to sudden attacks of disabling giddiness or fainting unless these can be controlled.

Those who have had a cardiac pacemaker fitted are advised to discontinue vocational driving, although driving may be permitted if a person who has disabling attacks which are controlled by a pacemaker has made arrangements for regular reviews from a cardiologist and will not be likely to endanger the public.

Notification of New or Worsening Medical Conditions

Once a licence has been granted (whether ordinary or covering vocational entitlements), holders are required to notify the Drivers Medical Group, DVLA at Swansea SA99 1TU (Tel: 0300 790 6806) of the onset, or *worsening*, of any medical condition likely to cause them to be a danger when driving – *failure to do so is an offence*. (The Medical Group is also the contact point for any enquiries relating to medical issues.)

Examples of what must be reported are:

- giddiness;
- fainting;
- blackouts;
- epilepsy;
- diabetes;
- strokes;

- multiple sclerosis;

- Parkinson's disease;

- OSAS (where symptoms are present);

- heart disease;

- angina;

- 'coronaries';

- high blood pressure;

- arthritis;

- disorders of vision;

- mental illness;

- alcoholism;

- drug-taking;

- loss, or loss of use, of any limb.

In many cases the person's own doctor will either advise reporting the condition to the DVLA, or the doctor (or hospital) may advise the DVLA direct. In either case the driving licence will have to be surrendered until the condition clears.

There is no requirement to notify the DVLA of temporary illnesses or disabilities such as sprained or broken limbs where a full recovery is expected within three months.

Most notifiable conditions are now able to be sent to the DVLA after downloading the notification form from the DVLA website. For example, OSAS is notified by completing form SL1 for car drivers and SL1V for vocational drivers.

EU Health Standards for Drivers from 2013

The UK aligned the driver health standards in 2013 with those contained in EU Directive 2006/126/EC. Principally, the changes concerned eyesight, diabetes and epilepsy as follows:

- The eyesight requirements were reduced – licence applicants now only have to read a number plate from 17.5 m instead of a distance of 20 m. Bus and lorry drivers are now able to take vision tests wearing glasses or contact lenses, and the rules for drivers who have reduced sight in one eye were relaxed.

- HGV drivers who are being treated with insulin are now able to apply to drive provided strict medical monitoring is carried out (as noted above). Previously they could only drive vehicles up to 7.5 tonnes gross weight.

- The 2013 rules set out a definition of epilepsy under which drivers will have to surrender their licence if they have two or more epileptic seizures in five years and they will not be able to reapply for their licence for a further five years. The UK proposed that two attacks in 10 years means the loss of a licence and a driver not being able to reapply for 10 years.

- Drivers are still required to notify the DVLA of any health issues, including heart problems, that their doctor has warned could affect their ability to drive.

Medical Appeals and Information

The final decision on any medical matter concerning driving licences rests with the Drivers Medical Group of the DVLA. However, there is the opportunity of appeal, within six months, in England and Wales to a magistrate's court, and within 21 days in Scotland to a sheriff's court. In other cases the refused driver may be given the opportunity to present further medical evidence which the medical advisor will consider.

Further information on medical conditions relating to driving are to be found in a Government booklet, 'Guide to the current medical standards of fitness to drive'. This can be found at GOV.UK. Useful information for diabetic drivers may also be obtained from Diabetes UK Central Office, Macleod House, 10 Parkway, London, NW1 7AA (tel: 0345 123 2399 or email: info@diabetes.org.uk).

Drugs and Driving

It is illegal to drive if either:

- you are unfit to do so because you are on legal or illegal drugs;
- you have certain levels of illegal drugs in your blood (even if they haven't actually affected your driving).

For these purposes, legal drugs are classed as prescription or what are known as over-the-counter medicines.

Should a driver be stopped by the police and it is suspected that drugs may be an issue, the police can make the driver perform a 'field impairment assessment'. This assessment is a series of physical tests to assess a driver's capability to perform certain tasks. Alternatively, the police may also use a roadside drug kit to screen for cannabis and cocaine.

Drivers who are suspected of drug-driving and being unfit to drive will be arrested and will have to take a blood or urine test at a police station.

Prescription Medicines

In England and Wales it is illegal to drive with legal drugs in the body if they impair driving. It is also an offence to drive in some European countries without carrying a medical prescription or if the driver has over the specified limits of certain drugs in their blood and hasn't been prescribed them.

Drivers need to consult their GP if they have been prescribed any of the following:

- amphetamine, eg dexamphetamine or selegiline;
- clonazepam;
- diazepam;
- flunitrazepam;
- lorazepam;
- methadone;
- morphine or opiate and opioid-based drugs, eg codeine, tramadol or fentanyl;
- oxazepam;
- temazepam.

Drivers can drive after taking these prescribed drugs providing advice on how to take them, by a healthcare professional, has been followed. Where a driver may have taken drugs which were not personally prescribed to them, and the levels are above certain limits for the drugs in question, prosecution is generally the resulting action.

At the roadside the police are now able to test for cannabis, cocaine, ecstasy, ketamine, benzodiazepines, methadone, morphine and opiates. If suspected of taking drugs, a 'field impairment test' is carried out and if the police are not satisfied with the results the driver is taken to a police station for tests of blood and urine.

Where prosecutions for drug-driving are made, drivers may receive a minimum driving ban of 12 months, an unlimited fine or up to six months in prison. In addition, the offence and conviction will be recorded on the driver's licence for a period of 11 years. If death is caused by dangerous driving while the driver is under the influence of drugs, a custodial sentence of up to 14 years can be given.

Note: The law does not apply to Scotland or Northern Ireland, although drivers in these countries who are deemed 'unfit' to drive may still be arrested.

Join the Fight against Drugs

If you have any information about drugs or drug smugglers, HM Revenue & Customs requests that you ring the 24-hour hotline 'Customs Confidential' on 0800 788 887. You don't have to tell them who you are, but for important information you may be eligible for a cash reward.

Eyesight Requirement

The statutory eyesight requirement mentioned above for ordinary (ie car and light goods vehicle) licence holders is for the driver to be able to read, in good daylight (with glasses or contact lenses if worn), a standard motor vehicle number plate from 20.0 metres (ie 65.6 feet). A 120°-wide field of view is also required. It is an offence to drive with impaired eyesight and the police can require a driver to take an eyesight test on the roadside. If glasses or contact lenses are needed for this, they must be worn at all times while driving. It is an offence to drive with impaired eyesight.

Eyesight Standards for Vocational Licence Holders

Drivers of vehicles in categories C, C1, CE, C1E, D, D1, DE and D1E (effectively trucks over 3.5 tonnes and passenger vehicles with more than nine seats) must have eyesight which is at least:

1 6/7.5 on the Snellen scale in the better eye.*

2 6/6.0 on the Snellen scale in the other eye.*

3 3/6.0 in each eye without glasses or contact lenses.

These standards may be met with glasses or contact lenses if worn but the glasses must not have a corrective power greater than (+8) dioptres.

To achieve these standards means being able to read the top line of an optician's chart (ie Snellen chart) with each eye from a distance of *at least* 3 metres without the aid of glasses or contact lenses – if it can only be read from, say, 2.5 metres or less, the test is failed. Wearers of spectacles or contact lenses must have vision of at least 6/7.5 in the better eye and at least 6/6.0 in the weaker eye, which means being able to read the sixth line of an optician's chart at 6 metres. Besides these requirements, all drivers must meet existing eyesight standards, which include having a field of vision of at least 120° (horizontal) and 20° (vertical) in each eye with no double vision.

Drivers who held a licence before 1 January 1997 and do not meet these higher standards are advised to check their licensing position with the Drivers Medical Group at the DVLA (see above for address and telephone number).

NB: Different EU/EFTA and EEA member states have different requirements relating to the need for a driver to carry a spare pair of spectacles in case the usual pair becomes lost or damaged. Drivers are advised to carry a spare pair for all EU member states, but this is compulsory in France, Spain and Switzerland.

Licence Fees and Validity

Fees for driving licences are as follows:

Licence type	Online	Post
First provisional		
Car	£34.00	£43.00
Bus or lorry (costs are taken in initial theory test, etc)	FREE	FREE

Licence type	Online	Post
First full		
Car	FREE	FREE (£17.00 to use a different photo from the provisional)
Bus or lorry	FREE	FREE
Renewal		
After expiry	£14.00	£17.00
From age 70	FREE	Free
For medical reasons	N/A	Free
Bus or lorry	N/A	Free
After disqualification	N/A	£65.00
HRO* disqualification	N/A	£90.00
After revocation	N/A	£50.00
Duplicate		
Replace lost or stolen licence	N/A	£20.00
Paper licence for photocard licence with no change of details	N/A	£20.00
Paper licence for photocard licence with change of name	N/A	Free
Paper licence for photocard licence with change of address	Free	Free
Exchange		
Add or remove entitlement	N/A	Free
Remove expired endorsements	N/A	£20.00
Change photo on licence	£14.00	£17.00
Northern Ireland licence for a full GB licence	N/A	Free
Other Fees		
Car theory test	£23.00	£23.00
Motorcycle theory test	£23.00	£23.00

*High-risk offender disqualified for drink-driving convictions.

Licence Validity

Vocational driving entitlements are normally valid for five years or until the holder reaches the age of 45 years under the self-certification scheme. After the age of 45 years, five-year entitlements are granted subject to medical fitness declared by a doctor, but may be for lesser periods where the holder suffers from a relevant or prospective relevant disability. From the age of 65 years, vocational entitlements are granted on an annual basis only.

Ordinary driving licences are valid until age 70 years after which they may be reviewed at three-yearly intervals subject to meeting the health requirements. Photocard driving licences need to be renewed at 10-yearly intervals and this can now be done online.

To renew online, you need:

- a valid UK passport;
- to be a resident of Great Britain (there's a different service in Northern Ireland);
- to pay £14 by MasterCard, Visa, Electron, Maestro or Delta debit or credit card (there's no fee if you're over 70);
- addresses of where you've lived over the last 3 years;
- your driving licence;
- your National Insurance number (if you know it);
- to not be disqualified from driving.

Tax Deductions

The cost of renewing vocational driving entitlements and of undergoing medical examinations in connection with licence renewals is income tax deductible against earnings – but not the cost of first obtaining such an entitlement.

Lost or Mislaid Licences

Drivers who lose or mislay their driving licence should apply for a duplicate licence in the normal way using the standard application form, form D2, at a cost of £20.00.

UK drivers moving to live abroad who have mislaid their driving licence may obtain a temporary 'Certificate of Entitlement' (commonly referred to as a cover note), valid for one month, from the DVLA at Swansea (free of charge), subject to proof of their identity. This document is valid for proving entitlement to drive to enable such persons to apply for and obtain an equivalent driving entitlement in their new country of residence. Applicants for these certificates will need to apply to the DVLA, or download an application from the website and then return it to the DVLA in Swansea for processing.

Production of Driving Licences

Both the police and enforcement officers of the DVSA can request a driver – and a person accompanying a provisional entitlement holder – to produce their licence showing ordinary and vocational entitlements to drive. If they are unable to do so at the time it may be produced without penalty, if the request was by a police officer, at a police station of choice within seven days.

If the licence cannot be produced within the seven days it can be produced as soon as reasonably practicable thereafter. A TC can also require the holder of any vocational driving entitlement to produce their licence at a Traffic Area Office for examination. Failure to produce a licence on request is an offence.

A police officer can ask a driver to state their date of birth – British ordinary driving licences carry a coded number which indicates the holder's surname and date of birth. The name and address of the vehicle owner can also be requested.

When required by a DVSA examiner to produce their licence, a vocational entitlement holder may be required to give their date of birth and to sign the examiner's record sheet to verify the fact of the licence examination. This should not be refused.

Licence holders apprehended for endorsable fixed-penalty (ie yellow ticket) offences are required to produce their driving licence to the police officer at that time or later (ie within seven days) to a police station and surrender the licence, for which they will be given a receipt. Failure to produce a licence in these circumstances means that the fixed-penalty procedure will not be followed and a summons for the offence will be issued requiring a court appearance. Drivers summoned to appear in court for driving and road traffic offences must produce their driving licence to the court on the day before the hearing at the latest.

International Driving Permits

An International Driving Permit (IDP) is not required to drive in the EU, Switzerland, Norway, Iceland or Liechtenstein if a UK-issued photocard driving licence is held. For all other countries an IDP is advisable.

There are three types of IDP:

1 1926;

2 1949;

3 1968.

Full details can be found at GOV.UK.

Exchange of Driving Licences

British driving licence holders can exchange their licence if necessary in order to:

- record changes of personal details;
- add new categories to a full licence;
- remove out-of-date endorsements or suspension details;
- add or take off provisional motorcycle entitlement;
- exchange an old-style pink or green licence for a new-style one.

Exchanging a Foreign Licence for a GB Licence

Northern Ireland Licences

Full NI driving licences or a test pass can be exchanged for a GB licence. Alternatively, a driver can continue to use an NI licence in Britain until it expires.

EU/EEA Licences

A valid full licence issued in any EU or EEA country (ie all EC countries plus Liechtenstein, Iceland and Norway) need not be changed immediately for a GB licence. So long as it remains valid, the holder can drive in Great Britain until 70 years of age or for three years after becoming resident in Great Britain, whichever is the longer period.

Foreign drivers of HGVs can drive in Great Britain until aged 45 or for five years after becoming resident, whichever is the longer period. Drivers aged over 45 years but under 65 can drive until their 66th birthday or for five years after becoming a GB resident, whichever is the shorter. Drivers aged 65 years or older may drive for 12 months after becoming a resident in Great Britain.

In order to continue driving after this time, a British driving licence must be obtained by making an application on form D2. Application can be made for a British licence at any time, even after expiry of the foreign national licence.

Non-EC (Designated) Countries and Gibraltar

A full valid car (Category B) licence issued in any of the following countries can be exchanged for a British licence: Australia, Barbados, British Virgin Islands, Gibraltar, Hong Kong, Japan, Kenya, New Zealand, Singapore and Zimbabwe.

Holders of any vocational licences from any of the above countries should contact DVLA Driver Licensing Enquiries on 0300 790 6801 for further information.

Full Jersey or Isle of Man car, lorry or bus licences, or a full Guernsey car licence, can be exchanged for a British licence if they were valid within the past 10 years.

Certain driving licences for vehicles up to 3.5 tonnes issued in South Africa and Canada may now be exchanged for an equivalent GB licence.

A foreign car (Category B) driving licence can be used in Great Britain for one year only provided it remains valid, but exchange of a driving licence issued in any of the above-listed countries can be done up to five years after taking up residence in Great Britain.

People from other countries not mentioned above cannot exchange their national licence for a British equivalent but they can drive Category B vehicles in Great Britain on such licences (or on an International Driving Permit) for up to one year.

All foreign licence holders who cannot obtain an exchange licence, or who wish to drive vehicles which their national licence does not cover, must apply for provisional entitlement in the normal way using form D1.

Full GB driving licences can only be issued to foreign nationals who become resident in Great Britain.

Visitors Driving in the UK

Visitors to the UK may drive vehicles in the UK provided they hold a domestic driving licence issued in their own country (ie outside the UK and the EU) or a Convention Driving Permit (issued under the 1949 Geneva Convention on Road Traffic by a country outside the UK). Holders of such permits are entitled to drive vehicles of a class which their own national or international licence covers for a period of 12 months from the date of their entry into the UK.

Driving While Tired

Drivers must be encouraged to *stop* when they feel tired, whether during the night-time hours or during daytime, and rest for a short while, no matter what the pressures of the job or the particular journey in which they are engaged. Employers have responsibilities under health and safety legislation to assess such potential risks and take proper action to eliminate them. (The *Highway Code* recommends that car drivers stop for a short break after every two hours of driving.)

THINK! – Driving Tiredness Campaign

Since tiredness has been established as the principal factor in around 10 per cent of all accidents, the DfT made obstructive sleep apnoea syndrome a notifiable condition and launched a THINK! campaign to combat tiredness among both car and vocational drivers. The main points for drivers to observe are that they should:

- Make sure they are fit to drive, particularly before undertaking any long journeys (over an hour) – avoid such journeys in the morning without a good night's sleep, or in the evening after a full day's work.

- Avoid undertaking long journeys between midnight and 6 am, when natural alertness is at a minimum.

- Plan their journey to take sufficient breaks. A minimum break of at least 15 minutes after every two hours' driving is advised.

- If they feel at all sleepy, stop in a safe place and either take a nap for not more than 15 minutes, or drink two cups of strong coffee.

Advice on taking regular breaks and not driving while tired is also regularly featured on information boards alongside motorways.

Driving Licence Penalty Points and Disqualification

In some circumstances, driving licence penalty points can be avoided if a driver agrees to attend a corrective 'workshop' where re-training and training is given in an attempt to prevent any re-occurrence of a similar contravention of the rules. 'Speed awareness workshops' and 'seat-belt awareness workshops' are offered to some drivers. This offer is dependent upon the nature of the offence and serious contraventions will not normally be eligible for this concession. The price for these workshops varies but is approximately £100 for speed awareness and £40 for seat-belt awareness. The speed awareness workshop requires the driver to attend a formal group workshop, while the seat-belt awareness workshop can be undertaken online. The seat-belt awareness workshop is an internet-based workshop which requires delegates to take, and pass, an assessment on completion.

In other cases, driving licence holders may be penalized following conviction by a court for offences committed on the road with a motor vehicle. These penalties range from the issue of fixed penalty notices for non-endorsable offences (which do not require a court appearance unless the charge is to be contested and incur no driving licence penalty points, although the relevant fixed penalty has to be paid) to those for endorsable offences when penalty points are added on the licence and the fixed penalty is incurred or a heavy fine imposed on conviction if a court appearance is made.

Licence disqualification for a period (extending to a number of years in serious cases) may also be an option – especially for drink-driving-related offences, and in very serious instances imprisonment of the offender may follow conviction in a magistrate's court or indictment for the offence in a higher court. Holders of vocational driving entitlements may be separately penalized for relevant offences, which could result in such entitlements being suspended or revoked and in serious circumstances the holder being disqualified from holding a vocational entitlement – see below.

The Graduated Fixed Penalty Scheme

The Graduated Fixed Penalty Scheme relates to a 'sliding scale' of penalties for breaches of regulations by commercial vehicles. It focuses on areas such as drivers' hours and tachograph infringements, loading and overloading, and roadworthiness. It allows DVSA officials and police officers to vary the fixed penalty levied in relation to the seriousness of the incident. It also allows the enforcement authorities to secure a financial guarantee of payment from foreign drivers who cannot supply a reliable address within the UK.

Fixed penalties can range from £50 to £300 and be non-endorsable or endorsable, with £100 and £200 fines also carrying three penalty points. This 'flexibility' allows the enforcement authorities to make allowances for minor infringements without having to treat each case using 'the full weight of the law'. Further information can be found at GOV.UK.

The Penalty Points System on Conviction and Disqualification

The penalty points system grades road traffic offences according to their seriousness by a number or range of penalty points, between 2 and 11, imposed on the driving licence of the offender. Once a maximum of 12 penalty points has been accumulated within a three-year period, counting from the date of the first offence to the current offence (not from the date of conviction), disqualification of the licence for at least six months will normally follow automatically (see below).

Most offences rate a fixed number of penalty points to ensure consistency, but a discretionary range applies to a few offences where the gravity may vary considerably from one case to another. For example, failing to stop after an accident which only involved minor vehicle damage is obviously less serious than a case where an accident results in injury.

Unless the court decides otherwise, when a driver is convicted of more than one offence at the same hearing, only the points relative to the most serious of the offences will normally be endorsed on the licence. Once sufficient points (ie 12) have been endorsed on the driving licence and a period of disqualification has been imposed (six months for the first totting-up of points), the driver will have his 'slate' wiped clean and those points will not be counted again. Twelve more points would have to be accumulated before a further disqualification would follow, but to discourage repeated offences the courts will impose progressively longer disqualification periods in further instances (minimum 12 months for subsequent disqualifications within three years and 24 months for a third disqualification within three years).

DVSA enforcement officers can issue fixed penalty notices for historic offences. This means that offences and infringements detected within the last 28 days can now be used to form a prosecution if a prosecution is to be brought for an offence being committed at the time the vehicle was stopped. The main reason for this change was to enable the DVSA to prosecute non-UK drivers at the roadside for offences committed while in the UK, a power it previously did not have.

Drivers caught using a mobile phone while driving now receive a fine of £200 (maximum £1,000) and get six penalty points on their licence. HGV drivers also receive six penalty points and a £200 fine but the maximum fine is £2,500. In addition, the Senior TC has issued guidance that HGV drivers should have their vocational entitlement suspended, with immediate effect, for 21 days for a first offence, 2 × 21 days for a second offence and 3 × 21 days for a third offence.

Licence Endorsement Codes and Penalty Points

Following conviction for an offence, the driver's licence record will be endorsed with both a code (to which employers and prospective employers should refer, with the driver's permission, so they can assess the offences which drivers have committed) and the number of penalty points imposed, as follows:

Code		Penalty points
Accident offences		
AC 10	Failing to stop after an accident	5–10
AC 20	Failing to report an accident within 24 hours	5–10
AC 30	Undefined accident offence	4–9
Disqualified driver		
BA 10	Driving while disqualified	6
BA 30	Attempting to drive while disqualified	6
BA 40	Causing death by driving while disqualified	3–11
BA 60	Causing serious injury by driving while disqualified	3–11
Careless driving		
CD 10	Driving without due care and attention	3–9
CD 20	Driving without reasonable consideration for other road users	3–9
CD 30	Driving without due care and attention or without reasonable consideration for other road users	3–9

Code		Penalty points
CD 40	Causing death through careless driving when unfit through drink	3–11
CD 50	Causing death by careless driving when unfit through drugs	3–11
CD 60	Causing death by careless driving with alcohol level above the limit	3–11
CD 70	Causing death by careless driving then failing to supply a specimen	3–11
CD 80	Causing death by careless, or inconsiderate, driving	3–11
CD 90	Causing death by driving: unlicensed, disqualified or uninsured drivers	3–11
Construction and use offences		
CU 10	Using a vehicle with defective brakes	3
CU 20	Causing or likely to cause danger by reason of unsuitable vehicle or using a vehicle with parts or accessories (excluding brakes, steering or tyres) in a dangerous condition	3
CU 30	Using a vehicle with defective tyre(s)	3
CU 40	Using a vehicle with defective steering	3
CU 50	Causing or likely to cause danger by reason of load or passengers	3
CU 80	Breach of the requirements as to control of the vehicle, mobile phone, etc	6
Reckless/dangerous driving		
DD 10	Causing serious injury by dangerous driving	3–11
DD 40	Dangerous driving	3–11
DD 60	Manslaughter or culpable homicide while driving a vehicle	3–11
DD 80	Causing death by dangerous driving	3–11
DD 90	Furious driving	3–9
Drink or drugs		
DG 40	In charge of a vehicle while drug level above specified limits	10
DG 60	Causing death by careless driving with drug level above the limit	3–11
DR 10	Driving or attempting to drive with alcohol level above limit	3–11
DR 20	Driving or attempting to drive while unfit through drink	3–11
DR 30	Driving or attempting to drive then failing to supply a specimen for analysis	3–11
DR 40	In charge of a vehicle while alcohol level above limit	10
DR 50	In charge of a vehicle while unfit through drink	10

Code		Penalty points
DR 60	Failure to provide a specimen for analysis in circumstances other than driving or attempting to drive	10
DR 70	Failing to provide a specimen for breath test	4
DR 80	Driving or attempting to drive when unfit through drugs	3–11
DR 90	In charge of a vehicle when unfit through drugs	10
Insurance offences		
IN 10	Using a vehicle uninsured against third-party risks	6–8
Licence offences		
LC 20	Driving otherwise than in accordance with a licence	3–6
LC 30	Driving after making a false declaration about fitness when applying for a licence	3–6
LC 40	Driving a vehicle having failed to notify of a disability	3–6
LC 50	Driving after a licence has been revoked or refused on medical grounds	3–6
Miscellaneous offences		
MS 10	Leaving a vehicle in a dangerous position	3
MS 20	Unlawful pillion riding	3
MS 30	Contravention of the Road Traffic Regulations provisions on street playgrounds	2
MS 50	Motor racing on the highway	3–11
MS 60	Offences not covered by other codes as appropriate	–
MS 70	Driving with uncorrected defective eyesight	3
MS 80	Refusing to submit to an eyesight test	3
MS 90	Failure to give information as to identity of driver, etc	3
Motorway offences		
MW 10	Contravention of Special Roads Regulations (excl speed limits)	3
Pedestrian crossings		
PC 10	Undefined contravention of Pedestrian Crossing Regulations	3
PC 20	Contravention of Pedestrian Crossing Regulations with moving vehicle	3
PC 30	Contravention of Pedestrian Crossing Regulations with stationary vehicle	3
Provisional licence offences		
PL 10	Driving without 'L' plates	3–6
PL 20	Not accompanied by a qualified person	3–6

Code		Penalty points
PL 30	Carrying a person not qualified	3–6
PL 40	Drawing an unauthorized trailer	3–6
PL 50	Undefined failure to comply with conditions of a provisional licence	3–6

Speed limits

SP 10	Exceeding goods vehicle speed limits	3–6
SP 20	Exceeding speed limit for type of vehicle (excluding goods or passenger vehicles)	3–6
SP 30	Exceeding statutory speed limit on a public road	3–6
SP 40	Exceeding passenger vehicle speed limit	3–6
SP 50	Exceeding speed limit on a motorway	3–6
SP 60	Undefined speed limit offence	3–6
	NB: Disqualification is obligatory where the relevant speed is in excess of 30 mph over the statutory limit.	

Traffic directions and signs

TS 10	Failing to comply with traffic-light signals	3
TS 20	Failing to comply with double white lines	3
TS 30	Failing to comply with a 'Stop' sign	3
TS 40	Failing to comply with direction of a constable or traffic warden	3
TS 50	Failing to comply with a traffic sign (excluding 'Stop' signs, traffic lights or double white lines)	3
TS 60	Failing to comply with a school crossing patrol sign	3
TS 70	Undefined failure to comply with a traffic direction or sign	3

Special code

TT 99	To signify a disqualification under 'totting up' procedure If the total of penalty points reaches 12 or more within three years, the driver is liable to be disqualified	

Theft or unauthorized taking

UT 50	Aggravated taking of a vehicle	3–11

NB: These codes relate to the driver only and do not take account of any subsequent effect the offence may have on the OCRS in cases such as vehicles with defective brakes, steering or tyres.

Where the offence is one of aiding or abetting, causing or permitting or inciting, the codes are modified as follows.

Aiding, Abetting, Counselling or Procuring

Offences as coded, but with zero changed to 2, eg UT 50 becomes UT 52.

Causing or Permitting

Offences as coded, but with zero changed to 4, eg LC 20 becomes LC 24.

Inciting

Offences as coded, but with zero changed to 6, eg DD 40 becomes DD 46. The length of time for periods of disqualification is shown by use of the letters D = days, M = months and Y = years. Consecutive periods of disqualification are signified by an asterisk (*) against the time period. The symbol + means that 3 to 11 points are added to a licence if for exceptional reasons disqualification is not imposed.

Disqualification

The endorsing of penalty points will also arise on conviction for offences where disqualification is discretionary and where the court has decided that immediate disqualification is not appropriate (for example if acceptable 'exceptional' reasons are put forward – see also below). In this case the offender's driving licence will be endorsed with four points. The courts are still free to disqualify immediately if the circumstances justify this. Offences carrying obligatory disqualification are shown in the following list:

- causing death by dangerous driving and manslaughter;
- dangerous driving within three years of a similar conviction;
- driving or attempting to drive while unfit through drink or drugs;
- driving or attempting to drive with more than the permitted breath-alcohol level;
- failure to provide a breath, blood or urine specimen;
- racing on the highway.

Driving while disqualified can result in a fine at level 5 on the standard scale (see below), ie £5,000 maximum, or six months' imprisonment, or both.

Special Reasons for Non-Disqualification

The courts have discretion in exceptional mitigating circumstances not to impose a disqualification. The mitigating circumstance must not be one which attempts to make the offence appear less serious and no account will be taken of hardship other than exceptional hardship. Pleading that the driver has a wife and children to support or will lose their job is not generally considered to be exceptional hardship.

If account has previously been taken of circumstances in mitigation of a disqualification, the same circumstances cannot be considered again within three years. Where a court decides not to disqualify a convicted driver, 3 to 11 penalty points will be added to the driver's licence in lieu of the disqualification.

Driving Offences

Dangerous Driving

A person is driving dangerously if the way they drive 'falls far short of what would be expected of a competent and careful driver, and it would be obvious to a competent and careful driver that driving in that way would be dangerous'. Driving would be regarded as dangerous 'if it was obvious to a competent and careful driver that driving the vehicle in its current state would be dangerous' – this obviously applies to the vehicle's mechanical condition or the way it is loaded. Also, 'dangerous' refers to danger either of injury to any person or of serious damage to property. The principal offences to which this relates are dangerous driving and causing death by dangerous driving.

Interfering with Vehicles, etc

It is an offence for any person to cause danger to road users by way of intentionally and without lawful authority placing objects on a road, interfering with motor vehicles, or directly or indirectly interfering with traffic equipment (road signs, etc).

Penalties

Causing death by careless driving while under the influence of drink or drugs carries a maximum penalty of up to five years in prison and/or a fine. For causing a danger to road users the maximum penalty is up to seven years' imprisonment and/or a fine. In addition to disqualification and the endorsement of penalty points on driving licences, courts may impose fines and, for certain offences, imprisonment. The maximum fine for most offences is determined by reference to a scale set out in the Criminal Justice Act 1991 as follows:

Level 1 £200

Level 2 £500

Level 3 £1,000

Level 4 £2,500

Level 5 Unlimited

Serious offences such as dangerous driving, failing to stop after an accident or failure to report an accident, and drink-driving offences, carry the maximum unlimited fine, as do certain vehicle construction and use offences (overloading, insecure loads, using a vehicle in a dangerous condition, etc) and using a vehicle without insurance.

The maximum penalty for the offence of causing death by dangerous driving is 14 years.

Driver Penalties for New Drivers

Where a new driver is awarded six or more penalty points on their licence within two years of passing their test, the DVLA will automatically revoke the licence on notification by a court or fixed penalty offence. Drivers have to surrender their full licence and obtain a provisional licence to start driving again as a learner. They have to pass both the theory and practical tests again in order to regain their full driving licence.

Penalty points counting towards the six include any incurred before passing the test, if this was not more than three years before the latest penalty point offence. Points imposed after the probationary period will also count if the offence was committed during that period.

Passing the re-test will not remove the penalty points from the licence; these will remain and if the total reaches 12, the driver will be liable to disqualification.

Removal of Penalty Points and Disqualifications

Penalty points endorsed on driving licences are removed automatically when they expire. They are valid for four years from the date of the offence, except in the case of reckless/dangerous driving convictions when the four years is taken from the date of conviction. Endorsements for alcohol-related and drug-related offences are valid for 11 years.

Application may be made by disqualified drivers for reinstatement of their licence after varying periods of time depending on the duration of the disqualifying period as follows:

- less than two years – no prior application time;
- less than four years – after two years have elapsed;
- between four years and 10 years – after half the time has elapsed;
- in other cases – after five years have elapsed.

The courts can make a disqualified driver retake the driving test before restoring a driving licence, and it is mandatory for them to impose 'extended' re-tests following disqualification for the most serious of driving offences, namely, dangerous driving, causing death by dangerous driving and manslaughter by the driver of a motor vehicle (in Scotland, the charge is culpable homicide).

The fees charged for replacement licences following disqualification are:

- £50 if disqualified under the New Drivers Scheme;
- £65 if disqualified for any reason except drink driving;
- £90 if disqualified for drink driving.

Re-Tests for Offending Drivers

Where drivers are disqualified due to manslaughter, death by dangerous driving or dangerous driving, an 'extended' re-test (involving at least one hour's driving) must be taken before the driving licence is restored. This also applies to drivers disqualified under the penalty points totting-up procedure. Courts may also order drivers disqualified for lesser offences to take an appropriate (ie ordinary) driving test.

Drink-Driving and Breath Tests

There are strict alcohol limits for drivers. However, the limits in Scotland are different to the rest of the UK.

Level of alcohol	Scotland	Rest of UK
Micrograms per 100 millilitres of breath	22	35
Milligrammes per 100 millilitres of blood	50	80
Milligrammes per 100 millilitres of urine	67	107

Failure to Produce a Breath Sample and Low Breath-Test Readings

If a driver cannot, due to health reasons, produce a breath sample, or if a breath test is failed, they are given the opportunity of an alternative test, either blood or urine. This test can only be carried out at a police station or a hospital and the decision as to which lies with the police.

Prosecution for Drink-Driving Offences

Prosecution follows failure to pass a breath test, which results in a fine or imprisonment and automatic disqualification from driving.

The police *do not have* powers to carry out breath tests at random but they *do have* powers to enter premises to require a breath test from a person suspected of driving while impaired through drink or drugs, or who has been driving or been in charge of a vehicle which has been involved in an accident in which another person has been injured.

Drink-Driving Disqualification

Conviction for a first drink-driving offence will result in a minimum one-year period of disqualification and for a second or subsequent offence of driving or attempting to drive under the influence of drink or drugs longer periods of disqualification will be imposed by the court. If the previous conviction took place within 10 years of the offence the disqualification must be for at least three years.

Drivers convicted twice for drink-driving offences may have their driving licence revoked altogether. Offenders who are disqualified twice within a 10-year period for any drink-driving offences and those found to have an exceptionally high level of alcohol in the body (ie more than 2½ times over the limit) or those who twice refuse to provide a specimen will be classified as high-risk offenders (HROs). They will be required to show that they no longer have an 'alcohol problem' by means of a medical examination by a DVLA-approved doctor before their licence will be restored.

Drink-Driving Rehabilitation Courses

Some drink-drive offenders may have the period of their disqualification reduced if they agree to undertake an approved rehabilitation course and satisfactorily complete it. The provision applies only where the court orders the individual (who must be over 17 years of age) to be disqualified for at least 12 months following conviction under the Road Traffic Act 1988 for:

- causing death by careless driving when under the influence of drink or drugs;
- driving or being in charge of a motor vehicle when under the influence of drink or drugs;
- driving or being in charge of a motor vehicle with excess alcohol in the body; or
- failing to provide a specimen (of breath, blood or urine) as required.

A number of approved courses have been established around the UK and can cost up to £250. These require attendance for at least 16 hours, which is normally spread over three days, over three weeks. Further details are available at GOV.UK.

Drug-Driving

Drug-driving includes driving while under the influence of prescription drugs and medicines as well as illegal drugs. Suspected drivers can be required to submit to a roadside impairment test by the police. Refusal to participate in the test will render a driver liable to the same penalty as refusal to undertake a breath test. This testing is in addition to the new drug testing equipment used by police traffic patrols at roadside checks and now carried in some police vehicles.

It should be noted that drug tests that indicate excessive use of prescription drugs are included in the overall drug testing scheme and drivers may be required to produce the prescription in order to prove that they have not exceeded a prescribed limit.

Penalties against Vocational Entitlements

Where a licence holder is disqualified from driving following conviction for offences committed with cars or other light vehicles, or as a result of penalty point totting-up, any vocational entitlement which that person holds is automatically lost until the licence is reinstated. Additionally, the holder of any vocational entitlement may have this revoked or suspended by the DVLA without reference to the TC – see below – and be disqualified from holding such entitlement, for a fixed or an indefinite period, at any time on the grounds of misconduct or physical disability. Furthermore, a person can be refused a new vocational driving entitlement following licence revocation, again either indefinitely or for some other period of time which the Secretary of State (ie via the DVLA) specifies. A new vocational test may be ordered before the entitlement is restored – see below.

Disqualification from holding a vocational entitlement as described above does not prevent licence holders from continuing to drive vehicles within the Category B entitlement that they hold.

The TCs continue to play a disciplinary role under the new licensing scheme with regard to driver conduct, but only at the request of the DVLA. They have powers under the new provisions to call drivers to public inquiry to give information and answer questions as to their conduct. Their duty is to report back to the DVLA if they consider that a vocational entitlement should be revoked or the holder disqualified from holding an entitlement. The DVLA must follow the TCs' recommendation in these matters.

Failure to attend a PI when requested to do so (unless a reasonable excuse is given) means that the DVLA will automatically refuse a new vocational entitlement or suspend or revoke an existing entitlement.

Rules on disciplining vocational entitlement holders require TCs to follow a set of recommended guidelines in imposing penalties against such entitlements. Under these rules, and where there are no aggravating circumstances, a driver being disqualified for 12 months or less should be sent a warning letter, with no further disqualification of the vocational entitlement. Where a driving disqualification is for more than one year, offenders should be called to appear before the TC and should incur an additional suspension of their vocational entitlement, amounting to between one month and three months. The intention here is to allow them to regain their driving skills and road sense in a car before driving a heavy vehicle again.

Where two or more driving disqualifications of more than eight weeks have been incurred within the past five years, and the combined total of disqualification exceeds 12 months, the driver should be called to a PI and a further period of vocational driving disqualification imposed amounting to between three and six months.

In the case of new vocational entitlements, for applicants who already have nine or more penalty points on their ordinary licence, the guidelines recommend that the TC should issue a warning as to future conduct or suggest that the applicant tries again when the penalty points total on their licence has been reduced.

Removal of Vocational Driving Licence Disqualification

Drivers disqualified from holding a vocational entitlement, as described above, may apply to have the disqualification removed after two years if it was for less than four years, or after half the period if the disqualification was for more than four years but less than 10 years. In any other case including disqualification for an indefinite period an application for its removal cannot be made until five years have elapsed. If an application for the removal of a disqualification fails, another application cannot be made for three months.

The DVLA will not necessarily readily restore vocational driving entitlements on application following disqualification of a driving licence. An applicant may be called to a PI by a TC, who will inquire into the events which led to the disqualification, and at which the TC may also decide that the applicant must wait a further period before applying again, must spend a period driving small (ie up to 3.5 or 7.5 tonnes) vehicles or must take a new vocational driving test in order to regain the vocational entitlement.

Appeals

If the DVLA refuses to grant an application for a vocational driving entitlement or revokes, suspends or limits an existing entitlement, the applicant or entitlement holder may appeal against the decision under the Road Traffic Act 1988. The first step is for them to notify the DVLA, and any TC involved in consideration of the applicant's conduct, of their intention to appeal. The appeal can then be made to a magistrate's court in England or Wales within six months of the DVLA decision, or in Scotland to the local sheriff's court within 21 days of the DVLA decision. However, the revocation will remain in force pending the outcome of the appeal.

Driver Testing and Training

07

This chapter deals with licence acquisition training, driving tests, HGV apprenticeships and training for the carriage of dangerous goods.

Driving Tests

The main purpose of driver testing is to ensure that all drivers taking a vehicle on the road:

- are safe and competent to do so;
- know the rules of the road and the significance of traffic signs and signals;
- appreciate the dangers arising from moving vehicles.

The objective of the vocational test is to ensure that HGV drivers have the skill to safely drive larger vehicles on the road. The test is more comprehensive than the ordinary (ie car and light goods) driving test and, consequently, demands greater skill and knowledge from the driver.

Proof of Identity

Candidates for both ordinary and vocational (ie C1, C1E, C, CE) driving tests must produce photographic evidence of identity when arriving for a test. Acceptable documents include existing photocard driving licences (ordinary, vocational or an overseas driving licence), a passport or an employer-issued identity card bearing the holder's name, signature and photograph. If a test candidate cannot produce satisfactory means of identification, the test will not be conducted and the fee will be forfeited.

HGV Driver Testing

In order to drive an HGV it is necessary to pass the large vehicle theory test and hazard perception test, a case study test, a practical demonstration and a practical driving test on either a large goods or passenger vehicle of the appropriate category for which a licence is required. These four elements of the driving test combine to meet the requirements of the Driver Certificate of Professional Competence initial qualification.

Some vocational drivers may not need a Driver CPC in order to drive a 'vocational' vehicle. Exemptions include:

- non-commercial carriage of passengers or goods for personal use;
- carrying material or equipment for the driver's use (but driving the vehicle can't be the main part of the driver's job);
- driving lessons for anyone who wants to get a driving licence or a Driver CPC;
- driving to or from pre-booked appointments at official vehicle testing centres;
- driving within 100 kilometres of base – but the vehicle can't be carrying passengers or goods, and driving a lorry, bus or coach can't be the driver's main job;
- maintaining public order – and the vehicle is being used or controlled by a local authority;
- rescue missions or in states of emergency.

In addition, the driver does not need the full Driver CPC if the vehicle is:

- limited to a top speed of 28 mph;
- being used or controlled by the armed forces, police, fire and rescue service, prison service or people running a prison or young offenders institution.

Theory and Hazard Perception Testing (Part One)

Large vehicle (ie HGV/PCV) driving test candidates must take and pass a 'touch screen' theory test, which has replaced the old, verbal, questioning to test the candidate's knowledge of technical and safety matters and the *Highway Code*. This test is in two parts – Module 1a and Module 1b – and includes fuel economy, environmentally sensitive driving and safety issues, and is conducted online at dedicated DVSA test centres available nationwide.

The theory test (Module 1a) takes 1 hour and 55 minutes and comprises 100 multiple-choice questions; a pass is achieved with 85 correct answers.

The hazard perception test (Module 1b) involves 19 video clips which include a total of 20 emerging hazards. Each hazard carries a maximum score of 5 and the pass mark is 67 out of 100.

The pass certificate issued for these tests is valid for two years.

The Case Studies (Part Two)

The case study test lasts for 1 hour and 15 minutes and comprises seven case studies that the candidate works through on a computer. The case studies are scenarios which have been developed to relate to real-life vocational driving and work situations. The candidate is asked six to eight multiple-choice questions on each case study and needs to score 40 marks from a total of 50 in order to pass.

The successful candidate needs the pass reference number in order to book Part Four of the overall test (Practical Demonstration). The pass reference number is valid for two years.

The Vocational Driving Test (Part Three)

In order to undertake a Category C1 or C driving test, candidates will need their HGV theory test pass certificate when booking.

The 90-minute practical driving test is conducted by DVSA examiners and booking is made directly through the DVSA. Certain test centres offer Saturday-morning vocational driver testing. The test must be taken within two years of the candidate passing the theory test.

The staged system of testing means that:

- applicants for vocational tests must already hold a full Category B (car and light vehicle) driving entitlement before taking a test to obtain a Category C entitlement;
- Category B entitlement holders must pass a test on a rigid goods vehicle in Category C before being able to take a test to qualify for driving articulated vehicles and drawbar combinations in Category CE;
- Category C1 entitlement holders wishing to drive vehicles in Category C1E must take a further test for this type of vehicle combination.

In each case, drivers must hold a provisional entitlement for the category of vehicle on which they want to be tested.

Application

Applications for the large vehicle practical driving test can be made online through the GOV.UK website or by contacting the DVSA on 0300 200 1122.

The lead time for an HGV driving test is approximately six to eight weeks.

Test Cancellation

Should a candidate need to cancel a test appointment, this should be done at least 10 clear working days in advance, otherwise the fee will be forfeited.

Identification

Test candidates must be able to produce satisfactory photographic identification on arrival at the test centre, otherwise the examiner may refuse to conduct the test and the fee will be forfeited.

The Practical Demonstration (Part Four)

The practical demonstration cannot be taken until the driver has completed Part Two of the driving test (Case Studies). The practical test is aimed at demonstrating that the driver is able to:

- load the vehicle following safety rules and keep it secure;
- stop trafficking of illegal immigrants;
- assess emergency situations;
- do a walkaround vehicle safety check.

The test, which takes approximately 30 minutes, is made up of five topics from the Driver CPC syllabus, and the driver is able to score up to 20 points for each topic. In order to pass, the driver must score at least 15 out of 20 in each topic area and have an overall score of at least 80 out of 100.

Vehicles for the Vocational Driving Test

The candidate has to provide the vehicle (or arrange for the loan of a suitable vehicle) on which they are to be tested and it must comply with the following requirements:

- be laden (see below) and of the category (ie a 'minimum test vehicle') for which an HGV driving entitlement is required – see below;
- display 'L' plates front and rear;
- be in a thoroughly roadworthy condition;
- have seating accommodation with a seat belt in the cab for the examiner;
- have sufficient fuel for a test lasting up to two hours.

Minimum Test Vehicles

All vehicles used for categories C1, 'C1E', C and 'CE' tests must have:

- externally mounted nearside and offside mirrors;
- seat belts fitted to seats used by the examiner or any person supervising the test;
- a tachograph fitted;
- an anti-lock braking system (ABS).

NB: Trailers don't need ABS.

All vehicle combinations must operate the appropriate service brakes and utilize a heavy-duty coupling arrangement suitable for the weight.

NB: An articulated tractor unit is not considered to be a suitable vehicle for Category C or C1 tests.

Category C1

- A medium-sized lorry with a gvw of at least 4 tonnes:
  - at least 5 metres in length;
  - capable of 80 kph (50 mph);
  - with a closed box cargo compartment at least as wide and as high as the cab.

Category C1E

- A drawbar combination comprising a Category C1 vehicle:
  - towing a trailer of at least 2 tonnes gvw;
  - with a combined length of at least 8 metres;
  - capable of 80 kph (50 mph);
  - with a closed box trailer slightly less wide than the towing vehicle, but rear view must be by external mirrors only;

or

- A medium-sized articulated lorry with a gvw of at least 6 tonnes:
  - with a combined length of at least 8 metres;
  - capable of 80 kph (50 mph);
  - with a closed box trailer slightly less wide than the towing vehicle, but rear view must be by external mirrors only.

Category C

- A rigid goods vehicle with a gvw of at least 12 tonnes:
  - at least 8 metres in length;
  - at least 2.4 metres in width;
  - capable of 80 kph (50 mph);
  - with at least eight forward gears or an automatic gearbox;*
  - a closed box cargo compartment at least as wide and as high as the cab;
  - a maximum length of 12 metres (39 ft 4 in).

Category CE

- A drawbar outfit comprising a combination of a Category C vehicle and trailer with a gvw of 20 tonnes:

- with a combined length of at least 14 metres;
  - with a trailer at least 7.5 metres in length from coupling eye to extreme rear;
  - at least 2.4 metres in width;
  - capable of 80 kph (50 mph);
  - with at least eight forward gears;*
  - with a closed box cargo compartment at least as wide and as high as the cab;
  - a maximum length of 18.75 metres (61 ft 5 in); or
- An articulated lorry with a gvw of at least 20 tonnes:
  - with a minimum length of 14 metres;
  - a maximum length of 16.5 metres (54 ft);
  - at least 2.4 metres in width;
  - capable of 80 kph (50 mph);
  - with at least eight forward gears or an automatic gearbox;*
  - with a closed box cargo compartment at least as wide and as high as the cab.

If an automatic gearbox is used, a successful candidate will gain a C or CE category entitling them to drive manual gearboxes in that category providing that they initially passed either a Category B, BE, C1, C1E, D, D1E or DE test in a vehicle with a manual gearbox. Existing drivers holding a manual entitlement in any of these categories may also upgrade to a full manual entitlement either by paying a fee or waiting until the next five-yearly renewal.

Real Total Mass

Some goods vehicles and/or trailers and some passenger-carrying vehicles used for practical driving tests need to be loaded to set minimum levels in order to achieve real total mass requirements.

These loading levels are as follows:

- Category BE – The trailer must be loaded with at least 600 kg in the form of sealed bags of sand or one intermediate bulk container (IBC) filled with water.
- Category C1 – No load requirement.
- Category C1E – The trailer must be loaded with at least 600 kg in the form of sealed bags of sand or one IBC filled with water.
- Category C – The vehicle must be loaded with at least 5,000 kg in the form of five IBCs filled with water.
- Category CE (artic.) – The trailer must be loaded with at least 8,000 kg in the form of eight IBCs filled with water.

- Category CE (drawbar) – The vehicle must be loaded with at least 5,000 kg in the form of five IBCs filled with water and the trailer must be loaded with at least 3,000 kg in the form of three IBCs filled with water.
- Category D1 – No load requirement.
- Category D – No load requirement.
- Category D1E – The trailer must be loaded with at least 600 kg in the form of sealed bags of sand or one IBC filled with water.
- Category DE – The trailer must be loaded with at least 600 kg in the form of sealed bags of sand or one IBC filled with water.

The Vocational Driving Test Syllabus

The recommended syllabus should be studied by candidates preparing for the C1, C1E or HGV driving test. It is available in the DVSA publication *The Official Guide to Driving Goods Vehicles* (available from The Stationery Office and most good bookshops) and *The Professional HGV Drivers' Handbook* (by David Lowe, available from Kogan Page).

Vocational Tests – Current Situation

Drivers seeking vocational licence entitlement are expected to be experienced and technically expert. Test candidates are asked at least one 'show me' and one 'tell me' question when taking the physical driving test, with a driving fault being recorded for each incorrect answer up to a maximum of four driving faults. If all five answers are given incorrectly, a serious fault will be recorded. These 'show me' and 'tell me' questions are necessary where a driver does not intend to drive professionally, or is exempted from Driver CPC, and does not require to pass Module 4 of the Initial Driver CPC, which includes the same types of questions.

Examples of safety check questions are as follows.

Identify where:

- you would check the engine oil level and tell me how you would check that the engine has sufficient oil;
- you would check the engine coolant level and tell me how you would check that the engine has the correct level;
- the windscreen washer reservoir is and tell me how you would check the windscreen washer level.

Tell me how you would check:

- your tyres to ensure that they are correctly inflated, have sufficient tread depth and that their general condition is safe to use on the road;

- that the brake lights are working;
- the condition of the reflectors on this vehicle;
- the condition of the windscreen and windows on this vehicle;
- the condition of the windscreen wipers on this vehicle;
- the condition of the suspension on this vehicle;
- that the condition of the body is safe on this vehicle;
- that the power-assisted steering is working.

Tell me:

- how you would operate the loading mechanism on this vehicle (vehicle-specific, ie tail-lift);
- the main safety factors involved in loading this vehicle.

Show me how you would check:

- that the headlamps, sidelights and tail lights are working;
- that the direction indicators are working;
- the operation (specify) of the audible warning devices on this vehicle;
- that the wheel nuts are secure on this vehicle;
- the condition of the mudguards on this vehicle;
- for the correct air pressure on this vehicle;
- for air leaks on this vehicle;
- that your cargo doors are secure;
- that your cab locking mechanism is secure.

Show me how you would:

- replace the tachometer disc on this vehicle;
- insert your driver digital tachograph card.

Show me:

- what instrument checks you would make before and after starting the engine on this vehicle;
- where the emergency exits are and how you would check that they are operating correctly;
- where the first-aid equipment is on this vehicle;
- where the fire extinguishers are on this vehicle.

The Braking Exercise

Braking tests are carried out on the road in normal traffic conditions. This is a more realistic test of a driver's ability to bring a vehicle to rest in a safe and timely manner, taking account of prevailing road and traffic conditions.

The Safe Parking Test

Candidates are asked to carry out the current reversing exercise, but at the end of the reversing bay there will be a simulated loading platform up to which the candidate will be required to reverse (stopping with the extreme rear of the vehicle within a stopping area marked by black and yellow hatched lines) and park safely for loading and unloading.

Stopping short of the marked stopping area will be assessed as a serious fault. Reversing through the marked stopping area and dislodging the simulated loading/unloading platform will be assessed as a serious fault. Stopping within the marked stopping area but unacceptably short of the platform will be assessed as a driving fault. A total loss of vehicle control, which causes actual danger to the driver, examiner or another road user, will be assessed as a dangerous fault.

It is recognized that some professional drivers reverse, under control, up to a loading/unloading platform until they gently touch the platform. This will be acceptable on test as long as the platform is not dislodged.

The Uncoupling and Recoupling Exercise

After uncoupling, the candidate will be required to park the towing vehicle alongside the trailer and then realign the towing vehicle with the trailer before recoupling. The competencies of control, accuracy and effective observation will be assessed during the exercise. A fault involving actual danger to the driver or another road user will be assessed as a dangerous fault. A fault that would be potentially dangerous to the driver or another road user will be assessed as a serious fault. Faults that reflect that the driver does not have the required competencies to carry out the exercise following industry best practice and recognized procedures will be assessed as driving or serious faults, depending upon the severity of the fault.

EU Vocational Driving Test Standards

The following text summarizes Annex II to the Directive in so far as it applies to vocational driving tests only.

Driving Skills and Behaviour for Vocational Drivers

Driving test candidates must demonstrate the following key skills:

- Preparation and technical check of the vehicle for the purposes of ensuring road safety. Applicants must demonstrate that they are capable of preparing to drive safely by satisfying the following requirements:
  - adjusting the seat as necessary to obtain a correct seated position;
  - adjusting rear-view mirrors, seat belts and head restraints if available;
  - random checks on the condition of the tyres, steering, brakes, lights, reflectors, direction indicators and audible warning device;
  - checking the power-assisted braking and steering systems;
  - checking the condition of the wheels, wheel nuts, mudguards, windscreen, windows and wipers, and fluids (eg engine oil, coolant, washer fluid);
  - checking and using the instrument panel, including the recording equipment (ie the tachograph);
  - checking the air pressure, air tanks and the suspension;
  - checking the safety factors relating to vehicle loading: body, sheets, cargo doors, loading mechanism (if available), cabin locking (if available), way of loading and securing load;
  - checking the coupling mechanism and the brake and electrical connections (categories CE, C1E only);
  - reading a road map route planning, including the use of electronic navigation systems (optional).
- Special manoeuvres to be tested with a bearing on road safety:
  - coupling and uncoupling, or uncoupling and recoupling a trailer from its motor vehicle;
  - the manoeuvre must involve the towing vehicle being parked alongside the trailer (ie not in one line) (categories CE, C1E only);
  - reversing along a curve;
  - parking safely for loading/unloading at a loading ramp/platform or similar installation.
- Behaviour in traffic. Applicants must perform all the following actions in normal traffic situations, in complete safety and taking all necessary precautions:
  - driving away: ie after parking, after a stop in traffic, when exiting a driveway;
  - driving on straight roads;
  - passing oncoming vehicles, including in confined spaces;
  - driving round bends;
  - crossroads: approaching and crossing of intersections and junctions;
  - changing direction: left and right turns and changing lanes;

- approach/exit of motorways or similar (if available): joining from the acceleration lane;
- leaving on the deceleration lane;
- overtaking/passing: overtaking other traffic (if possible);
- driving alongside obstacles, eg parked cars;
- being overtaken by other traffic (if appropriate);
- special road features (if available): roundabouts;
- railway level crossings;
- tram/bus stops;
- pedestrian crossings;
- driving up/downhill on long slopes;
- taking the necessary precautions when alighting from the vehicle.

Marking of the Skills and Behaviour Tests

In assessing driver competence, the examiner will be looking for the ease with which the applicant handles the vehicle controls and their capacity to drive in complete safety in traffic. Importantly, the examiner must be made to feel safe throughout the test. The examiner will also pay special attention as to whether the applicant shows defensive and social driving behaviour, in particular ensuring the safety of all road users, especially those who are the weakest and most exposed, by showing due respect for others. Overall, drivers are expected to make progress in an economic and environmentally friendly manner.

During the test, the examiner will be checking to ensure that the test candidate makes proper use of safety belts, rear-view mirrors, head restraints, driving seat, lights and other equipment, clutch, gearbox (if applicable), accelerator, braking systems (including third braking systems, if available) and the steering. They will also be checking the driver's control of the vehicle under different circumstances and at different speeds, their steadiness on the road (this means no fast acceleration, smooth driving and no hard braking), the weight and dimensions and characteristics of the vehicle and the weight and type of load.

Additionally, drivers must show that they are capable of detecting any major technical faults in their vehicles, especially those posing a safety hazard, and know how to have them remedied in an appropriate fashion.

Vocational Test Passes and Failures

A driver who passes the vocational driving test is issued with a certificate to that effect, valid for a period of two years, and the holder can apply for a vocational driving entitlement of the appropriate category to be added to their unified driving licence.

A driver who fails the vocational driving test is given a written statement of failure and an oral explanation of the reasons for failure. They may apply for an immediate re-test to be taken after an interval of at least three days.

Advanced Commercial Vehicle Driving

Commercial vehicle drivers who wish to show that they have attained an exceptional level of proficiency can take advanced driving courses and tests designed especially for commercial vehicles.

The advanced commercial vehicle driving test is organized by IAM RoadSmart (www.iamroadsmart.com) and is open to any HGV driver, subject to certain conditions:

- Loads, if carried on test vehicles, must be properly secured.
- A safe seat at the front of the vehicle, including seat belt, must be available for the examiner.
- The driver must not, by taking the test, contravene the drivers' hours and record-keeping rules.

On passing the test, the applicant becomes eligible for membership of the IAM.

Fees

The IAM has introduced a combined fee of £149, which includes the following:

- a copy of the IAM's *Advanced Driving Manual*;
- associate membership of one of the many local IAM groups;
- a place on an IAM course to prepare for the Advanced Driving Test;
- the fee for the IAM Advanced Test;
- first-year membership of the IAM after passing the Advanced Test.

It also offers a number of courses and tests as packages, all at different prices. Details on IAM RoadSmart tests and courses can be found on the IAM website.

Exemption from the Test

Certain specially qualified drivers may apply to become members of IAM without taking the advanced driving test, including:

- Royal Navy, army and Royal Air Force HGV instructors and Defensive Driving Examiners who have passed an HGV instructor's course and whose application is supported by the recommendation of the applicant's commanding officer;

- holders of the Road Transport Industry Training Board Instructor's Certificate;

- fire service HGV instructors who have completed an HGV instructor's course, and whose application is supported by the senior instructor;

- HGV driving examiners.

The Advanced Test

To pass the test the driver should show 'skill with responsibility', and any driver of reasonable experience and skill should be able to pass without difficulty. The IAM RoadSmart examiners test candidates on routes located all over Britain.

The test lasts about two hours, during which a test route of some 35–40 miles is covered. The route incorporates road conditions of all kinds, including congested urban areas, main roads, narrow country lanes and residential streets. Candidates are not expected to display elaborate driving techniques. Examiners prefer to see the vehicle handled in a steady manner without exaggeratedly slow speeds or excessive signalling. Speed limits must be observed (driving in excess of any limit results in test failure) and the driving manner must take into consideration road, traffic and weather conditions. However, the examiners expect candidates to drive briskly within the limits and to cruise at the legal limit (ie the limit either on the road or the vehicle, whichever is lower) whenever circumstances permit.

Drivers will be asked to make a hill start. There will be spot checks on the driver's power of observation (ie the examiner will ask questions about road signs or markings recently passed, or about other significant landmarks).

Test Requirements

The examiner will consider the following aspects of driving:

- *Acceleration*: must be smooth and progressive, not excessive or insufficient, and must be used at the right time and place.

- *Braking*: must be smooth and progressive, not fierce. Brakes should be used in conjunction with the driving mirror and signals. Road, traffic and weather conditions must be taken into account.

- *Clutch control*: engine and road speeds should be properly coordinated when changing gear. The clutch should not be 'ridden' or slipped and the vehicle should not be coasted with the clutch disengaged.

- *Gear changing*: should be smooth and carried out without jerking.

- *Use of gears*: the gears should be correctly selected and used and the right gear engaged before reaching a hazard (obviously where a vehicle with an automatic gearbox is used, some of these requirements are not applicable).

- *Steering*: the wheel should be correctly held with the hands and the 'crossed-arm' technique should not be used except when manoeuvring in confined spaces.

- *Driving position*: the driver should be alert and should not slump at the wheel. Resting an arm on the door while driving should be avoided.

- *Observation*: the driver should 'read' the road ahead and show a good sense of anticipation and the ability to judge speed and distance.

- *Concentration*: the driver should keep his or her attention on the road and should not be easily distracted.

- *Maintaining progress*: taking account of the road, traffic and weather conditions, the driver must keep up a reasonable pace and maintain good progress.

- *Obstruction*: the candidate must be careful not to obstruct other vehicles by driving too slowly, taking up the wrong position on the road or failing to anticipate and react correctly to the traffic situation ahead.

- *Positioning*: the driver must keep to the correct part of the road, especially when approaching and negotiating hazards.

- *Lane discipline*: the driver must keep to the appropriate lane and be careful not to straddle white lines.

- *Observations of road surfaces*: the driver must keep an eye on the road surface, especially in bad weather, and should watch out for slippery conditions.

- *Traffic signals*: signals, signs and road markings must be observed, obeyed and approached correctly and the driver should show courtesy at pedestrian crossings.

- *Speed limits and other legal requirements*: these should be observed. The examiner cannot condone breaches of the law.

- *Overtaking*: this must be carried out safely and decisively, maintaining the right distance from other vehicles and using the mirror, signals and gears correctly.

- *Hazard procedure and cornering*: road and traffic hazards must be coped with properly, and bends and corners taken in the right manner.

- *Mirror*: the mirror must be used frequently, especially in conjunction with signals and before changing speed or course.

- *Signals*: direction indicators, and hand signals when needed, must be given at the right place and in good time. The horn and headlamp flasher should be used as per the *Highway Code*.

- *Restraint*: the driver should show reasonable restraint, but not indecision, at the wheel.

- *Consideration*: sufficient consideration and courtesy should be shown to other road users.

- *Vehicle sympathy*: the driver should treat the vehicle with care, without overstressing it by needless revving of the engine and by fierce braking.

- *Manoeuvring*: this should be performed smoothly and competently.

Large Goods Vehicle Driver Apprenticeship

The goods driver apprenticeship was one of three apprenticeships developed as part of the Trailblazer programme. It provides the knowledge and skills for driving and delivering goods across all sectors and distances for a range of customers, from private individuals and sole traders through to large global organizations.

The apprenticeship is level 2 (equivalent to GCSE grades A* to C or 9 to 4) and the typical length is 12 months. The current funding band is up to £5,000 per apprentice. Candidates must hold at least a valid UK Category B driving licence and be 18 years old before they gain a provisional vocational licence.

Alongside attaining a Category C driving licence, apprentices learn:

- road safety practices, procedures and legislation – including goods vehicle and working time restrictions and vulnerable road users;
- vehicle safety and preparation – including checks and inspections, defect reporting and load security;
- safe and fuel-efficient driving techniques – including restricted space manoeuvres and using public and private roads;
- transport planning – including route selection and vehicle selection;
- industry-recognized systems and technology – including adaptive braking, hand-held scanners, on-board telematics and tachographs;
- communicating effectively with colleagues and customers – including customer service and establishing rapport;
- health and safety practices, procedures, regulations and legislation within a supply chain environment.

Employers must pay the apprentice at least the minimum wage and apprentices must:

- work with experienced staff;
- learn job-specific skills;
- get time for training or study during their working week (at least 20 per cent of their normal working hours).

Apprenticeships are managed by the Education and Skills Funding Agency and administered by the National Apprenticeship Service. For advice or help contact the National Apprenticeship Service on 0800 015 0600.

Specialist Training

Driver Training for Lorry Loaders

No recognized requirement exists for drivers to hold certificates of competence to operate lorry-mounted cranes. However, they do need to be 'competent' and under the Health and Safety at Work Act 1974 employers have a statutory duty to provide adequate instruction and safety training for all employees. Details of training providers can be obtained from the Association of Lorry Loader Manufacturers and Importers (ALLMI).

There is also a voluntary certification scheme run by the Construction Industry Training Board (CITB) to improve safety on construction sites. This scheme is strongly supported by the construction industry, which may refuse entry to its own sites to non-certified lorry drivers. Mainly, the Board's scheme is concerned with ensuring a sound understanding of safety procedures for the use of a wide range of equipment, including lorry-mounted cranes and skip loaders. Under the scheme, the Board provides certification of existing lorry-loader and skip-loader operators who can show, by means of employer confirmation, that they are experienced in the use of such equipment.

Newcomers seeking first-time certification and drivers renewing grandfather rights certificates have to undergo (re-)training and site-based assessment to show that they can operate such equipment with complete safety. CITB safety certificates are renewable at five-yearly intervals.

Another scheme is run by the Contractors' Mechanical Plant Engineers (CMPE), although this requires no specific training, certification being based solely on employers' references. Training is also provided by most member firms of ALLMI. Additionally, the Association itself publishes a Code of Practice for safe application and use of loaders. ALLMI has also been issued with the Health and Safety Executive's logo of recognition to reflect the standards of the training courses offered by its members. ALLMI offers a 15-module suite of operator training courses as well as slinger and crane supervisor training, appointed person, load test course and courses aimed at instructor accreditation and managers. Details of ALLMI training courses are available from the Association at Unit 7b, Cavalier Court, Bumpers Farm, Chippenham, Wiltshire SN14 6LH (0844 858 4334) www.allmi.com. Other organizations providing suitable lorry-loader training include Logistics UK (formerly the FTA), the RTITB Instructor Academy and a number of commercial training firms.

Driver Training for ADR

The Carriage of Dangerous Goods and Use of Transportable Pressure Equipment Regulations 2009 (regulation 5) require that dangerous goods drivers are trained in accordance with section 8.2.1 of the European Agreement Concerning the International Carriage of Dangerous Goods by Road (commonly referred to as the ADR 2017) and that they hold vocational training certificates issued by the DVLA, Swansea, and gained by attending an approved course and passing a written examination. Courses are offered by most transport training providers and the trade associations.

Relevant Vehicles

The regulations apply broadly to the carriage of specified dangerous goods in:

- road tankers with a capacity exceeding 1,000 litres;
- tank containers with a capacity greater than 3,000 litres (with certain exceptions);
- vehicles carrying radioactive materials or explosives;
- vehicles carrying packed dangerous goods the amount of which exceeds certain thresholds, as set down by the ADR regulations.

Driver Responsibilities

Vocational training certificates are valid for a period of five years and are renewable, subject to the holder attending an approved refresher course and taking a further examination within the 12 months prior to the expiry date of an existing certificate. The driver must hold a valid certificate for the actual class and group of dangerous goods being carried at the time. Drivers must carry the certificate with them when driving relevant vehicles and must produce it on request by police or a goods vehicle examiner. It is an offence to drive a dangerous goods vehicle without being the holder of a certificate, or to fail to produce such a certificate on request.

Employer Responsibilities

It is the responsibility of the employer to ensure that dangerous goods drivers receive training so they understand the dangers arising from the products they are carrying and what to do in an emergency situation, and that they hold relevant certificates covering the vehicle being driven and the products carried. The employer has a duty to provide necessary training leading to the certificate. The employer must retain records of all instruction and training given to drivers.

Approved Training and Examination

The Department for Transport has approved suitable establishments where dangerous goods driver training and dangerous goods safety advisor (DGSA) training can be obtained. These include the CILT, Logistics UK, RHA and many private training organizations. ADR training is also now able to be delivered as DCPC training offered by some JAUPT-approved training centres.

The syllabus for the examination involves both theoretical sessions and practical exercises. The examination itself comprises a core element designed to assess candidates' practical and legal knowledge, plus a specialist element for either road tanker and tank container drivers or packaged goods drivers (or both if required). Additionally, candidates have to pass individual 'dangerous substance' examination papers, which cover each of nine classes of dangerous goods, to test their specialist knowledge of the products they carry in their work.

Candidates who pass the examination (by achieving a pass mark of at least 75 per cent in each element – ie core, tanker/package and substance) will receive their certificate (similar to a photocard-style driving licence) direct from the DVLA, Swansea. Those who fail can apply to resit the examination without further training within a period of 16 weeks from receipt of the notification of failure.

Continuing Professional Development

Constant changes in business, industry and technology mean that staff at all levels need to keep their skills and knowledge up to date in order to maximize professional opportunities. Continuing professional development (CPD) schemes, such as those operated by the Chartered Institute of Logistics and Transport in the UK (CILT) for its members, enable individuals to improve their knowledge and competence systematically throughout their working life – a concept supported by the government.

Professional development is the key to career enhancement. Although it is possible to train as and when suitable courses become available, this approach can leave the individual with key needs unfulfilled. A CPD scheme offers personal development solutions structured to fit around a certain career and lifestyle. Planning career development in this systematic way brings the following developments:

- It makes the best use of training and learning opportunities.
- It encourages the individual to look for alternative ways of meeting training/learning needs.
- It enables the individual to become aware of less obvious knowledge or skills gaps.

- By periodic evaluation of development individuals can judge whether they are meeting their personal objectives.

- Records are kept to track progress.

Learning Activities

Formal learning usually comprises:

- company training;
- study courses including open learning;
- teaching and making presentations;
- attendance at conferences, seminars and meetings related to the individual's work or professional interests.

Informal learning includes:

- reading;
- networking;
- mentoring and coaching;
- project work.

CPD places emphasis on helping individuals to plan and progress their professional future. Normally, schemes focus on outputs without prescribing a minimum number of hours or particular courses to attend; professional persons are expected to take responsibility for their own learning. The CILT, for example, helps members to identify opportunities and provides accreditation of their learning log.

Further details of the CILT and its CPD scheme can be obtained from www.ciltuk. org.uk

Vehicle Registration, HGV Road User Levy, Excise Duty and Trade Licences

08

Vehicle Registration

New vehicles must be registered with the DVLA and issued with a vehicle registration mark (VRM). A one-off first registration charge of £55 is made to cover the DVLA's administrative costs. A list of new vehicle registration marks is also described in the section Vehicle Markings in Chapter 13.

The registration number must be displayed on plates mounted on the front and rear of the vehicle. These must conform to legal requirements as specified in the Road Vehicles (Display of Registration Marks) Regulations 2001 as amended.

Registration-plate format comprises two letters representing the place of registration (ie one of 19 areas followed by a letter for the office of registration). Two numbers denote the year of registration. The last three letters are randomly selected.

Form V55/4 (Application for first vehicle tax and registration of a new motor vehicle) is completed and sent to the DVLA and forms part of the national vehicle statistics.

The form includes questions about the purchaser's occupation and previous vehicle and about the main use for the new vehicle, and detailed information on the vehicle design and construction.

While most of the main vehicle manufacturers and importers will have entered the details of each vehicle on the form before it reaches the dealer, the purchaser will also need to complete details. If the manufacturer or importer has not completed the form in advance, copies are available at licensing offices.

Documents

A completed form V55/4, a copy of the supplier's invoice and an appropriate Type Approval Certificate for goods vehicles subject to the type-approval regulations are required when first registering a new goods vehicle (a certificate of insurance is only required if registering a new vehicle in Northern Ireland). When vehicle tax is required for vehicles exempt from annual testing, a completed form V112G (declaration of exemption from goods vehicle testing) must also be produced.

Vehicle Approvals

A new vehicle may be certificated under one of three approval methods:

- Individual Vehicle Approval (IVA) – a UK national scheme and the most likely route for those manufacturing or importing single vehicles or very small numbers.

- EC Whole Vehicle Type Approval (ECWVTA) – based around EC Directives and provides for the approval of large numbers of whole vehicles, in addition to vehicle systems and separate components, that are manufactured and sold across Europe. This certification is accepted throughout the EU without the need for further testing until a standard is updated or your design changes.

- National Small Series Type Approval (NSSTA) – a UK national scheme for low-volume manufacturers who intend to sell only in the UK. The advantages of NSSTA are relaxed technical requirements for some subjects, a more pragmatic approach to the Conformity of Production (CoP) requirements, and reduction in administrative requirements. Like ECWVTA, once the design is approved, individual vehicles do not need to be tested.

Type approval is the confirmation that production samples of a design meet specified performance standards. The specification of the product is recorded and only that particular specification is approved.

The general rules for vehicle and component approvals from 1 January 2021 after the Brexit transition period are:

- Manufacturers need to make sure they have the correct type approval for each market – the EU and the UK.

- Type approvals issued in the UK are no longer valid for sales or registrations on the EU market.

- European Community type approvals (EC type approvals) issued in the UK are no longer valid for sales or registrations on the EU market.

- EC type approvals issued outside of the UK are no longer automatically accepted for registering vehicles on the UK market.

- The UK continues to recognize United Nations Economic Commission for Europe (UNECE) approvals for systems and components. The EU continues to recognize UNECE approvals issued by the UK.
- The Vehicle Certification Agency (VCA) remains a technical service and type approval authority for the testing of UK and UNECE type approvals.

UK and EU technical standards are now aligned. As such, the UK can issue provisional UK type approvals, upon application, to manufacturers that can prove they hold valid EC type approvals. This is an administrative conversion of EC type approvals into UK type approvals. This streamlined approach avoids costly re-testing and re-design for manufacturers and also ensures that products can continue to be sold and registered in the UK.

The provisional UK type approval is valid for two years from the date of issue. It must be converted into a full UK type approval during this period or it will become invalid. Legislation to allow the VCA to convert provisional type approvals into full type approvals is expected to be in place during 2021.

Vehicle Registration Documents

A Registration Document/Certificate shows the registered keeper of a vehicle. The registered keeper is the person who keeps the vehicle on a public road, but is not necessarily the legal owner. The certificate gives the keeper's name and address, the registration mark and other details of the vehicle, including engine, VIN and type approval numbers, the category into which it falls, its body type, maximum mass (ie weight), etc. A new Registration Certificate is issued each time the DVLA updates the record with any change to the existing details. The vehicle keeper should make sure that the details on this certificate are accurate and must tell the DVLA immediately if any changes are necessary. It may be difficult to sell the vehicle if any of the information is inaccurate. However, it is important to note that the Registration Document/Certificate is not a document of title (ownership).

Anyone registering a vehicle will be issued with a Vehicle Registration Certificate (V5C). The V5C also shows (where applicable) the vehicle engine's Euro emissions standard (eg currently Euro VI for new vehicles). This enables operators to show the vehicle's compliance with emission standards for road tax and toll-charging purposes.

NB: *While the statutory charge of £55.00 is made by the DVLA for first registration of a new vehicle, the DVLA also charges £25.00 for replacing a lost, stolen, destroyed or damaged vehicle registration document.*

Police officers and enforcement officers of the DVSA may request production of the registration document for inspection at any reasonable time.

Vehicle Registration Plates

Vehicle registration plates (commonly referred to as 'number plates') are used to display the VRM and must be fitted to vehicles used on public roads. Vehicle registration plates must be displayed at the front and rear of the vehicle and:

- be made from a reflective material;
- display black characters on a white background (front plate);
- display black characters on a yellow background (rear plate);
- not have a background pattern.

As part of the DVLA's measures to combat vehicle crime, vehicle registration plates can only be produced by registered number plate suppliers, who must keep records of the plates they sell, to whom they are sold and whether that person is authorized to require the plates. Purchasers of plates need to produce evidence as to who they are (a passport or photocard driving licence) and that they have a right to the plates for the vehicle in question (generally by producing the V5C or a letter of authorization from the vehicle owner). Drivers of vehicles with dirty, unreadable number plates caught on ANPR (Automatic Number Plate Recognition) systems may be prosecuted.

After the Brexit transition period the Euro symbol and Great Britain (GB) national identifier on a vehicle registration plate remains valid. However, it is unclear whether a separate GB sticker is required or not when travelling within EU member states. If GB national flags, letters or identifiers are used, a GB sticker must be displayed at the rear of the vehicle or trailer.

Trailer Registration

Registration applies to all trailers used commercially over 750 kg and is optional for non-commercial trailers 750 kg to 3,500 kg. Registration can be done online at GOV.UK and by submitting the application to the Technical Application System (TAS). The registration document will be issued and sent via the post.

Details required to register a trailer include the keeper's details, trailer manufacturer, trailer VIN/chassis number, trailer gross vehicle weight and trailer unladen weight, number of axles, etc. Details of any change of ownership are also to be recorded. Costs are £26.00 for first registration, £21.00 for following registrations and £10.00 for a replacement certificate.

When the Trailer Registration Certificate is issued, it is to travel with the trailer and a trailer identity registration plate with one alpha and seven numeric figures on it is to be displayed at the rear of the trailer in addition to the number plate of the drawing vehicle. Forms to be used to apply for a new trailer ID number for a new-build trailer and for a 'Ministry Number' for a new trailer to be used on the road are Forms TES1 and TES2 respectively.

Advice and further details are available at GOV.UK or on 0300 123 9000.

Registration of 'O' Licence Vehicles

Vehicles specified on British 'O' licences must be registered in the UK. Vehicle tax must also be paid in the UK unless an operator has a genuine business abroad.

HGV Road User Levy

> The HGV levy is suspended from 1 August 2020 to 31 July 2022 to support the haulage sector and aid pandemic recovery efforts.

The HGV Road User Levy ensures HGV operators contribute to the wear and tear of the road network. It applies to HGVs with a gross weight of 12,000 kg or above and is based on vehicle weight and number of axles.

Operators that use less polluting vehicles benefit from a lower road user levy. Euro-VI vehicles attract a 10 per cent discount on the levy, whereas older vehicles attract up to 20 per cent more. Payments are collected by the DVLA. UK-registered vehicles pay levy costs at the same time and in the same transaction as vehicle tax.

Foreign operators pay the levy before they enter the UK. Their charges vary from around £10 per day up to around £1,000 per year. They are able to purchase short-term vignettes (daily, weekly, monthly, etc) and there are surcharges for the shorter terms. Payment can be made online but there are also payment facilities at truck-stops close to the Channel ports, at the ports, on the ferries and on the Eurotunnel link.

Enforcement is generally in relation to non-payment, or under-payment, of the levy. There are no discs or documentation (except proof of payment); enforcement is carried out through ANPR cameras. A £300 fixed penalty is charged and the vehicle can be immobilized if the driver cannot pay at the roadside, cannot pay a fixed penalty deposit (FPD) or cannot provide details of a suitable UK address.

Vehicle Tax

All HGVs, whether used for private or business purposes, which are used or parked on public roads in Great Britain must be taxed – except when a vehicle is travelling to or from a pre-arranged MOT appointment or to or from a pre-arranged repair appointment to have defects remedied that were discovered on a previous test.

Vehicle tax is an excise duty paid for most types of vehicles used on public roads in the UK. Vehicle tax is also referred to as Vehicle Excise Duty (VED). HGVs are taxed on their gvw, number of axles and any trailer drawn; since 2017 the vehicle's emission standard determines the first-year vehicle tax.

Taxing a vehicle

The registered keeper of a vehicle (named on the V5C) is responsible for taxing a vehicle:

- on the purchase of a new vehicle;
- when vehicle tax expires;
- when a vehicle is returned to the road after a Statutory Off Road Notification (SORN).

Vehicle tax is due annually but can be paid six-monthly or monthly. It can be renewed at a post office using DVLA form V85 (Application to tax an HGV) or taxed online at GOV.UK. Both processes require reference details from either:

- a renewal reminder (V11) or 'last chance' warning letter from the DVLA;
- the vehicle log book (V5C); or
- the green 'new keeper' slip from a V5C.

If a vehicle is taxed in person at a post office, one of the above forms must be presented with a valid MOT (annual test) certificate. If a vehicle is taxed online, payment is either by debit or credit card, or a direct debit can be set up. A tax disc is not issued (these were withdrawn in 2014).

For first registrations, form VE 55/4 is required for new vehicles and form 55/4 is required for imported and rebuilt vehicles.

Operators can find out if a vehicle is taxed or has been registered as off the road (SORN) at GOV.UK. However, it can take up to five working days for the records to update.

Cancelling vehicle tax

Operators can cancel a vehicle's tax by informing the DVLA they no longer have the vehicle or have declared it as SORN. A refund is issued for any full months of remaining tax.

Vehicle tax can be cancelled by informing the DVLA that the vehicle has been:

- sold or transferred to someone else;
- taken off the road, for example you're keeping it in a garage – this is called a SORN;
- written off by your insurance company;
- scrapped at a vehicle scrapyard;
- stolen – you'll have to apply for a refund separately;
- exported out of the UK;
- registered as exempt from vehicle tax.

A refund cheque is issued automatically for any full months left on the vehicle tax. The refund is calculated from the date the DVLA gets your information. The cheque is sent to the name and address on the V5C. If vehicle tax is paid by direct debit, the direct debit is cancelled automatically.

Vehicle tax is not transferred to a new owner when a vehicle is sold or bought.

Exemptions

Exemption from vehicle tax (as specified in the Vehicle Excise and Registration Act 1994) applies to the following:

1 Vehicles used for police, fire brigade, ambulance or health services (including veterinary ambulances).
2 Mines rescue vehicles.
3 Vehicles used for the haulage of lifeboats and lifeboat gear.
4 Vehicles for disabled people, including mobility scooters and powered wheelchairs with a maximum speed of 8 mph for road use.
5 Vehicles used solely for forestry, agriculture or horticultural purposes travelling on public roads to pass between land occupied by the same person and the distance travelled on public roads is not more than 1.5 km per journey.
6 Vehicles travelling to or from a place where they are to have an annual roadworthiness test by prior appointment.
7 Vehicles for export.

8 Vehicles in the service of a visiting force or headquarters.

9 Historic vehicles manufactured before 1 January 1976.

The special concessionary rate which formerly applied has been abolished and the following vehicles that were included in this class are now exempt from vehicle tax:

- An agricultural or off-road tractor, which is one used on public roads only for purposes relating to agriculture, horticulture, forestry or cutting verges, hedges or trees bordering public roads. An off-road tractor is one which is not an agricultural tractor but which is designed and constructed primarily for use otherwise than on roads and is incapable of exceeding 25 mph on the level.

- A light agricultural vehicle which is a vehicle with a revenue weight not exceeding 1,000 kg, which is designed and constructed to seat only the driver and primarily for use otherwise than on roads, and is used only for agriculture, horticulture or forestry.

- An agricultural engine.

- Mowing machines.

- Steam-powered vehicles.

- Electrically propelled vehicles where the source of power is not connected to any other source of power when the vehicle is moving.

- Vehicles when used, or going to or from a place for use, or kept for use, for clearing snow on public roads by means of a snow plough or similar device.

- Vehicles constructed or adapted and used only for the conveyance of machinery for spreading material on roads to deal with frost, ice or snow.

Special Vehicles

For special vehicles over 3.5 tonnes the current and annual rate of duty is £165. Special vehicles means mobile cranes, digging machines, works trucks, road rollers, mobile pumping vehicles and showmen's goods and haulage vehicles. Due to new equipment continually being developed, the list of special vehicles changes from time to time.

Concrete-pumping vehicles are not classified as special vehicles and must be taxed at the goods vehicle rate of duty, and not at the reduced rate applicable to mobile cranes.

Don't confuse special vehicles with Special Types.

Rates of Vehicle Tax

The rate of vehicle tax varies depending on the way in which the vehicle is constructed, the way that it is used and the gross weight and the number of axles.

Revenue Weight

Revenue weight means either the:

- gross vehicle weight as determined under the plating and testing regulations; or
- design weight for vehicles not subject to plating and testing and currently known as restricted HGVs.

Gross vehicle weight is the maximum laden weight at which non-plated vehicles can legally operate on roads in the UK.

Downplating

If operationally acceptable, and to lower the rate of vehicle tax, an HGV may be downplated to reduce the maximum weight it can work at. The vehicle may be required to pass an official weight test before the DVSA issues a new plate with the new weights.

Reduced Pollution Certificates

The Reduced Pollution Certificate (RPC) scheme to reduce vehicle tax ended on 31 December 2016.

Articulated Vehicles

In the case of articulated vehicles, which can be used with various trailer types, the vehicle tax is determined by the maximum number of axles on any trailer likely to be used.

Drawbar Trailers

In the case of vehicle combinations with drawbar trailers, tax is payable on the trailer if the gross weight of the trailer exceeds 4 tonnes and the gross weight of the towing vehicle exceeds 12 tonnes.

Goods-Carrying Vehicles

The goods vehicle rate of duty is payable if the vehicle is built or has been converted to carry goods, and is actually used to carry goods in connection with a trade or business. In general this rate of duty applies to all types of lorries, vans, trucks, estate cars, dual-purpose vehicles and also passenger vehicles if they are converted for carrying goods. If, however, dual-purpose vehicles (see below) and goods vehicles (over 3.5 tonnes) are never used for carrying goods in connection with a trade or business, they may be licensed at the private HGV rate of duty, which is currently £165 per year if paid as a single payment.

Vehicles carrying wide loads in excess of 4.3 metres must be taxed at the 'Special Types' rate of duty, irrespective of their gross weight. This duty is based on the use of a vehicle rather than its construction, and when carrying a wide load under the Motor Vehicles (Authorisation of Special Types) General Order 2003, the relevant Special Types duty rate must be applied.

Driver Training and Non-Goods-Carrying Vehicles

HGVs which are used exclusively for driver training purposes may be licensed at the private heavy goods rate of duty even if they carry ballast (eg IBCs filled with water, or other loads such as bags of sand) to simulate driving under loaded conditions – *but not other 'commercial' loads*. Similarly, other goods vehicles used for private purposes (ie carriage of goods but not in connection with a trade or business – for example, privately used horseboxes) may be licensed at the private HGV rate of duty – currently £165 for vehicles over 3.5 tonnes (note the point about single payment above).

Dual-Purpose Vehicles

A dual-purpose vehicle (as referred to above) is defined as a vehicle built or con-verted to carry both passengers and goods of any description, which has an unladen weight of not more than 2,040 kg and has either four-wheel drive or:

- has a permanently fitted roof;
- is permanently fitted with one row of transverse seats (fitted across the vehicle) behind the driver's seat (the seats must be cushioned or sprung and have upholstered back-rests);
- has a window on either side to the rear of the driver's seat and one at the rear.

The majority of estate cars, SUVs, station wagons, hatchbacks, certain Land Rovers and Range Rovers are dual-purpose vehicles under this definition. It should be noted, however, that vehicles used for *dual operations* are not dual-purpose vehicles in terms of the legal requirements.

VED Tables for Goods Vehicles Exceeding 3,500 kg gvw, Including Details of VED and Levy Bands

Table 8.1 VED and levy rates Euro-VI

VED band and rate	Total 12 months VED and levy	Total 6 months VED and levy	12-month VED rate	6-month VED rate	Levy bands	12-month levy rate (Euro-VI)	6-month levy rate (Euro-VI)	12- and 6-months Euro-0–V	6-month RPC discount or grant
AO	N/A	N/A	£165	£90.75	N/A	N/A	N/A	N/A	£2.75
BO	N/A	N/A	£200	£110	N/A	N/A	N/A	N/A	£22
A1	£156.50	£87.90	£80	£40	A	£76.50	£45.90	£102 and £61.20	£2.50
A2	£160.50	£87.90	£84	£42	A	"	"	"	"
A3	£176.50	£95.90	£100	£50	A	"	"	"	"
A4	£222.50	£118.90	£146	£73	A	"	"	"	"
A5	£227.50	£121.40	£151	£75.50	A	"	"	"	"
B1	£189.50	£104.20	£95	£47.50	B	£94.50	£56.70	£126 and £75.60	£20
B2	£199.50	£109.20	£105	£52.50	B	"	"	"	"
B3	£219.50	£119.20	£125	£62.50	B	"	"	"	"
C1	£426	£234.60	£210	£105	C	£216	£129.60	£288 and £172.80	£120
C2	£481	£262.10	£265	£132.50	C	"	"	"	"
C3	£505	£274.10	£289	£144.50	C	"	"	"	"
D1	£615	£339	£300	£150	D	£315	£189	£420 and £252	£185
E1	£1,136	£625.60	£560	£280	E	£576	£345.60	£768 and £460.80	£250
E2	£1,185	£650.10	£609	£305.50	E	"	"	"	"
F	£1,419	£782.40	£690	£345	F	£729	£437.40	£972 and £583.20	£250
G	£1,750	£965	£850	£425	G	£900	£540	£1,200 and £720	£250

NB: Inverted commas (") indicate the same cost as in the last figure above. For example, all levy Band A vehicles pay the same levy rates irrespective of whether or not they are banded as A1 or A5. This follows for the other bands where the band is sub-divided.

Table 8.2   Rigid goods vehicles

Weight over (kg)	Weight not over (kg)	Two axles	Three axles	Four or more axles
3,500	7,500	AO	AO	AO
7,500	11,999	BO	BO	BO
11,999	14,000	B1	B1	B1
14,000	15,000	B2	B1	B1
15,000	19,000	D1	B1	B1
19,000	21,000	D1	B3	B1
21,000	23,000	D1	C1	B1
23,000	25,000	D1	D1	C1
25,000	27,000	D1	D1	D1
27,000	44,000	D1	D1	E1

NB: The bands above also apply to rigid goods vehicles that are used to pull trailers that do not exceed 4,000 kg. Where rigid vehicles do tow trailers exceeding a weight of 4,000 kg a different banding system is used and a higher rate of duty is applied. These bands and rates are below.

Table 8.3   Levy bands for rigid vehicles towing trailers exceeding 4,000 kg

Weight of vehicle (not trailer) over (kg)	Weight of vehicle (not trailer) not over (kg)	Two axles	Three axles	Four axles
11,999	15,000	B(T)	B(T)	B(T)
15,000	21,000	D(T)	B(T)	B(T)
21,000	23,000	E(T)	C(T)	B(T)
23,000	25,000	E(T)	D(T)	C(T)
25,000	27,000	E(T)	D(T)	D(T)
27,000	44,000	E(T)	E(T)	E(T)

Table 8.4 Rigid vehicles towing trailers exceeding 4,000 kg levy rate and RPC grant

Levy band	Euro-VI levy rate for 12 months	Levy rate 6 months	Euro-0–V levy rate for 12 months	Levy rate 6 months
B(T)	£121.50	£72.90	£162	£97.20
C(T)	£279	£167.40	£372	£223.20
D(T)	£405	£243	£540	£324
E(T)	£747	£448.20	£996	£597.60

Table 8.5 Tractive unit with two axles

Weight over (kg)	Weight not over (kg)	Two axles	Three axles	Four or more axles
3,500	11,999	AO	AO	AO
11,999	22,000	A1	A1	A1
22,000	23,000	A2	A1	A1
23,000	25,000	A5	A1	A1
25,000	26,000	C2	A3	A1
26,000	28,000	D1	B3	B1
28,000	31,000	D1	C1	B1
31,000	33,000	E1	E1	C1
33,000	34,000	E1	E2	C1
34,000	38,000	F	F	E1
38,000	44,000	G	G	G

Table 8.6 Tractive unit with three or more axles

Weight over (kg)	Weight not over (kg)	Two axles	Three axles	Four or more axles
3,500	11,999	AO	AO	AO
11,999	25,000	A1	A1	A1
25,000	26,000	A3	A1	A1
26,000	28,000	A4	A1	A1
28,000	29,000	C1	A1	A1
29,000	31,000	C3	A1	A1

Table 8.6   *continued*

Weight over (kg)	Weight not over (kg)	Two axles	Three axles	Four or more axles
31,000	33,000	E1	C1	A1
33,000	34,000	E2	D1	A1
34,000	36,000	E2	D1	C1
36,000	38,000	F	E1	D1
38,000	44,000	G	G	E1

Table 8.7   VED and levy costs for rigid vehicles pulling trailers exceeding 4,000 kg with road-friendly suspension

HGV axles	Levy band	Trailer weight (kg)	Gross train weight not over (kg)	VED band and rate number	VED and levy 12 months (Euro-VI)	VED and levy 6 months (Euro-VI)	VED and levy 12 months (Euro-0–V)	VED and levy 6 months (Euro-0–V)
2	B(T)	4,001–12,000	27,000	B(T)1	£351.50	£187.90	£392	£212.20
2	B(T)	12,000+	33,000	B(T)3	£416.50	£220.40	£457	£244.70
2	B(T)	12,000+	36,000	B(T)6	£522.50	£273.40	£563	£297.70
2	B(T)	12,000+	38,000	B(T)4	£440.50	£232.40	£481	£256.70
2	B(T)	12,000+	40,000	B(T)7	£565.50	£294.90	£606	£319.20
2	D(T)	4,001–12,000	30,000	D(T)1	£770	£425.50	£905	£506.50
2	D(T)	12,000+	38,000	D(T)4	£835	£458	£970	£539
2	D(T)	12,000+	40,000	D(T)5	£849	£465	£984	£546
3	B(T)	4,001–12,000	33,000	B(T)1	£351.50	£187.90	£392	£212.20
3	B(T)	12,000+	38,000	B(T)3	£416.50	£220.40	£457	£244.70
3	B(T)	12,000+	40,000	B(T)5	£513.50	£268.90	£554	£293.20
3	B(T)	12,000+	44,000	B(T)3	£416.50	£220.40	£457	£244.70
3	C(T)	4,001–12,000	35,000	C(T)1	£584	£319.90	£677	£375.70
3	C(T)	12,000+	38,000	C(T)2	£649	£352.40	£742	£408.20
3	C(T)	12,000+	40,000	C(T)3	£671	£363.40	£764	£419.20
3	C(T)	12,000+	44,000	C(T)2	£649	£352.40	£742	£408.20
3	D(T)	4,001–12,000	33,000	D(T)1	£770	£425.50	£905	£506.50

Table 8.7 *continued*

HGV axles	Levy band	Trailer weight (kg)	Gross train weight not over (kg)	VED band and rate number	VED and levy 12 months (Euro-VI)	VED and levy 6 months (Euro-VI)	VED and levy 12 months (Euro-0–V)	VED and levy 6 months (Euro-0–V)
3	D(T)	4,001–12,000	36,000	D(T)3	£806	£443.50	£941	£534.50
3	D(T)	10,001–12,000	38,000	D(T)1	£770	£425.50	£905	£506.50
3	D(T)	12,000+	44,000	D(T)4	£835	£458	£970	£539
4	B(T)	4,001–12,000	35,000	B(T)1	£351.50	£187.90	£392	£212.20
4	B(T)	12,000+	44,000	B(T)3	£416.50	£220.40	£457	£244.70
4	C(T)	4,001–12,000	37,000	C(T)1	£584	£319.90	£677	£375.70
4	C(T)	12,000+	44,000	C(T)2	£649	£352.40	£742	£408.20
4	D(T)	4,001–12,000	39,000	D(T)1	£770	£425.50	£905	£506.50
4	D(T)	12,000+	44,000	D(T)4	£835	£458	£970	£539
4	E(T)	4,001–12,000	44,000	E(T)1	£1,282	£715.70	£1,531	£865.10
4	E(T)	12,000+	44,000	E(T)2	£1,347	£748.20	£1,596	£897.60

Table 8.8 VED and levy costs for rigid vehicles pulling trailers exceeding 4,000 kg without road-friendly suspension

HGV axles	Levy band	Trailer weight (kg)	Gross train weight not over (kg)	VED band and rate number	VED and levy 12 months (Euro-VI)	VED and levy 6 months (Euro-VI)	VED and levy 12 months (Euro-0–V)	VED and levy 6 months (Euro-0–V)
2	B(T)	4,001–12,000	27,000	B(T)1	£351.50	£187.90	£392	£212.20
2	B(T)	12,000+	31,000	B(T)3	£416.50	£220.40	£457	£244.70
2	B(T)	12,000+	33,000	B(T)6	£522.50	£273.40	£563	£297.70
2	B(T)	12,000+	36,000	B(T)10	£730.50	£377.40	£771	£401.70
2	B(T)	12,000+	38,000	B(T)7	£565.50	£294.90	£606	£319.20
2	B(T)	12,000+	40,000	B(T)9	£725.50	£374.90	£766	£399.20

Table 8.8 *continued*

HGV axles	Levy band	Trailer weight (kg)	Gross train weight not over (kg)	VED band and rate number	VED and levy 12 months (Euro-VI)	VED and levy 6 months (Euro-VI)	VED and levy 12 months (Euro-0–V)	VED and levy 6 months (Euro-0–V)
2	D(T)	4,001–12,000	30,000	D(T)1	£770	£425.50	£905	£506.50
2	D(T)	12,000+	33,000	D(T)4	£835	£458	£970	£539
2	D(T)	12,000+	36,000	D(T)8	£1,014	£547.50	£1,149	£628.50
2	D(T)	12,000+	38,000	D(T)5	£849	£465	£984	£546
2	D(T)	12,000+	40,000	D(T)7	£1,009	£545	£1,144	£626
3	B(T)	4,001–12,000	29,000	B(T)1	£351.50	£187.90	£392	£212.20
3	B(T)	4,001–12,000	31,000	B(T)2	£410.50	£217.40	£451	£241.70
3	B(T)	10,001–12,000	33,000	B(T)1	£351.50	£187.90	£392	£212.20
3	B(T)	12,000+	36,000	B(T)3	£416.50	£220.40	£457	£244.70
3	B(T)	12,000+	38,000	B(T)5	£513.50	£268.90	£554	£293.20
3	B(T)	12,000+	40,000	B(T)8	£663.50	£343.90	£704	£368.20
3	C(T)	4,001–12,000	31,000	C(T)1	£584	£319.90	£677	£375.70
3	C(T)	10,001–12,000	33,000	C(T)4	£680	£367.90	£773	£423.70
3	C(T)	4,001–12,000	35,000	C(T)1	£584	£319.90	£677	£375.70
3	C(T)	12,000+	36,000	C(T)2	£649	£352.40	£742	£408.20
3	C(T)	12,000+	38,000	C(T)3	£671	£363.40	£764	£419.20
3	C(T)	12,000+	40,000	C(T)5	£821	£438.40	£914	£494.20
3	D(T)	4,001–12,000	31,000	D(T)1	£770	£425.50	£905	£506.50
3	D(T)	4,001–12,000	33,000	D(T)3	£806	£443.50	£941	£524.50
3	D(T)	4,001–12,000	35,000	D(T)8	£1,014	£547.50	£1,149	£628.50
3	D(T)	12,000+	36,000	D(T)1	£770	£425.50	£905	£506.50
3	D(T)	12,000+	37,000	D(T)2	£797	£439	£932	£520
3	D(T)	12,000+	39,000	D(T)1	£770	£425.50	£905	£506.50

Table 8.8 *continued*

HGV axles	Levy band	Trailer weight (kg)	Gross train weight not over (kg)	VED band and rate number	VED and levy 12 months (Euro-VI)	VED and levy 6 months (Euro-VI)	VED and levy 12 months (Euro-0–V)	VED and levy 6 months (Euro-0–V)
3	D(T)	12,000+	40,000	D(T)4	£835	£458	£970	£539
4	B(T)	4,001–12,000	35,000	B(T)1	£230	£115	£135	£81
4	B(T)	12,000+	40,000	B(T)3	£295	£147.50	£135	£81
4	C(T)	4,001–12,000	37,000	C(T)1	£444	£222	£135	£81
4	C(T)	12,000+	40,000	C(T)2	£649	£352.40	£742	£408.20
4	D(T)	4,001–12,000	36,000	D(T)1	£770	£425.50	£905	£506.50
4	D(T)	4,001–12,000	37,000	D(T)5	£849	£465	£984	£546
4	C(T)	10,001–12,000+	39,000	D(T)1	£770	£425.50	£905	£506.50
4	D(T)	12,000+	40,000	D(T)4	£835	£458	£970	£539
4	E(T)	4,001–10,000	38,000	E(T)1	£1,282	£715.70	£1,531	£865.10
4	E(T)	4,001–10,000	40,000	E(T)3	£1,351	£750.20	£1,600	£899.60
4	E(T)	10,001–12,000	40,000	E(T)1	£1,282	£715.70	£1,531	£865.10

NB: It is noticeable that these tables are quite complex and it is possible for operators to make mistakes and to risk underpaying the correct VED/levy fee. Operators who may be uncertain are advised to contact the DVLA (DVA in Northern Ireland) to seek clarification. There is also help on the Government website to help operators calculate the correct tax: www.gov.uk/calculate-vehicle-tax-rates. Operators can also download form V149, which gives expanded views of all the VED tables.

DVLA Fleets Scheme

The DVLA fleets scheme helps deal with the administrative burden that accompanies maintaining fleets of 50 or more vehicles. The scheme is free to join and provides:

- a dedicated helpdesk – providing direct access to a dedicated fleet helpdesk by telephone and email;
- bulk dispatch – all V5Cs and tax reminders processed on any single day are combined and sent in bulk;

- bulk processing – notification of changes to multiple vehicles can be submitted without the need to fill in each V5C;

- bulk taxing – multiple vehicles can be taxed in one transaction;

- View Vehicle Record (VVR) – quick and easy online access to view information relating to any vehicle registered to the fleet;

- V5C On Demand – a service that saves unnecessary storage and distribution costs;

- online services – inform the DVLA online when a vehicle is sold or if changing a registration mark.

Statutory Off-Road Notification

If a vehicle is removed from operation and not used on the road for any reason, SORN may be applied for. The vehicle cannot be used on the road until it is taxed again. When SORN is granted, a refund will be issued for any full months of remaining tax.

Failure to tax a vehicle can attract an £80 fixed penalty notice, and persistent offenders can be prosecuted and awarded a minimum fine of £1,000. If fines are not paid, vehicles can be clamped or crushed, and owner details passed to a debt collection agency.

Making a false SORN declaration can result in prosecution and a maximum fine of £5,000 or two years' imprisonment on conviction.

Alteration of Vehicles

The vehicle registration certificate (V5C) must be updated if any changes are made to an HGV. Changes include:

- chassis or body type;

- chassis number;

- colour;

- cylinder capacity (cc);

- engine;

- fuel type;

- seating capacity;

- weight;

- wheel plan;

- VIN.

The DVLA requires evidence or written confirmation of any changes to a vehicle and may need to inspect the change.

Sale of Vehicles

When a vehicle is sold, the seller must notify the DVLA by completing the bottom tear-off portion of the registration document (form V5) with the name and address of the new owner of the vehicle. It is an offence to fail to notify a change of vehicle ownership (maximum fine £1,000) and it can lead to the original owner being prosecuted for offences committed with the vehicle by the new owner and leaving the previous owner to pay any fixed penalty fines incurred. The new owner has to fill in their name and address in the changes section of the registration document and send the document to the DVLA. If a vehicle is sold for scrap or is broken up, the registration document has to be sent to the DVLA.

Under a new vehicle keepership scheme, the police and the DVLA will combine reporting of the offences of failing to register a vehicle (ie by the new owner) and vehicle tax evasion. This scheme is intended to clamp down on those who fail to notify disposal or acquisition of a vehicle.

Where a vehicle is sold, the DVLA will refund any full months' vehicle tax remaining to the seller and the new owner must re-tax the vehicle before using it.

Vehicles Exempt from Plating and Testing

When applying to tax an HGV that is exempt from plating and testing, a declaration must be made using form V112G (declaration of exemption from goods vehicle testing) to cover the non-production of a valid test certificate.

Penalties and Payment of Back Duty

HGV operators prosecuted for tax evasion face fines of up £25,000. This also applies to payment at an incorrect (ie too low) rate of duty or payment by means of a cheque which defaults. Making a false SORN declaration can lead to a fine of up to £5,000 or two years' imprisonment on conviction. Failure by a vehicle keeper to notify the DVLA of a change of name or address can result in a fine of up to £1,000.

Trade Licences

Trade licences (trade plates) are available for use by motor traders and vehicle testers to save them having to license individually every vehicle.

Different forms are required for new and existing trade licence applications and changes. For example:

- Form VTL301 to apply for a first trade licence;
- Form VTL305 to renew an existing trade licence;
- Form VTL308 to surrender a trade licence (refund of duty);
- Form VTL310 to apply for a duplicate or replacement trade licence or trade plates.

A trade licence can be obtained from the DVLA. Replacements for lost or defaced trade plates (which remain the property of the DVLA) cost £13.50. Besides the 12-month and six-month licences, it is now possible to obtain such a licence for periods between seven months and 11 months at pro-rata rates to the six-monthly rate (ie 55 per cent of the annual rate for six months, plus one-sixth of this amount for every month in excess of six months). See Table 8.9.

Table 8.9   Trade licences

Month you apply	When the licence expires	How long it is valid for	Rate of duty for all vehicles
January	June	6 months	£90.75
January	December	12 months	£165
February	December	11 months	£165
March	December	10 months	£151.25
April	December	9 months	£136.10
May	December	8 months	£121
June	December	7 months	£105.85
July	December	6 months	£90.75
August	June	11 months	£165
September	June	10 months	£151.25
October	June	9 months	£136.10
November	June	8 months	£121.00
December	June	7 months	£105.85

Display of Trade Licences

The DVLA will issue a pair of special number plates with the registration number in red letters on a white background – an additional plate is available in certain circumstances.

Issue of Licences

There are restrictions on the issue and use of trade licences; they are issued only to:

- motor traders, defined as 'manufacturers or repairers of, or dealers in mechanically propelled vehicles' (this also includes dealers who are in business consisting mainly of collecting and delivering mechanically propelled vehicles), and those who modify vehicles (eg by fitting accessories) and those who provide valet services for vehicles, who may use the licence for all vehicles which are from time to time temporarily in their possession in the course of their business as motor traders;
- vehicle testers, for all vehicles which are from time to time submitted to them for testing in the course of their business as vehicle testers.

Vehicles such as service vans or general runabout vehicles owned by motor traders cannot be used under trade licences; the full rate of vehicle tax must be paid.

Use of Trade Licences

The following are the purposes for which vehicles operated under a trade licence may be used by a motor trader or vehicle tester:

- for test or trial in the course of construction or repair of the vehicle or its accessories or equipment and after completing construction or repair;
- travelling to or from a weighbridge to check the unladen weight or travelling to a place for registration or inspection by the council;
- for demonstration to a prospective customer and for travelling to or from a place of demonstration;
- for test or trial of the vehicle for the benefit of a person interested in promoting publicity for the vehicle;
- for delivering the vehicle to a purchaser;
- for demonstrating the accessories or equipment to a prospective purchaser;
- for delivering a vehicle to, or collecting it from, other premises belonging to the trade licence holder or another trader's premises;

- for going to or coming from a workshop in which a body or equipment or accessories are to be or have been fitted, or where the vehicle is to be or has been valeted, painted or repaired;

- for delivering the vehicle from the premises of a manufacturer or repairer to a place where it is to be transported by train, ship or aircraft or for returning it from a place to which it has been transported by these means;

- travelling to or returning from any garage, auction room or other place where vehicles are stored or offered for sale and where the vehicle has been stored or offered for sale;

- travelling to a place to be tested (and returned), dismantled or broken up.

It should be noted that the use of a vehicle on trade plates does not exempt the driver or operator from the need to ensure that it is in sound mechanical condition when on the road, even if being driven for the purposes of road testing or fault-finding prior to repair or after repair. The police can prosecute if they find trade-licensed vehicles on the road in an unsafe or otherwise illegal condition.

Carriage of Goods on a Trade Licence

Goods may only be carried on a vehicle operating under a trade licence:

- when a load is necessary to demonstrate or test the vehicle, its accessories or its equipment – the load must be returned to the place of loading after the demonstration or test unless it comprised water, fertilizer or refuse;

- when a load consists of parts or equipment designed to be fitted to the vehicle being taken to the place where they are to be fitted;

- when a load is built in or permanently attached to the vehicle;

- when a trailer is being carried for delivery or being taken to a place for work to be done on it;

- if the goods are another fully licensed vehicle being carried for the purpose of travel from or to the place of collection or delivery (ie the driver's own transport to get him or her out or back home).

Carriage of Passengers on a Trade Licence

The only passengers who are permitted to travel on a trade-licensed vehicle are:

- the driver of the vehicle, who must be the licence holder or their employee – other persons may drive the vehicle with the permission of the licence holder but they must be accompanied by the licence holder or their employee (this latter proviso does not apply if the vehicle is only constructed to carry one person);

- persons required to be on the vehicle by law – a statutory attendant, for example;

- any person carried for the purpose of carrying out their statutory duties of inspecting the vehicle or trailer;
- any person in a disabled vehicle being towed including persons from the disabled vehicle being carried, provided this is not for hire or reward;
- a prospective purchaser or their servant or agent;
- a person interested in promoting publicity for the vehicle.

NB: It is illegal for operators to road-test their own vehicles on trade plates. This is on the grounds that the vehicles are not 'temporarily' in their possession and are therefore outside the permitted terms of trade licence use.

Recovery Vehicles

A separate class of vehicle tax at an annual rate of duty of £165 or £410* currently applies to recovery vehicles. Any vehicle used for recovery work which does not conform to the definition given below must be licensed at the normal goods vehicle rate according to its class and gross weight.

The total annual rates of duty for recovery vehicles based on design weights are as follows although these fees can be paid in monthly instalments in the same way as vehicle tax:

- *3.5 to 25 tonnes: £165.00 (£90.75 for six months);*
- *over 25 tonnes: £410.00 (£225.50 for six months).*

Definition of Recovery Vehicle

A recovery vehicle is one which is 'either constructed or permanently adapted primarily for the purpose of lifting, towing and transporting a disabled vehicle, or for any one or more of those purposes'. A recovery vehicle is defined as one that:

- recovers a disabled vehicle (a maximum of two disabled vehicles may be recovered at any one time);
- removes a disabled vehicle from the place where it became disabled to premises at which it is to be repaired or scrapped;
- removes a disabled vehicle from premises to which it was taken for repair to other premises at which it is to be repaired or scrapped;
- carries fuel and other liquids required for its propulsion and tools and other articles required for the operation of, or in connection with, apparatus designed to lift, tow or transport a disabled vehicle;

- travels to a place where it will be available to recover or remove a disabled vehicle and to go from a place where it has recovered a disabled vehicle or to any place to which it has removed a disabled vehicle;

- repairs a vehicle at the place at which it became disabled or to which it had been taken for safety;

- tows or carries one trailer which had previously been towed or carried by the vehicle immediately prior to it becoming disabled;

- removes a vehicle from the road to a nominated place on the instruction of a police constable or a local authority under their statutory powers.

The carriage of passengers and/or goods on a recovery vehicle under the first two items listed above is permitted, provided they are either a driver or passenger in the vehicle immediately prior to it becoming disabled, or goods being carried on the vehicle immediately prior to it becoming disabled. The driver and/or passenger of a disabled vehicle (and their personal effects) may also be carried from the place where the disabled vehicle is to be repaired or scrapped to their original destination.

Operation of Recovery Vehicles

Recovery vehicles licensed under the recovery vehicle taxation class are not exempt from goods vehicle plating and testing unless they satisfy the definition of a 'recovery vehicle' (see above). In addition, recovery vehicles exceeding 12,000 kg gvw are subject to type approval at first registration. Such vehicles, however, are currently exempt from 'O' licensing. Recovery vehicles exceeding 7,500 kg are subject to speed restrictions:

- vehicles exceeding 7,500 kg but not exceeding 44,000 kg: 60 mph on motorways, 50 mph on dual carriageways and 40 mph on any other roads;

- vehicles exceeding 44,000 kg: 40 mph on motorways, 30 mph on dual carriageways and 30 mph on any other roads.

Recovery vehicles operating within 100 km of their base are also exempted from EU drivers' hours rules and the tachograph requirements but drivers must comply with the British domestic driving hours rules (see the section GB Domestic Rules in Chapter 3 for details). The driver must also be in possession of a driving licence that enables them to drive a vehicle at a weight that equals the combined weight of the recovery vehicle and any vehicle being towed. For example, the driver of a rigid (Category C) 12,000 kg gvw recovery vehicle performing a suspended tow of a vehicle exceeding 750 kg must be in possession of a Category CE licence.

Rebated Heavy Oil (Red Diesel)

HGVs powered by diesel (heavy oil) engines and used on the road must use fuel taxed at the appropriate rate of fuel duty. A lower rate of duty is payable on fuel used for purposes other than driving road vehicles, such as driving auxiliary equipment, for contractors' plant which does not use public roads, bench-testing of engines and space heating. Fuel on which the lower rate of duty has been paid is known as rebated heavy oil but is more commonly called gas oil or red diesel. It is illegal to use this red diesel, or kerosene, in road vehicles, or any other marked diesel such as Solvent Yellow used in most EU member states. Other dyes are used across Europe and are mostly primary colours.

The following vehicles may use rebated heavy oil as fuel:

- vehicles not used on public roads and not licensed for road use;
- road rollers;
- road construction machinery (vehicles used or kept on a road solely for carrying built-in road construction machinery);
- vehicles licensed as 'limited use vehicles' and used for agriculture, horticulture or forestry, which pass only between areas of land occupied by the same person and which travel on public roads between such places for no more than 1.5 km;
- agricultural machines (ie tractors);
- trench digging and excavating machines;
- mobile cranes;
- mowing machines;
- works trucks.

All other vehicles must use fuel taxed at the appropriate rate of fuel duty.

Road fuel testing units staffed by HMRC officers operate throughout the UK to test fuel in vehicles and in storage tanks. Under the Hydrocarbon Oil Regulations 1973 and the Hydrocarbon Oil (Marking) Regulations 2002, HMRC officers are empowered to examine any vehicle and any oil carried in it or on it and may also enter and inspect any premises and inspect, test or sample any oil on the premises, whether the oil is in a vehicle or not. Vehicle owners and drivers must give the officers facilities for inspecting oils in vehicles or on premises.

Penalties, including fines of up to £5,000, repayment of duty and impounding of vehicles, are imposed on offenders convicted of using rebated diesel illegally.

It should be noted, particularly by international hauliers, that use of 'red diesel' carried in reserve or 'belly' tanks or fed from diesel tanks on refrigerated semi-trailers and used once outside the UK is illegal (NB: red diesel can legally be used for powering refrigeration units on vehicles). It is also illegal to carry red diesel in unconnected or disconnected additional vehicle tanks. Although customs checks abroad on vehicle fuel tanks are limited, any operator found running on or illegally carrying such fuel overseas may face penalties.

Customs may question operators with unusually large diesel tanks mounted on reefer semi-trailers to determine whether such fuel is being illegally used to power the vehicle as well as the fridge unit.

The maximum legal capacity for an engine-connected diesel tank on a vehicle is 1,500 litres. HMRC policy is that vehicle manufacturer-fitted fuel tanks are acceptable, but any additional tank fitted to the vehicle, or the exchange of a standard manufacturer tank for a large-capacity tank, infringes the rules and can incur a penalty. Above 1,500 litres it is considered that the vehicle would have to operate under ADR regulations (see Chapter 20). It should also be noted that transferring fuel purchased abroad for use in another vehicle is illegal and may result in charges for evasion of duty.

HM Treasury consulted on the reforms to the tax treatment of red diesel and other rebated fuels in 2020. The outcome is yet to be published.

Operators in doubt about the use of rebated fuel or wishing to report illegal use of rebated fuel should contact the HMRC Tax Evasion Hotline on 0800 788 887 or go online at GOV.UK.

Oil Storage

Operators that store oil or fuel in bulk must comply with the Control of Pollution (Oil Storage) (England) Regulations 2010. These regulations apply to all types of oil (with the exception of waste mineral oil) stored above ground in containers of more than 200 litres at industrial or commercial premises. There are minimum standards for oil storage (ie tanks to have a 110 per cent bund capacity) to help prevent pollution and protect the environment. Oil is a major pollutant of watercourses and toxic to plants and animals. Fines for non-compliance are up to £5,000, but if pollution is caused then fines can be up to £20,000 or three months' imprisonment. In addition, a 'polluter' may be ordered to pay the costs of remedial actions, such as soil sterilization or the replacing of poisoned plant life. Further information can be found at GOV.UK.

Insurance (Vehicles and Goods in Transit) and Conditions of Carriage

09

Operators of motor vehicles using the public highway must insure against third-party* claims. It is also wise to be protected against claims made by third parties for compensation following injury to themselves or damage to their property as a result of some occurrence involving you, your employees, your property or taking place on your premises.

*The insurance company is the first party, the insured person(s) is the second party and anybody else involved (particularly if they make a claim for compensation) is termed the third party.

Motor Vehicle Insurance

Third-Party Cover

The Road Traffic Act 1988 (as amended) (s143) requires that all motor vehicles, except invalid carriages and vehicles owned by local authorities or the police, used on a road must be covered against third-party risks. (Exact details of bodies exempted under these broad categories can be found in the Act itself.) This can be achieved by means of a conventional insurance policy or, alternatively, by a deposit of £500,000 in cash or securities to the Accountant-General of the Supreme Court (only applicable if authorization is granted by the Secretary of State for Transport). Normally, authorization is only granted to public bodies and authorities and to major organizations with access to the substantial funds which may be needed to meet major accident claims.

Where the cover is obtained by conventional insurance, the Road Traffic Act 1988 stipulates that such cover is valid only if taken out with insurers which are members of the Motor Insurers' Bureau (MIB), a body established to meet claims for compensation (in respect of death or personal injuries only) by third parties involved in accidents with motor vehicles which subsequently prove to be uninsured against third-party risks.

Sections 145 (3a) and (3c) of the 1988 Act state that the insurance policy:

> must insure such person, persons or classes of persons as may be specified in the policy in respect of any liability which may be incurred by him or them, in respect of the death or bodily injury to any person or damage to property caused by, or arising out of, the use of the vehicle on a road in Great Britain [and] must also insure him or them in respect of any liability which may be incurred by him or them... relating to payment for emergency treatment.

NB: *The term 'on a road' also includes 'or other public place'.*

Passenger Liability

Third-party insurance cover must extend to authorized passengers (other than employees of the insured, who are covered separately by the compulsory employers' liability insurance), other non-fare-paying passengers and also to what may be termed 'unauthorized passengers' such as hitchhikers and other people who are given lifts.

Unauthorized Passengers

The display in a vehicle of a sign which reads 'No passengers' or 'No liability' does not indemnify a vehicle operator or driver from claims by so-called 'unauthorized' passengers who may claim for injury or damage received when travelling in or otherwise in connection with the vehicle resulting from the driver's or vehicle operator's negligence. Passenger liabilities are covered within a vehicle insurance policy.

Property Cover

All UK motor insurance policies are required to cover liability for damage to property (up to a maximum liability of £1,000,000) arising from one accident or a series of accidents from one cause. Damage to property in this context includes that caused by the weight of the vehicle (eg to road surfaces, paving slabs, etc), height of the vehicle (eg bridge strikes) and by vibration which may damage services (eg gas and water mains, gullies and sewers, telephone cables, etc) below the road surface, and third parties whose property is damaged in a vehicle accident have the right to request details of the vehicle insurance. Additional insurance cover may be necessary should these types of damage be caused by vehicles operating under Special Types General Orders (STGOs).

Certificate of Insurance

An insurance policy does not provide insurance cover until the insured person or organization has a Certificate of Insurance in their possession. The policy itself is not *proof* of insurance cover; it only sets out the terms and conditions for the cover and the exclusion and invalidation clauses.

The Certificate (or a temporary cover note until the Certificate is issued), which is *proof* (or evidence) of cover, must show the dates between which the cover is valid, give particulars of any conditions subject to which the policy is issued (eg the permitted purposes for which the vehicle may be used or not permitted) and relate to the vehicles covered, either individually by registration number or by specification, and to the persons who are authorized to drive them.

Note: Where the vehicles are covered by the operator depositing £500,000 with the Supreme Court, a Certificate of Deposit is issued and rules relating to production, etc, are the same.

Production of Insurance Certificate

Unless applying online to the DVLA or at a main post office, it is necessary to produce a current Certificate of Insurance when making an application for an excise licence (road tax) for a vehicle. Alternatively, a temporary cover note may be used, but the insurance policy document itself is not acceptable.

Note: Under the Vehicle Excise and Registration Act 1994, where a fleet comprises 250 vehicles or more, the normal requirement for the production of individual Certificates of Insurance for fleet vehicles when applying for vehicle excise licences does not apply.

The owner (ie registered keeper) of a motor vehicle must produce a Certificate of Insurance relating to the vehicle if required to do so by a police officer. If they are not able to produce the Certificate on the spot (or an employed driver is required to produce a Certificate of Insurance for the vehicle being driven), it may be produced no later than seven days from the date of the request, at a police station of the owner's or driver's choice. This also applies to the production of Certificates of Deposit. The person to whom the request is made does not have to produce the Certificate personally, but may have somebody else take it to the nominated police station. A valid temporary cover note would suffice if the Certificate has not yet been issued.

Duty to Give Information

If requested to do so, the owner of a vehicle must give the police any information to help determine whether a vehicle was driven without third-party insurance cover. The owner must also give information about the identity and address of a driver who may at any time have been driving a vehicle which is registered in their name, or information which may lead to identification of a driver if asked to do so by the police.

When the vehicle or vehicles concerned in such a request are the subject of a hiring agreement, the term 'owner' for the purposes of these insurance provisions includes each and every party to the hiring agreement.

The Motor Insurance Database

Under European law (the Fourth Motor Insurance Directive), vehicle fleet operators are required to register with the Motor Insurance Database (MID), which will hold details of the insurance arrangements for every vehicle on our roads. Failure to register will result in prosecution for the fleet operator, whose duty it is to provide details of the current fleet and any subsequent changes, including the use of any temporary vehicles. Information about privately owned vehicles is provided to the MID directly by the insurer and vehicle owners can access the MID by using the Motor Insurers' Bureau (MIB), although there are charges for some enquiries.

Registration of details may be made via the internet to, and further details obtained from, the Motor Insurers' Bureau at: www.mib.org.uk.

NB: Failure to notify the MIB can lead to a fine of up to £5,000, and while it is the motor insurer who will normally notify the MID, individual operators should check that this is the case.

Continuous Insurance Enforcement

Registered vehicle keepers must insure any vehicle(s) used on the road. It is an offence to *keep* a vehicle without insurance unless the DVLA has been notified that the vehicle is declared SORN. It is estimated that there are over 1 million uninsured people driving on UK roads. The police have powers and the technology to enforce remotely to identify offenders. The registered keeper does not have to be driving the vehicle to be caught and uninsured vehicles can be seized.

The MIB and the DVLA work in partnership to identify uninsured vehicles by comparing DVLA vehicle records against those held on the MID. The registered keeper will be sent an Insurance Advisory Letter (IAL) telling them that their vehicle appears to be uninsured and warning them that they will be fined unless they take action. If the keeper fails to comply with the advice in the letter the possible outcomes are:

- the vehicle being clamped, seized and disposed of;
- prosecution with an unlimited maximum fine.

The driver will face:

- a fixed penalty notice of £300 and six penalty points;
- possible disqualification from driving.

Operators can check if their vehicles are recorded as insured at GOV.UK.

Invalidation of Cover

Insurance cover may be invalidated and claims for compensation refused if policy conditions are not strictly adhered to. In particular, these circumstances may arise if the vehicle is operated:

- illegally (for example, in excess of its permissible weight);
- without a valid test certificate, in an unsound mechanical condition;
- outside the terms of an 'O' licence;
- with replacement components fitted to the vehicle which are not to the manufacturer's specification.

Or if the driver is:

- impaired through drink or drugs;
- medically unfit to drive;
- incorrectly licensed or unlicensed;
- disqualified.

In some cases, where authorized drivers are named on a policy, an un-named driver would also invalidate cover. A full list of insurance invalidation examples can be found within the Road Traffic Act 1988.

It is important to stress the need to examine carefully all the clauses contained in a motor insurance policy and to take steps to avoid any action which may invalidate the policy. This can include ascertaining whether or not a spouse or partner, who is a named driver but not an actual policy holder, is covered to drive other vehicles with the owners' consent when not holding an actual policy in their own name.

The employment of unlicensed or incorrectly licensed drivers or the use of unroadworthy vehicles (ie vehicles which do not comply with legal requirements or are found to be on the road in a dangerous condition) are two examples of the most likely ways of invalidating a motor insurance policy. Similarly, the policy should cover *all persons* who may be required (or may need in an emergency) to drive vehicles, not just employees.

Use of Unfit Drivers

It is important not to use drivers who are, or who are believed to be, medically unfit to drive. Insurance companies have a duty to notify the Secretary of State for Transport of the names and addresses of people refused insurance cover on medical grounds so their driving licences can be withdrawn. The medical standards to drive can change from time to time and operators must know what constitutes a 'notifiable' condition. Details can be found at GOV.UK.

Cancellation of Insurance

When an insurance policy is cancelled, the Certificate of Insurance – there may be one or more depending on the number of vehicles covered by the policy – relating to that policy must be surrendered or returned to the insurer within seven days of the cancellation date. Certificates issued by email can be surrendered by email as evidence of policy cancellation.

Cover in EU Countries

Motor insurance policies issued in an EU country or the EEA must include cover against those liabilities which are compulsorily insurable under the laws of every other member state (*Article 7 (2) of the EEC Directive on Insurance of Civil Liabilities arising from the use of Motor Vehicles (No 72/166/EEC)*).

Motor insurance policies issued in the UK include these provisions but this only provides very limited legal (usually third-party only) minimum cover, and while an international motor insurance Green Card may not be necessary for some European countries, it is strongly recommended that one is obtained prior to driving in mainland Europe. Following the Brexit transition period EU member states are free to decide whether or not UK insurance meets their requirements.

Possession of a Green Card provides adequate evidence of a minimum of third-party insurance when abroad and it also eliminates problems of language and different procedures in foreign countries. However, drivers and/or operators may wish to check the level of cover they will be provided with by their insurers when planning to go abroad; it may not reflect the level of cover they enjoy within the UK as many 'comprehensive' UK policies only offer third-party cover when the vehicle is used abroad.

European Accident Statement

The European Accident Statement (EAS) is a two-part form allowing each driver to complete the required sections and exchange them with the other party. In this way the insurance companies get the information they require and the whole process is speeded up and simplified. The EAS is normally provided by insurance companies, and is a common format throughout Europe for submitting accident details. Once completed, the form should be signed by both drivers, with one copy kept by each.

The statement includes a series of key information, including:

- vehicle and driver details;
- details of the accident (including time and place, sketches, etc);
- any injuries or damage caused and witnesses;
- insurance details for both parties.

The copy should then be sent to the vehicle insurance company. This effectively ensures a commonly agreed statement of facts before being submitted.

Fleet Insurance

Most large fleet operators obtain insurance cover on a 'blanket' or 'umbrella' basis. Under this arrangement, vehicles are not specified on the Certificate of Insurance by registration number, but there is a statement on the Certificate to the effect that cover is provided for any vehicle owned, hired or temporarily in the possession of the insured person or company. With blanket insurance it is normal to advise the insurance company by means of a quarterly return of the registration numbers of all vehicles added to, or deleted from, the fleet during that period.

The basic insurance premium is calculated on the total fleet at the beginning of the policy year and adjustments are made by the insurance company issuing debit or credit notes as necessary following receipt of the quarterly returns. This system saves the insurance companies having continually to issue and cancel cover notes and Certificates for vehicles in fleets where there may be many changes during a year because of staggered replacement programmes. The insured company also benefits by not having to get in touch with its insurers every time a vehicle is obtained or disposed of and, further, by being able to obtain an excise licence for a new vehicle without having to wait to receive a cover note from the insurance company.

Additional Insurance Cover

Extended Cover

The minimum cover against third-party risks mentioned above is not sufficient protection for the owner of a vehicle in the event of it being involved in an accident. To obtain extra protection it is necessary to extend the cover beyond the third-party legal minimum. This can be done in varying stages. The basic policy can be extended to:

- cover loss of any no-claims bonus;
- give additional limited cover (fire and theft);
- give comprehensive cover which provides protection against third-party claims, fire and theft risks, and accidental damage to the vehicle itself.

Guaranteed Auto Protection (GAP) Cover

This is an extra insurance policy, usually taken out when buying a vehicle by means of hire purchase. In the event of a total loss claim, it is intended to cover the difference between the current market value of the vehicle (ie the amount the insurance company pays out) and the amount still owing under the finance agreement.

Loading and Unloading Risks

Goods vehicle insurance policies should include clauses which give protection against claims arising from the loading or unloading of vehicles or the activities of employees engaged in such work.

Loss of Use

An extension to a policy can include protection against loss of use when a vehicle cannot be used due to damage and use of a hire vehicle is not taken. This 'loss of use' is similar to the loss-of-use charges made by hire companies while repairs are made to their vehicles following damage caused by the hirer.

Mechanical Failure

Mechanical failure is not normally included in motor insurance policies and generally it is not possible to obtain this type of cover for motor vehicles (although it is possible for some items of heavy engineering plant). Damage to engines caused by frost is covered in the majority of commercial vehicle insurance policies, although there are certain qualifications. It is necessary, for example, if a claim is to be met, for the vehicle to have been sheltered in a properly constructed garage between specified hours of the night and for the anti-freeze solution to be of a set level of concentration. This type of policy extension will specify the exact types of oils, fuel, spare parts, etc, that need to be used in order for the extension to be valid.

Windscreen Damage

Insurance companies normally provide cover for windscreen damage. Claims made for damaged windscreens are generally limited to a fixed amount (often set at a level where the vehicle owner will be expected to pay a proportion of the cost), but are paid to the policy holder without detriment to any existing no-claims bonus and irrespective of whether or not an 'excess' clause is in force on the policy. Similar cover applies on most goods vehicle policies, providing for the cost of replacement of the broken windscreen and for repairs to paintwork damaged by the broken glass.

Medical Expenses

When professional drivers are required to travel abroad they should be covered for medical expenses incurred in foreign countries, for compensation for taking relatives out to visit them if they stay in hospital and for bringing the patient back to the UK for further treatment. Compensation for the loss of drivers' personal effects and baggage can also usually be included in this type of policy.

The Transmed scheme rescues drivers from abroad and is available through insurance brokers.

This extended cover is over and above the level of cover provided by the European Health Insurance Card (EHIC), which only covers the driver for the cost of 'emergency' treatment in EEA member states. In relation to 'emergency' this means that things like mountain rescue costs, repatriation flight costs and costs of any lost or stolen property are not covered.

The cost of treating existing conditions is not covered by the EHIC and the EHIC will need to be renewed at five-yearly intervals. It should also be noted that EHIC only covers the costs of state-provided healthcare on a 'national basis', so if nationals have to pay for emergency treatment then the EHIC holder will also have to pay at the same rate.

Although EHIC is recognized across the EEA, it may not be recognized in all EU member states after the Brexit transition period.

Towing

Insurance cover for towing a vehicle which has broken down is normally provided under a goods vehicle policy, but the cover does not extend to damage caused to the vehicle while it is being towed, or to loss or damage of any goods being carried by the broken-down vehicle.

Damage by Weight

A goods vehicle insurance policy should provide cover against claims for damage caused to roads, bridges, manhole covers, etc, by the weight of the vehicle passing over them. Some policies have a limit on the maximum liability acceptable for damage to property and this amount should be checked to ensure that it is adequate to meet likely claims in this respect.

Defence Costs

A motor insurance policy can be extended to cover legal costs incurred in defending a driver faced with manslaughter or causing death by reckless driving charges.

Goods in Transit Insurance

Claims made for damage or loss to goods carried on or in the vehicle require goods in transit (GIT) insurance cover. In fact many own-account operators, carrying their own goods, include GIT insurance within their general business insurance.

Most GIT insurance policies provide cover in accordance with the limits established by the Road Haulage Association, or Freight Transport Association/Chartered Institute of Purchasing and Supply, Conditions of Carriage, which is normally a maximum liability of £1,300 per tonne for goods carried within the UK. If goods are of relatively low value (bulk traffics, such as coal, gravel and other excavated materials), a lower limit of liability and consequently a lower premium can be considered. However, in many cases the £1,300 per tonne limit can be totally inadequate. Many loads are valued at tens of thousands of pounds with an equivalent value per tonne way in excess of the RHA or FTA/CIPS level, and it is necessary to ensure that the insurance is adequate to cover the value of such loads. Owner–drivers, in particular, are advised to examine their GIT policies; many policies become automatically invalidated if high-value loads are left unattended (some loads must be accompanied *at all times*), approved routes are not taken or approved stopping points are not used, etc.

Some GIT policies specifically exclude certain high-risk loads such as cigarettes, tobacco, spirits, livestock, computers, etc, so the operator should check that the policy covers the value before accepting an order to move the goods.

Such liabilities may be accepted under conditions of carriage (see later in this chapter) or under a contract or agreement or, in the absence of any specific contract or conditions, at common law. If the operator is carrying own goods in addition to other people's, they should make sure that these are also covered under the policy.

Carrier Liability for Goods

It is important to consider and limit the liabilities for goods handled on behalf of customers and ensure that there is full understanding of the GIT insurance cover.

If operators assume total responsibility for high-value goods and do not limit their liability, claims handled by insurers will be unlimited and will impact on insurance premiums.

Operators under contract to distribute goods for a specific client may be able to negotiate that the client remains responsible for their own goods while in transit, although this fact must be ascertained and not assumed.

High-Value Loads

There may be a temptation for haulage contractors to accept high-value loads because the freight rate being offered by the consignor is generous in comparison with normal haulage rates. Such loads, however, are notoriously attractive to thieves, so it is important before accepting them to examine the GIT insurance policy to make sure that such high-value goods are not specifically excluded and that any special requirements which the insurance company may have imposed regarding routes, schedules, overnight parking and general vehicle specification, security and protection are complied with.

Night Risk and Immobilizer Clauses

Insurance policies frequently contain clauses requiring vehicles carrying high-value goods to be securely parked in locked or guarded premises overnight (known as the 'Night Risk' clause) or to be of a secure nature (box body), fitted with approved vehicle protection devices such as steering column and fifth-wheel locks, engine immobilizers and alarm systems (known as the 'Immobilizer' clause). It is a condition of the insurance that such devices must be maintained in good working order and must be put into effect when the vehicle is left unattended. Failure to comply with such conditions can render the cover invalid.

Note: Other policies may insist that tracker devices and electronic seals are used.

Sub-Contracting

Care must also be taken when an operator uses a sub-contractor to move, or carry, goods on their behalf, as the sub-contractor must have adequate insurance to meet the terms of any contract formed between the principal carrier and the owner of the goods. This is particularly important in the UK as it is the principal carrier who will be liable and, in the case of any problems, will then need to pursue the sub-contractor in order to try to recover any financial losses incurred through a claim.

GIT insurers may not accept responsibility for any losses involving sub-contracted loads unless they have had prior notification of the loads and the circumstances.

GIT on Hired Vehicles

The increasing use of vehicles on contract hire raises an important issue regarding liabilities for goods carried. Normally, under the terms of the hire contract it is made quite clear by the hire company supplying the vehicle that it assumes no responsibility for loss or damage to the goods which are carried on the vehicle.

Vehicles Hired with Drivers

If, however, under the terms of the contract the hire company offers to provide a driver, the driver acts under its instructions. Should the driver act in a way which would be considered contrary to normal reasonable action (for example, leaving a fully laden vehicle overnight in the open when they had been specifically instructed to empty the vehicle or to place it in a locked garage), the hire company may find itself held liable for a 'fundamental breach of contract' and be faced with having to pay the full amount of any loss incurred. A method of overcoming this is for the hire company to arrange with the owner of the goods for a GIT insurance policy to be effected in their joint names and for the owners of the goods to pay the premium in the contract hire agreement.

Conditions of Carriage

An operator carrying goods for hire or reward is advised to set out conditions of carriage under which they contract to carry goods. In these conditions the carrier can define liabilities by stipulating limits on the value of goods for which they will normally accept responsibility, with goods of higher value being carried only on special terms, and stating circumstances and provisions under which no compensation is payable. For example, an operator could make it a condition that they accept no liability under the following circumstances:

- force majeure;

- act of war or civil war;

- seizure under legal process;

- act or omission of the trader, their employees or agents;

- inherent liability to wastage in bulk, or weight; latent defect, inherent defect, criminal or natural deterioration of the merchandise;

- insufficient or improper packing;

- insufficient labelling or addressing;

- riots, civil commotions, strikes, lock-outs, stoppage or restraint of labour from whatever cause;

- consignee not taking or accepting delivery within a reasonable time;

- loss of a particular market whether held daily or at intervals;

- indirect or consequential damages;

- fraud on the part of the trader (in this context trader means either consignor or consignee);

- if non-delivery of a consignment, whether in part or whole, is not notified in writing within a specified number of days of dispatch and a claim made in writing within a further specified number of days of dispatch;

- if pilferage or damage is not notified in writing within a specified number of days of delivery and a claim made in writing within a further specified number of days of delivery.

A note to the effect that goods are carried only under the Conditions of Carriage should be made on all relevant business documents, particularly consignment and delivery notes, invoices and quotations. Conditions of Carriage should always be drawn to the customer's attention and copies made available for customers to examine before they give orders for movements to commence. Conditions of carriage are 'usually' found on the reverse side of quotations or other paperwork used by hauliers and/or on their websites.

RHA and FTA/CIPS Conditions of Carriage

The majority of transport contractors find it sensible to limit their liability in accordance with Conditions of Carriage such as those published by the RHA (these are the copyright of the RHA and may not be used by non-members), where the liability is based on a value of £1,300 per tonne on the actual weight of the goods carried or on the computed weight if the volume of the goods exceeds 80 cubic feet per tonne. This limit can be varied on the insurance policy to suit individual demands but otherwise retaining for the operator the legal liability limitations. Further sets of conditions for livestock carrying and sub-contracting are also prepared for members.

Conditions have also been drawn up by the FTA in conjunction with the CIPS, and these also specify a liability limit of £1,300 per tonne. These are not copyright and may be used by hauliers, although legal difficulties may arise where RHA conditions and the new FTA/CIPS conditions are applied to the same movement contract (ie one set by the customer and one by the haulier).

Cover for International Haulage Journeys (not Own-Account)

GIT cover is not sufficient or even legally acceptable where vehicles are engaged on international haulage work. In most cases, such operations are governed by the provisions of the Convention on the Contract for the International Carriage of Goods by Road, commonly known and referred to as the CMR Convention. This Convention automatically applies where an international haulage journey takes place between different countries at least one of which is party to the Convention (with the exception of UK–Eire and UK mainland–Channel Islands journeys, which are ruled not to be international journeys for this purpose).

Road hauliers who carry goods on any part of an international journey fall within the legal confines of the CMR Convention under which compensation levels for loss of or damage to goods are much higher than the standard Conditions of Carriage GIT cover applicable in national transport operations. CMR levels of cover vary according to a set standard, which is published daily in the financial press. For this reason it is important to obtain adequate cover when involved in international transport.

While cabotage activity may be minimal following the Brexit transition period, operators involved in cabotage should discuss the levels of cover required with their insurers. Difficulties may arise where local conditions of carriage are imposed, and claims and legal wrangling arise under law other than English law. For example, under French law, minimum liability is set at such a high value that it may well exceed the amount per tonne covered by a UK haulier's CMR policy (see the section Basic Requirements of CMR in Chapter 25).

Own-Account

The GIT cover for hauliers is not necessarily required by own-account operators, although it could be used if the operator felt it appropriate. However, most own-account operators limit the value of the load to the actual value of their goods being carried, or to another set limit below that of the requirements under CMR. Some actually set the limit extremely low, as many own-account loads of items such as component parts or raw materials have little monetary value until later in the production cycle.

Security

Thousands of HGVs are stolen in the UK each year and there is a range of best practice initiatives in place to counter this, including the Joint Action Group On Lorry Theft (JAGOLT), the Metropolitan Police's Operation Grafton, TruckWatch and the RHA Security Committee.

To protect against insurance loss, operators should minimize security risk and help safeguard against security breaches, unauthorized vehicle access and theft of vehicles, loads and equipment. To demonstrate this, a fleet security policy should be in place that outlines the commitment to raising awareness, security and vigilance across the organization. It should describe the:

- safety and security of vehicles and keys;
- driver security measures when stopping for breaks, rests and overnight parking;
- rules for unauthorized passengers;
- reporting of theft attempts and suspicious activity.

Insurers may refuse to pay out on loss or theft claims if keys are left in or on a vehicle, if a fitted immobilizer or tracker is not used or if the driver fails to undertake a check or security procedure that they were supposed to.

Road Traffic Law   10

Road traffic law is a complex set of regulations aimed at reducing road casualties, environmental impact and congestion. The principal law on the road is the Road Traffic Act 1988. A comprehensive list of laws includes:

- Motorways Traffic (England & Wales) (Amendment) Regulations 2004
- Motorways Traffic (Scotland) Regulations 1995
- Motorways Traffic (Scotland) (Amendment) Regulations 2004
- Motor Vehicles (Driving Licences) Regulations 1999
- Motor Vehicles (Variation of Speed Limits) (England & Wales) Regulations 2014
- Motor Vehicles (Wearing of Seat Belts) Regulations 1993
- Motor Vehicles (Wearing of Seat Belts) (Amendment) Regulations 2006
- New Roads and Streetworks Act 1991
- Road Safety Act 2006
- Road Traffic Act 1984, 1988 and 1991
- Road Traffic Act 1988 (Prescribed Limit) (Scotland) Regulations 2014
- Road Traffic (New Drivers) Act 1995
- Road Traffic Offenders Act 1988
- Road Vehicles (Display of Registration Marks) Regulations 2001
- Road Vehicles Lighting Regulations 1989
- Road Vehicles (Registration & Licensing) Regulations 2002
- Smoke-free (Exemptions and Vehicles) Regulations 2007 SI 2007/765
- Smoke-free (Private Vehicles) Regulations 2015
- Traffic Management Act 2004
- Traffic Signs Regulations & General Directions 2002
- Vehicle Excise and Registration Act 1994
- Zebra, Pelican and Puffin Pedestrian Crossings Regulations and General Directions 1997

To simplify matters, the most relevant rules relating to road traffic law are included in the *Highway Code*, which provides information, advice, guidance and mandatory rules for all road users in the UK.

Definition of a Road

In England and Wales a 'road' is defined as *'any highway and any other road* to which the public has access, and includes bridges over which a road passes'.

In Scotland, a 'road' is defined as *'any road and any other way* to which the public has access, and includes bridges over which a road passes'.

The term 'road' generally includes footpaths, bridleways and cycle tracks, and many roadways and driveways on private land (including car parks). In most cases, the law will apply to them and there may be additional rules for particular paths or ways.

The Highway Code

The *Highway Code* is a guide to some of the important points of road traffic law. For the precise wording of the law, the various Acts and Regulations should be referred to. Most of the provisions apply on all roads throughout Great Britain, although there are some exceptions. The Road Traffic Act 1988 states:

> A failure on the part of a person to observe a provision of the *Highway Code* shall not of itself render that person liable to criminal proceedings of any kind but any such failure may in any proceedings… be relied upon by any party to the proceedings as tending to establish or negative any liability which is in question in those proceedings.

The *Highway Code* is available in print as an HMSO publication, latest edition 2015, or online at GOV.UK where the latest revision was published in March 2021. The online edition is always the most up to date and should be the main reference point. There is a separate *Highway Code* for Northern Ireland available at NIDIRECT. GOV.UK

The *Highway Code* is broken down into numbered rules and annexes:

- Introduction.
- Rules for pedestrians (1 to 35).
- Rules for users of powered wheelchairs and mobility scooters (36 to 46).
- Rules about animals (47 to 58).
- Rules for cyclists (59 to 82).
- Rules for motorcyclists (83 to 88).
- Rules for drivers and motorcyclists (89 to 102).
- General rules, techniques and advice for all drivers and riders (103 to 158).
- Using the road (159 to 203).
- Road users requiring extra care (204 to 225).

- Driving in adverse weather conditions (226 to 237).
- Waiting and parking (238 to 252).
- Motorways (253 to 273).
- Breakdowns and incidents (274 to 287).
- Roadworks, level crossings and tramways (288 to 307).

In addition it covers:

- light signals controlling traffic, including traffic-light signals, flashing red lights, motorway signals and lane control signals;
- signals used to alert other road users, including direction indicator signals, brake light signals, reversing light signals and arm signals;
- signals used by authorized persons, including police officers, arm signals by persons controlling traffic, Driver and Vehicle Standards Agency officers and traffic officers and school crossing patrols;
- traffic signs used, including signs giving orders, warning signs, direction signs, information signs and roadworks signs;
- road markings used, including those across the carriageway, along the carriageway, along the edge of the carriageway, on the kerb or at the edge of the carriageway and other road markings;
- vehicle markings used, including large goods vehicle rear markings, hazard warning plates, projection markers and other markings;
- Annex 1: You and your bicycle. An annex of the *Code* with information and rules about you and your bicycle;
- Annex 2: Motorcycle licence requirements. An annex of the *Code* with information and rules about motorcycle licence requirements;
- Annex 3: Motor vehicle documentation and learner driver requirements. An annex of the *Code* with information and rules about motor vehicle documentation and learner driver requirements;
- Annex 4: The road user and the law. An annex of the *Code* with information about the road user and the law;
- Annex 5: Penalties. An annex of the *Code* with information and rules about penalties, including penalty points and disqualification, a penalty table, new drivers and other consequences of offending;
- Annex 6: Vehicle maintenance, safety and security. An annex of the *Code* with information and rules about vehicle maintenance, safety and security;
- Annex 7: First aid on the road. An annex of the *Code* with information about first aid on the road, including dealing with danger, getting help, helping those involved, and providing emergency care;

- Annex 8: Safety code for new drivers. An annex of the *Code* with information about the safety code for new drivers, including the New Drivers Act and further training;
- other information provided by the *Code*, including metric conversions, useful websites, further reading, the blue badge scheme and code of practice for horse-drawn vehicles.

The following three changes to the Highway Code were consulted on in 2020:

- introducing a hierarchy of road users to ensure those who can do the greatest harm have the greatest responsibility to reduce the danger or threat they may pose to others;
- clarifying existing rules on pedestrian priority on pavements and that drivers and riders should give way to pedestrians crossing or waiting to cross the road;
- establishing guidance on safe passing distances and speeds when overtaking cyclists or horse riders, and ensuring they have priority at junctions when travelling straight ahead.

In 2021, the D*f*T announced that the consultation highlighted overwhelming support for the changes and the *Highway Code* will be amended following due process.

Speed Limits

Excessive speed is a major factor in road casualties. Drivers must not drive faster than the speed limit for the type of road and type of vehicle. The speed limit is the absolute maximum and it doesn't mean it's safe to drive at this speed in all conditions.

There are five levels of speed limit:

- limits applying to vehicles using particular roads;
- limits applying to particular classes of vehicle (including limits imposed by the mandatory fitment of speed-limiter devices);
- temporary speed limits on vehicles introduced for special reasons such as in potentially hazardous situations;
- average speed limits for vehicles transiting hazards and sites such as roadworks;
- variable speed limits, which are set on major routes and determined by the volume of traffic and/or a temporary hazard at a given location.

Speed Limits on Roads

On roads where street lights are positioned at intervals of not more than 200 yards (defined as a 'restricted' road), an overall speed limit of 30 mph applies to all classes of vehicle, unless alternatively lower speeds are indicated by signs or the vehicle itself is subject to a lower limit by reason of its construction or its use. In some instances, speeds in excess of 30 mph are permitted on such roads and this is indicated by appropriate signs. A speed limit of 20 mph is being imposed in towns and cities by many authorities in a bid to reduce road deaths.

The maximum speed limits on roads outside built-up areas for cars and car-derived vans are 60 mph on single-carriageway roads and 70 mph on dual-carriageway roads and motorways, except where specified temporary or permanent lower limits are in force.

Other traffic-calming measures being increasingly used to improve road safety include road-narrowing chicanes, enforcement cameras and reductions from 60 mph to 50 mph on sections of roads with sharp bends. A 50 mph limit is also used as a measure to improve air quality.

Advisory speed limits on motorways should be observed. These are shown by illuminated signs which indicate hazardous situations and roadworks ahead and by temporary speed-limit signs at roadworks. The amber flashing warning lights positioned on the nearside of motorways (two lights, one above the other) indicate an advisory slowing down until the danger, and the next non-flashing light, is passed. Mandatory speed limits may also be seen where 'variable' speed limits are enforced, especially on motorways at peak travel times or at roadworks sites on motorways (indicated by white signs with black letters and a red border). There are also an increasing number of roadworks where average speed limits apply. These speed limits calculate the time it takes for a vehicle to travel between two, or more, set points, thereby enabling the average speed to be calculated for the distance travelled. Failure to comply with these mandatory motorway speed warning signs and limits can result in prosecution. Average speed limits are also used extensively in Europe for measuring average speeds between toll booths.

Speed Limits on Vehicles

Vehicles are restricted to certain maximum speeds according to their construction, weight or use, but when travelling on roads which themselves are subject to speed restrictions it is the lowest permitted speed (ie of the vehicle or of the section of road) which must be observed (see Table 10.1).

Table 10.1 Table of vehicle speed limits

	Motorway (mph)	Dual carriageway (mph)	Other roads (mph)
Private cars			
– solo	70	70	60
– towing caravan or trailer	60	60	50
Buses and coaches			
– not over 12 metres length	70 (65)*	60	50
– over 12 metres length	60	60	50
Coaches over 7.5 tonnes subject to speed-limiter legislation are restricted to 65 mph.			
Goods vehicles			
Car-derived vans			
– solo	70	70	60
– towing caravan/trailer	60	60	50
Not exceeding 7.5 tonnes gvw			
– solo	70	60	50
– articulated	60	60**	50
– drawbar	60	60**	50
**In Northern Ireland the speed limit for vehicles in these two categories is 50 mph only.*			
Over 7.5 tonnes gvw (England and Wales)	60	60	50
Over 7.5 tonnes gvw (Scotland)	60	50	40

Special Types Vehicles

Vehicles operating outside the Road Vehicles (Construction and Use) Regulations 1986 (C&U) for the purposes of carrying abnormal indivisible loads come within scope of the STGO as described in Chapter 19 and must conform to specified speed limits depending on their category. These speed limits are in Table 10.2.

Table 10.2 Special types vehicles

Vehicle category	Motorways	Dual carriageways	Single carriageways
1	60 mph	50 mph	40 mph
2 and 3	40 mph	35 mph	30 mph

Works Trucks and Industrial Tractors

The maximum speed limit for works trucks and industrial tractors is 18 mph but the latter are not permitted on motorways.

Wheeled Vehicles not Fitted with Pneumatic Tyres on All Wheels and Track-Laying Vehicles

There is a 20 mph speed limit on all types of roads, although permission is normally required for these vehicles to use motorways.

Emergency Vehicles

Fire, police and ambulance service vehicles are exempt from all speed limits if, by observing the speed limit, they would be hampered in carrying out their duties. Drivers have a duty to take particular care when exceeding statutory limits and could face proceedings if a collision results while exceeding the limits.

Speed Enforcement

Speed can be enforced using a RADAR or LIDAR speed gun operated by an enforcement officer or by a speed camera. Safety cameras can also be used to enforce other moving traffic offences, such as yellow box offences, illegal bus lane use and traffic-light jumping.

As technology has advanced, digital speed-enforcement cameras have been progressively introduced. These include average speed cameras where speeds are recorded between two cameras mounted on distinctive columns a distance apart, which create Speed Controlled Zones.

Where the statutory speed limit has been exceeded, the vehicle and registered keeper are identified from DVLA records and a relevant penalty is imposed. In the case of hire vehicles, the hire company, as the registered owner, is informed and the driver contacted. There is usually an administration fee levied by the hire company in these cases.

The fixed penalty for most speeding offences is £100 and three penalty points. In some cases, however, the punishment can be more severe, leading to more points, disqualification and fines totalling 50 per cent, 100 per cent and 150 per cent of the offender's weekly income dependent on the severity.

Lighting-Up Time

All mechanically propelled vehicles must display front and rear position lights and headlamps (where required by regulations) between sunset and sunrise and during daytime hours when visibility is seriously reduced (see Chapter 13 for lighting details).

Night Parking

Goods vehicles not exceeding 2,500 kg gross vehicle weight do not require lights at night when parked on restricted roads (ie on which a 30 mph speed limit – or lower limit – is in force) if they are parked either in a recognized parking place (ie outlined by lamps or traffic signs) or on the nearside, close to and parallel to the kerb, facing the direction of travel and with no part of the vehicle within 10 metres of a junction (ie on the same side as the vehicle or on the other side of the road). On any road where these conditions are not met, lights must be shown (ie front and rear position lights).

All goods vehicles exceeding 1,525 kg unladen weight must display lights at all times when parked on roads between sunset and sunrise. Trailers and vehicles with projecting loads must not be left standing on roads at night without lights.

Vehicles should be parked on the nearside of the road when left standing over-night except when parked in a one-way street or in a recognized parking place and they must not cause obstruction.

Parking in lay-bys separated from the main carriageway only by a broken white line, without sidelights and other obligatory lights as appropriate being lit after lighting-up time, is illegal. This does not apply where the lay-by is segregated from the highway.

Stopping, Loading and Unloading

Leaving Engine Running

Whenever a driver leaves a vehicle on a road, the engine must be stopped (except in the case of fire, police or ambulance service vehicles or when the engine is used to drive auxiliary equipment or to power batteries to drive such equipment).

Increasing numbers of vehicles are fitted with stop–start technology and locally introduced stop–start areas are to be found in many UK cities and London boroughs, where failure to comply by switching the engine off if the vehicle is to be stationary for more than one or two minutes can incur a fine.

A word of caution could be noted here as some people who have stopped a vehicle and left the engine running while they either made or received a mobile phone call while in the driving seat have been deemed to have been driving as they were deemed to have been 'at the controls of the vehicle for the purpose of controlling the motion'.

Obstruction

A vehicle must not be left in a position where it is likely to cause obstruction or danger to other road users, eg near an entrance to premises, a school, a zebra crossing or a road junction.

Trailers (including articulated semi-trailers) must not be left on a road when detached from the towing vehicle.

Where a vehicle left in a dangerous position is found to have been the cause of a collision, the driver can be prosecuted irrespective of whether or not they were actually in the vehicle at the time of the collision.

Loading and Unloading Restrictions

Vehicles must not stop or park on clearways to load or unload unless specifically authorized to do so. In some areas loading and unloading restrictions are indicated by yellow lines painted on the kerb at right angles, as follows:

- A single yellow line at intervals indicates a ban on loading and unloading between the times shown on a nearby plate (eg Mon–Sat, 0830–1830).
- Double yellow lines at intervals indicate a complete ban on loading and unloading at any time.

The precise terms of the restriction are indicated on signs mounted on nearby lamp posts, walls, etc. Delivery drivers should check these carefully to avoid any infringement of the law. Delivery drivers may also need to contact the local police or traffic warden in order to get permission to load or unload if there is no alternative location to undertake these tasks. Operators also need to note the move towards low-emission vehicles being required in order to load, or in some areas where Ultra-Low Emission Zones (ULEZs) have been created.

Waiting and Parking Restrictions

Single, double or broken yellow lines painted on the road parallel to the kerb apply to waiting and parking at various times, but they do not indicate a ban on loading or unloading and the same applies to 'no waiting' prohibitions indicated by 'no waiting' signs (see the *Highway Code* for full details of waiting and parking restrictions).

Drivers should also be aware that loading and unloading and waiting and parking restrictions also apply to Red Routes where red lines are painted on the road at the kerbside, especially in cities such as London, areas such as the West Midlands, and the Greenways of Edinburgh, to allow traffic to flow more freely on major routes into, and out of, the cities and areas. There are also similar restrictions applying to bus lanes and multi-occupancy vehicle (MOV) lanes.

Parking Meter Zones

Loading and unloading in parking meter zones during the working day (the times are indicated on signs) is not allowed unless a gap between meter areas or a vacant meter space can be found. A vehicle using a meter space for loading or unloading can stop for up to 20 minutes without having to pay the meter fee (this does not apply when parking for any purpose other than loading or unloading the vehicle).

Tramways

With the increased use of trams in many towns and cities, the Government has issued rules for all drivers in relation to what actions to take, and not to take, when driving on roads that are also tramways. There is also guidance to be found in the *Highway Code*.

In summary, the rules state:

- You **MUST NOT** enter a road, lane or other route reserved for trams. Take extra care where trams run along the road. You should avoid driving directly on top of the rails and should take care where trams leave the main carriageway to enter the reserved route, to ensure you do not follow them. The width taken up by trams is often shown by tram lanes marked by white lines, yellow dots or by a different type of road surface. Diamond-shaped signs and white-light signals give instructions to tram drivers only. Take extra care where the track crosses from one side of the road to the other and where the road narrows and the tracks come close to the kerb. Tram drivers usually have their own traffic signals and may be permitted to move when you are not. Always give way to trams. Do not try to race or overtake them or pass them on the inside, unless they are at tram stops or stopped by tram signals and there is a designated tram lane for you to pass.

- You **MUST NOT** park your vehicle where it would get in the way of trams or where it would force other drivers to do so. Do not stop on any part of a tram track, except in a designated bay where this has been provided alongside and clear of the track. When doing so, ensure that all parts of your vehicle are outside the delineated tram path. Remember that a tram cannot steer round an obstruction.

- Tram stops. Where the tram stops at a platform, either in the middle or at the side of the road, you **MUST** follow the route shown by the road signs and markings. At stops without platforms you **MUST NOT** drive between a tram and the left-hand kerb when a tram has stopped to pick up passengers. If there is no alternative route signed, do not overtake the tram – wait until it moves off.

- Look out for pedestrians, especially children, running to catch a tram approaching a stop.

- Always give priority to trams, especially when they signal to pull away from stops, unless it would be unsafe to do so. Remember that they may be carrying large numbers of standing passengers who could be injured if the tram had to make an emergency stop. Look out for people getting off a bus or tram and crossing the road.

- All road users, but particularly cyclists and motorcyclists, should take extra care when driving or riding close to or crossing the tracks, especially if the rails are wet. You should take particular care when crossing the rails at shallow angles, on bends and at junctions. It is safest to cross the tracks directly at right angles. Other road users should be aware that cyclists and motorcyclists may need more space to cross the tracks safely.

- Tramway overhead wires are normally 5.8 metres above any carriageway, but can be lower. You should ensure that you have sufficient clearance between the wire and your vehicle (including any load you are carrying, or fixed equipment) before driving under an overhead wire. Drivers of vehicles with extending cranes, booms, tipping apparatus or other types of equipment should ensure that the equipment is fully lowered. Where overhead wires are set lower than 5.8 metres, these will be indicated by height clearance markings – similar to 'low bridge' signs. The height clearances on these plates should be carefully noted and observed. If you are in any doubt as to whether your vehicle will pass safely under the wires, you should always contact the local police or the tramway operator. Never take a chance as this can be extremely hazardous.

Motorway Driving

Motorway driving requires special care and observance of the motorway regulations. In particular, vehicles not capable of exceeding 25 mph on the level are generally prohibited from using motorways, including vehicles operating under the Special Types General Order (see Chapter 19) if they cannot exceed this speed.

Vehicles must not stop on motorways except when instructed to by a police or traffic officer, through mechanical defect or lack of fuel, water or oil, due to a collision, the illness of a person in the vehicle or for other emergency situations (including giving assistance to other persons in an emergency), or to permit a person from the vehicle to recover or remove objects from the carriageway. It is illegal to drive on the hard shoulder (unless the hard shoulder is being used as an additional traffic lane during peak periods) or the central reservation, to reverse or to make a 'U-turn' on a motorway. Vehicles which must use the hard shoulder for emergency reasons as described above must remain there only for so long as is necessary to deal with the situation and the driver and any passengers should move away from the vehicle and stay behind the protective barrier of the hard shoulder.

Use of Lanes

Goods vehicles with maximum laden weights in excess of 7.5 tonnes and vehicles drawing trailers (and certain other heavy motor cars not included in the categories mentioned) must not use the outer or offside lane of three- and four-lane motorways.

On some steep slopes of two-lane motorway sections, large goods vehicles (ie over 7.5 tonnes) are banned from using the outside lane; these bans are clearly signposted on the approaches to the appropriate section indicating the extent of the banned section and the vehicles prohibited from using the outer lane.

Goods vehicles with a maximum laden weight exceeding 3.5 tonnes which are fitted with speed limiters as required by the Road Vehicles (Construction and Use) Regulations 1986 (see also the section Speed Limiters in Chapter 12) are also prohibited from using the outer lane of three-lane motorways.

Note: Lane departure warning systems (LDWS) need to be fitted to all new goods vehicles over 3,500 kg gvw. These systems warn the driver that they have strayed out of the limits of the lane they are travelling in. This is a requirement under EC Regulation 661/2009, which also brought advanced emergency braking systems (AEBS) to the UK.

Temporary Speed Limits

Where carriageway repairs take place on motorways or where contraflow traffic systems are used, an *advisory* 50 mph speed limit is usually imposed. The 50 mph limit can be lowered if the workforce needs to work in close proximity to the passing traffic. These limits are considered by the police to be a maximum speed, and they may prosecute drivers found speeding in these sections for a 'driving without due consideration' type of offence. However, it is becoming more common for a *mandatory* temporary speed limit to be imposed in such cases, and where drivers are detected speeding in these sections they will be prosecuted for this offence.

Other Vehicles on Motorways

Vehicles that do not comply with C&U Regulations, dump trucks, engineering plant and vehicles for export may be driven on motorways provided they are capable of attaining a speed of 25 mph on the flat when unladen and not drawing a trailer.

Learner Drivers on Motorways

HGVs may be driven on motorways on 'L' plates provided all provisional conditions are met and the driver is accompanied by a suitably qualified driver.

Lights, Markings and Signs on Motorways

Hazard Warning

Motorways are equipped with amber hazard warning lights located on the nearside verge and placed at one-mile intervals. When these lights flash, vehicles must slow down until the danger which the lights are indicating, and a non-flashing light, has been passed.

Rural Motorways

Rural motorways have amber lights, placed at not more than two-mile intervals and usually located in the central reservation, which flash and indicate either a maximum speed limit or, by means of red flashing lights, that one or more lanes ahead are closed. The speed limit indicated applies to *all* lanes of the motorway and should not be exceeded.

Urban Motorways

Urban motorways have overhead warning lights placed at 1,000-yard intervals. Amber lights flash in the event of danger ahead and indicate a maximum speed limit or an arrow indicating that drivers should change to another lane. If red lights flash above any or all of the lanes, vehicles in those lanes must stop at the signal. It is as much of an offence to fail to stop at these red lights as it is to ignore automatic traffic signals.

Information Signs

Overhead information signs are installed on many of the UK's motorways. These are generally controlled from control centres operated by Highways England or Transport Scotland and the police to notify drivers of incidents and conditions on the road ahead and warn of delays, closures and diversions. They are also used to inform drivers of times and distances to major junctions.

Motorway Road Markings

Road markings designed to reduce the risk of nose-to-tail collisions are used on some sections of the motorway network. The chevron-shaped markings are painted on the road surface at ten-metre intervals for five kilometres (ie three miles). Drivers are advised to keep at least two chevrons (ie two seconds) between themselves and the vehicle in front.

Local Radio Station Frequency Signs

Under arrangements with the D*f*T, local radio stations can have their broadcasting frequencies indicated on motorway signs. It is a condition of such signposting that the station in question provides traffic news relevant to the location of the signs and of benefit to long-distance travellers 24 hours a day, seven days a week, with at least four broadcasts per hour at peak times and two per hour during off-peak times, with programme interruptions for important announcements.

Emergency Telephones on Motorways

Emergency telephones are located at 1-mile intervals on the hard shoulders of each side of motorways. It is illegal to cross the carriageways to reach an emergency telephone. Arrows on the back of posts on the hard shoulder indicate the direction to the nearest telephone. The telephone box itself also has a code number written on it and the caller will be asked for this code number when making the call. The code number tells the operator the exact location of the telephone and on which carriageway it is sited. This enables the emergency services to attend with minimal delay. The use of the telephone is free, and it connects directly to the police, who should be given full details of the emergency, who is calling and the vehicle involved. A person travelling alone or drivers with a young child or children are advised to tell the police of this fact. After making the call you should return immediately to the location of your vehicle to await help but stand behind the crash barrier, where one is fitted.

Driving in Fog

To help drivers avoid the hazards of driving in fog, the *Highway Code* clearly advises, in Rule 235, that drivers should:

- use headlights as required by the *Code* (ie switch them on when visibility is reduced to 100 m – 328 ft);
- keep a safe distance behind the vehicle in front, remembering that the other vehicle's rear lights can give a false sense of security;

- be able to pull up within the distance they can see clearly, especially on motorways and dual carriageways, where vehicles are travelling much faster;
- use the windscreen wipers and demisters;
- beware of other drivers not using headlights;
- not accelerate to get away from a vehicle which is being driven too close behind;
- check mirrors before slowing down and use the brakes so the brake lights warn drivers behind that the vehicle is slowing down;
- stop in the correct position at a road junction with limited visibility and listen for traffic until it is safe to cross, then do so positively without hesitating in a position directly in the path of approaching vehicles.

The *Code* also states that drivers MUST NOT use front or rear fog lights unless visibility is seriously reduced as they dazzle other road users and can obscure the brake lights. These lights must be switched off when visibility improves.

Automatic Fog-Warning System

Automatic fog-warning systems operate on several motorways. Detectors installed alongside the motorway identify when visibility falls below 300 metres and automatically switch on the existing matrix signals to display the message 'FOG'. These systems are now largely incorporated into the 'Variable Message' systems used on many motorways and major trunk roads. The signals are located at strategic points where unexpected pockets of fog may occur, as identified by the Meteorological Office. When the fog signs are on, drivers should slow down and proceed at a speed where they can safely stop within their range of vision.

Hazard Warning Flashers

Four-way direction indicator flasher systems may be legally used to indicate that a vehicle is approaching slowed or stationary traffic, when a vehicle is temporarily obstructing the road or any part of the carriageway either while loading or unloading, when a vehicle is broken down or for any other emergency reasons (previously their use was only permitted in emergencies). Further details of vehicle lighting requirements are to be found in Chapter 13.

Temporary Obstruction Actions

The *Highway Code* gives the following advice for when a vehicle breaks down:

- Get your vehicle off the road if possible.
- Warn other traffic by using your hazard warning lights if your vehicle is causing an obstruction.
- Help other road users see you by wearing light-coloured or fluorescent clothing in daylight and reflective clothing at night or in poor visibility.
- Put a warning triangle on the road at least 45 metres (147 feet) behind your broken-down vehicle on the same side of the road, or use other permitted warning devices if you have them. Always take great care when placing or retrieving them, but never use them on motorways.
- If possible, keep your sidelights on if it is dark or visibility is poor.
- Do not stand (or let anybody else stand) between your vehicle and oncoming traffic.
- At night or in poor visibility do not stand where you will prevent other road users seeing your lights.

Drivers can also place, on the vehicle itself, a 'Road Vehicle Sign', described as a highly visible flexible yellow sheet depicting a red warning triangle.

The person in charge of, or accompanying, an emergency or breakdown vehicle that is causing an obstruction is authorized to place a 'keep right' sign to indicate a route past the vehicle.

In the case of an HGV breaking down, the following is recommended:

- If the ground is sufficiently firm, get the vehicle off the road if possible, preferably at least 3 metres from any passing traffic.
- Put the hazard warning lights on.
- Exit the vehicle on the side away from passing traffic, wearing a hi-visibility vest or tabbard.
- Don't stand in front of your lights and obscure them from other road users.
- Place hazard warning triangles at 100–200 metres behind the vehicle and one at the rear of the vehicle but don't use hazard warning triangles on a motorway if they are likely to impede any recovery vehicles.

NB: Goods vehicles operating under ADR carrying dangerous goods must also carry warning triangles or amber flashing lights in order to conform with these regulations.

Lights During Daytime

If visibility during the daytime is poor because of adverse weather conditions, drivers of all moving vehicles must switch on both front position lights and headlamps or front position lights and matched fog and spotlights. This applies in the case of heavy rain, mist, spray, fog or snow or similar conditions. When vehicles are equipped with rear fog lights (see the section Rear Fog Lamps in Chapter 13), these should be used when the other vehicle lights are switched on in poor daytime visibility conditions. Further details of vehicle lighting requirements are to be found in Chapter 13.

Parking

Drivers who park their vehicles in a position which causes danger or obstruction to other road users can be prosecuted and their driving licence endorsed with penalty points on conviction (usually three), or they can be disqualified from driving. This rule applies even if the driver is not in the vehicle at the time of any collision that may be caused.

The *Highway Code* lists the many places where drivers should not or must not park.

There are not many parking places for the goods vehicle driver who has collections or deliveries to make, particularly in town, and for this reason drivers should be instructed to take reasonable care when parking in congested areas to avoid causing obvious obstruction or danger. Drivers needing to park to unload heavy items or high-value items should enlist the help of the police, traffic wardens or a local authority parking enforcement officer in order to make a space available. In any case, drivers should not double-park, block entrances and exits of business or private premises, or park near dangerous junctions or near pedestrian crossings, as well as avoiding the areas mentioned in the *Highway Code*.

Parking on Verges

The Road Traffic Act 1988 (sections 19 and 20) makes it an offence to park a heavy commercial vehicle (ie a vehicle over 7.5 tonnes maximum laden weight including the weight of any trailer) on the verge of a road, on any land between two carriageways or on a footway, whether the vehicle is totally parked on those areas or only partially so.

There are exemptions to this: when a vehicle is parked on such areas with the permission of a police officer in uniform, or in the event of an emergency, such as for the purposes of saving life or extinguishing fire, or for loading and unloading, provided that the loading or unloading could not have been properly performed if the vehicle had not been so parked and that the vehicle was not left unattended while it was parked.

It is an offence (under the Road Traffic Act 1988 section 34) for any person to drive a motor vehicle onto common land, moorland or other land which does not form part of a road, or on any footpath or bridleway beyond a distance of 15 yards, except where legal permission exists to do so, but then only for the purposes of parking or to meet an emergency such as saving life or extinguishing fire.

Lorry Routes and Controls

While there are many major route markers with the green capital 'R', many local authorities identify preferred routes for heavy vehicles passing through their areas and display on them appropriate signs that:

- mark the most suitable route between dock areas and the nearest convenient connection with the primary route/motorway network;
- mark a suitable alternative route at any place on the primary route network where drivers of goods vehicles might be advised to avoid a particular part of that route, but where it is not appropriate to direct all traffic onto the alternative route, or to the primary route itself;
- mark routes from the primary/motorway route system to local inland centres which generate a high level of goods vehicle traffic (industrial estates, for example).

Certain areas, especially London and an increasing number of towns and cities, impose controls on the movement of goods vehicles and the parking of goods vehicles. These controls and restrictions are always marked with appropriate signs and operators are advised to ensure that their drivers observe them.

London Lorry Control Scheme

The London Lorry Control Scheme (LLCS) restricts the movement of HGVs over 18 tonnes gvw in London. It operates at night and at weekends on specific restricted roads in London with the aim of minimizing noise pollution.

The LLCS is often, mistakenly, referred to as the London lorry ban. However, it is actually a control which manages the environmental impact of HGV journeys in London. There is an Excluded Route Network (ERN), which is not controlled, but if operators need to gain access via a restricted road, each vehicle requires a permit within the hours of control. All journeys can be undertaken by using a compliant route.

Application for LLCS permits should be made to the London Lorry Control Team at londoncouncils.gov.uk.

Contraventions of LLCS are enforced through Penalty Charge Notices (PCNs) for both the operator and driver:

- Operator PCN is £550.
- Driver PCN is £130.
- Payment reduction of 50 per cent is applied if the PCN is paid within 14 days.

The LLCS applies at the times shown in Table 10.3.

Table 10.3 London Scheme times

Sunday	at all times
Monday to Friday	midnight to 7 am and 9 pm to midnight
Saturday	midnight to 7 am and 1 pm to midnight

Red Routes

Red Routes are a type of clearway that aims to prevent traffic congestion on primary routes. They are identified by red no-stopping lines on the highway and signs along the route. Single and double red lines ban all stopping, parking and loading. Double red lines apply at all times and single red lines usually apply during the working day. The times that single red line prohibitions apply are shown on nearby signs. The restrictions apply to the carriageway, pavement and verge.

Red Routes are enforced by traffic officers and often monitored by traffic enforcement cameras.

Red Routes are prevalent in London on the strategic route network but also used in other cities and private highway authorities such as airports. In 2020 Leicester City Council announced its Red Route trial.

London Congestion Charging

Congestion charges of £15 on the day (but only £14 for fleet vehicles using Auto Pay), and £17.50 per day if made by midnight on the third day following entering the Congestion Zone area, apply in a central area of London every day except Christmas Day between the hours of 7.00 am and 10.00 pm.

The charging zone covers any route that crosses the River Thames by Lambeth, Westminster, Waterloo, Blackfriars, Southwark or London Bridges. Not included in the charging area are Euston Road, Tower Bridge, Elephant and Castle, and Vauxhall Bridge. Cameras are located at 85 per cent of the boundary intersections

andom points within the zone. These cameras record vehicle registration
s and cross-check via computer with records of charges paid.

ers who regularly enter the charging zone may pre-register and Auto Pay,
otherwise payment of the daily fee may be made by credit card – a call centre
processes credit card numbers. Any driver who has not paid prior to entry into
the charging zone may pay later that day – up to midnight – or pay £17.50 until
midnight on the following third charging day. Payment can be made by calling 0343
222 2222 or at TfL.gov.uk.

Failure to pay the daily charge will result in a £160 penalty, issued to the vehicle
owner (not necessarily the driver). This is reduced to £80 if paid within two weeks,
but increased to £240 if it is not paid within 28 days. There is an appeals procedure.

Low and Ultra-Low Emission Zones (LEZ and ULEZ)

London Low Emission Zone (LEZ) applies across Greater London and operates
24 hours a day, every day of the year. It encourages the most polluting vehicles
driving in London to become cleaner.

Vehicles need to meet the specified Euro standard or pay a substantial daily charge
to drive within the LEZ boundary. From March 2021, HGVs must meet the Euro-VI
emission standard. Vehicles do not need to register with TfL before driving within
the LEZ. The charges and penalties are:

- HGVs – daily charge of £200 per day, penalty charges £1,000 per day (£500 if
  paid within 14 days).
- Larger vans – daily charge of £100 per day, penalty charges £500 per day (£250
  if paid within 14 days).

In addition to the LEZ, TfL also operates the Ultra-Low Emission Zone (ULEZ);
the Euro-VI emission standard is the same as LEZ. The charges and penalties are:

- HGVs – daily charge of £100 per day, penalty charges £1,000 per day (£500 if
  paid within 14 days);
- Larger vans – daily charge of £12.50 per day, penalty charges £500 per day (£250
  if paid within 14 days).

Currently the ULEZ boundary is the same as for the Congestion Charge. ULEZ
fees (and penalties) are in addition to any Congestion Charge or LEZ charges that
already apply.

Both LEZ and ULEZ daily charges must be paid for non-compliant vehicles.

Once the day has been paid for, the vehicle can be driven within LEZ/ULEZ
as many times as the operator wishes on that particular day. Payment will need to
be made for every day that the vehicle is used in either zone. Payment can be made
online, by phone, via autopay or through a road user charging account.

Clean Air Zones (CAZ)

Many other city councils are following TfL's lead to improve air quality by introducing clean air zones (CAZ). There are four types of Clean Air Zones, Classes A to D:

Class	Vehicle type
A	Buses, coaches, taxis, private hire vehicles
B	Buses, coaches, taxis, private hire vehicles, HGVs
C	Buses, coaches, taxis, private hire vehicles, HGVs, vans, minibuses
D	Buses, coaches, taxis, private hire vehicles, HGVs, vans, minibuses, cars (motorcycles are optional)

To avoid being charged, the minimum emission standards for HGVs is Euro-VI. Cities in the UK that have implemented a CAZ include:

- Bath – Class C;
- Birmingham – Class D.

More cities are expected to implement CAZs in 2022.

Exemptions

Certain vehicles are exempt from the zones, as follows:

- specialist non-road-going vehicles designed and built for mainly off-road use, but which may use the road for limited purposes (including agricultural and forestry tractors, mowing machines, agricultural and farm machinery and equipment, mobile cranes, and road and building construction machinery);
- historic vehicles built before 1 January 1973;
- vehicles operated by the Ministry of Defence.

If such vehicles meet any of the above criteria and are registered in Great Britain, they are automatically exempt and need not be registered with TfL. Such vehicles meeting any of the above criteria which are registered *outside* Great Britain (including Northern Ireland) are also exempt, but need to be registered with TfL. However, operators need to ensure that local London boroughs do not introduce their own exemptions.

Discounts

Some showman's vehicles are eligible for a 100 per cent discount from the daily charges if they are registered to a person following the business of a travelling showman and have been modified or specially constructed.

London Safer Lorry Scheme

London's Safer Lorry Scheme uses a combination of powers held by all highway authorities in London to deliver a simple, quick and complete road safety solution. It ensures that only HGVs with basic safety equipment fitted will be allowed on London's roads. Under the scheme, most vehicles that are exempt from national legislation for basic safety equipment will have to be retrofitted. This includes construction vehicles, which are involved in a disproportionate number of fatal collisions involving cyclists and pedestrians.

Under the scheme, vehicles over 3.5 tonnes gvw that are currently exempt will be required to:

- be fitted with Class V and Class VI mirrors giving the driver a better view of cyclists and pedestrians around their vehicles;
- be fitted with sideguards to protect cyclists from being dragged under the wheels in the event of a collision.

The scheme operates across London, 24 hours a day, seven days a week, covering the same area as the Low Emission Zone. It came into force on 1 September 2015 and is enforced by the police and the DVSA.

Drivers found to be in charge of a non-compliant vehicle may be issued with a £50 Fixed Penalty Notice and the offence carries a potential fine of £1,000 at magistrate's court. The Traffic Commissioners are also notified of operators in breach of the scheme.

NB: In the case of fitting sideguards, it has been agreed that extendible trailers (trombones) will only need to 'fully comply' when the trailer is in the closed (unextended) position and that only the actual extended section will be subject to the exemption. This exemption is also subject to review and technological advances which may enable extended trailers to be fully fitted with sideguards in the future.

Announced for 2020 and postponed until 2021 is London's HGV Direct Vision Standard (DVS) and Safety Permit Scheme. This means that an HGV Safety Permit is required before an HGV in excess of 12 tonnes gvw is operated on any public road in Greater London. The HGV Safety Permit is issued to a vehicle either:

- meeting the minimum One Star HGV DVS requirement rating unless exempt from the scheme; or
- meeting HGV Safe System Conditions:
  - A Class V mirror shall be fitted to the nearside of the vehicle.
  - A Class VI mirror shall be fitted to the front of the vehicle.

- Side under-run protection shall be fitted to both sides of the vehicle (except where this is impractical or proves to be impossible).

- External pictorial stickers and markings shall be displayed on vehicles to warn vulnerable road users of the hazards around the vehicle.

- A sensor system that alerts the driver to the presence of a vulnerable road user shall be fitted to the nearside of the vehicle.

- An audible vehicle manoeuvring warning shall be fitted to warn vulnerable road users when a vehicle is turning left.

- A fully operational camera monitoring system shall be fitted to the nearside of the vehicle.

For left-hand-drive vehicles, mirrors, cameras and sensors must be fitted appropriately to account for the blind spot on the right-hand side of the vehicle.

DVS star rating is to ensure a minimum standard of a driver's direct field of view and reduce the risk of close-proximity blind spot collisions. The rating is determined by the vehicle's manufacturer using the approved HGV DVS technical protocol. Where this rating is one star or above, operators will be able to apply for a safety permit with no further mandatory action required. Where this rating is zero star, or where a vehicle is unable to be rated, the vehicle shall be fitted with Safe System Conditions.

A record of star ratings will be kept by the vehicle manufacturer and passed on to TfL. Permits will not be automatically issued; operators will still be required to apply for a permit when a new vehicle is procured.

For existing vehicles, manufacturers may consider ratings based on the vehicle chassis number as provided by the operator. Any DVS rating advised will reflect the specification of the vehicle at first-stage manufacture; multi-stage manufacture and later modifications are not reflected in the DVS rating. Manufacturers should be able to advise.

Operators are advised to check TfL.gov.uk for updates and announcements.

Bus Lanes

Traffic lanes on urban roads reserved solely for use by buses are a common feature in many towns and cities. Uniform traffic signs and road markings indicate bus lanes. A single wide solid white line is used to mark the edge of the reserved lanes. Upright signs incorporating international symbols combined with arrows show to other traffic the number of lanes available for their use. When the signs and restrictions are in operation on a road, all other vehicles, except for pedal cycles (and taxis if signed to this effect), are prohibited from using the bus lane. Although contraflow bus lanes are still used, increasingly many towns and cities have ceased to use them on road safety grounds.

High-Occupancy Vehicle (HOV) Lanes

HOV lanes are a method of utilizing spare capacity in existing bus lanes used by some UK towns and cities. They are also used where bus-only lanes cannot be justified on bus frequency grounds, or as part of a policy to encourage car sharing. The basic principle is that only vehicles carrying two or more people, buses and two-wheeled vehicles are permitted to use the lanes during the hours of operation. Large goods vehicles may or may not be allowed access.

Level Crossings

Most railway level crossings are now fitted with automatic half-barrier crossing gates and appropriate warning signs are given in advance. When a train is approaching such crossings, red lights flash and a bell rings to warn drivers and pedestrians. Once these warnings start, the barrier comes down immediately, and drivers should not zig-zag around the barriers. When the train has passed, the barriers will rise unless another train is following, in which case the warnings will continue.

Drivers of vehicles which are large or slow (ie that with their loads are more than 2.9 metres (9 ft 6 in) wide or more than 16.8 metres (55 ft) long or weighing more than 38 tonnes gross or incapable of a speed of more than 5 mph) wishing to cross one of these crossings must, before attempting to cross, obtain permission to do so from the signalman by using the special telephone which is provided at the crossing. Failure to do this is an offence. In the event of a vehicle becoming stuck on the crossing, the driver should advise the signalman immediately by using the telephone.

Level and Tram Crossings

The *Highway Code* treats level crossings and tram crossings in similar ways. The rules state that a driver crossing a level crossing or tramway must take care when approaching a crossing point, never enter a crossing unless the exit is clear, never get too close to the vehicle in front and never park or stop on a crossing.

In addition, in relation to trams, where they share the road with other vehicles, the rules state that care must be taken not to enter a road reserved for trams, not to park where it could obstruct a tram, to take care where tramways cross from one side of the road to another, to be aware of overhead clearance of any electrical wires and to look out for pedestrians who may be running to catch a tram.

Weight-Restricted Roads and Bridges

Where signs indicate that a particular section of road or a bridge is restricted to vehicles not exceeding a specified weight limit or axle weight limit, unless otherwise expressly stated, the weight limit shown relates to the actual weight of the vehicle or to an individual axle of the vehicle, not the relevant plated weights.

Signs protect weak bridges by restricting vehicles according to their maximum authorized gross weight (ie their plated weight) – indicated as 'mgw'. The signs apply even if the vehicle, with a plated weight greater than the limit shown, is unladen at the time and therefore well below the maximum weight limit for the bridge (unless the sign permits 'empty vehicles'). Where doubt exists about any particular sign, it is advisable to consult the local authority responsible for its erection and to determine the precise wording of the Traffic Management Order under which authority the sign would have been erected.

Note: The Forth Road Bridge authority in Scotland currently enforces a maximum weight limit of 196 tonnes on the bridges for a single movement. In addition, vehicles exceeding 80 tonnes are subject to a speed limit and need to be escorted, while vehicles exceeding 44 tonnes or more than 27.4 metres in length need to notify and have indemnity in advance of crossing, and vehicles over 2.9 m wide or over 18.65 m in length just need to give notification. Further information is available at theforthbridges.org or by calling 0131 319 3083.

Owner Liability

Under the Road Traffic Offenders Act 1988, responsibility for payment of fixed penalty fines or excess parking charges, etc, rests with the registered vehicle owner (ie the keeper of the vehicle, not necessarily the legal owner) if the driver who committed the offence cannot be identified or found. The registered owner of the vehicle is sent details of the alleged offence and is obliged to pay the fine or submit a 'Statutory Statement' of ownership in which they state whether they were the vehicle owner at the time of the alleged offence (in which case the driver should be named), had ceased to be the owner at that time or had not yet become the owner at that time. Where the person was not the owner, they must give the name of the previous owner or the new owner to whom the vehicle was transferred, if known.

When a vehicle is hired out for less than six months and such an incident arises, the hiring company can declare that the vehicle was on hire and send a copy of the hiring agreement together with a signed statement of liability from the hirer accepting responsibility for the fine or excess parking charge. Such a clause is normally included in the hiring agreements which the hirer signs. Failure to pay a fixed penalty or excess charge, or to give information as required by the police in such matters, can result in a fine of up to £1,000 on conviction (or even £5,000 in certain circumstances).

Fixed Penalties

In order to reduce the pressure on the courts, a system of fixed penalties exists by which both civil enforcement officers (CEOs) (see below) and, in a limited way, police community support officers (PCSOs), as well as the police, can issue fixed penalty notices requiring the vehicle driver or owner to pay the fixed penalty or to elect to have the case dealt with in court in the normal way. The fixed penalty system operates on two levels: non-endorsable offences (mainly dealt with by CEOs) and driving licence endorsable offences, which only the police can deal with since CEOs have no general authority to request the production of driving licences.

Non-Endorsable Offences

For non-endorsable offences a white ticket/notice (penalty £50) is either issued to the driver if present or fixed to the vehicle windscreen. Since no driving licence penalty points are involved for such offences, there is no requirement to examine the licence. CEOs have authority to issue PCNs for the following non-endorsable offences:

- leaving a vehicle parked at night without lights or reflectors;
- waiting, loading, unloading or parking in prohibited areas;
- unauthorized parking in controlled parking zone areas;
- contravention of the Vehicle Excise and Registration Act 1994 by not displaying a current licence disc;
- making 'U' turns in unauthorized places;
- lighting offences with moving vehicles;
- driving the wrong way in a one-way street;
- overstaying on parking meters, returning to parking places before the expiry of the statutory period or feeding meters to obtain longer parking facilities than those permitted in a meter zone;
- parking on pavements or verges by commercial vehicles exceeding 3,050 kg unladen weight (see the Parking section above).

Endorsable Offences

The extended fixed penalty system covers driving licence endorsable offences, which can be dealt with only by the police (ie not PCSOs) – this includes some driving and vehicle use offences. For endorsable offences a yellow ticket/notice with a different level of penalty applies, as described below.

For driving licence endorsable offences the police issue a yellow ticket/notice, for which a penalty of £100 is payable and three penalty points are issued. These tickets are only issued after the police officer has seen the offender's driving licence and has established that the addition of penalty points appropriate to the current offence, when added to any points already on the licence, will not result in automatic dis-qualification under the 12-point totting-up procedure. If this is the case, the ticket will be issued and the driving licence will be confiscated (an official receipt, covering the holder for non-possession or production of their licence, will be given – valid for two months), being returned to the holder with the appropriate penalty points added when the penalty has been paid.

If the offender does not have their driving licence with them at the time, the penalty notice will not be issued on the spot but will be issued at the police station if the driving licence is produced there within seven days – subject again to the number of penalty points already on the licence.

Where the addition of further points in respect of the current offence would take the total of penalty points on the licence to 12 or more, thus leading to automatic disqualification, the ticket will not be issued and the offence will be dealt with by the offender being summoned to appear in court in the normal manner.

Note: There are a limited number of non-endorsable and endorsable offences that carry a £100, £200 or even £300 fine.

London Area Parking Offences

The fixed penalty system includes specific London area parking offences, namely parking on a Red Route (see the Red Routes section earlier in this chapter), for which the penalty is currently up to £130 (this is reduced to £65 if the fine is paid within 14 or 21 days – this time limit will be entered into the PCN), and parking in other prohibited places, for which the penalty is levelled by the borough concerned. Currently these offences attract a fine of between £80 and £130.

Payment or Election to Court

PCNs must be paid in accordance with the instructions on the notice and, in any case, within the specified time limit of 28 days. Alternatively, offenders can elect to have the charge dealt with by a court so they have the opportunity of defending themselves against the charge or, even if they accept that they are guilty, of putting forward mitigating circumstances which may lessen any penalty which may be imposed.

The address of the fixed penalty office to which the penalty payment should be sent is given in the notice, together with instructions for making application for a court hearing if this course of action is chosen.

Failure to Pay

With both the white and yellow ticket systems, failure to pay the statutory penalty within the requisite period of 28 days will result in the offender being automatically considered guilty and the penalty being increased by 50 per cent (ie a £50 fixed penalty increases to £75 and a £100 fixed penalty increases to £150). These increased amounts become fines and continued non-payment may lead to the arrest of the offender and appearance before a court in the district where the offence was committed.

Summary of Offences

Among the many offences covered by the fixed penalty scheme are the following:

- parking at night without lights or reflectors;
- waiting, parking, loading or unloading;
- breach of controlled parking zone regulations;
- failing to display a current excise licence disc;
- making 'U' turns in unauthorized places;
- lighting offences with a moving vehicle;
- driving the wrong way in a one-way street and making banned right turns;
- contravening traffic regulation orders;
- breach of experimental traffic orders;
- breach of experimental traffic schemes in Greater London;
- contravening motorway traffic regulations;
- using a vehicle in contravention of a temporary prohibition or restriction of traffic on a road;
- driving in contravention of an order prohibiting or restricting driving on certain classes of road;
- breach of pedestrian crossing regulations;

- contravention of a street playground order;
- breach of parking orders on roads, and of parking place designation orders and other offences committed in relation to them, except failing to pay an excess charge;
- contravening minimum speed limits;
- speeding;
- driving or keeping a vehicle not showing a registration mark;
- driving or keeping a vehicle with a registration mark or hackney carriage sign obscured;
- failing to comply with traffic directions or signs;
- leaving a vehicle in a dangerous position;
- failing to wear a seat belt;
- breach of a restriction on carrying children in the front or rear of vehicles;
- driving a vehicle elsewhere than on the road;
- parking a vehicle on a footpath or verge;
- breach of Construction and Use Regulations;
- contravening lighting restrictions on vehicles;
- driving without a licence;
- driving whilst using a mobile phone;
- breach of provisional driving licence conditions;
- failing to stop when required to do so by a uniformed police officer;
- obstructing the highway with a vehicle;
- overtaking on a pedestrian crossing;
- failing to display a registration mark (ie number plate) on a vehicle;
- driving on a footpath.

NB: The DVSA can issue fixed penalty notices for offences detected on a driver's tachograph records at any time over the previous 28 days. However, this can only be done in cases where the DVSA is conducting a roadside check and finds, at the time, that there is a current offence being committed and that that offence is prosecutable.

The Graduated Fixed Penalty and Deposit Scheme

There is a scheme of graduated fixed penalties (GFPs) and deposits for both UK and foreign truck drivers who break the law. It is operated by the police and by DVSA examiners.

Fixed penalties, issuable by police, exist for a range of traffic and roadworthiness offences for all categories of vehicle. They provide a quick and effective method of dealing with minor offences, which reduces the burden on the courts and saves police time. Acceptance of a fixed penalty provides offenders with the opportunity of discharging all liability for that offence, requires no admission of guilt, results in no criminal record and saves them the need to attend court.

The fixed penalty provisions created powers to introduce graduated fixed penalties for commercial vehicles as a means of dealing effectively with cases such as multiple offences arising from the commercial operation of vehicles, which proved cumbersome and time-consuming to process. Certain penalties are now graduated to reflect the number and severity of the offences.

The scheme covers offences, mainly relating to commercial vehicles, as follows:

- drivers' hours and tachograph record offences;
- overloading;
- roadworthiness;
- construction and use of vehicles;
- driver licensing;
- community authorizations;
- goods vehicle plating and testing;
- Vehicle Excise Duty;
- vehicle exhaust emissions.

The amounts of the graduated fixed penalty payable vary according to the type and degree of the alleged offence at three main levels, namely, £100, £200 and £300.

Additionally, powers are included in the legislation to:

- enable the number of penalty points endorsed on driving licences to be varied according to type, location and severity of offence;
- require operators to notify the TC of fixed penalty notices issued against them under the new GFP scheme;
- allow enforcement officers to issue endorsable fixed penalties to non-GB driving licence holders through checks of their 'driving record';
- require financial deposit payment (£300 up to £900) by drivers who do not have a satisfactory UK address (intended to enforce against foreign drivers who otherwise have been able to avoid a fixed penalty or prosecution in the UK);
- immobilize vehicles subject to a prohibition (again, primarily directed at foreign drivers).

NB: Where these requirements cannot be met, the police and DVSA officials have the right to impound the vehicle concerned.

Civil Enforcement Officers

Civil Enforcement Officers (CEOs), commonly known as traffic wardens, have powers to issue PCNs as described in the previous section, they have powers to act as parking attendants at street parking places, to carry out special traffic control duties, to inquire into the identity of drivers of vehicles, to act in connection with the custody of vehicles at car pounds and to act as school crossing patrols.

They may demand to know the names and addresses of those believed to have committed parking, obstruction, traffic sign and excise licence offences and to see the driving licence of any person who is reasonably suspected of such offences. If the licence cannot be produced at that time, the CEO may issue a form HO/RT 1 requiring its production at a police station within seven days. CEOs have no powers to request the production of insurance certificates or vehicle test certificates.

CEOs' powers were extended to include stopping vehicles for testing and other purposes and escorting abnormal loads.

Pedestrian Crossings

There are several types of pedestrian crossing. Zebra crossings are bounded on either side by areas indicated by zig-zag road markings in which overtaking, parking and waiting are prohibited. The marked areas extend to about 60 ft on either side of the crossing. A 'give way' line 3 ft from the crossing is the point at which vehicles must stop to allow pedestrians to cross. Pelican crossings are controlled by traffic lights which vehicle drivers must observe, and pedestrians should cross only when the green light signal indicates that they should do so (at many pelican crossings an audible bleeper is provided to assist blind people to cross in safety). With this type of crossing, if there is a central refuge for pedestrians, each side of the refuge is still considered to be part of a single crossing. Only if the two parts of the crossing are offset does it become two separate crossings. There are other types of pedestrian crossing in the UK, including 'puffin' crossings with red and green figures above the control box and 'toucan' crossings (where both pedestrians and cyclists may cross). Further information is available in the *Highway Code*.

Builders' Skips

Provisions are contained in the Highways Act 1980 to control the placing of builders' skips on the road. Before a skip is placed on the road, permission must be obtained from the local authority. This will be given subject to conditions relating to the size of the skip, its siting, the manner in which it is made visible to oncoming traffic, the care and disposal of its contents, the manner in which it is lit or guarded and its removal when the period of permission ends.

Owners must ensure that skips carry proper reflective markers (see Chapter 13), are properly lit at night, are clearly marked with their name and telephone number or address, and are moved as soon as is practical after they have been filled.

The police and highway authorities have powers to reposition or remove a skip from the road and recover the cost of doing so from the owner, and a penalty may be imposed.

The definition of a builder's skip is 'a container designed to be carried on a road vehicle and to be placed on a highway or other land for the storage of builders' materials, or for the removal and disposal of builders' rubble, waste, household and other rubbish or earth'.

Abandoned Motor Vehicles

It is an offence under the Road Traffic Regulation Act 1984 to abandon a motor vehicle or any part of, or part removed from, a motor vehicle in the open air or on any other open land forming part of a highway. Such offences, on conviction, can lead to fines for a first offence and fines and a term of up to three months' imprisonment or both for a subsequent offence.

Vehicles which are illegally or obstructively parked can be removed and a statutory charge imposed. An additional charge for storage of a removed vehicle can be made and, since the de-criminalization of many parking offences, many local authorities have their own levels of charges. Removed and impounded vehicles are not released until all relevant charges have been paid.

Retention and Disposal of Seized Vehicles

Where a police officer has seized and removed a vehicle as authorized under section 165A of the Road Traffic Act 1988, certain legal procedures must be followed: namely, the constable must give a seizure notice to the driver (unless it is impracticable to do so) and must also give a seizure notice to the registered keeper and the owner (where that appears to be someone different) requiring them to claim the vehicle within a specified period (but not less than seven working days). The notice must indicate the charges payable to reclaim the vehicle. These vary depending on the police authority concerned but comprise a seizure fee and a charge for each 24 hours or part thereof that the vehicle is in custody when the vehicle is claimed back after 24 hours of seizure, counting from noon on the first day after the seizure – and the person claiming the vehicle must produce a valid driving licence and certificate of insurance at a specified police station, the vehicle being retained until these conditions are met. Where the police cannot issue a seizure notice or the conditions of the notice are not met, the vehicle may be disposed of after 14 days. If disposal is by means of a sale, the net proceeds must be paid to the owner if they make a claim within one year of the sale.

Wheel Clamps

Vehicles which are illegally parked or which cause obstruction in a wide area of Central London, and in some other towns and cities, will be immobilized by the police or by contractors on their behalf. A wheel clamp will be fixed to one wheel of the vehicle preventing it being driven away. A notice will be stuck to the vehicle giving the driver notice of the offence committed and instructions for securing release from the clamp.

It is an offence to try to remove a wheel clamp or to attempt to drive off with one fitted. In London, vehicle drivers finding a clamp fixed to their vehicle must go to the Metropolitan Police pound and request removal of the clamp. Both a removal charge and a fixed penalty have to be paid before the clamp is removed. If the vehicle has been removed by the police a removal charge is payable, in addition to any fixed penalty, to secure its release.

The actual rates for the removal of wheel clamps fitted by the police vary across the country but information on where to contact to have the clamp removed, the fees and any fixed penalty will be available on the INF32 leaflet which is left on the vehicle by the wheel-clamping team.

Many local authorities remove illegally parked vehicles and impound them as opposed to fitting wheel clamps to vehicles which may be causing an obstruction.

Overloaded Vehicles

It is an offence to drive an overloaded vehicle on a road. Under the Road Traffic Act 1988 (sections 70 and 71), an authorized examiner or police officer may prohibit the use of an overloaded vehicle on the road until the weight is reduced to within legal limits and may direct, in writing, the person in charge of an overloaded vehicle to remove the vehicle to a specified place. See also the section on Weight Offences in Chapter 11.

Drivers may be instructed (normally by the issue of a form GV3) to drive for a distance of up to five miles to a weighbridge for the weight of their vehicle and load to be checked. If they are directed to drive more than five miles to the weighbridge and the vehicle is found to be within the maximum permitted weights, then a claim may be made against the appropriate highway authority for the costs incurred.

The DVSA and police also use mobile vehicle weighing equipment for roadside checks and a 'weighing in motion' system, which operates by having 'weigh strips' in the surface of the road and number plate recognition cameras. In practice, the axle weights are recorded as the vehicle passes over the weigh strip (an electronic strain gauge) in the road and the registration number is recorded at the same time. This enables enforcement officers to identify overloaded vehicles and to later pull them over at a suitable stopping place in order to carry out a full weight check.

The maximum fine for an overloading offence is £5,000 but any one instance of an overloaded vehicle could result in conviction for more than one offence, each of which carries this maximum penalty. Subsequent convictions for such offences could lead to higher fines. Convictions for overloading offences also jeopardize the operator's licence (see Chapter 11).

Road Traffic Collision Procedure

Any driver involved in a road collision in which personal injury is caused to any other person, or damage is caused to any vehicle or any animal* other than animals carried on their vehicle, or to any roadside property (see below for definition), MUST STOP. Failure to stop after a collision is an offence and fines of up to £5,000 can be imposed.

The driver of a vehicle involved in a collision must give, to anybody having reasonable grounds for requiring them, their name and address, the name and address of the vehicle owner and the registration number of the vehicle.

If the collision results in injury or damage to any person other than the driver or to any other vehicle or to any reportable animal,* or to roadside property, then the details of the collision must be reported to the police *as soon as reasonably practicable afterwards, but in any case no later than 24 hours after the event.* This obviously does not apply if police at the scene of the collision take all the necessary details. Failure to report a collision is an offence which also carries a maximum fine of £5,000.

For these purposes an animal means any horse, ass, mule, cattle, sheep, pig, goat, dog (in Northern Ireland only, a 'hinnie' is added).

Reportable incidents include those that occur 'in any public place' as well as on the road. Any public place would include, for example, supermarkets, railway stations and multi-storey car parks.

Under the Road Traffic Act 1988, the need to stop following collisions extends to cover any damage caused to any property 'constructed on, fixed to, growing on, or otherwise forming part of the land in which the road is situated or land adjacent thereto'. This means that if a vehicle runs off the road and no other vehicles or persons are involved, the driver still has to report damage to fences, hedges, gateposts, street bollards, lamp posts, etc.

Third parties injured in collisions who find that the vehicle was uninsured can make a claim for their personal injuries to the MIB (see Chapter 9). The MIB compensation scheme also covers claims for damage to property by uninsured vehicles. Such claims for property damage will only be accepted if the vehicle driver is traced and provided no claim for the damage can be made elsewhere. There is a limit of £250,000 on claims and they are subject to a £300 excess clause.

Road Humps – Traffic Calming

Regulations permit the construction of road humps on sections of the highway where a 30 mph speed limit or less is in force. The road hump will be treated as part of the highway provided it complies with the regulations. Some roads at the entrance to villages on 'A' class roads now also have raised areas to act to slow traffic down as it enters the built-up area.

Increasing use is being made of a variety of traffic-calming measures to reduce vehicle speeds and cut collision risks. Besides road humps, other measures include rumble strips, mini-roundabouts and 'pinch points' using steel poles to produce a narrow access point.

Sale of Unroadworthy Vehicles

It is an offence to sell, supply, offer to sell or expose for sale a vehicle in such a condition that it does not comply with the Construction and Use Regulations and is therefore legally unroadworthy. Under the Road Traffic Act 1988, offenders are liable to a fine of up to £5,000.

This means that to display a vehicle for sale which needs attention to bring it up to the required standard is an offence, even though the intention would have been to remedy any defects before a purchaser paid for or took the vehicle away. However, it would not be an offence if the buyer was made aware of the defects and intended to remedy them or have them remedied before using the vehicle on the road.

It is also an offence to fit any part to a vehicle which, by its fitting, makes the vehicle unsafe and causes it to contravene the regulations. For example, fitting a tyre which is below the limits regulating tread depth would be to commit such an offence.

Under the Road Traffic Act 1991, the law relating to the sale of unroadworthy vehicles has been tightened: in particular, the seller of such a vehicle now has a statutory duty to take steps to ensure that the buyer is aware that the vehicle is in an unroadworthy condition. Previously, sellers could rely on the defence that they believed that the vehicle was not to be used on the road until made roadworthy.

Seat Belts

Drivers must wear a seat belt if one is fitted in the seat they are using – there are only a few exceptions. Also, only one person is allowed in each seat fitted with a seat belt.

While children should not be passengers in commercial vehicles, if they are they must be:

- in the correct seat type for their height or weight until they reach 135 centimetres tall or their 12th birthday, whichever is first;
- wearing a seat belt if they are 12 or 13 years old, or younger and over 135cm tall.

Bench-Type Seats

Where a light goods vehicle is fitted with a bench-type or double front passenger seat, it is illegal to occupy the centre part of the seat (ie next to the driver), where a lap belt or no belt may be provided, if the outer part of the seat with the full belt provided is unoccupied.

Failure to Wear Seat Belts

Failure by a person to wear a seat belt as required by law could result in a fixed penalty (currently £100) or a fine of up to £500 if convicted by a court. In a case relating to illegally carrying an unrestrained child, a fine of up to £200 could be imposed.

A court has ruled that if, as a result of a collision, injuries were sustained which might have been prevented or lessened had the injured person been wearing a seat belt, then the damages awarded to that person in any claim should be reduced by an appropriate amount. Subsequently, other cases involving motor collision claims have followed the same lines.

Drivers caught not wearing a seat belt can, in some circumstances, elect to complete a seat-belt awareness course instead of paying the fine and having penalty points added to their driving licence. The internet-based 'Your Belt – Your Life' programme is offered by the police, and the driver in question needs to score a minimum of 7/10 on an assessment at the end of the course. The fee is currently £36.

Exemptions

Exemption from seat-belt wearing applies:

- when holding a valid medical certificate giving exemption (see further details below);
- when driving a vehicle constructed or adapted for the delivery or collection of goods or mail to consumers or addresses, while engaged in making local rounds

of deliveries or collections, but only where such journeys do not exceed 50 metres in length;

- when driving a vehicle at the time of carrying out a manoeuvre which includes reversing;

- when accompanying a learner driver as a qualified driver and supervising the provisional entitlement holder while that person is performing a manoeuvre which includes reversing;

- in the case of a driving test examiner (but *not* an instructor) who is conducting a test of competence to drive and who finds that wearing a seat belt would endanger himself or any other person;

- in the case of a person who is driving or riding in a vehicle being used for fire brigade or police purposes, or for carrying a person in lawful custody, including a person being so carried;

- in the case of a driver of a licensed taxi who is seeking hire, answering a call for hire, or carrying a passenger for hire; or of a driver of a private hire vehicle which is being used to carry a passenger for hire;

- when *riding** in a vehicle being used under a trade licence for the purposes of investigating or remedying a mechanical fault in the vehicle;

- in the case of a disabled person, wearing a disabled person's seat belt;

- in the case of a person *riding* (see note below) in a vehicle while it is taking part in a procession organized by or on behalf of the Crown. This exemption also applies to a person riding in a vehicle which is taking part in a procession held to mark or commemorate an event which is commonly or customarily held in the police area in which it is being held, or for which a notice has been given under the Public Order Act 1986.

*This particular exemption refers specifically to 'riding' in a vehicle and does not include 'driving' a vehicle for the same or similar purposes – therefore, it must be concluded that the driver of a vehicle using it for the purpose described would not be exempt from wearing a seat belt, whereas a passenger riding in the vehicle for the same purpose would be exempt.

The regulations also do not apply to a person who is:

- driving a vehicle if the driver's seat is not provided with an adult seat belt;

- riding in the front of a vehicle in which no adult belt is available to them;

- riding in the rear of a vehicle in which no adult belt is available to them.

It should be noted that these exemptions relate to the non-wearing of seat belts where they are not provided, but this circumstance may involve other infringements of the law relating to the non-fitment of seat belts.

Stowaways

The UK Border Force manages border control and enforces immigration and Customs regulations – including dealing with applications for permission to enter or stay in the UK, citizenship and asylum issues, smuggling and border tax fraud.

Concern about the number of illegal immigrants (legally termed 'clandestine entrants') entering this country stowed away in heavy goods vehicles has resulted in severe penalties being imposed on drivers and operators caught with such stowaways hidden in their vehicles. The Immigration and Asylum Act 1999 sets penalties of £2,000 for each immigrant found in a lorry trailer, with confiscation of the vehicle as the sanction should the fine not be paid. However, under existing legislation (ie the Immigration Act 1971, section 25) it is already an offence to aid illegal immigrants to enter Great Britain. On conviction, an offending driver could face a heavy fine or up to seven years' imprisonment.

Proof of 'due diligence' may be accepted in defence of any charges under the legislation, but it is important for accused drivers to clearly show that they followed one of the Codes of Practice produced by the Border Force, HMRC or the trade associations. In the meantime, the RHA provides the following advice to its members to pass on to their drivers:

- Never leave ignition keys in the vehicle. Lock cab doors and secure the vehicle's load space whenever the vehicle is unattended.
- Avoid routine stops for papers, cigarettes, etc, particularly within 100 km of Channel ports.
- Always ensure windows are closed when away from your vehicle.
- If sleeping in the vehicle, lock all doors and try to block access to the rear doors by parking up against a wall or other secure barrier.
- Be on the lookout for bogus officials or staff.
- Never leave keys hidden for a relief driver.
- On arrival at your destination, do not leave your vehicle in someone else's care.
- Look out for and report any security defects on your vehicle, such as faulty locks or straps.
- Use pre-planned secure overnight parking wherever possible.
- Try to keep your vehicle in sight if you leave it unattended.
- Make sure your vehicle is correctly loaded.
- If you make the same journey frequently, consider whether the route or schedule can be varied.
- Report any irregularity of loading, sealing or documentation.

- Never accept unsolicited offers of assistance.

- Avoid talking about your route over the radio.

- When returning to a vehicle, check for suspicious vehicles/people nearby and, if concerned, note descriptions, registration numbers, etc.

- After every stop, and throughout the journey, look for signs of tampering with doors, straps, curtains, etc.

- Ensure that you properly record all the checks you make in order to provide an audit trail.

- Managers should ensure that operational procedures are constantly reviewed.

- Report to base when you arrive at an unoccupied site, or when you see suspicious activity.

- If you are concerned that there may be illegal stowaways on the vehicle, report to the nearest authorities and, at ports, make use of any detection facilities available.

- If you are uncomfortable opening your vehicle for potentially bogus authorities, ask for their details so you can check up on them and offer to open your vehicle at the nearest police station.

HMRC summarizes these procedures with its own 'Secure – Check – Record' advice for drivers. In addition, in an attempt to reduce the problem, the UK's Border Force has increased investment in enforcement and is now using drones to detect 'illegals' who would otherwise not be detected from the ground.

Operators are advised to turn in any stowaways found in their vehicles, despite the onerous civil penalties involved. Facilitating the entry of illegal immigrants is a serious criminal offence that carries a maximum prison sentence of 10 years.

Home Office Civil Penalty Code of Practice

This Code of Practice is issued in accordance with section 33 of the Immigration and Asylum Act 1999, now amended by the Immigration, Asylum and Nationality Act 2006. This sets out the measures to be taken and the procedures to be followed by persons operating a system for preventing the carriage of clandestine entrants to the United Kingdom in respect of road vehicles.

Under section 34(3) of the 1999 Act, where it is alleged a person is liable to a penalty under section 32 of that Act for bringing a clandestine entrant to the United Kingdom, it is a defence to show that:

- they did not know and had no reasonable grounds for suspecting that a clandestine entrant was, or might be, concealed in the vehicle;

- there was an effective system in operation in relation to the vehicle to prevent the carriage of clandestine entrants;

- on the occasion concerned, the person or persons responsible for operating that system did so properly.

Part 1: Road Haulage and Other Commercial Vehicles

'Commercial vehicle' means any vehicle excluding buses, coaches, cars, taxis, mobile homes and caravans. 'Vehicle' refers to the entire vehicle, including any attached trailer(s) and any container carried. It also refers to a detached trailer, in the case of which any reference to 'driver' is to be read as 'operator'.

1.1 Measures to be taken to secure vehicles against unauthorized entry

1.1.1 Before final loading takes place, all existing cuts or tears in the outer shell or fabric of the vehicle that exceed 25 centimetres in length must be repaired and sealed so as to prevent unauthorized entry. If present at the time of final loading, the owner, hirer or driver of the vehicle must check it to ensure that no persons have gained entry and are concealed within. It must then be locked, sealed or otherwise made secure to prevent unauthorized entry.

1.1.2 If not present at the time of final loading, the owner, hirer or driver must, where possible, ensure that such checks are conducted at that point by reputable persons. The owner, hirer or driver must then obtain written confirmation from those persons that these checks were properly conducted and that the vehicle did not contain concealed persons at the time of final loading and securing.

1.1.3 When the final loading has been completed, the load space must be secured immediately by lock, seal or other security device that will prevent unauthorized entry.

1.1.4 Tilt cords and straps, where used, must be undamaged, pass through all fastening points, made taut and be secured by lock, seal or other security device.

1.1.5 There must be no means of entry to the load space, other than via access points which have been secured by lock, tilt cord/strap and seal, or other security device.

1.1.6 Locks, tilt cords, straps and other devices used to secure the load space must be effective and of robust quality.

1.1.7 Seals, other than Customs seals, must be distinguished by a number from a series that is unique to the owner, hirer or driver. This must be recorded in the documentation accompanying the vehicle.

1.1.8   When a sealed container (except a container sealed by Customs) is loaded onto a vehicle, the owner, hirer or driver must, where possible, check to ensure that it does not contain unauthorized persons. It must then be resealed and made secure in accordance with the above requirements. These actions and the number of the new seal used must be recorded in documentation accompanying the vehicle.

1.1.9   The same checking, securing and recording procedure detailed in paragraph 1.1.8 above must be followed when the load space in the vehicle has been opened by the owner, hirer, driver or any other person before the final checks detailed in section 1.2 below are carried out.

1.1.10   Where a new driver becomes responsible for the vehicle en route to the United Kingdom, they should ensure that it does not contain unauthorized persons and that the requirements detailed above have all been met.

1.1.11   Paragraphs 1.1.1–1.1.10 above will not apply in relation to any vehicle that it is not possible to secure by means of lock, seal or other security device. However, in such circumstances, it will be for the owner, hirer or driver concerned to establish alternative arrangements to prevent unauthorized entry, and to be able to demonstrate that such arrangements have been made and complied with.

1.2 Measures to be taken immediately prior to the vehicle boarding the ship, aircraft or train to the United Kingdom, or before arrival at immigration departure/control location in mainland Europe

1.2.1   Where used, check tilt cords and straps for evidence of tampering, damage or repair.

1.2.2   Where used, check that seals, locks or other security devices have not been removed, damaged or replaced. In order to ensure that there has been no substitution, numbers on seals must be checked to confirm that they correspond with those recorded on the documentation accompanying the vehicle.

1.2.3   Check the outer shell/fabric of the vehicle for signs of damage or unauthorized entry, paying particular attention to the roof, which may be checked from either inside or outside the vehicle.

1.2.4   Check any external storage compartments, toolboxes, wind deflectors and underneath the vehicle.

1.2.5   Check inside the vehicle. Effective detection devices may be used for this purpose at the discretion of the owner, hirer or driver, but this will not obviate the requirement that the other checks be carried out (detailed above). Where it is not possible to secure a vehicle lock, seal or other security device, a thorough manual check of the load and load space must be conducted.

1.2.6 Use any of the available facilities at the port that are in place to help detect clandestine entrants (X-ray, CO_2 detectors, etc).

1.3 General principles

1.3.1 Vehicles should be checked regularly en route to the United Kingdom to ensure that they have not been entered, particularly after stops when left unattended. These checks need to be effective and comprehensive.

1.3.2 A document detailing the system operated to prevent unauthorized entry must be carried with the vehicle, so that it may be produced immediately on demand to an immigration officer in the event of a possible liability to a penalty.

1.3.3 A report detailing the checks that were carried out must be kept with the vehicle. If it is possible to arrange it, the report should be endorsed by a third party, who has either witnessed or carried out the checks themselves by arrangement with the owner, hirer or driver, as the report will then be of greater evidential value.

1.3.4 While owners, hirers or drivers may contract with other persons to carry out the required checks on their behalf, they will nevertheless remain liable to any penalty incurred in the event of failure to have an effective system in place or to operate it properly on the occasion in question.

1.3.5 Where the checks conducted suggest that the security of the vehicle may have been breached, or the owner, hirer or driver otherwise has grounds to suspect that unauthorized persons have gained entry to the vehicle, it must not be taken onto the ship, aircraft or train embarking area in Europe for the journey to the United Kingdom. Any such circumstances must be reported to the police in the country concerned at the earliest opportunity, or at the latest to the passport control authorities at the port of embarkation. In the event of difficulties arising, owners, hirers or drivers should contact the UK Immigration Service at the proposed port of arrival for advice.

Smuggling

The Customs authorities are becoming increasingly concerned about the volumes of smuggled goods, particularly tobacco products, being brought into the UK. It is estimated that tobacco smuggling alone amounts to some £3.5 billion annually.

Besides new measures to detect smuggling, such as the use of sophisticated X-ray equipment, tougher new penalties have been introduced which could result in convicted offenders losing their vehicles (all goods vehicles found to be carrying contraband goods are seized: 300 HGVs were impounded in the first year of operation) and their driving licences, and facing up to seven years in prison. Smuggling also applies to 'people trafficking', where custodial sentences are the usual penalty for any driver who knowingly attempts to traffic illegal immigrants into, or out of, the UK.

The limits* for personal importation of goods into the UK are as follows.

Currently from within the EU:

Table 10.4   Personal importation of goods

800 cigarettes	400 cigarillos
200 cigars	1 kg of smoking tobacco
110 litres of beer	10 litres of spirits
90 litres of wine	20 litres of fortified wine (eg port or sherry)

Although there are no actual 'maximum' limits in place, you are likely to be asked questions if you carry more than the figures above.

Post-Brexit, the levels for bringing in duty-free items from Europe will be:

Table 10.5   Personal importation of goods post-Brexit

200 cigarettes or 100 cigarillos
50 cigars or 250 grams of tobacco
2 litres of fortified wine
16 litres of beer
4 litres of non-sparkling wine
1 litre of spirits

These figures are those 'expected' to be used unless individual EU member states decide to set individual specific limits for the UK post-Brexit.

Any amounts of such goods brought in exceeding these limits may be confiscated and penalties imposed.

Use of Radios and Telephones in Vehicles

It is illegal to hold a phone, satnav or other communication device while driving. This law also applies when a driver is stopped at traffic lights, queuing in traffic and supervising a learner driver. Drivers should not stop on the hard shoulder of a motorway to answer or make a call, no matter how urgent.

Penalties for Mobile Phone Use

Penalties for the illegal use of mobile phones or other similar hand-held devices by vocational drivers are a fine of £200 and six penalty points. Should offenders decide to take the case to court rather than accept the fixed penalty, on conviction they could face a maximum fine of £1,000 but, with penalty points, this could also mean disqualification.

Drivers who stop the vehicle, even in a safe place such as a lay-by, must apply the handbrake, switch off the engine and remove the ignition keys, if possible, in order to avoid any charge that they were 'driving' when using the telephone.

Traffic and Weather Reports

Drivers concerned about prevailing or likely weather conditions prior to making a journey, or even while en route, can check forecasts from local and national newspapers and get an update of the current situation by using a laptop, smartphone or listening to radio and television bulletins. In particular, the following are useful for traffic and weather forecasts.

Radio

Most radio stations broadcast regular weather and traffic bulletins.

Highways England often signposts frequencies for local radio stations on some motorways. These are broadcast 24 hours a day, seven days a week.

Online

AA Roadwatch (www.theaa.com/traffic-news) provides national motorway and A-road information, also call 84322 – 'the AA' on your mobile – or 0906 88 84322 from a land line.

The RAC Traffic News (www.rac.co.uk/route-planner/traffic-news) also provides information on route planning and traffic throughout the UK.

In addition there are online information systems, available with a smartphone or laptop, operated by national broadcasters (BBC, etc), local and regional government, and others covering individual motorways. They are even available through commercial organizations such as Michelin.

On-Board Traffic Information

AA Roadwatch Twitter

The AA Roadwatch Twitter page displays dynamic traffic news on the screen and provides live information and advice from fellow travellers.

Goods Vehicle Dimensions and Weights

11

The normal maximum permitted dimensions and maximum weight limits for goods vehicles and trailers in Great Britain are set out in the Road Vehicles (Construction and Use) Regulations 1986 (C&U Regulations), as amended, and the Road Vehicles (Authorised Weight) Regulations 1998, which specify the following weight limits:

- two-axle rigids (including buses) 18 tonnes;
- three-axle goods vehicles (without road-friendly suspension) 25 tonnes;
- three-axle goods vehicles (with road-friendly suspension) 26 tonnes;
- three-axle articulated buses 28 tonnes;
- four-axle goods vehicles (without road-friendly suspension) 30 tonnes;
- four-axle goods vehicles (with road-friendly suspension) 32 tonnes;
- four-axle combinations 36 tonnes;
- four-axle articulated vehicles fitted with road-friendly suspension on the drive axle, where the tractor unit does not exceed 18 tonnes and the trailer does not exceed 20 tonnes, 38 tonnes;
- four-axle articulated vehicles fitted with road-friendly suspension on the drive axle 38 tonnes;
- five-axle combinations 40 tonnes;
- five-axle (3+2) articulated vehicles at 44 tonnes permitted for the carriage or delivery of 'loading units' (a loading unit is normally an ISO container, swap-body or semi-trailer) on international combined transport operations;
- drive axles at 11.5 tonnes for all the above except 41-tonne combinations.

A 10.5-tonne maximum drive axle weight applies to vehicles grossing 40 tonnes or more; otherwise the limit is 11.5 tonnes. Tractive units of combinations operating at 44 tonnes gross weight must have engines that are regarded as meeting low pollution emission standards – ie either a gas-fuelled or dual-fuelled engine or a diesel engine that complies with at least the Euro-II emission standard.

European limits on vehicle weights and dimensions are detailed in EC Directive 96/53/EC of 25 July 1996.

Definitions

The following definitions apply when considering the lengths, widths and weights of goods vehicles and trailers:

- **Overall length** – the distance between the extreme forward and rearward projecting points of the vehicle/trailer inclusive of all parts, but excluding load-securing sheets and flexible coverings, receptacles for Customs seals and tailboards (provided they are not supporting the load, in which case they are included in the overall length). In the case of drawbar trailers overall length excludes the length of the coupling.

- **Overall width** – the distance between the extreme projecting points on each side of the vehicle/trailer inclusive of all parts but excluding driving mirrors, distortion of the tyres caused by weight, receptacles for Customs seals, load-securing sheets and flexible coverings.

- **Weight** – the maximum gross (or design) weight (gvw) for a vehicle/trailer is that at which it has been designed to operate. The permissible maximum weight for a vehicle/trailer is the limit set by law (and is shown on the 'Ministry' plate attached to the vehicle), which must not be exceeded on the road in Great Britain.

Length

Rigid Vehicles

The maximum overall length permitted for rigid vehicles, including draw bar trailers, is 12 metres.

Articulated Vehicles

For certain articulated vehicles the maximum permitted length is 16.5 metres (see below), provided the combination can turn within minimum and maximum swept inner and outer concentric circles of 5.3 metres radius and 12.5 metres radius respectively (see Figure 11.1); otherwise the maximum permitted length is 15.5 metres. The swept circle requirements do not apply to:

- low-loader or step-frame low-loader combinations;
- car transporters;

- articulated vehicles constructed to carry indivisible loads of exceptional length;
- articulated vehicles with semi-trailers built or converted to increase their length prior to 1 April 1990;
- articulated vehicles not exceeding 15.5 metres overall length.

Figure 11.1 The maximum and minimum outer and inner swept circles within which articulated vehicles over 15.5 metres long and certain other vehicles (see text for details and exceptions) must be able to turn

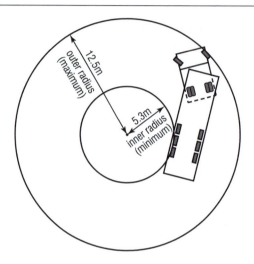

Articulated vehicles first used since 1 June 1998 which are fitted with a lift axle must meet the turning circle requirement (see below) both with and without all the wheels in contact with the ground.

For the purposes of enforcement of the turning circle requirements, the DVSA has notified vehicle manufacturers that it will take a notional measurement from the kingpin to the centre line of the semi-trailer bogie. Where such a dimension does not exceed 8.155 metres, the combination will be assumed to comply in the case of 2.5-metre-wide semi-trailers; 8.135 metres if 2.55 metres wide and 8.115 metres if 2.6 metres wide. Where this dimension exceeds 7.8 metres, the DVSA reserves the right to demand a turning circle demonstration on a steering pad.

The maximum overall length for an articulated vehicle incorporating a low-loader semi-trailer, manufactured after April 1991 (but not a step-frame semi-trailer), is 18 metres. Such vehicles do not have to meet the turning circle requirements described above.

Where an articulated vehicle is designed to carry indivisible loads of exceptional length, there is no length restriction (an indivisible load means 'a load which cannot without undue expense or risk of damage be divided into two or more loads for the purpose of conveyance on a road').

Longer Semi-Trailer Trial

Longer semi-trailers are a new type of HGV trailer that has been on trial since 2012. They are up to 2.05 metres longer than the current standard semi-trailers on our roads (15.65 metres instead of 13.6 metres). While the trailers are longer than existing HGV trailers, they cannot be heavier. The total weight of the trailer, the goods and the tractor unit must still be within the UK domestic weight limit of 44 tonnes. They must also pass the turning circle test applied to the existing 13.6-metre trailers. To achieve this, longer semi-trailers usually have a steering rear axle. By making the trailer 2 metres longer, a vehicle can carry two more rows of pallets or three more rows of goods cages on each journey compared with existing trailers.

The 10-year trial was initiated in 2012 for 1,800 trailers. This was extended by an additional five years in 2017 and an additional 1,000 longer semi-trailers. Operators participate voluntarily, at their own cost and risk, and there is no guarantee that longer semi-trailers will be permitted on the road beyond the end of the trial period. Any licensed HGV operator is eligible to apply to join the trial and the DfT's aim has been to include a mix of large and small operators. All participants must submit detailed data about the journeys their longer semi-trailers make and about all incidents (not just those resulting in injury) on the public road or in public areas (such as services).

Vehicle and Trailer Drawbar Combinations (Road Trains)

When a rigid motor vehicle is drawing a trailer, the maximum overall length for the combination is 18.75 metres, subject to certain other minimum dimensional requirements being met (see below).

The 18.75-metre maximum length for road train combinations incorporates:

- a maximum load space of 15.65 metres to be shared between the two bodies;
- a minimum gap of 0.75 metres (to provide a 16.4-metre 'envelope' of load and coupling space); and
- a minimum cab length of 2.35 metres (see Figure 11.2).

Figure 11.2 The maximum dimensions for drawbar vehicle combinations

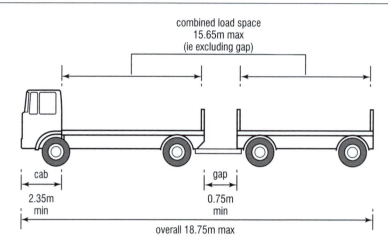

NB: The term 'loading area' includes the thickness of the bulkhead. Towing equipment is not counted in the measurement of the truck–trailer gap.

When a trailer is designed for carrying indivisible loads of exceptional length, the length of the drawing vehicle must not exceed 9.2 metres and the whole combination must not exceed 25.9 metres.

When two or more trailers are drawn, the overall length of the combination must not exceed 25.9 metres unless an attendant is carried and two days' notice is given to the police. When two trailers are drawn within the 25.9 metre limit mentioned here (ie only legally permissible with a vehicle classed as a motor tractor or locomotive), only one of the trailers may exceed an overall length of 7 metres. When three trailers are drawn (ie only legally possible with a vehicle classed as a locomotive), none of the trailers may exceed a length of 7 metres.

The limits do not apply when a broken-down vehicle (which is then legally classed as a trailer) is being towed.

Trailers

The maximum length for any drawbar trailer which has four or more wheels and is drawn by a vehicle which has a maximum gross weight exceeding 3,500 kg is 12 metres. The same 12-metre maximum length limit also applies to agricultural trailers.

NB: *Although the maximum individual lengths for both rigid drawing vehicles and trailers are 12 metres as stated, two such maximum-length units obviously cannot be combined within the overall 18.75-metre limit for drawbar combination described above.*

The maximum permitted length for all other drawbar trailers is 7 metres.

Composite trailers (see the Composite Trailers section in Chapter 12) having at least four wheels and drawn by a goods vehicle over 3,500 kilograms permissible maximum weight, or by an agricultural vehicle, may be up to 14.04 metres long.

Articulated Semi-Trailers

The maximum permitted length for certain articulated combinations is 16.5 metres. This applies where such vehicles include a semi-trailer with a distance from the centre line of the kingpin to the rear of the trailer which does not exceed 12 metres and where the distance from the kingpin (or foremost kingpin if more than one) to *any point* on the front of the trailer does not exceed 2.04 metres. Car transporter semi-trailers are slightly different insofar that the distance from the kingpin to the rear of the trailer can be up to 12.5 metres and the distance from the kingpin to any point on the front of the trailer can be up to 4.19 metres – see Figure 11.3.

Figure 11.3   The maximum dimensions for articulated vehicles and semi-trailers (see above for details and exceptions)

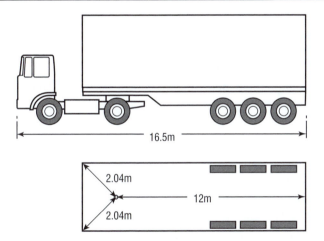

Articulated semi-trailers built since 1 May 1983 are limited to a maximum length of 12.2 metres. There is no specified length limit for semi-trailers built prior to this date. In measuring the 12.2-metre dimension, no account need be taken of the thickness of front or rear walls or any parts in front of the front wall or behind the rear wall or closing device (ie door, shutter, etc). The thickness of any internal partitions must be included in the length measurement. This means effectively that the dimension relates only to load space between the front and rear walls.

The 12.2-metre length limit for semi-trailers as described does not apply to a trailer which is normally used on international journeys, part of which is outside the

UK. Similarly, articulated vehicles operating within the 15.5-metre limit on international journeys do not have to meet the turning circle requirements described above for 16.5-metre-long vehicles.

The 13.7-Metre Container Problem

The carriage of standard 13.7-metre pallet-wide ISO-type shipping containers cannot be carried out legally on maximum-length articulated vehicles on account of the limitation on swing radius as set out in Community Directive 96/53/EC. This was particularly worrying for European intermodal road hauliers who needed to use the 13.7-metre pallet-wide container, the only size longer than 12.1 metres that would enable them to compete effectively against the traditional road hauliers using 13.6-metre-long semi-trailers. However, this problem has been overcome by use of the Geest (ie Geest North Sea Line bv)-designed 'Euro-Casting' fitted to the front end of a 13.7-metre container, which successfully meets the crucial swing radius of 2.04 metres – measured from the centre of the kingpin to any point at the front end of the container or skeletal semi-trailer – as well as the 12.0-metre length requirement measured from the centre of the kingpin to the rearmost point of the semi-trailer (see Figure 11.3).

Measurement of Length

In measuring vehicle or trailer length, account must be taken of any load-carrying receptacle (eg demountable body or container) used with the vehicle and any bridging plates used for loading and unloading, but not for carrying the load. Excluded from the overall length measurement are such things as rubber or resilient buffers and receptacles for Customs seals. Also excluded are forklifts that fit onto the rear of trailers for unloading and which are carried at the rear of the trailer when the vehicle is in motion; these are commonly used for unloading palletized loads. In the case of drawbar combinations, the length of the drawbar is excluded from overall length calculations. With dropside-bodied vehicles, the length of the tailboard in the lowered (ie horizontal) position is excluded unless it is supporting part of the load, in which case it must be included in the overall length measurement and for the purposes of establishing overhang limits (see below).

Overhang

Overhang is the distance by which the body and other parts of a vehicle extend beyond the rear axle. The maximum overhang permitted for rigid goods vehicles (ie cars) is 60 per cent of the distance between the centre of the front axle and the point from which the overhang is to be measured. The point from which the overhang is measured is, in the case of two-axled vehicles, the centre line through the rear axle, and in the case of vehicles with three or more axles, two of which are non-steering rear axles, 110 millimetres to the rear of the centre line between the two rear axles (Figure 11.4).

Figure 11.4 How to measure body overhang on vehicles with two axles, three axles and more (this measurement applies equally to two- and three-axle tractive units) (see details and exceptions in text above)

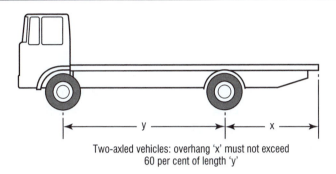

Two-axled vehicles: overhang 'x' must not exceed
60 per cent of length 'y'

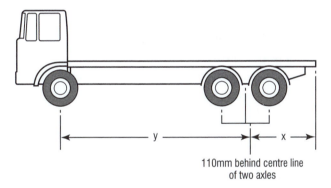

110mm behind centre line
of two axles

Vehicles with three axles or more: overhang 'x' measured
from 110mm behind the centre line of the two rear axles
must not exceed 60 per cent of the length of 'y', which is
the distance between the centre line of the front wheel to
the centre line of the two rear axles plus 110mm

This regulation does not apply to: vehicles used solely in connection with street cleansing; the collection or disposal of refuse; the collection or disposal of the contents of gullies or cesspools; works trucks; or tipping vehicles, provided the total overhang does not exceed 1.15 metres (3 ft 9 in approx). There is no specified overhang limit on trailers.

NB: *Overhang is not always measured from the rear axle but from the turning axis of the vehicle. In other words, this is not always the middle of the rear bogie of a six- or eight-wheeler: when one of the axles steers or is lifted, the turning centre becomes the driven axle. There is also an alternative to the 60 per cent of the distance from front axle to vehicle turning point. It can instead conform to European Directive 92/27/EEC, in accordance with which the swing-out of a rear corner is limited to 0.8 metres when the vehicle is following the 12.5-metre radius swept circle.*

Width

Motor Vehicles

The overall width of motor tractors, motor cars and heavy motor cars (most goods vehicles are included in these classifications) must not be more than 2.55 metres (see note below about refrigerated vehicles), and the maximum width of locomotives must not be more than 2.75 metres.

Trailers

The maximum permissible width for standard trailers is 2.55 metres (also note refrigerated vehicles below), provided the drawing vehicle has a maximum permissible weight exceeding 3,500 kg. If the towing vehicle is below this weight, the width of the trailer must not exceed 2.3 metres.

Refrigerated Vehicles

The maximum permitted width for refrigerated (ie reefer) vehicles, semi-trailers and drawbar trailers is 2.6 metres provided that the thickness of the side walls (inclusive of insulation) is at least 45 millimetres. For the purposes of this regulation, 'refrigerated vehicle' means a vehicle (or trailer) specially designed to carry goods at low temperature.

Height

There are currently no legal maximum height limits for goods vehicles or for loads in Britain (see below), but these are governed by the height of bridges on the routes on which the vehicles are operated. For general information, the minimum height of bridges on motorways is normally 4.8 metres to 5 metres and the maximum height for buses is 4.57 metres (see also the section on High Loads in Chapter 19).

NB: The Blackwall Tunnel (on the A102(M)), the River Thames crossing to the east of London, is limited to a maximum height of 4 metres northbound and 4.70 metres southbound. The Dartford Tunnels are also subject to a 4.8 metre height limit (west tunnel) and a 5.0 metre height limit (east tunnel).

EU regulations specify a general height limit of 4 metres, but this does not apply in the UK and some member states continue to have their own height limits, such as Sweden where, although the height is unrestricted, most main routes have a practical height limit of 4.5 metres.

Height Marking and Route Descriptions

All vehicles with an overall travelling height of more than 3 metres must have a notice prominently displayed in the driver's cab indicating the actual travelling height of the vehicle and its load or equipment in feet and inches (or in both feet and inches and metres).

The height marking, where this is shown in feet and inches only, must be in letters and figures at least 40 mm tall. Where the height is shown in both imperial and metric measures the figures shown must not differ by more than 50 mm.

As an alternative to the height marking described above, in circumstances where drivers are operating on a particular journey during which they are unlikely to be confronted with any bridge or overhead structure which does not exceed the maximum travelling height by at least 1 metre, a document may be carried on the vehicle (within easy reach of the driver) which describes the route, or a choice of routes, the driver must follow in order to avoid any risk of the vehicle, its load or equipment colliding with any bridge or overhead structure.

Where vehicles are fitted with 'high-level equipment' (defined as power-operated equipment) with a maximum height of more than 3 metres, they must have a warning device which gives visible warning to the driver if the height of the vehicle exceeds a predetermined level. This applies to vehicles first used and trailers first made from 1 April 1998.

Bridge Strikes

Loading a vehicle to a height which could cause danger or where the load hits a bridge is an offence under the Construction and Use Regulations. Network Rail reports an average of 1,800 bridge strikes every year, with the average cost being £550,000. Network Rail also states that there are an average of five strikes every day, costing the taxpayer around £23 million a year. Some key railway bridges have been identified as providing risk of potential disaster, should they be struck by a large vehicle. Infrared warning systems have been installed at many of these key sites, which trigger alarms when over-height vehicles approach. To prevent bridge strikes drivers must:

- check the maximum height of the vehicle, its load or its equipment;
- advise if the measured height is different from the height shown on the headboard;
- check the maximum height again after loading, unloading or reloading;
- display the correct height in the cab (over 3 metres) at the start of every journey and following any change in the load.

In the event of a bridge strike, drivers must report the incident – failure to do so is an offence. Most rail bridges have a sign indicating the Network Rail Helpline contact number (03457 11 41 41).

Vehicles for Combined Transport

Swap-body and container-carrying goods vehicles running to and from rail terminals on intermodal operations may operate at up to 44 tonnes gross weight provided they are:

- articulated vehicles and drawbar combinations equipped with:
  - at least six axles;
  - road-friendly suspensions (or having no axle exceeding 8.5 tonnes);
- articulated vehicles comprising specially built bimodal semi-trailers (ie capable of running on road or rail).

For these purposes, containers and swap-bodies are defined as being receptacles at least 6.1 metres long designed for repeated carriage of goods and for transfer between road and rail vehicles.

To comply with the law, the driver must carry documentary evidence to show that the swap-body or container load is on its way to a rail terminal (the document must show the name of the rail terminal, the date of the contract and the parties to it), or is on its way back from a rail terminal (in which case the document must show the terminal and the date and time that the unit load was collected). There is no restriction on the distance that may be travelled to or from a rail terminal for the purposes of complying with this legislation.

Authorized Weight Regulations

UK HGV weights are aligned with EC Directive 96/53/EC under the Road Vehicles (Authorised Weight) Regulations 1998 (SI 1998 No 3111). This specifies maximum authorized weights for vehicles (ie weights not to be exceeded in any circumstances).

It also makes provision for the weights of vehicles and trailers of the types defined in EC Directive 70/156/EEC (see below). The regulation does not apply to vehicle combinations that meet the requirements for combined transport in the C&U Regulations. Vehicles that comply with C&U are taken to comply with the Authorized Weight Regulations.

The vehicle and axle weight limits set out in the C&U Regulations (as amended) remain in force largely unchanged, apart from three particular provisions listed below, which were implemented when these regulations were amended in consequence of the making of the new authorized weight regulations:

- an increase in the maximum total weight of all trailers drawn at any one time by a vehicle;
- an increase in the maximum weight permitted for uncompensated steering axle from 7,120 kg to 8,500 kg;
- amendments to the provisions relating to vehicles used in combined transport operations.

Maximum Weight Determined by Axle Spacing

The authorized weight (in kg) for the vehicles shown below must equal the sum of the distance measured in metres between the foremost and rearmost axles of the vehicle multiplied by the factor specified in the third column and rounded up to the nearest 10 kg, if that number is less than the 'maximum authorized weight' (ie in accordance with Table 11.1).

Table 11.1   Maximum weight determined by axle spacing

Description of vehicle	Number of axles	Factor to determine maximum authorized weight (kg)
Rigid motor vehicle	2	6,000
Tractor unit	2	6,000
Trailer which is not a semi-trailer or centre-axle trailer	2	6,000
Rigid motor vehicle	3	5,500
Tractor unit	3 or more	6,000
Trailer which is not a semi-trailer or centre-axle trailer	3 or more	5,000
Rigid motor vehicle	4 or more	5,000
Articulated bus	any number	5,000

Maximum Authorized Weights for Vehicle Combinations

Table 11.2   Maximum authorized weights for vehicle combinations

Description of combination	Number of axles	Maximum authorized weight (kg)
Articulated vehicle	3	26,000
Rigid motor vehicle towing a trailer	3	22,000
Rigid motor vehicle towing a trailer (1)	3	26,000
Articulated vehicle	4	36,000
Articulated vehicle (2)	4	38,000
Rigid motor vehicle towing a trailer	4	30,000
Rigid motor vehicle towing a trailer (1)	4	36,000
Articulated vehicle	5 or more	40,000
Rigid motor vehicle towing a trailer	5 or more	34,000
Rigid motor vehicle towing a trailer (1)	5 or more	40,000
Articulated vehicle (3)	6 or more	41,000
Rigid motor vehicle towing a trailer (1 & 3)	6 or more	41,000
Rigid motor vehicle towing a trailer (1, 3 & 4)	6 or more	44,000

1. Applies to vehicles that have a distance between the rear axle of the motor vehicle and the front axle of the trailer of not less than 3 m.
2. Applies to combinations where:
   a. the combination is a 2-axle tractor unit and 2-axle semi-trailer;
   b. the weight of the tractor unit comprised in the combination does not exceed 18,000 kg;
   c. the sum of the axle weights of the semi-trailer does not exceed 20,000 kg; and
   d. the driving axle is fitted with twin tyres and road-friendly suspension.
3. Applies to vehicles where:
   a. the weight of each driving axle does not exceed 10,500 kg;
   b. either:
      i. each driving axle is fitted with twin tyres and road-friendly suspension; or
      ii. each driving axle that is not a steering axle is fitted with twin tyres and does not exceed 8,500 kg;
   c. each axle of the trailer is fitted with road-friendly suspension; and
   d. each vehicle comprised in the combination has at least three axles.
4. Applies to vehicles powered by low pollution engines (ie gas or diesel complying with emission requirements).

Weight by Reference to Axle Spacing

The maximum authorized weight in kg for an articulated vehicle shall be the sum of the distance measured in metres between the kingpin and the centre of the rearmost axle of the semi-trailer multiplied by the factor specified and rounded up to the nearest 10 kg, if that number is less than the 'maximum authorized weight' (ie in accordance with Table 11.3).

Table 11.3   Weight by reference to axle spacing

Description of vehicle combination	Number of axles	Factor to determine maximum authorized weight (kg)
Articulated vehicle	3 or more	5,500

Maximum Authorized Axle Weights

Table 11.4   Maximum authorized axle weights

Description of axle	Maximum authorized weight (kg)
Single driving axle	11,500
Single non-driving axle	10,000
Driving tandem axle	18,000
Driving tandem axle (1)	19,000
Non-driving tandem axle	20,000
Tri-axle	24,000

1. Applies to axles where:
   a. the driving axle is fitted with twin tyres and road-friendly suspension; or
   b. each driving axle is fitted with twin tyres and no axle has an axle weight exceeding 9,500 kg.

Where maximum weights are less than those in Table 11.4, see Table 11.5.

Table 11.5   Maximum authorized axle weights

Description of axle	Specified dimension	Length (metres)	Maximum authorized weight (kg)
Driving tandem axle	Distance between the 2 axles	Less than 1	11,500
Driving tandem axle	Distance between the 2 axles	Not less than 1 but less than 1.3	16,000
Non-driving tandem axle	Distance between the 2 axles	Less than 1	11,000
Non-driving tandem axle	Distance between the 2 axles	Not less than 1 but less than 1.3	16,000
Non-driving tandem axle	Distance between the 2 axles	Not less than 1.3 but less than 1.8	18,000

Table 11.5 *continued*

Description of axle	Specified dimension	Length (metres)	Maximum authorized weight (kg)
Tri-axle	Distance between any 1 axle and the nearer of the other 2 axles	1.3 or less	21,000

Overall Weight Limits

The total weight of the load on a vehicle, together with the weight of the vehicle itself, must not exceed the maximum permitted weight for each individual axle or for the vehicle.

NB: *In relation to both length and weight limits, EU rules on weights and dimensions limits were revised. The directive allows HGV and PSV manufacturers to exceed current length and weight limits in order to use designs to improve road safety and/ or environmental performance, such as 'crumple zones', rounded front cabs and alternative fuels.*

Load Movements – C&U Regulations Versus Special Types Order

Most general haulage loads moved in the UK fall within scope of the weights, lengths and width limitations set out in the Road Vehicles (Construction and Use) Regulations 1986. However, long, heavy and/or wide loads transported that exceed C&U rules are required to be moved under the abnormal indivisible loads (AIL) provisions of the Road Traffic Act 1988 Section 44(1) detailed in the Motor Vehicle (Authorization of Special Types) General Order 2003, as outlined in Chapter 19. Maximum vehicle and load lengths permitted under Regulation 7 of C&U must not be confused with those authorized under the STGO.

ISO Container Dimensions and Weights

Shipping containers to ISO standards present a complexity of dimensions and weights, mainly identified by a 'Type Designation'. A table showing the relevant internal and external heights, widths and lengths plus maximum gross weights and cubic capacity in metric and imperial measures is to be found in Appendix IX. Since July 2016, it is also now a requirement that ISO containers that are to travel by sea (but not ro-ro or short sea ferry crossings) must have proof of a certified gross weight before they will be loaded onto the container ship.

Weight Offences

It is an offence on the part of both the driver and the vehicle operator to operate a goods vehicle on a road laden to a weight above that at which it has been plated by the DVSA (ie above the maximum permitted gross and individual axle weights), and both are liable to prosecution. Such offences are 'absolute', in that once the actual overweight has been established, the fact that it was a deliberate action to gain extra revenue or purely accidental, unintentional, outside the driver's or vehicle operator's control, or loading was in a place where no weighing facilities existed, is of no consequence in defending against the charge.

Currently, the policy adopted by the DVSA is that if a vehicle exceeds its weight limits by more than 5 per cent (up to a maximum of 1 tonne), it will be prohibited from proceeding on its journey until the weight is reduced to within legal limits – see below. Where an overload exceeds 10 per cent of the vehicle's legal limits or a maximum of 1 tonne, a prosecution will follow, with heavier penalties being imposed on conviction. Trading Standards Officers may not take such a lenient view in their dealing with overloaded vehicles.

Vehicles can be diverted to a point of weighing by the enforcement authorities issuing a form PG3. This form gives the issuing officer the right to divert the vehicle for up to a distance of five miles. Should that distance be exceeded and the vehicle is found not to be overloaded, then the operator may claim for the disruption caused.

Defence

It is a defence under the Road Traffic Act 1988 (section 42) to prove that at the time the contravention was detected, the vehicle was proceeding to the nearest available weighbridge or was returning from such a weighbridge to the nearest point at which it was reasonably practicable to remove the excess load.

It is also a defence, where the weight exceeds maximum limits by not more than 5 per cent, to prove that the weight was within legal limits at the time of loading the vehicle and no person has added anything to the load. This defence is typically aimed at protecting loads that may have been subject to rain, hail, sleet or snow while in transit and absorbed the moisture.

Penalties

Overloading offences are taken very seriously. Both a driver and operator can be prosecuted and substantial fines can be imposed by the criminal courts for each offence of exceeding maximum axle weight (MAW), axle weight or gvw. Overloading offences will also affect the operator's OCRS.

Prohibition of Overweight Vehicles

Any vehicle on a road found by a vehicle examiner to be overloaded to the extent that it could endanger public safety will be ordered off the road immediately. The necessary powers to enable this step to be taken are included in sections 70 (2) and (3) of the Road Traffic Act 1988 and they empower an authorized officer to prohibit the driving of a goods vehicle on a road if, after having it weighed, it appears that the vehicle exceeds the relevant weight limits imposed by the Construction and Use Regulations 1986 and as a result would be an immediate risk to public safety if it were used on a road. The officer may be one of the DVSA's examiners or a specially authorized weights and measures inspector or a police constable.

A prohibition notice, Form TE160, is issued to the driver of a vehicle found to be overweight and it is the driver's responsibility to remove the excess weight to their own satisfaction and clear the TE160 before proceeding. The penalty for ignoring a prohibition notice is a fine of up to £5,000.

Under changes to the OCRS system, serious cases of overloading can now constitute a Most Serious Offence (MSO). These are classed as offences where:

- a vehicle with a gross weight not exceeding 12,000 kg is overloaded by a factor of 25 per cent or more; or where
- a vehicle with a gross weight exceeding 12,000 kg is overloaded by a factor of 20 per cent or more.

In these cases the operator's OCRS will be seriously affected and the operator and driver will usually face prosecution.

Official Weighing of Vehicles

Under the Road Traffic Act 1988, an authorized officer can request the person in charge of a vehicle to drive it to a weighbridge to be weighed. It is an offence to refuse to go to a weighbridge if requested (maximum fine currently £5,000). Once a vehicle has been weighed, the official in charge should give the driver a 'certificate of weight' (whether it is overloaded or not) and the vehicle will be exempt from further requests for weighing while carrying the same load on that journey.

The following Codes of Practice are currently in use by the DVSA for vehicle weighing.

Code of Practice for Conventional Weighing

The procedure will be as follows:

- Normally only one authorized officer will check-weigh a vehicle.
- The driver and any passengers should remain in the vehicle during weighing as they are part of the weight transmitted to the road.
- When requested, the driver should move the vehicle smoothly onto the weighbridge plate or pads.
- The engine should be switched off but left in gear during weighing. When a vehicle's individual axles are being check-weighed, both the hand and foot brakes should be released.
- If the vehicle is too long to go on the weighing plate or is over the weight capacity of the machine, it may require two or more weighings to get a total weight for the vehicle.
- The driver may be required to have the axle weights checked, and in positioning the vehicle he or she should carefully follow instructions given by the authorized officer.
- A certificate of weight will be issued for each vehicle weighed and will be handed to the driver. In some cases, where circumstances permit, the driver may be invited to see the weight recorded on the indicator. The certificate of weight exempts a vehicle from being weighed again on the same journey *with the same load* if stopped at another weight check. Drivers should give the certificate of weight to their employer as soon as they reach their base (see below).
- Drivers should also note that previous overloading offences may be detected by checks on weighbridge records.

Dynamic Weighing

The use of dynamic axle-weighing machines is permitted under regulations (the Weighing of Motor Vehicles (Use of Dynamic Axle Weighing Machines) Regulations 1978), which specify that an enforcement officer can require a vehicle to be driven across the weighing platform of a machine. The permitted weights for the vehicle are measured to within plus or minus 150 kg for each axle and within plus or minus 150 kg multiplied by the total number of axles to determine the tolerance on the total vehicle weights.

The DfT has a consolidated code of practice: enforcement weighing of vehicles, which must be followed by enforcement officers to secure a successful prosecution for vehicle overloading. This Code supplements the regulations and provides enforcement officers as well as vehicle operators and drivers with information on the correct setting up and operational use of weighing machines and on periodic (ie maximum six-monthly) accuracy tests which must be carried out. Among other things, the Code specifies standards for the approach and exit from the concrete apron of the equipment (ie plus or minus 3 mm for a distance of 8 metres on each side of the weigh beam, and the finished surface must not deviate from the level by more than 3 mm under a 3-metre-long straight edge).

Operators should be familiar with the consolidated code of practice and, if subjected to this enforcement process, must retain any printed records for two years.

Portable Weighers

Trading Standards Officers and DVSA inspectors can use portable axle weigh-pads as a means of checking vehicle/axle weights.

On-Board Vehicle Weighing

Operators of tippers and other vehicles where it is often impossible to measure the weight of the load being loaded may wish to fit an on-board weighing system, which is capable of measuring gross weight and/or individual axle weights. These systems are widely available and, over the life of the vehicle, could prove cost-effective if they prevent even a single prosecution. They operate in different ways, with some being operated by hydraulics and others by systems of sensors.

Construction and Use of Vehicles

12

In constructing goods vehicles and trailers, manufacturers and bodybuilders must observe requirements regarding the specification and standards of construction of components and the equipment used in the manufacture. While some of these items are covered by the type-approval schemes (see the Type Approval section later in this chapter), the majority are included in the Road Vehicles (Construction and Use) Regulations 1986, Statutory Instrument (SI) 1078/1986 (available from The Stationery Office or free to download from the GOV.UK website) and the many subsequent amendments to these regulations, which, collectively, are commonly referred to as the C&U Regulations. Certain EU legislation also applies, as indicated in the text.

Once a goods vehicle or trailer has been built and put into service, it is the operator as the vehicle user (see The Vehicle User section in Chapter 1) who must then ensure that it complies fully with the law regarding its construction and use when on the road.

Definitions of Vehicles

For the purpose of these regulations the following definitions, as given in the Road Traffic Act 1988, apply:

- A **goods vehicle** is a vehicle or a trailer adapted or constructed to carry a load.

- A **motor car** is a vehicle which, if adapted for the carriage of goods, has an unladen weight not exceeding 3,050 kg but otherwise has an unladen weight not exceeding 2,540 kg.

- A **heavy motor car** is a vehicle constructed to carry goods or passengers with an unladen weight exceeding 2,540 kg. Note: This definition may change when alternatively fuelled vehicles are allowed to operate at 4,250 kg, up from 3,500 kg, and operators need to monitor this situation.

- A **motor tractor** is a vehicle which is not constructed to carry a load and has an unladen weight not exceeding 7,370 kg.

- A **light locomotive** is a vehicle which is not constructed to carry a load and which has an unladen weight of more than 7,370 kg but not exceeding 11,690 kg.

- A **heavy locomotive** is a vehicle which is not constructed to carry a load and which has an unladen weight exceeding 11,690 kg.

- An **articulated vehicle** as defined in the C&U Regulations is a motor car or heavy motor car with a trailer so attached that when the trailer is uniformly loaded at least 20 per cent of the weight of the load is imposed on the drawing vehicle.

- A **composite trailer** is a combination of a converter dolly and a semi-trailer, and is treated as one trailer only when considering the number of trailers which may be drawn.

- **Engineering plant** means movable plant or equipment in the form of a motor vehicle or trailer which is specially designed and constructed for the purposes of engineering operations and which cannot, for this reason, comply with the C&U Regulations. Also, it is constructed to carry only materials which it had excavated from the ground and which it is specially designed to treat while being carried. It also means mobile cranes which do not conform in all respects with the C&U Regulations, but not mobile cranes based on a LGV chassis.

- An **agricultural motor vehicle** means a motor vehicle that is constructed or adapted for use off roads for the purposes of agriculture, horticulture or forestry and which is primarily used for one or more of those purposes.

- A **pedestrian-controlled vehicle** means a motor vehicle which is controlled by a pedestrian and which is not constructed or adapted to carry a driver or passenger.

- A **works truck** means a motor vehicle (other than a straddle carrier) designed for use in private premises and used on a road only in delivering goods from or to such premises, or from a vehicle on a road in the immediate neighbourhood, or in passing from one part of the premises to another or to other private premises in the immediate neighbourhood, or in connection with roadworks or in the immediate vicinity of the site of such works.

- A **works trailer** means a trailer used for the same purposes as a works truck.

International Vehicle Classifications

Goods vehicles are classified according to the following international categories:

- Category M: Motor vehicles having at least four wheels, or having three wheels when the maximum weight exceeds 1 metric ton, and used for the carriage of passengers:
  - *Category M1*: Vehicles used for the carriage of passengers and comprising no more than eight seats in addition to the driver's seat;

- *Category M2*: Vehicles used for the carriage of passengers, comprising more than eight seats in addition to the driver's seat, and having a maximum weight not exceeding 5 metric tons;

- *Category M3*: Vehicles used for the carriage of passengers, comprising more than eight seats in addition to the driver's seat, and having a maximum weight exceeding 5 metric tons.

- Category N: Motor vehicles having at least four wheels, or having three wheels when the maximum weight exceeds 1 metric ton, and used for the carriage of goods:

- *Category N1*: Vehicles used for the carriage of goods and having a maximum weight not exceeding 3.75 metric tons;

- *Category N2*: Vehicles used for the carriage of goods and having a maximum weight exceeding 3.75 but not exceeding 12 metric tons;

- *Category N3*: Vehicles used for the carriage of goods and having a maximum weight exceeding 12 metric tons.

- Category O: Trailers (including semi-trailers):

- *Category O1*: Trailers with a maximum weight not exceeding 0.775 metric tons;

- *Category O2*: Trailers with a maximum weight exceeding 0.775 metric tons but not exceeding 3.75 metric tons;

- *Category O3*: Trailers with a maximum weight exceeding 3.75 but not exceeding 10 metric tons;

- *Category O4*: Trailers with a maximum weight exceeding 10 metric tons.

Constructional and Maintenance Requirements

Brakes

All goods vehicles must meet specified braking efficiencies. The regulations state minimum efficiencies for the service brake, for the secondary brake and for the parking brake or handbrake. On pre-1968 vehicles the secondary brake can be the handbrake and on post-1968 vehicles it can be a split or dual system operated by the footbrake. If it is the latter it must be capable of meeting the secondary requirement if part of the dual system fails. The parking brake must achieve the required efficiency by direct mechanical action or by the energy of a spring without the assistance of stored energy.

Every vehicle must have a parking brake system to prevent at least two wheels from turning when it is not being driven. All vehicles first used after 1 January 1968 must have an independent parking brake.

Anti-lock (ie anti-skid) braking systems are required on certain later articulated vehicles and drawbar trailer combinations under EU legislation (for which Category 1 – wheel-by-wheel – systems are necessary) and under British C&U Regulations. The vehicles affected are articulated tractive units and rigid goods vehicles over 16 tonnes equipped to draw trailers and first used from 1 April 1992, and trailers over 10 tonnes built on or after 1 October 1991.

From 1 March 2002 anti-lock braking systems were required to be fitted on all newly registered HGVs over 3.5 tonnes gross weight. Today these ABS systems have been superseded by electronic braking systems (EBS), which are found on most new HGVs produced by the major manufacturers.

Advanced Emergency Braking Systems

The AEBS is a semi-automated braking system designed to help prevent collisions or to limit their consequences. Under EC Regulation 661/2009, there has been a phased-in introduction of AEBS on HGVs, minibuses, buses and coaches. AEBS warn the driver of a possible collision and, if the driver fails to take action, apply the brakes automatically.

Phasing in means:

- Level 1 AEBS systems are required to be fitted to all new HGVs exceeding 8,000 kg gvw from November 2015, fitted with a pneumatic/air or hydraulic braking system and pneumatic rear-axle suspension.

- Level 2 AEBS are required to be fitted to all new HGV types (vehicles launched for the first time) from November 2016 and all new vehicles (vehicles registered for the first time) from November 2018.

Lane departure warning systems must also be fitted to all new HGVs from November 2015.

Specified Braking Efficiencies

Goods vehicles used before 1 January 1968:

Table 12.1   Specified braking efficiencies

Two-axle rigid vehicles	Service brake	45%
	Secondary brake	20%
Multi-axled rigid vehicles, trailer combinations and articulated vehicles	Service brake	40%
	Secondary brake	15%

Goods vehicles first used on or after 1 January 1968:

Table 12.2 Specific braking efficiencies

All vehicles	Service brake	50%
	Secondary brake	25%
	Parking brake must be capable of holding the vehicle on a gradient of at least 1 in 6.25 without the assistance of stored energy (1 in 8.33 with a trailer attached)	16%

Maintenance of Brakes

The braking system on a vehicle, including all of its components and means of operation, must be maintained in good and efficient working order and must be properly adjusted at all times.

Braking Standards

The regulations reflect the requirements for braking standards laid down in EC Directives 320/1973, 524/1975 and 489/1979 (as amended). These call for the fitment of load-sensing valves or anti-lock braking on drive axles – most modern tractive units already comply with these requirements – and the overall emphasis is on stability, eliminating jack-knifing and trailer swing. EU rules permit the use of two-line air braking systems instead of the traditional British three-line systems. Most older tractive units in the UK have three-line braking systems fitted with yellow, blue and red couplings.

Vehicles built to the European standard have only two lines (red and yellow or two black). Coupling three-line tractive units to three-line trailers, two-line tractive units to two-line trailers and two-line tractive units to three-line trailers presents no difficulties. Problems arise when coupling three-line tractive units to two-line trailers. Such combinations must not be used unless they are specially designed or modified by fitting a fourth coupling or internal valves and connecting pipework.

Failsafe Handbrake Alarms

While still not mandatory, these alarms are often fitted as standard by some manufacturers and are also available from several different suppliers. They are available as either electronic alarms or as real-speech alarms.

Anti-Lock Brakes

The following goods vehicles must be fitted with anti-lock brakes:

- Motor vehicles first registered on or after 1 April 1992 with design gross vehicle weight greater than 16,000 kg and authorized to tow trailers with total design axle weight exceeding 10,000 kg.

- Trailers with total design axle weight exceeding 10,000 kg manufactured on or after 1 October 1991.
- New Category N vehicles from 1998 were required to have anti-lock braking fitted as part of their type approval.
- All Category N2 and N3 vehicles and Category O3 and O4 trailers registered from April 2002 were required to have anti-lock braking systems fitted.

Anti-lock systems must conform to Annex 10 of the EU braking directive (Council Directive 71/320/EEC).

A journey in a vehicle with a faulty anti-lock braking system may be completed if the fault arose en route, or the vehicle may be driven to a place where the fault is to be repaired. However, this does not apply if the defective braking system does not meet specified braking efficiency requirements.

Endurance Braking Systems

Endurance braking technology has become a standard fitment to most new vehicles and has developed into sophisticated systems able to stop a loaded vehicle effectively, reduce fuel usage, reduce brake pad wear and reduce general wear and tear on braking system components. Many systems now automatically apply retardation whenever pressure is taken off the accelerator pedal.

Automatic Brake Adjusters

N1 vehicles (light goods vehicles) first used since 1 April 1995 must have automatic brake adjusters on the front axle. All goods vehicles and trailers exceeding 3,500 kg gvw first used since that date are required to be fitted with automatic brake adjusters on all brakes. There are a few limited exceptions for specialized vehicles and electrically powered vans operating at 4,250 kg.

Brakes and Couplings on Trailers

Trailers must be fitted with brakes operating on all wheels which are capable of being applied by the driver of the drawing vehicle and having maximum efficiencies matching the braking requirement for the drawing vehicle, emergency brakes operating on at least two wheels and a parking brake capable of holding the trailer on a gradient of at least 1 in 6.25.

New lightweight trailers (ie weighing not more than 750 kg) made after 1 January 1997 must be fitted with a secondary safety coupling. Such trailers must also be marked with their date of manufacture.

Note: Trailers constructed before 1 January 1968 must have an efficient braking system on half the number of wheels.

Overrun Brakes

Overrun brakes may be fitted to trailers not exceeding 3,500 kg gross weight (or 3,560 kg if made before 27 February 1977). Overrun brake couplings must be damped and matched with the brake linkage. Normally, to ensure that these standards are met, the coupling design needs to be type-approved. Trailer braking efficiency must be at least 45 per cent and the parking brake must be capable of holding the laden trailer on a gradient of 1 in 6.25 (ie 16 per cent). Modern braked trailers must also be fitted with an emergency device (normally operated by a wire) which automatically applies the brakes if the trailer becomes uncoupled from the towing vehicle. This does not apply to single-axle trailers up to 1,500 kg gross weight provided they are fitted with a safety chain or cable to stop the coupling head touching the road if the trailer becomes detached.

Light Trailer Brakes

Light trailers must be fitted with brakes if:

- their maximum gross weight exceeds 750 kg and their unladen weight exceeds 102 kg;
- their maximum gross weight exceeds 750 kg and they were built on or after 1 October 1982;
- their laden weight on the road exceeds half the towing vehicle's kerbside weight (this does not apply to agricultural trailers or to trailers whose unladen weight does not exceed 102 kg and which were built before 1 October 1982).

Parked Trailers

When trailers are detached from the towing vehicle, they must be prevented from rolling by means of a brake, chain or chock applied to at least one of their wheels.

Braking Coils

Braking coils to ISO 7638 standard (standards for trailer connectors) must be used when both drawing vehicle and trailer are fitted with suitable electrical connections. A prohibition notice will be issued where these coils are found unconnected in roadside checks.

Exhaust Emissions

European emission standards define the acceptable limits for exhaust emissions of new vehicles sold in the EU and EEA member states. Since 1 April 1991, newly registered diesel HGVs have been required to comply with EC Directive 88/77, which sets gaseous emission (ie exhaust emission) limits (see Chapter 21 for details of emission requirements for fleet cars and light vans). These limits are applied in type-approval regulations to vehicles first used from 1 April 1991 (later for cars/vans with engines over 1,400 cc and those with diesel engines).

The purpose of the EU's legislative programme (under EC Directive 91/542) was to reduce the amount of nitrogen oxide (NO_x), carbon monoxide (CO) and unburned hydrocarbons (HC) blown into the atmosphere from vehicle exhausts. The first stage of this programme (ie the Euro-I standard) applied to all new type-approved goods vehicles from 1 July 1992 (and to earlier type-approved vehicles from 1 October 1993). Tougher Euro-II standards applied to new vehicles over 3.5 tonnes gvw from 1 October 1996, and progressively more stringent emission controls have applied since 1 October 2000. Euro-IV limits have been in force since 1 October 2005. The Euro-V standard came into force from 1 October 2008. Euro VI has applied since 1 January 2014.

The following table indicates the relevant emissions standards with the date of implementation and the emissions and smoke limits.

Current standards for new vehicles are:

- Euro 6 for cars and vans;
- Euro VI for HGVs and PSVs.

Table 12.3   Emissions standards

Tier	Date	CO	HC	NO_x	PM	Smoke
Euro IV	10.2005	1.5	0.46	3.5	0.02	0.5
Euro V	10.2008	1.5	0.46	2.0	0.02	0.5
Euro VI	01.2014	1.5	0.13	0.4	0.01	–

Vehicle users are required by law to keep the engine of their vehicle and any emission control equipment (ie catalytic converter) in good working order and in tune.

Euro-VI Standard

The **Euro-VI** requirement applies from 31 December 2012 for new types of vehicles and from 31 December 2013 for all new registered vehicles. It seeks to achieve a halving of particle emissions from the previous Euro-V standard of 0.02 g/kWh to a maximum of 0.01 g/kWh and a reduction in nitrogen oxide (NO_x) of some 77 per cent. These reductions are important because they are the component gases of the exhaust emission that do most harm both to people and to the atmosphere, plus, of course, there are the emissions of unburnt hydrocarbons (reduced to 0.13 for Euro VI from 0.46 for Euro V) and carbon monoxide (a greenhouse gas). As a notable point, they are also the gases that most town and city authorities target when considering low-emission solutions, and the Euro-VI standard is normally a prerequisite for vehicles hoping to enter such zones. In addition, some ECMT permits will be limited to vehicles able to meet Euro-VI emission standards (see Chapter 25).

To put these reductions into context, information disseminated by Volvo Trucks via the internet shows that, whereas the environmental footprint of exhaust emissions for a Euro-I diesel engine in 1993 equated roughly to the area of a tennis court, the exhaust emissions for a Euro-VI diesel engine will equate to the miniscule area of a postage stamp. The technology needed to achieve this reduction involves the use of existing exhaust gas recirculation (EGR) systems combined with selective catalyst reduction (SCR) technology, together with variable geometry turbo-charging, a diesel particulate filter and an ammonium slip catalyst to effect a further clean-up of NO_x emissions at the tailpipe.

Emissions Developments

The Euro-VI standards saw the legislation change from an EU Directive to an EU Regulation and it is expected that this will remain a regulatory standard for future UK domestic legislation, thereby aligning the UK standards with those of the EU in order to reduce possible 'incompatibility' problems when UK vehicles are operating in Europe. However, the EU Commission dropped the idea of proposing Euro VII at the same time as Euro VI but the drive towards reduced emissions will continue.

EGR v SCR

For vehicles to achieve the Euro-IV standard from 1 October 2005 and Euro V from 1 October 2008, necessary for all vehicles over 7.5 tonnes gross weight, operators have needed to choose between two technologies: EGR, which requires no additions to either engine or silencer box, or SCR, which achieves its effect through the addition of a chemical substance generally called 'AdBlue'. Current opinion suggests that EGR is preferable because it is cheaper, has no additional maintenance, has an absence of moving parts and is a proven technology. AdBlue is a synthetic urea solution which, when used with SCR engine technology, converts exhaust pollutants (mainly nitrogen oxides and particles) into water vapour and harmless nitrogen. It requires intervention from the driver, by way of regular topping up of the AdBlue tank, otherwise the engine will run at reduced power. It also relies on the driver being able to source AdBlue when away from base.

Euro VI and EGR/SCR

By way of an example of manufacturers meeting the tough Euro-VI emission standard, in some of its most developed engines Swedish manufacturer Scania uses the vehicle's existing EGR system and is also using variable geometry turbo-charging, a diesel particulate filter, SCR and an ammonium slip catalyst to clean up exhaust emissions. The new engines are designed to give the same performance and fuel efficiency as their older Euro-V counterparts. These engines, Scania says, make it possible for operators to take the next step and invest in the greenest technology available. This enables them to benefit from lower motorway charges and other incentives that may be introduced by the authorities and also commands a higher second-hand value on resale.

On-Board Diagnostic Equipment

All heavy diesel-engine vehicles complying with Euro-IV, Euro-V and Euro-VI emissions standards must be fitted with on-board diagnostics (OBD) or on-board management (OBM) equipment to monitor their emissions performance. If this diagnostic equipment fails or it records a malfunction in the emissions system, the vehicle can only be operated at very much reduced power levels.

Local Authority Emissions Testing

Throughout the UK, local authorities are empowered to operate roadside emissions testing schemes under section 83 of the Environment Act 1995. Drivers of vehicles that fail the test are issued with a prohibition notice giving them 10 days to fix the problem and (usually) a fixed penalty notice requiring payment of £60, rising to £90 if unpaid within 28 days. The test levels are the same as those that vehicles would be expected to meet at annual test. The scheme covers all types of vehicles, including commercial vehicles, but excludes hybrid engines, three-wheeled vehicles and two-stroke engines.

Smoke

Vehicles must not emit smoke, visible vapour, grit, sparks, ashes, cinders or oily substances that might cause damage to property or injury or danger to any person.

Excess Fuel Devices

Excess fuel devices must not be used on diesel vehicles while the vehicle is in motion. Such devices are incorporated in the vehicle fuel pump to enable extra fuel to be fed to the engine to aid cold-starting. Their use when the engine is warm slightly increases the power of the engine, but in doing so black smoke is emitted from the exhaust. For this reason their use is forbidden while the vehicle is in motion. These devices are not now commonly found on modern diesel engines with improved fuel management technology.

Smoke Opacity Limits

Diesel-engined vehicles first used after 1 April 1973 (but not manufactured before 1 October 1972) must comply with smoke opacity limits specified in BS AU 141a/1971. Engines fitted to such vehicles must be of a type for which a type test certificate in accordance with the British Standard Specification for 'The Performance of Diesel Engines for Road Vehicles' has been issued by the Secretary of State. The certificate indicates that engines of that type do not exceed the emission of smoke limits set out in the BS Specification.

Offences

It is an offence to use a vehicle to which this type test applies if the fuel injection equipment, the engine speed governor or other parts of the engine have been altered or adjusted in such a way that the smoke emission of the vehicle is increased. An offence is committed if a vehicle emits black smoke or other substances even without alteration or adjustment of the parts (eg as a result of lack of maintenance). The DVSA has promised tougher enforcement of goods vehicle smoke emissions, particularly at the time of submitting vehicles for annual test, and operators are encouraged to use Euro-VI standard vehicles if at all possible.

Control of Fumes

Petrol-engined vehicles first used after 1 January 1972 must be fitted with a means of preventing crankcase gases escaping into the atmosphere except through the exhaust system.

Fuel Tanks

Vehicle fuel tanks must be constructed so as to prevent any leakage or spillage of fuel. In particular, there is concern about leakage from heavy vehicle fuel tanks onto the road, where it causes exceptional danger to cyclists, motorcyclists and other road users. Checking the fuel tank filler cap seal is now included as a part of many drivers' daily checks.

NB: Drivers operating internationally are also advised to check the tank by opening the filler cap in order to ensure that no drugs/packages have been lowered into the tank prior to border crossings.

Failure to maintain diesel fuel tanks in good condition (and especially filler caps) is now an offence in its own right and gives the police the opportunity to prosecute without having to actually observe spillage from the tank. Fines of up to £2,000 could be imposed on conviction for such offences.

Vehicles first used since 1 July 1973 and manufactured since 1 February 1973 that are propelled by petrol engines must have metal fuel tanks fitted in a position to avoid damage and prevent leakage. This provision does not apply where the vehicle complies with relevant EU regulations (EC 221/70) and is marked accordingly.

Ground Clearance for Trailers

Minimum ground clearances are specified for goods-carrying trailers manufactured since 1 April 1984. Such trailers must have a minimum ground clearance of 160 mm if they have an axle interspace of more than 6 metres and not more than 11.5 metres. If the interspace is more than 11.5 metres, the minimum clearance is 190 mm.

Measurement of the axle interspace is taken from the point of support on the tractive unit in the case of semi-trailers or the centre line of the front axle, and in other cases to the centre line of the rear axle or the centre point between rear axles if there is more than one.

In determining the minimum ground clearance, no account should be taken of any part of the suspension, steering or braking system attached to any axle, any wheel and any air skirt. Measurement of the ground clearance is taken in the area formed by the width of the trailer and the middle 70 per cent of the axle interspace.

Horn

All vehicles with a maximum speed exceeding 20 mph, except works trucks and passenger-controlled vehicles, must be equipped with an audible warning instrument. The sound emitted by a horn must be continuous and uniform and not strident. Gongs, bells, sirens and two-tone horns are only permitted on emergency vehicles, though a concession allows similar instruments, except two-tone horns, to be used on vehicles from which goods are sold to announce the presence of the vehicle to the public. Any vehicle first used since 1 August 1973 must not be fitted with multi-toned or musical horns.

Restriction on Sounding Horns

Audible warning instruments must not be sounded at any time while the vehicle is stationary or in a built-up area (ie where a 30 mph speed restriction is in force) between 11.30 pm and 7.00 am (see also the Reversing Alarms section found later in this chapter). The use of the horn on a stationary vehicle in an emergency situation (ie 'at times of danger due to another, moving vehicle on or near the road') is allowed.

Horns Used as Anti-Theft Devices

Audible warning instruments that are gongs, bells or sirens may be used to prevent theft or attempted theft of a vehicle provided a device is fitted that will stop the warning sounding continuously for more than five minutes. Hazard lights and interior lights may be set to operate continuously for (a maximum of) five minutes if the vehicle is tampered with.

Mirrors

Goods vehicles and dual-purpose vehicles must be fitted with at least two mirrors. One of these must be fitted externally on the offside and the other must, in the case of vehicles first used since 1 June 1978, be fitted in the driver's cab or driving compartment. When an interior mirror does not provide an adequate view to the rear, a mirror must be fitted externally on the nearside. The mirrors must show traffic to the rear or on both sides rearwards. Mirrors fitted to vehicles over 3,500 kg must conform to at least Class II and those fitted to other vehicles to Class II or III, as described in EC Directive 2003/97/EC. Since 2012 it has been compulsory for all LGVs to be fitted with 'Cyclops mirrors', which are front-facing mirrors, to eliminate the driver's blind spot directly in front of the vehicle. These Class-VI mirrors are now fitted to all new HGVs over 7,500 kg.

Definitions for Classes of Mirrors

Classes of mirrors are defined in EC Directive 2003/97/EC as follows:

- Class I – being an interior rear-view mirror;
- Classes II and III – being main exterior rear-view mirrors;
- Class IV – being a wide-angle exterior mirror;
- Class V – being a close-proximity exterior mirror;
- Class VI – being a front mirror (ie one that gives a view across the front of the vehicle).

In all these cases, very specific and detailed indirect fields of vision are prescribed and illustrated in the Directive.

Mirrors can be conventional mirrors, camera monitors or other devices able to present information about the indirect field of vision to the driver.

Fitment of Mirrors

Type-approved external mirrors with a bottom edge less than 2 metres from the ground (when the vehicle is loaded) must not project more than 20 cm beyond the overall width of the vehicle or vehicle and trailer. Mirrors fitted on the offside must be adjustable from the driving seat unless they are of the spring-back type. Type-approved internal mirrors fitted to vehicles first registered on or after 1978 must be framed with material (usually plastic beading) which will reduce the risk of cuts to any passenger who may be thrown against the mirror.

Close-Proximity and Wide-Angle Mirrors

Goods vehicles over 12 tonnes maximum permissible weight first used since 1 October 1988 must be fitted with additional mirrors that provide close-proximity and wide-angle vision for the driver in accordance with EC Directives 205/85 and 562/86.

Since January 2007 all new trucks have required more mirrors as a result of two EU Directives (ie Directive 2003/97/EC as amended by Directive 2005/27/EC). Besides the existing requirements described in this section:

- vehicles between 3.5 tonnes and 7.5 tonnes gross weight need two Class-IV (wide-angle) mirrors and a Class-V (close-proximity) mirror;
- vehicles between 7.5 tonnes and 12 tonnes gross weight need two Class-IV (wide-angle) mirrors, a Class-V (close-proximity) mirror and a Class-VI (front) mirror;
- heavy vehicles over 12 tonnes gross weight need additional Class-IV (wide-angle) and Class-V (close-proximity) mirrors plus a Class-VI (front) mirror.

Safety Glass

Goods vehicles must be fitted with safety glass (ie toughened or laminated glass which, when fractured, does not fly into fragments likely to cause severe cuts) for windscreens and windows in front of and on either side of the driver's seat. The windscreen and all windows of dual-purpose vehicles must be fitted with safety glass. Glass bearing an approval mark under EC Directive 92/22 is regarded as meeting the requirement stated above for safety glass.

The glass must be maintained so as not to obscure the vision of the driver while the vehicle is being driven on the road. This means that a driver could be prosecuted for having a severely misted-up, iced-up or otherwise dirty windscreen.

Seat Belts

Seat belts for the driver and one front-seat passenger must be fitted to goods vehicles not exceeding 1,525 kg unladen registered since 1 April 1967 and goods vehicles not exceeding 3,500 kg gross weight first used since 1 April 1980. From 1 October 1988 goods vehicles over 3,500 kg must be fitted with seat-belt anchorage points for each forward-facing seat to which lap-strap-type seat belts can be fixed (see Chapter 10 for details of seat-belt fitment requirements in fleet cars).

Since 1 March 2001 seat belts have been required by law to be fitted in new goods vehicles over 3.5 tonnes gross weight (although many new vehicles were fitted with seat belts by manufacturers on a voluntary basis long before this date).

Vehicles to which this regulation applies, first used since 1 April 1973, must be fitted with belts that can be secured and released with one hand only and also with a device to enable the belts to be stowed in a position where they do not touch the floor. Vehicles to which this requirement applies will fail the annual test if seat belts are not fitted, are permanently obstructed or are not in good condition.

Sideguards

Most heavy vehicles and trailers must be fitted with sideguards to comply with legal requirements, except for certain vehicles and trailers that are exempt from the fitting requirement as listed at the end of this section.

Sideguards must be fitted to the following vehicles and trailers:

- goods vehicles exceeding 3.5 tonnes maximum gross weight manufactured since 1 October 1983 and first used since 1 April 1984;

- trailers exceeding 1,020 kg unladen weight manufactured since 1 May 1983 and which, in the case of semi-trailers, have a distance between the foremost axle and the centre line of the kingpin (or rearmost kingpin if there is more than one) exceeding 4.5 metres (Figure 12.1);

- semi-trailers made before 1 May 1983 with a gross weight exceeding 26,000 kg and used in an articulated combination with a gross train weight exceeding 32,520 kg.

Figure 12.1 Measurements of relevant distance between foremost axle and centre of kingpin for semi-trailers to determine if sideguards must be fitted

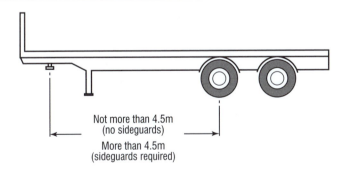

Not more than 4.5m
(no sideguards)

More than 4.5m
(sideguards required)

NB: The IVA type-approval scheme takes the definition of 'unprotected road users' from Directive 89/297/EEC and enforces the need for sideguards that protect these users (cyclists, pedestrians, motorcyclists) from falling under the sides of the vehicle to be caught in the wheels of the vehicle.

In line with the London Safer Lorry Scheme covered in Chapter 10, the sideguard requirement for sliding bogie/extendible trailers (trombones) only applies to when they are in the non-extended (closed) position. Sideguards are not required on vehicles and trailers, other than semi-trailers, where the distance between any two consecutive (ie front and rear) axles is less than 3 metres (Figure 12.2).

Figure 12.2   Measurements of two consecutive axles on drawbar trailers – the same dimension applies to rigid vehicles – to determine if sideguards must be fitted

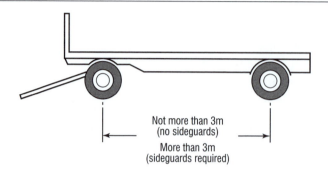

Not more than 3m
(no sideguards)
More than 3m
(sideguards required)

Strength of Sideguards

Sideguards must be constructed so they are capable of withstanding a force of 200 kg (2 kilonewtons) over their length, apart from the rear 250 mm, without deflecting more than 150 mm. Over the last 250 mm the deflection must not be more than 30 mm under such force (Figure 12.3). These force resistance requirements *do not* apply where sideguards were fitted to existing semi-trailers (ie those built before 1 May 1985, and which were used at weights above 32,520 kg).

Figure 12.3   How force resistance applies to sideguard on new vehicles and trailers (it does not apply to sideguard fitted to existing semi-trailers)

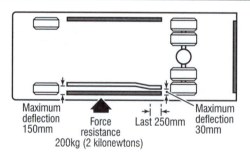

Maximum
deflection
150mm
Force
resistance
200kg (2 kilonewtons)
Last 250mm
Maximum
deflection
30mm

Fitment of Sideguards

The fitting position for sideguards depends on the type of vehicle or trailer as follows:

- Rigid vehicles: at front – not more than 300 mm behind the edge of the nearest tyre and the foremost edge of the sideguard; at rear – not more than 300 mm behind the rearmost edge of the sideguard and the edge of the nearest tyre (Figure 12.4).

Figure 12.4 Fitting position for sideguard on rigid vehicles

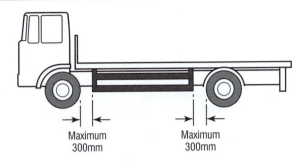

- Trailers: at front – not more than 500 mm behind the edge of the nearest tyre and the foremost edge of the sideguard; at rear – not more than 300 mm behind the rearmost edge of the sideguard and the edge of the nearest tyre (Figure 12.5).

Figure 12.5 Fitting position for sideguard on trailers

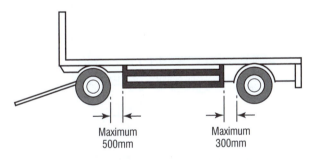

- Semi-trailers with landing legs: at front – not more than 250 mm behind the centre line of the landing legs and the foremost edge of the sideguard; at rear – not more than 300 mm behind the rearmost edge of the sideguard and the edge of the nearest tyre (Figure 12.6).

Figure 12.6 Fitting position for sideguard on semi-trailers with landing legs

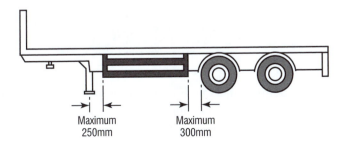

- Semi-trailer without landing legs: at front – not more than 3 metres behind the centre line of the rearmost kingpin and the foremost edge of the sideguard; at rear – not more than 300 mm behind the rearmost edge of the sideguard and the edge of the nearest tyre (Figure 12.7).

Figure 12.7 Fitting position for sideguard on semi-trailers without landing legs

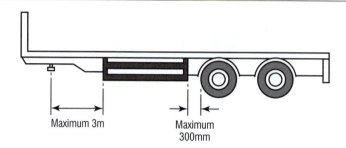

Maximum 3m   Maximum 300mm

In all cases sideguards must be fitted so they are not inset more than 30 mm from the external face of the tyre, excluding any distortion due to the weight of the vehicle (Figure 12.8).

Figure 12.8 Inboard mounting position for sideguards – all vehicles and trailers

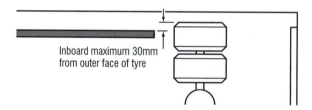

Inboard maximum 30mm from outer face of tyre

The upper edge of sideguards must be positioned as follows:

- In the case of vehicles or trailers with a body or structure that is wider than the tyres, no more than 350 mm from the lower edge of the body or structure (Figure 12.9).

Figure 12.9 Fitting position for sideguards where body or structure is wider than the tyres

Maximum 350mm

Maximum 550mm

- In the case of vehicles or trailers with a body or structure that is narrower than the tyres or that does not extend outwards immediately above the wheels, a vertical plane taken from the outer face of the tyre must be measured upwards for

1.85 metres above the ground. If this plane is dissected by the vehicle structure within 1.85 metres from the ground, the sideguard must extend up to within 350 mm of the structure where it is cut by the vertical plane (Figure 12.11); if the vertical plane is not dissected by the vehicle structure, the upper edge of the sideguard must extend to be level with the top of the vehicle structure to a minimum height of 1.5 metres from the ground (Figure 12.10).

Figure 12.10   Fitting position for sideguards where body or structure is narrower than the tyres up to a height of 1.85 metres

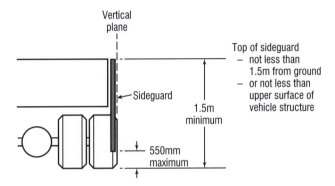

The lower edge of sideguards must not be more than 550 mm from the ground. This dimension is to be measured on level ground and, in the case of a semi-trailer, when its load platform is horizontal.

Figure 12.11   Fitting position for sideguards where body or structure is narrower than the tyres

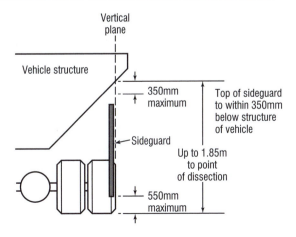

When sideguards are to be fitted to extendible trailers and to vehicles and trailers designed to carry demountable bodies or containers, the following fitting provisions apply:

- Sideguards must be fitted to extendible trailers in compliance with the original fitting specifications in regard to spacings from the nearest wheel, kingpin or landing leg when the trailer is at its shortest length. When the trailer is extended beyond its minimum length, the spacings between the front edge of the sideguard and the semi-trailer landing legs or kingpin (if it has no landing legs) and the rear edge of the sideguard and the foremost edge of the tyre nearest to it are no longer applicable.
- Sideguards must be fitted to vehicles and trailers that are designed and constructed (not merely adapted) to carry demountable bodies or containers so that when the body or container is removed the sideguards remain in place.

This means that if the vehicle runs without a body or container, it must still comply with the sideguard requirements.

Vehicles that are fitted with sideguards complying with EC Directive 89/279 do not have to comply with the fitting requirements specified in the UK regulations as detailed above.

Construction of Sideguards

All parts of the sideguard that face outwards must be 'smooth, essentially rigid and either flat or horizontally corrugated'. Each face of the guard must be a minimum of 100 mm wide (including the inward face at the forward edge) and the vertical gaps between the bars must not be more than 300 mm wide.

Maintenance of Sideguards

Sideguards must be maintained free of any obvious defect that would impair their effectiveness. It is important to ensure that the fitting dimensions are observed, particularly when the sideguards are damaged (eg by forklift truck impact).

Exemption to Fitting Dimensions

The specific requirements relating to the fitting positions for sideguards as previously described only apply so far as is practicable in the case of the following vehicles and trailers:

- those designed solely for the carriage of a fluid substance in closed tanks permanently fitted to the vehicle and provided with valves and hose or pipe connections for loading and unloading;

- those vehicles that require additional stability during loading and unloading or while working and which are fitted with extendible stabilizers on either side (eg lorry-mounted cranes, tower wagons, inspection platforms).

Exemptions

Sideguards do not have to be fitted to vehicles and trailers in the following list:

- vehicles incapable of a speed of more than 15 mph on the level under their own power;
- agricultural trailers;
- engineering plant;
- fire engines;
- land tractors;
- side- and end-tipping vehicles and trailers;
- vehicles with no bodywork fitted and being driven or towed for the purposes of a quality or safety check by the manufacturer, distributor or dealer in such vehicles, or being driven by prior arrangement to have bodywork fitted;
- vehicles being driven or towed to a place by prior arrangement to have sideguards fitted;
- vehicles designed solely for use in connection with street cleansing, the collection or disposal of refuse or the collection or disposal of the contents of gullies or cesspools;
- trailers specially designed and constructed to carry round timber, beams or girders of exceptional length;
- articulated tractive units;
- naval, military or air-force vehicles;
- trailers specially designed and constructed (not merely adapted) to carry other vehicles loaded from the front or rear (eg car transporters);
- temporarily imported foreign semi-trailers;
- low-loader trailers where:
  - the upper surface of the load platform is not more than 750 mm from the ground; and
  - no part of the edge of the load platform is more than 60 mm inboard from the external face of the tyre (discounting the distortion caused by the weight of the vehicle).

Note the possible requirement in order to comply with the London Safer Lorry Scheme (as mentioned previously).

Silencer

An adequate means of silencing exhaust noise and of preventing exhaust gases escaping into the atmosphere without first passing through a silencer must be fitted to all vehicles. Silencers must be maintained in good and efficient working order and must not be altered so as to increase the noise made by the escape of exhaust gases.

Speedometer

Speedometers (and/or tachographs, as appropriate – see Chapter 5) must be fitted to all vehicles registered since 1 October 1937 except those that cannot or are not permitted to travel at more than 25 mph, agricultural vehicles that are not driven at more than 20 mph and works trucks first used before 1 April 1984. In the case of vehicles first used since 1 April 1984, the speedometer must indicate speed in both miles per hour and kilometres per hour. The instrument, either mechanical or electronic, must be maintained in good working order at all material times and kept free from any obstruction that might prevent it being easily read.

Defence

It is a defence to be able to show that a defect to a speedometer or a tachograph occurred during the journey when the offence was detected or that at that time steps had been taken to get the defect repaired with all reasonable expedition (ie as soon as reasonably practicable). In relation to tachographs, the defect must be rectified within seven days and if the vehicle is not expected to return to base within that time the repair must be undertaken en route.

Speed Limiters

In a move to reduce the number and severity of road accidents, legislation requires certain heavy vehicles to be fitted with speed limiters. The EU requires certain vehicles also to be fitted with speed limiters set to a maximum of 90 kph (approx 56 mph).

The UK regulations, which came into effect on 1 August 1992, limited relevant vehicles to a maximum speed of 60 mph (ie 96.5 kph). They applied to all new goods vehicles exceeding 7.5 tonnes permissible maximum weight that were capable of a speed in excess of 60 mph on the flat and which were first registered on or after 1 August 1992.

Some operators have reduced the set maximum speed to 50 mph for vehicles operating in the urban cycle or on relatively local work. In a similar way, some van operators have also voluntarily fitted speed limiters to delivery vans.

Vehicles not capable of travelling at or above 60 mph (eg some highway maintenance vehicles) are exempt from the regulations, as are the following vehicles:

- those being taken to a place to have a speed-limiter device fitted or calibrated;
- those owned and being used by the army, navy or air force;
- those being used for military purposes while driven by a person under military orders;
- those being used for fire brigade, ambulance or police purposes;
- those exempt from excise duty because they do not travel more than six miles per week on public roads.

Speed-limiter equipment must comply with BS AU 217 (or some acceptable equivalent), be calibrated to a set speed not exceeding 60 mph and be sealed by an 'authorized sealer'.

Speed limiters must be maintained in good working order, though it is a defence to show that where a vehicle is driven with a defective limiter, the defect occurred during that journey or that at the time it is being driven to a place for the limiter to be repaired.

EU Requirements

The speed-limiter requirements of EC Directive 92/6/EEC apply from 1 January 1994 and require new goods vehicles first registered from this date and which exceed 12 tonnes gvw to be fitted with speed limiters. Speed limiters should be set at a speed of not more than 85 kph (52.8 mph), allowing a stabilized speed of not more than 90 kph (56.0 mph). An extension to the regulations in 2007 saw goods vehicles first used on or after 1 October 2001 up to and including 31 December 2004, exceeding 3.5 tonnes, also brought into scope. Speed limiters for these vehicles needed to be set at 90 kph (56 mph) and goods vehicles exceeding 7.5 tonnes gvw up to 12 tonnes gvw were required to have their speed limiters re-set at 90 kph from 100 kph. It is unlikely that the UK will change these current requirements.

Speed Limiter Plates

Vehicles that are required to be fitted with speed limiter equipment must carry a plate (fitted in a conspicuous and readily accessible position in the vehicle cab) on which are shown the words:

- 'SPEED LIMITER FITTED' (in large letters at the top);
- the Standard with which the installation complies (eg BS AU 217 Part 1A 1987);
- the speed setting in mph/kph;
- the vehicle registration number;

- the name/trademark of the firm which carried out the calibration;
- the place where the speed limiter was fitted and the date of fitment.

Plates that referred to a maximum speed of 56 mph had to be changed (as of 1 September 1997) to show 85 kph.

Speed Limiters for Larger Vans and Light Trucks

Since 1 January 2007, all HGVs fitted with Euro-III engines and first registered from 1 October 2001 to 31 December 2004 should have been fitted with a speed limiter calibrated to a maximum speed not exceeding 56 mph (90 kph). Euro-III vehicles already have the facility to have a top-speed limiter built into the engine electronic control unit, thus ensuring that the calibration procedure does not involve the fitment of brackets, air cylinders or piping.

The same date, 1 January 2007, was also the date from which any vehicle over 3.5 tonnes gvw has been prohibited from using the outside lane of a motorway with three or more lanes.

Spray Suppression

Regulations require certain vehicles and trailers to be equipped with anti-spray devices. The following vehicles and trailers must be fitted with approved equipment from the date shown:

- N2: Motor vehicles for transporting goods with a maximum mass exceeding 7.5 tonnes.
- N3: Motor vehicles for transporting goods with a maximum mass exceeding 12 tonnes.
- O3: Trailers and semi-trailers with a maximum mass between 3.5 and 10 tonnes.
- O4: Trailers and semi-trailers with a maximum mass exceeding 10 tonnes.

These requirements came into force with effect from 9 April 2011.

Exemptions

Anti-spray requirements do not apply to those vehicles and trailers that are fitted with such devices in accordance with EC Directive 91/226 (and marked accordingly) and to those that are exempt under the C&U Regulations from the need for wings. Further exemptions are as follows:

- four-wheel- and multi-wheel-drive vehicles;
- vehicles with a minimum of 400 mm (approx 16 in) ground clearance in the middle 80 per cent of the width and the overall length of the vehicle;

- works trucks;
- works trailers;
- broken-down vehicles;
- vehicles that cannot exceed 30 mph on the level under their own power owing to their construction;
- vehicles specified in regulations as exempt from sideguards:
  - agricultural trailers and implements;
  - engineering plant;
  - fire engines;
  - side and end tippers;
  - military vehicles used for military, naval or air-force purposes;
  - vehicles with no bodywork fitted being driven on road test or being driven by prior appointment to a place where bodywork is to be fitted or for delivery;
  - vehicles used for street cleansing, or the collection or disposal of the contents of gullies or cesspools;
  - trailers designed and constructed to carry round timber, beams or girders of exceptional length;
  - temporarily imported foreign semi-trailers;
- concrete mixers;
- vehicles being driven to a place by prior arrangement to have anti-spray equipment fitted;
- land locomotives, land tractors and land implement conveyors;
- trailers forming part of an articulated vehicle or part of a combination of vehicles having, in either case, a total laden weight exceeding 46,000 kg.

British Standard

In order to comply with the law, relevant vehicles and trailers must be fitted with anti-spray systems that fall into one of two main categories:

- a straight valance across the top of the wheel and a flap hanging vertically behind the wheel, all made from approved spray-suppressant material;
- a semi-circular valance following the curvature of the wheel, with either:
  - air/water separator material round the edge;
  - a flap of spray-suppressant material hanging from the rear edge.

Spray-Suppressant Material

Two types of material are referred to in the Standard. These are generally identifiable as follows:

- spray-suppressant material – designed to absorb or dissipate the energy of water thrown up from the tyre in order to reduce the degree to which water shatters into fine droplets on hitting a surface;
- air/water separator – 'a device forming part of the valance and/or wheel flap which permits air to flow through while reducing the emission of spray'.

Maintenance of Anti-Spray Equipment and Devices

The regulations stipulate that all devices fitted to comply with the legal requirement (and every part of such a device) must be maintained, when the vehicle is on the road, so that they are free from 'any obvious defect which would be likely to affect adversely the effectiveness of the device'. It is also important that fitting dimensions are maintained, especially if the flaps are damaged.

Fitment – Valances and Flaps

Where the choice is for spray suppression to be achieved by the use of valances and flaps (particularly on rear vehicle wheels and trailer wheels), the specific requirements for fitment are as follows:

- Valances of spray-suppressant material must extend across the top of the tyre from a line vertical with the front edge of the tyre (A) to a line beyond the rear wheel which will allow the rear flap to be suspended no more than 300 mm from the rear edge of the tyre (B). The valance must be at least 100 mm deep (C).

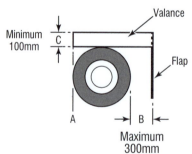

- The valance must extend downwards to be level with the top of the tyre (D) or it may overlap the top of the tyre (E).

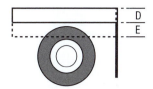

- In the case of multiple-axle bogies the relevant dimensions are shown below with the additional requirement that where the gap between the rear edge of the front tyre and the front edge of the rear tyre is greater than 250 mm (F), a flap must be fitted between the two. No middle flap is required if the distance does not exceed 250 mm.

NB: *The top of the valance may be in two separate sections (see shaded part) so long as it otherwise conforms to the dimensions.*

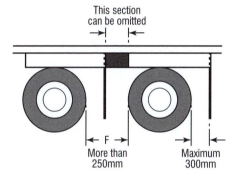

- Valances must extend the full width of the tyre and beyond to a maximum of 75 mm (G) in the case of the rear wheels (non-steerable) and 100 mm (H) in the case of steered wheels.

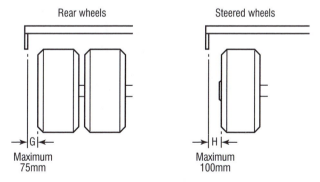

If the valance extends below the level of the tyre on fixed wheels, the gap between the tyre face and the valance can be extended to 100 mm (J). There must be no gaps between the valance and the vehicle body.

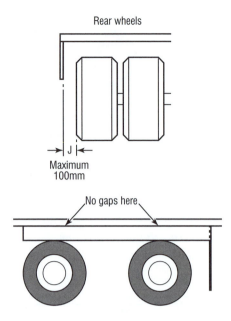

- Flaps used in conjunction with valances as described above must conform to the following dimensions:
  - They must extend to the full width of the tyre/tyres (K).
  - They must reach down to within 200 mm of the ground (L) when the vehicle is unladen (300 mm on rearmost axles of trailers used on roll-on/roll-off ferries or on any axle where the radial distance of the lower edge of the valancing does not exceed the radius of the tyres fitted).

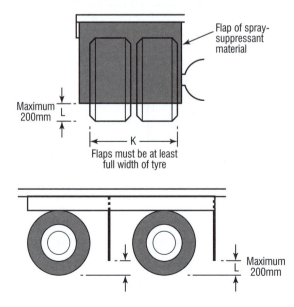

- When flaps are used in conjunction with mudguard valances the top of the flap must extend upwards at least to a point 100 mm above the centre line of the wheel irrespective of the position of the lower edge of the mudguard.

- Where the flap extends inside the guard it must be at least the width of the tyre tread pattern.

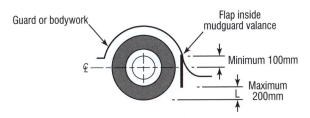

Flap used in conjunction with mudguard valance

- If the flap used is of a type with an air/water separator device (ie bristles) fitted to the bottom edge, the following dimensions apply:

  - Rear edge of tyre to flap – maximum distance 200 mm (M).

  - The edge of the device must come to within 200 mm of the ground (N).

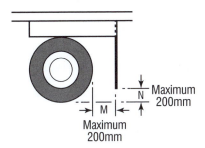

Deflection of Flaps

Wheel flaps must not be capable of being deflected rearwards more than 100 mm when subjected to a force of 3N (ie 4 lb) applied near the bottom of the flap.

Fitment – Mudguards and Air/Water Separator Devices

Where the choice for compliance with the regulations is by means of conventional mudguarding, there are specific dimensions to be observed:

- If the mudguard is covering a steerable wheel (see later note about steerable axles on drawbar trailers), the radius of the edge of the valance must be not more than 1.5 times the radius of the tyre measured at three points (P) and in the case of non-steerable wheels, 1.25 times the same radius:

- vertically above the centre of the tyre;

- a point at the front of the tyre 20 degrees above the horizontal centre line of the tyre (non-steerable wheels) or a point 30 degrees above the horizontal centre line of the tyre (steerable wheels);

- a point at the rear of the tyre 100 mm above the horizontal centre line of the tyre.

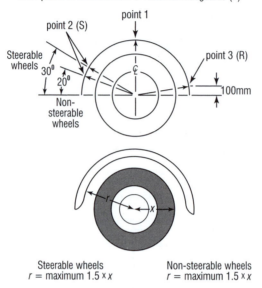

Three points of measurement of radial for mudguards (P)

Steerable wheels
r = maximum 1.5 × x

Non-steerable wheels
r = maximum 1.5 × x

- Mudguard valances must be at least 45 mm deep behind a point vertically above the wheel centre. They may reduce in depth forward of this point (Q).

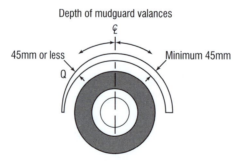

Depth of mudguard valances

- In the case of drawbar trailers and rear-steer trailers, the 1.5 times radius dimension applies as above for the front steerable axle or rear steering axle unless the mudguards are fitted to the turntable and/or can turn with the wheels, in which case the maximum radius for the valance is 1.25 times the tyre radius.

- If the valancing on fixed wheel mudguards is provided by means of air/water separator material (ie bristles), the edge must follow the periphery of the tyre. On steerable wheels the edge must be not more than 1.05 times the tyre radius.

- The valances on mudguards must extend downwards at the front and rear to at least the following dimensions:
  - at rear – to within 100 mm above the centre line of the axle (point 3) (R);
  - at front – to within a line 20 degrees above the centre line of the axle. In the case of steerable wheels this dimension is raised to 30 degrees (point 2) (S).

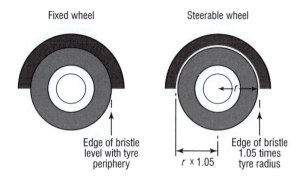

Fixed wheel

Steerable wheel

Edge of bristle level with tyre periphery

r × 1.05

Edge of bristle 1.05 times tyre radius

- In the case of multi-mudguarding over tandem axles or bogies, the intersection of the guards between the wheels must conform to one of the two dimensions:
  - the gap between the guards at the valance edges must not exceed 60 mm; or
  - the edges must come down to within 150 mm of the horizontal centre line across the wheels.
- If the gap between the tyre edges is greater than 250 mm, a flap must be provided between the wheels. If the gap is more than 300 mm, the wheels should be treated as though separate for mudguarding purposes.

Notes

- All dimensions in the regulations are to be taken when the vehicle is unladen, when steerable wheels are straight ahead and when the load platforms of articulated semi-trailers are level.
- All suppression material or devices and air/water separator material or devices must be permanently and legibly marked with the following mark: BS AU 200/2, plus 'the name, trademark or other means of identification of the responsible manufacturer'.

Tyres

It is an offence to use, or cause or permit to be used on a road, a vehicle or a trailer with a pneumatic tyre which is unsuitable for the use to which the vehicle is being put. It is also an offence to have different types of tyres fitted to opposite wheels of the vehicle or trailer; for example, radial-ply tyres must not be fitted to a wheel on the same axle as wheels already fitted with cross-ply tyres and vice versa. Tyres must be inflated to the vehicle or tyre manufacturers' recommended pressures so as to be fit for the use to which the vehicle is being put (for example, motorway work or cross-country work). No tyre must have a break in its fabric or a cut deep enough to reach the body cords, more than 25 mm or 10 per cent of its section width in length, whichever is the greater; also there must be no lump, bulge or tear caused by separation or partial fracture of its structure; neither must there be any portion of the ply or cord structure exposed.

As at 1 February 2021 C&U Regulations do not allow tyres aged over 10 years old to be used on the front-steered axles of HGVs. If used it will mean a dangerous fail at annual test and a prohibition.

If inspected at a DVSA enforcement check, tyres aged over 10 years old found on these positions will be considered dangerous and attract an 'S'-marked immediate prohibition notice.

It is also a requirement for the manufacturer's date code to be legible on all tyres fitted to HGVs and trailers. If a tyre is a retread then the manufacturer date is taken from when the retread was carried out.

Approval Marks on Tyres

It is an offence to sell motor car tyres unless they carry an 'E' mark to show compliance with EU load and speed requirements. It is also an offence to sell re-tread car or lorry tyres unless they are manufactured and marked in accordance with British Standard BS AU 144b 1977.

Since 1 October 1990 it has been a requirement for tyres on heavy goods vehicles to show load and speed markings in accordance with UNECE Regulation 30 or 54. It is a legal requirement that these limits of both loading and speed performance are strictly observed. Failure to do so can result in prosecution and could invalidate insurance claims in the event of an accident involving a vehicle loaded above the weight limit of the tyres or travelling at a speed in excess of the tyre limit.

Tread Depth

All tyres on goods vehicles of over 3,500 kg gross weight must have a tread depth of at least 1 mm across three-quarters of the breadth of the tread and around the entire circumference of the tyre. This 1 mm tread depth must be in a continuous band around the entire circumference of the tyre. Further, on the remaining one-quarter of the width of the tyre, where there is no requirement for the tread to be 1 mm deep, the base of the original grooves must be clearly visible.

Most tyres for heavier vehicles have a depth/wear indicator bar in the bottom of the tread. This gives a quick check on tyre wear but it must be remembered that on tyres which have been re-cut the wear bars will not be present.

The minimum tread depth for cars, light vans (not exceeding 3,500 kg gross weight) and light trailers was increased to 1.6 mm from 1 January 1992, and this applies across the central three-quarters of the width of the tyre and in a continuous band around the entire circumference. The 1 mm limit stated above remains in force for heavy goods vehicles.

Re-Cut Tyres

Re-cut tyres may be fitted to goods vehicles of over 2,540 kg unladen weight which have wheels of at least 405 mm rim diameter, to trailers weighing more than 1,020 kg unladen weight and to electric vehicles. They must not be used on private cars, dual-purpose vehicles, goods vehicles or trailers of less than the weight or wheel size specified.

Run-Flat and Temporary-Use Spare Tyres

The regulations permit the legal use of 'run-flat' tyres in a partially inflated or flat condition and what are described as temporary-use spare tyres. Where a temporary-use spare tyre is being used the vehicle speed must not exceed 50 mph, otherwise the legal provision which permits their use ceases to apply. The temporary-use spare tyre or the wheel to which it is fitted must be of a different colour to the other wheels on the vehicle and a label must be attached to the wheel giving clear information about the precautions to be observed when using the wheel. There are also compounds available (for smaller vehicle tyres) that can be used to fill the tyre to enable it to be used following a puncture, although many of these compounds cannot be removed from the tyre and, once the vehicle gets to a suitable tyre replacement facility, the tyre with the compound must be replaced.

Lightweight Trailer Tyres

Tyres fitted to lightweight trailers since 1 April 1987 must be designed and maintained to support the maximum axle weight at its maximum permitted speed (ie 60 mph).

Front Under-Run Protection

Under EC Directive 2000/40/EC all goods vehicles exceeding 3.5 tonnes gvw should be fitted with an approved form of front under-run protection (ie bumper) system (FUPS). This bumper must extend to the full width of the vehicle, must be fitted no higher than 400 mm from the ground when the vehicle is unladen and must meet the same strength requirements specified for rear under-run bumpers (see below). Vehicles over 16 tonnes gross weight used for off-road purposes (ie principally tippers – in European Categories N2G and N3G) and vehicles whose 'use is incompatible with the provisions of front under-run protection' are exempt from the legal requirements.

Rear Under-Run Protection

Rear under-run protection systems (RUPS) must be fitted to most rigid goods vehicles over 3.5 tonnes gvw manufactured since 1 October 1983 and first used since 1 April 1984. Trailers, including semi-trailers, over 1,020 kg unladen weight manufactured since 1 May 1983 must also be fitted with rear under-run protection. Certain vehicles and trailers are exempt (see below) from the fitting requirements and there were no retrospective fitting requirements for existing vehicles.

Strength of RUPS

RUPS bumpers must be constructed so they are capable of withstanding a force equivalent to half the gross weight of the vehicle or trailer or a maximum of 10 tonnes, whichever is the *lesser*, without deflecting more than 400 mm measured from the rearmost point of the vehicle or trailer – not from the original vertical position of the bumper.

Fitment of RUPS

RUPS must be fitted as near as possible to the rear of the vehicle and the lower edge must be not more than 550 mm from the ground (see Figure 12.12). Normally, only one bumper would be fitted, but where a tail-lift is fitted or the bodywork or other parts of the vehicle make this impracticable, two or more bumpers may be fitted. When a single full-width bumper is fitted it must extend on each side of the centre to within at least 100 mm from the outermost width of the rear axle, but must not in any case extend beyond the width of the rear axle measured across the outermost face of the tyres. When two or more bumpers are fitted, for the reasons mentioned above, the space between each part of the bumper must not exceed 500 mm and the outermost edge of the bumpers must extend to within at least 300 mm from the outermost width of the rear axle (see Figure 12.13). Bumpers must not protrude beyond the width of the vehicle or trailer and the outside ends of the bumper must not be bent backwards.

Figure 12.12 Illustration of the rear under-run bumper force resistance requirements and ground clearance dimension

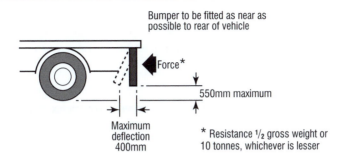

Bumper to be fitted as near as possible to rear of vehicle

Force*

550mm maximum

Maximum deflection 400mm

* Resistance ½ gross weight or 10 tonnes, whichever is lesser

Figure 12.13 Illustrations of the fitting dimensions for single and multiple rear under-run bumpers

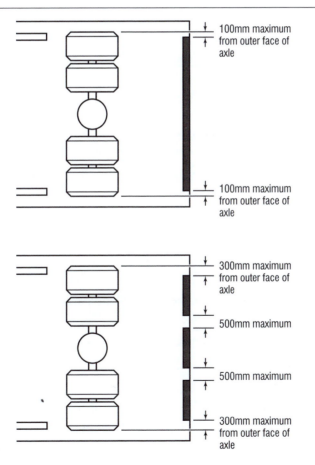

100mm maximum from outer face of axle

100mm maximum from outer face of axle

300mm maximum from outer face of axle

500mm maximum

500mm maximum

300mm maximum from outer face of axle

Maintenance of Bumpers

Rear bumpers must be maintained free from any obvious defect that would adversely affect their performance in giving resistance to impact from the rear. It is also important to ensure that the dimensional requirements are met, particularly if the bumper is damaged (for example by forklift truck impact or reversing onto loading bays).

Exemptions

Rear under-run bumpers do not have to be fitted to vehicles and trailers in the following list:

- vehicles incapable of a speed exceeding 15 mph on the level under their own power;
- tractive units of articulated vehicles;
- agricultural trailers, trailed appliances and agricultural motor vehicles;
- engineering plant;
- fire engines;
- road-spreading vehicles (ie for salt and grit);
- rear-tipping vehicles;
- military, naval or air-force vehicles;
- vehicles being taken to have bodywork fitted, or being taken for quality or safety checks by the manufacturer, distributor or dealer in such vehicles;
- vehicles being driven or towed to a place to have a rear under-run bumper fitted by prior arrangement;
- vehicles designed to carry other vehicles which are loaded from the rear (eg car transporters);
- trailers designed and constructed (not just adapted) to carry round timber, beams or girders of exceptional length;
- vehicles fitted with tail-lifts where the tail-lift forms part of the floor of the vehicle and extends to a length of at least 1 metre;
- temporarily imported foreign vehicles and semi-trailers;
- vehicles specially designed (not just adapted) for carrying and mixing liquid concrete;
- vehicles designed and used solely for the delivery of coal by means of a conveyor fixed to the vehicle so as to make the fitment of a rear under-run bumper impracticable.

View to the Front

Drivers must have a full view of the road and traffic ahead at all times when driving. Obstructing the windscreen with mascots, stickers, stone guards and other such things could result in prosecution and/or failure of the vehicle when it is presented for annual test.

Vehicles with closed-circuit television (CCTV) rear-view monitors mounted in the cab in such a position that the driver's view to the front is obscured, or partly obscured, will normally be failed in their annual test. This particularly applies to refuse collectors and ambulances, which traditionally use such equipment (see also the Televisions in Vehicles section found later in this chapter).

Windscreen Wipers and Washers

Windscreen Wipers

All vehicles must be fitted with one or more efficient automatic windscreen wipers capable of clearing the windscreen to provide the driver with an adequate view to the front and sides of the vehicle. They must be maintained in good and efficient working order and must be adjusted properly. This provision does not apply if the driver has an adequate view of the road without looking through the windscreen.

Windscreen Washers

Vehicles required to be fitted with windscreen wipers must be fitted with a windscreen washer that is capable, in conjunction with the wipers, of clearing mud or dirt from the area of the windscreen swept by the wipers. Washers are not required on land tractors, track-laying vehicles and vehicles that cannot travel at more than 20 mph.

A vehicle should not be driven on the road with defective windscreen wipers or washers. This is an offence which could result in a fine of up to £1,000 (as with many other C&U regulation offences). Washers and wipers which may be frozen and unable to operate can be deemed to be defective and also be subject to enforcement.

Note: Many operators now insist that drivers only use a proper screen wash solution, and not tap water, following concerns about the possibility of contracting Legionnaire's Disease from coming into contact with water which may have been in the washer system for some time whilst also having been warmed by the heat of the engine.

Wings

Goods vehicles and trailers must be fitted with wings to catch, as far as practicable, mud and water thrown up by the wheels, unless adequate protection is provided by the bodywork.

Articulated vehicles and trailers used for carrying round timber are exempt from these requirements except on the front wheels of the tractive unit. Vehicles and trailers in an unfinished condition that are proceeding to a bodybuilder for work to be completed and works trucks are also exempt from the need to have wings.

Use of Vehicles

There are requirements regarding the use of vehicles which are the responsibility of the operator.

These requirements cover such items as vehicle weights (which were dealt with earlier), towing, fumes, the condition and maintenance of vehicles and their components, noise, smoke and general safety in the use of vehicles. They also include the regulations regarding the number of trailers which a vehicle may draw. The regulations also clearly state that any vehicle used must be 'fit for purpose' and not present any hazard to any other road users.

Gas-Powered Vehicles

C&U Regulations specify technical standards for fuel tanks or containers, the filling system and valves and general requirements for gas propulsion systems in motor vehicles. The regulations permit the use of LPG only in gas-propelled vehicles, though this may be combined with petrol fuel systems, and the sole use of methane or hydrogen is prohibited. The DfT publishes free guides on fitting and operating both LPG and CNG (see below) and information is available at GOV.UK.

Article (17A) and schedules (5A and 5B) to the Motor Vehicles (Authorisation of Special Types) General Order 1979 – inserted by virtue of Amendment No 2 of 1 December 1998 to the Order – authorize the use on roads of vehicles propelled by compressed natural gas (CNG), notwithstanding that they do not comply with the requirements of the C&U Regulations. They must, however, comply with the provisions of the new schedules as to constructional requirements and the requirements for testing gas containers used in these systems.

Since that date, CNG engines and multi-fuel vehicles have been introduced as research and development continues in an attempt to reduce the use of carbon-based liquid fuels. However, while the C&U Regulations will apply to these alternative fuel engines, Commission Regulation (EU) No 630/2012 also covers the specification of vehicles powered by all types of gas and mixtures of hydrogen with natural gas.

Electric-Powered Vehicles

More and more electric goods vehicles are entering service and, while originally exempted from many regulations, they are now increasingly included in C&U standards and operators need to be aware of changing standards for these vehicles. That said, it is to be noted that electrically powered vans are now permitted to operate at weights up to 4,250 kg and not 3,500 kg in order to take account of the additional weight of the batteries without reducing payload.

Noise

It is an offence to use, or cause or permit to be used, on a road a motor vehicle or trailer which causes an excessive noise because of a defect, lack of repair or faulty adjustment of components or load. Also, no motor vehicle must be used on a road in such a manner as to cause any excessive noise which could have been reasonably avoided by the driver. Noise for these purposes is the combined noise emitted by the exhaust plus that from the tyres, engine, bodywork and equipment, and the load. Noise levels for goods vehicles are measured by special meters either by the police or by DVSA examiners at goods vehicle testing stations and occasionally on roadside tests. The noise measured is that of the 'whole' vehicle, not just the exhaust and engine. Refrigerator compressors, reversing bleepers (see below) and warning devices also constitute noise emitted from a vehicle and care needs to be taken if these are used during the silent hours and/or in residential areas.

Reversing Alarms

Operators may fit reversing alarms to certain goods and passenger vehicles. Such alarms are voluntarily fitted and may be either a warning buzzer or horn, or a verbal recording. They may be used on the following vehicles:

- commercial vehicles over 2 tonnes gross weight;
- passenger vehicles with nine or more seats;
- engineering plant;
- works trucks.

Time Restriction on Use of Reversing Alarms

The alarms are subject to the same night-time restrictions that apply to the sounding of horns in built-up areas (ie not after 11.30 pm and before 7.00 am) and the sound emitted must not be capable of being confused with the pelican crossing 'safe to cross' signal. If a vehicle fitted with a reversing alarm is to be used during these 'silent hours', the alarm must be capable of being switched off.

Restriction on Fitment of Reversing Alarms

Such alarms *must not* be fitted to light goods vehicles below 2 tonnes gross weight or to motor cars.

Televisions in Vehicles

It is illegal for a vehicle to be fitted with television receiving apparatus where the driver can see the screen either directly or by reflection, except where such equipment displays nothing other than information:

- about the state of the vehicle or its equipment;
- about the location of the vehicle and the road on which it is located;
- to assist the driver to see the road adjacent to the vehicle (eg to the rear when reversing);
- to assist the driver to reach their destination.

Towing

Goods vehicles (not showmen's vehicles) may draw (ie tow) only one trailer. An exception to this is when a rigid goods vehicle tows a broken-down vehicle on a towing ambulance or dolly, in which case, although this is counted as towing two trailers, it is allowed. In a case where an articulated vehicle has broken down, this may be towed by a rigid goods vehicle so long as the articulated vehicle is not loaded. In these circumstances the outfit is treated as one trailer only, but if it is loaded, an articulated outfit being towed is considered to be two trailers and it would be illegal for a normal goods vehicle (ie a heavy motor car) to tow it. Only a locomotive (this definition normally applies to recovery vehicles which can only tow and that are unable to carry goods; further information can be found in the VOSA publication *Guide for Recovery Operations* or in the *Association of Vehicle Recovery Operators (AVRO) Guide*) can tow a broken-down articulated vehicle which is laden (see below).

Motor tractors may draw one laden or two unladen trailers, and locomotives may draw three trailers (see Definitions of Vehicles at the beginning of this chapter).

Composite Trailers

The C&U Regulations make it permissible for rigid goods vehicles (apart from locomotives and motor tractors) to draw two trailers instead of only one, when one of the trailers is a towing implement (ie a dolly) and the other is an articulated-type semi-trailer secured to and resting on, or suspended from, the dolly. This combination of dolly and semi-trailer is known as a composite trailer (Figure 12.14).

Figure 12.14 A conventional six-wheeled rigid vehicle drawing a dolly mounted semi-trailer for which the maximum overall length is 18.35 metres

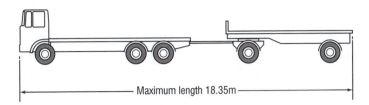

Maximum length 18.35m

To comply with the regulations, the dolly needs to have two or more wheels and be specifically designed to support a superimposed semi-trailer. Dollies must display a manufacturer's plate and they are subject to the annual heavy goods vehicle test.

Towing Distance

The distance between the nearest points of two vehicles joined by a tow rope or chain must not exceed 4.5 metres. When the distance between the two vehicles exceeds 1.5 metres, the rope, chain or bar must be made clearly visible from both sides of the vehicles. There is no specified maximum distance limit if a solid tow bar is used for towing.

Trailer and Semi-Trailer Coupling and Uncoupling

A Code of Practice ensures that safe practices are adopted and followed by drivers and others when carrying out the high-risk procedure of coupling and uncoupling. The Code is divided into five sections dealing with safe procedures for standard and close-coupled semi-trailers and both centre-axle and turntable drawbar trailers.

Copies of the Code are available from the SOE and online at: www.soe.org.uk. Copies of an HSE guide and the HSE 2016 *Safe Coupling and Uncoupling Guide* are available on the HSE website: hse.gov.uk.

Type Approval

Type approval is a scheme which requires vehicle manufacturers to submit new vehicles (ie new designs, new models and changes of specifications for existing approved models) for approval before they are put on the market. The Department for Transport examines the vehicle submitted to ensure that it meets all legal requirements and also meets minimum standards of construction and performance. When a vehicle has been approved, the manufacturer is then required by law to build all vehicles of a similar type to exactly those standards and certify this fact to the customer by the issue of a Certificate of Conformity.

An EU directive lays down the basic procedures for the type-approval schemes for vehicles and components. Subsidiary directives have also been issued setting out agreed standards on some aspects of vehicle safety or pollution. They cover the same ground as existing national regulations. The directives do not yet cover all vehicle features which need to be regulated, so until the programme is complete both EU directives and national regulations apply to relevant items. The UK established a non-compulsory scheme to enable exporting vehicle manufacturers to gain the necessary type approval in order to sell their products in EU countries.

Vehicles Covered

EC approval of most road vehicles is based around a 'Whole Vehicle' framework directive, Directive 70/156/EEC as most recently amended by Directive 2007/46/ EC – implemented in all EU member states from 29 April 2009 – which specifies the range of aspects of the vehicle that must be approved under separate technical directives.

This Directive is known as EC Whole Vehicle Type Approval (ECWVTA) and applies to manufacturers of large numbers of vehicles. Where a manufacturer may only produce a few vehicles, the type-approval procedure is known as National Small Series Type Approval. Both these schemes are overseen in the UK by the VCA, which is an executive agency of the DfT.

In order to gain ECWVTA, a vehicle must first be approved in regard to its brakes, emissions, noise, etc – in fact, up to 48 different standards for a typical vehicle. The issuing of the whole vehicle approval does not in itself involve testing, but *a production* sample of the complete vehicle is inspected to check that its specification matches the specifications contained in all the separate directive approvals.

Broadly, the whole vehicle framework document covers any vehicle with four or more wheels intended for use on roads, except agricultural or forestry tractors, mobile machinery and vehicles with a design maximum speed of less than 25 kph. Separate technical directives and regulations allow (or require) the approval of individual vehicles and systems as part of a type of vehicle, and some allow for the approval of separate devices. Where this is used for 'one-off' vehicles it is known as Individual Vehicle Approval (IVA). System and component approval requires that a sample of the type to be approved is tested by the Technical Service to the requirements of the relevant directive. Its technical specification is documented and that specification forms part of the approval.

From 29 October 2014, before a vehicle can be registered at the DVLA it has to be able to prove that it complies with ECWVTA in at least one of the following ways:

- It complies with full EU type approval through the VCA.
- It complies with NSSTA through the VCA.
- It complies with the rules of the IVA scheme through the DVLA.

Exemptions from Type Approval

Type approval does not apply to the following vehicles:

- vehicles manufactured before 1 October 1982, whenever they are first registered;
- vehicles manufactured on or after 1 October 1982, providing they were first licensed before 1 April 1983;
- temporarily imported vehicles;
- vehicles proceeding for export from the UK;
- vehicles in the service of visiting forces or headquarters;
- certain vehicles which are, or were formerly, in use in the public service or the Crown;
- prototypes which are not intended for general use on the roads;
- motor tractors, light locomotives and heavy locomotives;
- engineering plant (provided it does NOT have a truck chassis), pedestrian-controlled vehicles, straddle carriers, works trucks and track-laying vehicles;
- vehicles specially designed and constructed for use in private premises for moving excavated materials, vehicles fitted with movable platforms and vehicles designed and constructed for the carriage of abnormal indivisible loads;
- tower wagons;
- fire engines;
- road rollers;
- steam-propelled vehicles;
- vehicles constructed for the purpose of preventing or reducing the effect of snow or ice on roads;
- two-wheeled motorcycles with or without sidecars;
- electrically propelled vehicles;
- breakdown vehicles (providing they are NOT recovery vehicles exceeding 12,000 kg gvw);

- any vehicle not exceeding 3,500 kg gvw which is constructed or assembled by a person not ordinarily engaged in the manufacture of goods vehicles of that description;
- vehicles not exceeding 3,500 kg gvw provided that:
  - the vehicle has been purchased outside the UK for the personal use of the individual importing it or their dependants;
  - the vehicle has been so used by that individual or their dependants on roads outside the UK before it is imported;
  - the vehicle is intended solely for such personal use in the UK;
  - the individual importing the vehicle intends, at the time when the vehicle is imported, to remain in the UK for not less than 12 months from that date.

For clarification purposes, the following vehicles which were exempted from type approval before October 2014 are now no longer excluded:

- crash cushion vehicles;
- vehicles used for AIL work;
- vehicles with moving mounted platforms on booms;
- highway testing vehicles based on a truck chassis.

Responsibility for Compliance

Responsibility for complying with the complex construction standards rests with the manufacturer, although users are still responsible for maintaining vehicles in roadworthy condition. The construction standards applied by the scheme are limited to those which can be approved during the primary stage of manufacture. The standards are identical to those already required under the Construction and Use Regulations but under this scheme vehicles have to be approved before they can be used on the road.

Effects on Plating and Testing

The scheme requires plated weights for heavy goods vehicles to be set during the type-approval process instead of waiting until the first annual plating and testing examination. This means that heavy vehicle operators need a Type Approval Certificate in order to get a Ministry plate for display in the vehicle cab (see Chapter 14). However, annual testing is retained so as to check the condition of vehicles and to ensure that plated weights are accurate.

Responsibility for Type Approval

All aspects of type approval are the responsibility of the DVSA, which reminds operators that in order to obtain an annual test or a plating certificate for a type-approved vehicle they need to use form VTG788 for ECWVTA and NSSTA vehicles and form VTG789 for IVA vehicles.

The Standards Checked

To obtain goods vehicle national type approval it is first necessary to obtain individual systems approvals for the following items:

- power-to-weight ratio (not applicable to petrol-engined vehicles or dual-purpose vehicles);
- gaseous exhaust emissions (petrol-engined vehicles only);
- particle emission (ie exhaust smoke) (diesel-engined vehicles only);
- external noise level;
- radio-interference suppression (petrol-engined vehicles only);
- brakes.

NB: As the whole type-approval scheme currently applying to UK vehicles and vehicle components is based on EU standards and requirements it is likely (depending upon a deal or no-deal Brexit) that the UK will have to develop its own new type-approval standards and regime, although it could simply adopt what we have. In any case, interested parties need to monitor this requirement closely either by contacting the trade associations or by following developments on the DVSA website https://www.gov.uk/vehicle-approval.

Arrangements for First Licensing of Vehicles

For vehicles over 1,525 kg unladen weight or which form part of an articulated vehicle, application for first licensing on form V55 must be accompanied by two copies of the Type Approval Certificate, which should have been supplied with the vehicle. On one of these the applicant must complete a declaration saying whether or not the vehicle is exempt from the plating and testing regulations (see Chapter 14 for full details) and whether it has been altered in any way that has to be notified to the DVSA under the type-approval regulations and, if so, whether any action arising from the notification has been satisfactorily completed.

Issue of Plates

When application is made for first licensing a vehicle which is subject to plating and testing in accordance with the Haulage Permits and Trailer Registration Act 2018, the DVLA will send a copy of the Type Approval Certificate and the Certificate of Conformity (CoC) with the applicant's declaration to the Goods Vehicle Centre (GVC). The second copy will be stamped and returned to the applicant to serve as a temporary Ministry plate. When the GVC receives the copy of the certificate, and if the details compare satisfactorily with those on the copy sent direct by the vehicle manufacturers, it will issue a Ministry plate and laminated plating certificate. These will be sent direct to the person or company in whose name the vehicle is registered. Thus, operators buying new vehicles receive their first plate and plating certificate for the vehicle from the GVC at the time of licensing rather than from the goods vehicle testing station when the vehicle is presented for its first annual test, as under previous arrangements. This also means that trailers will be issued with paper plates and not paper discs and that the plates will need to travel with the trailers and that the trailers will also require their own registration plates. When an application is made for licensing a vehicle which is exempt from plating and testing, a copy of the certificate and the declaration will be sent to the GVC so that it is aware that it is exempt.

Refusal to Licence

No vehicle subject to the type-approval regulations will be first licensed unless the DVLA registration form V55 has a valid type-approval number on it or it is an exempt vehicle.

Alteration to Vehicles

If a vehicle which has been issued with an Approval Certificate and supplied to a dealer or direct to an operator is modified by them, prior to first licensing, they must notify the VCA at Bristol (Vehicle Certification Agency, 1, The Eastgate Office Centre, Eastgate Road, Bristol, BS5 6XX (0300 330 5797), www.dft.gov.uk/vca) and send the certificate for the vehicle together with a completed VTG10 form, full technical details, drawings of the alterations and details of the weights on the certificate which need, or may need, changing.

The VCA will judge whether the alterations affect the vehicle's compliance with the regulations; if they do not affect compliance, the certificate will be returned so the vehicle can be licensed. If they do contravene compliance, the certificate will be cancelled and fresh approval will need to be obtained before the vehicle can be licensed. This is a complex and costly procedure that most operators will want to avoid; they can do so by registering and licensing the vehicle before any alterations are carried out.

Vehicle Lighting and Marking   13

The legal requirements for vehicles to be fitted with and to display lights at night and other times, and for the fitment of reflectors and other markings on vehicles, are detailed in the Road Vehicles Lighting Regulations 1989 (as amended). These are also complemented by UNECE Regulation 48 on conspicuity marking. These regulations specify the requirements for the position of lamps and reflectors and the angles from which they must be visible. Advice can also be found in the revised *Heavy Goods Vehicle (HGV) Inspection Manual* at GOV.UK.

The lighting regulations require that lights and reflectors which are fitted to vehicles must be maintained so as to enable them to be driven on a road between sunset and sunrise, or in seriously reduced visibility between sunrise and sunset, or to be parked safely on a road between sunset and sunrise. All lights must be kept clean and in good working order. It is an offence to cause undue dazzle or discomfort to other road users by the use of lights or through their faulty adjustment, or to have defective or obscured lighting on a vehicle.

Obligatory Lights

Between sunset and sunrise, vehicles used on a public road must display the following obligatory lights, other lights and reflectors:

- Two front position lamps (ie sidelamps) showing white lights to the front.
- Two rear position lamps (ie rear lamps) showing red lights to the rear.
- Two headlamps showing white lights to the front (alternatively, the light may be yellow).
- Illumination for the rear number (ie registration) plate when the other vehicle lights are on.
- One or two red rear fog lamps on post-1 April 1980 vehicles.
- Two red reflex retro-reflectors at the rear.
- End-outline marker lamps.

- Any other lights or lighting devices with which the vehicle is fitted (eg stop lamps, hazard warning signals, running lamps, dim-dip devices and headlamp levelling devices). Certain goods vehicles and trailers additionally require side marker lamps plus side-facing reflectors and rear reflective markings.

It is illegal except in certain specified cases for a goods vehicle to show a white light to the rear (showing such a light when reversing and indirect illumination of the rear registration plate are permitted, for example) or a red light to the front.

Daytime running lamps (DRLs), which switch on automatically when the vehicle ignition is switched on, have been required on new HGVs since August 2012.

Headlamps

Motor vehicles must be fitted with two headlamps capable of showing a white or yellow light to the front – both lamps must emit the same colour light. Headlamps must be either permanently dipped or fitted with dipping equipment. Vehicles first used since 1 April 1987 must have dim-dip lighting devices unless their lighting equipment complies with EU requirements (see below). Vehicles must also have a warning device for the driver that indicates when full beam, and not dipped beam, is selected.

Headlamps must be mounted so that they are not lower than 500 mm from the ground and not higher than 1,200 mm. They must be placed on either side of the vehicle with their illuminated areas not more than 400 mm from the side of the vehicle. They must be equipped with bulbs or sealed-beam units of not less than 30 watts in the case of vehicles first used before 1 April 1986. For vehicles used since this date no minimum wattage requirement is specified.

Vehicles that are used on international operations are often fitted with headlamps that can be set by operating a switch in the cab for either right-hand-side or left-hand-side driving.

Headlamp Exemptions

Certain vehicles are exempt from the headlamp requirements. These include vehicles with fewer than four wheels, pedestrian-controlled vehicles, agricultural implements, land tractors, works trucks, vehicles not capable of travelling at a speed of more than 6 mph and some military vehicles.

Headlamps on Electric Vehicles

Electrically propelled goods vehicles with four or more wheels registered before October 1969 and electric vehicles with two or three wheels first used before 1 January 1972 and capable of a speed of more than 15 mph are required to comply with the headlamp requirements. Those electrically propelled vehicles which are incapable of speeds of more than 15 mph are exempt from the headlamp requirements.

Use of Headlamps

Headlamps must be adjusted so that they do not cause undue dazzle or discomfort to other road users. When vehicles which require headlamps are being driven on unlit roads between sunset and sunrise and in seriously reduced daytime visibility, the headlamps must be illuminated. They must be switched off when the vehicle is stationary except at traffic stops.

HGVs presented for annual test that require the headlights adjusting at the time of the test will be recorded as a PRS (pass after rectification at the station). In effect, this notes that the vehicle arrived at the test station in a 'fail' state and this is recorded and counts towards an operator's OCRS even if the vehicle is prepared and presented by a maintenance contractor.

NB: Unlit roads are roads on which there are no street lamps or on which the street lamps are more than 200 yards apart.

Headlamps in Daylight

It is a legal requirement for vehicles to use side-position lights (ie sidelights) and dipped headlights when travelling in seriously reduced daytime visibility conditions such as in fog, smoke, heavy rain, spray or snow. If matching fog or fog and spotlights are fitted in pairs, these may be used instead of headlights, but sidelights must still be used and the other vehicle lights must be on (eg side marker lights).

Dim-Dip Lighting

Newly registered vehicles (since 1 April 1987) must be fitted with dim-dip lighting devices which operate automatically when the obligatory lights of the vehicle are switched on and ensure that either 10 per cent (with halogen) or 15 per cent (with grading filament lamps) of the normal dipped-beam intensity shows when the vehicle ignition key is switched on or the engine is running.

Front Position Lamps (Sidelamps)

Two front position lamps (ie sidelamps) emitting a white light through a diffused lens must be fitted to all motor vehicles with three or more wheels and trailers (except those not more than 1,600 mm wide), those no longer than 2,300 mm (excluding the drawbar) built before 1 October 1985 and those used for carrying and launching boats. These are now usually incorporated into the headlight assembly. If such lamps are incorporated within a headlamp showing a yellow light then the side-position lamps may be yellow. No minimum wattage is specified for these lights. The lights must be equal in height from the ground and mounted not more than 1,500 mm from the ground (in exceptional circumstances this height can be increased to 2,100 mm) in the case of vehicles first used on or after 1 April 1986 and 2,300 mm in other cases, and not more than 400 mm from the outer edge of the vehicle for vehicles first used since 1 April 1986 and 510 mm in other cases. No minimum height above the ground is specified.

Rear Position Lamps (Rear Lamps)

Two red rear position lamps (ie rear lamps) must be fitted to all motor vehicles and trailers. There is no specified wattage for these lights. They must be mounted not less than 350 mm and not more than 1,500 mm (2,100 mm in exceptional circumstances) from the ground. They must be at least 500 mm apart (no specified distance on pre-1 April 1986 registered vehicles) and not more than 400 mm (800 mm on pre-1 April 1986 registered vehicles) from the outside edge of the vehicle.

Stop Lamps

All goods vehicles (except those not capable of more than 25 mph) must be fitted with red stop lamps which are maintained in a clean condition and in good and efficient working order. Vehicles registered before 1 January 1971 need only one such lamp, which must be fitted at the centre or to the offside of the vehicle, although a second matching lamp may be fitted on the nearside. Vehicles registered since that date need two such lamps (specified wattage 15 to 36 watts except with pre-1 January 1971 registered vehicles) mounted not less than 350 mm from the ground and not more than 1,500 mm (in exceptional circumstances this may be increased to 2,100 mm) and they must be at least 400 mm apart. Such lamps must be visible horizontally from 45 degrees on either side and normally from 15 degrees above and below vertically (from only 5 degrees below where fitted less than 750 mm from the ground and only 10 degrees below when fitted not more than 1,500 mm from the ground).

Reversing Lamps

White reversing lamps (not more than two) may be fitted to vehicles provided they are only used while the vehicle is reversing and operate automatically only when reverse gear is selected. Alternatively, they may be operated manually by a switch (which serves no other purpose) in the driver's cab provided that a warning device indicates to the driver that the lights are illuminated. The lights must be adjusted so as not to cause dazzle to other road users. Such lamps when bearing an 'e' approval mark do not have to meet minimum wattage requirements but those without approval marks must not exceed 24 watts.

Number Plate Lamp

Rear number plates (ie registration plates) on vehicles must be indirectly illuminated when the other obligatory lamps on the vehicles are lit. The light must be white and must be shielded so that it only illuminates the number plate and does not show to the rear.

Rear Fog Lamps

Rear fog lamps (at least one, but two may be fitted) must be fitted to new vehicles and trailers manufactured on or after 1 October 1979 and first used since 1 April 1980. There is no legal requirement to fit such lamps on pre-1 October 1979 registered vehicles, but if they are fitted voluntarily they must comply with the regulations in regard to mounting position, method of wiring and use.

Rear Fog Lamps on Articulated and Towing Vehicles

In the case of articulated vehicle combinations, if a tractive unit registered after April 1980 is coupled to a trailer built before October 1979 there is no requirement for the vehicle to be fitted with rear fog lamps.

A broken-down vehicle being towed does not need rear fog lamps. However, it is important to remember the dangers which arise if such a combination is used when the tractive unit or towing vehicle itself has rear fog lamps which would, in some instances, be visible to following motorists who, in bad visibility, might not be aware of some 12 metres of trailer or another vehicle on tow behind the lights.

Mounting of Rear Fog Lamps

Rear fog lamps must be mounted either singly in the centre or on the offside of the vehicle or in a matched pair not less than 250 mm and not more than 1,000 mm from the ground (in the case of agricultural vehicles this height limit is increased to 1,900 mm or, in cases where (because of the shape of the vehicle) 1,000 mm is not practical, it may be increased to 2,100 mm). The lamps must be at least 100 mm from existing stop lamps.

Restriction on Wiring of Rear Fog Lamps

The lights must be wired so that they only operate when the other statutory lights on the vehicle are switched on; they must not be wired into the brake/stop light circuit and the driver must be provided with an indicator to show him when the lights are in use.

Use of Rear Fog Lamps

The lights should only be used in conditions affecting the visibility of the driver (ie in fog, smoke, heavy rain or spray, snow, dense cloud, etc), when the vehicle is in motion or during an enforced stoppage (a motorway hold-up, for example). They must not cause dazzle. The *Highway Code* recommends these lights should not be used unless visibility is below 100 metres (328 feet).

Side Marker Lamps

Side marker lamps must be fitted on vehicles and trailers as follows:

- Vehicles first used on or after 1 April 1991 and trailers made from 1 October 1990 and being over 6 metres long:
  - one lamp on each side within 4 metres of the front of the vehicle;
  - one lamp on each side within 1 metre of the rear of the vehicle;
  - additional lamps on each side at 3-metre intervals (or, if impracticable, 4 metres) between front and rear side marker lamps.
- Vehicles (including a combination of vehicles) over 18.3 metres long (including the length of the load):
  - one lamp on each side within 9.15 metres of the front of the vehicle;
  - one lamp on each side within 3.05 metres of the rear of the vehicle;
  - additional lamps on each side at 3.05-metre intervals between front and rear side marker lamps.
- Vehicles in combination between 12.2 metres and 18.3 metres long (but not articulated vehicles) carrying a supported load:
  - one lamp on each side within 1,530 mm of the rear of the rearmost vehicle in the combination;
  - one lamp on each side within 1,530 mm of the centre of the load, if the load extends further than 9.15 metres to the rear of the drawing vehicle.
- Trailers more than 9.15 metres long (6 metres for post-1 October 1990 trailers):
  - one lamp on each side within 1,530 mm of the centre of the trailer length.

Side marker lamps fitted to trailers built before 1 October 1990 may show white side marker lights to the front and red lights to the rear; in all other cases such lights must be amber. They must be positioned not more than 2,300 mm from the ground.

End-Outline Marker Lamps

Vehicles (except those less than 2,100 mm wide and those first used before 1 April 1991) and trailers (except those less than 2,100 mm wide and those built before 1 October 1990) must be fitted with two end-outline marker lamps visible from the front and two visible from the rear. They must be positioned no more than 400 mm in from the outer edges of the vehicle/trailer and mounted at the front at least level with the top of the windscreen. They must show white lights to the front and red lights to the rear.

Lighting Switches

On vehicles first used since 1 April 1991, a single lighting switch only must be used to illuminate all front and rear position lamps, side and end-outline marker lamps and rear number plate lamp, although one or more front or rear position lamps may be capable of being switched on independently.

Visibility of Lights and Reflectors

A part, at least, of each front and rear position light, front and rear-mounted direction indicator lamp and rear retro-reflector required to be fitted to a vehicle/trailer must be capable of being seen from directly in front of or behind the lamp or reflector when the vehicle doors, tailgate, boot lid, engine cover or other movable part of the vehicle is in a fixed open position.

Direction Indicators

All goods vehicles must be fitted with amber-coloured direction indicators (on pre-September 1965-registered vehicles, indicators can be white facing to the front and red facing to the rear) at the front and rear which must be fixed to the vehicle not more than 1,500 mm (2,300 mm in exceptional cases) and not less than 350 mm above the ground, at least 500 mm apart and not more than 400 mm from the outer edges of the vehicle. Side repeater indicators are required on vehicles first used since 1 April 1986 and these must be fitted within 2,600 mm of the front of the vehicle. Normally vehicles should have one indicator on each side at the front and rear but may have two on each side at the rear. They must not have more than one on each side at the front.

Indicators bearing approval marks do not have to meet minimum wattage requirements but those without such marks must be between 15 and 36 watts. They must flash at a rate of between 60 and 120 times a minute and a visible or audible warning must indicate to the driver when they are operating. The flash may be a single flash or a staggered sequence. The indicators must be maintained in a clean condition and in good and efficient working order.

Hazard Warning

Direction indicators operating on both sides of the vehicle simultaneously as a hazard warning to other road users are required by law on all vehicles first used since 1 April 1986. They must be operated by a switch solely controlling that device and a warning light must indicate to the driver that the device is being operated. The hazard indicators may be used when the vehicle is stationary on a road, or any part of the road (ie not just the carriageway), because of a breakdown of it or another vehicle, an accident or other emergency situation, when encountering and slowing down for a barrier or slow or stationary traffic or when the vehicle is causing a temporary obstruction on a road when loading or unloading.

Emergency Warning Triangles

As an additional warning of a hazard, drivers *may* (ie it is not compulsory to do so in the UK) place a red warning triangle on the road to the rear of a vehicle when causing a temporary obstruction (eg through breakdown). The triangle must be made and marked to British Standard Specification BS AU 47: 1965. It must be placed upright on the road, 45 metres to the rear of the obstruction and on the same side. This requirement is compulsory in many EU member states and the requirements do vary in relation to both the distance the triangle(s) must be placed from the vehicle and the number of triangles to be used. Many EU countries also require the driver to wear a hi-visibility vest if they leave the cab in order to set out any triangle(s). Further advice can be obtained from the RHA or FTA.

Other safety devices may be used to warn of vehicles broken down on the roadside. These include traffic cones, warning lamps and traffic pyramids.

Optional Lamps

Optional main-beam headlamps (which includes spot lamps) may be fitted to a vehicle but they must be capable of being dipped, and if fitted as a matched pair they must also be capable of being switched off together – not individually. They must emit either a white or yellow light, must be adjusted so that they do not cause dazzle to other road users and must not be lit when the vehicle is parked. If optional front fog lamps are fitted and used singly, the headlamps must also be illuminated.

These optional lamps should be positioned not more than 1,200 mm from the ground and not more than 400 mm from the sides of the vehicle. They should be aligned so that the upper edge of the beam is, as near as practicable, 3 per cent below the horizontal when the vehicle is at its kerbside weight and has a weight of 75 kg on the driver's seat.

Vehicles first registered since 1 April 1991 may be fitted with only one pair of extra dipped-beam headlamps and then only on vehicles intended to be driven on the right-hand side of the road. They must be wired so that only one pair of dipped-beam headlamps can be used at any one time. Pre-April 1991-registered vehicles may have any number of additional dipped-beam headlamps.

Any number of extra main-beam headlamps (including spot/driving lamps) may be fitted and there is no restriction on their fitment or use except that they must not cause dazzle to other road users.

Warning Beacons

Amber warning beacons must be fitted to vehicles with four or more wheels and having a maximum speed no greater than 25 mph when using unrestricted dual-carriageway roads, except where such use is merely 'for crossing the carriageway in the quickest manner practicable in the circumstances'.

Amber warning beacons may also be fitted to vehicles used at the scene of an emergency, when it is necessary or desirable to warn of the presence of a vehicle on the road (eg Special Types vehicles carrying abnormal loads), and to breakdown vehicles used at the scene of accidents and breakdowns and when towing broken-down vehicles.

Blue warning beacons and other special warning lamps may only be used on emergency vehicles (ie ambulance, fire brigade or police service vehicles; Forestry Commission fire-fighting vehicles; military bomb disposal vehicles; RAF Mountain Rescue vehicles; Blood Transfusion Service vehicles; Mines Rescue Service vehicles; HM Coastguard vehicles; RNLI vehicles; and those used primarily for transporting human tissue for transplanting).

Green warning beacons may be used on vehicles by medical practitioners when travelling to or dealing with an emergency.

In all cases, such beacons should be fitted with their centres no less than 1,200 mm from the ground and visible from any point at a reasonable distance from the vehicle. The light itself must show not less than 60 and not more than 240 times per minute.

Swivelling Spotlights (Work Lamps)

White swivelling spotlights may be used only at the scene of an accident, breakdown or roadworks to illuminate the working area or work in the vicinity of the vehicle, provided they do not cause undue dazzle or discomfort to the driver of any vehicle.

Working lights may also be fitted to articulated units in order to help the driver connect the air and electrical connections. These must also be actuated by a switch solely controlling them and a warning light must indicate to the driver that the device is being operated in order to prevent it being left on when the vehicle is in motion.

Rear Retro-Reflectors

Motor vehicles must be fitted with two red reflex retro-reflectors facing squarely to the rear. Reflectors must be fitted not more than 900 mm and not less than 350 mm from the ground. For normal goods vehicles and trailers they must be within 400 mm of the outer edge of the vehicle or trailer and not less than 600 mm apart. Reflectors must be capable of being seen from an angle of 30 degrees on either side.

Triangular Rear Reflectors

Triangular rear reflectors must not be used other than on trailers or broken-down vehicles being towed.

Side Retro-Reflectors

Vehicles more than 6 metres long first used since 1 April 1986 (more than 8 metres long if first used before 1 April 1986) and trailers more than 5 metres long must be fitted with two (or more as necessary) amber side retro-reflectors on each side. One reflector on each side must be fitted not more than 1 metre from the extreme rear end of the vehicle and another no more than 4 metres from the front of the vehicle, with further reflectors at minimum 3-metre intervals (or can be 4-metre intervals) along its length. They must be mounted not more than 1,500 mm and not less than 350 mm from the ground. On pre-April 1986 vehicles, one reflector must be positioned in the middle third of the vehicle length and the other within 1 metre of the rear. Where such reflectors are mounted within 1 metre of the rear of the vehicle/trailer they may be coloured red instead of amber.

Front Retro-Reflectors

Trailers built since 1 October 1990 must be fitted with two obligatory front retro-reflectors, white in colour and mounted facing forward, at least 350 mm but not more than 900 mm from the ground and no more than 150 mm in from the outer edges of the trailer and at least 600 mm apart.

Vehicle Markings

Number (Registration) Plates

All vehicles first registered since 1 January 1973 and all registered semi-trailers and trailers must be fitted with number plates made of reflecting material complying with BS AU 145a. This requirement does not apply to HGVs over 7.5 tonnes gvw, which are required to display rear reflective markers (see the Rear Reflective Markings section later in this chapter), or works trucks, agricultural machines and trailers or pedestrian-controlled vehicles. If a vehicle over 3,050 kg unladen weight is exempt from the requirement to fit rear reflective markers then it must be fitted with reflective number plates. Regulations specify the precise style of letters and numerals to be used on vehicle registration plates, in particular the spacing between each individual character. It is an offence to alter, rearrange or misrepresent the characters or to alter the spacings to form words or names. It is also an offence to use a number plate with a patterned or textured background. Three possible repercussions may result from the illegal presentation of vehicle registration numbers:

- A fine of up to £1,000 may be imposed on conviction.
- The registration number (mark) may be withdrawn.
- The vehicle may fail its MOT test.

The DVLA requires number plate manufacturers to be registered to help prevent vehicle crime. Lists of authorized number plate manufacturers can be found on GOV.UK.

Vehicle Registration Numbers

All registration plates for vehicles registered after 1 September 2001 must comply with the following format:

AB69 DVL

The letters 'AB' identify the local area in which the vehicle is registered. The number '69' identifies the date of first registration (ie 69 representing vehicles first registered on, or after, 1 September 2019) and will change every six months in September and March each year (eg 19 being March 2019 and 69 being September 2019, etc). The last three letters are random.

All registration plates must display the mandatory fonts (in both style and size – see below) specified in the Road Vehicles (Display of Registration Marks) Regulations 2001. No lettering other than in the specified standard font may be used. The name and trademark of the maker and the postcode of the supplying outlet may be used.

Mandatory Character Font

Registration plates must display the mandatory font as shown here and characters must be of the regulation size:

Table 13.1   Mandatory character font

123456789
ABCDEFGH
JKLMNOPQ
RSTUVWXYZ

Height	79 mm
Width	50 mm
Stroke	14 mm
Side margin	11 mm
Top and bottom margin	11 mm
Space between characters	11 mm
Space between groups	33 mm
Vertical space between age and random numbers	19 mm

NB: Applicable to all vehicles except motorcycles and vehicles manufactured before 1973.

Existing registration plates do not have to be changed to conform to the 2001 style provided the font used is 'substantially the same' as the new style. However, registration plates must be replaced if they have been customized with either:

- stylized letters and figures such as italics; or
- registration-plate fixing bolts that alter the appearance of the letters or numbers.

Failure to replace such number plates may result in the vehicle keeper risking prosecution.

Nationality Symbols

It is a requirement (under the Vienna Convention on Road Traffic) for vehicles travelling in a country other than that in which they are registered to display at the rear a nationality plate showing the official symbol for the country of registration (eg GB for Great Britain, F for France and D for Germany). These plates, usually in the form of a self-adhesive or magnetic sticker, should be of an approved pattern, oval in shape (at least 17.5 cm by 11.4 cm) and contain the relevant national symbol in black letters on a white background. A GB plate will need to be fitted to the vehicle if it is to travel abroad if the number plate does not include the EU symbol. Where the EU symbol is included in the number plate and contains a GB symbol, these plates will be accepted by EU authorities but an additional GB plate will still be required for travel beyond or outside of the EU.

Vehicle owners/operators who wish to do so may display their national flag on number plates (ie the union flag with 'GB' for Great Britain; the cross of St George with 'ENG' for England; the Saltire – the cross of St Andrew – with 'SCO' for Scotland; or the Red Dragon for Wales or Cymru). However, this must be in addition to displaying GB if travelling abroad.

Weight Markings

Goods vehicles must not display any weight markings other than their plated weights, any weights required to be displayed under the C&U Regulations, or weights required under other regulations (eg the Motor Vehicles (Authorisation of Special Types) General Order). This means that maximum weights shown on 'Ministry' plates and maximum laden weights (so long as these do not exceed 'Ministry' plated weights) may be shown on either one or both sides of a vehicle.

Motor tractors and locomotives must have their unladen weight shown in a conspicuous place on the outside of the vehicle where it can easily be seen.

Dimensions Marking

Goods vehicles over 3.5 tonnes and trailers built after 31 May 1998 must be fitted with a plate showing their length and width, unless this information is already shown on either the manufacturer's plate or a 'Ministry' plate.

Plating Certificates

Plating involves the DVSA issuing a plating certificate, in advance of a vehicle's first test. This is attached to the vehicle and denotes maximum weights. This assists with vehicle testing and enforcement. Goods vehicles over 3,500 kg gvw and trailers over 1,020 kg unladen weight must display a plating certificate or a manufacturer's plate showing the maximum permissible gross vehicle weight and individual axle weights at which the vehicle or trailer is allowed to operate within Great Britain.

Special Types Plates

Vehicles carrying abnormal indivisible loads must display a manufacturer's plate showing the maximum weights at which the vehicle can operate and the relevant speeds for travel at those weights. The weights shown must be those approved by the vehicle or trailer manufacturer and the vehicle must not exceed specified Special Types speed limits when travelling loaded to the weight shown on the plate.

Food Vehicles

Vehicles which are used in connection with a food business or from which food is sold must display in a clearly visible place the name and address of the person carrying on the business and the address at which the vehicle is kept or garaged. If the vehicle bears a fleet number and is kept or garaged on that person's premises, the garage address is not required but the local authority must be notified. Most vehicles operating under ATP regulations must also show ATP approval marks of blue letters on a white background, although they may carry a certificate within the vehicle as an alternative.

Height Marking

The travelling height of vehicles and trailers carrying engineering equipment, containers and skips, where the height of the vehicle and load exceeds 3 metres, must be marked in the cab where the driver can see it. Further provisions extend this by requiring the fitment of warning devices where vehicles carry 'high-level equipment' (see Height Marking and Route Descriptions in Chapter 11 for further details).

Hazard Marking

Vehicles which carry hazardous, radioactive or explosive loads must display appropriate hazard warning symbols on the vehicle, whether a bulk tanker, a tank container or a normal delivery vehicle used for carrying hazardous consignments, and on the individual packages too in the latter case. Further details are given in Chapter 20.

Rear Reflective Markings

All vehicles with a maximum permissible weight exceeding 7,500 kg and trailers with a maximum permissible weight exceeding 3,500 kg must be fitted with rear reflective markers which make them more conspicuous at night and in poor visibility (Figures 13.1 and 13.2). The markers may also be displayed on loads such as builders' skips (see below).

For new vehicles first used from 1 April 1996 and trailers manufactured on or after 1 October 1995, which under the regulations require the fitment of rear reflective markings as described below, fitment of a new type of rear marking (in accordance with ECE Regulation 70) is necessary.

Types of Markers

For pre-1 April 1996-used vehicles and pre-1 October 1995-built trailers, there are two types of markings, each in two sizes:

- alternating red fluorescent and yellow reflective diagonal strips – diagrams 1, 2, and 3 in Figure 13.1a;
- a central yellow reflective panel overprinted with the words LONG VEHICLE and having a red fluorescent surround – diagrams 4 and 5 in Figure 13.1a.

For post-1 April 1996-used vehicles and post-1 October 1995-built trailers, the markings comprise two types:

- alternating red fluorescent and yellow retro-reflective diagonal strips – diagrams 1, 2, 3 and 4 in Figure 13.1b;

Figure 13.1a Rear reflective markers required on certain goods vehicles. The plates comprise red fluorescent material background. The lettering is in black on yellow reflex reflecting material

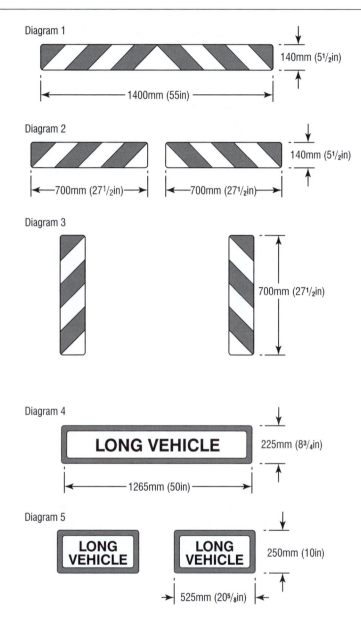

Figure 13.1b Rear markings for post-1 April 1996-used vehicles and post-1 October 1995-built trailers

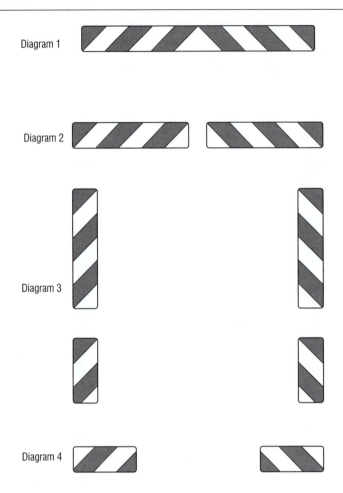

- a central yellow retro-reflective panel surrounded by a red fluorescent border – diagrams 5, 6, 7 and 8 in Figure 13.1c.

Figure 13.1c New-type rear markers for use on long vehicles first used from 1 April 1996 and trailers built since 1 October 1995

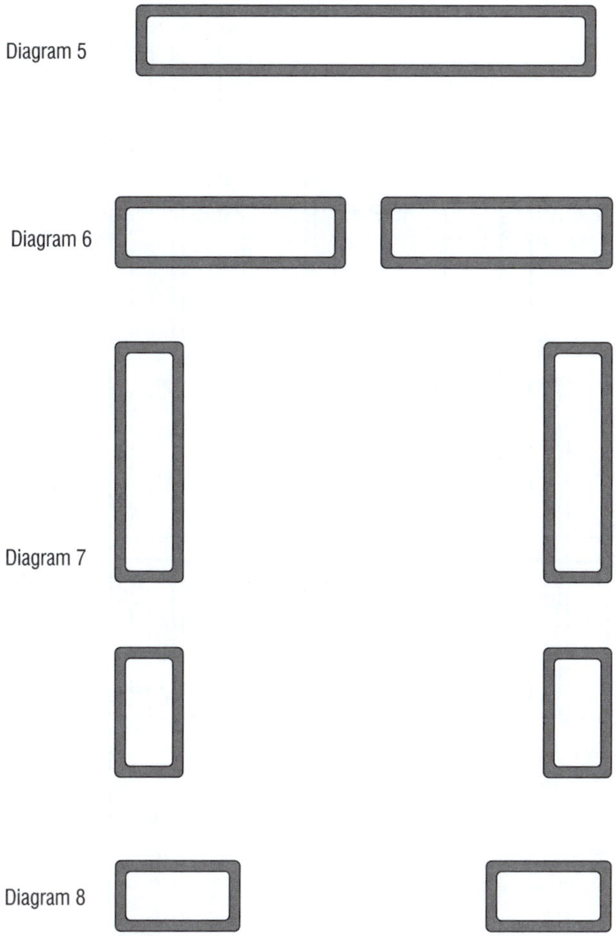

Diagram 5

Diagram 6

Diagram 7

Diagram 8

Figure 13.2 Vehicles which must carry reflective rear markers and the alternative fitting arrangements

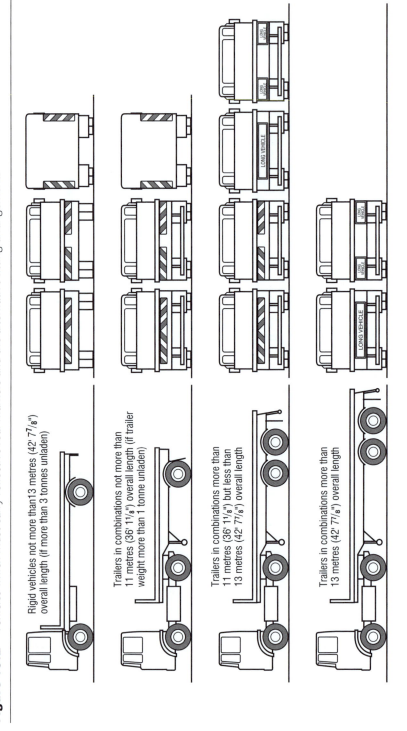

Rigid vehicles not more than 13 metres (42' 7⁷/₈") overall length (if more than 3 tonnes unladen)

Trailers in combinations not more than 11 metres (36' 1¹/₈") overall length (if trailer weight more than 1 tonne unladen)

Trailers in combinations more than 11 metres (36' 1¹/₈") but less than 13 metres (42' 7⁷/₈") overall length

Trailers in combinations more than 13 metres (42' 7⁷/₈") overall length

Specification for Markers

Markers of the type illustrated in Figure 13.1a must comply with the regulations regarding size and colour and they must be in the form of durable plates stamped with the mark BS AU 152/1970. Those of the type illustrated in Figures 13.1b and 13.1c must also comply with the regulations as above and be stamped with a designated approval mark. They must not be simulated by being painted on the vehicle and the plates must not be defaced, cut or modified to aid fitting to the vehicle.

Which Markers to Be Fitted

Pre-1 April 1996-used Vehicles and Pre-1 October 1995-built Trailers

Vehicles not exceeding 13 metres in length and trailers in combinations not exceeding 11 metres must be fitted with the markers shown in diagrams 1, 2 or 3 in Figure 13.1a. Alternatively, they may be fitted with the markers shown in diagrams 1, 2, 3 or 4 in Figure 13.1b.

Vehicles more than 13 metres long and trailers in combinations more than 13 metres long must be fitted with the markers shown in diagrams 4 or 5 in Figure 13.1a (or alternatively those shown in diagrams 5, 6, 7 or 8 in Figure 13.1c).

Trailers in combinations of more than 11 metres but not more than 13 metres may be fitted with the markers shown in diagrams 1, 2, 3, 4 or 5 in Figure 13.1a or those in diagrams 1 to 8 in Figure 13.1b and 13.1c.

Post-1 April 1996-used Vehicles and Post-1 October 1995-built Trailers

Vehicles not exceeding 13 metres in length and trailers in combinations not exceeding 11 metres must be fitted with a marker or set of markers of the types shown in diagrams 1, 2, 3 or 4 in Figure 13.1b.

Vehicles more than 13 metres long and trailers in combinations more than 13 metres long must be fitted with the markers shown in diagrams 5, 6, 7 or 8 in Figure 13.1c. Trailers in combinations of more than 11 metres but not more than 13 metres must be fitted with a marker or set of markers of the types shown in diagrams 1 to 8 in Figure 13.1b and 13.1c.

Fitting Position

The height from the ground to the lower edge of the marker when fitted must not exceed 1,700 mm but must be at least 400 mm. It must be fitted parallel to the ground and be facing square to the rear.

Alternative Fitting Position

When a vehicle which by law requires rear reflective markers to be displayed is carrying a load which obscures partly or wholly the markers so that they are not clearly visible from the rear, the reflective markers may be fitted to the rear of the load.

Exemptions

Certain vehicles as indicated in the following list are exempt from the requirement to fit these markers:

- vehicles having a maximum speed not exceeding 25 mph;
- vehicles with a maximum gross weight not exceeding 7,500 kg;
- passenger vehicles other than articulated buses;
- land tractors, land locomotives, land implements, land implement conveyors, agricultural tractors or industrial tractors;
- works trucks or works trailers;
- vehicles in an unfinished condition proceeding to a works for completion or to a place where they are to be stored or displayed for sale;
- motor vehicles constructed or adapted for the purpose of forming part of articulated vehicles;
- broken-down vehicles while being drawn in consequence of the breakdown;
- engineering plant;
- trailers, not being part of an articulated bus, drawn by public service vehicles;
- vehicles designed for fire-fighting or fire-salvage purposes;
- vehicles designed and used for the purpose of servicing or controlling aircraft;
- vehicles designed and used for the transportation of two or more motor vehicles carried thereon, or of vehicle bodies or two or more boats;
- vehicles proceeding to a place for export;
- vehicles brought temporarily into Great Britain by persons residing abroad;
- vehicles in the service of a visiting force or of a headquarters;
- motor vehicles first used before 1 January 1940;
- vehicles owned or in the service of the army, navy or air force;
- vehicles designed for heating or dispensing tar or similar material for road construction or maintenance;
- trailers designed for the production of asphalt, bitumen or tarmacadam;
- trailers made before 1 August 1982 with an unladen weight not exceeding 1,020 kg;
- trailers with a gross weight not exceeding 3,500 kg.

Previously it was illegal to fit the markers to these vehicles, but a change in the regulations permits the fitting of such markers to exempt vehicles on a voluntary basis, provided the vehicles exceed the specified weight limit. It is illegal to display these markers on vehicles which do not require them by law, except as mentioned above.

Builders' Skips

Rear reflective markings of the type described above (as shown in diagram 3, Figure 13.1a) must be fitted to the ends of builders' skips which are placed on the highway. They must be fitted as a matched pair as near to the outer edge as possible, mounted vertically and no more than 1.5 metres from the ground to the top edge. They must be kept clean, in good order and be visible from a reasonable distance. They must also be illuminated when standing on roads at night.

Conspicuity Markings

The legislation covers the following vehicles:

- goods vehicles with a gross vehicle weight exceeding 7,500 kg first used on or after 10 July 2011;
- trailers with a gross vehicle weight exceeding 3,500 kg manufactured on or after 10 July 2011.

Certain vehicles are exempt from the requirements, as follows:

- a vehicle which is not a goods vehicle;
- goods vehicles not exceeding 7,500 kg gvw;
- trailers not exceeding 3,500 kg gvw;
- chassis cabs;
- incomplete vehicles proceeding to a works for completion or to a place where they are to be stored or displayed for sale;
- articulated tractive units;
- vehicles/trailers with an overall width not exceeding 2.1 metres do not require rear markings;
- vehicles/trailers with an overall length not exceeding 6 metres do not require side markings.

In addition to covering the specification of lights and light components for new vehicles exceeding 7,700 kg gvw and trailers exceeding 3,500 kg gvw, the regulations state that, where applicable, vehicles and trailers must be fitted with horizontal and vertical reflective markings to the rear outline of the vehicle or trailer, as close to the edge of the vehicle or trailer as possible. Where the actual shape is impossible to define, lines produced by reflective tape are acceptable. Reflective tape needs to be red or yellow for rear markings and yellow or white for side markings and the tape must be at least 60 mm in width.

Goods Vehicle Plating, Annual Testing and Vehicle Inspections

14

Most goods vehicles are required to be tested annually to ensure they are safe to operate on the road and meet the legal requirements relating to mechanical condition. In particular, this annual inspection is intended to determine whether vehicles and trailers meet the standards specified in the Road Vehicles (Construction and Use) Regulations 1986 (as amended). Additionally, it is necessary for certain goods vehicles and trailers to be 'Ministry plated' to show the gross vehicle weight and maximum axle weights at which they may be operated. The requirement for annual plating and testing of goods vehicles is contained in the Road Traffic Act 1988 and is detailed in the Goods Vehicles (Plating and Testing) Regulations 1988 as amended.

The DVSA is responsible for the operation of goods vehicle testing stations. There are DVSA goods vehicle testing stations (GVTSs) and privately operated but DVSA-controlled 'designated premises' known as Authorized Testing Facilities (ATFs).

NB: Details of GVTSs or ATFs can be found at GOV.UK.

Annual Testing

All HGVs and semi-trailers and drawbar trailers over 1,020 kg unladen weight must be tested annually at either a GVTS or an ATF. The different levels of annual test for goods vehicles are:

- Class VII = goods vehicles exceeding 3,000 kg and up to 3,500 kg gvw.
- HGV test = goods vehicles over 3,500 kg gvw and trailers over 1,020 kg unladen weight or 3,500 kg gvw.

Certain specialized vehicles are exempt from the test, as shown in the Exemptions from Plating and Testing section found later in this chapter, and the regulations do not apply to vehicles used under a trade licence.

The minimum acceptable test standards for each vehicle component are detailed in the DVSA's HGV inspection manual at GOV.UK. HGV annual test history can be checked online at GOV.UK.

It should be noted that annual test standards do not necessarily allow for further deterioration when the vehicle is in service.

Types of Annual Test

There are various types of HGV annual test, as follows:

- *First test*: the first annual test of the vehicle or trailer carried out no later than the end of the anniversary month in which it was first registered.
- *Parts 2 and 3 re-tests*: re-examination of vehicles which have failed their first test or a re-test.
- *Periodical test*: the annual test which applies to all relevant vehicles after the first test.
- *Part 4 test*: a test which may be required if a notifiable alteration has been made to the vehicle, such as different tyres being fitted, or amending the plating certificate to show different weights as a result of a notifiable alteration.
- *Re-test following appeal*: re-tests carried out following an appeal to the test station manager or subsequently the DVSA regional manager.

Test Fees

The appropriate test fee(s) should be sent to the Goods Vehicle Centre with the first test application form (VTG1 or VTG2), while fees for subsequent tests should be sent direct to the test station. (Operators can open a direct debit account with the DVSA to enable any fee to be collected for any test station.)

The fees for various HGV and trailer tests, re-tests and other services are detailed in Tables 14.1 to 14.4.

Table 14.1 Test fees

NB: *Previous charges relating to the cost of enforcement and compliance functions in relation to motor vehicles and trailers have been abolished.*

Test type	Vehicle type	DVSA – normal hours	DVSA – out of hours	ATF – normal hours	ATF – out of hours
Motor vehicles					
1st test, annual tests, prohibition clearances (full inspections), re-tests after 14 days	2 axles	£112.00	£150.00	£91.00	£129.00
1st test, annual tests, prohibition clearances (full inspections), re-tests after 14 days	3 axles	£144.00	£182.00	£113.00	£151.00
1st test, annual tests, prohibition clearances (full inspections), re-tests after 14 days	4+ axles	£177.00	£215.00	£137.00	£175.00
Re-tests within 14 days, prohibition clearances (partial inspections)	2 axles	£49.00	£69.00	£35.00	£55.00
Re-tests within 14 days, prohibition clearances (partial inspections)	3 axles	£69.00	£89.00	£49.00	£69.00
Re-tests within 14 days, prohibition clearances (partial inspections)	4+ axles	£91.00	£111.00	£65.00	£85.00
Part-paid re-tests*	Any number of axles	£13.00	£13.00	£13.00	£13.00
Notifiable alterations		£27.00	£40.00	£27.00	£40.00
Replacement documents	£13.00				
Trailers					
1st test, annual tests, prohibition clearances (full inspections), re-tests after 14 days	1 axle	£51.00	£75.00	£41.00	£65.00
1st test, annual tests, prohibition clearances (full inspections), re-tests after 14 days	2 axles	£70.00	£94.00	£54.00	£78.00

Table 14.1   *continued*

Test type	Vehicle type	DVSA – normal hours	DVSA – out of hours	ATF – normal hours	ATF – out of hours
1st test, annual tests, prohibition clearances (full inspections), re-tests after 14 days	3+ axles	£84.00	£108.00	£64.00	£88.00
Re-tests within 14 days, prohibition clearances (partial inspections)	1 axle	£25.00	£38.00	£18.00	£31.00
Re-tests within 14 days, prohibition clearances (partial inspections)	2 axles	£35.00	£48.00	£25.00	£38.00
Re-tests within 14 days, prohibition clearances (partial inspections)	3+ axles	£46.00	£59.00	£33.00	£46.00
Part-paid re-tests*	Any number of axles	£7.00	£7.00	£7.00	£7.00
Notifiable alterations		£27.00	£40.00	£27.00	£40.00
Replacement documents	£13.00				

*Part-paid re-tests are for failure items marked on the inspection document (PG14), which are re-tested on the same day as the test, or the next working day.

Table 14.2   Appeals

Fee type	Fee
Appeal fee	£39.00

Table 14.3   TIR and ADR

TIR fee type	Fee
Initial application	£106.00
Re-inspection	£70.00
Type approval	£644.00
Type variation	£106.00

Table 14.3 *continued*

TIR fee type	Fee	
Certificate of conformity	£14	
Duplicate certificate	£14	

ADR fee type	Fee at DVSA site	Fee at ATF site
Initial application and full re-test	£116.00	£83.00
Re-test within 14 days	£63.00	£39.00
New type-approved artic tractor certificate	£28.00	
Duplicate certificate	£14.00	

Hire of loaded trailers for solo tractor unit tests – all types of test £29.50 plus VAT.

Table 14.4 Pit fees which may be charged by some ATFs

Fee type	Fee
Where a test is being carried out on an HGV	£55.00 + VAT*
Where a test is being carried out on a trailer	£40.00 + VAT*

*This fee, which is not always charged, is capped at these rates.

Test Dates

Vehicles may be submitted for test at any one of the full-time or part-time goods vehicle test stations selected by the vehicle operator. Vehicles are due for test each year no later than the end of the anniversary month in which they were first registered (eg a vehicle registered on 1 January 2019 would be due for its first test no later than 31 January 2020 and for subsequent tests by 31 January in each following year).

Trailer Test Dates

The DVSA issues form VTG5B to the supplier of a new trailer prior to the trailer going to the customer. This form has a unique ID number, which must be prominently displayed on the trailer. The first annual test then becomes due before the end of the month of the anniversary of the issue of the form to the customer when the trailer is actually supplied.

Year of Manufacture/Registration

There is an anomaly with due test dates when a vehicle or trailer is manufactured in one year and is not registered before 1 July of the following year. In this case it must be tested by the end of December in the year in which it was first registered or sold.

Phased Programmes and Missed Test Dates

The DVSA allows vehicle operators the facility of having vehicles tested before their due date to accommodate phased programmes of test preparation, rather than having a large number of vehicles due for preparation and test in any particular month of the year.

Test Applications

Initial application for a first test of vehicles and trailers, and subsequent applications, can be made at any GVTS or ATF, or online at GOV.UK.

Annual tests can be booked direct with a test station or online. Tests can be booked through the DVSA Contact Centre on 0300 123 9000. There are two ways to book tests at DVSA test stations online:

- Single vehicles – no registration required with DVSA.
- Multiple vehicles – registration with the DVSA online services (Transport Office Portal) is required.

ATF bookings must be made with the ATF direct.

Register with DVSA online or contact the Transport Office Portal helpdesk at GOV.UK.

Application for subsequent tests can be made either to the Goods Vehicle Centre or direct to any test station/facility. The forms available at GOV.UK used for making the application are:

VTG1   First test of a vehicle

VTG2   First test of a trailer

VTG10 To inform of notifiable alterations to a vehicle

VTG40 For subsequent tests of both vehicles and trailers

VTG15 To be completed and submitted every time a dangerous goods vehicle is presented for test.

Time for Application

Applications can be made up to 93 days in advance of the due date. The DVSA recommends that applications for tests should be made as early as possible. It also states that, if this is the case, the testing station will try to arrange for a test within one month of receipt of the application.

Saturday and Out-of-Hours Testing

Saturday and out-of-hours testing is available at most test stations and facilities for an additional fee. Operators wishing to take advantage of this facility must mark their applications very clearly 'SATURDAY TEST' and show the appropriate date.

Testing for LEZ/CAZ Compliance

Low-emission certificate tests can be booked at a GVTS or ATF to confirm whether older vehicles comply with low emission and clean air zone standards. The cost for a test during normal working hours is £30 at an ATF or £42 at a GVTS.

Trailer Testing

Many operators have more semi-trailers and trailers than tractive units or drawing vehicles, and in order to have these additional trailers tested it may be necessary for them to be submitted for test with a vehicle which has already been tested and has a current valid test certificate. In these cases, only the trailer will be examined and the fee payable will be the trailer fee only.

Cancellations

If it is necessary to cancel a test booking then, provided seven days' notice is given to the test station, either a new test date will be arranged or the fee will be refunded. In exceptional circumstances, such as an accident to the vehicle on the way to the test station, if notification is given to the station within three days of the accident the fee will be carried forward or refunded.

Temporary Exemption

Should it ever be necessary for a test station or facility to cancel a test through exceptional circumstances such as a fire, severe weather conditions, flood, staff sickness, etc, if an alternative station or facility cannot be found in time before the test is due, the station or facility concerned can issue a certificate of temporary exemption (form VTG33), which allows the vehicle to be used until a test can be arranged. This form can be produced either to the police or to examiners of the DVSA if they ask for the test certificate, or when applying for an excise licence for the vehicle.

Refusal to Test

Test station officials have the right to refuse to test a vehicle or trailer for the following reasons, in which circumstances form VTG12 will be issued:

- Arrival after the appointed time.
- Appointment card or vehicle registration document not produced.
- If it is found that the vehicle brought to the test station does not conform to the details given on the application form.
- If the vehicle was booked for the test with a trailer but the trailer is not taken to the test station.
- If the chassis number cannot be found by the examiner or if the serial number given for the trailer by the DVSA is not stamped on it.
- If the vehicle is in a dirty or dangerous condition.
- If the vehicle does not have sufficient fuel or oil to enable the test to be carried out.
- If the test appointment card specified that the vehicle should be loaded for the test and it is taken to the test station without a load. Under normal circumstances the decision whether the vehicle is to be tested in a laden or unladen condition is left to the owner to suit his or her convenience, but in some circumstances the test station may request that the vehicle is fully or partially loaded to enable the brakes to be accurately tested on the roller brake tester.
- In the case of a trailer, if the vehicle submitted with it is not suitable to draw it.
- If the vehicle breaks down during the test.
- If the vehicle is submitted for its annual test (ie not for the first test) or a re-test and the previous test and plating certificates are not produced.
- If the vehicle arrives and is loaded with some dangerous or toxic goods or goods that are comprised of human or animal waste, etc.

Test Procedure

Goods vehicle test stations and ATFs vary in size and in the number of examination staff. Testing normally takes approximately 45 minutes, during which time the driver must be available to assist and move the vehicle as required. Examination of vehicles is carried out by DVSA examiners based at the station, or ATF, in accordance with the *Heavy Goods Vehicle Inspection Manual* published by the DVSA and available free online at GOV.UK. All items which have to be inspected are listed in the *Manual* together with, where necessary, details of how the inspection of each item should be carried out and the reasons for failing the item. Under the 'reasons for rejection' column in the *Manual*, where the item inspected is one that is subject to wear, the maximum tolerance will be indicated. Also shown are the standards at which a prohibition notice may be issued during the annual test.

The Diesel Smoke Test

As part of the annual test, vehicle exhaust emissions are tested using an approved and calibrated smoke meter. This is the statutory smoke meter test and referred to as the smoke test. Smoke tests are carried out to make sure the vehicle's engine is operating efficiently and operating to the relevant emission standard.

Smoke tests are taken after a total of six accelerations have been completed. A visual smoke check may be carried out but only in exceptional circumstances when it is not possible to use the smoke meter or where there is a risk to health and safety. A Low Emissions Vehicle (LEV) smoke test is also available but this is not part of the statutory test.

Inspection Card

During the annual test an inspection card is used with a list of all inspection items. In the case of failure of any item the card is marked accordingly.

A computerized test card is used, which allows the examiner to produce:

- a test 'pass' certificate;
- an advice note (for action required);
- a failure notice;
- a PG9 prohibition notice;
- a PG14 refusal of test certificate.

Tachograph Testing

Tachograph testing is part of the annual test. Tachograph testing will check the unit has been inspected, calibrated and sealed at an approved tachograph calibration centre.

Analogue

The annual test for analogue systems comprises an inspection of the:

- tachograph scale marking in kph (additional mph marking is allowed);
- presence of the tachograph serial number and appropriate 'e' marking;
- tachograph installation/calibration plaque (its presence, condition and calibration date);

- 'K factor' plaque to ensure its presence, condition and that the 'K factor' is clearly visible;
- condition and presence of seals (checking particularly for evidence of interference).

The analogue tachograph must be inspected every two years and recalibrated and resealed every six years.

Digital

As a part of the annual test, the integrity of the installation will be checked, and that it has not been the subject of tampering or manipulation. In particular the test will check that:

- seals on the recording equipment/installation are not missing/improperly fitted or ineffective;
- the 'K factor' setting has not been altered, and that it corresponds to the vehicle parameters;
- there are no manipulation devices connected between the sender/motion sensor and the tachograph head/vehicle unit.

The digital tachograph must be inspected and recalibrated every two years.

The 'K factor' is the parameter for tachograph calibration. It is the number of pulses received by the tachograph when the vehicle travels 1 km.

Tachograph-Exempt Vehicles Using a Tachograph as a Speedometer

A vehicle must have a tachograph fitted unless the person presenting the vehicle for test claims that it is exempt from the tachograph regulations. If a tachograph is fitted on an exempt vehicle and used in place of a speedometer, the tachograph must be calibrated and sealed in accordance with the Community Recording Equipment Regulations. However, provided the seals remain intact, there will be no requirement for two-yearly inspections or further calibration. If the above vehicle legally requires a speed limiter and has the speed signal operating the limiter transmitted from the tachograph head, then all the seals including the gearbox sender unit must remain intact to avoid the requirement for recalibration. If the vehicle does not legally require a speed limiter (or the speed limiter does not receive the speed signal from the tachograph head) then the tachograph head seals (excluding the gearbox sender unit seal) must remain intact to avoid the requirement for recalibration.

Speed Limiter Checks

An electronic device is used during testing to check the function and setting of the speed limiter under test item 33 and failure of the item will jeopardize the whole vehicle test.

ABS/EBS Cables

Where tractive units and trailers are fitted with ISO 7638 sockets to power ABS and/or EBS braking systems, these sockets must be connected by a dedicated ABS cable (where one or the other does not have an ISO 7638 socket, the ABS is powered through the stop light circuit). Vehicles presented for test without a cable will be refused a test. Vehicles stopped at roadside checks without a cable will also receive a prohibition notice (PG9 – see the section on Prohibition Notices later in this chapter).

Where a vehicle and trailer are fitted with EBS as well as ABS, a seven-core cable connection must be used. Vehicles found during roadside checks to have only a five-core instead of the requisite seven-core cable will receive a Defect Note (PGDN 35). On presentation at the test station or ATF such vehicles will receive an advisory notice to replace the cable.

Test Pass

Test certificates are issued by the test station or ATF. For goods vehicles the certificate is form VTG5 and for goods-carrying trailers it is VTG5A. The trailer test disc is included with the certificate and this must be fixed onto the trailer in a protective holder in a position where it is conspicuous, readily accessible and clearly visible from the nearside.

Replacement Documents

Replacement test certificates, replacement plates and plating certificates (see later in chapter) may be obtained from local test stations or the GVC at Swansea at a cost of £14.00 each. Application in both cases should be made on form VTG59, obtainable from goods vehicle test stations or the GVC. Automatic replacement of lost or defaced documents is not guaranteed. The Secretary of State has powers to order a re-test before issuing such replacements, in which case full test fees become payable.

Test Failure and Re-tests

When the vehicle is sent for test, it is recommended that a mechanic with a toolkit and minor spares items (light bulbs, for example) accompanies it so that any minor defects can be rectified on the premises and the test can be completed. The examiner may allow certain minor defects to be repaired during the test. In some instances the vehicle may be allowed to be taken out of the test line for minor repairs to be carried out but this is at the discretion of the examiner.

If minor repairs are allowed to be made at the time of the test, the fact that the vehicle arrived for test in a 'fail state' will be recorded and applied to the OCRS.

If it is necessary to take the vehicle away to get the defects rectified and it is submitted again later that day or during the next working day, no additional charge is made. These free re-tests are restricted to those cases where the vehicle failed because of certain prescribed defects in items as follows:

- legal plate position;
- legal plate details;
- bumper bars;
- spare wheel carrier;
- cab doors;
- mirrors;
- view to front;
- speedometer;
- audible warning;
- oil leaks;
- fuel tanks, pipes and system;
- obligatory sidelamps;
- obligatory rear lamps;
- reflectors;
- direction indicators;
- headlamps – vertical aim;
- obligatory headlamps;
- obligatory stop lamps.

If the vehicle which fails the test is submitted to the same test station again within 14 days, a reduced re-test fee is charged and only the items on which the test was failed are re-examined. Arrangements for re-tests have to be made with the manager of the test station or ATF concerned. As with minor defects repaired at the time of the test, any test failure will also be recorded and applied to the operator's OCRS.

Appeals against Test Failure

If a vehicle or trailer undergoing test or re-test failed for a reason which the operator believes is not justified, there is a right of appeal to the test station or ATF manager or DVSA regional manager, by completing form VT17 within 14 days. The form can be found on the GOV.UK website and can be emailed to csccomplaints@dvsa.gov.uk or posted to the DVSA in Swansea. The fee is usually the same as the cost of a test or re-test.

Reduced Pollution Examination of Vehicles

Although reduced pollution certificates and grants are no longer generally used, they may be required for vehicles operating in LEZs and CAZs and operators may still submit their vehicles to a goods vehicle testing station for examination by the DVSA.

The reduced pollution requirement may be satisfied by:

- a new vehicle meeting the required standard;
- the fitting of a new engine to a vehicle; or
- the fitting of a type-approved device for which there is a Certificate of Conformity issued by the vehicle manufacturer.

The reduced pollution requirements are satisfied if the rate and content of a vehicle's particulate emissions do not exceed the number of grams per kilowatt-hour specified in the tables below.

Table 14.5 EU emission standards for HD diesel engines, g/kWh (smoke in m^{-1})

Tier	Date	CO	HC	NO_x	PM	Smoke
Euro IV	October 2005	1.5	0.46	3.5	0.02	0.5
Euro V	October 2008	1.5	0.46	2.0	0.02	0.5
Euro VI	January 2014	1.5	0.13	0.4	0.01	

Table 14.6 Emission standards for diesel and gas engines, transient test, g/kWh

Tier	Date	CO	NMHC	CH4a	NO_x	PMb
Euro IV	October 2005	4.0	0.55	1.1	3.5	0.03
Euro V	October 2008	4.0	0.55	1.1	2.0	0.03
Euro VI	January 2014	4.0	0.16	0.5	0.46	0.01

Reduced Pollution Schemes for Lighter Vehicles

The introduction of the Euro-VI standards and the continuing move towards reducing emissions is being extended to include lighter vehicles. The EU intends to introduce stricter limits on emissions from light road vehicles by making manufacturers change existing engine specifications and maintenance regimes for specifications and maintenance regimes that will make the vehicles more fuel efficient. Most manufacturers have already confirmed that they will be introducing or have introduced AdBlue and/or selective catalytic reduction (SCR) systems for light vehicles. Other considerations include fitting lighter vehicles with exhaust gas recirculation (EGR) systems in order to help meet the proposed new standards.

Plating of Goods Vehicles and Trailers

Manufacturer's Plating

All new goods vehicles and new trailers over 1,020 kg unladen weight must be fitted with a plate by the manufacturer which shows specified information as follows:

- the manufacturer's name;
- the date of manufacture;
- vehicle type;
- engine type and power rating;
- chassis or serial number;
- number of axles;
- maximum weight allowed on each axle;
- maximum gross weight for the vehicle (including the weight imposed on the tractive unit by a semi-trailer in the case of articulated vehicles);
- maximum train weight.

The plate containing this information is normally fitted inside the driver's cab on the nearside.

For trailers, the information shown on the plate is:

- the manufacturer's name;
- date of manufacture;
- chassis or serial number;
- number of axles;
- maximum weight allowed on each axle;
- maximum weight imposed on the drawing vehicle in the case of semi-trailers;
- maximum gross weight for the trailer.

The plate for trailers is usually riveted to the chassis frame on the nearside.

Design Weights

The weights stated are those at which the manufacturer has designed the vehicle to operate. Where these weights exceed those permitted by law (ie in the C&U

Regulations) for the type of vehicle in question, then, until such time as the vehicle is plated by the DVSA, the lower statutory weight limits apply. Similarly, if the manufacturer's design weight is lower than that permitted by law for the type of vehicle, then it is still the lower limit which applies.

Vehicle Dimensions

Goods vehicles over 3.5 tonnes gross weight and trailers manufactured since 31 May 1998 must be fitted with a plate showing their length and width, unless this information is already shown on either the manufacturer's plate or a 'Ministry' plate.

Plating Certificates

Plating involves the DVSA issuing a plating certificate, in advance of a vehicle's first test. This is attached to the vehicle and denotes maximum weights. This assists with vehicle testing and enforcement. Goods vehicles over 3,500 kg gvw and trailers over 1,020 kg unladen weight must display a plating certificate or a manufacturer's plate showing the maximum permissible gross vehicle weight and individual axle weights at which the vehicle or trailer is allowed to operate within Great Britain.

A plating certificate (form VTG7 – for all vehicles and trailers) and a plate (form VTG6 – for pre-1 April 1983 vehicles; VTG6T – for post-1 April 1983 vehicles; VTG6A – for all trailers) and, on special request (apply on form VTG101), for older goods vehicles used in international operations, giving similar details to those on the manufacturer's plate, are issued by the Goods Vehicle Centre after receipt of the necessary documents (including the Type Approval Certificate) when a new vehicle is first registered. The plating certificate must be retained by the vehicle operator but the plate must be fixed to the vehicle in an easily accessible position. Generally, it should be fitted inside the cab of vehicles on the nearside (but not affixed to the door) and in a suitable position on the nearside of trailers (it is usually fitted to the chassis frame). In all cases the plates should be protected against the weather, kept clean and legible, and secure against accidental loss.

Tractive units and semi-trailers in articulated outfit combinations are plated separately and the individual plates must be fixed separately to the tractive unit and the trailer.

Downplating of Vehicles

Downplating enables lower rates of vehicle tax and HGV Road User Levy. This may be requested using form VTG10.

Where no alteration has been made to the vehicle, inspection by the DVSA will not normally be necessary. For example, in cases where:

- an articulated vehicle is downplated to 23 tonnes gvw;
- a four-axle rigid vehicle is downplated to 27 tonnes gvw;
- a three-axle rigid vehicle is downplated to 19 tonnes gvw;
- a two-axle rigid vehicle is downplated to 12 tonnes gvw,

the DVSA will not require any further information or action to be taken. Where these limits are exceeded, the DVSA may request the reason for operating at such low weights.

In no circumstances will a vehicle be plated at lower weights to compensate for defects such as inefficient braking performance or if it is not maintained to required safety standards or otherwise does not comply with legal requirements. In such cases examiners at the goods vehicle testing station/ATF will refuse to issue the vehicle with a test (pass) certificate.

The procedure for downplating is to complete the form for notifiable alterations (VTG10), obtainable from goods vehicle test stations and the Goods Vehicle Centre, and then:

- hand it in at the time of presenting the vehicle for its annual goods vehicle test;
- contact the local goods vehicle test station at any time for an appointment to submit the vehicle for downplating;
- send the form and the fee (see below) to the Goods Vehicle Centre.

The statutory fee is £27 if the downplating is done at the time of the annual test. If not, then the fee is £40. The old vehicle plate will need to be returned and a new vehicle plate (to be fitted in the vehicle cab) and plating certificate will be issued.

International Plates

Since 2014, international plates are automatically produced for all new vehicles as part of the ECWVTA and the international plate application form (VTG101) has been withdrawn.

Notifiable Alterations

In addition to downplating, operators who make any alteration to the structure of their vehicles must notify the DVSA before the vehicle is used on the road. Details of the alterations which require notification, on form VTG10, are as follows:

a *Alterations to the structure or fixed equipment of a vehicle which vary its carrying capacity*
These include alterations to any of the following items:

(i) *Chassis frame or structure*

Any alteration which increases or decreases the front or rear overhang by more than 1 foot. Any structural alteration (other than normal adjustment of an extensible structure) which reduces or extends the wheelbase (or in the case of a semi-trailer the equivalent distance). Any other extension, deletion or alteration including cutting, welding, riveting, etc, which materially weakens the chassis frame or structure or changes its torsional stiffness.

(ii) *Steering suspension, wheels and axles (including stub axles and wheel hubs)*

The fitting of steering gear, axles, hubs or road springs of a different design or load-bearing capacity. The fitting of additional wheels and axles, or the removal of such items. Any addition, deletion or alteration which reduces the inherent strength of the above components.

(iii) *The fitting of an alternative body of different design, construction or type*

Any alteration which reduces materially the strength of the body structure or the means by which it is attached to the chassis. Any alteration which causes the body to extend beyond the rear of the chassis frame.

b *Alterations to braking system*

These comprise alterations which adversely affect either the braking system or the braking performance of the vehicle. They include the addition or deletion of components such as reservoirs, servomotors, brake actuators, exhausters and compressors. They would also include the addition of any equipment which it is necessary to connect to any part of the braking system, and the fitting of different brake drums or shoes or liners of a smaller contact area.

c *Other alterations to the structure or fixed equipment*

Any other alteration made in the load-bearing structure or fixed equipment of the vehicle, eg the coupling gear, which could make the vehicle unsafe to travel on roads at any weight shown on the plate and plating certificate. In the case of a motor vehicle this could include such alterations as changing the type of engine or repositioning the engine or its mountings (eg petrol to diesel, normal control to forward control, etc). Notifiable alteration inspections and certification also attract a fee of £27.00 during normal working hours or £40.00 if conducted out of hours at DVSA test stations or ATFs.

NB: *Any trailer that is over eight years old submitted for examination under the notifiable alterations procedure must have its braking system brought up to the latest standard applicable at the time of its rebuilding.*

Exemptions from Plating and Testing

Vehicles which are subject to the Goods Vehicle (Plating and Testing) Regulations 1988 (as amended) are exempt from the need to hold current plating and testing certificates while being taken to a test station, when used on a road during the test, returning to base from the test station after a test and being taken (unladen) to a working or repair centre for work to be carried out on them in connection with the test.

Exempt Vehicles

Vehicles to which the regulations do not apply are as follows:

- dual-purpose vehicles not constructed or adapted to form part of an articulated vehicle;
- road rollers;
- vehicles designed for fire-fighting or fire-salvage purposes;
- works trucks, straddle carriers used solely as works trucks and works trailers;
- motor vehicles used solely for clearing frost, ice or snow from roads by means of a snow plough or similar contrivance, whether forming part of the vehicle or not;
- vehicles constructed or adapted for, and used solely for, spreading material on roads to deal with frost, ice or snow;
- motor vehicles used for no other purpose than the haulage of lifeboats and the conveyance of the necessary gear of the lifeboats which are being hauled;
- living vans not exceeding 3,500 kg design weight;
- vehicles constructed or adapted for, and used primarily for the purpose of, carrying equipment permanently fixed to the vehicle which equipment is used for medical, dental, veterinary, health, educational, display or clerical purposes, such use not directly involving the sale, hire or loading of goods from the vehicle;
- trailers which have no other brakes than a parking brake and brakes which automatically come into operation on the overrun of the trailer;
- vehicles exempted from duty because they do not travel on public roads for more than 6 miles in any week and trailers drawn by such vehicles (Vehicle Excise and Registration Act 1994, Schedule 3);
- agricultural motor vehicles;
- agricultural trailers and trailed appliances drawn on roads only by a land tractor;
- passenger-carrying vehicles and hackney carriages;
- vehicles used solely for the purpose of funerals;
- goods vehicles proceeding to a port for export and vehicles in the service of a visiting force;
- unladen vehicles operating under a trade licence;

- vehicles equipped with new or improved equipment or types of equipment and used solely by a manufacturer of vehicles or their equipment or by an importer of vehicles, for or in connection with the test or trial of any such equipment;

- motor vehicles temporarily in Great Britain;

- motor vehicles for the time being licensed in Northern Ireland;

- trailers temporarily in Great Britain, a period of 12 months not having elapsed since the vehicle in question was last brought into Great Britain;

- track-laying vehicles;

- steam-propelled vehicles;

- motor vehicles manufactured before 1 January 1960 used unladen and not drawing a laden trailer, and trailers manufactured before 1 January 1960 and used unladen;

- three-wheeled vehicles used for street cleansing, the collection or disposal of refuse and the collection or disposal of the contents of gullies;

- vehicles designed and used for the purpose of servicing or controlling aircraft, while so used on an aerodrome within the meaning of the Civil Aviation Act 1982 or on roads to such extent as is essential for the purpose of proceeding directly from one part of such an aerodrome to another part thereof or, subject as aforesaid, outside such an aerodrome unladen and not drawing a laden trailer;

- vehicles designed for use, and used, on an aerodrome mentioned in the preceding paragraph, solely for the purpose of road cleansing, the collection or disposal of refuse or the collection or disposal of the contents of gullies or cesspools;

- vehicles provided for police purposes and maintained in workshops approved by the Minister as suitable for such maintenance, being vehicles provided in England and Wales by a police authority or the receiver for the Metropolitan Police or, in Scotland, by a police authority or a joint police committee;

- heavy motor cars or motor cars constructed or adapted for the purpose of forming part of an articulated vehicle which are used for drawing only a trailer of a type described above or a trailer being used for, or in connection with, any purpose for which it is authorized to be used on roads under the Special Types General Order;

- play buses.

NB: *The following definition applies in the above exemptions: 'works truck' means a motor vehicle designed for use in private premises and used on a road only in delivering goods from or to such premises, to or from a vehicle on a road in the immediate neighbourhood, or in passing from one part of any such premises to another or to other private premises in the immediate neighbourhood, or in connection with roadworks while at or in the immediate neighbourhood of the site of such works.*

Taxing Exempt Vehicles

When applying for a vehicle excise licence for a vehicle exempt from plating and testing, it is necessary to complete declaration form V112G (available from the GOV.UK website, the DVLA and main post offices) in order to obtain the licence without a valid test certificate.

Tachograph Testing

Operators submitting vehicles for test which are exempt from the requirement for tachograph fitment must declare the exemption on the appropriate form, which is form DVSA 75. The form is available on the GOV.UK website, which lists the exempt categories (see the Exemptions section in Chapter 5 for a list of tachograph exemptions).

Production of Documents

The police and DVSA examiners can request production of both test and plating certificates for goods vehicles when such vehicles have been involved in an accident or if they believe an offence has been committed. If these documents cannot be produced at the time, they may be produced within seven days at a police station convenient to the person to whom the request was made, or as soon as reasonably practicable thereafter.

Enforcement Checks on Vehicles

Operator Compliance Risk Score

The OCRS is a key element of 'targeted enforcement'. The DVSA scores each 'O' licence holder from 0 to 10 to indicate how many times the operator has been caught breaking the rules. Operators are rated red, amber and green – those with a higher score and red rating will be targeted for enforcement activity. The scores are based on results from annual tests, vehicle inspections and prosecution records.

Currently, the historic score for an operator is calculated on data gathered over a three-year rolling period. There are actually two scores used to arrive at a historic score. There is a 'roadworthiness' score where points are issued for test failures, PG9s, etc, and there is an 'enforcement' score for issues such as drivers' hours and tachograph offences.

Points for offences vary according to their severity and are banded. For example:

Table 14.7 Points for offences

Points	Offence	Band
300	Prosecution	5
200	£300 fixed penalty	4
100	£200 fixed penalty	3
50	£100 fixed penalty	2
25	£50 fixed penalty	1
0	Verbal warning	0

The actual historic score is arrived at by dividing the number of points accrued by the number of events over a three-year rolling reference period. Once this is done, each operator is allocated a 'risk band'. There are separate risk bands for roadworthiness and traffic enforcement scores as detailed in Table 14.8.

Table 14.8 Risk band

Risk Band	Roadworthiness	Enforcement
Grey	no score	no score
Green	<10	<5
Amber	10–25	5–30
Red	>25	>30

The DVSA also uses a 'weighting factor' in relation to the length of time since an offence was recorded. By doing this, older offences accrue fewer points. Currently offences are weighted as follows:

- up to 12 months – multiplied by 1;
- over 12 months and up to two years – multiplied by 0.75;
- over two years – multiplied by 0.5.

Regulation EC 1071/2009 and regulation EU 2016/403 categorize offences deemed as Most Serious Infringements (MSI). These are:

- exceeding the six-day or fortnightly driving limits by more than 25 per cent;
- exceeding the maximum daily driving limit by a margin of more than 50 per cent without taking a break or uninterrupted rest period of at least 4.5 hours;
- driving without a valid roadworthiness 'annual test' certificate;
- driving with a very serious component defect, such as braking, steering, wheels/tyres, suspension or chassis;

- not having a speed limiter or using a fraudulent device that modifies the speed limiter;
- using a fraudulent device able to modify the tachograph records;
- driving with a driver tachograph card that has been falsified or belonging to another driver;
- transporting regulated dangerous goods without identifying them on the vehicle as dangerous goods;
- serious overloading of a vehicle with a gross weight:
  - up to 12 tonnes by a factor of 25 per cent or more;
  - more than 12 tonnes by a factor of 20 per cent or more.

Operators can find out their current OCRS for the three-year period up to the end of the previous calendar month by emailing top.registrations@dvsa.gov.uk. As OCRS figures are updated weekly, it is not possible to obtain backdated reports, and operators wishing to keep track of their performance should obtain their OCRS reports regularly. Information relating to OCRS is also available from the DVSA on 0300 123 9000.

Earned Recognition

DVSA earned recognition is a voluntary scheme for operators to prove they meet driver and vehicle standards. Operators share performance information with the DVSA, such as their MOT initial pass rates and if their drivers have broken drivers' hours rules. In return, their vehicles are less likely to be stopped for roadside inspections, saving them time and money. This allows the DVSA to target more of its enforcement activities at the high-risk operators who put other road users in danger.

Operators need to have undergone an audit of their transport management processes and use a DVSA-validated IT system for vehicle maintenance and drivers' hours. This will monitor whether a set of key performance indicators (KPIs) is being met. Every four weeks, the system informs the DVSA if any of the KPIs have been missed. Further information is available at GOV.UK.

Roadside Checks

In addition to carrying out annual vehicle tests at the GVTS, DVSA examiners operate roadside checks on commercial vehicles. They are carried out at intervals on main roads. Typically, vehicles which are required for examination are directed into a lay-by, where they are inspected mainly for visible wear and defects of the brakes, steering gear, silencers, tyres, lights and reflectors, and for the emission of black smoke when the engine is revved up.

The *DVSA Categorization of Defects* guide promotes consistency among vehicle examiners and provides guidance on the action to take when roadworthiness defects are found during vehicle inspections, either at the roadside or at annual test. The guide is available at GOV.UK.

Vehicle Inspections on Premises

DVSA examiners and police officers are, at any reasonable time, free to enter any premises on which goods vehicles are kept and to examine goods vehicles. The owner's consent is not needed. However, to examine any vehicle other than a goods vehicle, the owner's consent must be obtained or they must be given at least 48 hours' notice; *if the notice is sent by recorded delivery post the period is increased to 72 hours*. In the latter case the consent of the owner of the premises, if different from the vehicle owner, must also be obtained. If on these inspections defects are found on the vehicles examined, the same procedure applies regarding the prohibition of their use as explained for roadside checks.

A police officer in uniform or a DVSA examiner, on production of suitable identification, can instruct a driver in charge of a stationary goods vehicle on a road (by the issue of form GV3) to take the vehicle to a suitable place to be examined, but this must not be for a distance of more than five miles.

Prohibition notices can be issued by examiners at a goods vehicle test station if defects of a serious enough nature are found. Also, the police may be notified if prosecution is warranted.

Powers of Police, DVSA Examiners and Certifying Officers

The Road Traffic Act 1988 gives authorized examiners powers to test and inspect vehicles (and examine vehicle records), on production of their authority, as follows:

- They can test any motor vehicle or trailer on a road to check that legal requirements regarding brakes, silencer, steering, tyres, lights and reflectors, smoke and fumes are complied with, and may drive the vehicle for this purpose.

- They can test a vehicle for the same purposes on premises if the owner of the premises consents or has been given at least 48 hours' notice, except where the vehicle has been involved in a notifiable accident, when there is no requirement to give notice. If the notice given is in writing it must be sent by recorded post and the time limit is extended to 72 hours.

- They may at any time enter and inspect any goods vehicle and goods vehicle records, and may at a reasonable time enter premises on which they believe a goods vehicle or goods vehicle records are kept.

- They can request a driver of a stationary goods vehicle to take the vehicle to a place for inspection up to five miles away.

- They can at any reasonable time enter premises where used vehicles are sold, supplied or offered for sale or supply or exposed or kept for sale or supply, to ensure that such vehicles can be used on a road without contravening the appropriate regulations. They may drive a vehicle on the road for this purpose.

- They may enter at any reasonable time premises where vehicles or vehicle parts are sold, supplied, offered for sale or supply, exposed or kept for sale or supply.

- They may require the person in charge of any vehicle to take it to a weighbridge to be weighed. If the vehicle is more than five miles from the place where the request is made and the vehicle is found not to be overloaded, the operator can claim against the highway authority for any loss sustained.

- When a goods vehicle has been weighed and found to exceed its weight limit and its use on a road would be a risk to public safety, they can prohibit its road use by the issue of form TE160P until the weight is reduced to within the legal limit.

- If they find that a goods vehicle is unfit or likely to become unfit for service, they can prohibit the driving of the vehicle on the road either immediately or from a later date and time by the issue of a prohibition notice (form PG9 – see later).

NB: Police powers in this respect are restricted under the provisions of the Road Traffic Act 1991 (effective from 1 July 1992) to the issue only of immediate prohibitions in circumstances where they consider that the driving of a defective vehicle would involve a 'danger of injury to any person' as opposed to the DVSA examiner's right to prohibit a vehicle which is 'unfit for service'.

- Where a prohibition order has been placed on a vehicle for various reasons, they are empowered to remove the prohibition (by the issue of form PG10) when they consider the vehicle is fit for use. *Where evidence of the vehicle's test certificate is required to be produced the vehicle will normally be subjected to a full roadworthiness test by the DVSA at a goods vehicle testing station or ATF – and payment of the current full test fee will be required.*

- They can ask the driver of a goods vehicle registered in an EU member state, fitted with a tachograph, to produce the tachograph record of the vehicle when it is used in this country and ask to examine the official calibration plaque in the instrument. They can at any reasonable time enter premises where they believe such a vehicle is to be found or that tachograph records are kept, and may inspect the vehicle and records (ie tachograph charts).

Police Powers

- A police officer or Highways England traffic officer *in uniform* can stop a moving vehicle on a road. They can direct the vehicle to a place of testing or test any motor vehicle or trailer on a road to check that legal requirements regarding brakes, silencer, steering, tyres, lights and reflectors, smoke and fumes are complied with. They may drive the vehicle for this purpose.

- They can test a vehicle for the same purposes on premises if the owner of the premises consents or has been given at least 48 hours' notice (or 72 hours if given by recorded post), except that consent is not necessary where the vehicle has been involved in a notifiable accident.

Enforcement Powers for DVSA Examiners

DVSA enforcement support officers (stopping officers) also have powers to stop moving vehicles. These officers are uniformed and operate with liveried and fully marked vehicles. DVSA stopping officers have the powers to:

- stop commercial vehicles;

- carry out vehicle roadworthiness inspections;

- carry out vehicle weight checks;

- inspect documents, records and tachograph equipment;

- ensure that 'O' licence discs are correctly exhibited;

- ensure that a valid 'O' licence is held;

- ensure that drivers carry evidence of their Driver CPC training, or exemptions from such.

Resisting or obstructing a DVSA stopping officer is a criminal offence and can carry a fine of up to £5,000. The DVSA publishes its *Enforcement Sanctions Policy* which may be applied when vehicles are stopped and problems, which may lead to action being taken against the driver and/or the operator, are encountered. This policy is available at GOV.UK.

Powers of Trading Standards Officers

Trading standards officers (ie employed by local authorities) can request an HGV driver who requires an official conveyance note (ie ballast which includes sand, gravel etc) to take the vehicle to a weighbridge to be weighed. Goods may have to be unloaded if necessary.

Inspection Notices and Prohibitions

Vehicle Inspection Notice – Form PGDN35

Following an inspection of a vehicle which is found to have no serious road safety defects, form PGDN35 (commonly known as an inspection notice) is issued to indicate to the user either that one or more minor defects were found which it is in their interest, and the interests of other road users, to have rectified at an early date – it is not actually a prohibition – or that the vehicle has no apparent defects (subject to a disclaimer) to save further inspection later on that journey or that day. This form is also issued when a vehicle is stopped but found to be defect-free to enable the driver to prove that this is the case should they be stopped again on the same journey.

NB: If this form is produced by a computer it is known as a form PG35ECDN.

Prohibition Notices

The driver of any vehicle found to have serious defects by an enforcement officer is issued form PG9. Form PG9 is the examiner's authority to stop the use of the vehicle on the road for carrying goods. Depending on how serious the defects are, the prohibition will either take effect immediately, in which case the vehicle, if loaded, has to remain where it is until either it is repaired or has been unloaded and then taken away for repair, for which the examiner will give authority by issuing form PG9B, or it may be delayed for 12 to 24 hours or more depending on the seriousness of the fault. In this case the vehicle may continue to operate until the limit of the period of exemption by which time, if it is not repaired and cleared, it must be taken off the road. If defects recorded as requiring immediate attention are repaired quickly on the roadside, the examiner may issue a variation to the PG9 notice with form PG9A, which then allows the vehicle to be removed and used until the new time specified on the variation notice (the forms are described further individually below). In all cases where a PG9 is issued, details will be recorded on the operator's OCRS.

C&U Offences

If defects are found at a roadside check which make the vehicle unsafe to be on the road (usually tyres, brakes, steering or suspension defects) or if the defects are such that an offence under the Construction and Use regulations is committed (particularly in respect of lights, reflectors, smoke emission or the horn), DVSA examiners will report these items to the police for consideration for prosecution and the matter will be recorded on the operator's OCRS.

Prohibition Forms

A number of official forms as described below are used by DVSA examiners in the process of inspecting vehicles, recording defects and prohibiting the use of those which are defective. Any PG forms, or TE forms (see below), retained by the operator should be filed in the vehicle history file in the same way as periodic vehicle inspection sheets and retained for 15 months.

Form PG9

When an inspection by a DVSA examiner reveals defects of a serious nature, form PG9 will be issued, specifying the defects and stating the precise time at which the prohibition preventing further use of the vehicle comes into force (which could be the time when the notice is written out – ie with immediate effect – or later). A copy of the PG9 is given to the driver and this must be carried on the vehicle until the prohibition is removed. Further copies of the notice are sent to the vehicle operator and, if the vehicle is specified on an 'O' licence, to the relevant TC.

If the PG9 has immediate effect, this means that the vehicle cannot be driven or towed away (see below).

Form PG9A

This form (Variation in the Terms of a Prohibition…) is issued if the DVSA examiner wishes to vary the terms of a PG9 notice by either suspending the PG9 until a future time (eg midnight on the day of issue), altering the time (which is effectively the same thing as suspending the notice as mentioned above) or altering the list of defects shown on the PG9 notice.

Form PG9B

A DVSA examiner may, after issuing a PG9, exempt the vehicle (Exemption from a Prohibition…) from the terms of the prohibition and permit its movement provided that the vehicle:

- is unladen;
- proceeds at a speed not in excess of a specified figure;
- does not tow a trailer;
- is towed on a rigid tow bar;
- is towed on a suspended tow;
- is not used after lighting-up time (if it has lighting defects);
- proceeds only between two specified points.

Other conditions may be added as appropriate.

Form PG9C

When a vehicle which is subject to a PG9 notice is presented to a DVSA examiner for clearance of the defect and the examiner is not satisfied that it is fit for service, he or she may issue form PG9C (Refusal to Remove a Prohibition…), which means that the original PG9 notice remains in force until the defects are satisfactorily rectified. (Forms PG9 A, B and C are all actually different parts of the same form, although they carry individual identities.)

Form PG10

If the defects specified in a PG9 notice have been repaired to the satisfaction of the DVSA examiner, a PG10 notice is issued, which removes the prohibition. The TC must be notified of the clearance if the vehicle is specified on an 'O' licence.

Form TE160

This relates to prohibition on the use of overweight vehicles. It effectively requires drivers of such vehicles to take the vehicle to a weighbridge and, if it is found to be overloaded, reduce the gross weight to legal limits before proceeding on their journey.

NB: It is a defence to a charge of overloading that the vehicle was on its way to the nearest practicable weighbridge or that at the time of loading the weight was within legal limits and was subsequently not more than 5 per cent heavier despite not having any additions to the load en route.

Form TE160DH

This notice relates to prohibition on the use of a vehicle for drivers' hours contraventions. It effectively requires the driver of the vehicle to park the vehicle and to take any statutory breaks, or rests, that are required before being allowed to continue their journey.

Effects of Prohibition

A vehicle must not, under any circumstances, be used to carry goods while it is the subject of a PG9 prohibition notice, but despite the prohibition notice a vehicle may be driven unladen to a goods vehicle test station or to a place agreed with a goods vehicle examiner (both by previous appointment only) in order to have the vehicle inspected. The vehicle may also be driven on the road for test purposes, provided it is unladen, within three miles of where it has been repaired.

Appeals against the Issue of Prohibition Notices

There is no appeal against the imposition of a PG9 prohibition notice, but there is a right of appeal against refusal to remove a prohibition after repair.

Northern Ireland Certification of Vehicles

Vehicle services available in Northern Ireland have been increased in recent years. This includes access to the DVLA to tax vehicles (form V85 for HGVs or online at GOV.UK), the DVLA's fleet scheme and simplification of the procedure to move vehicles between GB and NI. In addition, an increased range of licensing transactions is now permitted at post offices in Northern Ireland.

The GB system of goods vehicle plating and annual testing does not fully apply in Northern Ireland. Northern Ireland has its own Goods Vehicle Certification scheme which requires HGVs to be submitted to the Department for Infrastructure (NI) for an annual mechanical examination. Under the Goods Vehicles (Certification) Regulations (Northern Ireland) 1982, owners of HGVs (other than those specifically exempted) must obtain a test certificate for each vehicle no later than one year from the date of first registration and annually thereafter.

Applications for a certificate can be made online, by post or in person to any of the test stations, or by telephone (0845 247 2471).

While the Driver and Vehicle Agency (DVA) controls enforcement and vehicle testing, the operator licensing role is run by the Department for Infrastructure, Transport Regulation Unit. Email: dcu@infrastructure-ni.gov.uk; tel: 028 9054 0540.

Applications and Certification by Non-NI-Based Bodies

Where an application is made by a corporate body with its principal or registered office outside Northern Ireland or by a person residing outside Northern Ireland, the following conditions must be observed:

- During the currency of the certificate a place of business must be retained in NI.
- They must be prepared to accept, at such a place of business, any summons or other document relating to any matter or offence arising in NI in connection with the vehicle the certificate is applied for.
- They must undertake to appear at any court as required by such a summons or by any other document.
- They must admit and submit to the jurisdiction of the court relative to the subject matter of such summons or other document.

Failure to comply with any of the above-mentioned requirements will involve immediate revocation of the certificate.

Examination of Vehicle

When notified by the DVA the applicant must present the vehicle for examination, in a reasonably clean condition, together with the registration document and previous certificate, if any, at the time and at the centre specified in the notice.

Issue of Certificate

If, after examining the vehicle, the DVA is satisfied that it complies in all respects with the regulations in respect of the construction, use, lighting and rear marking, etc, of vehicles, a certificate will be issued.

Refusal of Certificate

If the vehicle does not meet the requirements of the regulations, a certificate will be refused and the applicant will be notified of the reasons why.

Re-examination of Vehicles

When a certificate has been refused and the defects specified in the notice have been put right, an application may be made for a further examination of the vehicle. A reduced re-test fee will be payable if the re-test is conducted within 21 days of the original test.

Refund of Fees

Prepaid test fees may be refunded in the following circumstances:

- if an appointment for an examination of a vehicle is cancelled by the DVA;
- if the applicant cancels the appointment by giving the DVA (at the centre where the appointment is made) three clear working days' notice;
- if the vehicle is presented to meet the appointment but the examination does not take place for reasons not attributable to the applicant or the vehicle;
- if the applicant satisfies the DVA that the vehicle could not be presented for examination on the day of the appointment because of exceptional circumstances which occurred no more than seven days before the day of the appointment, and providing notice is given to the centre where the examination was to take place within three days of the occurrence.

Duplicate Certificates

Duplicate certificates may be issued in replacement of those which have been accidentally lost, defaced or destroyed. A fee is payable for replacement certificates. If subsequently the original certificate is found, it must be returned to the nearest DVA examining centre or to any police station. Duplicates can also be obtained by completing Section 5 of form VT3 (MOT) or by calling the DVA on 0300 200 7861.

Display of Certificates

Since April 2015, there is now no requirement to display the certificate in the windscreen of the vehicle.

Conditions of Certificate

It is a condition of the certificate that the vehicle owner:

- must not permit the vehicle to be used for any illegal purpose;
- must not deface or mutilate the certificate or permit anybody else to do so;
- must, at all reasonable times, for the purpose of inspection, examination or testing of the vehicle to which the certificate relates:
  - produce the vehicle at such a time and place as may be specified by any inspector of vehicles;
  - afford to any inspector of vehicles full facilities for such inspection, examination or testing, including access to his or her premises for that purpose;
  - ensure that the vehicle and all its fittings are maintained and kept in good order and repair and must take all practical steps to ensure that all parts of the mechanism, including the brakes, are free from defects and are in efficient working order;
  - immediately notify the nearest examination centre of any alteration in design or construction of the vehicle since a certificate was issued.

Transfer of Certificates

If vehicle owners sell or change the ownership of a vehicle, they must pass on the certificate or the new owner will need to apply for a duplicate.

If a vehicle owner dies or becomes infirm of mind or body, on application of any person the DVA may transfer the certificate to such a person.

Change of Address

If certificate holders change their address during the currency of a certificate, they must notify details of such changes to the nearest examination centre.

Offences

It is an offence to operate when a certificate has expired, or to alter, deface, mutilate or fail to display a certificate. Failure to observe such rules will result in the certificate being declared invalid. It is also an offence to assign or to transfer a certificate to another person without notification to the DVA, with the same resultant penalty. Fines or six months' imprisonment may be imposed on summary conviction for such offences, or up to two years' imprisonment upon any further conviction or indictment.

Renewal of Certificates

Reminders of a forthcoming test are usually sent out about seven weeks before the test is due. However, they must be submitted at least one month before the expiry date of a certificate. If no reminder is sent, or if the vehicle has not been certificated in Northern Ireland previously, the holder should apply for a certificate using an application form obtainable from any examination centre or the DVA office in Belfast.

Exemptions from Certification

The following vehicles are exempt from the requirements of NI certification:

- vehicles constructed or adapted for the sole purpose of spreading material on roads or used to deal with frost, ice or snow;
- a land tractor, land locomotive or land implement;
- an agricultural trailer drawn on a road only by a land tractor;
- a vehicle exempted from duty under section 7(i) of the Vehicles (Excise) Act (Northern Ireland) 1972 and any trailer drawn by such a vehicle;
- a motor vehicle for the time being licensed under the Vehicles (Excise) Act 1971, paragraph (a);
- a trailer brought into NI from a base outside NI if a period of 12 months has elapsed since it was last brought into NI;

- a pedestrian-controlled vehicle;

- a track-laying vehicle;

- a steam-propelled vehicle;

- a vehicle used within a period of 12 months prior to the date of it being registered for the first time in NI or the UK; or, where a vehicle has been used on roads in NI or elsewhere before being registered, the exemption applies for the period of 12 months from the date of manufacture rather than from the date of registration (for this purpose any use before the vehicle is sold or supplied retail is disregarded).

Light Vehicle (MOT) Testing

15

Private cars, motor caravans (irrespective of weight), dual-purpose vehicles (see Chapter 8 for definition) under 2,040 kg unladen weight and light goods vehicles not exceeding 3,500 kg gvw are subject to MOT testing at DfT-approved MOT test stations, starting on the third anniversary of the date of their first registration and each year thereafter. (This is the fourth anniversary after registration for cars in Northern Ireland, although light goods vehicles are tested on their third anniversary in the same way as in the rest of the UK.) The weight threshold for goods vehicles powered by alternative fuels and for electrically powered vehicles is 4,250 kg gvw.

Cars and light goods vehicles may be tested up to one month before the due date of their first test and the test certificate will extend for 13 months to expire on the anniversary of the first registration date.

Testing is carried out at garages displaying the blue-and-white MOT triple-triangle symbol, and appointments are made direct with the garage.

The maximum fees for the light vehicle MOT– payable to the garage at the time of the test – are as follows:

Table 15.1 Class IV & IVa (Class IVa includes seat-belt installation check)

Vehicle type	Age first test certificate required (years)	Fee
Cars (up to 8 passenger seats)	3	£54.85
Motor caravans	3	£54.85
Dual-purpose vehicles	3	£54.85
PSVs (up to 8 seats)	3	£54.85
Ambulances and taxis	1	£54.85
Private passenger vehicles and ambulances (9–12 passenger seats)	1	£57.30
Class IVa	–	£64.00

Table 15.2   Class V (with more than 13 passenger seats)

Vehicle type	Age first test certificate required (years)	Fee
13–16 passenger seats	1	£59.55
More than 16 passenger seats	1	£80.65

Table 15.3   Class Va (includes seat-belt installation check)

Vehicle type	Age first test certificate required (years)	Fee
13–16 passenger seats	–	£80.50
More than 16 passenger seats	–	£124.50

Table 15.4   Class VII

Vehicle type	Age first test certificate required (years)	Fee
Goods vehicles (over 3,000 kg up to 3,500 kg gvw)	3	£58.60

Duplicate test certificates cost £10 or half of the above amounts.

Vehicle Classes

Vehicles subject to the MOT test are classified as follows:

Table 15.5   Vehicle classes

Class I	Light motor bicycles not exceeding 200 cc cylinder capacity with or without sidecars
Class II	All motor bicycles (including Class I) with or without sidecars
Class III	Light motor vehicles with three or more wheels (excluding Classes I and II) not exceeding 450 kg unladen weight

Table 15.5 *continued*

Class IV	Heavy motor cars and motor cars (excluding Classes III and V); ie any vehicle with an unladen weight of more than 450 kg which is: (a) a passenger vehicle (ie private car, taxi, vehicle licensed as private, with 12 passenger seats or fewer, or small public service vehicle with fewer than eight passenger seats) (b) a dual-purpose vehicle not exceeding 2,040 kg unladen weight (see Chapter 8 for definition) (c) a goods vehicle not exceeding 3,000 kg gross weight (d) a motor caravan irrespective of weight
Class V	Large passenger-carrying vehicles; ie motor vehicles which are constructed or adapted to carry more than 12 seated passengers in addition to the driver, and which are not licensed as public service vehicles
Class VI	Public service vehicles other than those in Class V above
Class VII	Goods vehicles of 3,001 kg to 3,500 kg gross weight* (these vehicles may be tested at MOT garages – where the facility to test such vehicles is available – or at goods vehicle testing stations)

*Note the increase for goods vehicles powered by alternative fuels and for electrically powered vehicles to 4,250 kg (above).

Exemptions

Public service vehicles with seats for eight or more passengers excluding the driver, track-laying vehicles, vehicles constructed or adapted to form part of an articulated vehicle, works trucks and all trailers are excluded from the above classes.

The following vehicles are also exempt from the MOT:

- heavy locomotives;
- light locomotives;
- goods vehicles over 3.5 tonnes (4.25 tonnes for alternative-fuel vehicles);
- articulated vehicles other than articulated buses;
- vehicles exempt from duty under the Vehicle Excise and Registration Act 1994;
- works trucks;
- pedestrian-controlled vehicles;
- vehicles temporarily in Great Britain;
- vehicles proceeding to a port for export;
- some vehicles adapted for use by invalids supplied by the Department of Health or the Department for Social Security, the Scottish Office or the Welsh Office;
- vehicles provided for use by the police force;

- imported vehicles owned or in the service of HM navy, army or air force;
- vehicles which have Northern Ireland test certificates;
- certain hackney carriages.

Many of these vehicles are exempt from MOT but subject to goods vehicle testing and plating (see Chapter 14). A full list of exemptions is available on form V112 (Declaration of exemption from MOT).

There is also an exemption which applies to vehicles which come within the MOT test scheme while they are being driven to a place by previous arrangement for a test or bringing it away, if it fails, to a place to have work done on it. This means that such vehicles can be driven on the road without a valid test certificate being in force, but only in the circumstances mentioned and no other.

The Test

When presenting a vehicle for test the following conditions must be observed:

- The vehicle must be sufficiently clean so as not to make the test unreasonably difficult.
- The vehicle must have sufficient petrol and oil to enable the test to be completed.
- If the vehicle is presented for the test in a loaded condition (ie in the case of light goods vehicles), the load must be properly secured or removed.

Refusal and Discontinuance of Test

Failure to observe any of the above conditions can lead to a refusal to test the vehicle, and the test fee will be refunded. Furthermore, if testers find a defect of a serious nature which, in their opinion, makes it essential to discontinue the inspection on the grounds of risk to their own safety, risk to the test equipment or to the vehicle itself, they may do so and issue form VT30 showing the defects which caused the test to be discontinued.

Items Tested

The following items are tested and must meet the conditions specified in *The MOT Tester's Manual*:

Table 15.6 Items tested

Interior checks	Seats and seat belts
	Warning lamps
	Switches (position lamp, headlamp, hazards)
	View to front, wipers and washers
	Brake controls, servo operation
	Steering wheel and column
	Doors, mirrors, horn
	Speedometer, driver controls
Exterior checks	Registration plates
	Lamps, registration-plate lamps
	Indicators, hazards
	Headlamps & aim
	Stop lamps, fog lamps, reflectors
	Wheels, tyres
	Shock absorbers
	Mirrors, wiper blades, fuel tank cap
	Glazing
	Doors, boot lid, loading doors, bonnet
	Towbars
	General condition of body
Under-bonnet checks	Vehicle structure
	Braking systems
	Exhaust systems, fuel system
	Speed limiter (if applicable)
	Steering & power steering components
	Suspension components
Under-vehicle checks	Steering including power steering
	Drive shafts (if applicable)
	Suspension, shock absorbers
	Wheel bearings
	Wheels & tyres
	Brake systems & mechanical components
	Exhaust system
	Fuel system & fuel tank
	Structure, general vehicle condition

Exhaust Emissions

A check is made on emissions from diesel-engined vehicles.

Cars, light goods vehicles and particularly goods vehicles within the weight range 3,001 kg to 3,500 kg gross weight, which fall within the Class VII MOT test, are subjected to exhaust emission checks as well as checks for excessively smoking exhausts. This involves measurement of the levels of CO and HC to ensure that engines are properly tuned.

Emission standards tests as described above do not apply to motorcycles or three-wheelers.

Seat-Belts

The condition of seat belts in all vehicles (whether required to be fitted mandatorily or fitted on a voluntary basis) is examined to determine whether the belts are likely to fulfil their intended function in the event of an accident. The checks on seat belts include the warning light and the automatic pre-tensioner.

Test Failure

If the vehicle fails to reach the required standard of mechanical condition, a 'Refusal of MOT test certificate' is issued. This indicates the grounds on which the vehicle failed the test (ie it names the faulty components or component area and the actual fault).

Re-tests

If a vehicle fails the test, no further test fee is payable if it is left at the garage for the necessary repairs to be carried out before the end of the 10th working day from the day of the initial test. However, if the vehicle is taken away following the test failure, a three-tier system of re-tests and fees applies as follows:

- Tier 1 Full Test. Where a vehicle is presented for re-test more than 10 working days after the day of the initial test, or if the original MOT tester is not available for a tier 2 test, a full test must be carried out and the full test fee is payable.

- Tier 2 Partial Re-test. Where a re-test is necessary that requires the use of a major piece of testing equipment (including hoist or pit, brake performance tester, exhaust gas analyser (EGA), diesel smoke meter (DSM) and headlamp aim equipment), or where a repair has been carried out by welding, or there has been a repair to the steering or braking system (excluding stop lamps), provided that the re-test is carried out by the same tester at the same MOT garage before the end of the 10th working day from the day of the initial test, a partial re-test will be carried out and only half of the full test fee will be payable.

- Tier 3 Partial Re-test. Where a re-test does not require the use of a major piece of testing equipment, provided it is carried out at the same MOT garage before the end of the 10th working day from the day of the initial test, half of the test fee will be due.

Where any vehicle does not fall into tier 2 or 3 above, a full re-examination in accordance with tier 1 must be carried out. Only one partial re-examination is permissible per full examination.

Issue of Test Certificate

On completion of the test, if the vehicle is found to meet the minimum standards, a printed MOT test certificate is issued. The certificate may be issued with 'no defects', minor defects or advisory items to point out components which may need attention in the future to keep it in good, safe working order.

Appeals

A vehicle owner can appeal, if they are not satisfied with the result of the test, using form VT17 and send it to the DVSA within 14 days of taking the test.

Vehicle Defect Rectification Schemes

Vehicle Defect Rectification Schemes (VDRS) are aimed at improving road safety and reducing the burden on the police of prosecuting motorists for minor offences that can be quickly rectified. However, failure to follow the procedure on receipt of a VDRS notice, or refusal to accept VDRS as a course of action, will result in pro-secution, and persistent offenders who are also operators will be reported to the Traffic Commissioner. Appeals are permitted under VDRS schemes.

Operators of light vehicles (up to 3,500 kg gross weight) found on the road with non-endorsable minor vehicle defects (ie lights, wipers, speedometer, silencer, etc) in certain areas may be offered the VDRS procedure by the police force in that area who will issue a defect form, but no prosecution will result if:

1 Arrangements are made for the repair of the defect within 14 days of the issue of the defect form.

2 The repaired vehicle and VDRS notice are presented to an MOT garage for examination and certification (usually by the use of a stamp) that the defects have been rectified.

3 The certificate is returned to the police within 14 days.

NB: *The Scottish VDRS allows 21 days for similar actions to be taken.*

Vehicle Maintenance and Maintenance Records

16

Vehicles and trailers must be kept in a safe, fit and roadworthy condition. Their maintenance, inspection, checks and records must meet the requirements covered in the:

- Road Traffic Act 1988;
- The Road Vehicles (Construction and Use) Regulations 1986;
- Transport Act 1968 which sets out the conditions relating to vehicle maintenance under which an O-Licence will be granted.

Operators must maintain their vehicles and trailers to a sufficiently high standard to enable them to pass the annual goods vehicle test, which they should be able to do on the test day *and on every other day when they are on the road*. An effective maintenance plan and ongoing maintenance regime needs to be in operation. Operators applying for an O-Licence will be expected to demonstrate a maintenance plan in place for at least six months, but preferably 12 months.

The DVSA *Guide to Maintaining Roadworthiness* and *Guide to Goods Vehicle Operators' Licensing* are available at GOV.UK.

The different types of vehicle inspections which must be carried out are:

- First use inspection – A safety inspection either for a vehicle brought into use, returned to use or on hire, loan or lease. A first use inspection is conducted by a workshop technician and must include all the items covered by the annual test. Do not get the first use inspection confused with the driver's walkaround check.
- Safety inspection – A routine inspection conducted at a periodic frequency providing an independent ongoing report on a vehicle's roadworthiness. A safety inspection is conducted by a workshop technician and must include all the items covered by the annual test. The frequency at which safety inspections are

undertaken is between 4 and 13 weeks, dependent on the level of mechanical degradation likely to be incurred as a result of the vehicle's use. The maximum safety inspection frequency for vehicles and trailers over 12 years old is 6 weeks. The safety inspection frequency is documented as a condition of the O-Licence.

- Walkaround check – A roadworthiness check conducted by the driver each time a vehicle is used. Any defects identified must be reported for a decision to be made on the roadworthiness of the vehicle. 'Nil' defects must also be recorded to confirm a walkaround check has been completed and that the driver has determined the vehicle roadworthy. The driver is always legally responsible for the condition of the vehicle while in use; therefore, the walkaround check is a vital part of a driver's core role.

Records

Records must be kept of all safety inspections to show the history of each vehicle and made available to the authorities 'upon request'. These records must be kept for at least 15 months. If vehicles from several operating centres are inspected and repaired at a central depot, the records may be kept at that depot, although DVSA examiners can request inspection of records at the operating centres where vehicles are based.

If a contractor does the inspections and repairs, operators must keep any records and make them available, if required.

Facilities

Facilities depend on the number, size and types of vehicles to be inspected. It must be possible to have a covered area to inspect the underside of a vehicle, with sufficient light and space to examine individual parts closely. Ramps, hoists or pits will usually be necessary, but may not be needed if the vehicles have enough ground clearance for a proper underside inspection to be made on hard-standing. Creeper boards, jacks, axle stands and small tools should be available.

As well as providing facilities for checking the underside of vehicles, operators should use equipment for measuring braking efficiency and headlight alignment. If many vehicles have to be inspected, it may be worthwhile providing a roller brake tester.

Driver Defect Reports

Drivers must report any defects or symptoms of defects that could adversely affect the safe operation of vehicles. Driver defect reports and details of any rectification work must be recorded. Owner-drivers must note faults as they arise and keep these notes as part of their maintenance record. Driver defect reports must form a part of the vehicle's maintenance record and be retained for 15 months.

Nil defects, where the driver finds no faults during their walkaround check, should be retained 'for as long as they are required'. It is recommended that this is until the next periodic safety inspection.

Hired Vehicles and Trailers

In the case of hired, rented or borrowed vehicles or those belonging to other operators used in inter-working arrangements, it is the user who is responsible for their mechanical condition on the road. If enforcement action is taken as a result of a mechanical fault, it is against the user's O-Licence, not the company from which the vehicle is hired, or the owner.

Generally, if a vehicle is hired with a driver, then the company employing the driver is the 'user'. If a vehicle is hired in without a driver, then the company hiring in the vehicle is the 'user'.

The Choice: In-House or Contract Out

Safety inspections and maintenance work can either be conducted in-house or be contracted out to someone else. All or part of the work may be contracted out. During the O-Licence application process, TCs will consider any proposed vehicle maintenance arrangements as part of the approval. If vehicle maintenance is contracted out, the TC must be provided with a copy of the contract. The operator is still responsible for the condition of their vehicles and trailers, even if they are maintained by someone else.

Contracted-out Maintenance

Operators using a contractor remain responsible for the condition of vehicles that are inspected or maintained by the contractor. It is essential to have a written contract that sets out precise details of vehicles covered and frequency and type of check, along with a repair policy. Care must be taken to ensure that the facilities used by the contractor are adequate and that the staff are competent. The contractor must also be in possession of the HGV inspection manual and have suitable inspection documentation.

The maintenance contract must be kept on the operator's maintenance file and produced on request. The maintenance provider details must also be up to date on the VOL system.

Even when a maintenance contract exists, the operator remains legally responsible for the condition of the vehicle, the authorization of any repair work undertaken and the retention of records. Operators need to be satisfied that the level of maintenance agreed matches the demands placed upon vehicles and that the standards achieved by the contractor are kept at a sufficiently high level. There should be regular contact with the contractor to ensure that they are familiar with the operational needs of the vehicles they are required to inspect and repair. This knowledge is important if the contractor is to be called upon to advise on a particular course of action – particularly if technical know-how is limited in an operation.

Even if the relationship with a contractor is good, operators should have a system for regularly monitoring the quality of work done. Obtaining first-time pass rate annual test data from the contractor is one way of checking that their performance is satisfactory, but this should be supplemented by other checks and references.

Any sign of unreliability, incompetence or other shortcomings causing a reduction in the standards expected should receive prompt attention. If problems persist, operators should consider a change of contractor.

A model agreement between an operator and contractor for vehicle maintenance and safety inspections is included in the DVSA *Guide to Maintaining Roadworthiness* found at GOV.UK.

In-House Maintenance

The advantages of operators running vehicle maintenance in-house are that it provides overall control, the flexibility to prioritize work and utilizes on-site staff who are familiar with the fleet. This control can lead to less vehicle downtime. However, running vehicle maintenance in-house does mean capital costs for facilities and equipment, stock costs, staff overheads, training and additional health and safety compliance.

Operators that provide their own safety inspection and maintenance facilities must ensure that they are suitable. It is strongly recommended that the suitability and competence of the maintenance facility are demonstrated by achieving a recognized accreditation for workshop standards. This can be gained through manufacturers' franchised workshop quality standards or by an independent assessment, such as the IRTE National Workshop Accreditation scheme.

In-house safety inspection and maintenance facilities must provide a safe working environment and include:

- undercover accommodation for the largest vehicle in the fleet, which is required to ensure that safety checks can be conducted satisfactorily in all weathers (depending on fleet size, the building may need room for more than one vehicle at a time);

- tools and equipment appropriate to the size and nature of the fleet;
- an adequate under-vehicle inspection facility;
- adequate lighting;
- access to:
  - brake test equipment (eg a roller brake tester, decelerometer);
  - headlamp test equipment;
  - emissions testing equipment;
  - steam or pressure under-vehicle washing facilities.

Safety Inspectors

The technician undertaking safety inspections must be technically competent and operationally aware of the safety standards that apply to the vehicles they inspect. They should have been trained in the techniques of vehicle examination, diagnosis and reporting, and possess a sound working knowledge of the relevant inspection manuals produced by the DVSA. A safety inspector may prove technical competence solely by time-served experience. However, with modern vehicle systems and working practices, it is strongly recommended that inspectors have relevant technical qualifications and achieve an automotive technical accreditation such as IRTEC (Inspection Technician Accreditation) or similar – meeting a recognized quality standard for the vehicles they inspect. A safety inspector should not be expected to carry out repair or servicing work during the course of the safety inspection.

Vehicle Servicing

Regular servicing should be carried out at predetermined intervals of time or mileage. Regular vehicle servicing is important because:

- many warranties and leasing agreements insist on the service intervals;
- the vehicle must meet minimum legal requirements;
- operators benefit by maximizing vehicle availability and minimizing vehicle failure and breakdowns;
- the life of vehicles and component parts is maximized.

Vehicle manufacturers usually provide a service schedule which operators should work to. Progressively, service intervals are being extended with the use of longer-life components, sealed units and particularly by improved filters and lubricating oils, which can go for very much longer periods these days without detriment to their lubricating properties.

Cleaning of Vehicles

Vehicles should be cleaned regularly on top, inside and underneath to make it easier to spot defects at safety inspections and during the daily walkaround checks. If vehicle maintenance is contracted out, the operator should arrange for the contractor to clean the vehicle before inspection.

Maintenance Records

Operators must keep records of maintenance work carried out on their vehicles.

In the O-Licence declaration of intent the operator promises to ensure that the following records will be kept:

- safety inspections;
- routine maintenance;
- repairs to vehicles.

The declaration includes a promise that drivers will report safety defects 'as soon as possible'; these must be in writing and therefore part of the vehicle record-keeping system. All defect reports must be given to a responsible person with authority to ensure that appropriate action is taken. This may include taking the vehicle out of service.

Records must be kept for a minimum period of 15 months and made available on request by enforcement officers. Records may be paper based or in an electronic format.

Driver Defect Reports

There must be a system of reporting and recording defects that may affect the roadworthiness of the vehicle. This must include how they have been rectified before the vehicle is used. Daily defect checks are vital, and the results of such checks must be recorded as part of the maintenance system.

Drivers must report any defects, or symptoms of defects, that could prevent the safe operation of the vehicle. In addition to the walkaround checks, drivers must monitor the roadworthiness of the vehicle when being driven, and be alert to any indication that the vehicle is developing a fault, eg warning lights, vibrations or other symptoms. If a vehicle is working in off-road conditions, a walkaround should be conducted before leaving the site to identify any defects. If any safety defects are found, they must be recorded and the vehicle must not be used on the road until it is repaired.

It is important that enough time is allowed for the completion of walkaround checks and that drivers are trained to carry them out thoroughly. Drivers should be made aware that daily defect reporting is one of the critical elements of any effective vehicle roadworthiness system.

Any defects found during the daily walkaround check, while the vehicle is in use or on its return to base, must be the subject of a written report by the driver or some other person responsible for recording defects.

The details recorded should include:

- vehicle registration or identification mark;
- date;
- details of the defects or symptoms;
- the reporter's name;
- who the defect was reported to;
- assessment of the defect;
- rectification work;
- date rectification work was completed.

Inspection Reports

Records of regular periodic safety inspections to vehicles must be made. For this purpose the vehicle inspector should have an inspection record which lists all items to be inspected (in accordance with *The Heavy Goods Vehicle Inspection Manual*).

The inspection record should cross-check with the *Inspection Manual* for the full details of the method of inspection to be determined – and any reason for its rejection or not being within acceptable limits. The record should have provision for the inspector to mark against each item whether it is 'serviceable' or 'needs attention' and space to comment on defects for immediate rectification and other items for attention. The record should enable the inspector to date and sign the document (this may be a digital signature).

Service Records

Records should be kept of all other work carried out on a vehicle, whether it is repair or replacement of working parts or normal servicing (oil changes and greasing, etc).

Contractor Maintenance Records

When vehicle safety inspections, servicing and repair work are carried out for the operator by a contractor, the operator should receive copies of records, either as a hard copy or digitally. It is acceptable for the contractor to retain maintenance records as long as they can be made available for examination when required. The operator must be certain, in these instances, that the garage is keeping proper records for a minimum period of 15 months, and that they are readily accessible and available for inspection.

Location of Records

Where companies hold O-Licences in a number of separate Traffic Areas, the maintenance records for the vehicles under each licence should be kept in the Traffic Area of each individual licence (preferably at the vehicle operating centre). Records may be kept centrally at a head office or central vehicle workshop with TC permission.

Maintenance Planning

Safety inspections must be planned at least 6 months (ideally 12 months) in advance. Planning can combine safety inspections, annual test and major servicing – to avoid duplication of work. Digital planning systems and electronic record storage are both acceptable but must be capable of providing records in 'real time' to the operator and include an audit process that shows date and time stamping.

Typical forward planning will include when each vehicle/trailer is due for:

- safety inspection;
- service;
- annual test;
- tax (VED) renewal.

Safety – on the Road and at Work

17

The safety of people must be an operator's top priority and safety is included in almost everything an operator does. However, workplace safety and work-related road safety are regulated, managed, investigated and enforced in completely different ways. The government agency responsible for workplace safety is the Health and Safety Executive, with the principal regulations being the Health and Safety at Work Act 1974 and Management of Health and Safety at Work Regulations 1999. The government agency responsible for operator road safety is the DVSA, with the principal regulations being the Road Vehicles (Construction and Use) Regulations 1986 (as amended) and the Road Traffic Act 1988.

Road Safety

Provisional government statistics show the following road casualties in Great Britain for 2020: 1,472 people killed and 23,486 people seriously injured. In all, there were 115,333 casualties. These numbers are a significant reduction based on previous years due to the COVID-19 lockdowns. In 2019, there were 67 goods vehicle occupant fatalities, of which 56 were goods vehicle drivers and 11 were goods vehicle passengers. Goods vehicle fatalities have fluctuated between 47 and 67 in the past 10 years.

Managing Road Risk

While knowledge of and compliance with the *Highway Code* is essential for both drivers and managers alike, the HSE guides *Driving at Work – Managing Work-Related Road Safety* and *Vehicles at Work: Driving at Work and Work-Related Road Safety* are essential reading for transport management and for anybody who drives on company business, ie managers and staff as well as commercial vehicle drivers. The guidelines show how legal responsibilities under health and safety at work provisions must be complied with in addition to existing road traffic and vehicle construction and use provisions. They describe how to manage, assess and evaluate work-related road risk. Overall, the aim is to cut the number of road accidents involving people at work in all sectors of industry.

THINK! Campaigns

The UK government has been running road safety campaigns for more than 75 years and THINK! was officially established in 2000 as the government's designated road safety campaign.

THINK! runs iconic and ground-breaking campaigns that challenge unsafe dangerous behaviour on the road. Campaigns have evolved from encouraging the use of seat belts to tackling excessive speed, drink and drugs, and the use of mobiles at the wheel. From 2000 to 2010 THINK! contributed to a reduction in UK road deaths by 46 per cent.

The latest THINK! resources and campaign assets are freely available and should be used to help educate drivers. Go to THINK.GOV.UK to sign up to receive updates.

Vehicle Safety

The Road Vehicles (Construction and Use) Regulations 1986 require that all vehicles and trailers, and all their parts and accessories, and the weight, distribution, packing and adjustment of their loads, shall be such that no danger is caused or likely to be caused to any person in or on the vehicle or trailer or on the road. Additionally, no motor vehicle or trailer must be used for any purpose for which it is so unsuited as to cause or be likely to cause danger or nuisance to any person in or on the vehicle or trailer or on the road.

Under the regulations, provisions relating particularly to bulk and loose loads make it an offence if a load causes a nuisance as well as a danger to other road users and such loads must be secured, if necessary by physical restraint, to stop them falling or being blown from a vehicle.

These regulations include specific terms relating to load safety. The term 'nuisance' is used in addition to the term 'danger' so that to commit an offence the operator does not have to go so far as causing danger; merely causing nuisance is sufficient to cause an offence. The other term is 'physical restraint', which clearly implies the need for sheeting and roping or strapping any load, such as sand or grain, hay and straw and even builders' skips carrying rubble that may be blown from the vehicle.

The Road Traffic Act 1988 further states that 'it is an offence to use a goods vehicle, or cause or permit it to be used when overloaded'. The maximum fine is £5,000.

Load Safety

Load Securing: Vehicle Operator Guidance and the code of practice, *Safety of Loads on Vehicles*, are available at GOV.UK. They both set out general requirements in regard to who is responsible for load securing, the issues related to poor load securing and the way that the DVSA responds to poor load security. They give advice on loading and carrying different types of loads and explain what the DVSA looks for when stopping a loaded vehicle and how different types of load restraints can be used. Neither guide is meant to contradict, undermine or replace the other, but they do cover some different areas.

Distribution of Loads

When loading a vehicle, care must be taken to ensure that the load is evenly distributed to ensure stability of the vehicle and to conform to the vehicle's individual axle weights as well as the overall gross weight, and is secure so it cannot move or transfer its weight during transit. It is important on multi-delivery work to make sure that when part of the load has been removed in the course of a delivery, none of the axles has become overloaded because of the transfer of weight. This can happen even though the gross vehicle weight is still within permissible maximum limits, and in such cases it is necessary for the driver to attempt to correct the situation by shifting the load, or part of it.

All loads should be securely and safely restrained. It is an offence to have an insecure load or a load which causes danger to other road users. Furthermore, it is a legal requirement of the C&U Regulations that loads must not cause or be likely to cause a danger or nuisance to other road users and that they should be restrained to avoid parts of the load falling or being blown from the vehicle. It is also an offence for the restraint equipment to cause nuisance or danger to other road users.

It should be noted that drivers who need to climb onto, or into, a vehicle to secure or sheet a load are subject to the Working at Height Regulations 2005 (see later).

Axle Load Calculations

Axle loads can be calculated to determine whether a vehicle is operating legally by using the following method:

- Determine the vehicle wheelbase.
- Determine the weight of the load (ie payload).

- Determine the centre of gravity of the load from the front or rear axle, depending upon which axle load you require.

Once you have these, the formula is:

$$\frac{\text{Weight of the load} \times \text{Distance of the centre of gravity of the load from the axle}}{\text{Wheelbase of the vehicle}}$$

It must be said that this formula relies on the centre of gravity of the load being able to be determined, which in many cases is not possible. However, for some bulk loads and/or large single items of a regular shape, the formula is very useful.

Workplace Transport Safety

Workplace transport is any vehicle or piece of mobile equipment used in any work setting. It covers a very wide range of vehicles, from cars, vans, HGVs, lift trucks and plant. Risk must be controlled and can be managed by considering a safe site, vehicle and driver.

Organization, Systems and Training

- Have all health and safety aspects of the transport operation been assessed?
- Has an organization (and arrangements) for securing such safety been detailed in the safety policy?
- Has a person(s) been appointed to be responsible for transport safety?
- Have risk assessments and safe systems of work been set up?
- Are all employees able to report safety incidents or issues?
- What monitoring is carried out to ensure that the systems are followed?
- Have all drivers been adequately trained and tested?
- Is there a satisfactory formal licensing or authorization system for drivers?
- Have all personnel been trained, informed and instructed about safe working practices where transport is involved?
- Is there an accident book and is it used?
- Are all accidents and near-misses reported?
- Is there sufficient supervision?
- What review procedures are in place?

External Roadways and Manoeuvring Areas

- Are they of adequate dimensions?
- Are they of good construction?
- Are they well maintained?
- Are they well drained?
- Are they scarified when smooth?
- Are they gritted, sanded, etc, when slippery?
- Are they kept free of debris and obstructions?
- Are they well illuminated?
- Are there sufficient and suitable road markings?
- Are there sufficient and suitable warning signs?
- Are there speed limits?
- Is there a one-way system (as far as possible)?
- Is there provision for vehicles to reverse where necessary?
- Is the area shared with cyclists?
- Are there pedestrian walkways and crossings?
- Are there barriers by exit doors leading on to roadways?
- Is there a separate vehicle parking area?
- Are there individual, clearly marked parking bays?
- Is there any storage positioned close to vehicle ways?
- Is the yard suitable for internal works transport, eg smooth surface, hard ground, no slopes?

Internal Transport

- Are internal roadways demarcated and separated where possible from pedestrian routes with crossings and priority signs?
- Are there separate internal doors for vehicles and pedestrians? Do these have vision panels?
- Are blind corners catered for by mirrors, etc?
- Are vehicles kept apart from personnel where possible?
- Do lift trucks use a satisfactory warning system?
- Are lift truck operators trained?
- Are lift trucks made unavailable when not in use?

Vehicles

- Are all staff properly trained on new vehicles before being allowed to use them?
- Is there a maintenance programme for vehicles and mobile plant?
- Is there a fault-reporting system?
- Are there regular checks to ensure that the vehicles are up to an acceptable standard?
- Are keys kept secure when vehicles and mobile plant are not in use?
- Are vehicles and mobile plant adequate and suitable for the work in hand?
- Is suitable access provided to elevated working places or vehicles?
- Are tractors and lift trucks equipped with protection to prevent drivers being hit by falling objects and from being thrown from their cab in the event of overturning?
- Are there any unfenced mechanical parts on vehicles, eg power take-offs?
- Are there fittings for earthing vehicles with highly flammable cargoes?
- Are loads correctly labelled (especially hazardous substances)?
- Are vehicles used to carry dangerous goods properly marked?
- Are the vehicles suitable for use in all the areas they enter?
- If passengers ride on vehicles, do they have a safe riding position?

Loading and Unloading

- Do loading positions obstruct other traffic? Do pedestrian ways need diverting?
- Are there special hazards, eg flammable liquid discharge? Do pedestrians need to be kept clear?
- Is there a yard manager to supervise the traffic operation, to control vehicular movement and to act as a banksman during reversing?
- Have yard managers received satisfactory training? Do they use recognized signals, do they have cover during absences?
- Are there loading docks? Will the layout prevent trucks falling off or colliding with objects or each other?
- Are there any mechanical hazards caused by dock levellers, etc?
- Are methods of loading and unloading assessed and drivers trained, as required?
- Are safe arrangements made for sheeting?
- Is there a pallet inspection scheme?
- Is personal protective equipment (PPE) available, if required?

Motor Vehicle Repair

- Are appropriate arrangements made for tyre repair and inflation?
- Are arrangements made for draining and repair of fuel tanks?
- Is access available to elevated working positions?
- Are arrangements made to ensure brakes are applied and wheels checked?
- Is portable electrical equipment low voltage and properly earthed?
- Are moving vehicles in the workshop carefully controlled?
- Are vehicles supported on both jacks and axle stands where appropriate?
- Are engines only run with the brakes on and in neutral gear?
- Are raised bodies always propped?
- Are there systems in place for recycling/disposal?

As stated above, these points are general in nature but they may provide the basis for a company to begin to work up its own safety reports.

Health and Safety at Work

The Health and Safety at Work Act 1974 is the main legislation for health and safety in the UK. It is supported by a range of supporting regulations. Some of the principal regulations are:

- Management of Health and Safety at Work Regulations 1999;
- Workplace (Health, Safety and Welfare) Regulations 1992;
- Manual Handling Operations Regulations 1992;
- Health and Safety (Display Screen Equipment) Regulations 1992;
- Provision and Use of Work Equipment Regulations 1998;
- Lifting Operations and Lifting Equipment Regulations 1998;
- Personal Protective Equipment at Work Regulations 2002;
- Control of Substances Hazardous to Health (COSHH) Regulations 2002, 2003 and 2004;
- Reporting of Injuries, Diseases and Dangerous Occurrences Regulations 2013 (RIDDOR).

NB: A full list of all Statutory Instruments managed and enforced by the HSE is available at GOV.UK.

The Health and Safety at Work Act 1974

The Health and Safety at Work etc Act 1974 is the primary legislation covering occupational health and safety in Great Britain. It sets out the general duties which:

- employers have towards employees and members of the public;
- employees have to themselves and to each other;
- certain self-employed have towards themselves and others.

Employers must have policy statements regarding health and safety at work, appoint safety representatives and establish safety committees, in addition to ensuring that workplaces meet all the necessary safety requirements of the law and apply to the transport operator's premises (ie offices, workshops, warehouses and yards) and to the vehicles which constitute the workplace of drivers.

There are four parts to the Act:

- Part I – Health, Safety and Welfare at Work;
- Part II – Employment Medical Advisory Service;
- Part III – Law Regarding Building Regulations;
- Part IV – General and Miscellaneous Provisions.

The main effects of the Act were:

- to maintain and improve standards of health and safety for people at work;
- to protect people other than those at work against risks to their health or safety arising from the work activities of others;
- to control the storage and use of explosives, highly flammable or dangerous substances, and to prevent their unlawful acquisition, possession and use;
- to control the emission into the atmosphere of noxious or offensive fumes or substances from work premises;
- to set up the Health and Safety Executive.

Duties of Employers

The Act prescribes the general duties of all employers towards their employees by obliging them to ensure their health, safety and welfare while at work. This duty requires that all plant (including vehicles) and methods of work provided are reasonably safe and without risks to health. A similar injunction relates to the use, handling, storage and transport of any articles or substances used in connection with the employer's work. Provisions contained in the Data Protection Act mean that employers are no longer permitted to design health questionnaires for completion by employees or to screen or interpret employees' medical data. Now, only qualified health professionals may carry out these functions.

Provision of Necessary Information

In order that employees are fully conversant with all health and safety matters, it is the duty of the employer to provide all necessary information and instruction by means of proper training and adequate supervision.

Employers must either: 1) display the 'Health and Safety Law' poster; or 2) distribute the 'Health and Safety Law' leaflet to employees. (Copies can be obtained from HSE Books: http://www.hse.gov.uk/pubns/books. Other leaflets and guides are free to download from this site.)

Condition of Premises

Workplaces generally, if under the employer's control, must be maintained in such a condition that they are safe and without risks to health, have adequate means of entrance and exit (again this applies as equally to vehicles as it does to 'premises') and must provide a working environment that has satisfactory facilities and arrangements for the welfare of everybody employed in the premises. In addition, site visitors must also be free from risks to their health or safety and may need safety briefings before entering some parts of the site.

Statements of Safety Policy

It is necessary for an employer of five or more employees to draw up and bring to the notice of the workforce *a written statement of company policy* regarding their health and safety at work, with all current arrangements detailed for the implementation of such a policy. Stress is laid on the necessity of updating the 'statement' as the occasion arises and of communicating all alterations to the personnel employed.

Appointment of Safety Representatives

Involvement of all employees in health and safety activities is envisaged by the appointment (by a recognized trade union) or election of safety representatives from among the workforce. A safety representative should be a person who has been employed in the firm for at least *two years* or who has had two years' similar employment 'so far as is reasonably practicable'. The broad duties of safety representatives are concerned with the inspection of workplaces, investigating possible hazards and examining the cause of accidents, investigating employees' complaints regarding health and safety matters, and making representations to their employer on matters of health and safety at work.

Safety Committees

At the written request of at least two safety representatives, employers must establish a safety committee, within a time limit of three months, to review health and safety at work matters. The establishment of a safety committee creates a joint responsibility with the employer for concern over all health and safety measures at the workplace, together with any other duties arising from regulations or codes of practice.

Duty to the Public

Employers and self-employed persons are required to ensure that their activities do not create any hazard to members of the general public. In certain circumstances, information must be made publicly available regarding the existence of possible hazards to health and safety.

Summary of Duties of Employers to their Employees

- It shall be the duty of every employer to ensure so far as is reasonably practicable the health, safety and welfare at work of all their employees. That duty includes, in particular:
  - the provision and maintenance of plant and systems of work that are so far as is reasonably practicable safe and without risks to health;
  - arrangements for ensuring so far as is reasonably practicable safety and absence of risks to health in connection with the use, handling, storage and transport of articles and substances;
  - the provision of such information, instruction, training and supervision as is necessary to ensure so far as is reasonably practicable the health and safety at work of employees;
  - so far as is reasonably practicable the maintenance of any place of work that is under the employer's control in a condition that is safe and without risks to health, and the provision and maintenance of means of access to and egress from it that are safe and without such risks;
  - the provision and maintenance of a working environment for employees that is so far as is reasonably practicable safe and without risk to health and adequate as regards facilities and arrangements for their welfare at work.
- Except in such cases as may be prescribed, it shall be the duty of all employers to prepare and as often as may be appropriate revise a written statement of their general policy with respect to the health and safety at work of their employees and the organization and arrangements for the time being in force for carrying out that policy, and to bring the statement and any revision of it to the notice of all employees.

- It shall be the duty of any person who erects or installs any article for use at work in any premises where the article is to be used by persons at work to ensure, so far as is reasonably practicable, that nothing about the way in which it is erected or installed makes it unsafe or a risk to health when properly used.

- No employer shall levy or permit to be levied on any employee any charge in respect of anything done or provided in pursuance of any specific requirement of the relevant statutory provisions.

As well as these statutory duties, employers have a common law duty of care. Where a breach of that care results in negligence (eg where careless conduct results in injury to a person), they may be liable to pay compensation, even if, in some cases, the injury was caused to a person who was acting illegally at the time.

Duties of Employees

The Act states in general terms the duty of employees to take reasonable care for their own safety and that of others who may be affected by their work activities and to cooperate with others in order to ensure that there is a compliance with statutory duties relating to health and safety at work. In this connection no person shall interfere with or misuse anything provided in the interests of health, safety or welfare either intentionally or recklessly.

Summary of Duties of Employees at Work

- It shall be the duty of all employees while at work:
  - to take reasonable care for their own health and safety and of other persons who may be affected by their acts or omissions at work; and
  - as regards any duty or requirement imposed on their employer or any other person, to cooperate with them so far as is necessary to enable that duty or requirement to be performed or complied with.

- No person shall intentionally or recklessly interfere with or misuse anything provided in the interests of health, safety or welfare.

General Duties of Employers and Self-Employed to Persons Other than Their Employees

- It shall be the duty of all employers and self-employed persons to conduct their undertaking in such a way as to ensure so far as is reasonably practicable that persons not in their employment are not thereby exposed to risks to their health and safety.

- It shall be the duty of all employers and self-employed persons to give to persons not in their employment, who may be affected, the prescribed information about such aspects of the way in which they conduct their undertaking as might affect such persons' health and safety.

The Management of Health and Safety

The Management of Health and Safety at Work Regulations 1999 require employers to put in place arrangements to control health and safety risks. As a minimum, operators must have the processes and procedures required to meet the legal requirements, including ensuring:

- a written health and safety policy is in place (five or more people);
- risks to employees, contractors, customers, partners, and any other people who could be affected by your activities are assessed and recorded;
- arrangements for the effective planning, organization, control, monitoring and review of the preventive and protective measures that come from risk assessment;
- access to competent health and safety advice;
- employees are provided with information about the risks in your workplace and how they are protected;
- instruction and training for employees in how to deal with the risks;
- there is adequate and appropriate supervision in place;
- consulting with employees about their risks at work and current preventive and protective measures.

Workplace Regulations

The Workplace (Health, Safety and Welfare) Regulations 1992 cover a wide range of basic health, safety and welfare issues and apply to most workplaces.
Specifically, the regulations impose requirements on the:

- maintenance of workplaces;
- ventilation of enclosed workplaces and temperatures of indoor workplaces and the provision of thermometers;
- lighting (including emergency lighting);
- cleanliness of the workplace, and of furniture, furnishings and fittings (also the ability to clean floors, walls and ceilings) and the removal of waste materials;
- room dimensions and unoccupied space;

- suitability of workstations (including those outside) and the provision of suitable seating;

- condition of floors, and the arrangement of routes for pedestrians or vehicles;

- protection from falling objects, and from persons falling from a height, or falling into dangerous substances;

- material of and protection of windows and other transparent or translucent walls, doors or gates, and to them being apparent;

- way in which windows, skylights or ventilators are opened and their position when left open and the ability to clean these items;

- construction of doors and gates (including the fitting of necessary safety devices), and escalators and moving walkways;

- provision of suitable sanitary conveniences, washing facilities and drinking water (including cups and drinking vessels);

- provision of suitable accommodation for clothing and for changing clothes, for rest and for eating meals.

Manual Handling

The Manual Handling Regulations 1992 are intended to reduce back and other injuries suffered through the manual handling of loads and to ensure that manual handling operations are properly risk assessed.

Where such activities must take place, the employer should ensure that employees:

- are well trained in good handling techniques;

- understand how operations have been designed to ensure their safety;

- make proper use of systems of work provided.

In particular, employees should understand:

- how potentially hazardous handling operations can be recognized;

- how to deal with unfamiliar operations;

- the proper use of handling aids;

- the proper use of personal protective equipment;

- features of the working environment that contribute to safety;

- the importance of good housekeeping;

- factors affecting individual capability;

- good handling techniques.

Training in good handling techniques should be tailored to the particular handling operations likely to be undertaken, beginning with relatively simple examples and progressing to more specialized handling operations.

It is especially useful to train employees to:

- recognize loads whose weight as well as their shape and other features, and the circumstances in which they are handled, might cause injury;
- treat unfamiliar loads with caution and not assume that apparently empty drums or other closed containers are in fact empty;
- test loads first by attempting to raise one end;
- apply force gradually when lifting or moving loads until either undue strain is felt, in which case an alternative method should be considered, or it is clear that the task can be accomplished without injury.

The HSE *Guide to Manual Handling at Work* is available at GOV.UK.

The Use of Display Screen Equipment

Operators must protect workers from the health risks of working with display screen equipment (DSE), such as PCs, laptops, tablets and smartphones.

The Health and Safety (Display Screen Equipment) Regulations apply to workers who use DSE daily, for an hour or more at a time. These workers are described as 'DSE users'. The regulations don't apply to workers who use DSE infrequently or only use it for a short time.

Operators must therefore:

- do a DSE workstation assessment;
- reduce risks, including making sure workers take breaks from DSE work or do something different;
- provide an eye test if a worker asks for one;
- provide training and information for workers.

DSE law applies if users are:

- at a fixed workstation;
- mobile workers;
- home workers;
- hot-desking (workers should carry out a basic risk assessment if they change desks regularly).

Provision and Use of Work Equipment

The Provision and Use of Work Equipment Regulations 1998 (PUWER) require employers and the self-employed to ensure that equipment provided for use at work complies with the regulations. The law applies to owned, hired, leased and second-hand equipment and all machinery, appliances (including cranes, lift trucks and vehicle hoists), apparatus, tools or component assemblies so arranged as to function as a whole unit. Work equipment must be:

- suitable for its intended purpose;
- assessed as to any risks associated with the equipment;
- subject to a recorded inspection where such an inspection would assist in identifying health and safety risks;
- maintained in efficient working order, in an efficient state and in good repair, and a maintenance log kept.

Personal Protective Equipment

Operators are required to provide suitable PPE to employees where there are risks to their health and safety which cannot be adequately controlled by other means – it is a last-resort measure. Self-employed persons must provide their own protective equipment where necessary and employees must report defective PPE. PPE is not suitable unless:

- it is appropriate for the identified risks;
- account has been taken of the environment that it will be used in, ergonomic factors such as the nature of the job, the need for communication and the health of the wearer;
- it fits the wearer correctly and comfortably and is capable of being adjusted;
- it is effective, so far as is practicable, against the risks it is intended to control;
- it is serviceable and in good condition.

The COSHH Regulations 2002 (as Amended)

These regulations are aimed at eliminating exposure, or controlling the degree of exposure, that workers are experiencing to hazardous substances. They do so by classifying the nature of the hazards as 'very toxic', 'toxic', 'harmful', 'corrosive' or 'irritant'.

Under the Act, employers are required to carry out adequate assessments before any employee is exposed to any hazardous substance, to eliminate the use of the substance or, where this is not possible, to control the exposure by whatever means possible and to issue PPE as a last resort in that control, to monitor employees' exposure to hazardous substances, to keep records of such monitoring and to provide employees with information and training in relation to hazards.

The Reporting of Injuries, Diseases and Dangerous Occurrences Regulations 2013 (RIDDOR)

RIDDOR covers certain accidents and incidents relating to the workplace and how these issues are reported and recorded.

RIDDOR is overseen by the HSE Incident Contact Centre (ICC) in South Wales and relates to accidents and incidents that occur in the workplace. These include:

- fatal accidents;
- accidents resulting in major injury (loss of a limb, fingers, or an eye and more than 24 hours' hospitalization);
- dangerous occurrences;
- accidents leading to seven consecutive days off work;
- some work-related diseases;
- most incidents relating to problems with natural gas and liquefied petroleum gas (LPG).

Reporting to the ICC:

1 For accidents where there is a fatality or a major injury or a dangerous occurrence, the incident has to be reported immediately by phone to the ICC (0345 300 9923) or by using the form on the HSE website.

2 For accidents causing more than seven days' incapacity for work, there is no requirement to make an immediate telephone notification, but the online form is still required to be completed within 15 days.

In cases where the accident or incident involves vehicles on the public highway, the Traffic Commissioner must also be informed. In addition, records of all reportable accidents and incidents must be kept for a minimum period of three years, while all minor accidents need to be recorded in an accident book. Completed books also need to be kept for three years.

Full contact details for the ICC, which is open 8.30 am–5.00 pm Monday–Friday, are as follows:

Telephone: 0345 300 9923

Email: riddor@natbrit.com

All incidents can be reported online but a telephone service is also provided for reporting fatal/specified incidents only – call the Incident Contact Centre on 0345 300 9923 (opening hours Monday to Friday 8.30 am to 5 pm).

Major Injury

For clarification, a 'major injury' is defined as follows:

- fracture of the skull, spine or pelvis;
- fracture of any bone:
  - in the arm other than a bone in the wrist or hand;
  - in the leg other than a bone in the ankle or foot;
- amputation of a hand or foot;
- the loss of sight of an eye;
- any other injury which results in the person injured being admitted into hospital as an inpatient for more than 24 hours, unless that person was detained only for observation.

Dangerous Occurrences

Dangerous occurrences must be reported even though no injury was actually caused to any person. Examples include:

- failure, collapse or overturning of lifts, hoists, cranes, excavators, tail-lifts, etc;
- explosion of boiler or boiler tube;
- electrical short circuits followed by fire or explosion;
- explosion or fire which results in stoppage of work for more than 24 hours;
- release of flammable liquid or gas (ie over 1 tonne);
- collapse of scaffolding;
- collapse or partial collapse of any building;
- failure of a freight container while being lifted;
- a road tanker to which the Hazchem regulations apply either overturning or suffering serious damage to the tank while a hazardous substance is being carried.

Lifting Operations

The Lifting Operations and Lifting Equipment Regulations 1998 (LOLER) apply to all lifting equipment which is defined as 'work equipment for lifting and lowering loads and includes its attachments used for anchoring, fixing or supporting it'. These regulations apply to forklift trucks and to automated goods storage and retrieval systems, and front-end loaders on tractors. These regulations also apply to tipping vehicles.

The regulations make provisions regarding:

- the strength and stability of lifting equipment;
- the safety of lifting equipment for lifting persons;
- the way lifting equipment is positioned and installed;
- the marking of machinery and accessories for lifting, and lifting equipment which is designed for lifting persons or which might so be used in error;
- the organization of lifting operations;
- thorough examination and inspection of lifting equipment in specified circumstances;
- evidence of examination to accompany it (ie the lifting equipment) outside the firm's premises;
- exceptions for winding apparatus at mines;
- the making of reports of thorough examinations and records of inspections;
- the keeping of information in the reports and records.

Additionally, operators must ensure that:

- lifting operations are planned, supervised and carried out in a safe manner by people who are competent;
- where equipment is used for lifting people it is marked accordingly, and it should be safe for such a purpose, eg all necessary precautions have been taken to eliminate or reduce any risk;
- where appropriate, before lifting equipment (including accessories) is used for the first time, it is *thoroughly examined*. Lifting equipment may need to be thoroughly examined in use at periods specified in the regulations (ie usually at least six-monthly for accessories and equipment used for lifting people and, at a minimum, annually for all other equipment) or at intervals laid down in an examination scheme drawn up by a competent person. All examination work should be performed by a competent person;

- following a thorough examination or inspection of any lifting equipment, a report is submitted by the competent person to the employer to take the appropriate action.

NB: *The Royal Society for the Prevention of Accidents (ROSPA) also produces a guide on these regulations. Both versions are free to download from the respective websites.*

Work-Related Stress

Employers have a legal duty to protect employees from stress at work by doing a risk assessment and acting on it. The HSE defines stress as 'the adverse reaction people have to excessive pressures or other types of demand placed on them'. Employees feel stress when they can't cope with pressures and other issues.

To manage stress, the demands of a role should be matched to an employee's skill, knowledge, ability and the resources available to them. For example, drivers can get stressed if they feel they don't have the resources or time to meet a delivery schedule. Good planning, training and support can reduce pressure and bring stress levels down.

Stress affects people differently. What stresses one person may not stress another, and stress in the workplace should be risk assessed. Stress is not an illness but it can make people ill. Recognizing the signs of stress will help operators to take steps to stop, lower and manage stress and help ensure a safer operation.

The HSE has guidance at GOV.UK for managers on how to have simple, practical conversations with staff to help prevent stress.

Smoking in the Workplace

Smoke-free legislation was introduced in England in 2007, banning smoking in nearly all enclosed workplaces and public spaces, following similar bans in Scotland, Wales and Northern Ireland. Local authorities are responsible for enforcing the legislation.

In relation to transport, these regulations also apply to vehicles and vehicle cabs which are deemed to be 'places of work'. In order to fully comply with the regulations, 'No Smoking' signs need to be placed in every compartment where people may be carried in, or on, a vehicle. These signs must be the EU-specified 'No Smoking' sign and be at least 70 mm in diameter.

There are three principal ways that the regulations are enforced. These are:

- fixed penalty notices for employees (including drivers) smoking in a place of work. However, if the person is taken to court and prosecuted, it can result in additional fines being levied;

- fixed penalty notices being issued to employers who fail to post 'No Smoking' signs when and where they are required. This can also result in additional fines if taken to court;
- fines being handed out to any person (director, manager, supervisor, etc) who is in a position to control smoke-free premises and fails to do so.

While considering smoking in the workplace, e-cigarettes must also be considered. These include both personal vaporizers (PVs) and electronic nicotine delivery systems (ENDS), which fall outside the scope of the regulations. However, the Health and Safety Executive and ACAS strongly advise employers to develop a policy, in conjunction with worker representatives if possible, in relation to the use of e-cigarettes (vaping) at work in order to protect any employees who may have concerns about related health issues, while taking into account any possible benefits there may be for people trying to give up smoking.

Vehicle Batteries

HSE guide INDG139 provides advice on how to use rechargeable batteries safely. Following it can greatly reduce the risks involved. The advice is aimed at supervisors, technicians and safety professionals in a range of sectors.

General Precautions

- Always wear goggles or a visor when working on batteries.
- Wherever possible, always use a properly designated and well-ventilated area for battery charging.
- Remove any metallic objects from hands, wrists and around the neck (eg rings, chains and watches) before working on a battery.

Disconnecting and Reconnecting Batteries

- Turn off the vehicle ignition switch and all other switches or otherwise isolate the battery from the electrical circuit.
- Always disconnect the earthed terminal first (often the negative terminal, but not always – check) and reconnect it last using insulated tools.
- Do not rest tools or metallic objects on top of a battery.

Battery Charging

- Always observe the manufacturer's instructions for charging batteries.
- Charge in a well-ventilated area.

- Do not smoke or bring naked flames into the charging area.

- Make sure the battery is topped up to the correct level.

- Make sure the charger is switched off or disconnected from the power supply before connecting the charging leads, which should be connected positive to positive, negative to negative.

- Vent plugs may need to be adjusted before charging. Carefully follow the manufacturer's instructions.

- Do not exceed the recommended rate of charging.

- When charging is complete, switch off the charger before disconnecting the charging leads.

Jump-Starting

Preparation:

- Before attempting to jump-start a vehicle, always check to see if the vehicle is capable of being jump-started without causing any damage to the vehicle or any of its components.

- Always ensure that both batteries have the same voltage rating.

- If starting by using a battery on another vehicle, check the earth polarity on both vehicles.

- Ensure the vehicles are not touching.

- Turn off the ignition of both vehicles.

- Always use purpose-made, colour-coded jump leads with insulated handles – red for the positive cable and black for the negative cable.

Connection for vehicles with the *same* earth polarity:

- First connect the non-earthed terminal of the good battery to the non-earthed terminal of the flat battery.

- Connect one end of the second lead to the earthed terminal of the good battery.

- Connect the other end of the second lead to a suitable, substantial, unpainted point on the chassis or engine of the other vehicle, away from the battery, carburettor, fuel lines or brake pipes.

Connection for vehicles with *different* earth polarity:

- First connect the earthed terminal of the good battery to the non-earthed terminal of the flat battery.

- Connect one end of the second lead to the non-earthed terminal of the good battery.

- Connect the other end of the second lead to a suitable, substantial, unpainted point on the chassis or engine of the other vehicle, away from the battery, carburettor, fuel lines or brake pipes.

The HSE warns that in view of the potential for confusion, this should be attempted only by skilled and experienced personnel.

Starting

- Ensure the leads are well clear of moving parts.
- Start the engine of the 'good' vehicle and allow to run for about one minute.
- Start the engine of the 'dead' vehicle and allow to run for about one minute.

Disconnection

- Stop the engine of the 'good' vehicle.
- Disconnect the leads in the reverse order to which they were connected.
- Take great care in handling jump leads; do not allow the exposed metal parts to touch each other or the vehicle body.

Always check the manufacturer's guidance before jump-starting a vehicle.

The Batteries Directive

The EU's Batteries Directive (2006/66/EC) provides for control of the environmental impacts of batteries, in particular setting limits for the content of certain heavy metals within batteries.

Two particular and connected environmental hazards are associated with batteries. First, they often contain heavy metals such as cadmium and mercury, which can pose a threat if released into the environment. Second, the disposal sources for many batteries are either landfill sites or incineration plants, the use of either being likely to lead to polluting releases into the environment.

The Directive includes all types of batteries and accumulators, and divides batteries into three main categories:

- Portable batteries: These include household batteries, such as those used to power portable electronic equipment and torches.
- Industrial batteries: These include lead-acid batteries used in heavy machinery and industrial power tools.
- Automotive batteries: All batteries used to power motor vehicles. These are commonly lead-acid batteries.

The main aims of the Directive include:

- restricting the use of mercury and cadmium in batteries;
- setting out labelling requirements for new batteries (to help consumers in choosing batteries and in deciding how to send them for recycling);
- setting targets for collecting waste portable batteries:
  - 45 per cent by September 2016 (figures of achievement or not were not available at the time of writing but in March 2018 there was a 57-tonne predicted shortfall announced, with the UK achieving a 28 per cent collection rate but with other European countries achieving 45 per cent);
- prohibiting the disposal by landfill or incineration of waste industrial and automotive batteries, which implies a 100 per cent collection and recycling target;
- introducing producer responsibilities.

Risk Management

Risk management may be defined as the process of measuring or assessing risks (ie in the workplace) and then developing strategies to manage those risks. Generally, the strategies adopted would include transferring the risk to another party, avoiding the risk, reducing the negative effect of a particular risk, or deciding to accept some or all of its consequences. Traditionally, risk management focuses on risks arising from physical or legal causes (eg natural disasters or fires, accidents, death and lawsuits) or malpractices in the workplace. Ideally, risk management should follow a prioritization process whereby the greatest risks (ie those likely to cause most harm to people or damage to equipment) are dealt with first, while those with a lower probability of occurrence and less likelihood to cause harm or damage are dealt with later. In practice, careful decisions need to be made about these issues. Most large companies have risk management teams, but even the smallest of firms and even one-man owner-driver businesses need to have focused risk management procedures.

Risk Management for Transport Operators

Running a safe operation is crucial in today's increasingly litigious world. When something goes wrong, particularly a serious accident or incident, it is increasingly the directors of a company who are held accountable, while the true costs of road traffic accidents are often overlooked when considering insured costs such as property damage and injury compensation. In any event, the impact on profitability of the following should not be underestimated:

- loss of revenue through vehicles being unavailable for use;
- the cost of replacement drivers following injury to regular drivers;
- loss of business through damage to customer relationships;
- damage to brand image if a liveried vehicle is involved in a fatal accident.

Risk Assessment

Many accidents could be prevented by simply examining what actually goes on in your business, removing and controlling hazards as far as possible and taking the necessary managerial and supervisory steps to make sure that what is supposed to happen does happen. For example:

STEP 1 Look for the hazards.

STEP 2 Decide who might be harmed and how.

STEP 3 Evaluate the risks and decide whether the existing precautions are adequate or whether more should be done.

STEP 4 Record your findings.

STEP 5 Review your assessment and revise it if necessary.

Source: HSE Guide to Risk Assessment.

NB: A hazard is simply something that can cause harm. Risk is the chance of anyone suffering harm from such a hazard.

Clearly, work activities need to be assessed for risk but it is not sufficient to 'assess and forget'. Risk assessments need to be ongoing and to change as activities change and new activities are introduced. In addition, workers undertaking the tasks need to be involved to give their feedback as to how risks can be reduced and eliminated. This is particularly important where the risk assessment is focused on technical tasks, complex tasks, specialized tasks, etc. Also note the new need for risk assessment when using tyres that are 10 years old or more, as mentioned in Chapter 12.

Fire Safety

All employers are required by law to carry out a fire risk assessment and introduce appropriate safety measures within their workplaces.

This regulatory Order is a fire risk assessment-based approach where the person responsible for the premises or area they control must decide how to address the risks identified, while meeting certain requirements. By adopting this fire risk assessment approach, the responsible person will need to consider how to prevent fire from occurring in the first place, by removing or reducing hazards and risks (such as ignition sources), then consider the precautions necessary to ensure that people are adequately protected if a fire were still to occur. The fire risk assessment must also take into consideration what effect a fire may have on any person in or around your premises, plus in neighbouring property.

While the Order is intended to be less burdensome and clearer than former legal provisions, the main emphasis of the regulations remains on fire prevention, so risk assessments will need to be kept under regular review.

The Order applies to all non-domestic properties, including those of voluntary organizations, and is subject to monitoring and, where appropriate, enforcement by the Local Authority Fire Service (LAFS).

Summary of the Order

- All existing fire legislation has now been repealed or revoked, which includes the Fire Precautions Act 1971, the amended 1997 Fire Precautions (Workplace) Regulations plus 100 other pieces of fire-related legislation.

- Fire certificates have been abolished and are no longer issued.

- A 'responsible person' is to be responsible for fire safety and they must conduct a fire risk assessment regardless of the size of the risk (see below).

- The identified responsible person(s) will carry full corporate liability.

- The Order extends the scope of consideration to include property safety, firefighter safety and the environment around the site. The responsible person has a duty to protect all risks.

- Unlike the previous legislation, this Order places emphasis on business continuity and containing and preventing the spread of small fires.

Protection is explicitly extended to occupants of all premises, including employees, visitors, contractors and passers-by, all of whom have to be considered in the fire risk.

The rules related to fire risk assessment and required actions are outlined below. Employers and building owners and occupiers must carry out a fire risk assessment and keep it up to date. Based on the findings of the assessment, adequate and appropriate fire safety measures must be put in place to minimize the risk of injury or death in the event of a fire.

The risk assessment needs to identify what could cause a fire (sources), substances that burn and people who may be at risk. The prime aim should be to eliminate risks, but where this is not possible the risks need to be minimized and properly managed. Managing also includes considering how people at work can be protected if there is a fire.

General considerations include:

- keeping sources of ignition and flammable substances apart;
- avoiding accidental fires;
- ensuring good housekeeping practices;
- considering fire-detection and fire-warning measures;
- having sufficient fire-fighting resources and equipment;
- having appropriate, fully operational fire-fighting equipment;
- ensuring staff are trained on actions to take in the event of a fire.

There is a whole range of fire prevention and risk guidance freely available on the GOV.UK and HSE websites covering many different work environments and requirements, depending upon the actual work sector.

First Aid

Employers must train members of staff in first-aid techniques and provide first-aid equipment and facilities under the Health and Safety (First Aid) Regulations 1981. An approved Code of Practice established by the Health and Safety Executive provides both employers and the self-employed with practical guidance on how they may meet the requirements of the regulations.

Regulations state that 'an employer shall provide, or ensure that there are provided, such equipment, information and facilities as are adequate and appropriate in the circumstances for enabling first aid to be rendered to his employees if they are injured or become ill at work'.

Trained First-Aiders

The employer must, in some cases, provide suitable persons to administer first aid and these persons must have had specific training or hold appropriate qualifications. This usually requires attending periodic training and refresher courses. The numbers of first-aiders required depends upon the work activity and the number of employees but there are no actual statutory number requirements. However, the HSE recommends that, generally speaking, one first-aider is required for every 50 workers in a company where there are no special risks or circumstances. Further advice is available on the HSE website.

First-Aid Boxes

First-aid boxes must be provided. These should be properly identified as first-aid containers, preferably with a white cross on a green background, and contain sufficient quantities of first-aid material *and nothing else*. In particular, the boxes should contain only material which a first-aider has been trained to use. There is no mandatory list of items to put in a first-aid box. It depends on what you assess your needs to be. As a guide, the HSE suggests that where work activities involve low-level hazards, a minimum stock of first-aid items would be:

- a leaflet giving general guidance on first aid (eg HSE's leaflet 'Basic Advice on First Aid at Work');
- 20 individually wrapped sterile plasters (of assorted sizes), appropriate to the type of work (you can provide hypoallergenic plasters if necessary);
- two sterile eye pads;
- four individually wrapped triangular bandages, preferably sterile;
- six safety pins;
- two large, individually wrapped, sterile, unmedicated wound dressings;
- six medium-sized, individually wrapped, sterile, unmedicated wound dressings;
- at least three pairs of disposable gloves.

Soap and water and disposable drying materials, or suitable equivalents, should also be available. Where tap water is not available, sterile water or sterile 9 per cent saline, in sealed disposable containers (refillable containers are banned) each holding at least 300 millilitres, should be kept easily accessible, and near to the first-aid box, for eye irrigation.

The contents of first-aid boxes should be replenished as soon as possible after use and items which deteriorate will need to be replaced from time to time. Items should not be used after the indicated expiry date on the packet. Boxes and kits should be examined frequently to make sure they are fully equipped.

Travelling First-Aid Kits

An employer does not need to make first-aid provisions for employees working away. However, where the work involves carrying passengers, travelling for long distances in remote areas, from which access to NHS accident and emergency facilities may be difficult, or where employees are using potentially dangerous tools or machinery, small travelling first-aid kits should be provided.

The regulations suggest that in general the following items should be sufficient to comply with BSI-8599 minimum contents:

- one pair of rust-proof, blunt-ended scissors;
- ten antiseptic wipes, foil packed;
- one conforming disposable bandage (not less than 7.5 cm wide);
- two triangular bandages;
- one packet of 24 assorted adhesive dressings;
- three large sterile unmedicated ambulance dressings (not less than 15 × 20 cm);
- two sterile eye pads, with attachments;
- assorted safety pins.

First Aid on the Road

The following guidelines have been established for dealing with casualties at the scene of a road accident:

1 Assess the situation:
   - What has happened?
   - Is there any further danger to you or the casualty? (Remember, roadsides are particularly dangerous places to treat a casualty.)
   - How many people are injured?
   - Is anybody else able to help?

2 Assess the casualty:
   - What is wrong with the casualty?
   - Is it necessary to move the casualty, or can he/she be left safely in his/her current position?
   - Remember, further injuries can be caused through unnecessary movement of the casualty.

3 Do you need assistance?
   - Do you need assistance from the emergency services?
   - Don't forget, other first-aiders/bystanders can help you.
   - When you ask for help from the emergency services they will need to know:
     - the precise location of the incident;
     - what happened;
     - the injuries involved;
     - how many people are injured.

4 Make a diagnosis:

– What happened to the casualty? Did he or she fall, faint or have a bump on the head?

– Look for signs such as bleeding, swelling or unaligned limbs.

– If the casualty is conscious, ask him or her where he or she feels pain or if he or she went dizzy before the accident.

5 Priorities:

– The priorities of first aid are usually referred to as the ABC of first aid:

– *Airway*: check inside the mouth and remove any visible obstruction. Put your fingertips under the point of the casualty's chin. Lift the chin to open the airway.

– *Breathing*: spend at least 10 seconds looking, listening and feeling for breathing. If the casualty is breathing, put him/her in the recovery position. Continue to monitor the patient's breathing.

– *Circulation*: look, listen and feel for normal breathing, coughing or movement by the victim. Only if you have been trained to do so, check the carotid pulse.

6 Priorities of general treatment (the three Bs):

– *Breathing* (see above).

– *Bleeding*: stop bleeding by raising the injured limb above the heart. Apply pressure to the wound with pad, bandage, clean handkerchief or towel.

– *Bones*: if necessary immobilize a broken arm in a sling. If a broken leg is suspected, keep the casualty still.

7 While you are waiting for the arrival of the emergency services:

– Look for changes in the casualty's condition, monitoring the vital signs.

– Check your treatment is adequate and successful.

– Cooperate with the emergency services when they arrive.

NB: *It must be stated that guidance on the actual procedures to be administered change frequently and regular first-aid training should be undertaken.*

Workplace Safety Signs

At work, a safety sign is defined as one which combines geometrical shape, colour and a pictorial symbol to provide specific health or safety information or an instruction as to whether or not any text is included on the sign. Regulations concerning the specification of safety signs in work premises have applied to all such signs since

1 January 1986. Specifications for various types of safety sign are given in BS 5378 (Part I). They are briefly described as follows:

- *Prohibition sign*: round in shape with a white background and a circular band and cross-bar in red. The symbol must be black and placed in the centre of the sign without obliterating the cross-bar. Typical examples of such signs are those prohibiting smoking, prohibiting pedestrians, or indicating the use of water for drinking purposes.

- *Warning sign*: triangular in shape with a yellow background and black triangular band. The symbol or words must be black and placed in the centre of the sign. Typical examples of such signs are those warning of the danger of fire, explosion, toxic substances, corrosive substances, radiation, overhead loads, industrial trucks, electric shocks, proximity of laser beams, etc.

- *Mandatory sign*: round in shape with a blue background, with the symbol or words placed centrally and in white. Typical examples of such signs are those advising that certain pieces of protective clothing must be worn (eg goggles, hard hats, breathing masks, gloves, etc).

- *Safety sign*: square in shape with a green background and white symbol or words centrally placed. Typical examples of such signs are those for fire exits, first-aid posts and rescue points.

Vehicle Reversing

Among the statistics of industrial accidents and road accidents, those resulting from vehicles reversing feature significantly. According to the HSE, nearly one-quarter of all deaths involving vehicles at work occur while vehicles are reversing. In a guide titled *Vehicles at Work – Reversing*, available from the HSE website, the HSE gives the following advice and information to those concerned:

- Remove the need for reversing altogether by setting up one-way systems, for example drive-through loading and unloading positions. Where reversing is unavoidable, routes should be organized to minimize the need for reversing.

- Ensure visiting drivers are familiar with the layout of the workplace, and with any site rules. Do drivers have to report to reception on arrival?

In locations where reversing cannot be avoided:

- 'Reversing areas and bays' should be planned out and clearly marked.
- People who do not need to be in reversing areas should be kept well clear.

- Consider employing a trained signaller (a banksman), both to keep the reversing area free of pedestrians and to guide drivers. Be aware: the use of signallers is not allowed in some industries due to the size of vehicles involved and the difficulty that drivers have in seeing them.

- A signaller:
  - will need to use a clear, agreed system of signalling;
  - will need to be visible to drivers at all times;
  - will need to stand in a safe position from which to guide the reversing vehicle without being in its way;
  - should wear very visible clothing, such as reflective vests, and ensure that any signals are clearly seen.

- If drivers lose sight of the signaller, they should know to stop immediately.

- Consider whether portable radios or similar communication systems would be helpful.

The following steps might help to reduce the risk of reversing accidents. The following are examples, but it is unlikely that any single measure will be enough to ensure safety:

- Site layouts can be designed (or modified) to increase visibility for drivers and pedestrians, for example:
  - by increasing the area allowed for reversing;
  - by installing fixed mirrors in smaller areas.

- Reducing the dangers caused by 'blind spots':
  - Install rear-view cameras to vehicles and trailers.
  - Most vehicles already have external side-mounted and rear-view mirrors fitted. These need to be kept clean and in good repair.
  - Refractive lenses fitted to rear windows or closed-circuit television systems can be used to help drivers to see behind the vehicle.
  - If drivers cannot see behind the vehicle, they should leave their cab and check behind the vehicle before reversing.

- Reversing alarms can be fitted:
  - These should be kept in working order.
  - Audible alarms should be loud and distinct enough that they do not become part of the background noise.
  - Where an audible alarm might not stand out from the background noise, flashing warning lights can be used.

- Other safety devices can be fitted to vehicles:
  - For example, a number of 'sensing' and 'trip' systems are available, which either warn the driver or stop the vehicle when an obstruction is detected close to, or comes in contact with, the reversing vehicle.
- Stops such as barriers or buffers at loading bays can be used. They should be highly visible and sensibly positioned.
- Where vehicles reverse up to structures or edges, barriers or wheel stops can be used to warn drivers that they need to stop.
- White lines on the floor can help the driver position the vehicle accurately.

It is in consequence of the dangers of reversing that legislation permits the voluntary fitment of reversing bleepers on certain goods and passenger vehicles (see the Reversing Alarms section in Chapter 12 for full details). It should be remembered that the use of reversing alarms is subject to the same rules for sounding the horn of the vehicle after 11.30 pm and before 7.00 am. With the introduction of these voluntary provisions, there is the risk that operators deciding not to fit such equipment on a voluntary basis, who then have one of their vehicles involved in a reversing accident, could face proceedings under the Health and Safety at Work Act for not taking sufficient care in safeguarding the health of others. A number of successful prosecutions on this account have been reported and in some cases very heavy fines were imposed.

Safe Tipping

Another area where concern has been expressed over safety measures involves the use of tipping vehicles (and vehicles with lorry-mounted cranes and suchlike) whereby elevated bodies (or crane jibs) come into contact with overhead power cables or are sufficiently close for arcing to occur in wet conditions. The specific danger lies in touching the vehicle body or tipping controls while in contact with the power cable. Drivers are safe when a cable is touched provided they remain in the cab, where the vehicle tyres prevent completion of an electrical circuit. This becomes difficult when many 'Hiab' systems are operated, as the driver needs to be out of the cab and is therefore at a greatly increased risk. A spokesperson for the electricity supply industry advises drivers, where possible, to remain in their cabs and drive clear. If this is not possible they should jump from the cab and NOT touch any part of the vehicle, remaining well clear until an electricity engineer has been contacted and reports that it is safe to return to the vehicle.

Tipper operators should also advise drivers to ensure the ground is firm before tipping to prevent the vehicle sinking and overturning as the weight of the load shifts to the rear during tipping, and to make sure the tipping gear is disengaged and the body is not in the raised position, or able to be raised, before driving off. Operators should also be aware of the provisions of the LOLER described in the Lifting Operations section earlier in the chapter.

Sheeting Loads

A variety of load types need to be sheeted for both legal and operational reasons, particularly loads comprising waste skips, bricks, sand, gravel, ash, grain and various types of agricultural produce. Other loads need to be sheeted for weather protection and security reasons.

Many aspects of health and safety legislation and various Codes of Practice are relevant and should be carefully observed to avoid any breach of health and safety law. Also, specifically, it is an offence under C&U Regulations to allow loose loads of any type to cause nuisance or danger to other road users as a result of such material falling or being blown from the vehicle. These loads must be adequately restrained by sheeting or by covering with netting, and 'auto-sheet' systems are now widely fitted to most tippers.

As we discussed earlier, 'working at height' legislation normally applies to these types of tasks, and health and safety guidelines suggest that priority should be given to the use of closed vehicles or, where this is not feasible, to vehicles with mechanically operated sheeting systems or, at the very least, with mechanical systems that can be operated from ground level. Alternatively, consideration should be given to the provision of gantries from which operatives can sheet loads with minimal risk to their personal safety.

Useful guidance on safe sheeting methods is to be found on the HSE and GOV.UK websites and in a number of official publications (as earlier) and as follows:

- Health and Safety Executive:
  - *Workplace Transport Safety* – HS(G)136.
- Department for Transport:
  - *Safety of Loads on Vehicles: Code of Practice* (third edition, 2003).
- DVSA:
  - *Load Securing: Vehicle Operator Guidance* (2015).

Safe Parking

Many accidents occur with parked vehicles and trailers. In particular, within transport depots there should be proper procedures for parking, especially in regard to parking areas and level standing for detached semi-trailers. A common failing is not ensuring that semi-trailers are dropped onto hard and level ground, allowing the landing gear on one side to sink and the trailer to topple over to the side. Nose-diving is another common accident, where nose-heavy semi-trailers are not supported with trestles when left detached. Ground sinkage can also be a cause of difficulty when recoupling tractive units.

Cases have been reported of unsafe parking practices resulting in driver deaths related to the braking of parked semi-trailers. When recoupling tractive units, drivers insert the red air hose which releases the emergency brakes on the semi-trailer without checking that both the semi-trailer ratchet brake (if fitted) and the tractive-unit handbrake are fully applied. In such circumstances the vehicle combination can move while the driver is out of the cab. To counter this risk, alarms are available to warn the driver that the unit handbrake has not been applied. Other potential sources of accidents are when articulated combinations are coupled near to walls and loading bays, where there is always a danger of an unseen person walking behind the trailer. Again, if brakes are not properly set, the semi-trailer is likely to shunt backwards as the tractive unit is driven under the coupling plate.

Work at Height

Falls from height remain the most common cause of workplace fatality. The Work at Height Regulations 2005 apply to any person who, whilst at work, may fall from a position above ground level and suffer personal injury. This means that there is a duty on employers and work controllers to ensure that:

- all work at height is properly planned and organized;
- persons working at height are competent to do so;
- the risks from work at height are assessed, and appropriate equipment is selected and used;
- the risks of working on or near fragile surfaces are properly managed;
- the equipment used for work at height is properly inspected and maintained.

The rules apply to most 'work at height' situations where there is a risk of a fall likely to cause injury to a person, such as climbing into or out of a vehicle cab or the load area. The employer's duty is to ensure that current practices are risk assessed and safe and to take steps to prevent falls and ensure that relevant staff are trained, that work is planned accordingly and that work is suspended when weather conditions endanger health or safety. Provision in these regulations also relates to falling objects, which should be safeguarded against. In the context of this legislation, 'at height' means a place from which a person falling could be injured.

Noise at Work

According to Action on Hearing Loss, around 900,000 people in Britain actually suffer severe or acute deafness, tinnitus and other hearing problems, much of which stems from work activities.

The Control of Noise at Work Regulations 2005 (Noise Regulations 2005) require employers to prevent or reduce risks to health and safety from exposure to noise at work. Employees have duties under the Regulations too. The Regulations require you as an employer to:

- assess the risks to your employees from noise at work;
- take action to reduce the noise exposure that produces those risks;
- provide your employees with hearing protection if you cannot reduce the noise exposure enough by using other methods;
- make sure the legal limits on noise exposure are not exceeded;
- provide your employees with information, instruction and training;
- carry out health surveillance where there is a risk to health.

Forklift Truck Safety

There has been much concern in recent years about the high level of industrial accidents which are caused by, or which result from, forklift truck misuse. In consequence of this, a system of forklift truck driver licensing has been established in order to ensure a safe standard of operation. However, the HSE is keen to point out that there is no such thing as a statutory forklift truck driver's licence, but under PUWER there are certain requirements on employers and this has driven the need for both training and voluntary licensing of forklift truck operators.

PUWER states that employers must make sure that all people who use, supervise or manage the use of work equipment have received adequate training, which includes the correct use of the equipment, any risks from its use and the precautions to take. These requirements are the driving force that ensures employers can avoid conflict with the Health and Safety Inspectorate (HSI), which has powers to issue improvement notices and prohibition notices to employers to have drivers trained, to order that the use of forklift trucks must be stopped immediately if they believe that danger is being caused and to take an employer to court if an untrained driver causes an accident with a forklift truck.

Further information can be downloaded from the HSE website or from publications such as:

- 'Consulting Employees on Health and Safety: A brief guide to the law.' Leaflet INDG232 (rev2) HSE Books 2013, www.hse.gov.uk/pubns/indg232.pdf.

- *Rider-operated Lift Trucks: Operator Training and Safe Use.* Approved Code of Practice and guidance L117 (third edition). HSE Books 2013 ISBN 978 0 7176 6441 2, www.hse.gov.uk/pubns/books/l117.htm.

- 'Use Lift Trucks Safely: A brief guide for operators.' Pocket card INDG457, HSE Books 2013, www.hse.gov.uk/pubns/indg457.htm.

Freight Container Safety Regulations

Owners and lessees and others in control of freight containers must ensure that they comply with the International Convention for Safe Containers – Geneva 1972. The Freight Containers (Safety Convention) Regulations 1984 apply to containers designed to facilitate the transport of goods by one or more modes of transport without intermediate reloading, designed to be secured or readily handled or both, having corner fittings for these purposes and which have top corner fittings and a bottom area of at least 7 square metres or, if they do not have top corner fittings, a bottom area of at least 14 square metres.

Containers must have a valid approval issued by the HSE or a body appointed by the HSE (or under the authority of a foreign government which has acceded to the Convention) for the purpose of confirming that they meet specified standards of design and construction and should be fitted with a safety approval plate to this effect. If they are marked with their gross weight, such marking must be consistent with the maximum operating gross weight shown on the safety approval plate. Containers must be maintained in an efficient state, in efficient working order and in good repair. Details of the arrangements for the approval of containers in Great Britain are set out in the document 'Freight Container Approval Arrangements in Great Britain', which is free to download from the HSE website.

The safety approval plate (issued by the HSE) as described in the regulations must be permanently fitted to the container where it is clearly visible and not capable of being easily damaged and it must show the following information:

CSC Safety Approval:

- approval reference;
- date manufactured;
- identification number;
- maximum gross weight... kg... lb;
- allowable stacking weight for ... g... kg... lb;
- racking test load value;
- next examination date.

Operation of Lorry Loaders

The use of hydraulically operated lorry loaders, or lorry-mounted cranes as they are more commonly called (the name Hiab becoming perhaps the most used term for this equipment), has reduced the risk of accident from the arduous and potentially injurious manhandling of loads, and these loaders reserve the strength of the driver for safe conduct of the vehicle, according to the Association of Lorry Loader Manufacturers and Importers (ALLMI). But, the Association says, despite the inherent safety of a properly designed and installed lorry loader, accidents still occur through lack of knowledge and understanding. For this reason ALLMI has published an excellent book called *Code of Practice for the Safe Installation, Application and Operation of Lorry Loaders*. ALLMI also produces a range of other products including a training DVD to complement formal training as a visual aid. Copies are available from the Association (tel: 0844 8584334), by contacting ALLMI on www.allmi.com or by writing to them at:

Unit 7b, Prince Maurice House
Cavalier Court
Bumpers Farm
Chippenham
Wiltshire
SN14 6LH

ALLMI also offers extensive training through a national network of approved training providers. Details of these training providers can also be found on the ALLMI website.

NB: See also Chapter 7 which deals with driver training for lorry-loader operatives.

Safety in Dock Premises

The Docks Regulations 1988 has now been repealed, with new guidelines having been produced by the HSE (see below). The HSE guidelines still require many of the old regulations to be observed, such as goods vehicle drivers working in or visiting docks premises, including roll-on/roll-off ferry ports, being provided with high-visibility clothing to be worn when they leave the vehicle cab. The clothing may take the form of fluorescent jackets, waistcoats, belts or sashes and must be worn at all times when out of the cab on such premises, including when on the vehicle decks of ferries. Protective headgear (hard hats) must also be supplied and worn in such areas where there is likely to be danger of falling objects from above (eg where cranes are working). Other requirements include drivers leaving the vehicle cab when parked on a straddle-carrier grid or where containers are being lifted onto or off the vehicle.

In September 2019 the HSE published an updated 'Code of Practice: Safety in Docks: Approved Code of Practice L148', which is free to download. This publication and further information relating to working in ports is available from the HSE website.

Health and Safety Enforcement

The HSE's emphasis is on prevention of incidents but, where appropriate, it enforces the law where it is found to be deliberately flouted. The aim of enforcement action is to ensure management deal immediately with serious risks (so they prevent harm), comply with the law and are held to account if they fail in their responsibilities. The HSE states its enforcement action is proportionate, targeted, consistent, transparent and accountable.

Improvement and Prohibition Notices

Improvement Notice

An improvement notice may be served on a person by health and safety inspectors in cases where they believe (ie are of the opinion) that the person is contravening or has contravened, and is likely to continue so doing or will do so again, any of the relevant statutory provisions. Inspectors must give details of the reason for their belief on these notices, which require the person concerned to remedy the contravention within a stated period.

Prohibition Notice

A prohibition notice with immediate effect may be served by inspectors on a person under whose control activities to which the relevant statutory provisions apply are being carried on, or are about to be carried on, if they believe that such activities involve or could involve *a risk of serious personal injury*. A prohibition notice must specify those matters giving rise to such a risk, and the reason why the inspector believes the statutory provisions are, or are likely to be, contravened, if indeed the inspector believes that such is the case. The notice must direct that the activities in question shall not be carried on unless those matters giving rise to the risk of serious personal injury, and any contravention of the regulations, are rectified.

Remedial Measures

Both improvement and prohibition notices may include directions as to necessary remedial measures and these may be framed by reference to an approved Code of Practice and may offer a choice of the actions to be taken. Reference must be made by the inspector to the fire authority before serving a notice requiring, or likely to lead to, measures affecting means of escape in case of fire.

Withdrawal of Notices and Appeals

A notice, other than a prohibition notice with immediate effect, may be withdrawn before the end of the period specified in the notice, or an appeal against it made. Alternatively, the period specified for remedial action may be extended at any time provided an appeal against the notice is not pending.

Penalties for Health and Safety Offences

Conviction for an offence under the Health and Safety at Work Act 1974 may lead to an unlimited fine. However, it should be stressed that while generally the fine imposed is intended to reflect the gravity of the particular offence and the employer's attitude towards health and safety matters, the Court will also bear in mind offenders' resources and the effects of a heavy penalty on their business, and may reduce the penalty accordingly.

Corporate Manslaughter

Where a death is caused through the negligence of an employer, whether health and safety related or as a result of a road accident, the employer risks facing a charge of corporate manslaughter.

It has been ruled by the courts that for an indictment on such a charge to be sustained, three key issues must be established by the jury as follows:

- The defendant owed a duty of care to the person killed.
- The defendant had breached his or her duty of care and that breach of care led to the death.
- The defendant's negligence was so gross that a jury would consider it justified to bring in a criminal conviction.

Loads – General, Livestock, Food, etc

18

This chapter deals with both the length and width of normal loads and also covers some of the special points applicable to carrying food, livestock, sand and ballast, solid fuel and containers.

Load Dimensions

Loads on normal goods vehicles (ie within C&U Regulations) that exceed the vehicle length and width dimensions may be carried provided that certain special conditions are met. The requirements for abnormal and projecting loads are covered in Chapter 19.

Length

Under C&U Regulations, the maximum length of a:

- rigid HGV and draw-bar trailer is 18.75 metres;
- tractor unit and semi-trailer is 16.5 metres.

If a long load is carried on a semi-trailer which is specially designed to carry long loads but in all other respects complies with the C&U Regulations, the 18.75-metre dimension is measured excluding the length of the tractor unit. The load itself must not project more than 2 metres to the front of the vehicle and 3.05 metres to the rear.

Under C&U rules, 27.4 metres is the maximum length of a trailer and its load (the length of the towing vehicle is excluded from this).

Width

Under C&U rules, the overall width of a load carried on a vehicle must not exceed 2.9 metres. The load itself must not project more than 305 millimetres on either side of the vehicle. There is an exception to this requirement when loose agricultural produce is carried.

Carriage of Livestock

'No animal shall be transported unless it is fit for the intended journey, and all animals shall be transported in conditions guaranteed not to cause them injury or unnecessary suffering' (Council Regulation 1/2005/EC on the protection of animals during transport and related operations and amending Directives).

All persons who take animals on a journey, whatever the length, should always apply the following good transport practice by ensuring that:

- the journey is properly planned and time is kept to a minimum and the animals are checked and their needs met during the journey;
- the animals are fit to travel;
- the vehicle and loading and unloading facilities are designed, constructed and maintained to avoid injury and suffering;
- the vehicle used is properly constructed, 'fit for purpose' and able to be cleaned effectively;
- those handling animals are trained or competent in the task and do not use violence or any methods likely to cause unnecessary fear, injury or suffering;
- water, feed and rest are given to the animals as needed, and sufficient floor space and height is allowed.

The Regulation applies to all those involved with the transport of live vertebrate animals in connection with an economic activity, for example:

- livestock and equine hauliers;
- farmers;
- commercial pet breeders.

The Regulation also applies to those working at:

- markets;
- assembly centres;
- slaughterhouses.

The Regulation does not apply to the transport of animals:

- where the transport is not in connection with an economic activity;

- to or from veterinary practices or clinics under veterinary advice, where the animal is an individual animal accompanied by its owner (or other responsible person) and is fit for the journey;
- where animals are pet animals accompanied by their owner on a private journey.

Animals that Cannot Be Transported

It is illegal to transport an animal 'unfit for travel'. These groups include:

- very young animals, eg calves less than 10 days old, pigs less than three weeks and lambs less than one week;
- calves less than 14 days old, for journeys over eight hours;
- cervine animals in velvet, ie deer with newly growing antlers;
- puppies and kittens less than eight weeks old, unless accompanied by their mother;
- newborn mammals where the navel hasn't completely healed;
- heavily pregnant females – where more than 90 per cent of the expected gestation period has passed – unless they are being transported for veterinary treatment;
- females who have given birth during the previous seven days;
- sick or injured animals where moving them would cause additional suffering, unless instructed by a vet;
- shorn sheep during cold weather, particularly from November to March.

Transporter Requirements for Journeys up to 65 Kilometres

Transporters are not required to have vehicle authorization or training and certificates of competence. However, they must comply with the technical rules on fitness to travel, means of transport and transport practices as set out in Annex 1 of Council Regulation 1/2005/EC. Where these journeys do not include a market, there is no need to clean the vehicle between each load, but this is required where any one point of the journey includes a market.

Transporter Authorization for Journeys Over 65 Kilometres and Under Eight Hours' Duration

A General Authorization will be granted by the Department of Environment, Food and Rural Affairs (DEFRA), and will be valid for five years, if transporters can comply with the following:

- They have an established business or, in the case of businesses established outside the UK, are represented in the UK.
- They can demonstrate that they have appropriate staff, equipment and operational procedures to transport animals in compliance with the new Regulation.
- They have no record of serious infringements of animal welfare legislation in the three years preceding application.
- They have a driver who has undergone assessment and holds a certificate of competence to care for animals.
- Records of these journeys must be retained by the operator for a minimum of six months.

Transporter Authorization for Journeys of Over Eight Hours' Duration

A Special Authorization, issued by DEFRA, will be valid for five years. Authorization will be granted if transporters can comply with the following:

- They have an established business or, in the case of businesses established outside the UK, are represented in the UK.
- They can demonstrate that they have appropriate staff, equipment and operational procedures to transport animals in compliance with the new Regulation.
- They have no record of serious infringements of animal welfare legislation in the three years preceding their application.
- They have a driver who has undergone assessment and holds a certificate of competence to care for animals.

The transporter must provide:

- valid certificates of approval for vehicles and containers;
- a route plan which has been approved by the DEFRA Divisional Veterinary Manager (DVM);
- details of procedures enabling transporters to trace and record the movement of road vehicles under their responsibility and to contact the drivers at any time;
- contingency plans in the event of emergencies;
- from 2008, valid certificates of competence for drivers and attendants.

In addition:

- The animals must have sufficient bedding and food.
- The vehicle must have fittings for drinking water.

- The vehicle must be compartmentalized.
- The driver/crew must have access to each level.

NB: *All cattle movements in Scotland require you to contact the British Cattle Movement Service usually at least three days before the cattle are moved. Other time limits do apply and further information is available from the British Cattle Movement Service (BCMS) at:*

BCMS
Curwen Road
Workington
Cumbria
CA14 2DD
Tel: 0345 050 1234 (Mon–Fri 0830–1700)

Training and Competence for Drivers and Attendants and Assembly Centre Personnel

Drivers or attendants responsible for the transport of farmed animals, horses and poultry over distances greater than 65 km are required to hold a certificate of competence. Assembly centre staff are *not* required to obtain a certificate of competence but will need to have undergone training.

Training courses will cover the technical and administrative aspects of the rules and regulations that apply to the protection of animals during transport and cattle passports. These include:

- general conditions of transporting animals;
- the documents that are required;
- fitness for transport;
- journey planning;
- animal physiology and feed needs, animal behaviour and the concept of stress;
- practical aspects of handling animals;
- impact of driving behaviour on welfare of animals and on the quality of meat;
- emergency care for animals;
- safety of personnel handling animals.

The certificate of competence will be awarded once an independent assessment of knowledge of the above has been made.

Exporting of Animals

When animals are exported out of Great Britain, the transporter must ensure that the journeys are properly planned and that a route plan is submitted to the Divisional Veterinary Manager at DEFRA for approval. Without this approval an export health certificate will not be issued. Operators based outside Great Britain will require an authorization from their own domestic authorities to transport animals.

Importing of Animals

When importing animals from the EU, every consignment must be accompanied by an Intra Trade Animal Health Certificate (ITAHC). Operators must also ensure that the person the animals are imported from has arranged the ITAHC in their own country. The importer is also legally required to send an importer notification form to the Animal and Plant Health Agency (APHA). This must be sent at least 24 hours before any animals are due to arrive in the UK.

When applying for an ITAHC, an official veterinarian must be nominated. For details contact APHA.

For animal movement licensing in England tel: 03000 200 301 or email: customeradvice@apha.gsi.gov.uk. (For enquiries in Wales and Scotland contact the local Field Services Office.) For animal transport tel: 03000 200 301 or email: WIT@ apha.gov.uk.

Journey Logs (Over Eight Hours)

Anyone exporting farm livestock or unregistered horses is required to complete a journey log. This needs to be approved by the relevant DVM for the place of departure within 28 days of the journey being completed. Journey logs need to be retained by the carrier for a minimum of three years.

Animal Transport Certificates (Under Eight Hours)

Animal Transport Certificates (ATCs) are required for journeys of any species of animal over any distance or duration *except* journeys involving farm livestock and unregistered horses on export journeys of over eight hours, which require a journey log instead (see above). The ATC is required to provide the following information:

- origin and ownership of animals;
- place of departure and destination;
- date and time of departure and expected duration of journey.

NB: *Farmers transporting their own animals in their own means of transport on journeys of up to 50 km from their holding are exempt from this requirement.*

Any other document containing the required information – such as an Animal Movement Licence – may be used, if preferred. In all cases, the ATC needs to be retained by the carrier for six months following the movement.

Vehicle Inspection and Approval

Vehicles used for transporting farm livestock and horses on long journeys (those in excess of eight hours) must be inspected and approved by the competent authority of a member state or a body designated by a member state. In the UK this will include such organizations as the FTA, the European Food Safety Inspection Service (EFSIS) (Agriculture) and CMI Certification. In Scotland it is Acoura, email info@acoura.com or call 0330 024 0255.

Since 1 January 2009, all new cattle and horse transport vehicles need to be fitted with a satellite navigation system. Older vehicles used for transporting livestock and horses nationally on journeys in excess of 12 hours and internationally on journeys in excess of eight hours are subject to mandatory retro-fitting of such systems.

Food

The Food Standards Agency controls and regulates food safety and standards in the UK, including the transport of livestock, fresh meat and other foods. It also has power to intervene if operators compromise food safety.

The Food Safety (General Food Hygiene) Regulations 1995 apply to vehicles used for the carriage of food, excluding milk and drugs.

Drivers of a food vehicle should wear clean overalls and if meat or bacon sides are carried, which they have to carry over their shoulder, they should wear a hat and/or hairnet to prevent the meat touching hair. Any cuts or abrasions on hands must be covered with waterproof dressings.

If a driver or any other person concerned in the loading and unloading of food develops any infectious disease, their employer must notify the local authority health department immediately.

Food vehicles must have the name and address of the person carrying on the business shown on the nearside and the address at which the vehicle is garaged if this is a different address. If a vehicle based in England or Wales has a fleet number clearly shown and is garaged at night on company premises, then the garage address is not required.

A wash hand basin and a supply of clean water must be provided on vehicles which carry uncovered food (except bread) unless drivers can wash their hands at both ends of the journey before they have to handle food. When meat is carried, soap, clean towels and a nail brush must be provided on the vehicle. In Scotland all food-carrying vehicles must also be provided with these items.

An authorized council officer may enter and detain (but not stop while it is in motion) any food-carrying vehicle except those owned by a rail company or vehicles operated by a haulage contractor.

Perishable Foodstuffs

A whole range of legislation covers the carriage of food, and particularly perishable food, both in the UK and in Europe. When perishable foodstuffs are carried on international journeys to and through all EU member states and a further 17 non-EU and EFTA countries, including, for example, countries such as Norway, Russia, Switzerland, Turkey and the Balkan states, the conditions of the UNECE Agreement on the International Carriage of Perishable Foodstuffs (known as the ATP agreement) must be observed. ATP also applies on short sea crossings up to 150 km.

As a signatory to the agreement, ATP also applies in Britain and under its provisions vehicles used to carry perishable food must be constructed to design standards and tested for thermal efficiency (the initial test lasts for six years, thereafter three-yearly tests are required) to certain specified standards and must display an ATP approval plate, or carry an ATP certificate, to this effect. Details of where to get these tests can be obtained through the trade associations.

The principal requirement is that vehicles carrying certain specified perishable foodstuffs must comply with the body and temperature control equipment test standards and must be certified to this effect and that records of movements under ATP are properly monitored and, where thermographs are used, that records be retained for at least 12 months. The ATP agreement applies broadly to quick-frozen, deep-frozen, frozen and non-frozen foodstuffs but not fresh vegetables and soft fruit.

Information relating to food transport as well as codes of practice may be obtained from DEFRA.

Chilled Food Controls (ie Temperature-Controlled Food)

The Food Hygiene (Amendment) Regulations 1990 apply to goods vehicles exceeding 7.5 tonnes gross weight carrying 'relevant food' products (which are listed in the schedules to the regulations). Such vehicles must have equipment capable of maintaining the temperature of the food at or below the specified temperature (–5 °C for certain foods as listed in the schedules and –8 °C for other 'relevant' foods) or at or above 63 °C as appropriate and be fitted with either a thermograph or have a visible thermometer.

Vehicles up to 7.5 tonnes used for local deliveries must be capable of keeping relevant food at or below the specified temperature or at or above 63 °C as appropriate. However, in a case where the Regulations specify that food is to be kept at 5 °C, provided it is not kept in the vehicle for more than 12 hours, it may be at a higher temperature, not exceeding 8 °C.

There are exemptions to these requirements: where food is to be sold within two hours (ie if prepared at 63 °C or over) or four hours (ie if prepared below 63 °C). Other variations (ie not exceeding 2 °C for a maximum of two hours) may be permitted in certain specified circumstances such as: variations in processing; while equipment is defrosted; during temporary breakdown of equipment; while moving food from one place or vehicle to another; or any other unavoidable reason.

Quick-frozen Foodstuffs

The UK Quick-frozen Foodstuffs (QFF) Regulations 1990 are effective in setting general conditions for the quality and use of equipment for storing and transporting food labelled 'quick-frozen' (but not ice cream). These regulations require certain temperatures to be maintained within a percentage range of –18 °C, or colder, as follows:

- during transport (other than local distribution): a tolerance for brief periods of 3 °C (but not warmer than –15 °C);
- during local distribution: 6 °C (but not warmer than –12 °C).

The Quick-frozen Foodstuffs (Amendment) Regulations 1994, which took effect from 1 September 1994, require refrigerated transport operators to fit temperature recorders to vehicles carrying frozen foodstuffs (but not chilled foods) and to keep the records for at least 12 months.

Waste Food

Vehicles used to collect unprocessed waste food must be drip-proof, covered and enclosed with material capable of being cleansed and disinfected.

Vehicles must be thoroughly cleansed and disinfected on the completion of unloading. No livestock or poultry or foodstuff or anything intended for use for any livestock or poultry may be carried in any vehicle which is carrying unprocessed waste food. Furthermore, processed and unprocessed waste food may not be carried in the same vehicle at the same time.

Grain Haulage

Grain trailers cannot be used for the carriage of other loads (such as glass, toxins, waste, bonemeal and manure) which may contaminate the trailer. Auditors from the

Agricultural Industries Confederation (AIC) monitor standards and check hauliers' records and invoices to ensure they have not broken the Association's code, which is based on provisions in the Food Safety Act 1990. A 'grain passport' must be carried on vehicles, otherwise loads may be rejected by consignees if they are not satisfied as to the origin or standard under which loads have been carried.

Sand and Ballast Loads

Schedule 4 of the Weights and Measures Act 1985 covers the movement of sand and ballast, which must be sold in weighed quantities (normally by volume in metric measures – in multiples of 0.2 cubic metres) and/or carried in calibrated vehicles which display a stamp placed on the body by the Trading Standards department of the local authority. In the cases where the vehicle is calibrated, the load must be levelled off and 'evened out' to ensure that the full load is carried.

When sand and ballast (including shingle, ashes, clinker, etc) loads are carried, the driver must have a signed note (ie conveyance note) from the supplier indicating the following facts:

- the name and address of the sellers;
- the name of the buyer and the address for delivery of the load;
- a description of the type of ballast;
- the quantity by net weight or by volume;
- details of the vehicle;
- the date, time and place of loading the vehicle.

Aggregates Levy

The Aggregates Levy of £2.00 per tonne applies to all primary aggregates such as sand, gravel and crushed rock taken from quarries. This is a levy on aggregates excavated from the ground, dredged from the sea or imported.

Landfill Tax

Landfill tax applies to most materials, including wastes from construction, demolition, clay and coal extraction, etc, that go to landfill. The tax is levied at two rates; from April 2021 the rates are:

- Standard rate: £96.70 per tonne for inactive waste such as brick, concrete and glass, etc.
- Lower rate: £3.10 per tonne for active waste such as wood and plastics.

Solid Fuel Loads

When solid fuel is carried, a document giving similar details to those mentioned above for sand and ballast carrying must be held by the driver of the vehicle. When solid fuel is carried for sale in open sacks, a notice on the vehicle in letters at least 60 mm high must contain the following words: 'All open sacks on this vehicle contain 25 kg.'

ISO Containers

The majority of containers in use are constructed to International (ISO 1496) or British (BS 3951) standards, hence the name ISO containers. ISO containers are secured to vehicles by container locks commonly known as twist locks. The Freight Containers (Safety Convention) Regulations 2017 cover the examination and plating of freight containers. ISO 1161 2016 covers the specification for series 1 container corner fittings. A minimum of four twist locks should be provided for each container carried. In most cases twist locks will be fitted to the vehicle during manufacture. Twist locks should be inspected regularly for wear, damage and correct operation. Locking devices which are intended to prevent the operating levers from moving during transit should be given special attention.

Fly-Tipping

Fly-tipping is an offence under The Environmental Protection Act 1990 and can result in fines of up to £50,000 to companies and individuals and a possible 12-month term of imprisonment for magistrate's court convictions. Where a case goes before a Crown Court, much higher penalties may be imposed, including unlimited fines and up to five years' imprisonment. Local authorities also have the powers to issue fixed penalty notices of between £150.00 and £400.00 to anyone caught fly-tipping.

NB: See Chapter 20 for more information on the carriage and disposal of waste materials.

Loads – Abnormal and Projecting 19

Abnormal Indivisible Loads

Abnormal indivisible loads (AILs) are loads which cannot, without undue expense or risk of damage, be divided into two or more loads and which cannot be carried on a vehicle operating under C&U Regulations.

Quantity of AILs on One Vehicle

While normally the carriage of only one AIL is permitted, two AILs may be carried on one vehicle within Category 1 or Category 2 (see below) provided the loads are collected from the same place and are to be delivered to the same destination.

Engineering Plant

In the case of engineering plant, such plant and parts dismantled from it may be carried on the same vehicle provided that the carriage of the parts does not cause the overall dimensions of the vehicle and the main load to be exceeded and that the parts are loaded and unloaded at the same place as the main load.

Special Types Vehicles

Dimensions

Special types vehicles are those which don't meet the C&U and AW Regs but can be used outside these rules under the authority of the Road Vehicles (Authorisation of Special Types) (General) Order 2003.

The maximum dimensions of Special Types vehicles, locomotives and trailers and their loads are:

Width – up to 2.9 metres wide but, if necessary to ensure the safe carriage of AILs, they may be up to a maximum of 6.1 metres wide.

Length – up to 27.4 metres, but where the AIL is carried on a combination of vehicles and trailers or on a long articulated vehicle, the dimension of 27.4 metres is measured excluding the drawing vehicle.

Weight – up to 150,000 kg. There is a limit on the maximum weight which may be imposed on the road by any one wheel of the vehicle of 8,250 kg, and the maximum weight imposed by any one axle must not exceed 16,500 kg.

Exceeding these limits requires authorization by Special Order through Highways England.

STGO (Special Types General Order) Categories

STGO specifies three separate weight categories for AIL vehicles as follows:

Category 1 – up to 50 tonnes gvw.

Category 2 – up to 80 tonnes gvw.

Category 3 – up to 150 tonnes gvw.

Table 19.1   Category 1 vehicles

Category 1 vehicles will normally fall within the C&U Regulations in regard to permissible maximum weight, axle spacings and axle weights, but where it is a five-axle articulated vehicle the weight may exceed 40 tonnes up to a maximum of 50,000 kg (ie 50 tonnes) provided the following minimum relevant axle spacings are observed:

Relevant axle spacing	Maximum weight
At least 6.5 metres	40,000 kg
At least 7.0 metres	42,000 kg
At least 7.5 metres	44,000 kg
At least 8.0 metres	50,000 kg

Table 19.2 a and b Category 2 vehicles

Category 2 vehicles may operate up to a maximum weight of 80,000 kg (ie 80 tonnes) but they must have a minimum of six axles with a maximum weight of 50,000 kg on any group of axles and they must meet the minimum axle spacing requirements specified below.

Individual wheel and axle weight limits are as follows:

Distance between adjacent axles	Maximum axle weight	Maximum wheel weight
At least 1.1 metres	12,000 kg	6,000 kg
At least 1.35 metres	12,500 kg	6,250 kg

Minimum axle spacings and applicable maximum weights are as follows:

Distance between foremost and rearmost axles	Maximum weight
5.07 metres	38,000 kg
5.33 metres	40,000 kg
6.00 metres	45,000 kg
6.67 metres	50,000 kg
7.33 metres	55,000 kg

Table 19.3 a and b Category 3 vehicles

A minimum of six axles are needed on Category 3 vehicles operating up to a permissible maximum weight of 150,000 kg (ie 150 tonnes) with a limit of 100,000 kg on any group of axles or 90,000 kg on any group of axles where the distance between adjacent axles is less than 1.35 metres. Vehicles in this category must meet the minimum axle spacing requirements specified below. Individual wheel and axle weight limits are as follows:

Distance between adjacent axles	Maximum axle weight	Maximum wheel weight
At least 1.1 metres	15,000 kg	7,500 kg
At least 1.35 metres	16,500 kg	8,250 kg

Table 19.3 a and b *continued*

Minimum axle spacings and applicable maximum weights are as follows:

Distance between foremost and rearmost axles	Maximum weight
5.77 metres	80,000 kg
6.23 metres	85,000 kg
6.68 metres	90,000 kg
7.14 metres	95,000 kg
7.59 metres	100,000 kg
8.05 metres	105,000 kg
8.50 metres	110,000 kg
8.95 metres	115,000 kg
9.41 metres	120,000 kg
9.86 metres	125,000 kg
10.32 metres	130,000 kg
10.77 metres	135,000 kg
11.23 metres	140,000 kg
11.68 metres	145,000 kg
12.14 metres	150,000 kg

Vehicle tax for Special Types

A separate vehicle taxation class applies to Special Types vehicles.

Braking Standards

Category 1 vehicles must meet the C&U regulation braking standard requirements and those operating within Categories 2 and 3 must meet the EU braking standards (ie EC Directive 71/320). In cases of Category 2 and 3 vehicles, wheel chocks may be used along with the parking brake in order to improve braking efficiency to meet the required EC standard.

Identification Sign

Vehicles operating under the STGO must display an identification sign at the front. This sign, on a plate at least 250 mm × 400 mm, must have white letters on a black background as follows:

Table 19.4 Identification sign

letters 105 mm high
letters and figures 70 mm high

NB: *A figure 1, 2 or 3 must follow the word 'CAT' as appropriate, depending on the category of vehicle.*

Special Types Plates

Categories 2 and 3 vehicles must display Special Types plates (in a conspicuous and easily accessible position) showing the maximum operational weights recommended by the manufacturer when travelling on a road at varying speeds as follows: 12, 20, 25, 30, 35, 40 mph. The weights to be shown are the permissible maximum gross and train weights and the maximum weights for each individual axle. Plates on trailers (including semi-trailers) must show the permissible maximum weight for the trailer and the maximum weights for each individual axle. The plates must be marked with the words 'Special Types Use'.

Speed Limits

Maximum permitted speeds* are specified for Special Types vehicles as follows:

Table 19.5 Speed limits

STGO category	Motorways	Dual carriageways	Other roads
1. Up to 50 tonnes	60 mph	50 mph	40 mph
2. Up to 80 tonnes	40 mph	35 mph	30 mph
3. Up to 150 tonnes	40 mph	35 mph	30 mph

Speeds for Wide Loads

Vehicles carrying loads over 4.3 metres but not over 6.1 metres wide are restricted to 30 mph on motorways, 25 mph on dual carriageways and 20 mph on other roads.

It is important to note that tyre equipment on vehicles and trailers must be compatible with both the gross weight of the vehicle and the authorized maximum speed of operation.

Attendants

An attendant must be carried on Special Types vehicles:

- when the vehicle or its load is more than 3.5 metres wide;
- if the overall length of the vehicle is more than 18.75 metres (not including the length of the tractive unit in the case of articulated vehicles);
- if the length of a vehicle and trailer exceeds 25.9 metres;
- if the load projects more than 2.00 metres beyond the front of the vehicle;
- if the load projects more than 3.05 metres beyond the rear of the vehicle.

If three or more vehicles carrying AILs or other loads of dimensions that require statutory attendants to be carried travel in convoy, attendants need only be carried on the first and last vehicles in the convoy.

Attendants must be at least 18 years of age and properly trained in their duties.

Police Notification

The police of every district through which a Special Types combination is to be moved must be given two clear days' notice excluding Saturdays, Sundays and bank holidays in the case of notification under the STGO, and excluding Sundays and bank holidays for notification under the C&U Regulations if:

- the vehicle and its load is more than 3.0 metres wide;
- the vehicle and its load (or trailer and load) is more than 18.75 metres long;
- a combination of vehicles and trailers carrying the load is more than 25.9 metres long;
- the load projects more than 3.05 metres to the front or rear of the vehicle;
- the gross weight of the vehicle and the load is more than 80,000 kg.

The notice given must include details of the vehicle and the weight and dimensions of the load, the dates and times of the movement through the police district and the proposed route to be followed through that district.

In the case where notice has been given to the police of the movement of an AIL, they have the power to delay the vehicle during its journey if it is holding up other traffic or in the interests of road safety.

Notification of Highway and Bridge Authorities

If a Special Types vehicle and its load weighs more than 80,000 kg, or the weight imposed on the road by the wheels of such a vehicle exceeds the maximum limit laid down in the C&U Regulations (see Chapter 11), five clear days' notice must be given to the highway and bridge authorities for the areas through which the vehicle is to pass. Two days' notice is required when only the C&U axle weight limit is exceeded. The operator of such a vehicle is also required to indemnify the authorities against damage to any road or bridge over which it passes. These requirements also apply to vehicles which exceed the C&U gross weight limits and those which exceed their plated axle weight limits, plus mobile cranes and engineering plant which exceed the limits specified. The contact details of the actual person(s) who need to be contacted are available through ESDAL (see Appendix V).

Stopping on Bridges

Drivers of vehicles carrying an AIL must ensure that no other such vehicle and load are on a bridge before they drive onto the bridge, and once on the bridge they must not stop unless forced to do so.

Where a vehicle weighing more than 44,000 kg gross has to stop on a bridge for any reason, it must be moved off the bridge as soon as possible. If it has broken down, the advice of the bridge authority (usually the Highways Department of the local authority) must be sought before the vehicle is jacked up on the bridge. In the event of damage being caused to a road or bridge by the movement of a heavy or large load over it, the highway authority can take steps to recover from the vehicle operator the costs of repairing the damage.

Notification to Network Rail

Network Rail monitors the movement of AILs over all rail structures. All movements of AILs over rail bridges, whether they are oversize or overweight, must be notified to Network Rail at: abnormalloadsenquiries@networkrail.co.uk, Tel 01908 783 140. For operators using ESDAL (see below), the system will automatically notify Network Rail.

Special Orders

Written approval has to be obtained from Highways England in cases where a Special Types vehicle and its load exceeds 5 metres in width. Application is made on form VR1 (ie the movement order) and a copy of this completed form must be carried on the vehicle. The route specified, and the date and timings for the journey notified in the application, must be adhered to, otherwise further approval will have to be sought.

Dump Trucks

When dump trucks (ie vehicles designed for moving excavated material) are used on the road, the maximum permissible gross weight is limited to 55,000 kg and the maximum axle weight allowed for such vehicles is 22,860 kg. They must not exceed a speed of 12 mph on normal roads and an attendant must be carried if the width exceeds 3.5 metres. If a dump truck is more than 4.3 metres wide, permission in the form of a Special Order from the Secretary of State is required before it is moved. Where three or more such vehicles over 3.5 metres wide travel in convoy, only the first and last vehicles need carry attendants.

Other Plant

The Special Types General Order also makes special provision for other items of plant such as grass-cutting machines and hedge trimmers, track-laying vehicles, pedestrian-controlled road maintenance vehicles, vehicles used for experimental trials, straddle carriers, land tractors used for harvesting, mechanically propelled hay and straw balers, vehicles fitted with movable platforms and engineering plant. Any person proposing to move such items on public roads is advised to check that the appropriate legal requirements are met.

ESDAL Abnormal Load Notification

Highways England's ESDAL service makes it easy for operators to find out who they must notify about a route. However, operators need to register before they can start using the service, allowing two to three working days for the application to be processed. Full details of ESDAL are at GOV.UK. (See also contact details in Appendix V.)

Escorts

An escort vehicle is required if an AIL or vehicle exceeds:

- 30.5 metres in length;
- 4.6 metres in width or 130 tonnes gvw on motorways;
- 4.1 metres or 100 tonnes gvw width on other roads.

This is general guidance and may be different across different police forces.

Where the operator escorts the load, the vehicle(s) used needs to be of a specification recommended in the Code of Practice published by Highways England and approved by the police.

An escort vehicle must be a uniform conspicuous colour of white, yellow or orange. It must also have:

- a minimum of four wheels and no open cargo space;
- 360-degree visible amber flashing full-roof-width warning light bar fitted to the roof;
- clear marking in solid black lettering to identify that it is an escort vehicle;
- a roof sign displaying 'Abnormal Load' in title case clearly visible from both the front and rear of the vehicle;
- a continuous 200 mm wide horizontal strip of yellow retroreflective material along the length of the vehicle to at least the front wheel arch;
- a 300 mm wide vertical chevron strip of retroreflective yellow and non-retroreflective red fitted at the rear of side of the vehicle;
- chevron markings of alternate red retroreflective material and yellow vinyl non-retroreflective material at the rear of the vehicle;
- no company livery displayed on the front or rear of the vehicle.

A placard may be fitted to the front and rear of the vehicle with the following in UPPER CASE:

'ABNORMAL LOAD' or 'WIDE LOAD' with 'SLOW LORRY' or 'LONG LOAD'

The sign should have black lettering on a yellow retroreflective background. Full details can be found at GOV.UK.

High Loads

Motorway bridges are built to give a clearance of 16 ft to 16 ft 6 ins and overhead power cables crossing roads are set at a minimum height of 19 ft (5.8 metres) where the voltage carried does not exceed 33,000 volts and at 6.0 metres where this voltage is exceeded (see also the note in the Safe Tipping section in Chapter 17 about tipping-vehicle dangers in regard to contact with overhead power cables). When planning to move loads above 19 ft, it is a legal requirement to make contact with the National Grid or the appropriate regional electricity distribution company (ie previously the regional electricity boards) beforehand. It is also recommended that contact should be made with British Telecom (BT) regarding the presence of its overhead lines on the routes to be used.

Projecting Loads

Projecting loads may be carried on normal C&U regulation vehicles as well as on Special Types vehicles as described above. A projecting load is one that projects beyond the foremost or rearmost points or the side of the vehicle and, depending on the length or width of the projection, certain conditions apply when such loads are carried on normal vehicles, including requirements for lighting and marking.

Side Projections

Loads more than 4.3 metres wide cannot be moved legally under the C&U Regulations, although they can be carried on vehicles which comply with those regulations. In such cases the provisions of the Special Types General Order apply (see above).

   The normal width limit for loads is 2.9 metres overall or 305 mm on either side of the vehicle except in the case of loose agricultural produce and indivisible loads. Where an indivisible wide load extends 305 mm or more on one or both sides of the vehicle or exceeds 2.9 metres overall, the police must be given two clear days' notice in advance and end marker boards must be displayed front and rear (fitted within 50 mm of the edge of the load), and if it exceeds 3.5 metres, police notification, end marker boards and an attendant are required.

Forward Projections

A load projecting more than 2.0 metres beyond the foremost part of the vehicle (on C&U vehicles) must be indicated by an approved side and end marker board (Figure 19.1) and an attendant must be carried. On Special Types vehicles only, where the load projects more than 1.83 metres to the front, an end marker must be displayed and an attendant carried.

   If a load projects more than 3.05 metres beyond the front (on both C&U and Special Types vehicles), the police must be given two days' notice of its movement, both side and end approved marker boards must be displayed and an attendant must be carried.

   If a load projects more than 4.5 metres beyond the front of the vehicle, the provisions mentioned above must be observed and additional side marker boards must be displayed within 2.5 metres of the first set of side markers.

Figure 19.1   The approved-type marker boards which must be displayed when projecting loads are carried

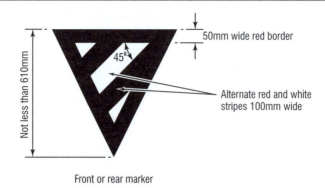

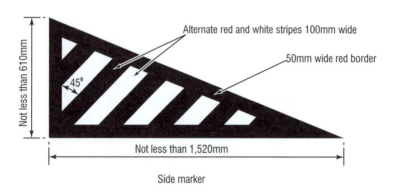

Rearward Projections

Where a load projects more than 1.0 metre beyond the rear of a C&U vehicle (1.07 metres on Special Types vehicles), it must clearly be marked (the form which this must take is not specified, but a piece of rag tied to the end is usually sufficient). If the rear projection is more than 2.0 metres on C&U vehicles (1.83 metres on Special Types vehicles), an end marker board must be displayed.

Where the rearward projection is more than 3.05 metres, the police must be notified, an attendant carried and approved side and end marker boards displayed. An end marker is not required if the projecting load is fitted with a rear reflective marker. If the rearward projection exceeds 5.0 metres, additional side marker boards must be displayed within 3.5 metres of the first set of side markers.

Marker Boards

Marker boards carried in accordance with the requirements described above must conform to the dimensions and colours shown in Figure 19.1 and they must be indirectly illuminated at night.

Lighting on Projecting and Long Loads

Rearward Projections

When carrying a load projecting more than 1.0 metre beyond the rear end of the vehicle, an additional red rear position light must be carried within 1.0 metre of the end of the load, or if the projecting load covers the rear lights and reflectors of the vehicle, additional lights and reflectors must be fixed to the load. This is usually best accomplished by having a complete lighting set and reflectors fitted to a board which can be fixed to the load.

Side Projections

When a load projects sideways more than 400 mm beyond the front and rear position lights of a vehicle, front position lights must be carried within 400 mm of the outer edges of the load and additional rear lights must also be carried within 400 mm of the outer edges of the load. White front and red rear reflectors must also be carried within 400 mm of the outer edges of the load.

Long Vehicles

A vehicle or combination of vehicles which, together with their load, are more than 18.75 metres long must, when on the road during the hours of darkness, carry side marker lights on each side positioned within 9.15 metres of the front of the vehicle or load and within 3.05 metres of the rear of the vehicle or load, and other lights positioned between these at not more than 3.05-metre intervals. These requirements do not apply if approved illuminated marker boards are carried or if the combination is formed of a towing vehicle and a broken-down vehicle.

In the case of a combination of vehicles carrying a supported load (a load not resting on a vehicle except at each end) when the total length of the combination exceeds 12.2 metres but not 18.75 metres, side marker lights must be carried when on the road during the hours of darkness, positioned not more than 1.53 metres behind the rear of the drawing vehicle, and if the load extends more than 9.15 metres beyond the drawing vehicle, an additional side marker light must be carried not more than 1.53 metres behind the centre line of the load.

All Vehicles

Where any projecting load or part load obscures, either completely or partially, an obligatory vehicle light or the vehicle registration plate, a replacement light or plate, fixed to the projection, must be used. This is normally achieved by attaching a trailer board to the end of the projection.

Loads – Dangerous Goods and Waste

20

Dangerous Goods by Road – UK

The Carriage of Dangerous Goods and Use of Transportable Pressure Equipment Regulations 2009 (SI 1348: 2009) deals with the carriage of dangerous goods (other than explosives and radioactive material) by road and rail, in packages or in bulk in any container, tank or vehicle.

SI 1348: 2009 implements European rules on the carriage of dangerous goods which are governed by the United Nations Economic Commission for Europe through the European Agreement Concerning the International Carriage of Dangerous Goods by Road (ADR). UK regulations cross-reference to the provisions set out in ADR and, in Part 2(5), it states that no person may carry dangerous goods, or cause or permit dangerous goods to be carried, where that carriage is prohibited by ADR or where that carriage does not comply with any applicable requirement of ADR. In other words, all carriage of dangerous goods by road in the UK must be in accordance with ADR.

ADR

ADR provides the prescriptive details for the carriage of dangerous goods by road. However, its enforcement of the requirements is subject to the relevant domestic laws.

ADR is relevant in over 50 European and central Asian countries known as competent authorities.

ADR is published in two volumes and is consistent with the United Nations' Model Regulations on the Transport of Dangerous Goods, the International Maritime Dangerous Goods Code and the International Civil Aviation's Technical Instructions for the Safe Carriage of Dangerous Goods by Air. It is fully harmonized with the Regulations concerning the International Carriage of Dangerous Goods by

Rail (RID). ADR is published every two years and the latest version is dated January 2021.

Volume 1 includes the text of the actual ADR Agreement, the Protocol of Signature and Parts 1 to 3 of Annex A, which cover the general provisions and provisions concerning dangerous substances and articles, as follows:

- Part 1 deals with the general provisions.
- Part 2 deals with classifications.
- Part 3 deals with the dangerous goods list, special provisions and exemptions related to limited and excepted quantities.

Volume 2 includes:

- Part 4 packing and tank provisions;
- Part 5 consignment procedures;
- Part 6 construction and testing of packaging and IBCs;
- Part 7 carriage by road, loading and handling of dangerous goods;
- Part 8 vehicle crews and equipment;
- Part 9 construction and approval of dangerous-goods-carrying vehicles.

Definition and Classification of Dangerous Goods

Definition

Dangerous goods are defined as being those substances and articles the carriage of which is prohibited by ADR (or RID in the case of carriage by rail), or authorized only under the conditions prescribed in these Agreements.

In general terms the following types of article and substance would be defined as dangerous goods:

- goods named in the ADR classification list as set out in ADR Part 2 (see also SI 2004/568, regulation 15);
- other goods which have one or more hazardous properties;
- explosives;
- radioactive material.

Dangerous articles or substances falling within the scope of the legal requirements include:

- quite small quantities of individually packaged goods such as domestic cleaning products;

- tanker loads of acids and corrosive substances;
- explosives (both substances and explosive articles – eg detonators, etc);
- radioactive substances.

Identification

The purpose of identifying dangerous goods is to determine their classification and identify their most hazardous properties and the dangers which may arise or be created when they are loaded, transported and unloaded.

It is for the manufacturer or consignor initially to determine the classification for dangerous goods intended to be consigned for carriage by deciding whether they are:

- explosives;
- radioactive material;
- named individually in ADR Chapter 2;
- not named individually in ADR Chapter 2.

Dangerous Goods Named Individually in the ADR Dangerous Goods List

Most dangerous goods are named in ADR under their proper name, in alphabetical order and with their UN number. If the goods comprise a mixture or preparation of substances, these too may be listed, as many dangerous goods have a generic name.

Dangerous Goods Not Named Individually in the ADR Dangerous Goods List

Where the dangerous goods are not 'named individually', the most appropriate generic entry (where the goods are of one chemical family) must be established or, alternatively, the relevant 'Not Otherwise Specified' (NOS) entry should be used for those goods. This is done by first establishing the hazardous properties of the goods and then checking to see whether any alternative name can be found in the list that could be used to classify the goods.

Classification

It is important to note that the carriage of dangerous goods is prohibited unless their classification, packing group and any subsidiary hazards have been determined. An established classification system applies in ADR Part 2.

The UN system classifies dangerous goods into:

- classes (of which there are nine);
- divisions;
- packing groups.

The nine classes cover the main types of dangerous goods (eg explosives, gases, flammable and oxidizing substances, etc) – see the full list below. Each of these classes is further sub-divided into a number of divisions which more specifically identify dangerous goods falling within each of the classes. A further degree of classification is achieved by assigning goods to a packing group according to the degree of danger they present.

Classes and Divisions

The following list shows the classes and divisions for dangerous goods:

- Class 1: Explosive substances and articles.
  - Division 1.1: Substances and articles which have a mass explosion hazard.
  - Division 1.2: Substances and articles which have a projection hazard, but not a mass explosion hazard.
  - Division 1.3: Substances and articles which have a fire hazard and either a minor blast hazard or a minor projection hazard or both, but not a mass explosion hazard.
  - Division 1.4: Substances and articles which present no significant hazard.
  - Division 1.5: Very insensitive substances that have a mass explosion hazard.
  - Division 1.6: Extremely insensitive articles that do not have a mass explosion hazard.
- Class 2: Gases.
  - Division 2.1: Flammable gases.
  - Division 2.2: Non-flammable, non-toxic gases.
  - Division 2.3: Toxic gases.
- Class 3: Flammable liquids.
- Class 4: Flammable solids, substances liable to spontaneous combustion and substances which, on contact with water, emit flammable gases.
  - Division 4.1: Flammable solids, self-reactive and related substances and desensitized explosives.
  - Division 4.2: Substances liable to spontaneous combustion.
  - Division 4.3: Substances which, on contact with water, emit flammable gases.

- Class 5: Oxidizing substances and organic peroxides.
  - Division 5.1: Oxidizing substances.
  - Division 5.2: Organic peroxides.
- Class 6: Toxic and infectious substances.
  - Division 6.1: Toxic substances.
  - Division 6.2: Infectious substances.
- Class 7: Radioactive material.
- Class 8: Corrosive substances.
- Class 9: Miscellaneous dangerous substances and articles.

UN Numbers and Proper Names

Dangerous goods are assigned a UN number comprising four digits which are used in conjunction with the letters 'UN' (eg UN1230) and a proper shipping name (eg Methanol).

UN Packing Groups

Dangerous substances are also allocated UN packing groups as follows:

- Packing group I: for goods presenting high danger.
- Packing group II: for goods presenting medium danger.
- Packing group III: for goods presenting low danger.

UN Table of Precedence

ADR sets out a table of precedence to take account of situations where dangerous goods not specifically identified in the Dangerous Goods List (in ADR Chapter 3.2) have more than one risk, or where dangerous goods have multiple risks. In such cases the most stringent packing group (ie Packing group I) takes precedence over other packing groups.

The following tables indicate the relevant classifications for dangerous goods, along with their packing group number (ie I, II or III), their class number and any optional lettering to be shown on packages (Table 20.1) and the relevant danger signs for dangerous goods indicating the symbol to be used and the colouring of the lettering and background (Table 20.2).

Table 20.1   Classifications for dangerous goods

Classification	Packing group	Class no	Optional lettering
Non-flammable, non-toxic gas	–	2.2	Compressed gas
Toxic gas	–	2.3	Toxic gas
Flammable gas	–	2.1	Flammable gas
Flammable liquid	I, II or III*	3	Flammable liquid
Flammable solid	I, II or III*	4.1	Flammable solid
Spontaneously combustible substance	I, II or III*	4.2	Spontaneously combustible
Substance which on contact with water emits flammable gas	I, II or III*	4.3	Dangerous when wet
Oxidizing substance	I, II or III*	5.1	Oxidizing agent
Organic peroxide	II	5.2	Organic peroxide
Toxic substance	I, II or III*	6.1	Toxic
Infectious substance	–	6.2	Infectious substance
Corrosive substance	I, II or III*	8	Corrosive
Miscellaneous dangerous goods	–	9	–

*Depending on its relevant properties.

Table 20.2   Danger signs for dangerous goods

Description of sign	Symbol	Lettering	Background
Non-flammable, non-toxic gas	Black gas cylinder	Black or white	Green
Toxic gas	Black skull & crossbones	Black	White
Flammable gas	Black flame	Black or white	Red
Flammable liquid	Black flame	Black or white	Red
Flammable solid	Black flame	Black	Vertical white/red stripes
Spontaneously combustible substance	Black flame	Black or white	White top/red bottom
Substance which on contact with water emits flammable gas	Black flame	Black or white	Blue
Oxidizing substance	Black 'O' & flame	Black (5.1)	Yellow
Organic peroxide	Black 'O' & flame	Black (5.2)	Red top/yellow bottom

Table 20.2 *continued*

Description of sign	Symbol	Lettering	Background
Toxic substance	Black skull & crossbones	Black	White
Infectious substance	Black symbol	Black	White
Corrosive substance	Black symbol	White	White top/black bottom
Miscellaneous			Vertical white/black stripes at top
Limited quantity	Plain	None	Horizontal black (2) and white (1) stripes
Environmentally hazardous substance	Black	None	White with picture of black fish and black tree

Dangerous goods being moved throughout the UK, and from the UK to mainland Europe, will also require 'tunnel codes'. All road tunnels are risk assessed and then classified and given codes which relate to any potential danger posed as well as any available or alternative routes in order to avoid them.

Tunnels are categorized as follows:

- Category A – no restrictions.
- Category B – risk of a large explosion.
- Category C – risk of a large or very large explosion or a large toxic release.
- Category D – risk of a large or very large explosion, a large toxic release or a large fire.
- Category E – restriction on the carriage of all dangerous goods in consignments of more than 8 tonnes.

Responsibilities

Responsibility for Classification of Dangerous Goods

Responsibility for the classification of dangerous goods rests with:

- the appropriate competent authority (eg the United Nations) in publishing the classification system;
- the manufacturer of the goods and the consignor (ie the sender) – these may be one or separate entities who must:

- identify their hazards;
- determine the most appropriate description for them;
- establish their correct UN identification number.

Legal Responsibilities

Responsibility for ensuring that legal requirements are met rests with:

- the competent national authority (the DfT in the UK);
- the HSE and the police;
- consignors of dangerous goods;
- those who load, unload and transport such goods, namely:
  - employers/carriers;
  - dangerous goods safety advisors (DGSAs);
  - drivers of dangerous-goods-carrying vehicles;
  - employees and other people.

Employer Responsibilities

Any 'undertaking' or individuals involved in the loading, unloading or carriage of dangerous goods by road must comply with statutory requirements and appoint a qualified DGSA (SI 2004 No 568, regulation [12] and ADR 1.8.3). An 'undertaking' is any legal body (eg limited liability company), association or group (eg voluntary and charitable organizations), or any official body that transports, loads or unloads dangerous goods.

Employers are responsible for ensuring that:

- a qualified DGSA is appointed, where relevant;
- dangerous goods vehicle drivers:
  - hold vocational training certificates;
  - are trained in emergency procedures;
- vehicles are approved and carry the correct emergency equipment.

Rules for Drivers

ADR drivers must not:

- carry unauthorized passengers (ADR 8.3.1);

- open any package containing dangerous goods unless authorized to do so (ADR 8.3.3);
- carry matches or lighters (or anything else capable of producing a flame or sparks) (ADR 8.3.4 and 8.3.5).

Responsibility for Safety

Responsibility for safety issues rests with the consignor, the carrier and the consignee together with other personnel such as loaders, fillers, packers, etc (ADR 7.5.1 and SI 2004 No 568, regulation 23[5]). In particular, they must take appropriate measures according to the nature and extent of foreseeable dangers, so as to avoid damage or injury and, if necessary, to minimize their effects. Where there is an immediate risk that public safety may be jeopardized, they must immediately notify the emergency services and make available to them the information they will need to take appropriate action. Chapter 1.4 of ADR specifies the individual responsibilities of the three main participants as outlined below.

The Consignor

The consignor must ensure, when handing over dangerous goods for carriage, that consignments conform to the requirements of ADR, in particular by:

- ensuring that the goods are classified and authorized for carriage in accordance with ADR;
- giving the carrier relevant information, data and the required transport documents;
- using only packaging, IBCs and tanks (ie tank vehicles, demountable tanks, battery vehicles, MEM, portable tanks and tank containers) approved for and suited to the carriage of the substances concerned and displaying the markings prescribed by ADR;
- complying with the requirements on the means of dispatch and on forwarding restrictions.

Where consignors use the services of other participants (packers, loaders, fillers, etc), they must still ensure that the consignment meets the requirements of ADR.

The Carrier

The carrier is the haulage operator and must establish that:

- the dangerous goods to be carried are authorized for carriage in accordance with ADR;
- the next due test date for tank vehicles, portable tanks and tank containers has not passed;

- vehicles are not overloaded;
- visually, vehicles and loads have no obvious defects such as leakages, cracks or missing equipment, etc;
- appropriate danger labels and prescribed markings have been affixed to the vehicle;
- prescribed documentation is being carried on board the vehicle;
- the equipment prescribed in the driver's written instructions is on board the vehicle.

If, in carrying out the above checks, the carrier observes any infringement of the ADR requirements, they must not allow the consignment to be shipped until the matter has been rectified. Similarly, if during the journey an infringement is detected which could jeopardize the safety of the operation, the consignment must be stopped as soon as possible, bearing in mind the requirements of traffic safety, the safe immobilization of the consignment and of public safety.

The Consignee

Consignees may not defer acceptance of a consignment of dangerous goods without compelling reasons. They must also, after unloading, verify that the requirements of ADR have been complied with.

Other Participants/DGSAs

Other participants may be involved with the carriage of dangerous goods consignments, such as employees described as tanker operators, loaders, packers, fillers, etc. Broadly, such employees have a duty to ensure that their actions and the loads they deal with comply in all relevant respects with the requirements of ADR.

In particular, a DGSA may be required. The DGSA needs to be qualified and able to provide advice and assistance, and an annual report relating to the types of dangerous goods carried (see later).

Exemptions

A number of exemptions to ADR are specified in Chapter 1.1 (ie 1.1.3) and in SI 2004 No 568, regulation 7, and are set out in simplified form in the publication *Working with ADR* as follows:

- the carriage of dangerous goods by private individuals where the goods are packaged for retail sale and are intended for their personal or domestic use or for their leisure or sporting activities;

- the carriage of machinery or equipment not specifically listed in the Dangerous Goods List and which contain dangerous goods in their internal or operational equipment;

- carriage undertaken by enterprises which is ancillary to their main activity;

- carriage by, or under the supervision of, the emergency services, in particular by breakdown vehicles carrying vehicles which have been involved in accidents or have broken down and contain dangerous goods;

- emergency transport intended to save human lives or protect the environment.

Special Provisions Exemptions

Certain special provisions of the ADR (ie Chapter 3.3) exempt, either partially or totally, the carriage of specific dangerous goods from the requirements of ADR, as identified in column 6 of the Dangerous Goods List (Chapter 3.2, Table A), against the appropriate entry for that article or substance.

Limited Quantities Exemptions

Exemptions relate to dangerous goods packed in limited quantities where a 'limited quantity' code Q1–Q29 (see table in ADR 3.4.6) appears in column 7 of the appropriate entry of the Dangerous Goods List, in which case that article or substance is exempted from the requirements of ADR, but only if it meets packaging and marking requirements, and if the prescribed maximum quantities per inner packaging, and per package, are not exceeded.

Table 20.3 Transport categories and maximum quantities per transport unit

Transport category	Max total quantity per transport unit*
0	0
1	20
1A	50
2	333
2A	500
3	1,000
4	unlimited

*For articles, gross mass in kg (for articles of Class 1, net mass in kg of the explosive substance); for solids, liquefied gases, refrigerated liquefied gases and dissolved gases, net mass in kg; for liquids and compressed gases, nominal capacity of receptacles (see definition in ADR 1.2.1) in litres.

When the code LQ0 appears in column 7 of the Dangerous Goods List (ADR 3.2), the substance or article is not exempted from any of the requirements of ADR (unless otherwise specified). Anyone involved in the carriage of Limited Quantity (LQ) packages must be given suitable and appropriate training as required by ADR Chapter 1.3. The training provisions must be complied with, for example, by those who simply place the goods on pallets ready for shipment (so that those people are aware of the obligations to ensure the LQ marks are visible or repeated on the over-package and marked also with the word 'OVERPACK') or those who drive vehicles that are delivering LQ packages.

Transport Unit Exemptions

This class of exemptions is sometimes also referred to as being a 'limited quantities exemption', but it should not be confused with the limited quantities exemption described above. In this case, the exemption applies where:

- a specified maximum total quantity per transport unit, depending on its transport category (ADR 1.1.3.6), is not exceeded;
- the dangerous goods carried in the transport unit are in more than one transport category and the total quantity carried does not exceed the value calculated in accordance with ADR 1.1.3.6.4.

If either of the two bullet point conditions (above) applies, the dangerous goods may be carried in packages in a single transport unit and the following requirements of ADR will not apply.

Table 20.4   Other exemptions

ADR	Covering
5.3	Placarding and marking of containers, etc
5.4.3	Documentation – instructions in writing
7.2 except for V5, V7 and V8 of 7.2.4	Carriage in packages
CV1 of 7.5.11	Prohibitions on loading and unloading in public places
Part 8, except for 8.1.4.2–8.1.4.5, 8.2.3, 8.3.4, 8.4 and S1(3), S1(6), S2(1), S4, S14–S21 of 8.5	Vehicle crews, equipment operation and documentation
Part 9	Construction and approval of vehicles

Other Exemptions

ADR also includes other exemptions relating to:

- gases;
- liquid fuels;
- empty uncleaned packaging;
- carriage in a transport chain including maritime or air carriage;
- the use of portable tanks approved for maritime transport;
- carriage other than by road.

A full list of exemptions can be found in the current version of ADR.

Transport Information and Documentation

Information to Be Provided

Consignors of dangerous goods must provide the carrier with a transport document (often referred to as the ADR note) showing:

- the designation, classification code, UN number and proper name for the goods;
- any additional information needed to determine their transport category and their control and emergency temperatures;
- the hazard class of the goods and any additional/associated hazards;
- the tunnel code for the goods;
- for packaged goods, the number and weight or volume of individual packages, or the total mass or volume in each transport category;
- for bulk loads, the weight or volume in each tank or container and the number of tanks or containers;
- the name and address of both consignor and consignee;
- any other information which the operator must give to the driver;
- a 'consignor's declaration' that the goods may be carried as presented, that they, their packaging and any container or tank in which they are contained are fit for carriage and are properly labelled.

It is an offence to provide false or misleading information and where one transport operator sub-contracts a dangerous goods consignment to another operator, they must, by law, pass on the information provided by the consignor.

Documentation to Be Carried

Drivers and crew members must be provided with the following 'transport documentation', in writing:

- the information provided by the consignor (see above);
- details of the weight or volume of the load;
- the relevant hazard identification number, tunnel code (if applicable) or the emergency action code (where appropriate);
- emergency information comprising:
  - the dangers inherent in the goods and safety measures;
  - what to do and the treatment to be given should any person come into contact with the goods;
  - what to do in the event of fire and what fire-fighting appliances or equipment must not be used;
  - what to do in case of breakage or deterioration of packaging or of the goods, particularly where this results in a spillage onto the road;
  - what to do to avoid or minimize damage in the event of spillage of goods likely to pollute water supplies;
- any relevant additional information about the particular type of dangerous goods being carried.

It is an offence to provide false or misleading information to drivers about the particular type of dangerous goods being carried.

Drivers must keep the transport documentation readily available and produce it on request by an enforcement officer. Where a dangerous-goods-carrying trailer is detached from the towing vehicle, the transport documentation (or an authenticated copy) must be given to the owner or manager of the premises where it is parked, or attached to the trailer in a readily visible position.

Documentation relating to dangerous goods no longer carried on a vehicle must be either removed completely, or placed in a securely closed container clearly marked to show that it does not relate to dangerous goods still on the vehicle.

Operators must keep a record of journey transport documentation for at least three months (SI 2004 No 568, regulation 54).

Note: vehicles using ferry services may need additional documentation to meet the International Maritime Dangerous Goods (IMDG) requirements.

Instructions in Writing

Operators must give drivers 'instructions in writing' to help them with any emergency that may arise. The key features are:

- They are to be issued by the carrier not the consignor.

- They must be in a language that the driver and/or crew members can read and understand before starting their journey and in the language of the country(ies) of origin, transit and destination (particularly for use by the emergency services).

- Vehicle crews are required to familiarize themselves with the emergency arrangements for the dangerous goods loaded *before* commencing a journey.

- A new four-page model of the revised instructions in writing consists of:

  - action to be taken in the event of an emergency;

  - guidance on the hazards and actions to be taken for each class of dangerous goods.

In addition to an instruction in the guidance to drivers that smoking is not permitted, new instructions in writing have been amended to include not using 'e-cigarettes'.

Information to be Displayed on Containers, Tanks and Vehicles

Containers, tanks and vehicles used for carrying dangerous goods must display information as described below.

It is an offence to display information when the container, tank or vehicle is not carrying dangerous goods, and to cause or permit the display of any information likely to confuse the emergency services.

Signs and panels relating to dangerous goods no longer being carried must be covered or removed. Where a panel is covered, the covering material must remain effective after 15 minutes' engulfment in fire. Danger signs, hazard warning panels, orange-coloured panels or subsidiary hazard signs need not be covered or removed if the mass or volume of dangerous goods in packages falls below the following limits:

Table 20.5 Limits

Transport category	Total mass/volume (kg/litres)
0	0
1	20
2	200
3	500
4	unlimited

It is an offence to remove panels or signs from a container, tank or vehicle carrying dangerous goods (except for updating the information) and to falsify information on any panel or sign.

Danger Signs and Panels

A reflective orange-coloured, black-bordered panel (plain with no letters or figures) must be displayed at the front of vehicles carrying dangerous goods. A similar panel must be attached to the rear of vehicles carrying dangerous goods in packages. If the vehicle, exceeding 12 tonnes unladen, is carrying more than 8 tonnes of packaged dangerous goods that are being carried as LQ goods, the orange panels can be used or they can be replaced with black-and-white diamond-shaped LQ plates.

Single Load Labelling

Where a *single load* of dangerous goods is carried in a container, tank or vehicle, an orange-coloured panel showing the appropriate UN number and emergency action code (see Figure 20.1) must be displayed:

- one at the rear of the vehicle;
- one on each side of the vehicle or the tank;
- one on each side, one at the rear and one at the front of a tank container;*
- and, in the case of a tank, one on each side of the frame of the tank, or on the vehicle positioned immediately below the tank.

Containers are marked on all four sides.

Figure 20.1   Orange panel showing the emergency action code and the UN number identifying the dangerous substance being carried

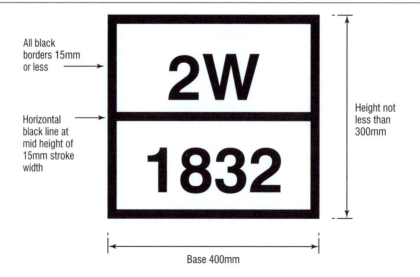

Multi-Load Labelling

Where a vehicle is carrying a *multi-load* in tanks, or in bulk in separate compartments of the vehicle, or in separate containers, an orange-coloured panel showing the appropriate emergency action code (see below) must be displayed at the rear of the vehicle.

Orange-coloured panels are required on both sides of each tank (or, if it has multiple compartments, on each compartment), on each compartment of the vehicle or on each container on the vehicle:

- at least one on each side showing the UN number and emergency action code (Figure 20.1);
- the remainder showing only the UN number.

Alternatively, for dangerous goods carried in a tank, the panels may be displayed on both sides of the frame of each tank, or on the vehicle positioned immediately below the tank or tank compartment.

Where diesel fuel, gas oil or heating oil (UN 1202), petrol, motor spirit or gasoline (UN 1203), or kerosene (UN 1223) is carried in a multi-compartment road tanker, it may be labelled as a single load only, showing the UN number and emergency action code for the most hazardous of the products carried.

Detail of Panels

The orange-coloured panels must be either:

- a rigid plate fitted as near vertical as possible; or
- in the case of a tank or bulk container:
  - orange-coloured self-adhesive sheets; or
  - orange-coloured paint (or equivalent), provided the material is weather-resistant and ensures durable marking.

UN numbers and emergency action codes must be shown in black, at least 100 mm high and 15 mm wide – but where the emergency action code is white on a black background, it must appear as orange on a black rectangle at least 10 mm greater than the height and width of the letter. Except where panels comprise self-adhesive sheets or are applied by paint, UN numbers and emergency action codes must be indelible and remain legible after 15 minutes' engulfment in fire.

Where there is insufficient space for full-sized panels, these may be reduced to 300 mm wide by 120 mm high with a 10 mm black border.

Emergency Action Codes

The emergency action codes are as follows:

By numbers 1 to 4 indicating the suitable fire-fighting and spillages equipment:

1 water jets;

2 water fog;

3 foam;

4 dry agent.

By letters indicating the appropriate precautions to take (as shown in Table 20.6).

Table 20.6 Emergency action codes

Letter	Danger of violent reaction	Protective clothing and breathing apparatus	Measures to be taken
P	Yes	Full protective clothing	Dilute
R	No	Full protective clothing	Dilute
S	Yes	Breathing apparatus	Dilute
S*	Yes	Breathing apparatus for fire	Dilute
T	No	Breathing apparatus	Dilute
T*	No	Breathing apparatus for fire	Dilute
W	Yes	Full protective clothing	Contain
X	No	Full protective clothing	Contain
Y	Yes	Breathing apparatus	Contain
Y*	Yes	Breathing apparatus for fire	Contain
Z	No	Breathing apparatus	Contain
Z*	No	Breathing apparatus for fire	Contain

*These symbols, shown as orange (or can be white) letters reversed out of a black background, remain valid but are not included in the latest versions of the EAC.

Where a letter 'E' is shown at the end of an emergency action code, this means that consideration should be given to evacuating people from an incident.

Display of Telephone Number

The Carriage of Dangerous Goods Regulations (CDG2009) allow a contact telephone number as a concession, comprising black digits at least 30 mm high on an orange background, which must be shown on vehicles carrying single or multi-loads of dangerous goods in tanks, within the UK, positioned:

- at the rear of the vehicle;
- on both sides of the tank (or each tank if more than one), the frame of each tank or the vehicle;
- in the immediate vicinity of the orange-coloured panels.

Instead of a telephone number, the words 'consult local depot' or 'contact local depot' may be substituted, but only if:

- the name of the operator is clearly marked on the tank or the vehicle; and
- the fire chief for every area in which the vehicle will operate has been notified in writing of the address and telephone number of that local depot, and has confirmed in writing that he or she is satisfied with the arrangements.

Display of Danger Signs and Subsidiary Hazard Signs

Where a vehicle is carrying:

- packaged dangerous goods in a container:
  - any danger sign or subsidiary hazard sign required on the packages must also be displayed on at least one side of the container;
- dangerous goods in a tank container or in bulk in a container:
  - any danger sign or subsidiary hazard sign required on the packages containing such goods must be displayed on each side of the tank container or container, and where such signs are not visible from outside the carrying vehicle, the same signs must also be shown on each side of and at the rear of the vehicle;
- dangerous goods in a tank, other than a tank container, or in bulk in a vehicle, but not in bulk in a container on a vehicle:
  - any danger sign or subsidiary hazard sign required on the packages containing such goods must be displayed on each side of and at the rear of the vehicle.

Danger signs for a particular classification, or subsidiary hazard signs, need not be shown more than once on the sides or rear of any container, tank or vehicle.

Danger signs and subsidiary hazard signs must have sides at least 250 mm long; have a line the same colour as the symbol 12.5 mm inside the edge and running parallel to it; and be displayed adjacent to one another and in the same horizontal plane.

Display of Hazard Warning Panels

Despite the requirements described above for the display of orange-coloured panels, the regulations permit (wherever such a panel is required on the sides or rear of a

Figure 20.2   Existing UK-type combined hazard warning panel which may be used on the sides and rear of a bulk chemical tanker vehicle or container

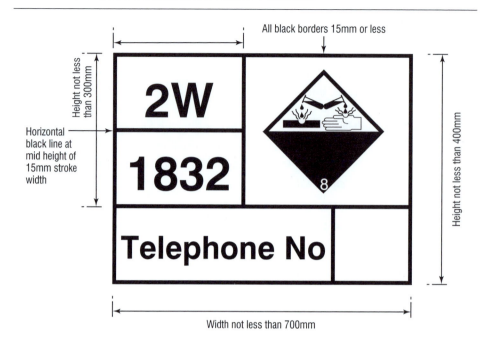

container, tank or vehicle) the alternative use of existing-type combined hazard warning panels (see Figure 20.2) on vehicles operating within the UK.

These are mainly orange with black borders and lettering – except for the white background where a reduced-size (ie 200 mm sides) danger sign is located and any subsidiary hazard sign must be the same size and displayed adjacent to it and in the same horizontal plane.

All danger panels and signs required on the front or rear of a vehicle must be positioned at right angles across its width, and those on the sides of a container, tank or vehicle at right angles along its length. All signs must be clearly visible.

Vehicles operating internationally under ADR may display a similar orange board with a three-digit ADR Kemler Code instead of an Emergency Action Code. The UN number is shown in the lower half of the panel.

Emergency Procedures

Vehicles carrying dangerous goods must be equipped so that the driver can take emergency measures, as follows:

- Vehicles up to 3.5 tonnes must have a minimum total of 4 kg of fire extinguishers with a minimum 2 kg cab extinguisher plus one other 2 kg extinguisher.

- Vehicles between 3.5 and 7.5 tonnes gvw must have a minimum 2 kg cab extinguisher, and one other extinguisher which must have a minimum capacity of 6 kg (totalling 8 kg).

- Vehicles exceeding 7.5 tonnes must carry a total capacity of 12 kg of fire extinguishers. This must include a minimum of a 2 kg cab extinguisher and at least one of the others must have a minimum capacity of 6 kg (totalling 12 kg).

- In all cases the vehicle crew must be trained to use the extinguishers carried and the extinguishers must be capable for use on class A, B and C fires as defined in Standard EN2-1992, 'Classification of Fires'.

Portable fire extinguishers must not be liable to release toxic gases into the driver's cab, or under the heat of a fire. They must be marked in compliance with a recognized standard fitted with a seal verifying they have not been used and be inscribed with the date for their next inspection.

A fire extinguisher is not needed where only infectious substances are carried.

Where toxic gases are carried, vehicles must carry respiratory equipment to enable the crew to escape safely.

Other equipment to be carried includes:

- a shovel and a plastic collecting container (eg a 9-litre bucket with lid);
- non-sparking torch;
- protective gloves;
- eye protection and eye-rinsing liquid;
- high-visibility clothing;
- two warning cones, triangles or flashing amber lights;
- at least one wheel chock for the unit or prime mover and at least one for any semi-trailer or trailer being drawn;
- any tools or equipment required for dealing with a spillage.

There are more stringent requirements relating to the vehicle batteries and wiring for vehicles exceeding 16 tonnes and trailers exceeding 10 tonnes gross weight. Also there are vehicle engine screening requirements for some tankers and vehicles pulling tank trailers where the contents of the tank are highly flammable.

Accidents and Emergencies

In accident or emergency situations drivers must comply with the emergency information given to them and apply the emergency procedures stated on the emergency action information (eg on the instructions in writing), including:

- notifying the relevant emergency services by the quickest practical means;
- taking steps to prevent chemical contamination of the environment (eg watercourses);
- taking steps to prevent the risk of fire;
- keeping the public away from the scene;
- applying first aid where necessary.

Accident Investigation and Reports

All accidents and dangerous goods incidents must be reported and investigated to determine how and why they were caused and to prevent recurrence.

DGSAs have a duty to prepare reports on serious accidents, incidents or legal infringements occurring during the loading, unloading and transport of dangerous goods and to implement measures to avoid recurrence.

Reporting to the Health and Safety Executive

Accidents and serious incidents involving dangerous goods must be reported to the HSE at the Incident Contact Centre as required under the Reporting of Injuries, Diseases and Dangerous Occurrences Regulations 1995 (SI 1995/3163 – RIDDOR). (See Chapter 17.)

Road Traffic Collisions

The procedures to be followed in the event of a road traffic collision, apart from the special considerations relating to the carriage of dangerous goods as set out above, are those described under Road Traffic Collision Procedure in Chapter 10.

Security Provisions

The security provisions relating to the carriage of dangerous goods (except nuclear materials) have requirements that fall into four groups: general provisions; provisions relating to high consequence dangerous goods; training requirements; and security plans.

General Provisions

These require that:

- all persons engaged in the carriage of dangerous goods must consider the security requirements for the carriage of dangerous goods commensurate with their responsibilities;

- dangerous goods may only be offered to carriers that have been appropriately identified;

- areas within temporary storage terminals, temporary storage sites, vehicle depots, berthing areas and marshalling yards used for temporary storage during carriage of dangerous goods must be properly secured, well lit and, where possible and appropriate, not accessible to the general public;

- each crew member of a vehicle carrying dangerous goods must carry photographic identification;

- safety inspections must cover security measures.

High Consequence Dangerous Goods

High consequence goods are those goods that may be used in a terrorist incident where there is a serious risk of danger, such as explosives, some flammable liquids and solids, and some toxic, corrosive and infectious substances. These goods require a security plan to be drawn up when they are moved by road.

Full details, instructions and a template to draw up a plan are available on the GOV.UK website.

Training Requirements

Additional provisions relating to training require that up-to-date registers of all valid training certificates must be maintained by the competent authorities and that relevant training, and refresher training, must include elements of security awareness, in particular addressing the following issues:

- the nature of security risks;

- how to recognize security risks;

- how to address and reduce such risks;

- what actions to take in the event of a breach of security.

Security Plans

A security plan must cover the following requirements:

- Responsibility for security must be allocated to competent and qualified persons with appropriate authority to carry out their responsibilities.

- Records must be kept of the dangerous goods or types of dangerous goods involved in the carriage.

- A review must be undertaken of current operations and assessment of security risks, including at any stops necessary to the transport operation, the keeping of dangerous goods in the vehicle, tank or container before, during and after the journey and the temporary storage of dangerous goods during the course of intermodal transfer or transhipment between units.

- A clear statement must be made of the measures that are to be taken to reduce security risks, commensurate with the responsibilities and duties of the participant, including:

  - training matters;

  - security policies;

  - operating practices;

  - equipment and resource use to reduce security risks.

- Effective and up-to-date procedures must be established for reporting and dealing with security threats, breaches of security or security incidents.

- Procedures must be put in place for the evaluation and testing of security plans and actions.

- Measures must be taken to ensure the physical security of transport information contained in the security plan.

- Measures must be taken to ensure that the distribution of information relating to the transport operation contained in the security plan is limited to those who need to have it.

- A process needs to be established to cooperate in the exchange of security threat information, to apply appropriate security measures and to respond to security incidents.

- Steps must be taken to prevent the theft of vehicles carrying high consequence dangerous goods or their cargo by means of suitable security devices, equipment or arrangements. These must be kept operational and effective at all times, but must not jeopardize any emergency response.

- Transport telemetry or other tracking methods or devices should be used to monitor the movement of high consequence dangerous goods, when it is appropriate to do so and when such systems are already fitted.

High consequence dangerous goods are those listed in Table 20.7 and carried in quantities greater than shown.

Table 20.7 High consequence dangerous goods

Class	Division	Substance or article	Quantity Tank (ltrs)	Bulk (kg)	Packages (kg)
1	1.1	Explosives	a	a	0
	1.2	Explosives	a	a	0
	1.3	Compatibility group C explosives	a	a	0
	1.5	Explosives	0	a	0
2	2.1	Flammable gases (classification codes including only the letter F)	3,000	a	b
	2.2	Toxic gases (classification codes containing the letters T, TF, TC, TO, TFC or TOC) excluding aerosols	0	a	0
3		Flammable liquids of packing groups I and II	3,000	a	b
		Desensitized explosives	a	a	0
4	4.1	Desensitized explosives	a	a	0
	4.2	Packing group I substances	3,000	a	b
	4.3	Packing group II substances	3,000	a	b
5	5.1	Oxidizing liquids of packing group I	3,000	a	b
		Perchlorates, ammonium nitrate and ammonium nitrate fertilizers	3,000	3,000	b
6	6.1	Toxic substances of packing group I	0	a	0
	6.2	Infectious substances of Category A	a	a	0
7		Radioactive material	3,000 A1 (special form) or 3,000 A2, as applicable, in Type B or Type C packages		
8		Corrosive substances of packing group I	3,000	a	b

Enforcement

The police and DVSA examiners are given wide-ranging powers to ensure compliance with the law on dangerous goods carriage.

The DVSA is empowered to enforce certain aspects of dangerous goods law relating solely to vehicles; the HSE has responsibility for premises-based inspections.

Offences and Penalties

For an offence under the HSWA 1974, a fine of up to £5,000 may be imposed, while in more serious cases an offence may lead to an unlimited fine and/or a two-year prison sentence.

Obstructing an inspector when fulfilling their statutory duties is an offence carrying a fine of up to £5,000, while breach of any notice served by an inspector can result in a fine of up to £20,000.

Carriage of Explosives

For non-armed forces movements and other non-exempt movements, European Regulation (EC) No 1272/2008 on classification, labelling and packaging of substances and mixtures (the CLP Regulation) applies. This also means that ADR crosses into the carriage of explosives, and operators are advised to refer to the ADR volumes at GOV.UK for further information.

Class 7: Radioactive Substances

Complex legislation controls the carriage of Class 7 radioactive substances. These include:

- Radioactive Material (Road Transport) Act 1991;
- Radioactive Material (Road Transport) Regulations 2002 (amended 2018);
- Ionizing Radiations Regulations 1985 and Ionizing Radiations (Outside Workers) Regulations 1993 (IRR).

Guidance in relation to the civil transport of radioactive material by road and rail is available from the Office for Nuclear Regulation (ONR). This guidance includes ONR's expectations in relation to 'suitable and sufficient' radiation risk assessment (RRA) and emergency planning and notification for the transport of Class 7 goods.

Operators transporting Class 7 goods should refer to onr.org.uk.

Driver Training

ADR drivers must be instructed and trained so they understand the dangers of the particular goods being carried and the emergency action to be taken, as well as their duties under the Health and Safety at Work Act 1974 and current dangerous goods legislation. Operators must keep training records.

The driver training specified in ADR 8.2 applies (from the time of loading until the goods have been unloaded and, where appropriate, the compartment has been cleaned or purged) to drivers of the following dangerous goods vehicles:

- road tankers exceeding 1 m^3 capacity;
- those carrying tank containers exceeding 3 m^3 capacity;
- those carrying dangerous goods:
  - in bulk;
  - in a road tanker with a capacity not exceeding 1,000 litres;
  - in a tank container with a capacity not exceeding 3,000 litres;
  - where any of the goods are in transport category 0;
  - comprising more than 20 kg/litres* of Category 1 goods in packages;
  - comprising more than 200 kg/litres* of Category 2 goods in packages;
  - comprising more than 500 kg/litres* of Category 3 goods in packages;
- those carrying explosives;
- those carrying radioactive materials.

This refers to 'total mass or volume' (ie as measured in kg or litres).

Vocational Training Certificates

Drivers must hold a valid vocational training certificate (ADR certificate) appropriate to the classes of dangerous goods they carry. ADR certificates are valid for five years.

Certificates to be Carried and Produced to the Police

Drivers must carry their ADR certificates on all dangerous goods journeys and produce them on request by the police or a goods vehicle examiner.

Minimum Training Requirements for Issue of Vocational Training Certificates

Approved training for drivers must cover at least:

- general requirements on dangerous goods carriage;
- main types of hazard;
- environmental protection in the control of the transfer of wastes;
- preventive and safety measures appropriate to various types of hazard;

- what to do after an accident (first aid, road safety, the use of protective equipment, etc);
- labelling and marking to indicate danger;
- what to do and not do when carrying dangerous goods;
- the purpose and operation of technical equipment on vehicles used for carrying dangerous goods;
- prohibitions on mixed loading in the same vehicle or container;
- precautions during loading and unloading of dangerous goods;
- civil liability;
- multi-modal transport operations.

For drivers of vehicles carrying packaged dangerous goods, training must also cover the handling and stowage of packages, and for road tanker or tank container drivers, training must cover the behaviour of such vehicles on the road, including load movement during transit.

Dangerous Goods Safety Advisor (DGSA)

Companies which load, unload or carry dangerous goods by road (and by rail and inland waterway) must appoint a qualified DGSA under provisions contained in EU Directive 96/35/EC. This also applies to self-employed persons. The person appointed must hold a valid vocational training certificate confirming they have passed the official DGSA examination conducted by the SQA (Scottish Qualifications Authority). (SQA is appointed by the DfT to conduct all UK DGSA examinations.)

To qualify as a DGSA it is necessary to study the subject material contained in the official syllabus, sit the relevant examinations and pass in at least three of the following subjects:

- the core examination, which is compulsory for all candidates;
- one modal paper covering either road, rail or inland waterways;
- at least one dangerous goods class paper covering either:
    - Class 1;
    - Class 2;
    - Class 3 (specifically UN 1202, 1203 and 1223 – ie mineral oils);
    - Class 7;
    - General Chemical Classes (3, 4.1, 4.2, 4.3, 5.1, 5.2, 6.1, 6.2, 8 and 9); or
    - all classes.

Tasks and Functions of DGSAs

Appointed DGSAs must effectively carry out the legal duties and bear the responsibilities set out in law as follows:

- monitor compliance with the law on the transport of dangerous goods;
- advise their employer on the transport of dangerous goods;
- prepare reports on any accidents involving dangerous goods;
- prepare an annual report to their employer on the firm's activities in transporting dangerous goods (to be kept for five years and made available to the authorities on request).

The DGSA must also monitor:

- procedures for identifying dangerous goods being transported;
- practices for taking account of any special requirements in connection with dangerous goods being transported;
- procedures for checking equipment used in the transport, loading or unloading of dangerous goods;
- employee training and maintenance of training records;
- emergency procedures to be taken in the event of accidents that may affect safety during the transport, loading or unloading of dangerous goods;
- investigation and preparation of reports on serious accidents or legal infringements during the transport, loading or unloading of dangerous goods;
- implementation of steps to avoid the recurrence of accidents, incidents or serious legal infringements;
- account taken of the legal requirements in the choice and use of sub-contractors;
- operational procedures and instructions that employees must follow;
- introduction of measures to increase awareness of the risks inherent in the transport, loading and unloading of dangerous goods;
- verification procedures to ensure that vehicles carry the documents and safety equipment required and that they comply with the law;
- verification procedures to ensure that the law on loading and unloading is complied with.

Controlled and Hazardous Waste

Controlled waste is classified as three types, domestic, commercial and industrial, but for disposal waste it may be considered in two forms:

- controlled waste, which comprises 'household, industrial and commercial waste or any such waste' (ie including waste paper, scrap metal and recyclable scrap);
- hazardous waste, which is material defined as 'special waste' in the controlled waste legislation, or material which falls within the classification of dangerous substances for the purposes of the road tanker or packaged dangerous goods legislation.

A range of legislation applies in this area of activity, including the Disposal of Poisonous Waste Act 1972 (which makes it an offence to dispose of poisonous waste in an irresponsible way), the Criminal Justice Act 1988 (which provides powers for the authorities to impound vehicles engaged in illegal fly-tipping), the Control of Pollution (Amendment) Act 1989, the Controlled Waste (Registration of Carriers and Seizure of Vehicles) Regulations 1991 and the Controlled Waste Regulations 2012. Other sets of regulations are also important, including the Environmental Protection Act 1994, the Waste Management Licensing Regulations 2011 and the Hazardous Waste Regulations 2016.

Controlled Waste

Controlled waste should not be disposed of, or transported away, by a person or firm not legally authorized for this purpose.

Registration of Operators

The 1990 Environmental Act Protection requires operators who transport controlled waste within Great Britain to register with the appropriate waste regulation authority (WRA), ie in the area in which they have their business. The relevant authorities are:

- the Environment Agency (EA) – England and Wales;
- the Scottish Environmental Protection Agency (SEPA);
- the Northern Ireland Environment Agency (NIEA).

It is an offence to fail to register or to carry controlled waste when not registered. Besides fines following prosecution and conviction for such offences, legislation provides powers for the seizure and disposal of vehicles used for such illegal purposes.

There are two tiers of licensing: 'upper tier' licences which are valid for three years and 'lower tier' licences which renew automatically.

Exemptions are provided for charities, voluntary organizations, domestic householders disposing of their own waste, waste collection authorities and producers of controlled waste. Builders and demolition companies are not exempt and must register and otherwise comply with the legislation.

Duty of Care

Companies and individuals that produce, import, store, treat, process, recycle, dispose of or transport controlled waste (see above for definition) have a statutory 'duty of care'. This places responsibility for the completion of paperwork (ie 'waste transfer notes'), taking all reasonable steps to stop waste escaping and ensuring its safety and security, recording all involved parties, taking waste to authorized sites and keeping records of waste transfers on parties involved with the carriage of controlled waste.

Waste Transfer Notes

Waste transfer notes comprise written descriptions of waste handed over to other persons to transport and/or dispose of, and a transfer note signed by both parties (allowable as a single document) containing the following details:

- what the waste is and the quantity;
- the type of container in which it is carried;
- the time and date of transfer;
- the place where the transfer took place;
- the names and addresses of both parties (ie consignor and recipient);
- detail as to which category each falls into (eg producer and registered waste carrier);
- a certificate number if either or both parties hold waste licences and the name of the authority from whom it/they was/were issued;
- reasons for any exemption from registration or waste licensing.

Copies of documents (ie descriptions of waste and/or transfer notes) given and received must be retained by carriers for at least one year and by waste dealers and brokers for at least three years. Both or either party may be required to produce these and prove in court where particular consignments of controlled waste originated. Operators can register online to fill in, sign and store waste transfer notes, using the Electronic Duty of Care (EDOC) system, or use alternative documentation with the required information.

Seizure of Vehicles

The law gives powers to waste regulation authorities to seize the vehicles of offenders, remove and separately store or dispose of loads as necessary, and dispose of (or destroy) vehicles following set procedures to publicize details of the seizure in local newspapers. Attempts will be made to seek out legitimate owners, who may reclaim their vehicles on satisfactory proof of entitlement and identification.

Hazardous Waste Disposal

Broadly, the law on hazardous and toxic waste requires that waste which is poisonous, noxious or polluting is not deposited on land where its presence is liable to give rise to an environmental hazard. And it is necessary for anyone removing or depositing poisonous material to notify both the local authority and the river authority before doing so.

An environmental hazard is defined as waste that is deposited in a manner or in such quantity that it would subject persons or animals to material risk of death, injury or impairment of health or threaten the pollution or contamination of any water supply. The European Commission has also produced a booklet on this subject for local authorities in EU member states.

There are additional controls over the carriage and disposal of particularly hazardous waste. The Control of Pollution (Special Waste) Regulations 1980 (amended in 1996) were introduced in order to comply with EU Directives and there is also the Hazardous Waste Regulations 2005.

The main requirements of these regulations are:

- Certain types of waste are to be regarded as special waste and subject to the additional controls. These are wastes that are regarded as dangerous to life as set out in the regulations.

- Waste producers have to give not less than three days' and not more than one month's notice to waste disposal authorities of their intention to dispose of a consignment of special waste.

- A set of consignment notes must be completed when special wastes are transported. This means that a consignment of special waste can be transported from the producer to the disposal site only if each person has signed for it and taken on responsibility for it. This is to ensure that waste disposal authorities know who is carrying the waste and they have to be informed within 24 hours of when it reaches the disposal site. Waste producers should take particular note of the requirement that all notices must be made on the statutory forms. Each form contains a unique reference number to assist an authority in making sure that waste is safely disposed of.

- A record of the location of the point of disposal on site of all special wastes must be kept in perpetuity. This is to ensure that proper arrangements can be made to bring the site back into use after the waste disposal operation has ceased.

- Proper registers of consignments must be kept by the producers, carriers and disposers.

- There will be a 'season ticket' arrangement for regular consignments of special wastes of similar composition disposed of at the same site. The waste disposal authorities will decide which producers and disposers in their areas qualify.

- The Secretary of State has emergency powers to direct receipt of special wastes at a particular site. This is likely to be rarely used.

- Radioactive waste which also has the characteristics of special waste will be subject to the new controls.

Advice on particular problems can be obtained from waste regulation authorities (see below) and details about the regulations are available at GOV.UK.

Waste Site Licensing

Waste regulation authorities (WRAs) must inspect sites regularly and make sure the operators are following the conditions of the licence. Failure to comply with licence conditions is a criminal offence carrying a fine of up to £20,000. This can be increased to five years' imprisonment where special waste rules are broken. In addition to prosecution, a WRA can amend or even revoke the licence. See also the section dealing with unauthorized tipping of waste (ie fly-tipping) in Chapter 18.

Packaging Waste

Waste Packaging

The Directive on Packaging Waste 94/62 EC sets out the definition of the materials covered and the target recycling percentages for producers of waste packaging. Registered businesses with a turnover of more than £2 million or who deal with more than 50 tonnes of packaging a year need to provide details of annual tonnages to be recycled or disposed of and to prove that they have achieved a target percentage. Under this scheme, waste producers are classed as 'large' or 'small' and pay fees accordingly.

Proof of packaging recycling and recovery is done by producing packaging recovery notes issued by the recycling/disposal organization. The UK itself has targets of recycling all types of packaging, with some targets changing year on year.

Further information on waste packaging is available at GOV.UK, the WRAs, the Waste and Resources Action Programme (WRAP) or from NetRegs, which provides environmental guidance for businesses in Northern Ireland and Scotland.

Light Vehicles 21

Light vehicles generally means cars, vans and dual-purpose vehicles not exceeding 3,500 kg gvw and alternatively fuelled goods vehicles not exceeding 4,250 kg gvw, ie vehicles under the O-Licence threshold. Much of the legislation applicable to the use of light vehicles regarding vehicle tax, insurance and moving traffic has been dealt with in earlier chapters.

However, some rules are worth emphasizing for the benefit of the light vehicle fleet manager.

Vehicle Roadworthiness

Operators should be aware that Traffic Commissioners can take account of failure to operate light vehicles safely and within the law when deciding whether an applicant is fit or is of sufficiently good repute to hold an O-Licence. In addition, the police and HSE may consider that safety, risk assessment or duty of care issues may be relevant in cases of light vehicles being involved in road traffic collisions or found to be unroadworthy.

Vehicle Tax

Light vehicles used for business purposes are taxed at the private/light goods (PLG) rate of duty (see Chapter 8).

Insurance

Light vehicles are required to be covered for third-party insurance risks as a minimum. In the case of fleet cars, additional cover may be taken out and in most instances comprehensive cover is advisable.

Correct Cover

It is essential to ensure that light vehicles are fully insured for 'business use' by employees.

All UK vehicle insurance provides the minimum third-party cover to drive in the EU and EEA countries. For other countries, a Green Card may be required. This provides proof of third-party liability cover. Checks with the insurer should be made for extra cover such as fire, theft or damage to the insured vehicle.

Grey Fleet

A grey fleet is where employees use their own vehicle for business purposes, even if only occasionally, and the fleet manager should ensure that they have adequate insurance cover. This usually means that employees' own policies must include provision for their car to be used in connection with the business of their employer.

The fleet manager should ask to see evidence of the cover (ie a valid Certificate of Insurance or a temporary cover note showing the conditions for use covered by the policy). Evidence should be checked periodically to ensure that cover is continually in place.

Fuel

Fuel Benefit Charge

If an employee doesn't pay for any fuel they use privately during a tax year, this is reported on form P11D and Class 1A National Insurance must be paid on the value of the fuel benefit.

Where a van is used solely for business travel to and from work, with only occasional private use, the benefit-in-kind rules do not apply.

Payment by passengers towards the cost of fuel consumed on a journey is permitted as long as the payment is proportionate to the fuel only. Charging more than the proportion of fuel can result in a fine of up to £2,500.

Construction and Use Regulations

The Road Vehicles (Construction and Use) Regulations 1986 require all vehicles to be maintained in such a condition that they shall not cause danger to people carried in the vehicle and other road users – this applies equally to all vehicles, irrespective of their size or weight.

Towing

All tow bars fitted to new light vehicles must be type-approved and marked accordingly. While light vehicle tow bars used before 1 August 1998 aren't required to be type-approved, fleet managers should consider this in their company fleet policies.

Local Authority Emissions Testing

Local authorities throughout England who have declared an Air Quality Management Area (AQMA), and all local authorities in Scotland, are operating their own schemes of roadside emissions testing. Drivers of vehicles which fail the test will be issued with a fixed penalty notice usually requiring payment of £60, rising to £90 if unpaid within 28 days, although these figures do change depending upon individual authorities. The test levels are the same as those that vehicles would be expected to meet at the annual test. Commercial vehicles that fail an emissions test invariably have poorly maintained engines. The scheme covers all types of vehicles, including commercial vehicles.

NB: Failing emissions tests during an annual MOT can result in a fine of up to £2,500.

Carrying Dangerous Goods in Light Vehicles

The rules on dangerous goods carried in light vehicles are determined by the type of goods carried, the size of the receptacles in which they are carried and the total size of the load. The quantity thresholds for UK carriage are shown in the CDG Road Regulations (Schedule 1, Table 2 – see the Exemptions section in Chapter 20 for further details).

For the most part, it is unlikely that sufficient quantities of such goods in Class 3 (Flammable), Packing Group III (Transport Category 3) would be carried in a private car to require the full legal gamut of vehicle placarding, the provision of Instructions in Writing and the need for driver training. Provided these goods are in receptacles with a volume of 25 litres or less, it would be difficult to exceed the quantity threshold of 500 litres above which these legal requirements apply.

However, should the samples fall within the requirements for Packing Group I substances (Transport Category 1), goods must then be in a receptacle with a capacity of 1 litre or less, with a total volume of 20 litres or less, to avoid these requirements.

So far as the risk element is concerned, it is necessary to consider what would happen in the event of a road accident. With no Instructions in Writing on the vehicle, there is no emergency information available for either the driver or the emergency services, nor, invariably, is there likely to be any emergency equipment such as the appropriate fire extinguishers, first-aid kit, respirator, gloves, spill kit or emergency warning triangle to place on the road.

Besides all the dangers implicit in the carrying of dangerous samples, there is the question of the vehicle insurance to consider. Generally, it may be expected that an insurance company would reject any claim if they were not advised beforehand of the carriage of such goods, especially if legal requirements were not being met at the time.

Drivers' Hours and Records

Drivers of light vehicles as defined in this chapter are exempt from the EU/AETR drivers' hours rules. However, British domestic drivers' hours rules apply in certain cases.

The applicable limits for drivers of light goods vehicles (not exceeding 3.5 tonnes gvw) are:

- maximum daily driving time: 10 hours;
- maximum daily duty time: 11 hours.

There are no specified break or daily or weekly rest period requirements; no limits on continuous duty or weekly limits on duty or driving. However, Working Time Regulations breaks are required (see Chapter 3).

Drivers of light goods vehicles and dual-purpose vehicles (see the Dual-Purpose Vehicles section in Chapter 8) used for certain specialized duties are only required to observe the daily maximum driving time of 10 hours. These include:

- doctors, dentists, nurses, midwives or vets;
- any service of inspection, cleaning, maintenance, repair, installation or fitting;
- a commercial traveller and carrying only goods used for soliciting orders;
- an employee of the AA, the RAC or the RASC;
- business of cinematography or of radio or television broadcasting.

Full details of drivers' hours and records can be found in Chapters 3 and 4.

Tachographs

Light goods vehicles are exempt from tachograph fitment and use. However, if a light goods vehicle is coupled to a goods-carrying trailer exceeding 750 kg in weight, so that the total of the combined gross weights exceeds 4.25 tonnes, then the vehicle is in the scope of the EU/AETR tachograph regulations, unless it is otherwise exempt due to special use. This means that a fully calibrated tachograph must be fitted and must be used by the driver when the trailer is drawn (see Chapter 5) and EU/AETR drivers' hours rules must be followed (see Chapter 3).

Speed Limits

Private cars and dual-purpose vehicles not drawing trailers are restricted to maximum permitted speeds on certain roads in accordance with the restriction signposted on the section of road and to overall maximum speeds of 60 mph on single-carriageway roads and 70 mph on dual carriageways and motorways.

Speed limits for cars and light goods vehicles are as follows:

Table 21.1 Speed limits for cars and light goods vehicles (mph)

	Motorways	Dual carriageways	Other roads
Cars and car-derived vans	70	70	60
Cars and car-derived vans towing trailer	60	60	50
Rigid goods vehicles not exceeding 7.5 tonnes	70	60	50
Articulated vehicles and rigid goods vehicles not exceeding 7.5 tonnes drawing trailer	60	60*	50

NB: In all cases of speed restrictions mentioned above, if specific lower limits are in force on any section of road, then it is the lower limit which must be observed. Lower limits also apply when towing trailers.
*In Northern Ireland the limit for this category of vehicle is 50 mph.

NB: *Many smaller vans are now fitted with side windows and at least one seat fixed behind the driving seat position. This allows those types of vehicles to travel at the same speeds as cars and car-derived vans and to pay lower tolls at crossings.*

Seat Belts

Compulsory fitment of seat belts applies in the case of the following light vehicles (see also the Seat Belts section in Chapter 10):

- goods vehicles not exceeding 1,525 kg unladen (first registered since April 1967);

- goods vehicles not exceeding 3,500 kg maximum gross weight (first registered since 1 April 1980);

- dual-purpose vehicles first registered since 1 January 1965;

- private cars first registered since 1 January 1965.

Vehicles to which the regulations apply must be fitted with seat belts which can be secured and released with one hand only and must also be fitted with a device to enable the belts to be stowed in a position where they do not touch the floor. The belts must be maintained in a fit and serviceable condition and kept free from permanent or temporary obstruction which would prevent their being used by a person sitting in the seat for which the belt is provided. In cases where the regulations apply, as above, belts must be provided for the driver and one front-seat passenger.

Wearing of Seat Belts

The driver and all passengers must wear a seat belt if one is fitted in the seat being used – there are only a few exceptions:

- driver reversing, or supervising a learner driver reversing;

- passenger in a trade vehicle who is investigating a fault;

- driver of a goods vehicle on deliveries and travelling no more than 50 metres between stops;

- licensed taxi driver who is 'plying for hire' or carrying passengers;

- driver in a vehicle being used for police, fire and rescue services;

- driver or passenger in possession of a 'Certificate of Exemption from Compulsory Seat Belt Wearing'.

There must only be one person in each seat fitted with a seat belt.

Heavy fines may be imposed on conviction for failing to wear a seat belt as required by law. The responsibility for seat-belt wearing rests with the person sitting in the seat for which the belt is provided, except that responsibility for ensuring that children wear seat belts as required by law either in the front or rear seats rests with the driver of the vehicle (ie not the parent or guardian who may be accompanying the child).

Vehicle Fuel Efficiency 22

Next to wages, fuel is normally the most expensive goods vehicle operating cost, accounting for an average of around 40 per cent of road transport operating costs for an articulated HGV. It is also subject to price fluctuations.

Fuel and Vehicle

Fuel consumption relates to vehicle type, its power unit and drive line, its mechanical condition, its use and how it is driven. For the most part, operators have to consider how improved fuel economy can be achieved with the existing vehicle fleet. Three principal areas exist for improvement in the vehicle itself. These are:

- mechanical condition;
- efficient use;
- retrofit fuel efficiency aids.

Mechanical Condition

A poorly maintained vehicle will consume more fuel. Particular attention should be paid to efficient maintenance of the following components:

- Fuel system (fuel tank, pipe lines, filters, pump and injectors). There should be no leaks and the vehicle should not emit black smoke. Drivers must check the fuel cap is in place and the seal in good condition during the walkaround check. Fuel pumps and injectors should be properly serviced as recommended by the manufacturers.

- Wheels and brakes. Wheels should turn freely and without any brake binding. Front wheels should be correctly aligned. Brake binding and misalignment cause unnecessary friction which affects fuel consumption. Lift axles and 'low running resistance' tyres are options to consider.

- Driving controls. Throttle, clutch and brake pedals should be correctly adjusted so the driver has efficient control over the vehicle. In particular, engine tick-over should be accurately adjusted to save throttle 'blipping' to keep it running when the vehicle is stationary. Stop–start technology is now standard on most new vehicles. Where the controls are controlled by an engine management system, these need to be checked regularly in order to ensure the controls are set for optimum performance.

Efficient Use

The way a vehicle is driven has the greatest impact on fuel consumption. The following activities should be avoided by careful route planning and scheduling:

- vehicles running long distances when only partially loaded;
- vehicles covering excessive distances to reach their destination;
- large vehicles being used for running errands or making small-item deliveries which could be accomplished more efficiently, and certainly more economically, by other means;
- unnecessary detours and extended, but preferred, routes taken by drivers;
- engine idling;
- excessive speed;
- harsh acceleration, braking and steering.

Vehicle telematics can be used to monitor speed, route and schedule compliance and manage customers' expectations.

Fuel Efficiency Aids

Fuel efficiency aids fall into six categories:

- Streamlining devices such as skirts, cab-top air deflectors, teardrop trailers, under-bumper air dams, front corner deflectors for high trailers and box vans, in-fill pieces for lorry and trailer combinations, and shaped cones for addition to the front of van bodies.
- Speed governors restricting maximum speed.
- Engine fans and radiator shutters designed to ensure engines operate at the correct temperature.
- Exhaust gas recirculation and selective catalytic reduction systems.
- 'Stop–start' technology to reduce engine idling.
- Dual fuel, alternative fuel and electric power to reduce conventional carbon-based fuel and emissions and, in some cases, engine noise and maintenance costs.

In addition, efficient scheduling, so as to avoid congestion and reduce engine idling, etc, can play a major part in reducing fuel usage.

Operators considering fuel reduction measures which may impact upon a vehicle's dimensions or weight, etc, should check with the DVSA before assuming they will be allowed to operate the vehicle once the modifications have been made.

Fuel and Tyres

The type and condition of tyres play a significant part in fuel consumption.

Tyre manufacturers claim that improvements in fuel consumption of 5 to 10 per cent can be expected from the use of radial-ply tyres. Low-profile tyres which offer a number of operational benefits over conventional radial tyres – such as reduced platform height and reduced overall height – also offer further possibilities for fuel saving. It is also possible to purchase 'low-resistance' tyres designed to reduce the level of friction between the tyres and the road surface.

Savings will only be achieved if tyres are in good condition, are correctly inflated and are properly matched, especially when used in twin-wheel combinations. Neglecting tyre pressures is common in fleets and under-inflation is one of the major causes of tyre failure.

Vehicles with lift axle options can also reduce fuel consumption as they drastically reduce resistance between the vehicle and the road surface.

Fuel and the Driver

Driving techniques, above all else, influence the overall fuel consumption of vehicles. A driver with a lack of compassion for the vehicle will negate all other fuel-saving measures. Drivers must be aware of the engine tachometer and that the amber, green and red bands all relate to engine performance. The monitoring of tracking and telematics systems can motivate drivers to stick to approved routes. Lockable fuel tanks and appropriate overnight parking procedures can help counter fuel theft. In larger vehicles, effective use of the exhaust brake helps reduce fuel usage. Inefficient driving falls into two categories:

- excessive speed;
- erratic, stop–go driving.

Excessive speed consumes more fuel: this fact is beyond question but the extent of the extra consumption is difficult to assess accurately. Tests have proven that at 40 mph, fuel consumption was 10.5 miles per gallon (mpg) but this was reduced by 2.6 mpg to 7.9 mpg at 50 mph. This represents a 24.76 per cent increase in fuel consumption.

The effects of erratic driving are more difficult to determine in quantitative terms, but it is sufficient to say that it results in abnormally high fuel consumption as well as causing excessive wear and tear on vehicle components. Impatience behind the wheel and an inability to anticipate the road ahead leads the driver to accelerate harshly to keep up with the traffic and brake suddenly.

More economical driving is achieved by concentration on the road and traffic conditions ahead, anticipating well in advance how the traffic flow will move and what is happening in front, so that acceleration and braking can be more progressive.

One other fuel-saving practice which drivers can adopt, if they do not have stop–start fitted, is to stop the engine while the vehicle is stationary rather than letting it tick over for unnecessarily long periods.

For fuel consumption, vehicle performance, safety and driver comfort, most new vehicles are fitted with automatic gearboxes.

Fuel and Fleet Management

Operators can implement other measures to manage fuel consumption.

Bulk Supplies/Buying

Operating bulk fuel on site can reduce costs and bulk tanks can become a complete fuel management system for refuelling and dispensing. They provide convenient fuelling points on site, reducing the risk of spills and unnecessary vehicle movements. Direct fuel suppliers provide the option to buy in bulk with flexing purchase volume to obtain cheaper price-per-litre rates.

Fuel Accounting

Accurate accounting of fuel issues against individual vehicles and/or drivers must be managed. Bulk fuel-dispensing systems prevent unauthorized access and track fuel issues to identified vehicles or keyholders.

Long-Range Tanks

Long-range tanks enable savings by using bulk-purchased supplies. However, extra fuel carried can compromise payload. There is also the cost of fuel levies or taxes to be borne in mind. These are chargeable when entering some countries (notably Norway) and are based on the amount of fuel in the tank. British hauliers returning to the UK may also find they have to pay an excess fuel tax on supplies bought outside the UK. However, long-range tanks do allow drivers to fill up in countries where fuel is cheaper.

Under Article 8a of Council Directive 92/81/EEC, the diesel tanks fitted to new vehicles are defined as follows:

> The tanks permanently fixed by the manufacturer to all motor vehicles of the same type as the vehicle in question and whose permanent fitting enables fuel to be used directly, both for the purpose of propulsion and, where appropriate, for the operation, during transport, of refrigeration and other systems.

HMRC warns that the focus of attention on fuel import issues is on the misuse of duty relief and has emphasized that fuel brought into the UK may only be used by the particular vehicle carrying it and should not be offloaded from that vehicle for use by other vehicles or for transfer to a bulk fuel installation.

Operators should be aware that some European countries do not recognize rebated fuel such as 'Red Diesel'. The Finance Bill 2021 and subsequent secondary legislation restricts the entitlement to use Red Diesel and rebated biofuels from April 2022. A new Schedule to the Hydrocarbon Oil Duties Act 1979 (HODA) will specify which vehicles and machines are 'excepted machines' for rebated fuel. Operators using Red Diesel should review these changes to determine their effect.

Route Planning and Scheduling

Better planning of vehicle schedules and routes and maximizing 'backloading' and cabotage possibilities offer the prospect of quite considerable fuel savings. A reduction in distances travelled will inevitably result in fuel savings. If the schedules can be planned so that fewer vehicles are needed to carry out the operation, then, besides the broader savings in vehicle costs, the fleet as a whole will use less fuel. Therefore, the elimination of unnecessary trips, or trips where vehicles are only partly loaded, is a major priority in the search for fuel cost savings.

Tachographs

Analysis of tachograph records helps provide operators with fuel savings and fuel consumption comparisons. In addition, data collection from the new fourth-generation tachographs will enable operators to better analyse routes and journeys.

Fuel Cards

There are a number of fuel cards available. They can be direct from a fuel provider or from other commercial third-party providers.

Fuel cards offer the opportunity to buy fuel at a pre-arranged rate and pay only when fuel is purchased. The difference in the various schemes is in the levels of service they offer. Operators may also need to consider availability when deciding on which card to select, as some cards may need drivers to divert in order to find a suitable place to purchase fuel if the card they have is not widely accepted.

Fuel Efficiency Checklist

Check

- Fuel systems (including filler cap) free from leaks.
- Filler cap lock fitted and operational.
- Fuel pump and injectors serviced and correctly adjusted.
- Exhaust not emitting black smoke.
- Air cleaners not blocked.
- Engine operating at correct temperature.
- Wheels turning freely.
- Controls properly adjusted and lubricated.

Tyres

- Condition and inflation pressures.
- Possibility of changing to low-resistance radials on all vehicles.
- Lifting/steering axle considerations.

Drivers

- Speed limits not being exceeded.
- Driving methods smooth and gentle.
- Engines stopped when vehicle standing.
- Authorized routes used.

Management

- Control over supplies and issues.
- Avoidance of spillage, loss and unauthorized use.

- Purchases from outside suppliers kept to a minimum.
- Record systems accurate and up to date.
- Possibility of installing fuel issue and monitoring systems.
- Use of vehicle trackers.
- Possibility of fitting fuel economy aids (alternative fuels, deflectors, engine fans, etc).
- Possibility of using long-range fuel tanks on vehicles.
- Routing and scheduling practices to reduce wasted journeys and unnecessary mileage.
- Fuel economy programme/training to ensure all possible steps being implemented efficiently and recorded accurately.

Energy Efficiency Best Practice Programme

The Government has produced a comprehensive guide outlining its energy efficiency strategy, and various sustainable transport bodies, including the respected Energy Saving Trust, produce guides and help. The guides cover many aspects of best practice in fuel efficiency, including easy methods of capturing and monitoring data, vehicle specification and maintenance as well as driver training. The Trust can be contacted at:

England
EST England
30, North Colonnade
Canary Wharf
London E14 5GP
Tel: 020 7222 0101

Northern Ireland
EST Northern Ireland
Titanic Suites, 55/59
Adelaide Street
Belfast BT2 8FE
Tel: 028 9072 6006

Scotland
EST Scotland
Second Floor, Ocean Point 1
94, Ocean Drive
Edinburgh EH6 6JH
Tel: 0131 555 7900

Wales
EST Wales
33, Cathedral Road
Cardiff CF11 9HB
Tel: 029 2046 8340

Reducing Fuel Bills

The following are key to improving fuel efficiency:

- Know your numbers. Fuel and mileage data are key to monitoring efficiency.
- Get the best from your fleet.
- Make fuel-efficient purchasing decisions when buying equipment.

A fuel efficiency action plan should include the following components:

- Check that weekly or monthly averages are produced by total distance divided by total fuel used rather than average of the daily averages. Quarterly summaries (using average of the daily averages) have been found to be inaccurate by as much as half a mile per gallon.
- In most cases there is a seasonal pattern to mpg, which peaks in July and August and bottoms out in December and February. It is very important to know this if you are going to test products that claim to improve mpg.
- When you find a large discrepancy in daily mpg, investigate it. Don't just average it or ignore it. Take measures to prevent it from happening again.
- Driver training/assessment consistently achieves better mpg, but it needs a reinforcement mechanism otherwise it will fail.
- Reinforcement mechanisms for fuel-efficient driving can be:
  - simple feedback on a noticeboard;
  - individual letters to drivers; or
  - a fuel bonus (however while an annual bonus can be based on the annual average mpg, shorter-term bonus systems (eg weekly or monthly) should not use the annual average mpg, and remember too that bonuses must not endanger road safety).
- The most senior person with an HGV licence should be trained first.
- Identify the most fuel-efficient vehicles and, if possible, bearing in mind other operational factors, place them on the operations or routes that use the most fuel.
- Think of aerodynamics. For example, ensure that the gap between the back of the cab and the front of the trailer is minimized to reduce aerodynamic

resistance. Tippers with easy sheets should have them closed when empty to prevent the airflow hitting the inside of the tailboard.

- If adjustable air deflectors are fitted, get the drivers to adjust them for maximum effect. If the deflector is too low, you will see a tidemark on the front of the trailer.
- Specify the correct bodywork – it should be no higher or wider than the job requires.
- Monitor maintenance records – poor mpg and short brake-lining life are good indicators of a driving style that wastes fuel.
- When buying new vehicles, calculate which is best for fuel over the life of the vehicle. Is there a better residual at the end of the vehicle's life from a larger engine, or are there reduced fuel costs from a smaller engine that is just as capable of doing the job?
- Specify trailers or bodywork with rounded leading edges (minimum 200 mm radius) or with curved roofs.
- Aerodynamic aids may not be cost-effective on vehicles that do not undertake long, high-speed journeys as part of their regular work.
- Beware of claims made for aerodynamic equipment tested at 56 mph and translating the saving to your vehicle(s). Aerodynamics is highly sensitive to speed. As a rough guide, calculate the average speed of your vehicle(s) and ask for test results conducted at that speed.
- Specify and activate an engine speed limiter. (In some vehicles these are a legal requirement.)
- When buying a second-hand vehicle, take it for a test drive and note the engine speed at 56 mph. If the vehicle is being purchased for medium- or long-distance work, you do not want to purchase a vehicle that is geared for local work. If you get this wrong, you will end up cruising at too high an engine speed and subsequently wasting a lot of fuel.
- When purchasing a new vehicle, get the manufacturer to provide free driver training. Most do, so take advantage of it.

Digital Communications and Technology

23

Never before has there been a more powerful influence on transport operations than the effect of digital technology. The pace of the digital revolution quickens daily and even more so in the sector's response to the COVID-19 pandemic. The fleet sector isn't new to technology though – telematics, tachographs and fleet management software are deeply entrenched in transport operations and even government services are now digital. The Government Digital Service has led to automated driver licence checking, paperless vehicle tax, DVSA VOL, Earned Recognition and remote enforcement.

Instant communications are a 21st-century expectation. Whether it's routing, scheduling, tracking, consignment notes, walkaround checks, defect reporting or even the driver's handbook – the digitized workplace is the new norm for transport operations.

Information Management Systems

The two main information management systems used in transport and logistics operations are the Transport Management System, which deals with the day-to-day processes of planning, execution and post-processing of consignments; and the Fleet Management System, which focuses solely on vehicle asset management and its visibility.

Transport Management System

The Transport Management System (TMS) is operations planning software that optimizes pickup/delivery routes and automated dispatching of tasks, and provides real-time visibility on job fulfilment. Most TMSs are equipped to handle consignment planning, execution, post-processing and reporting metrics. Planning will conduct, or integrate with, route optimization and scheduling for each vehicle in the fleet. Execution is the automated dispatch to drivers providing documentation, vehicle and driver tracking, and electronic proof-of-delivery via mobile communication device. Post-processing automates physical administrative work such as invoicing, billing, customer feedback and consolidating documentation. Finally, reporting provides a live dashboard, and automated KPI reports for operations, customer service and account managers help them make more informed decisions.

Fleet Management System

The Fleet Management System (FMS) is asset management software that generally exchanges information between a vehicle and the transport office. Information can also be transmitted from and to drivers and maintenance staff. While specific FMS features vary dependent on the service provider, its main purpose is to gather, store, process, monitor, report on and export information about the vehicle fleet. A constant stream of data is collected in a vehicle via its telematics and sent over a mobile network. Depending on how advanced the FMS is, a typical system will track the physical location of the vehicle, perform vehicle diagnostics and monitor the lifecycle of a vehicle. Some systems can improve security and control by immobilizing vehicles if they're stolen. The FMS can also be used as an office planning tool, keeping track and records of vehicle maintenance, safety inspections, annual tests, tax and insurance.

Digital routing and scheduling systems are FMSs that use mapping algorithms to optimize routes. Inputs include delivery addresses, order volumes, time windows, vehicle sizes and driver shifts. The result is an immediate transport routing plan that is compliant, cost-effective and efficient, meeting customer delivery requirements and making best use of available resources. Historical data can also be used to carry out what-if scenario exercises to inform resource planning, such as using larger vehicles or smaller vehicles, or adjusting delivery frequency.

Mobile Communications Devices

The fundamental tool in a digital operation is the mobile communication device. Devices can be smartphones, tablets, personal digital assistants (PDAs) or satnavs, completely mobile or fitted in the vehicle. While they provide the benefits of instant communications and visibility of the operation, they also present risks.

Safety Policy

Operators must ensure that drivers issued with mobile communication devices are not distracted, they exercise proper control of the vehicle and have full view of the road and traffic ahead. Key to this is not causing or permitting a driver to use a hand-held communication device while driving. A company policy should be in place covering the use of mobile communications devices while driving. The policy should cover two main areas:

- unlawful use of hand-held mobile communication devices whilst driving;
- the responsibilities of office staff making, receiving and ending calls to and from drivers.

The only exception to these rules is to call 999 or 112 in a genuine emergency when it is unsafe or impractical to stop.

Consideration should also be given to any conditions of use for hands-free mobile communication devices, such as safe stowage, field of view, length of calls and any restrictions on making and receiving personal calls. It is the driver's responsibility to remain in full control of the vehicle and not get distracted from driving. If hands-free mobile communication devices are permitted in an operation, their use should be fully risk assessed.

PDAs

PDAs connect a driver and driver functions with the operating centre and often the customer. Driver tasks and schedule can be on the device within seconds. Drivers can accept new jobs, record track and trace, read barcodes and record signatures. They have GPS tracking, allowing operators to geographically view the fleet and its activity. They help operators respond and make business decisions instantly and accurately. PDAs can integrate with most transport and fleet management systems and can be loaded with a range of apps and functions.

Digital Driver Walkaround Checks

Digital driver walkaround check systems store a complete record of a driver's daily safety check and enable instant defect reporting. They allow photographs of defects to be added to a check, which can be viewed on the device and within its reporting system. Drivers' safety checks can be completed manually through the app or electronically by scanning QR codes placed around the vehicle. If the driver identifies a defect, they send it electronically to the operator who then schedules the relevant repairs. Any systems used should be checked as to whether they meet DVSA guidelines on walkaround checks.

Digital Driver Handbook

The DVSA advises that drivers should have their responsibilities documented as 'instructions in writing'; the common method for providing this is through a driver handbook. With printed documents outdating quickly, a digital driver handbook ensures availability of the most up-to-date information, policies, safe operating procedures, toolbox talks and regular communications on current topics and campaigns. Digital driver handbooks range from the more straightforward PDF documents loaded into tablets or smartphones, through to mobile apps which record and monitor drivers' progress, knowledge and understanding.

Satellite Navigation Systems (Satnavs)

Standard satnavs don't account for larger vehicles in terms of their height, width, length and weight, particularly in terms of road restrictions. There are also other restrictions not included in standard systems, such as the Safer Lorry Scheme, LLCS and CAZs.

HGV-specific satnavs are available and have a range of features designed for larger vehicles, and provide turn-by-turn navigation instructions to drivers. Many new vehicles come factory fitted with a navigation device, but when selecting a retrofit navigation device for an HGV, operators must ensure the mapping and routing software includes HGV restriction data. Company policies and instructions to drivers should also prohibit the use of standard satnavs in HGVs.

Tachograph Analysis

The digital tachograph is an important compliance tool, but it also collects, stores and makes available extremely valuable data, including vehicle speed, distance travelled, driver activity, and events such as speeding, driving without a driver card, errors and tampering. It also logs information on enforcement checks. Data are stored as a file that can be downloaded and imported into tachograph analysis software. Tachograph analysis software services help manage tachograph data to identify driver infringements and enable transport managers to take action to ensure drivers' hours and working time compliance.

Online Services

Driver Licence Checking

The DVLA provides an online driver licence-checking service (for licences issued in England, Wales or Scotland). Drivers can view or share their driving licence information with their employer by creating a licence 'check code'. This service provides information on driving licence categories, licence codes and penalty points or disqualifications. The check code generated is valid for 21 days. To use this service, drivers will need their driving licence number, National Insurance number and the postcode on their driving licence. There are also commercial driving licence-checking services available which keep operators fully informed of driver licence risk factors and compliance issues.

Driver CPC Recording and Evidencing System

The Driver CPC Recording and Evidencing (R&E) system is the DVSA central training record database service for UK vocational driving licence holders. JAUPT-approved training providers upload the records of course attendees and their periodic training. To record a driver's training hours on the R&E system, the training provider must upload the course details and the driver's licence number within five days of course completion. The upload fee for training is £8.75 for seven hours of training per driver, and no VAT is charged. Training can only count towards the driver's 35 hours once it has been validated and the DVSA has received payment. Data held within the R&E system informs the online Driver CPC enquiry service.

Online Driver CPC Enquiry

The DVSA provides an enquiry online service for Driver CPC periodic training records. This service is used to check how many Driver CPC periodic training hours a driver has completed, which courses they have attended and when the next Driver CPC qualification card is due to be issued. Drivers can also create a temporary password for employers to view their Driver CPC records. Temporary passwords are valid for 21 days.

MOT, Annual Test and Tax Checking

The DVLA provides an online service to check the MOT, annual test and tax status of a vehicle. Enter a vehicle's details to see whether it has an MOT or annual test certificate and when it expires, whether a vehicle is taxed and when it expires, or whether a vehicle is SORN. There is a separate DVSA service to check the MOT and annual test history of a vehicle, including whether it passed or failed, the mileage recorded when it was tested, where each test was done and what parts failed at each test, and if any parts had minor problems. You can also check if a vehicle has outstanding manufacturer recalls.

Vehicle Insurance Checking

The Motor Insurance Database (MID) provides insurance information about a vehicle. Any person checking the insurance details of a vehicle must be the registered keeper, owner, insured party or driver of that vehicle. It is an offence to wrongfully obtain insurance information without any of these reasons. There is separate access to MID to enable individuals to conduct vehicle insurance checks in the event of a road traffic collision. MID information is not proof of insurance. More information on this service is at ownvehicle.askmid.com.

Vehicle Operator Licensing

Vehicle Operator Licensing is a DVSA service that can be used by O-Licence applicants and holders, transport managers and DVSA examiners. Using VOL, operators can apply for and apply to make changes to O-Licences. Registration and login are required. Also, DVSA enforcement staff have access to live data from VOL at the roadside; when a vehicle is stopped they're able to instantly check if it's properly licensed.

Transport Office Portal

Transport Office Portal (TOP) is a DVSA service that can be used by O-Licence holders and transport managers. Using TOP, operators can view the DVSA's online report services, which include vehicle annual test histories, roadside check reports and the OCRS. Registration and login are required using the O-Licence number. On registration, the DVSA checks that the details match the operator licence records, and within five working days the DVSA will send a membership and confirmation letter by post, with information on how to use TOP.

Electronic Service Delivery for Abnormal Loads (ESDAL)

ESDAL is a DfT service. It is managed under protocol by Highways England as it covers the whole of the GB road network. It is a database and mapping service enabling operators to provide a notification and planned route for AILs. ESDAL also informs which authorities may need to be notified about the route and can be accessed by structure authorities, highway authorities and the police. To use ESDAL, operators need to register and applications can take two to three working days to be processed.

New Computerised Transit System

The New Computerised Transit System (NCTS) is an online system that traders must use to submit union transit and Transports Internationaux Routiers (TIR) declarations to HMRC. Operators need a Government Gateway user ID and password to sign in to the service. NCTS processes the declaration and controls the transit movement. It is used by the UK, EU member states and signatories to the Common Transit Convention. Common Transit countries are the EFTA countries.

The TIR procedure is used for transit operations that begin, end or transit a third (non-EU) country. You'll also have to declare such goods to the NCTS for any part of the journey taking place within the UK and the EU.

Intelligent Transport Systems

Intelligent transport systems (ITS) is a generic term used across all modes of transport. It uses technology to make transport networks more efficient, safer and smarter. In road transport, typical ITS functions include:

- smart motorways and variable speed limit;
- variable message signs (VMS);
- on-board route and traffic information;
- traffic control and enforcement;
- digital speed and average speed cameras;
- electronic road charging and toll collection;
- dynamic traffic lights.

Data Protection (GDPR)

The Data Protection Act 2018 is the UK's implementation of the General Data Protection Regulation. Unless the Data Protection Act 2018 is repealed or amended after the Brexit transition period, the UK's rules on data protection will remain in line with GDPR.

The ICO (Information Commissioner's Office) recommends that organizations should follow a 12-step approach to data protection:

1 Awareness. This focuses on the need for decision makers within organizations to be aware of the changes in order to properly assess their impact.

2 Holding Information. The new rules require organizations to hold accurate files on personal data held and that these files and the way in which they are compiled should be properly recorded as company policy.

3 Communication. When collecting personal data, organizations need to make sure that they explain who they are, what they want the data for and how long they intend to hold them. This ensures legality and gives individuals the right to make complaints to the ICO.

4 Individuals' Rights. Individuals have the right to know the format of the data, a right to access them, a right to have them amended or deleted and a right to object to how they may be used.

5 Access. Organizations holding personal data cannot charge a fee for access and they have one month to comply with a request for access. If a request is not granted, they have one month to explain to the individual concerned why this is so.

6 Data Processing. Processing must be lawful and only done with the consent of the individual; to do otherwise is illegal. Organizations also need to ensure that their data processing procedures comply with GDPR.

7 Consent. Organizations must gain and manage consent to hold personal data. Consent must be given freely and openly.

8 Children. Under GDPR rules a child of 16 can give consent. This is reduced to 13 in the UK. This may not apply often, but could apply where temporary employment is offered over school holidays, etc.

9 Data Protection Breaches. Breaches must be detected, reported and investigated and notice given to the ICO, within 72 hours, of any breach where a risk to the 'rights and freedoms of individuals' is possible. The individuals concerned must also be notified. Fines are levelled both for breaches and for failure to report them.

10 Data Protection and Data Protection Impact Assessments (DPIA). While data protection is a legal requirement under GDPR, impact assessments are also mandatory. Organizations with 'high risk' data being protected may need to contact the ICO for advice on DPIAs.

11 Data Protection Officers (DPOs). In organizations where high levels of data are held, there should be a DPO nominated to have overall responsibility for data protection. This person can be either an employee or an external consultant.

12 International Aspects. Organizations operating in more than one EU member state must appoint a lead authority where they have their main activity.

The Department for Digital, Culture, Media and Sport (DCMS) has the overall responsibility for data protection, but information should be sought from the ICO at GOV.UK, by calling 0303 123 1113 or emailing casework@ico.org.uk.

Operators must pay a data protection fee to the ICO if they are processing personal data such as driver licence details. This is an annual fee and depends on the size and turnover of the organization. It's £40 or £60 for most organizations, including charities and small and medium-sized businesses. The fee can be up to £2,900 for businesses that employ many people and have a high annual turnover.

CCTV

Rules relating to CCTV are directly linked to data protection. All CCTV systems need to be accompanied by signs clearly stating that they are fitted and in operation and you should also note that if a person who has been filmed on CCTV requests to see the footage that was taken, you must show it to them within 40 days; a charge may be requested.

Transport and the Environment 24

One of the most important and widely discussed issues in transport continues to be the impact the industry has on the environment. The environment features in almost every aspect of a transport operation, from the siting of vehicle depots to the routing of HGVs, tailpipe emissions and noise, and the disposal or recyclability of vehicles and loads and waste.

Road transport is a major source of air pollution that harms human health and the environment. Vehicles emit a range of pollutants, including nitrogen oxides and particulate matter. There are limits for the maximum amount of air pollution people should breathe, but urban populations in the UK are exposed to toxic levels above these limits. See Chapter 10 for details on clean air zones and London's Low and Ultra-Low Emissions Zones.

Impact of Transport

Transport impacts on the environment in a variety of ways; some are more distinctly controllable by fleet operators than others; some produce more tangible benefits both to the vehicle operator and to the community than others; but it has to be remembered that, inevitably, any form of transport, serving any and every need imaginable, has an adverse impact on the environment. There is no such thing as a totally environmentally acceptable form or means of transport. What there can be, however, are means and systems of transport which are more 'friendly' towards the environment, and which can be controlled and managed in such a way that the environmental impact is minimized.

Some of the main areas of environmental impact are as follows.

Principal Emissions

Balancing a transport operation with the need to protect the environment is a challenge. There are two major impacts HGVs have on the environment: greenhouse gas – CO_2; and air pollution – NO_2, NO_x, PM:

- CO2 Carbon Dioxide: Principal greenhouse gas related to climate change.
- NO2 Nitrogen Dioxide: A gas formed by combustion, identified as an air pollutant harmful to human health. The European limit values measure concentrations of NO2 in the air.
- NOx Nitrogen Oxides: A generic term for Nitrogen Dioxide (NO2) and Nitrogen Monoxide (NO), which can form NOx in the atmosphere. Euro standards set limits for vehicle emissions of NOx.
- PM Particulate Matter: A mixture of various solid and liquid particles of various chemical compositions suspended in the air. PM is rated by the size of harmful particles:
  - PM10 Particulate Matter;
  - PM2.5 Particulate Matter.

Vehicle Depots

- Size, siting, access and egress
- Noise, fumes, vibration and light emitted
- Obstruction
- Disposal of waste
- Recycling levels
- Energy use
- Pollution
- Material handling equipment (MHE) operation
- Times of operation

Vehicle Operations

- Engine, exhaust, tyre, body and loading/unloading noise
- Smoke, fumes, gases, spray emitted
- Fuel/oil consumption
- Visual impact
- Driver standards
- Routes and schedules
- Load and vehicle utilization
- Waste and general recycling
- Vehicle and component recyclability

Oil Storage

The Control of Pollution (Oil Storage) Regulations 2001 apply to operators who store more than 200 litres of oil on any site that is located near to a river, waterway, borehole or even close to the water table. These regulations require the person with custody of the oil to carry out such works or to take such precautions or actions as are necessary to minimize the risk of oil-related water pollution. The regulations specify technical details relating to the storage facility, particularly its bund base and wall, which must have a capacity of 110 per cent of the capacity of the tank and be checked regularly, along with the pipework, valves and gauges. It is essential that the tank or its pipework are not positioned where there is a risk from vehicle impact, especially when reversing. To prevent oil-contaminated water entering the public surface water sewer, an 'interceptor' should be incorporated into the operating centre's internal drainage system.

Possible Solutions

Transport managers and small fleet operators are undoubtedly limited in the steps they can individually take towards improving the environment, but this does not mean they should take no steps at all. Simple measures are available to them which will make a valuable contribution. The following list provides just a few examples.

In the Depot

- Examine the way that waste material is stored, recycled and disposed of.
- Ensure that controlled waste (see Chapter 20) is correctly and safely stored on site and then handed over to licensed disposal contractors.
- Avoid burning of waste, which can cause pollution and lead to complaints.
- Ensure that recyclable material is identified and saved for proper disposal – including waste paper and packing materials from office and stores.
- Take steps to ensure that vehicle washing does not result in dirty (ie grease-laden) water draining on to neighbouring properties as well as into sewage systems.
- Ensure that oil and fuel spillages do not pollute drains and are cleaned up immediately.
- Consider the use of recycled products such as paper for administrative uses and packing.
- Undertake regular depot clean-up campaigns (in particular, ensuring that the outside appearance of the depot is 'environmentally friendly' to local residents, business visitors and others).

- Consider involving customers and suppliers in developing more environmentally acceptable ways of working.
- Ensure noise from reversing alarms, site music and Tannoy systems and vehicle in-cab radios, etc, is not excessive or generated outside of normal working hours.
- If possible, also try to engage local residents and businesses and develop discourse.

On the Vehicle

- Ensure that legal requirements regarding noise, smoke, exhaust emissions and spray suppression are fully complied with.
- Take steps to economize on fuel consumption (see Chapter 22).
- Invest in the latest alternative-fuel technology.
- Provide driver training to ensure fuel-efficient driving.
- Fit body skirts and air deflectors and use aerodynamic 'curve top' trailers and bodies.
- Specify lifting and/or steering axles, where possible.
- Ensure that drivers obey rules about parking and causing obstruction with their vehicles, and are aware of the problems of visual intrusion, noise and vibration on domestic properties (contravention of these matters can jeopardize O-Licences – see Chapter 1).
- Route vehicles and plan journeys to avoid congestion – ensure full utilization of vehicles to avoid extra or unnecessary journeys (which add to congestion, air pollution and the operator's own costs).
- Fit rubber 'buffers' to tail-lifts and roller doors, and switches to reversing alarms to reduce noise during the 'silent hours'.
- Consider the visual impact of vehicles in terms of their general appearance and livery (change aggressive liveries to present a 'softer' image).

In the Community

- Consider the sponsorship of local community efforts to improve the environment and encourage staff to undertake environmental protection projects.
- Make it known that local residents are able and welcome to discuss issues with management.

The International Organization for Standardization (ISO) has developed a set of internationally recognized standards so that businesses can monitor and control the environmental effects of their activities. The key stages in developing an environmental management system in compliance with the ISO 14001 Standard are as follows:

- Draw up an environmental policy.
- Carry out environmental impact assessments (EIAs) as a part of expansion and new-build projects.
- Set targets and make plans to achieve those targets.
- Implement the plans and ensure that information is communicated to all relevant staff.
- Measure results and compare these to the set targets, take corrective action where necessary and implement a system for regular reviews of the policy.
- Invite local community members to visit the depot and discuss their concerns (work with them, not in isolation).

Alternative Fuels

The UK has an ambition to reach net zero emissions by 2050. In November 2020, as part of the Prime Minister's Ten Point Plan for a Green Industrial Revolution, the Government announced that it would end the sale of new petrol and diesel cars and vans from 2030, with all new cars and vans being zero emission at the tailpipe from 2035.

At the time of writing (September 2021), the Government was consulting on when to end the sale of new non-zero emission HGVs in the UK and whether to increase the GVW for zero emission and alternatively fueled HGVs completing domestic journeys.

Some of the main alternative cleaner fuels available are as follows.

Battery Electric

Pure battery electric vehicles (EV) are powered entirely by an electric motor using energy stored in a battery.

Current models are best suited for city or suburban driving although this is changing as battery technology improves.

Drivers can charge vehicles at home provided they have access to off-road parking and a charging point or an on-street charging bay. BEVs have zero tailpipe emissions, although if charged from the UK grid there will be emissions associated with the electricity generation.

Hydrogen Fuel Cell

Hydrogen is used to generate electricity through an electrochemical process in a fuel cell.

The electricity drives an electric motor and the only waste output is water. Fuel cells can be retrofitted to battery electric vehicles. The OEM hydrogen fuel cell market in the UK is emerging very slowly.

Hydrogen Diesel Hybrid

If you burn hydrogen (H_2), you get water (H_2O). It is possible to construct a dedicated hydrogen-powered internal combustion engine.

However, the ICE engine is not very efficient when run on hydrogen and the vehicle's range is limited by the size of the hydrogen storage tank. A viable alternative is a hydrogen–diesel hybrid and there are companies who offer dual-fuel conversions.

Compressed Natural Gas

Compressed Natural Gas (CNG) vehicles use mains gas and can be refuelled from an on-site refuelling facility if the local gas network can supply the required pressure.

CNG is stored on the vehicle in pressurised cylinders and used in a spark ignition engine. CNG is a fossil fuel but biomethane is available which is a renewable and sustainable version.

Biomethane is produced from organic waste and injected into the national gas grid in the same volume that you are drawing methane from the grid.

Liquefied Natural Gas

Liquefied Natural Gas (LNG) vehicles have achieved steady growth in recent years and are already very popular in Europe. At least three major truck manufacturers already offer, or plan to offer, gas-powered vehicles. Retrofit conversions are also possible.

Biodiesel

Biodiesel can be a sustainable and renewable source of energy if it is made using waste products such as vegetable oils and fats. First-generation biofuels which involved growing crops to produce fuel should not be used. Instead, only biodiesel made from waste products, such as used cooking oil, should be used.

Fuel suppliers can blend biodiesel into regular diesel up to seven per cent, known as B7, and that is compatible with any vehicle.

Higher blends such as B20 and B30 are widely available and can be used in most engines requiring no modifications. Hydrotreated Vegetable Oil (HVO) can be used in blends up to 100 per cent.

Always contact the vehicle manufacturer before using a high-blend biofuel.

International Operations

25

Although the UK has withdrawn from the European Union, it remains a member of many collective international agreements, such as EFTA, EEA, AETR and UNECE.

The Brexit transition ended on 31 December 2020 and the UK dropped out of the European Single Market and Customs Union. On 30 December 2020, after eight months of negotiation, the EU–UK Trade and Cooperation Agreement (TCA) was signed, which has been applied provisionally since 1 January 2021. The TCA provides for free trade in goods and limited mutual market access in services, but does not allow for the free movement of UK citizens into and between EU member states.

Most EU regulations are incorporated into UK statute as part of the European Union (Withdrawal) Act 2018. So the basic rule book for transport operators remains. Drivers require passports, driving licences, Driver CPC and have to adhere to drivers' hours rules – whilst vehicles must be type approved, taxed, tested, insured and roadworthy. However, the process for exporting goods to EU member states has seen a significant change.

This chapter includes the new rules and latest information for conducting international road haulage operations.

Operators

Operator Licensing

UK operators undertaking international journeys continue to require a Standard International Operator Licence. The Community Licence for transporting goods to or through the EU, Liechtenstein, Norway and Switzerland has been replaced with the 'UK Licence for the Community'. It is issued with the International Operator Licence and a certified copy must be carried on all vehicles when operating internationally.

Transport Manager Certificate of Professional Competence

The UK Transport Manager CPC continues to be valid for transport managers working for UK operators.

Drivers

Driving Licences and International Driving Permits

Drivers must have the correct category of driving licence for the vehicle they are driving. For drivers with photocard driving licences issued in the UK, an International Driving Permit (IDP) is not required to drive in the EU, Switzerland, Iceland or Liechtenstein. An IDP may be required to drive in other countries, if a paper driving licence is issued or if a licence has been issued in Gibraltar, Guernsey, Jersey or the Isle of Man. IDPs can be purchased over the counter at many UK Post Office branches.

Driver Certificate of Professional Competence

Drivers require a Driver Certificate of Professional Competence (CPC) in order to operate in the UK and EU. Drivers need to carry their Driver CPC qualification card while driving in the EU. A UK Driver CPC is valid for drivers of all journeys that UK operators are entitled to undertake, whether as a result of an agreement with the EU or on the basis of ECMT permits.

UK legislation currently allows EU drivers working for UK operators to continue doing so with a Driver CPC awarded by EU member states. If such drivers wish to have long-term certainty on their ability to work for UK operators, they should exchange their EU Driver CPC for a UK Driver CPC.

ADR Qualification Card

Drivers of vehicles carrying dangerous goods must hold an ADR qualification card valid for the correct category of dangerous goods they are carrying.

Visas, Passports and Identity Cards

Drivers must have at least six months on a UK passport to travel to the EU. A visa is not required for travel in the EU providing drivers do not spend more than 90 days in the EU within any 180-day period. Visa rules for each country are listed on the travel advice pages at GOV.UK.

Vehicles

Motor Insurance Green Card

An international certificate of motor insurance is required for vehicles operating in the 48 countries that are part of the Green Card scheme. Green Cards are issued by the insurance company insuring the vehicle or trailer.

Vehicle Registration Documents

Drivers must carry a vehicle registration document when driving abroad. This can be either:

- the vehicle log book (V5C); or
- a vehicle on hire certificate (VE103) to show the vehicle is allowed to be used abroad.

National Identifier

A national identifier (GB sticker) must be fixed to the rear of the vehicle and trailer, unless the vehicle and trailer registration plates includes the GB identifier on its own or with the Union Flag. Vehicles operated in Spain, Cyprus or Malta must display a GB sticker no matter what is on the registration plate. UK-registered vehicles are not required to display a GB sticker in Ireland.

Cross-Border Readiness

New rules are in place and new documentation is required to move goods between the UK and EU. Operators should use the 'Check an HGV is ready to cross the border' service to check if all documentation is in order to cross the border between Great Britain and the EU. Documentation is required even if a vehicle is not carrying goods. This service has replaced the previous Smart Freight service. For countries without a customs control system in place, a pre-notification procedure applies.

Inland Border Facilities

Inland border facilities (IBFs) are UK Government sites where customs and document checks can take place away from port locations. IBFs act as a Government Office of Departure (for outbound journeys) and as Government Office of Destination (for inbound journeys). Operators can start and end journeys at IBFs when moving goods in and out of the UK and checks for the following movements are conducted:

- ATA carnet – Admission Temporaire/Temporary Admission;
- TIR carnet – Transport Internationaux Routiers;
- CTC – Common Transit Convention;
- CITES – Convention on International Trade in Endangered Species of Wild Fauna and Flora.

Vehicles may also be directed to an IBF because they are not border ready or for a physical inspection of their load and or documentation. A full list of UK IBF locations and their functions is in Table 25.1

Table 25.1 UK IBF locations and their functions

IBF site	Location	Functions
Sevington inland border facility (inbound and outbound)	Mersham, Ashford TN25 6GE	Start transit movement (Office of Departure) End transit movement (Office of Destination) ATA carnets stamp CITES Traffic management If Sevington IBF is closed, Waterbrook will be made available as a contingency site
Ebbsfleet (outbound)	International Way Ebbsfleet Valley DA10 1EB	Start Transit movement (Office of Departure) ATA and TIR carnets stamp CITES licence check defra prioritization (seafood and day-old chicks) Physical checks and inspections
North Weald Airfield (outbound)	North Weald Airfield Merlin Way North Weald Bassett Epping CM16 6GB	Start Transit movement (Office of Departure) ATA and TIR carnets stamp Physical checks and inspections
Birmingham Airport (inbound and outbound)	Birmingham International Airport BHX Car Park 6 B26 3QY	Start Transit movement (Office of Departure) End Transit movement (Office of Destination) ATA and TIR carnets stamp Physical checks and inspections

Table 25.1 *continued*

IBF site	Location	Functions
Warrington (inbound and outbound)	Barley Castle Lane Appleton Thorn Warrington WA4 4SR	Start Transit movement (Office of Departure) End Transit movement (Office of Destination) ATA and TIR carnets stamp Physical checks and inspections
Dover Western Docks (inbound)	Dover Western Docks Lord Warden Square Dover CT17 9DN	End Transit movements (Office of Destination) ATA and TIR carnets stamp CITES licence check Physical checks and inspections
Stop 24 (inbound)	Folkestone Services Junction 11 M20 Hythe CT21 4BL	End transit movement (Office of Destination) ATA and TIR carnets stamp Physical checks and inspections
Holyhead – Port of Holyhead (inbound and outbound)	Port of Holyhead Holyhead LL65 1DJ	Office of Transit CITES checks
Holyhead – RoadKing Truckstop (inbound and outbound)	RoadKing Truckstop Parc Cybi Kingsland Holyhead LL65 2YQ	Start Transit movement (Office of Departure) End Transit movement (Office of Destination) ATA carnet stamp Booking is required for these services At least 24 hours before due to arrive: let Border Force know when expect to arrive Tell Border Force if transporting live animals Notify Border Force of arrival by emailing BFHolyhead@HomeOffice.gov.uk Get ready before travelling to Holyhead – use an Authorised Consignor/Consignee to start or end transit movement

Trader Responsibilities

It is the trader's or consignor's responsibility to make customs declarations and provide the haulage company and driver with the correct documents. This can be done directly or via a third party, for example a freight forwarder, logistics company or customs agent.

Operator Responsibilities

The operator must ensure their driver has all the necessary customs information and documents and other paperwork. Drivers must also know what documents to present at each stage of the journey, including:

- on-road pre-departure inspections – checks to demonstrate border readiness;
- at ports or train terminals;
- at customs posts.

Driver Responsibilities

As each movement of goods is both an export and import movement, drivers must carry the relevant documentation for the duration of the journey. This also includes information and documentation necessary to meet different EU member state requirements. It is important that drivers know what information and documentation is needed, and where, when and how documentation will be checked.

Drivers travelling to the EU must also be made aware of additional restrictions to personal imports. This includes personal goods containing meat or dairy (eg a ham and cheese sandwich). Find out more on the rules and exemptions on personal imports to the EU at EUROPA.EU.

Kent Access Permit (KAP)

A KAP is no longer needed to enter Kent.

Ways to Move Goods Across a Border

There are four ways to transport goods across a border. These are:

- CTC – Common Transit Convention;
- ATA – Admission Temporaire/Temporary Admission;
- TIR – Transports Internationaux Routiers;
- Pre-notification.

The consignor selects the most appropriate method dependent on the type of consignment.

CTC Convention

The CTC is used to ease the movement of goods between or through any common transit countries. If a consignor arranges for goods to move into the EU under the CTC, the driver must be given either:

- a Transit Accompanying Document (TAD) from the consignor, and be informed that the movement has been released to the transit procedure and they can proceed to the place of exit from GB;
- a Local Reference Number (LRN) or a TAD that hasn't been released to the transit procedure, and be informed to present the goods and the LRN or TAD to the UK Border Force at a nominated UK office of departure – the goods will then be released, and a TAD will be given to the driver.

The exporter or agent is responsible for updating the operator and driver on the status of the TAD. Consignors moving goods under CTC must ensure that the appropriate safety and security declarations are made in both the EU and in GB where required.

At the EU border, the TAD must be presented by the driver to the EU customs authorities in line with the EU's procedures. After the EU border, the driver must present the TAD at an EU office of destination or to an authorized consignee, where the transit procedure will be closed. The goods will then be subject to EU import procedures.

If a consignor arranges for goods to move into GB under the CTC, the operator must follow the same procedure for moving goods into the EU but instructing the driver to present documentation to the relevant EU customs authority.

After the UK border, operators must follow either the paper-based process or the Goods Vehicle Movement Service (GVMS) process to complete the transit movement on entry to GB. Which process applies will depend on the location the goods arrive at.

Consignors must provide the operator with a TAD MRN for each CTC consignment. The reference number proves that the driver has the right declaration to move goods under transit. The paper TAD must also travel with the goods moving via transit.

Operators must use GVMS to link all the TAD reference numbers into one GMR for each trailer movement. They can use GVMS in two ways:

- a direct link from their own system into the GVMS;
- through the Government Gateway at GOV.UK.

For each trailer movement, operators or drivers update the GMR with the correct VRN for accompanied movements or TRN for unaccompanied movements. The

VRN/TRN can be updated to cater for any changes but must be correct when the GMR is presented to the cross-Channel carrier at the point of departure.

Drivers will not be able to board international ferries or Eurotunnel without a complete GMR. They must not proceed to the border:

- before all the necessary references are added into a GMR;

- if any declaration reference has not been accepted onto the GMR.

Drivers must present the GMR to the cross-Channel carrier on arrival at the point of departure to show that they have the necessary evidence to legally move goods. They must comply with instructions issued by border authorities to proceed to a specific location for checks as required.

ATA Carnet

ATA Admission Temporaire/Temporary Admission carnets are international customs documents used for the temporary export or import of goods. If a consignor arranges for goods to move under the ATA into the EU, the driver must:

- be issued the ATA carnet document by the consignor;

- be instructed to take the goods and the ATA carnet to the UK Border Force at UK office of departure;

- check that the EXS declaration requirements have been met for the movement and for the country the goods are being moved to.

At the EU border, the driver must present the ATA carnet and ensure it is stamped by the EU customs authorities in line with EU procedures. After the EU border, the driver must give the ATA carnet to the consignee on delivery.

If the consignor arranges for the goods to move under the ATA Convention into GB, the driver must obtain the ATA carnet document, present it to EU customs authorities and ensure it is stamped in line with the EU's procedures. At the UK border, the driver must follow the port's local procedures for the presentation of an ATA carnet.

TIR Carnet

TIR carnets are international customs documents used for the transport of goods across borders. The TIR system allows customs officials to pack and seal goods before they are transported outside the UK. This means that the load will not need to be opened and inspected by customs officials at border crossings.

If a consignor arranges for goods to move into the EU under TIR the operator must hold a TIR authorization and the vehicle must hold a TIR approval certificate for transporting goods under customs seal. The operator must:

- give the TIR carnet to the driver;
- ensure that arrangements have been made, to declare the movement on the New Computerised Transit System (NCTS) and have the LRN/MRN reference numbers required to present the goods to EU customs officials;
- instruct the driver to take and present the goods and the TIR carnet to the UK office of departure – page 1 of the carnet will be stamped and detached and the vehicle will be sealed;
- instruct the driver to take and present the goods and the TIR carnet to the UK Border Force at a UK office of departure – page 2 of the carnet will be stamped and detached and the vehicle seal will be checked;
- check with the consignor that the EXS and ENS declaration requirements have been met for the movement.

At the EU border, the driver must present the TIR carnet and ensure it is stamped by the EU customs authorities in line with EU procedures. After the EU border, the driver must present the TIR carnet and ensure it is stamped either when the goods leave the customs territory of the EU, at an EU office of destination or at an EU-TIR authorized consignee's premises.

If a consignor arranges for goods to move into GB under TIR the operator must hold a TIR authorization and the vehicle must hold a TIR approval certificate for transporting goods under customs seal. To move goods into GB the operator must follow the same procedure for moving goods into the EU. At the EU border, the driver must present the TIR carnet and ensure it is stamped by the EU customs authorities in line with the EU's procedures.

At the UK border, the driver must follow the port's local procedures for the presentation of the TIR carnet, presenting the TIR carnet to the port customs office. Customs will check the documents, the seal, stamp and detach the relevant page of TIR carnet.

The driver will go to the customs office of destination or TIR authorized consignee's premises to ensure that the TIR carnet is handled. After that, the customs seals can be removed and goods unloaded.

Once a vehicle has completed its journey, either to the EU or GB, the driver must return the TIR carnet to their transport office.

Pre-Notification

The pre-notification procedure applies at locations without customs control systems. If a consignor arranges for goods to move under the pre-notification procedure, the driver must be given all the relevant customs documentation and confirm that:

- the consignor has completed the relevant export procedures;
- the exporter has met all relevant import requirements.

For moving goods from GB, the exporter must complete the EXS declaration. The driver must be told if the goods need to be presented to a UK customs office. Once this has been done, the exporter is given Permission to Progress (P2P) and any additional documentary checks are conducted at the National Clearance Hub. The driver can then collect and take the goods to the GB port or terminal of departure. If the goods are selected to undergo a physical check the P2P process, outlined at the GB customs procedure must be followed.

There is a different customs requirement for controlled goods and non-controlled goods:

- Controlled goods – customs declarations are required for all goods on the controlled goods list and operators must have an MRN.
- Non-controlled goods – the importer can record the movement in their commercial log, and then submit a supplementary declaration to HMRC within six months of the import. Operators must have the consignor's Economic Operator Registration and Identification (EORI) number.

At the EU border, the EU customs procedure and country-specific procedures must be followed.

Safety and Security Declarations

A safety and security declaration (or entry and exit summary declaration) is required for all goods movement types. The legal requirement to submit a declaration lies with the operator transporting the goods into a customs territory. An EORI number is required to make safety and security declarations.

There are two safety and security declarations:

- EXS – Exit Summary Declaration submitted to the customs authority of the country from which the goods are being exported;
- ENS – Entry Summary Declaration submitted to the customs authority of the country of which the consignment is entering into the import control system (ICS).

For goods exported from the UK the EXS data is normally merged with the export customs declaration.

On some routes into the Netherlands and Belgium, the ferry operator performs the ENS procedures on behalf of the operator. Safety and security data must be provided at the time of the booking.

For goods imported to the UK, operators and drivers must provide and produce the ENS declaration. The operator can agree to pass the safety and security requirement onto the consignor but the operator retains legal responsibility:

- for Eurotunnel, ENS declarations submitted at least one hour before arrival;
- for short sea journeys, ENS declarations submitted at least two hours before arrival.

For imports to GB, the submission of the ENS declaration must be made in the new UK safety and security system (S&S GB). S&S GB handles digital communications between customs administrators and carriers and APIs providing declarations, notifications and outcomes are available to link to third-party software.

At the EU border, drivers must have a customs declaration for each consignment from the consignors and consignee (in the EU and the UK). This will be in the form of an MRN (or the consignor's EORI number) and the EU export declaration MRN.

UK and EU Customs Procedures

UK Customs Procedure

When collecting goods for transit to the EU, the driver must be given all customs documents necessary. The exporter must complete the UK export procedures including the combined customs and safety and security EXS declaration. The driver must be informed if the goods are required to be presented to a UK customs office.

Once the exporter has P2P and having completed any additional documentary checks requested by the National Clearance Hub, the driver can collect and take the goods to the GB port or terminal of departure.

If the exporter is told that the goods must undergo a physical check, the driver can collect the goods but must take them to a Designated Export Place (DEP) or to an approved inland location for appropriate checks. Only after P2P is granted following completion of those checks can the driver take the goods to the GB port or terminal of departure.

It is the responsibility of the exporter to inform the operator about the P2P situation. The driver must carry evidence that a UK combined customs and safety and security EXS declaration has been made and they will be required to carry EU import documentation.

At the UK border, authorities will not routinely stop vehicles on their way into the UK to check that they have the correct import customs documents. However, on arrival, UK Border Force officers may stop vehicles to carry out checks for other customs offences, such as breaches of security and smuggling.

EU customs procedure

The driver must have all necessary reference numbers or documents to meet the import requirements of the EU country they are entering. It is the responsibility of the GB exporter, their customs agent and the operator to ensure this is done.

A consignor exporting goods from GB must:

- confirm with the EU importing consignee that all customs requirements have been met;
- provide complete instructions and documentation to the operator and driver, such as the Movement Reference Number (MRN), and hard copies of any licences, permits or certificates;
- ensure the safety and security EXS and ENS declaration requirements have been met for the movement.

At the EU border the driver must follow EU import and border requirements for the country they are entering.

Customs Procedures by Country

There are different procedures for entering the EU dependent on the country of entry. However, once the goods have passed EU customs they can proceed to their final destination.

Entering via France

France uses a smart border system for processing HGVs using ferry and Eurotunnel crossings. It pairs customs declaration data with the vehicle registration number transporting the consignment(s).

At check-in at ferry terminals or at the 'pitstop' at Eurotunnel, the driver will hand in the MRN. The MRN will be scanned and matched with the VRN or TRN. For goods from multiple consignors, either the exporter or the driver can scan all the barcodes from the separate documents, using the Prodouanes app. This will create an MRN envelope. The driver will then only need to present one single MRN from the load they are carrying.

The driver will be informed en-route if:

- they can proceed;
- they need to declare for customs and/or Sanitary and Phytosanitary (SPS) checks;
- there are any problems which need to be addressed before they can continue.

ENS declarations must be made by electronic data interchange. For accompanied freight, the operator makes the ENS declaration entry into the French Import Control System (ICS). For unaccompanied freight, the ferry operator makes the ENS declaration entry into the French ICS.

Entering via The Netherlands

The Netherlands uses a paid- for pre-registration service via Portbase for all customs declaration numbers for UK export and imports. Drivers will not be able to access Dutch terminals if they have not pre-registered via Portbase. The driver must present MRNs at UK check-in.

ENS declarations are also submitted via Portbase at the time of booking the crossing. The submission is completed by the ferry operator for both accompanied and unaccompanied freight.

Entering via Belgium

The Port of Zeebrugge uses the RX/SeaPort eDesk for imports and exports which joins up the data submitted and required by all parties at the Port of Zeebrugge. This can be done manually, through a linked data connection or through customs software. Drivers cannot proceed to the Zeebrugge Terminal if customs declarations have not been pre-notified through the RX/SeaPort e-Desk.

The Port of Antwerp uses the Port Community system C-point for imports and exports. Pre-notification can be lodged by the exporter, the freight forwarder, customs agent or the operator.

In Belgium, the ENS declaration is submitted into the import clearance system via an EDI interface to the Customs Computer Paperless Customs and Excises (PLDA) system. It is submitted by the ferry operator or shipping company for both accompanied and unaccompanied freight.

Entering via Spain

The Spanish ports of Santander and Bilbao are yet to establish a port community system. Whereas the ports in the south of Spain, such as Algeciras Port Authority, use the port community system Teleport 2.0. Operators travelling from GB to Spain should obtain the MRN, log into the carrier system and link the vehicle registration number to the MRN. The system checks the first four digits of the Integrated Tariff of the European Communities (TARIC) code, number of packages and weight.

ENS declarations must be lodged for all consignments. The ferry operator must be satisfied that this requirement has been met before loading will be authorized. For accompanied freight, the haulage operator makes the ENS declaration entry into the Spanish ICS but this doesn't rule out the possibility of a private agreement between the haulage operator and the ferry operator to submit it on their behalf. For unaccompanied freight, the ferry operator makes the ENS declaration entry into the Spanish ICS.

The ferry operator sends the manifest (including references to previous ENS declarations) to the operatives in the Spanish ports. The operatives then send the documents to Aduanas (Spanish customs).

Entering via Ireland

Ireland uses a new Automated Import System (AIS) for EU import declarations. The Irish Revenue Customs RoRo Service provides three functions to facilitate the flow of goods vehicles into and out of Irish ports:

1 Pre-Boarding Notification (PBN) – customs declarations are made in advance of arrival at the port of departure in GB. The PBN is a virtual envelope that links together the details of all the goods being carried on a vehicle. Operators can track the progress of the PBN via the Customs RoRo Service so that they know when to arrive at the terminal and the customs authority provides a single instruction to be followed by the driver on arrival at an Irish port.

2 Channel Look-Up (CLU) – the CLU service provides information on whether a vehicle can directly exit the port or if the goods need to be brought to customs for checking. This information will be made available via the Customs RoRo Service 30 minutes prior to arrival of the ferry into Ireland and can be accessed by anyone in the supply chain.

3 Parking self check-in – drivers whose vehicles have been called for a physical inspection will remain in their vehicle and inform Revenue that the goods are available for inspection using this function. When an examination bay becomes available the driver will receive a text message advising where to attend for inspection.

Using the Customs RoRo Service is a pre-requisite to receiving the PBN, without which access to the ferry will be denied.

Returning from Ireland

All goods being moved from Ireland to GB require an export EXS declaration completed by the exporter and submitted using the existing Automated Entry Processing (AEP) system. The AEP system handles the validation, processing, duty accounting and clearance of customs declarations. For goods exported via RoRo, a Pre-Boarding Notification must be completed prior to arrival at the port of departure in Ireland.

New Registration Rules

As at 2 February 2022

From 2 February 2022, operators need to register the details of HGV journeys within the EU, Iceland, Liechtenstein and Norway before the journey starts.

Journeys must be registered if goods are transported between two points in the EU, Iceland, Liechtenstein and Norway for hire or reward. This means loading goods at one point and unloading them at another point in any of those countries. This type of journey includes:

- cabotage journeys – loading goods in one of these countries and unloading them at a different place in the same country, using a vehicle registered in the UK;
- cross-trade journeys – loading goods in one of these countries and unloading them in a different one of these countries, using a vehicle registered in the UK;
- own-account journeys – moving goods for an operator's own business use between these countries.

Both GB and Northern Ireland operators need to register journeys within Ireland.

Registering the journey is referred to as a 'postings declaration' and there's no fee. The online service is being developed by the EU.

When registering a journey, operators will need:

- O-Licence number;
- transport manager contact details;
- driver names, addresses and driving licence numbers;
- driver employment contract date (or agency contract date);
- driver employment contract type;
- estimated start and end dates of the journey;
- VRM and trailer identification number.

On the journey, drivers must carry a digital or physical copy of the information used to register the journey, in addition to all other documents drivers need for international journeys.

The enforcement authorities in EU countries, Iceland, Liechtenstein and Norway may also ask for:

- copies of the documents that drivers have to carry;
- information about the driver's pay during the journey;
- drivers' hours and working time records.

Information must be uploaded within eight weeks of it being asked for.

As at 21 May 2022

From 21 May 2022, operators of light commercial vehicles need a standard international goods vehicle operator licence to transport goods in the EU, Iceland, Liechtenstein, Norway and Switzerland.

This will apply to you if you're based in Great Britain or Northern Ireland, transporting goods for hire or reward and using a:

- van exceeding 2,500kg gvw;
- van or car towing a trailer exceeding 2.5 tonnes gtw.

These vehicles can have a new O-Licence application or be added to an existing O-Licence.

UK Licence for the Community

Operators need a UK Licence for the Community if journeys for hire or reward are made within the EU, Liechtenstein, Norway and Switzerland. Operators must have a standard international vehicle operator licence for Great Britain or standard international vehicle operator licence for Northern Ireland to apply for a UK Licence for the Community.

The UK Licence for the Community has replaced the EU Community Licence. It's a single permit that covers trips between these countries. It also allows transit traffic through these countries to and from non-EU countries – but extra permits may be needed for journeys to non-EU countries.

The UK Licence for the Community also allows drivers to carry out a limited number of cabotage journeys inside an EU country or cross-trade journeys between two EU countries.

There are no limits on the number of available licences.

Operators that had an EU Community Licence before 2021 received a replacement UK Licence for the Community by 31 December 2020. Old EU Community Licences should be destroyed.

For further information, email the DVSA at notifications@vehicle-operator-licensing.service.gov.uk quoting the relevant operator licence number.

UK Licence for the Community Exemptions

It is unclear whether transport operations that are exempt from the Community licences will remain so after the transition period. These operations are:

- carriage of mail as a public service;
- carriage of vehicles which have suffered damage or breakdown;
- carriage of goods in vehicles with a permissible gross weight exceeding 3.5 tonnes;
- carriage of goods* in vehicles owned (including hired) by an own-account firm solely for its own purposes and where the transport is no more than ancillary to its overall activities and where the vehicle is driven only by an employee of the firm;
- carriage of medicinal products, appliances, equipment and other articles required for medicinal care in emergency relief, in particular for natural disasters.

*The goods concerned may be the property of the firm, or have been sold, bought, let out on hire or hired, produced, extracted, processed or repaired by the firm. Although exempt, the company may need to carry 'own-account' documentation in order to prove the status of the goods in question.

International Permits

Bilateral Permits

Certain road haulage operations from the UK to non-EU member states require a bilateral road haulage permit. A bilateral road haulage permit is required for some non-EU countries the UK has agreements with. These countries are Belarus, Georgia, Kazakhstan, Morocco, Russia or Tunisia. A bilateral road haulage permit is also required if travelling:

- through Turkey to another country;
- in Ukraine using a Euro III or Euro IV vehicle.

International permits are applied for on DVSA Form 0433, through:

DVSA International Road Haulage Permits Office

irhp@dvsa.gov.uk

Telephone: 0330 678 1117

A road haulage permit is not required for transporting goods to, through or from Albania, Moldova, Montenegro, North Macedonia, Serbia, Turkey and Ukraine.

ECMT Multilateral Permits

It is these permits which, post-Brexit, will form the 'lion's share' required by UK-based international haulage operators seeking to move goods out of the UK into the EU member states.

Currently, a number of ECMT permits are allocated to the UK for EU transit and haulage journeys between the 43 ECMT member countries.

These ECMT permits allow journeys between member countries, including laden or empty transit journeys and third-country journeys to other ECMT countries which are prohibited by certain bilateral agreements. However, they cannot be used for transit of ECMT countries on journeys to non-ECMT states or for cabotage. The normal permits are for hire or reward journeys only and may not be used by unaccompanied trailers or semi-trailers. They are valid for one calendar year (Dec–Jan) and allow an unlimited number of journeys within that period, but they may be used with only one vehicle at a time. Journey logs are required when operating under ECMT permits. They need to be sent to the IRFO on a monthly basis while the permit is valid. The permits and any outstanding logs have to be returned to the IRFO within 15 days of expiry of the permit. The quota for their issue is limited, so these permits are allocated before the beginning of the year in which they are issued. Usually no further supplies are available during the course of the year, but should the quota be increased an announcement is made in the trade press.

ECMT Removals Permits

These permits are quota-free and can be used for international removals between, or crossing, ECMT member countries. They are available only to firms employing the specialized equipment and staff needed to undertake such operations and are valid for one year from the date of issue.

Permit Checks

As a result of the exposure of a number of cases of permit frauds, stringent regulations exist to prevent vehicles on international journeys travelling without valid permits and checks are made on vehicles to ensure that these regulations are complied with. A vehicle will be prevented from continuing its journey if it does not carry a valid permit. In the UK it is an offence to forge or alter permits, to make a false statement to obtain a permit or to allow one to be used by another person.

Validity of Permits

Where bilateral road haulage permits are required, such permits are available covering single journeys only, allowing just one return journey to be undertaken between the UK and the nominated country on the dates shown on the permit. Outside of these dates the permit is invalid and it would be illegal to commence or continue the journey.

Issue of Permits

Road haulage permits are issued by the relevant authority in each member state. Normally, this involves completion of application forms, advance payment of the relevant fee and submission by the applicant of a copy of their authority to operate (eg the UK Licence for the Community). Application needs to be made 7–10 days before the permit is required.

Permits may be quota (limited numbers issued) or non-quota (unlimited issue). Where quota permits are issued but not used, operators may have the number requested on their next request reduced as quota permits are often in short supply. The issue of non-quota permits is via VOL.

Return of Used Permits

Used and expired bilateral permits must be returned to the issuing authority not later than 15 days after the relevant journey has been completed as they are 'single journey' permits.

ECMT permits used for tramping operations and EU transit, are valid for 12 months and must be returned to IRFO within 15 days of the expiry date. The terms of these permits also require the haulier to use log books and submit monthly returns to IRFO giving details of work carried out under the permit.

Lost or Stolen Permits

Road haulage permits are valuable transit documents. They are not transferable to another operator. Replacement of lost or stolen permits is not normally automatic, and in any case a full written explanation of the circumstances surrounding the loss or theft is required, together with a copy of the police report.

Journeys to or through Non-Agreement Countries

If vehicles are to travel to or through a country with which an EU member state has no agreement, permission to operate in that country has to be sought direct from its transport authority. Application should be made well before the journey is due and full details of the vehicle, the load and the route should be given. Advice is available through the trade associations, IRFO or embassies of the countries concerned.

Own-Account Operations

'Own account' is where either a vehicle is only carrying goods in connection with its own business or delivery contents are not for hire or reward. A UK Licence for the Community is not required for own-account journeys between the UK and EU if the:

- goods carried are the operator's property, or have been sold, bought, let out on hire or hired, produced, extracted, processed or repaired by the operator;
- journey's purpose is to carry the goods to or from the operator's premises or to move them for the operator's own requirements;
- driver is employed, or is at the operator's disposal for their own requirements;
- vehicles carrying the goods are owned by the operator or they have bought them on deferred terms, or hired them;
- goods only support the operator's main business activity.

Own-account operators who are carrying goods for a commercial purpose will still be subject to cabotage and cross-trade rules when operating in the EU.

For own-account journeys between the UK and Cyprus or Hungary, drivers must carry documents in the vehicle that show:

- the name and address of the operator;
- the operator's trade or business;
- the nature of the goods being carried;
- loading and unloading points;
- registration number of the vehicle being used;
- the route the haulage takes.

Drivers may be asked to provide evidence of the ownership of the goods.

A bilateral international road haulage permit for own-account journeys may be required for some non-EU countries with which the UK has agreements.

International Carriage of Goods by Road – CMR

Operators carrying goods for hire or reward on international journeys must comply with the Convention on the Contract for the International Carriage of Goods by Road 1956 (*Convention Relative au Contrat de Transport International de Marchandises par Route* – commonly referred to as the CMR Convention). This Convention is applied in the UK by the provisions of the Carriage of Goods by Road Act 1965. The Convention defines the carriers' liability and the documents to be carried on vehicles engaged in the international movement of goods between different countries, of which at least one is a party to the CMR Convention.

CMR is the standard contract used by companies who want to use a transport operator to move goods by road internationally. The CMR confirms that the operator has received the goods and has a contract from the supplier to carry them. A CMR must be carried on all commercial international journeys. It can be completed by either:

- the operator;
- the company sending the goods abroad;
- a freight forwarder.

Three copies are required, one each for:

- the supplier of the goods;
- the eventual customer;
- to accompany the goods while they are being transported.

Non-CMR Operations and Journeys

For the CMR Convention to apply, there must be clear evidence of a contract for the international carriage of goods for reward. In other words, the carriage of goods on an international journey at no charge, and therefore outside of a contract for carriage as specified in the Convention, would not be covered by CMR. Furthermore, the carriage must be of *goods* to allow the Convention to apply.

Besides these exclusions arising from defining the precise terms of applicability, the Convention has a number of more specific exemptions. Namely, its terms do not apply to:

- own-account operations which involve international journeys;
- furniture removals;
- funeral consignments which are transported abroad;
- carriage under an International Postal Convention.

The Convention is also *not* applicable in respect of international haulage operations between the UK and the Channel Islands (ie Guernsey, Jersey, Alderney, Sark and Herm). Cabotage journeys (ie internal journeys within a country by a road haulier from another country) are also outside the provisions of the CMR.

Basic Requirements of CMR

The CMR Convention automatically applies to every contract for the international carriage of goods by road in vehicles for reward, even when the vehicle containing the goods is carried over part of its journey by sea, rail or inland waterway, providing that the goods concerned are not unloaded from the vehicle in transit at any point. Other conventions may also apply and take precedence over CMR. A CMR-type consignment note must be completed for the journey.

CMR Conditions for International Road Haulage Journeys

An outline of the principal conditions of the Convention is given here:

1   The Convention applies to every contract for carriage of goods, whether wholly by road or partly by road and partly by rail, sea or inland waterway, as long as the goods remain in the original vehicle, on a journey from one country to another, one of which is a contracting party to the Convention (with the exception of UK–Eire and UK mainland–Channel Islands journeys which are ruled not to be international journeys for this purpose). Exemptions to CMR apply to carriage under international postal conventions, funeral consignments and furniture removals.

2   Carriers (ie road hauliers) are responsible under the Convention for the actions and omissions of their agents and any other persons whose services are used in carrying out the movement. Even if the original road haulier contracted to undertake the movement sub-contracts the whole of the operation to another road haulier (whose name appears on the CMR consignment note), the first (original) haulier remains fully liable under CMR should a dispute or claim arise. This can present problems in a case where, for example, the first (original) haulier operates only in domestic transport and thus is covered only by, say, Road Haulage Association Conditions of Carriage and is insured accordingly – not being insured to the much higher CMR level of liability.

3   A contract for the international carriage of goods for reward is confirmed by making out a CMR consignment note in at least four original copies which should be signed by the sender and carrier. Each keeps a copy, a copy travels on the vehicle with the goods and the final copy is retained by the carrier at base. While a CMR consignment note confirms that a contract exists, the absence of, or failure to raise, such a note does not invalidate the contract or dis-apply the terms of the Convention.

4   If the goods are carried under a single contract in different vehicles or are divided owing to their different nature, the carrier or the sender can specify that a separate consignment note should be made out for each vehicle or each load of goods.

5   The consignment note must contain certain specified details and may also contain additional information of use to the parties to the contract. It must state that the carriage is subject to CMR. Although not a 'title' to the goods, the consignment note is evidence of the facts it contains (ie the details shown are presumed to be correct), such as the number of packages, etc, and any claim which disputes such facts would have to be backed by substantial independent evidence to the contrary. Normally a standard note such as that available from the IRU is used (or in the UK from the Road Haulage Association or the Freight Transport Association – both IRU members).

6   The sender is responsible for all expenses, loss and damage sustained by the carrier as a result of inaccuracies in completion of the consignment note in relation to information supplied by the sender – even if the road haulier completes the note from information supplied by the sender.

7   On receipt of the goods, the carrier must check the accuracy of the details shown in the consignment note, particularly, for example, as to the number of packages, the apparent condition of the goods, their packaging and how they are marked. Any discrepancies or comments about other relevant matters such as the condition of the goods or packages or not being able to physically check the goods should be noted by a 'reservation' on the note. Should the sender request the carrier to check the contents of packages or to have the consignment weighed, the sender must reimburse the carrier for any costs incurred in doing so.

8   The sender is liable to the carrier for damage and expenses due to defective packing of the goods unless the defects were known to the carrier when taking over the goods and the carrier indicated this fact by way of a 'reservation' on the note. The absence of such a reservation means that the carrier, if aware of the damage, accepted any likely risks of subsequent claims.

9   The sender must attach to the consignment note or make available to the carrier the necessary documents to complete Customs formalities. The sender is liable to the carrier for any damage caused by the absence, inadequacy or irregularity of such documents.

10 The sender has the right of disposal of the goods and may stop transit of the goods or change the delivery address up to the time of delivery to the consignee unless the sender has stated on the consignment note that the consignee has this right. Once the goods are delivered to the address on the consignment note, the consignee has the right of disposal.

11 A carrier who fails to follow the instructions on the consignment note or who has followed them without requesting the first copy of the consignment note to be produced is liable for loss or damage caused by such failure.

12 The carrier must provide the consignee with a second copy of the consignment note at the time of delivering the goods.

13 If the carrier cannot follow the instructions on the consignment note for any reason, they must ask the sender or the consignee, depending on who has the right of disposal.

14 The carrier is liable for the total or partial loss of the goods and for any damage to them occurring between the time when the carrier takes over the goods and the time of their delivery unless the loss, damage or delay was caused by a wrongful act or neglect of the claimant. The burden of proof in this case rests with the carrier. However, the carrier is not bound to pay any compensation for delay where they do not receive a 'reservation' from the consignee within 21 days of the date of delivery.

15 Failure to deliver goods within 30 days of a specified time limit, or within 60 days from the time when the first carrier took them over if there is no time limit for delivery, results in the goods being considered to be lost.

16 When goods of a dangerous nature are consigned, the carrier must be informed of the nature of the danger and the precautions to be taken.

17 Calculation of compensation in the event of loss or damage is related to the value of the goods at the place and time they were accepted for carriage but will not exceed a set value.

18 Carriage charges, customs duties and other charges in respect of the carriage are refunded in the case of total loss of the goods and proportionately in the case of partial loss.

19 Higher levels of compensation may be claimed where the value or a special interest in delivery has been declared or where a surcharge has been paid in respect of a declared value exceeding the set limit.

20 In the case of damage the carrier is liable for the amount by which the value of the goods has diminished.

21 The claimant may demand interest in respect of the amount of any claim at 5 per cent per annum from the date on which the claim was sent to the carrier.

22 Carriers cannot avail themselves of exclusions or limiting clauses if damage to goods was caused by their wilful misconduct or default which constitutes wilful misconduct.

23 The consignee is considered to have accepted the goods in a satisfactory condition if they do not indicate their reservations at the time of delivery or within seven days (excluding Sundays and public holidays).

24 In legal proceedings, the plaintiff may bring an action in any court or tribunal of a contracting (ie CMR contracting) country, or of a country in which the defendant is normally resident or has their principal place of business, or of a country where the goods were taken over by the carrier or where they were designated for delivery, and in no other courts or tribunals.

25 The period of limitation for an action under the Convention is one year, or three years in the case of wilful misconduct.

26 Where successive road carriers are involved in a contract under the Convention, each one of them is responsible for the whole operation as a party to the contract. Each successive carrier must give the previous carrier a dated receipt and must enter their name and address on the second copy of the consignment note.

27 A carrier who has paid compensation arising from a claim may recover the compensation plus interest, costs and expenses from other carriers who were parties to the contract subject to:

(a) the carrier responsible for the loss or damage paying the compensation;

(b) each carrier responsible for loss or damage jointly caused shall be liable to pay proportionate compensation, or compensation proportionate to their share of the carriage charges, if responsibility cannot be apportioned.

28 If a carrier who is due to pay compensation is insolvent, their share must be paid by the other carriers who are party to the contract.

In particular, operators should note that the terms of the carriage contract require the carrier taking over the goods to check the accuracy of the statements in the consignment note as to the number of packages, their marks and numbers, the apparent condition of the goods and their packaging. Under the Convention the carrier is responsible for loss, damage or delay from the time of taking over the goods until the time of their delivery.

Furthermore, where goods are handled by a number of carriers on an international journey, provisions are contained in CMR to apportion the liability for loss or damage between all the carriers.

CMR Liability

International carriage automatically comes within the terms of CMR under which the carrier's liability for claims resulting from loss of or damage to the goods carried is determined by comparison with a measure known as 'Special Drawing Rights' (SDRs), whereby compensation must not exceed 8.33 units of account per kg of gws (gross weight short). SDRs are defined by the International Monetary Fund (IMF) as being a unit for converting currency values based on a 'basket' of the currencies of the key member states of the IMF and are converted to the national currency of the country in which any claim is dealt with in court, and are assessed as to value on the date of the judgment, or on a date agreed to by the parties. A treasury certificate stating the value for that day is taken to be conclusive proof of that fact.

CMR Consignment Notes for International Haulage Journeys

Operators carrying goods under CMR must complete special CMR consignment notes to be carried on the vehicle.

The CMR consignment note is made out in four copies all of which should be signed by both the carrier and the consignor of the goods. One copy of the note (with red lines) is retained by the consignor, the second copy (with blue lines) is for the consignee and the third copy (with green lines) is for the carrier and must travel forward with the vehicle and remain with it while the goods are on board – the fourth copy (with black lines) may be retained on file by the originator of the document.

Where a consignment is divided to travel by different vehicles or by separate means, separate CMR consignment notes should be completed for each individual part of the consignment.

The following details must be entered on CMR consignment notes:

Box 1   Sender (name, address, country)
Box 2   Customs reference/status
Box 3   Sender's/agent's reference
Box 4   Consignee (name, address, country)
Box 5   Carrier (name, address, country)
Box 6   Place and date of taking over the goods
Box 7   Successive carriers
Box 8   Place designated for delivery of goods
Box 9   Marks and numbers; number and kind of packages; description of goods*
Box 10   Gross weight (kg)
Box 11   Volume (m³)
Box 12   Carriage charges
Box 13   Sender's instructions for Customs
Box 14   Reservations
Box 15   Documents attached
Box 16   Special agreements
Box 17   Goods received
Box 18   Signature of carrier
Box 19   Company completing the note
Box 20   Place, date, signature
Box 21   Copies to:
- Sender'
- Consignee'
- Carrier.

For dangerous goods indicate:

1 correct technical name (ie proper shipping name);

2 Hazchem class;

3 UN number;

4 flashpoint (°C), if applicable.

Box 14 (Reservations) is required so that the driver can make a statement that they could not check or confirm some item of detail (condition, volume, shortages, etc) relating to the consignment at the time of taking over the consignment. This can be a very important element of CMR when claims are made against the carrier.

Where applicable, the consignment note must also contain the following particulars:

- a statement that transhipment to another vehicle is not allowed;
- the charges which the sender undertakes to pay;
- the amount of 'cash on delivery' charges;
- a declaration of the value of the goods and the amount representing special interest in delivery;
- the sender's instructions to the carrier regarding insurance of the goods;
- the agreed time limit within which the carriage is to be carried out;
- a list of documents handed to the carrier.

The consignor or consignee can also add to the consignment note any other particulars which may be useful to the road haulier.

Authorized Economic Operators

The aim of the AEO is to provide businesses with an internationally recognized quality mark that will demonstrate that they operate within a secure supply chain and that their internal Customs controls and procedures are sufficiently efficient and compliant for them to conduct 'self-clearance' for customs purposes. Under the legislation, businesses that satisfy certain EU-wide criteria may apply for, and be granted, the status of AEO by HMRC. When a member state has granted a business AEO status, this status is currently recognized across all member states. AEOs will be able to benefit from facilitation of Customs controls or simplifications of Customs rules or both, depending on the type of AEO certificate.

Application forms for AEO status and further details on the benefits and criteria are available at GOV.UK.

Community Transit

Community transit (CT) is a UK and EU customs procedure that allows non-community goods on which duty has not been paid to move from one point in the UK or EU to another (including from one point to another in an individual member state). It's also used for the movement of goods to, from or between the 'special territories' of the EU and between the UK, or EU, and Andorra or San Marino.

The 'common' transit procedure is used for the movement of goods between the UK, or EU, and the other contracting parties to the Common Transit Convention ('common transit countries') or between the common transit countries. The common transit countries are:

- EFTA countries (Switzerland, Norway, Iceland and Lichtenstein);
- Macedonia and Serbia.

The UK, all EU member states and common transit countries have designated customs offices where movements under the community or common transit procedure must begin and end. These offices are called 'offices of departure' and 'offices of destination' respectively. Offices where goods may leave or enter the territory of the UK, EU or a common transit country in the course of a CT movement are called 'offices of transit'.

Any person acting as the principal of a transit movement must provide a guarantee to ensure payment of the customs duties and other charges if the CT requirements are not fulfilled.

The CT guarantee must be valid for the UK, all EU member states, and any other countries (common transit countries, San Marino or Andorra) involved in the movement.

A guarantee is usually an acceptance by an independent party (usually a bank, insurance company or similar organization) for liability, jointly and severally with the principal. Traders who meet special requirements may qualify for a guarantee waiver, avoiding the need for a guarantor.

CT declarations must be made electronically, using the New Computerised Transit System (NCTS).

The Tariff

All the information and advice needed to help with importing and exporting procedures is to be found in 'The Tariff' (ie 'The Integrated Tariff of the United Kingdom'). This document contains all the relevant commodity codes (more than 65,000 of them); duty rates; procedures, including a box-by-box completion guide for C88 Single Administrative (SAD) documents; as well as references to the legal provisions.

Customs Documentation

An eight-part Customs document (C88) known as the 'Single Administrative Document' is used throughout the EU and EFTA countries for the purposes of non-NCTS (see Chapter 23) import, export and transit controls. A CT declaration comprises completed copies of pages 1, 4 and 5 of the SAD. In certain circumstances a Community status document (T2L) may be used where required to provide evidence to Customs of EU status. A T2L can be either a copy of page 4 of the SAD, or a commercial document such as an invoice, a transport document or a manifest.

The following copies are required:

Copy 1 Copy for the Customs office of departure

Copy 3 Consignor/exporter's copy

Copy 4 For Customs office of destination, or T2L declaration

Copy 5 Return copy from Customs office of destination to prove that the goods arrived intact

Copy 7 Statistical copy for Customs in the country of destination.

Copies 1 and 3 remain in the country of origination (ie export) and copies 4, 5 and 7 travel forward with the goods, copy 5 eventually being returned to the office of departure.

NB: Whilst the term 'community transit' is used throughout this section, the European Community (EC) is now almost exclusively referred to as the European Union (EU).

Community Transit Movements

There are two types of CT procedure:

1 *The external CT procedure.* This is mainly used to control the movement of non-EU goods and to control the movement of EU goods which are subject to EU measures involving their export to a third country, eg CAP goods which are liable to an export refund. This procedure is also known as the 'T1' procedure.

2 *The internal CT procedure.* This procedure controls the movement of free circulation goods to or from the special territories, to or via the EFTA countries and between the EFTA countries. This procedure is also known as the 'T2' procedure (or the 'T2F' procedure for goods moving to or from the special territories).

These status classifications could be subject to change for UK goods post-Brexit, but it seems likely that T1 and T2 status may actually largely remain in their current formats although declared differently.

Control Procedures

All transit movements are the responsibility of a 'principal', who is the person or company which undertakes to ensure that the goods are delivered to the office of destination within the prescribed time limit. The principal must put up a guarantee to secure the relevant duties and other charges in case the goods do not arrive intact at the office of destination. The guarantee can be cash (lodged at the office of departure), vouchers (purchased from a guaranteeing association) or a guarantee undertaking (provided by a guarantor).

To start a CT movement the completed declaration must be presented to Customs at an 'office of departure' where it will be authenticated and a time limit for completing the movement will be set. The goods may also be sealed and an itinerary set. Copies 4 and 5 of the CT declaration (ie the SAD) must travel together with the goods until they reach the EU member state or EFTA country where the movement is to end. Here the declaration and goods must be presented to the appropriate Customs at the 'office of destination'. This office will then stamp copy 5 of the SAD and return it to the office of departure so that the movement can be discharged. If copy 5 is not received within two months the principal is contacted and asked to provide proof that the procedure has ended correctly. If proof is not provided within four months, the enquiry procedure is initiated to recover the potential debt.

There is a range of transit simplifications available for use by compliant and reliable traders. These include the use of comprehensive and reduced guarantees or waivers, becoming authorized consignors and consignees, using trader seals on vehicles, special loading lists, having an exemption from prescribed itineraries, goods moved by pipeline, use of other simplified procedures and being able to use commercial documentation instead of the SAD in the case of air, rail and sea environments. All of these simplifications are subject to authorization by the Customs authorities.

Customs Declaration Service

The Customs Declaration Service supports the UK's trade with the EU and the rest of the world. It also plays an essential role in GB freight movements to Northern Ireland. HMRC is closing the Customs Handling of Import and Export Freight (CHIEF) system on 31 March 2023. The Customs Declaration Service is replacing it as the UK's single customs platform. All businesses will need to declare goods using the Customs Declaration Service.

HMRC will gradually reduce CHIEF services, with functionality switched off in two phases:

- 30 September 2022, import declarations using CHIEF will cease;
- 31 March 2023, export declarations using CHIEF and the National Export System (NES) will cease.

Cabotage

Cabotage is domestic haulage conducted by foreign operators – the collection and delivery of goods by road within a country by a road haulier whose business is established in another country. Up to two cabotage or cross-trade movements (moving goods between two EU countries) may be undertaken following a laden journey from the UK. However, there is a maximum of one cabotage movement within a seven-day period. For Northern Ireland operators, two cabotage movements may be conducted in Ireland within a seven-day period provided they follow a journey from Northern Ireland. Operators may apply to undertake up to three cross-trade movements but must be in possession of an ECMT permit. There are 43 ECMT member countries; details can be found at GOV.UK.

Cabotage by EU own-account road transport operators is permitted, but only on the same basis as defined above.

VAT on Cabotage Operations

Internal transport operations under cabotage authorization require operators to comply with national VAT regulations. For this purpose, if cabotage is permitted in any EU member state post-Brexit transition, operators may need to register in the member states in which they are operating or appoint a suitable VAT agent or fiscal representative to handle these matters on their behalf.

The TIR Convention

The TIR Convention system applies to road journeys to all countries (except for journeys between member states of the EU and EFTA made by EU and EFTA operators) which are party to the Convention but only where the haulier elects to conform to the Convention's requirements. TIR is being seen as a good 'backstop' for UK hauliers to use post-Brexit in order to reduce delays at borders, as it is a UNECE Convention and not an EU Convention and it is expected that many UK operators will select TIR as a preferred way forward post-Brexit.

Under the Customs Convention on the International Transport of Goods by Road (TIR Carnets) 1959, to which the UK is party, goods in Customs-sealed vehicles or containers may travel through intermediate countries en route to their final destination with the minimum of Customs formalities provided a TIR Carnet has been issued in respect of the journey (UK vehicles may currently operate on international haulage journeys outside the EU without the protection of TIR but in this case they will be subject to the full weight of Customs formality and bureaucracy (and delay) at each border crossing and on arrival at destination).

The Carnet is a recognized international Customs document intended purely to simplify Customs procedures; it is not a substitute for other documents, nor is it mandatory for operators to use it; it does not give operators the right to run vehicles in any European country. Use of a Carnet frees operators from the need to place a deposit of duty in respect of the load they are carrying in each country through which the vehicle is to pass.

The issuing authorities for the Carnets (Logistics UK and the RHA) act as guarantors on behalf of the IRU – the international guarantor, and for this reason Carnets are issued only to bona fide members of these two associations.

Goods may only be carried under a TIR Carnet provided the vehicle in which they are carried has been specifically approved by the DVSA. This means complying with constructional requirements so that the load-carrying space can be sealed by Customs, after which it must not be possible for any goods to be removed from or added to the load without the seals being broken, and there must be no concealed spaces where goods may be hidden.

The DVSA examines vehicles (by appointment at goods vehicle test stations) to ensure that they meet the technical requirements for operation under the TIR Convention and issues a certificate of approval (GV 60), which must be renewed every two years and must be carried on the vehicle when it is operating under a TIR Carnet. This point is particularly important as Customs authorities carry out checks on vehicles leaving the UK to ensure that this certificate is being carried where necessary.

Application for TIR Certification

Application for the examination of vehicles or containers must be made as early as possible and in any case not less than one month before inspection is required. The application form (GV62) can be downloaded from the GOV.UK website. The application should be forwarded to the test station for the area in which the vehicle is available for inspection and postage must be prepaid. A separate application must be submitted for each vehicle/trailer.

If a TIR-approved vehicle is sold to another operator, the TIR certificate (form GV60) is not transferable and the new owner must have the vehicle re-certified if they wish to use it for TIR operations.

The fee for examination of a vehicle for TIR purposes is £106.00, unless it is not of a previously approved TIR design type, in which case the fee is £644.00. The fee for a TIR certificate is £14.00. For a re-inspection of a failed vehicle, the fee is £70.00.

TIR Plates

When a vehicle has been approved it must display at the front and the rear a plate showing the letters 'TIR' in white on a blue background. Such plates are obtainable from the Logistics UK and RHA. They should be removed or covered when the vehicle is no longer operating under TIR.

TIR Carnets

TIR Carnets are internationally recognized Customs documents. Carnets are in pairs and have counterfoils in a bound cover. They are in four parts and contain 6, 14 or 20 pages. A six-page Carnet is valid only for a journey between the UK and one other country. Journeys to more than one other country require 14- or 20-page Carnets, which are valid for two months and three months respectively. A Carnet covers only one load and if a return load is to be collected, a separate Carnet is needed (each individual voucher covers one frontier crossing).

Carnets are valid for limited periods only, and if not used they must be returned to the issuing authority for cancellation. Those which are used and which bear all the official stampings acquired en route must also be returned within 10 days of the vehicle's return.

The four parts of the Carnet comprise the following:

1 Details of the issuing authority, the Carnet holder, the country of departure, the country of destination, the vehicle, the weight and the value of the goods as shown in the manifest.

2 A declaration that the goods specified have been loaded for the country stated, that they will be carried to their destination with the Customs seals intact and that the Customs regulations of the countries through which the goods are to be carried will be observed.

3 A goods manifest giving precise details of the goods, the way in which they are packed (the number of parcels or cartons) and their value.

4 Vouchers which Customs officials at frontier posts will remove, stamping the counterfoil section which remains in the Carnet.

Before obtaining a Carnet, the applicant must sign a form of contract with the issuing authority, agreeing to abide by all the necessary legal and administrative requirements. A financial guarantee is required to ensure that any claims which may be made against the applicant will be met. Logistics UK and RHA both act as guarantors for members.

Seal Breakage

If a Customs seal on a TIR vehicle is broken during transit (as a result of an accident for example), Customs or the police must be contacted immediately to endorse the Carnet to this effect and to re-seal the vehicle and, if required, amend the load documentation.

Carnets de Passage en Douane

Most countries to which vehicles are likely to travel permit the temporary importation and re-exportation of foreign vehicles and containers (not to be confused with the loads they carry) free of duty or deposit and without guaranteed Customs documents.

However, a Customs document known as a *Carnet de Passage en Douane* (CPD) is required for vehicles and trailers intending to transit or visit Africa, Asia, the Middle East, Oceania (the Pacific) or South America.

Further information is available from the motoring associations in each of these countries.

Road Tolls

The Austrian 'Maut' System

The former Austrian Eco-points system described in some earlier editions of this Handbook has been abolished and replaced by a new 'Maut' (toll) 'per mile' system for trucks over 3.5 tonnes gross weight, similar in concept to the German LKW-Maut system. This system is based on day and night charges and varies according to certain zones within the country. The previous Austrian 'Vignette' sticker system has also been replaced. The system requires relevant vehicles to be fitted with an easy-to-install DSRC-TAG electronic (microwave) transponder, colloquially called a 'GO-Box', and payment is via the internet (www.go-maut.at) or at point-of-sale terminals, located mainly at roadside fuel-filling stations.

All 2,000 km of Austria's motorways are wired for DSRC (short-range electronic tolling) to operate the nationwide toll system, which is achieved with the aid of an electronic transponder or by off-road payment, normally by internet or at one of 200-odd point-of-sale terminals, mostly located at fuel-filling stations. When paying the toll, truck drivers enter their registration number, which is recorded on a list of payers. When the vehicle is seen on the road by cameras mounted on some 400 over-head gantries, it is matched against the so-called 'white' payment list.

Tariff group	Category 2 2 axles		Category 3 3 axles		Category 4+ 4 & more axles	
	Day	Night*	Day	Night*	Day	Night*
A Euro emission class Euro VI	0.18820	0.18860	0.26411	0.26503	0.39443	0.39559
B Euro emission classes Euro V and EEV	0.20240	0.20280	0.28399	0.28491	0.41875	0.41991
C Euro emission class Euro IV	0.20870	0.20910	0.29281	0.29373	0.42883	0.42999
D Euro emission classes Euro 0 to Euro III	0.22870	0.22910	0.32081	0.32173	0.46083	0.46199

NB: Prices in euros per kilometre, excluding 20 per cent VAT.
*The night tariff applies between 2200 and 0500 hours.

A higher toll rate is charged for use of a number of special road sections on the A9, A10, A11, A13 (the Brenner Pass) and A16 motorways. VAT at the local rate is added to the tolls.

The German LKW-Maut System

Germany's distance-based LKW-Maut road toll system, operated by Toll Collect, applies to all HGVs, domestic and foreign, exceeding 7.5 tonnes gvw.

Toll payments can be made in several alternative ways as follows:

- LogPay plan (direct debit);
- Road Account;
- fuel card payment;
- credit account payment;
- EC card payment;
- credit card payment;
- cash payment.

The total cost is broken down into infrastructure, pollution and noise. Details are:

Infrastructure
gvw 7.5 t–12 t   8.0 cents per km
gvw 12 t–18 t   11.5 cents per km

gvw less than 4 axles and less than 18 t   16.0 cents per km
gvw with more than 4 axles and more than 18 t   17.4 cents per km

Pollution

Euro 0, 1	8.5 cents per km
Euro 2	7.4 cents per km
Euro 3	6.4 cents per km
Euro 4	3.2 cents per km
Euro 5	2.2 cents per km
Euro 6	1.1 cent per km

Noise

0.2 cents per km for all vehicles.

Eurovignettes

Motorway charges (ie tax) must be paid for HGVs exceeding 12 tonnes gvw, including those towing trailers where the combined maximum weight is 12 tonnes or more, when travelling in or through the Netherlands, Luxembourg, Denmark and Sweden. The tax is charged in euros (a), payable in advance, and is based on a sliding scale according to the pollution emission rating of the vehicle engine (ie Euro-0, Euro-I or Euro-II/III – see Chapter 11), the number of axles and the amount of time during which the motorways will be used (eg day, week, month, etc). Payment covers journeys in all four countries.

When the fees are paid, a certificate/receipt called a Eurovignette is issued, showing the vehicle registration number, the date and period of validity, and the amount paid. The Eurovignette must be carried on the vehicle at all times as proof of payment. Failure to obtain a Eurovignette or to be able to produce it on request can result in a fine of up to £5,000.

Eurovignettes should be purchased online by going to the Eurovignette home website (www.eurovignettes.eu) and following a link to 'AGES', the service provider responsible for selling Eurovignettes.

Other Motorway Tolls in Europe

All goods vehicles over 3,500 kg gvw travelling in Belgium need to have an On Board Unit (OBU) which operates through a system using ANPR cameras and mobile enforcement. Penalties of up to €1,000 can be levied for non-compliance and drivers without OBUs can be made to obtain one within three hours. The toll charges are based on the gross weight of the vehicle, the vehicle's emissions and the type of road.

Hungary has an electronic payment toll system for trucks weighing more than 7.5 tonnes on all its main roads (mostly trans-border routes). France, too, has an e-toll system ('TIS PL') for trucks over 3.5 tonnes using its motorways, with automatic billing via an electronic box system. The TIS PL system in France is also valid for use on Spanish motorways by some HGVs. Contact https://vrioeurope.com for more details. However, use of the system is not compulsory, although frequent users who sign up to the system will be eligible for rebates.

The French HGV transit tax, called the 'péage de transit poids lourds', is charged on major transit routes that carry more than 2,500 lorries a day and is applied to vehicles exceeding 3,500 kg.

Norway's 'bar-tag' is required by vehicles over 3.5 tonnes and applies to most of the roads in Norway and not just the main routes.

There are also automated billing arrangements across most of the EU, including Autopass in Italy and even the Heavy Goods Vehicle Road User Levy and some estuarial crossing charges in the UK and péage, autobahn and Autostrada charges throughout Europe, so it is important when travelling abroad to check the requirements for every country you may want to enter or transit.

European Lorry Restrictions

Some European countries impose restrictions on the movement of commercial vehicles exceeding 7.5 tonnes gvw. The main restrictions are:

- France – from 22.00 Saturday and the eve of public holidays until 22.00 Sundays and public holidays.
- Germany – from 00.00 to 22.00 on Sundays and public holidays (includes any vehicle with a trailer, regardless of weight).
- Italy – from 08.00 to 22.00 on Sundays between October and May, and from 07.00 to 24.00 from June to September. Also applies on public holidays and days of heavy traffic. There are exceptions for HGVs carrying perishable produce or fuels.
- Spain – from 08.00 to 24.00 on Sundays and on public holidays and from 13.00 to 24.00 on the eve of public holidays. There are exceptions for HGVs carrying livestock or fresh milk, on certain roads and on certain dates. Regional and date restrictions can be extensive and fines can be severe.

Miscellaneous Requirements

Trailer Registration and Certification

UK international road hauliers travelling to the EU need to ensure that commercial trailers over 750 kg and all trailers over 3,500 kg are registered with their own registration number plate consisting of one alpha and seven numeric figures if they are to travel to Europe and that a trailer 'MoT' type certificate is gained to prove the trailer has a valid annual test.

Registration details required will include the operator's details, trailer manufacturer, VIN/chassis number, gvw and ULW and, once registered, any change in ownership will need to be declared.

Costs are £26.00 for first-time registration, £21.00 for subsequent registrations and there is a £10.00 administration charge for a replacement certificate.

The physical plates must be displayed at the rear of the trailer, although they do not have to be lit. They do, however, need to be in a set format. This requires the plate to have one letter and seven figures (for example B2345678). In addition, the number plate of the drawing vehicle is still required on the rear of the trailer and this must be lit.

Austria

In Austria, drivers carrying out cabotage operations within that country must produce proof that they are in receipt of wages at least equal to those set by the Austrian minimum wage levels. This requirement has now also become a requirement in France and Germany.

France

Speed-limit offenders in France face instant loss of their driving licence if they exceed statutory limits by more than 40 kph (ie approximately 25 mph). Heavy vehicles in France are restricted to 90 kph (ie approx 56 mph) on motorways, 80 kph (ie approx 50 mph) on dual carriageways, 80 kph on country roads (only 60 kph, ie 37 mph, for vehicles drawing trailers) and 50 kph (ie approx 31 mph) in built-up areas.

NB: Many telepéage systems in France and other EU member states actually time the vehicle between ticket issue and pay points and, where the vehicle arrives at a pay point and it must have exceeded the speed limit in order to arrive so quickly, on-the-spot fines can be levied.

Drivers travelling to or through France must carry either:

- a copy of their contract of employment with their current employer;
- a letter of engagement from their employer (attestation of employment); or
- a valid recent (ie their last) payslip.

Operators also need to provide details of the carbon used in the supply of the goods to their customers as part of the French 'Carbon Reporting Scheme'. In addition, the French authorities are trying to enforce proof of minimum wage requirements and are enforcing this by fines of up to €4,000 for drivers not able to produce the required evidence. Failure to pay these fines results in the driver being banned from driving in France.

Germany

The German authorities require the drivers of small goods vehicles between 2,800 and 3,500 kg to keep driver's record books. In addition, there is a requirement for all drivers delivering goods to Germany (not in transit through Germany) to carry evidence that they are being paid at least at the same rate as the German national minimum wage. Record books are available through the UK trade associations, if required.

The Netherlands

If the authorities in the Netherlands require proof that a UK driver's earnings exceed the Netherlands minimum wage level, they contact the driver's employer for this information and do not ask the driver themselves for documentary evidence.

Attestation of Drive, Work and Rest Activities

UK HGV drivers, particularly on international journeys, may be asked to provide evidence of their activities that are not covered by a valid tachograph record. For this purpose the EU has devised an official form of activity attestation (not to be confused with a driver's employment attestation). However, this form was required under EEC Regulation 3821/85 which has now been superseded by Regulation EU 165/2014. In Regulation 165/2014 there is no requirement to use a letter of attestation for activities, although drivers are still expected to produce records of their activities to the authorities. Until such time that the EU or DfT produces an acceptable replacement form, it seems logical for UK operators to continue to use the old-style letters of attestation in order for the driver to be able to provide a record of the past 28 days of activity. A version of this form should be completed by the employer and issued to drivers on such journeys. Copies can be downloaded from the United Road Transport Union (URTU) website at: www.urtu.com.

Attestation (2)

HGV drivers who are non-EU nationals employed to drive EU-owned and EU-based vehicles are required to carry a letter of attestation affirming their employment status as required under EU Regulation 1072/2009/EC. This document (commonly referred to as the 'third country' attestation) certifies that the driver of a vehicle carrying out road haulage operations between member states is either 'lawfully employed by the EU transport operator concerned in the member state in which the operator is established, or is lawfully placed at the disposal of that operator'. Normally, it should be accompanied by a valid and current work visa or permit for the individual driver.

Drink-Driving Limits

The blood alcohol limit is 80 mg per 100 ml of blood in England, Wales and Northern Ireland. In Scotland, it is 50 mg of alcohol in 100 ml of blood. Some of the variations across Europe are:

- 0 mg – Estonia, Lithuania, Romania, Slovakia, Czech Republic, Hungary (this means zero tolerance);
- 20 mg (0.02 per cent) – Croatia, Norway, Poland, Sweden;
- 50 mg (0.05 per cent) – Belgium, Bulgaria, Denmark, Germany (Germany is 30 mg (0.03 per cent) if you're in an accident), Finland, France, Greece, Italy, Scotland, Serbia/Montenegro, Latvia, Macedonia, Netherlands, Austria, Portugal, Slovenia, Spain, Turkey, Cyprus (North);
- 80 mg (0.08 per cent) – England, Ireland, Luxembourg, Malta, Switzerland, Wales;
- 90 mg (0.09 per cent) – Cyprus (South).

More information on safe driving in Europe can be found on the Safe Travel website at: http://www.safetravel.co.uk.

Driver Health Cover Abroad

Drivers engaged on international journeys should carry their own personal EHIC to provide cover for any medical treatment required as a result of accident or illness while in any European Economic Area country. The card (which replaced the former E111 document) is obtainable free of charge from the NHS and can be applied for online. The card enables holders to obtain some free emergency medical attention from state-run hospitals and medical centres on the same basis as the local populace. The EHIC does not cover:

- treatment in private medical facilities abroad;
- repatriation when the patient is well enough to travel;
- the cost of recovering the vehicle;
- the cost of hospital visits by relatives;
- the costs of funeral transport from abroad.

All these additional items, if required, should be covered by private medical insurance taken out by the driver or the employer.

The position of EHIC post-Brexit may change after the transition period.

Single European Emergency (Phone) Number 112

Lorry and coach drivers on international journeys are advised that using this telephone number will provide them with a rapid and effective response in case of a road accident. In the UK either 999 or 112 will alert the emergency services.

The number can be dialled from fixed and mobile phones free of charge throughout the EU.

INDEX

Note: page numbers in *italic* indicate figures or tables

abnormal loads 470–82
   abnormal indivisible loads (AIL) 296, 470
   escorts 477–78
   high loads 478
   Highways England's ESDAL notification
      service 477, 536–37
   legislation 470, 473, 479
   lighting on projecting and long loads 481–82
   projecting loads 479–81, *480*
   special types vehicles 470–77, *471, 472, 473,*
      474
Access to Driver Data (ADD) system 136
AdBlue 309
Admission Temporaire/Temporary Admission
      (ATA) 551, 553
agency drivers 8–9
Air Quality Management Area (AWMA) 518
alcohol 153, 167–68, 173–74
Animal and Plant Health Agency (APHA) 464
annual testing 371–84
   ABS/EBS cables 381
   applications 376–77
   dates 375–76
   failure and re-tests 381–82
   fees 372, *373–75*
   pass 381
   procedure 378–79
   reduced pollution examination of vehicles
      383–84, *384*
   refusal to test 378
   speed limiter checks 380
   tachographs 379–80
   types 372
Association of Lorry Loader Manufacturers and
      Importers (ALLMI) 455
Authorized Testing Facilities (ATFs) 371
Automated Entry Processing (AEP) system
      559–60

Brexit
   AETR rules 84
   cabotage 235, 576
   community transit (CT) movements 574
   data protection 537
   drivers' hours rules 69
   ECMT multilateral permits 563
   EU-UK Trade and Cooperationa Agreement
      (TCA) 546

European Health Insurance Card (EHIC)
      251, 586
   foreign vehicles in UK 50
   insurance 227
   national identifiers 199
   personal importation of goods 279
   Type Approval 345
   vehicle approvals 197
British Association of Removers (BAR) 34, 53
British Cattle Movement Service (BCMS) 463
bus lanes 259–60

Carriage of Goods by Road Act (1965) 565–75
Central Licensing Office (CLO) 3
Channel Look-Up (CLU) service 559
Chartered Institute of Logistics and Transport
      (CILT) 53, 54, 62, 194
clean air zones (CAZ) 257, 534
closed-circuit television (CCTV) 337, 539
codes of practice 451
   conventional weighing 299
   dock premises 456
   dynamic weighing 299–300
   escorts 477
   first aid 444
   forklift trucks 454
   health and safety 457
   Home Office Civil Penalty 275–76
   horse-drawn vehicles 240
   load safety 421, 451
   lorry loaders 192, 455
   trailer/semi-trailer coupling/uncoupling 341
collision procedures 270–71
Common Transit Convention (CTC) 551, 552–53
construction, maintenance and use of vehicles
      301–47
   alterations 346–47
   brakes 303–07
   C&U Regulations 301, 332, 337, 338, 340
   definitions of vehicles 301–02
   electric-powered 339
   Euro-VI standard 308–09
   exhaust emissions 307–08, *307*
   exhaust gas recirculation (EGR) vs selective
      catalyst reduction (SCR) 309–10
   first licensing arrangements 345–46
   front under-run protection system
      (FUPS) 333–34

fuel tanks 311–12
gas-powered 338
ground clearance for trailers 312
horn 312–13
international vehicle classifications 302–03
light vehicles 517–19
mirrors 313–14
noise 339
plating and testing 344
rear under-run protection system (RUPS)
  334, 335, 336
responsibility for compliance 344
responsibility for type approval 345
reversing alarms 339–40
safety glass 314
seat belts 314–15
sideguards 315–22, 315, 316, 317, 318, 319
silencer 322
smoke 310–11
speed limiters 322–24
speedometer 322
spray suppression 324–31, 327, 328, 329,
  330, 331
standards checked 345
televisions in vehicles 340
towing 340–41, 341
trailer/semi-trailer coupling/uncoupling 341
type approval 341–44
tyres 331–33
view to the front 337
windscreen wipers and washers 337
wings 338
Control of Pollution (Amendment) Act (1989)
  512
Convention on the Contract for the International
  Carriage of Goods by Road (CMR)
  235
COSHH Regulations 2002 (as Amended)
  433–34
COVID-19 419, 531
Criminal Justice Act (1988) 512
criminal offences 16–17

dangerous goods transportation 483–511
carriage of explosives 508
Dangerous Goods Safety Advisor
  (DGSA) 510–11
definition and classification 484–89, 488,
  489
driver training 508–10
emergency procedures 502–04
enforcement 507–08
European Agreement Concerning the
  International Carriage of Dangerous
  Goods by Road (ADR) 483–84
exemptions 492–95, 493, 494
information to be displayed 497–502, 497,
  498, 500, 502

International Maritime Dangerous Goods
  (IMDG) 496
legislation 483–84, 504, 508, 514
in light vehicles 518–19
radioactive substances 508
responsibilities 489–92
security provisions 504–07, 507
transport information and documentation
  495–97
data protection 43–44
CCTV 539
legislation 537–39
Data Protection Act (2018) 44
Department for Digital, Culture, Media and
  Sport (DCMS) 539
Department of Environment, Food and Rural
  Affairs (DEFRA) 461–63, 464, 466
digital communications and technology
  531–39
data protection 537–39
driver handbook 534
driver walkaround check systems 533
Fleet Management System (FMS) 532
information management systems 531
intelligent transport systems (ITS) 537
legislation 537–39
mobile communication devices 532–34
online services 535–37
personal digital assistants (PDAs) 533
satnavs 534
tachograph analysis 534
Transport Management System (TMS)
  531–32
display screen equipment (DSE) 432
Disposal of Poisonous Waste Act (1972) 512
Driver Certificate of Professional Competence
  (CPC) 547
driver licensing 136–76
applications 148–50
checking licenses 136–38
definitions 138
driving while tired 163–64
exchanging foreign for GB 162–63
fees 158–59
insurance, invalidation of 137
International Driving Permit (IDP) 161
issuing authority 138–39
legislation 137
lost/mislaid 160
medical requirements 150–58
minimum driver age 139–42
online checking 535
organ donor option 138
penalty points and disqualification 164–76
production of 161
validity 159–60
vehicle categories/groups 142–47
visitors driving in UK 163

driver training 192–94
  approved establishments and examination
      194
  carriage of dangerous goods 193–94
  continuing professional development (CPD)
      194–95
  Driver CPC Recording and Evidence (R&E)
      system 535
  lorry loaders 192
  responsibilities 193
Driver and Vehicle Standards Agency (DVSA) 3,
      265–66, 297, 332, 411, 414
drivers' hours records (EU/AETR rules) see
      tachographs
Driving at Work – Managing Work-Related Road
      Safety 419
driving hours rules 68–92
  AETR rules 84
  British domestic rules 81–83, 93–96
    driving and duty definitions 82
    emergencies 82–83
    exemptions and concessions 81, 94
    light goods vehicles 83
    record books 94–96, 97
    summary 82
  enforcement and penalties 91
  European Union and AETR rules 69–81
    amendments 79–80
    break periods 75
    driving limits 75
    employers' responsibilities 74
    exemptions 69–72
    prohibition on certain payments 81
    rest periods 76–78
    summary 78–79
    terminology 73–74
    unforeseen circumstances 81
    vehicles covered 69
  legislation 68–69
  light vehicles 519–20
  mixed EU/AETR and British domestic rules
      81–84
  national minimum wage 87–88
  regulations 85–87
  reporting illegal operations 91–92
  self-employment 88–89
  tax relief on driver allowances 89–90
  working time 85
driving tests 177–95
  advanced commercial vehicle driving 188–90
  HGV 177–80
    application 179
    case studies 178–79
    identification 179
    practical demonstration 160
    test cancellation 179
    theory and hazard perception 178
    vocational driving test 179
  large goods vehicle driver apprenticeship
      191
  proof of identity 177
  real total mass 182–83
  vocational 180–88
    current situation 183–85
    EU standards 185–87
    passes and failures 187–88
    syllabus 183
    vehicles 180–82
drugs 153, 156, 157, 167–68
dual-purpose vehicles 205, 519

electric vehicles (EV) 544
Electronic Duty of Care (EDOC) 513
enforcement checks on vehicles 390–95
  earned recognition 392
  operator compliance risk score 390–92, 391
  powers of police, DVSA examiners and
      certifying officers 393–95
  roadside checks 392–93
  vehicle inspection on premises 393
Environment Act (1995) 310
Environment Agency (EA) 512
environmental impact 540–45
  alternative fuels 544–45
  in the community 543–44
  oil storage 542
  principal emissions 540–41
  solutions 542–44
  vehicle depots 541, 542–43
  vehicle operations 541, 543
Environmental Protection Act (1990) 469, 512
Environmental Protection Act (1994) 512
EU-UK Trade and Cooperation Agreement (TCA)
      546
European Accident Statement (EAS) 228
European Agreement Concerning the
      International Carriage of Dangerous
      Goods by Road (ADR 2017) 193,
      483–87, 491–92, 492–93, 494, 495,
      502, 509, 547
European Agreement Concerning the Work
      of Crews of Vehicles Engaged in
      International Road Transport (AETR)
      68–81
European Food and Safety Inspection Service
      (EFSIS) 465
European Health Insurance Card (EHIC)
      230–31
European Union (Withdrawal) Act (2018) 1, 546

Fire Precautions Act (1971) 443
fly-tipping 469
food transportation 465–68
  grain haulage 467–68
  legislation 465, 466, 467
  perishable food 466

temperature-controlled food 466–67
wast food 467
Freight Transport Association/Chartered Institute
        of Purchasing and Supply (FTA/
        CIPS) 231, 234–35
fuel alternatives 544–45
    batteries 544
    biodiesel 545
    compressed natural gas (CNG) 545
    hydrogen diesel hybrid 545
    hydrogen fuel cell 544–45
    liquefied natural gas (LNG) 545
fuel benefit charge 517
fuel efficiency 522–30
    aids to 523–24
    best practice programme 528–29
    checklist 527–28
    driving techniques 524–25
    efficient use 523
    fleet management 525–27
    mechanical condition 522–23
    reducing fuel bills 529–30
    tyres 524

General Data Protection Regulation (GDPR) 44
goods in transit (GIT) 231
goods vehicle dimensions and weights 282–300
    13.7-metre container problem 288
    authorized weight regulations 292–96
    bridge strikes 291–92
    definitions 283
    dynamic weighing 299–300
    height 290–92
    ISO shipping containers 296–97
    length 283–90
    longer semi-trailer trial 285
    offences 297–300
    on-board vehicle weighing 300
    portable weighers 300
    width 290
goods vehicle testing stations (GVTSs) 371
Goods Vehicles (Licensing of Operators) Act
        (1995) 2, 51
Government Digital Service 531
graduated fixed penalty (GFP) 265–66
Green Card 227–28, 517, 548
grey fleet 517
Guide to Goods Vehicle Operators' Licensing
        411
Guide to Maintaining Roadworthiness 411, 414

Health and Safety at Work Act (1974) 419, 425,
        426–29, 457
Health and Safety Executive (HSE) 454, 456
Health and Safety Inspectorate (HSI) 453–54
Heavy Goods Vehicle Inspection Manual 417
high-occupancy vehicle (HOV) lanes 260

Highway Code
    2021 revision 238–40
    driving in fog 250–51, 353
    driving tests 178, 190
    driving when tired 163
    level crossings 260–61
    managing road risk 419
    in Northern Ireland 48
    pedestrian crossings 267
    road traffic law 237
    temporary obstruction actions 252
    tramways 246–47
    waiting and parking restrictions 245, 253
Highways England 473, 477
Hydrocarbon Oil Duties Act (HODA) (1979)
        526

Immigration Act (1971) 274
Immigration and Asylum Act (1999) 274,
        275–76
Immigration, Asylum and Nationality Act (2006)
        275
impounding of vehicles 50–51
Information Commissioner's Office (ICO) 43
inland border facilities (IBFs) 548–49, 549–50
inspection notices and prohibitions 396–99
Inspection Technician Accreditation (IRTE)
        scheme 411, 415
Institute of Advanced Motorists (IAM)
        RoadSmart 188, 189
Institute of the Furniture Warehousing and
        Removing Industry (IFWRI) 53
Institute of Transport Administration 53
insurance 222–36
    additional cover 229–31
    conditions of carriage 233–36
    fleet operators 228–29
    goods in transit (GIT) 231–33
    Green Card 227–28, 548
    Guaranteed Auto Protection (GAP) 229
    Insurance Advisory Letter (IAL) 226
    invalidation of 137
    light vehicles 516–17
    motor vehicles 222–28
        cancellation 227
        Certificate of Insurance 224–25
        duty to give information 225
        enforcement 225–26
        EU countries 227–28
        European Accident Statement 228
        invalidation of cover 226–27
        Motor Insurance Database 225
        passenger liability 223
        property cover 223–24
        third-party cover 222–23
    night risk and immobilizer clauses 232
    online checking 536

security 236
sub-contracting 233
International Carriage of Perishable Foodstuffs
    (ATP) 466
International Chamber of Commerce (ICC) 58
International Commercial Terms (Incoterm) 58
International Driving Permit (IDP) 547
international operations 546–86
    attestation of drive, work and rest activities
        584–85
    Austria 579–80, 583
    Belgium 558
    cabotage 576
    Carnets de Passage en Douane (CPD) 579
    Convention on the Contract for the
        International Carriage of Goods by
        Road (CMR) (1956) 565–75
    cross-border readiness 548–51, *549–50*
    drink-drive limits 585
    driver health cover 585–86
    drivers 547, 551
    EU customs procedure 557
    European lorry restrictions 582
    France 557–58, 583–84
    Germany 580–81, 584
    insurance 548
    Ireland 559–60
    Kent Access Permit (KAP) 551
    legislation 546
    national identifier (GB sticker) 548
    Netherlands 558, 584
    new registration rules 560–61
    operators 546–47, 551
    own-account operations 565
    permits 547, 562–65
    pre-notification 554–56
    registration documents 548
    responsibilities 550–51
    road tolls 579–82
    safety and security declarations 555–56
    single European emergency (phone) number
        586
    Spain 558–59
    TIR convention 576–79
    trailer registration and certification 582–83
    UK customs procedure 556
    UK licence for the Community 561–62
    vehicles 548
    visas, passports, identity cards 547
    ways to move goods across a border
        551–54
Intra Trade Animal Health Certificate (ITAHC)
    464
ISO containers 469

Joint Action Group On Lorry Theft (JAGOLT)
    236

Joint Approvals Unit for Periodic Training
    (JAUPT) 65

Kent Access Permit (KAP) 551

landfill tax 468- solid fuel loads 469
learner drivers 145–46
leasing 10–11
legislation/regulation 1–2, 14–16, 50, 51, 60
level crossings 260
Light Commercial Vehicles (LCV) 49–60
light vehicles 516–21
    construction and use regulations 517–19
    drivers' hours and records 519–20
    fuel 517
    insurance 516–17
    legislation 517
    roadworthiness 516
    seat belts 520–21
    speed limits 520, *520*
    vehicle tax 516
lighting 348–58
    direction indicators 354–55
    end-outline marker lamps 354
    front retro-reflectors 358
    obligatory 348–53
    optional lamps 355–56
    rear retro-reflectors 357
    side marker lamps 353
    side retro-reflectors 357
    switches 354
    swivelling spotlights (work lamps) 357
    visibility of lights and reflectors 354
    warning beacons 356
livestock, carriage of 460–65
    Animal Transport Certificates (ATCs) 464–65
    animals that cannot be transported 461
    exporting of animals 464
    importing of animals 464
    journey logs 464
    legislation 460–61
    training and competence of personnel 463
    transporter requirements and authorization
        461–63
    vehicle inspection and approval 465
load dimensions 459–60
Load Securing: Vehicle Operator Guidance 421,
    451
London 246
    area parking offences 263
    congestion charging 255–56
    Excluded Route Network (ERN) 254
    fixed penalties 263
    HGV Direct Vision Standard (DVS) 258–59
    lorry routes and controls 254–56, 258–59
    low and ultra-low emission zones (LEZ and
        ULEZ) 256

Red Routes 255
  Safer Lorry Scheme 258–59
London Lorry Control Scheme (LLCS) 254–55,
    255
Low Emission Zone (LEZ) 256
Low Emissions Vehicle (LEV) 379

Maritime and Coastguard Agency (MCA) 5
medical requirements 150–57
  driving following disqualification 150–57
    alcohol and drug-related problems 153
    appeals and information 156
    category C1 drivers 151
    coronary health problems 152–53
    diabetes 151–52
    epilepsy 152
    EU health standards 155–56
    medical examination fees 151
    notification of new/worsening conditions
      154–55
    other medical conditions 154
    prescription medicines 156–57
  eyesight requirement 157–58
Metropolitan Police's Operation Grafton 236
mobile phones 280
Most Serious Offence (MSO) 298
MOT testing (light vehicle) 404–10, *404, 405*
  failure 409
  issue of test certificate 410
  items tested 407–09, *408*
  online checking 535–36
  re-tests 409–10
  refusal and discontinuance of test 407
  vehicle classes 405–07, *405–06*
  Vehicle Defect Rectification Scheme (VDRS)
    410
Motor Insurance Database (MID) 225, 536
Motor Insurers' Bureau (MIB) 223
motorways 247–51
  bridge clearance 478
  driving in fog 250–51
  emergency telephones 250
  international toll systems 579–82
  learner drivers 249
  lights, markings, signs 249–50
  other vehicles 249
  temporary speed limits 248
  use of lanes 248
multi-occupancy vehicle (MOV) lanes 246

national minimum wage 87–88
National Union of Rail, Maritime and Transport
    Workers (RMT) 34
Network Rail 476
New Road and Streetworks Act (1991) 237
Northern Ireland
  Certification of vehicles 399–403

Environment Agency (NIEA) 512
  licensing 47–49

offences 311
  buffer period *17–18*
  criminal 16–17
  Most Serious Infringements (MSI) 392
  rehabilitation period *18–19*
  serious 16
  spent convictions 17–19
oil storage 221
on-board diagnostics (OBD) 310
Operator Compliance Risk Score (OCRS) 16
operator licensing ('O'licensing) 1–52, 411
  additional vehicles 36–38
    hired vehicles 37
    number of extra vehicles 37
    replacement vehicles 37
    seeking a margin 36–37
  administration of system 2–3
  application procedure 21–36, *25, 27*
  definition 1
  drivers' hours/records 29
  exemptions 1, 4–7
  foreign vehicles in UK 50–51
  guideline hours per week *23*
  hire and contract hire 10
  leasing 10–11
  legislation/regulation 1–2
  licence variation 38
  light commercial vehicles 49–50
  national electronic registers 41–42
  in Northern Ireland 47–49
  not for sale 4
  notification of changes 39
  penalties 41–44
  production of licence 40
  rental of vehicles 9
  requirements 12–21
    applications/decisions 33
    financial standing 30
    good repute 13–19
    grant/refusal of licence 35
    licence grant with conditions 35–36
    objections 33–34
    operating centres 21
    overloading 29
    professional competence 29–30
    representations by local residents
      34–35
    restricted licenses 12
    sustainability of operating centres
      32–33
  restricted licenses 11
  revocation of licences 42–43
  standard licences
    national transport operations 11–12

national/international transport
operations 13
own-account operators 12
subsidiary companies 39
surrender of licence 38
TCs power of review 40
temporary derogation 39–40
transfer of vehicles 38
Upper Transport Tribunal 44–47
Vehicle Operator Licensing (VOL) system 3
'vehicle user' definition 7–8
overloaded vehicles 269–70

parking 253
London area offences 263
night 244
parking charge notices (PCNs) 263–64
parking meter zones 246
on verges 253–54
waiting and parking restrictions 245–46
pedestrian crossings 267
periods of availability (POA) 75
plating of goods vehicles and trailers 384–90
certificates 385
downplating 385–86
exemptions 387–90
international 386
manufacturer's 384–85
notifiable alterations 386–87
production of documents 390
vehicle dimensions 385
Pre-Boarding Notification (PBN) 559
professional competence 52–67
Certificate of Professional Competence
(CPC) 52, 62–66
examination syllabus 54–62
minimum training/qualification
requirements 66–67
proof of 53
qualification by exemption 53–54
transfer of qualifications 62
Provision and Use of Work Equipment
Regulations (1998) 453
public inquiry (PI) 44–45

Radioactive Material (Road Transport) Act
(1991) 508
radios 280
rebated heavy oil (red diesel) 220–21, 526
recovery vehicles 218–19
Red Routes 246, 255, 263
Reporting of Injuries, Diseases and Dangerous
Occurrences Regulations (2013)
(RIDDOR) 434–38
rest periods 76–78
Road Haulage Association (RHA) 34, 231,
234–35, 236, 274–75

Road Safety Act (2006) 237
Road Traffic Act (1984) 237
Road Traffic Act (1988) 222–23, 237, 268, 269,
296, 297, 298, 301, 393, 411, 419,
420
Road Traffic Act (1991) 237, 271, 394
road traffic law 237–81
abandoned motor vehicles 268
builders' skips 267–68
bus lanes 259–60
civil enforcement officers 267
driving in fog 250–51
fixed penalties 262–66
hazard warning flashers 251
high-occupancy vehicle (HOV) lanes 260
Highway Code 238–40
level crossings 260
level and tram crossings 260–61
lighting-up time 244
lights during daytime 253
lorry routes and controls 254–58
motorways 247–51
night parking 244
overloaded vehicles 269–70
owner liability 261–62
parking 253–54
pedestrian crossings 267
retention/disposal of seized vehicles 268–69
road, definition of 238
road humps/traffic calming 271
road traffic collision procedure 270–71
sale of unroadworthy vehicles 271
seat belts 272–73
smuggling 278–79
speed limits 240–43
stopping, loading, unloading 244–46
stowaways 274–78
temporary obstruction actions 252–53
traffic/weather reports 280–81
tramways 246–47
use of radios/telephones in vehicles 280
weight-restricted roads/bridges 261
wheel clamps 269
Road Traffic (New Drivers) Act (1995) 237
Road Traffic Offenders Act (1988) 237, 261
Road Transport Act (2013) 2
Road Transport Directive (RTD) 75
Road Transport (Working Time) Regulations
(2005) 86–87
Royal National Lifeboat Institution (RNLI) 5

Safer Lorry Scheme (LLCS) 534
safety 419–58
distribution of loads 421–22
dock premises 456
fire safety 442–44
first aid 444–47

forklift trucks 453–54
freight container regulations 454–55
health and safety at work 425–33
    corporate manslaughter 457–58
    dangerous occurrences 435
    employee duties 429
    employer duties 426–29
    enforcement 456–58
    improvement notices 456
    legislation 425, 426, 430, 431, 433–35,
        437
    management of 430
    manual handling 431–32
    penalties for offences 457
    personal protective equipment (PPE) 433
    prohibition notices 457
    provision and use of work equipment 433
    remedial measures 457
    use of display screen equipment 432
    workplace 430–31
international operations 555–56
lifting operations 436–37
load safety 421
lorry loaders 455
mobile communication devices 532–33
noise at work 453
parking 452
reporting of injuries, diseases and dangerous
        occurrences 434–38
responsibility for 491–92
reversing vehicles 448–50
risk management 441–42
road safety 419–20
sheeting loads 451
smoking and vaping 437–38
tipping vehicles 450–51
vehicle batteries 438–41
vehicle safety 420
work at height 452–53
work-related stress 437
workplace signs 447–48
workplace transport safety 422–26
Safety of Loads on Vehicles: Code of Practice
        421, 451
sand and ballast loads 468
    aggregates levy 468
    legislation 468
satellite navigation systems (satnavs) 534
Scania 309–10
Scottish Environmental Protection Agency
        (SEPA) 512
Scottish Qualifications Authority (SQA) 510
seat belts 272–73
    bench-type seats 272
    exemptions 272–73
    light vehicles 520–21
    wearing of 272, 521

self-employment 88–89
smuggling 278–79, 279
Society of Operations Engineers (SOE) 55
speed limits 240–43, 520
statutory off-road notification (SORN) 213, 225
stowaways 274–78

tachographs 98–135
    analogue 109–18
        calibration plaques 107–08
        completion of centre field 109–10
        dirty/damaged charts 109
        EU instruments and charts 117–18
        faults 116
        fiddles 116–17
        instrument itself 114–18
        making recordings 110–11
        manual records 111–12
        official inspection 113–14
        part-time driver records 112
        recordings 115–17
        retention, return, checking 112–13
        sealing of 106–07
        time changes 109
    analysis software services 534
    breakdown 108–09
    calibration 105–06
    chart analysis 118
    digital 118–33, 125
        definitions 119–20
        displaying/printing for authorized
            examiner 123–24, 126
        fees (digi-cards) 129
        functions and use 120–24
        legislation 135
        operator responsibility 129–32
        production of records 129–34
        recording rules 128
        recording and storing 120–22
        regulations 119
        signing and returning records 132–33
        smart cards 124, 127, 128
        smart tachographs 133–34
        storage on driver card 122
    drivers' responsibilities 104–05
    employers' responsibilities 102–03
    exemptions 99–102
    fuel efficiency 526
    installation offences 105
    legal requirements 98–99
    light vehicles 519–20
    offences 134–35
    records as evidence 135
    testing 379–80
tax records, retention of tachograph charts
        112–13
tax relief on driver allowances 89–90

benchmark scale rate payments 90
    personal incidental expenses 90
    sleeper cab allowances 89–90
television 340
THINK! campaign 420
trade licences 215–18, *215*
    displaying 216
    issue of 216
    use of 216–18
Traffic Area Offices (TAOs) 2
traffic calming 271
Traffic Commission (TC) 2–3, 40
Traffic Management Act (2004) 237
traffic reports 280–81
tram crossings 260–61
tramways 246–47
Transport Act (1968) 411
Transport and General Workers' Union
    (TGWU) 34
transport managers 30, *31*
Transport Office Portal (TOP) 536
Transports Internationaux Routiers (TIR) 551,
    553–54, 576–79
TruckWatch 236
Type Approval scheme 341–44
    alteration to vehicles 346–47
    exemptions 343–44
    first licensing of vehicles 345
    issue of plates 346
    plating certificates 385
    refusal to licence 346
    responsibility for 345
    standards checked 345
    vehicles covered 342–43

UK Border Force 274
UK Licence for the Community 560–61
Ultra-Low Emission Zone (ULEZ) 256
Ultra-Low Emission Zones (ULEZs) 245
Union of Shop, Distributive and Allied Workers
    (USDAW) 34
United Road Transport Union (URTU) 34
unroadworthy vehicles 271
Upper Transport Tribunal 44–47

vehicle Excise and Registration Act (1994) 224,
    237, 388
vehicle maintenance 411–18
    cleaning of vehicles 416
    contracted-out 413–14
    driver defect reports 412–13, 416–17
    facilities 412

hired vehicles and trailers 413
    in-house 414–15
    inspection reports 417
    planning 418
    records 412, 416
    safety inspectors 415
    service records 417–18
    vehicle servicing 415
vehicle markings 358–70, *359, 363, 364, 365,*
    366
vehicle registration 196–200
    approval methods 197–98
    documents 197
    HGV road user levy 200
    number (registration) plates 199
    'O licence vehicles 200
    registration document/certificate 198
    trailers 199–200
vehicle tax 201–14
    alteration of vehicles 213–14
    cancelling 202
    exemptions 202–03, 214
    light vehicles 516
    penalties and payment of back duty 214
    rates 204–05, *206–12*, 212–13
    rebated heavy oil (red diesel) 220–21
    recovery vehicles 218–19
    sale of vehicle 214
    special vehicles 203
    statutory off-road notification (SORN) 213
    VED and levy rates *206–12*
Vehicles at Work: Driving at Work and Work-
    Related Road Safety 419
Vehicles at Work – Reversing 448
Vehicles (Excise) Act (1971) 402

waste disposal 511–15
    controlled 512–13
    fly-tipping 469
    hazardous waste 514–15
    legislation 512, 513, 514
    packaging waste 515
    waste food 467
Waste regulation authority (WRA) 512, 515
Waste and Resources Action Programme
    (WRAP) 515
weather reports 280
weight-restricted roads/bridges 261
wheel clamps 269
Working with ADR 492
Working Time (Amendment) Regulations
    (2003) 85–86